WASHINGTON
THE INDISPENSABLE MAN

Other Books by James Thomas Flexner

AMERICAN PAINTING
I. First Flowers of Our Wilderness
II. The Light of Distant Skies
III. That Wilder Image

AMERICA'S OLD MASTERS

THE POCKET HISTORY OF AMERICAN PAINTING
(also published as *A Short History of American Painting*)

JOHN SINGLETON COPLEY

GILBERT STUART

THE WORLD OF WINSLOW HOMER
(with the editors of Time-Life Books)

NINETEENTH CENTURY AMERICAN PAINTING

DOCTORS ON HORSEBACK: PIONEERS OF AMERICAN MEDICINE

STEAMBOATS COME TRUE
(also published as *Inventors in Action*)

THE TRAITOR AND THE SPY
(also published as *The Benedict Arnold Case*)

MOHAWK BARONET: SIR WILLIAM JOHNSON OF NEW YORK

WILLIAM HENRY WELCH AND THE HEROIC AGE OF AMERICAN MEDICINE
(with Simon Flexner)

GEORGE WASHINGTON
I. The Forge of Experience (1732–1775)
II. In the American Revolution (1775–1783)
III. And the New Nation (1783–1793)
IV. Anguish and Farewell (1793–1799)

WASHINGTON

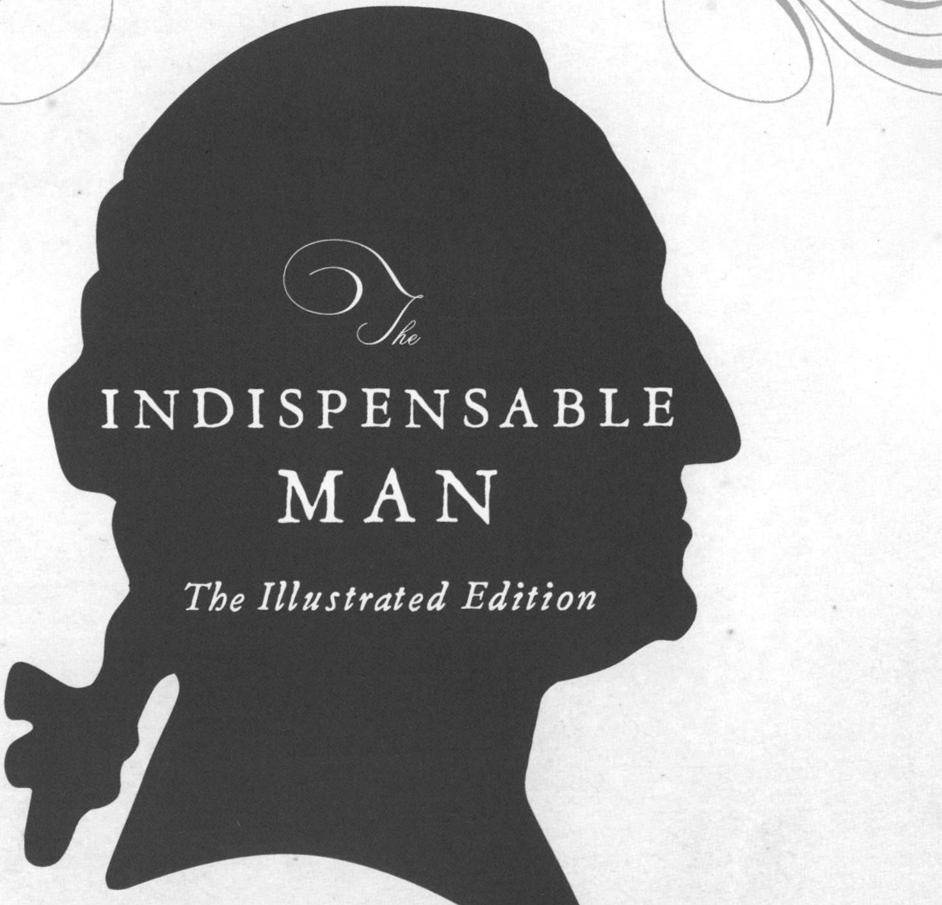

The INDISPENSABLE MAN

The Illustrated Edition

JAMES THOMAS FLEXNER

Sterling Signature
NEW YORK

Sterling Signature
NEW YORK

An Imprint of Sterling Publishing
387 Park Avenue South
New York, NY 10016

Book design by Kimberly Glyder

ISBN 978-1-4027-7821-6
ISBN 978-1-4549-0484-7 (book club)

Distributed in Canada by Sterling Publishing
c/o Canadian Manda Group, 165 Dufferin Street
Toronto, Ontario, Canada M6K 3H6
Distributed in the United Kingdom by GMC Distribution Services
Castle Place, 166 High Street, Lewes, East Sussex, England BN7 1XU
Distributed in Australia by Capricorn Link (Australia) Pty. Ltd.
P.O. Box 704, Windsor, NSW 2756, Australia

For information about custom editions, special sales, and premium and corporate purchases, please contact Sterling Special Sales at 800-805-5489 or specialsales@sterlingpublishing.com.

Manufactured in China

2 4 6 8 10 9 7 5 3 1

www.sterlingpublishing.com

To Beatrice, my wife

Contents

Foreword

When James Thomas Flexner embarked on his landmark study of George Washington, he intended it to come out as a single volume. He soon determined, however, that one book, even a substantial one, couldn't do justice to the significance and richness of his subject; the project became a four-volume work published between 1965 and 1972.

Luckily for the general reader who might be daunted by the scope and sheer size of the multi-volume work, Flexner didn't leave it at that. Relenting under pressure, he subsequently wrote the one-volume edition that forms the basis of the book you hold in your hands. In no way a condensation of the larger work, *The Indispensable Man* is a fully reconceived whole. Upon its publication in 1974, it was heralded by *The Los Angeles Times* as "the most convincing evocation of the man and his deeds in one book" and by the *New York Times* as "the most satisfying biography of Washington between two covers."

In the nearly four decades since its publication, Flexner's epic character study has lost none of its authority, readability, or relevance, and is still considered among the finest works within the huge body of literature on the Founding Fathers.

So . . . why this new volume? It is our hope that the diverse array of materials, both written and visual, that we have integrated into Flexner's original work (which appears here unexpurgated) will enhance his text and reveal new dimensions of the story of Washington's life and times. Among the many treasures you will find reproduced here are:

★ Portraits and sculptures of Washington and all of the major figures from his military, political, and personal life, created by the most prominent artists of his day and beyond, including Junius Brutus Stearns, Gilbert Stuart, Charles Willson Peale (who painted Washington from life more than any other painter), Joshua Reynolds, and Jean-Antoine Houdon.

★ Maps of all kinds, from battle plans for crucial engagements of the Revolution to surveys of Washington's Mount Vernon home.

★ Original documents and ephemera, including Washington's commission as commander in chief of the army; a draft and the final version of the Declaration of Independence; the 1778 Treaty of Alliance with France; speeches, editorial cartoons, posters, and excerpts from Washington's own diaries.

★ Letters to and from Washington, including the precious few bits of correspondence that remained between him and his wife, Martha, after she obeyed his request to destroy it all.

★ Prints and engravings from the eighteenth, nineteenth, and twentieth centuries depicting the major events of Washington's day, from local rebellions and strikes to major war battles, treaty signings, and other historic moments. In the time before photography and film, these images were widely disseminated in order to provide a (sometimes romanticized or stylized) record for all to share.

★ Photographs of key artifacts and objects, including Washington's own camp cot, canteen, battle sword, portable liquor case, books, coat buttons, and décor items. These simple objects speak volumes of their own on the details of day-to-day life during times of war and peace. They also provide a window into Washington's personal taste and sense of style.

★ Contemporary photographs of key sites from Washington's life story as they appear today, linking our own time with his and offering a sense of what we might see if we were to walk in his footsteps.

★ And finally, numerous sidebars throughout the text that expand and comment upon various themes, movements, and ideas touched upon by Flexner in the course of his narrative. Primary texts excerpted here include Thomas Paine's pamphlet series, *The Crisis*; *The Federalist Papers*; and Washington's first State of the Union Address (establishing that tradition for all time) and his 1796 Farewell Address. In addition, historian Jimmy Napoli has contributed brief, enlightening essays on the topics of Washington's illnesses, the strategic burning of New York City in 1776, and Washington's spy network.

As a whole, *Washington: The Indispensable Man, the Illustrated Edition* endeavors to set one of the great American biographies of all time within a rich context of artwork, artifacts, and documentation, bringing it to life for new generations of readers interested in the birth of our great nation.

I must give the final word of introduction to this monumental biography to Willard M. Wallace, writing in the *New York Times Book Review* on October 20, 1974: "Mr. Flexner brings Washington amazingly alive without recourse to sensationalism and without violating the integrity of his subject. He has a keen understanding of the issues and personalities of the era and Washington's position with respect to them. . . . This book deserves a place on every American's bookshelf, but first it should be read with mind and heart."

—Laura Ross

Preface

When more than a dozen years ago I began my biographical study of George Washington, I intended to encompass his life in a single volume such as this one. But I then concluded that so short a work could not be written without being superficial or incomplete.

Compare, for instance, the magnitude of the tasks faced by biographers of Washington and Lincoln. Washington lived eleven years longer than Lincoln. While Lincoln was a major national figure for only some seven years (from the Douglas debates to his assassination), Washington was for twenty-four years (from his election as commander in chief to his death) the most conspicuous and influential man in the United States. For seventeen of those years, comprising the war, the Constitutional Convention, and the presidency, he was from day to day actively engaged in great events. Before all that, his role in the French and Indian War made him internationally known when he was hardly twenty, an age at which Lincoln was still an obscure frontiersman.

The scope of my studies was almost doubled by a determination to describe Washington's indispensable role in the creation of the United States and yet not lose the man in the leader. Events indicative of character were as important to my work as world-shaking decisions. I thus found myself writing a four-volume biography of Washington, published between 1965 and 1972.

After these books had been happily received, pressure on me was renewed to prepare a biography of Washington that would be available to a broader public than any four-volume life could be. And to my surprise, I concluded that all the previous effort had made it possible for me to distill, at long last, what I had discovered into a single volume, one that would, without entirely omitting anything of importance, present in essence Washington's character and career.

The fact that the longer work stands on many shelves has contributed to the possibility of achieving the shorter. Knowing that further facts, more personal details, deeper analyses, and also justifications for my conclusions can be found in the apposite original volumes, I have felt enabled to move rapidly from one high point to another. The bibliographies and source references, which in the original work totalled 112 pages, make it unnecessary to append here more than a brief essay and list.

Despite its relation to the longer biography, this one-volume life is by no means a series of patched-together extracts. The extreme reduction of scale—to about one-fifth—dictated that, if the shorter work were to have its own integrity and literary effect, the material would have to be revisualized and rewritten. Except for the account of Washington's death, the text is almost altogether new.

—J. T. F.

A 1778 mezzotint of Washington by Charles Willson Peale.

Introduction

During my years of work on a biography of Washington, I have made various unexpected discoveries. Surely the most surprising was that George Washington is alive. Or, to put it more accurately, millions of George Washingtons are alive. Washingtons have been born and have died for some two centuries.

Almost every historical figure is regarded as a dead exemplar of a vanished epoch. But Washington exists within the minds of most Americans as an active force. He is a multitude of living ghosts, each shaped less by eighteenth-century reality than by the structure of the individual brain in which he dwells. An inhabitant of intimate spaces, Washington is for private reasons sought out or avoided, loved or admired, hated or despised. I have come across almost no Americans who prove, when the subject is really broached, emotionally indifferent to George Washington.

The roles played by the mythological George Washingtons fall into two major categories: one Freudian, the other a procession of mirrors reflecting people's attitudes towards the situation of the United States at their time.

In an essay that had no specific reference to Washington, Freud described how "infantile fantasies" concerning people's own fathers can shape their conceptions of historical figures. "They obliterate," Freud wrote, "the individual features of their subject's physiognomy, they smooth over the traces of his life's struggles with internal and external resistances, and they tolerate in him no vestiges of human weakness or imperfection. Thus, they present us with what is in fact a cold, strange, ideal figure instead of a human being to whom we might feel ourselves distantly related."

This is an exact description of the marble image of Washington which so many Americans harbor—and dislike. I have been amazed by the infantile glee with which people I have met made fun of my writing a biography of Washington. Was I recording the clacking of wooden false teeth? Had I ever tried to envision how Washington would have looked in long winter underwear? These mockers often dance up and down with self-satisfaction, like a small child who has dared express an impious thought about his father.

Down the years, Washington's second mythological role has been as a national symbol, an alternate to the American flag. In periods when Americans were happy with their society, they have thought of Washington with adulation. At times of resentment and self-distrust, the mythological Washingtons have been resented and distrusted. I have discovered, sometimes to my considerable embarrassment, that the current attitude towards Washington—and towards me as his biographer—is often hostile.

My continuing effort has been to disentangle the Washington who actually lived from all the symbolic Washingtons, to rescue the man and his deeds from the layers and layers of obscuring legend that have accreted around his memory for more than two hundred years. This involved, in the first place, an act of will. I tried to forget everything I had ever heard about George Washington. Rather than endeavor to emend old images, I determined to start with a blank canvas.

Beginning thus, as it were, anew, I found a fallible human being made of flesh and blood and spirit—not a statue of marble and wood. And inevitably—for that was the fact—I found a great and good man. In all history, few men who possessed unassailable power have used that power so gently and self-effacingly for what their best instincts told them was the welfare of their neighbors and all mankind. Most of the brickbats now being thrown at Washington are figments of the modern imagination. In being ourselves untrue to the highest teaching of the American tradition, we of this generation have tended to denigrate that tradition, to seek out all that was unworthy, to emphasize whatever justifies national distrust. In so doing, we have discarded an invaluable heritage. We are blinding our eyes to stars that lead to the very ideals many of us most admire: the sanctity of the individual, the equality of all men before the law, government responsive to the people, freedom for all means of communication, avoidance of what Washington denounced as international "ambition," the self-determination of people everywhere.

Almost every historical figure is regarded as a dead exemplar of a vanished epoch. But Washington exists within the minds of most Americans as an active force.

George Washington *(Lansdowne portrait) by Gilbert Stuart, oil on canvas, 1796.*

To find again the American ideals we have lost, we may not return to our national beginnings with the blinded eyes of idolatry or chauvinism. Let us examine deeply every flaw, every area, where George Washington and his fellow Founding Fathers were untrue to what they professed. Let us examine Washington not as the spotless figure delineated by infantile fantasies or by self-seeking wavers of the flag. Let us determine without prejudice exactly what happened, exactly how men behaved. If we do this we shall, so I am profoundly convinced, find, in the dark valley where we often stand, inspiration.

George Washington *after Samuel King (1748/49–1819), oil on canvas.*

WASHINGTON
THE INDISPENSABLE MAN

One

A POWERFUL APPRENTICESHIP

(1732–1753)

No American is more completely misunderstood than George Washington. He is generally believed to have been, by birth and training, a rich, conservative, British-oriented Virginia aristocrat. As a matter of fact, he was, for the environment in which he moved, poor during his young manhood. He never set foot in England or, indeed, any part of Europe. When at seventeen he began making his own living, it was as a surveyor, defining tracts of forest on the fringes of settlement. Soon the wilderness claimed him, first as an envoy seeking out the French in frozen primeval woods and then, for almost five years, as an Indian fighter.

No other president of the United States before Andrew Jackson was as much shaped by the wilderness as Washington, and he had less formal education than did Jackson, than Lincoln even. Both Jackson and Lincoln studied law, while Washington's total schooling hardly went beyond what we should consider the elementary grades.

In all his long life, Washington never heard of Sulgrave Manor, the ancient British house far back in his lineage, which has been reverently restored as a relic of his transatlantic ancestry. By the time he was born, the family had lost all memory of their British origin. The first settler, John Washington, was an impoverished adventurer who reached Virginia in 1675. The "Wild West" was then on the Atlantic seacoast, and John might have been a character—not the hero—in a modern Western. He was implicated in the murder of five Indian ambassadors; he was a most unscrupulous businessman; and after the wife who was George's ancestress died, he married in succession two sisters who had been accused before him, when he had sat as justice of the peace, one with keeping a bawdyhouse and the other with being the governor's whore.

As Virginia grew, the Washington family prospered modestly. No member ever reached the social and political pinnacle of serving on the King's Council, but they associated with members and sometimes

A surveyor's compass and staff, c. 1750–1800. Washington's first career as a surveyor was brief but successful, endowing him with an intimate knowledge of the backcountry and its inhabitants, a small fortune in land, and a reputation for courage and integrity. After establishing himself as a gentleman farmer at Mount Vernon, he continued to employ his surveying skills to lay out fields and verify disputed boundary lines. One of the most important tools of the trade was a surveyor's compass.

even married their daughters. Had George's childhood proceeded smoothly, he would have been raised in the conventional manner of the minor Virginia gentry. But his childhood did not proceed smoothly.

Legend has clustered around George's father, Augustine Washington, but we know for sure little about him beyond what is revealed in business records. These show him to have been restless, apprehensive, unsure, making deals which he subsequently denied making. He was often in the law courts. He married twice. Two sons survived from his first marriage, and from his second, five children, of whom George was the oldest.

The future hero saw the light on February 11, 1732,* in a cheaply built house, now long vanished, near where Pope's Creek empties into the Potomac. As an infant, he was carried some forty miles upriver to a story-and-a-half farmhouse on a bluff (eventually to be known as Mount Vernon). When the boy was six, the family moved again, this time to the farm across the Rappahannock from Fredericksburg that was to be George's childhood home. An inventory made when he was eleven reveals modest comfort. The house had six rooms, four below and two above, into which were crowded thirteen beds and one couch. To service these, the Washingtons owned six good pairs of sheets, ten inferior pairs, and seventeen pillowcases. Their proudest possessions were described as "plate": one soup spoon, eighteen small spoons, seven teaspoons, a watch, and a sword, for a total value of £25 10s. Although they owned two china tea sets, they had only eleven china plates; most of the Washingtons' utensils were whittled from wood. However, Augustine owned twenty slaves: seven able-bodied, eight of moderate value, and five not capable of work.

This Memorial House at George Washington Birthplace National Monument in Westmoreland County, Virginia, was constructed in 1931 to re-create the home in which Washington was born.

* A change in the calendar during George's lifetime pushed his birth date ahead to the 22nd.

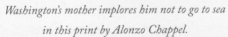

Washington's mother implores him not to go to sea in this print by Alonzo Chappel.

A portrait of George's beloved, older half brother, Lawrence Washington, by an unknown artist, detail, c. 1743.

Washington spent his childhood in what was for rural Virginia a lively place. Transatlantic vessels beat up the Rappahannock outside his windows to Fredericksburg, and a ferry plied across to the town from the Washington property. There was a perpetual trickle of travelers, some of whom found a temporary haven in the Washingtons' many beds.

The intention was that George would, like his father and two older half brothers, go to school in England. He was later to disapprove of foreign schooling as weakening the passion of Americans for freedom. In his case, the test was not made. When he was eleven, his father died, carrying away with him any hope of George's receiving education abroad. The disappointment haunted George for years.

Augustine Washington left the major parts of his modest property to his two older sons, George's half brothers. The house in which the family lived, Ferry Farm, was eventually to come to George, but his mother was in control, and throughout a long life she refused to relinquish the property.

Mary Ball Washington was given neither to acquiescence nor compromise. Orphaned early, she had grown up largely independent, and by the time she married, at twenty-five, she had been an old maid (according to Virginia mores) for a number of years. After the death of Augustine Washington she never married again. The passion of her life became her son George, and it was a very possessive passion. Even when he was commander in chief, even when he was president, she objected to his occupations, complaining violently that he was ungratefully neglecting his duties to her.

After his father's death, George was cast, under his mother's demanding eyes, as the captain of a household team made up of his younger brothers and sister. At the age of eleven, himself a substitute father, the mainstay and main victim of a termagant mother, the future father of his country escaped as often as he could. He found a substitute father of his own in his half brother Lawrence, who was his elder by fourteen years.

Lawrence had already fired George with martial ardor by becoming an officer in an American regiment enrolled in the British regular army for an expedition against the Spanish West Indian stronghold of

Cartagena. How the boy, who was all his life to have a passion for military regalia, must have admired his brother's red uniform! Then there had been the exciting departure, followed by rumors and dispatches concerning the brother's adventure, and at last a happy homecoming. Lawrence's complaints of how the officers from Great Britain had humiliated the American regiment did not (although they surely remained in George's memory) prevent the boy from visualizing for himself a career in the British regular army.

> At the age of eleven, himself a substitute father, the mainstay and main victim of a termagant mother, the future father of his country escaped as often as he could.

Probably owing to the passion of his mother, Washington's childhood schoolbooks have been preserved. At their most advanced, they show him studying elementary geometry and the zodiacal configuration of the stars.

Concerning where Washington received instruction, there is only one solid piece of evidence. It shows him attending an unnamed school while he was staying at the farm Lawrence had inherited and renamed Mount Vernon, after Admiral Edward Vernon, who had commanded the Cartagena expedition.

Surely more important to Washington's education than this or any school was a nearby mansion called Belvoir. Although its inhabitants described it as "a tolerable cottage" in a "wooded world," Washington considered the handsome brick structure, with its two elaborately furnished sitting rooms, the height of elegance and grandeur. This was the American headquarters of the great English Fairfax family. Under a royal grant, which Virginians were perpetually protesting, Lord Fairfax owned a sizable section of the colony. The master of Belvoir, William Fairfax, was a cousin of his Lordship, his Lordship's American agent, and consequently one of the most powerful men in Virginia. Perhaps the first indication of George's unusual qualities was the way in which the young boy was taken into the bosom of the Fairfax clan.

At Belvoir, the future revolutionary had his first close view of British upper-class life. Even if he did not realize it at the time, the vision was equivocal. However well placed he was now in Virginia, William Fairfax had been born into his aristocratic family as the insignificant younger son of a younger son. Prevented by his elevated caste from struggling for his own living but with practically no inheritance, he had been completely dependent on having the grander members of his family use their influence to keep him employed in ways suited to his station. Although he made his motto "I trust in God I shall never procure the disesteem of any relation," he was given a tremendous kicking around before he finally found his seemingly safe position in Virginia. His son George William Fairfax (who might inherit the title and the great estates if certain deaths were not counteracted by births in certain bedchambers) had been so maltreated by toplofty relatives that he had been beaten into a cringing weakling who became a disciple to the much younger—by seven years—George Washington. And when the great Lord Fairfax came himself to Belvoir, he proved to be entirely dominated by three obsessions: a consciousness of power, a hatred of women, and a love of foxhunting. He treated the William Fairfaxes—and also Lawrence Washington, who had married one of William's daughters—with an offhand mixture of generosity and brutality which they had to put up with since their prosperity depended on his whims.

His Lordship was taken with young George, who was so naturally gifted at riding to hounds. The Fairfax influence would have got the lad into the

GEORGE WASHINGTON IN HIS BOYHOOD.

Washington's interest in military strategy emerged at a tender age. Here, he leads friends in a mock charge as another group of boys advances in the background.

Colonel George Washington the fox hunter, artist unknown, c. 1857.

British navy—with what effect on future history?—if his mother had not made such a fuss at his deserting her that he unpacked bags already shut. Next, the Fairfaxes propelled him in the exactly opposite direction. He accompanied a surveying party assigned to lay out Fairfax land on the frontier over the Blue Ridge in the Shenandoah Valley. Washington was then sixteen. It was his first real adventure. Here is how he described his initial encounter with a backwoods lodging:

"We got our supper and was lighted into a room and I, not being as good a woodsman as the rest of my company, stripped myself very orderly and went in to the bed, as they called it, when to my surprise, I found it to be nothing but a little straw matted together, without sheets or anything else, but only one threadbare blanket, with double its weight of vermin, such as lice, fleas, etc., and I was glad to get up, as soon as the light was carried from us. [He does not seem to have wanted to offend the landlord by leaping out of bed.] I put on my clothes, and lay as my companions [on the floor]."* The next day they found a more civilized inn where "we cleaned ourselves to get rid of the game we catched the night before."

Washington studied practical surveying; swam horses across a river swollen by snow melting in the mountains; met a party of Indians carrying one scalp who, when inspired by a gift of rum, performed a war dance; got lost in the Blue Ridge Mountains, where he encountered a rattlesnake. He found it all exhilarating. During thirty-one days of blustery March and April weather, he gave to the American West a part of his heart he was never to regain.

Washington had gone along on this trip largely for the fun of it. However, it was clear to the teenager that he had to make some money. He was to write again and again that men judged their condition less by what it actually was than by comparison. Although he never lacked for food or warm clothes, he would have been ashamed to take the friends he was making to his mother's rundown farm. On one recorded occasion, he could not get away to some dances because he could not buy feed for his horse. And so at the age of seventeen he set himself up as a surveyor over the Blue Ridge. At eighteen, he was able to make his first land purchase: 1,459 acres on Bullskin Creek, a tributary of the Shendandoah.

When staying at Lord Fairfax's hunting lodge, he wrote "Dear friend Robin" that he might, "was my heart disengaged, pass my time very pleasantly, as there's a very agreeable young lady lives in the same house . . . but as that's only adding fuel to the fire, it makes me the more uneasy for, by often and unavoidably being in company with her, revives my former passion for your Low Land Beauty, whereas was I to live more retired from young women, I might in some measure alleviate my sorrows by burying that chaste and troublesome passion in the grave of oblivion or eternal forgetfulness," etc.

The Low Land Beauty could have been any one of many girls, for Washington was in love with love. He even wrote poetry—and very badly, it turned out. He was not, indeed, much of a success with girls. Very tall for his generation—over six feet—with reddish hair and gray-blue eyes, his face massive, his shoulders narrow for his height but his hands and feet tremendous, George exuded such masculine power as frightens young women just wakening to the opposite sex. He enjoyed making playful compliments and flirting in a ritualistic manner, yet his gaiety was seemingly belied by a slowness of speech more suited to the careful expression of profound thought. His lack of surface vivacity allowed other young men to cut him out with many a pretty girl.

* The spelling and punctuation of all quotations have been modernized.

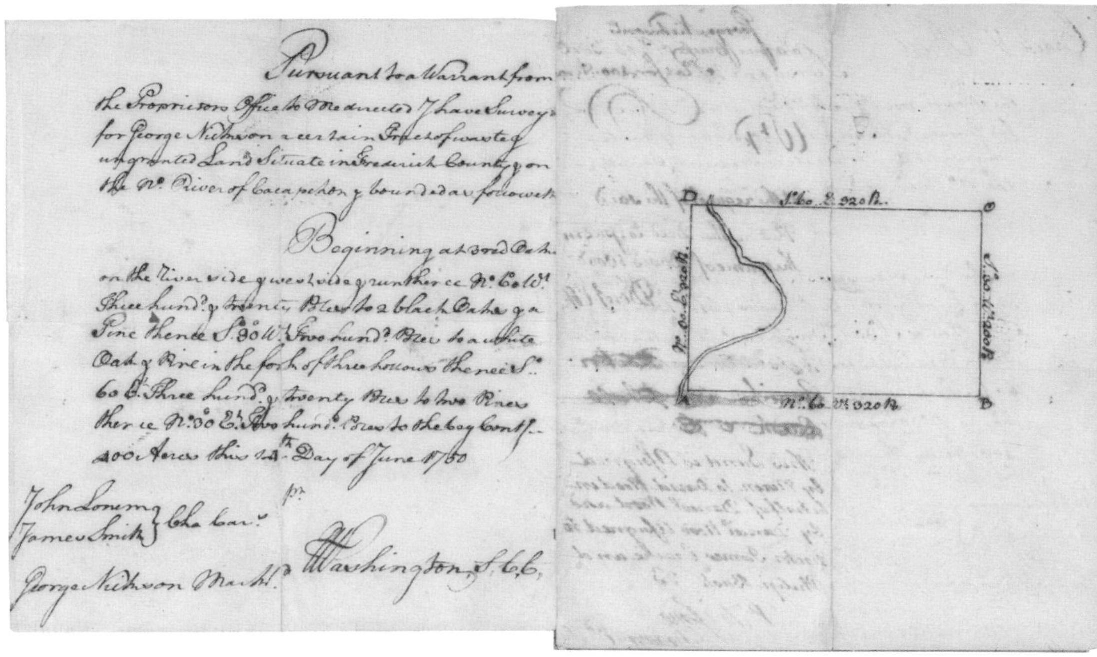
Pursuant to a Warrant from the Proprietors Office to me directed I have Surveyd for George Nixon a certain Tract of waste & ungranted Land Situate in Frederick County on the No. River of Cacapehon & bounded as followeth

Beginning at 3 red Oaks on the River side ...

400 Acres this 14th Day of June 1750

John Lonem, James Smith } Cha: Carrs

George Nixon Markr

pr G Washington S.C.C.

George Washington's Survey for George Nixon, April 14, 1750. *Signed "Washington, SCC" (for Surveyor of Culpeper County), this survey details 400 acres of Frederick County along the North River. These lands originally belonged to George Nixon, and in 1771 were assigned to Dr. James Craik, George Washington's friend and physician, and Philip Bush. Washington recorded the survey in his field book on April 14, 1750, but may have incorrectly dated the finished document June 14, 1750.*

As Washington was beginning to find his way in the world, a slow and excruciating tragedy darkened over him. His beloved brother Lawrence came down with virulent tuberculosis. George accompanied his dying friend to Barbados, in the hope that a tropical climate would help. This was the only ocean trip Washington ever took, the only occasion on which he went outside the limits of the future United States. He kept a boyish diary, but in all his later writings, he never mentioned the journey or used a metaphor that revealed he had been in the tropics. As Lawrence coughed his life away, the experience had been too sad. Washington himself sickened with smallpox. This (since he recovered) was a hidden boon: it made him immune to the greatest killer of the American Revolution.

In Virginia, as in all the colonies, every community supported a volunteer militia company, presumably a military force but more closely resembling a men's drinking and political club. Appointed adjutant general of Virginia, Lawrence had been supposed to see that the militiamen possessed such martial skills as the ability to turn in formation without falling over each other. On Lawrence's death, George sought the office. He went after it in the Fairfax manner: not by becoming proficient in military matters, but by paying semi-social calls on influential members of the government. Thus following the mores of an aristocratic world, he secured, at the age of twenty, the title of major and the responsibility of training militia in skills he did not himself possess.

Hardly anyone could have sounded more insignificant if mentioned in the chancelleries of Europe. Yet in his obscure forests, Washington was soon to fire the first shots in what became a world war.

Two

A CLUMSY ENTRANCE ON THE WORLD STAGE

(1753–1754)

England and France were engaged in a cold war, each trying to contain the other. The Ohio Valley was among the globally scattered areas claimed by both rivals. France impinged from Canada, the British from across the Allegheny Mountains. Indians inhabited the valley. Although the few white men who traversed the paths and watercourses were mostly French, English land speculators had visions. The highest resident crown official in Virginia, Lieutenant Governor Robert Dinwiddie, joined with influential men (including the Fairfaxes) in his colony and in London to secure for their "Ohio Company" a grant of half a million acres.

What was Dinwiddie's horror to hear rumors that the French, who controlled the Great Lakes, were fortifying a route from Lake Erie to the Ohio River system so that their troops could float into the areas to the west of Virginia that the Ohio Company wanted. The lieutenant governor complained to his sovereign. George II ordered the building of a fort and also that an envoy be sent through the wilderness to search out the French position. If the French were really on land the British claimed, the envoy was to warn the intruders away. If the miscreants would not withdraw, Dinwiddie should use force.

To find a possible envoy presented Dinwiddie with serious problems. Whoever was chosen would have to travel first north against the rivers and then south with them, for some five hundred miles through an unbroken, Indian-haunted forest. The way back would go quickly if the rivers remained open, but winter was so close that the waters might harden into ice. The paths would then become almost impassable with snow. And no Virginian whose social position was commensurate with acting as a royal emissary possessed wilderness experience.

Yet the Fairfax connection boasted a physical giant who, even if he had never crossed the Alleghenies, had surveyed in the semi-wild Shenandoah Valley. Furthermore, although only twenty-one, George Washington carried the manifest air of one born to command. He was assigned two interpreters: a Dutchman, Jacob van Braam, whose knowledge of French was testified to by the badness of his English; and a fur trader, Christopher Gist, who was to prove less conversant with Indian tongues than he should have been. Add four backwoodsmen of low degree who acted as "servitors," some riding horses, and a flock of packhorses, and you had the expedition which in October 1753, already fighting through heavy snow, descended from the mountains into the wild Ohio Valley. The French wilderness masters, so numerous and so familiar with Indian trails and embassies, would have regarded this tiny, amateur force as comic. Yet the tenderfoot who led it was no ordinary man.

Washington soon dashed ahead of his party to where the Monongahela joined the Allegheny to form the lordly Ohio. Although "the Forks of the Ohio"

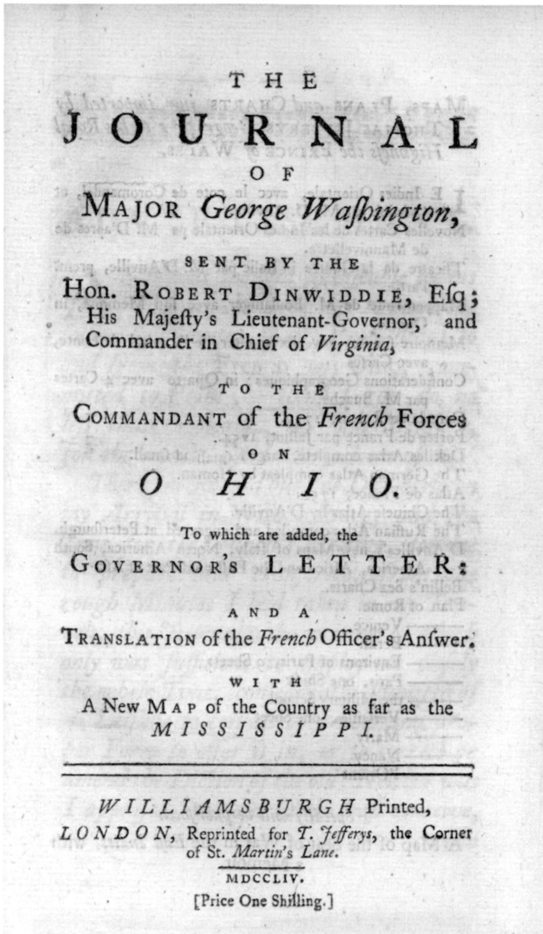

THE

JOURNAL

OF

MAJOR *George Washington*,

SENT BY THE

Hon. ROBERT DINWIDDIE, Esq;
His Majesty's Lieutenant-Governor, and
Commander in Chief of *Virginia*,

TO THE

COMMANDANT of the *French* Forces

ON

OHIO.

To which are added, the

GOVERNOR'S LETTER:

AND A

TRANSLATION of the *French* Officer's Answer.

WITH

A New MAP of the Country as far as the
MISSISSIPPI.

WILLIAMSBURGH Printed,
LONDON, Reprinted for *T. Jefferys*, the Corner
of St. *Martin's Lane*.

MDCCLIV.

[Price One Shilling.]

In 1753–1754, a twenty-two-year-old George Washington traveled as emissary and diplomat deep into the Ohio Territory to deliver Governor Robert Dinwiddie's order for the French forces to evacuate. The French commander's refusal to move would plunge England and her colonies into the French and Indian War. Washington kept a diary of his arduous journey, from which he prepared a report to Governor Dinwiddie upon his return. Much to his surprise, Dinwiddie immediately had it printed in Williamsburg. A London edition appeared later that same year.

(now Pittsburgh) was the strategic position that controlled thousands of miles of wilderness, he found there no signs of humanity except empty trails. For two days he explored by himself through the tangled forest, seeking, despite his military ignorance, the best location for a fort. His judgment was confirmed by both the French and the English, who were in succession to erect major works at the spot he chose.

After Washington's expedition had reassembled, they advanced to the Indian village of Logtown where they hoped to pick up an escort of warriors. Washington now met the Iroquois chief the British called the Half-King, who was to play a greater part in his destiny than he could possibly have realized. The greenhorn now tried his hand at the exquisite art of Indian diplomacy: he proceeded brashly and made a fool of himself. He began by reminding the Indians that they had made a treaty of alliance with the British. This the Half-King did not deny, but he went on to state that the treaty had been based on assurances that the British merely wished to trade, having no designs on the land which "the Great Being above allowed . . . to be a place of residence to us." He then asked the nature of Washington's mission to the French.

Realizing that it would never do to admit that he was claiming the valley for George II, but unwilling to make up an excuse, Washington gave a noncommittal reply. He was pleased when the Indian statesman seemed satisfied by the evasion. However, the Half-King soon opined that it would be safer not to provoke the French, by having Washington accompanied by a military escort. Three old chiefs, including the Half-King, would go along. One able-bodied hunter would serve to supply the party with meat.

The weather had abated, and the trip to the first of a sequence of French forts, at the confluence of French Creek with the Monongahela (now Franklin, Pennsylvania), was not arduous. Ordering his Indian companions to camp outside, Washington entered to find gathered in a log room France's most expert Indian negotiators. They told Washington he would have to carry his message further, and then expressed concern that he had not felt free to bring in his Indians. Washington, who wanted to protect the chiefs from what he considered subversive influences, made lame excuses. The Frenchmen must have been amused at his dismay when the old braves, taking matters in their own hands, filed in, and also at the young Virginian's inability to stick out the party that followed. (It took years of practice to be able to enjoy the company of drunken Indians.) Washington did, however, stay in the fort long enough to hear the French officers, who were more interested in frightening the tribes than soothing Virginia, announce over their wine that their sovereign intended to establish his control over the Ohio Valley.

Washington now met the Iroquois chief the British called the Half-King, who was to play a greater part in his destiny than he could possibly have realized.

Eventually reclaiming his Indians, Washington proceeded through what he called "excessive" rain and snow some sixty miles up French Creek to Fort Le Boeuf (near Waterford, Pennsylvania). He saw a rectangular log enclosure, almost completely surrounded by swirling water. It bristled with cannon. Washington was received at this outpost hundreds of miles from civilization with ceremony that would have done credit to Versailles. After he had donned the dress uniform of a Virginia major, which he had packed along the Indian trails for the occasion, he met officially with the even more elegantly attired Legardeur de St. Pierre, Knight of the Military Order of St. Louis. The Virginia stripling presented George II's ultimatum. The elderly Frenchman brushed it aside. No effort was made to hide from Washington the more than two hundred canoes that lay in the snow beside the creek, ready to drift down to the Forks of the Ohio.

But—it was now mid-December. Drifting home was not possible for Washington. French Creek could, it is true, be fought through, but the Monongahela was frozen solid. Nothing to do but to attempt to traverse the trails! His horses' legs sank deep into snowdrifts and were cut at the ankle by sharp crusts of ice. The horses staggered with hunger because all forage was frozen over. Thirst became a horror for man and beast: all water had turned to ice so cold that, if sucked, it would burn the mouth. In the midst of this utter desolation, the cavalcade moved more and more slowly.

Finally, Washington, anxious to warn Dinwiddie of an approaching invasion, decided that he and Gist would push ahead on foot. The woodsman objected that the tenderfoot "had never been used to walking before this time." But Washington overruled Gist's doubts, and overruled them again by picking up, at an Indian village called Murthering Town, an Indian guide whom Gist distrusted but who offered to lead them on a shortcut through pathless woods.

The ice-covered wilderness glowed like a hall of mirrors, but dimly, since the high trees shut out the sun. Suddenly they came out into a clearing where sunlight dazzled. The Indian ran ahead about fifteen paces, turned, raised his gun, and fired at his companions. The bullet moved through utter emptiness without changing the history of the world.

Springing forward, Gist and Washington leapt on the Indian before he could reload. Since the hostile brave might have companions to whom he would betray them, Gist wished to kill him. Washington could not bear to see a man killed. So the brave was sent off in one direction, while Gist and Washington ran in another. For a long time they dared not light a campfire. Moving sometimes separately, sometimes together,

Lieutenant Governor of Virginia Robert Dinwiddie, artist unknown, detail of painting, c. 1760–1765.

WASHINGTON'S LETTER TO GOVERNOR DINWIDDIE

IN APRIL OF 1754, WASHINGTON WROTE THE FOLLOWING LETTER to Lieutenant Governor Robert Dinwiddie to give an account of his campaign to order the French out of the Ohio Valley. Captain Trent was the commander of the Virginia Regiment and had established both Fort Prince George and Fort Hanger. After Fort Hanger was surrendered to the French, the military strategy was to attack and recapture the Forks of the Ohio after reinforcements arrived. Washington describes his efforts to build a wagon road at Redstone Creek to allow artillery to pass and to prepare for more men and supplies. It would be from Wills Creek that Washington, his men, and Indian allies would meet and defeat a French party during a surprise attack.

Will's Creek, 25 April, 1754

Sir,

Captain Trent's ensign, Mr. Ward, has this day arrived from the Fork of the Monongahela and brings the disagreeable account that the fort on the 17th instant was surrendered at the summons of Monsieur Contrecoeur to a body of French consisting of upwards of one thousand men, who came from Venango with eighteen pieces of cannon, sixty batteaux, and three hundred canoes. They gave him liberty to bring off all his men and working-tools, which he accordingly did the same day.

Immediately upon this information I called a council of war to advise on proper measures to be taken in this exigency. A copy of their resolves, with the proceedings, I herewith enclose by the bearer, whom I have continued express to your Honor for more minute intelligence.

Mr. Ward has the summons with him and a speech from the Half-King, which I also enclose with the wampum. He is accompanied by one of the Indians mentioned therein, who were sent to see where we were, what was our strength, and to know the time to expect us out. The other young man I have prevailed upon to return to the Half- King with the following speech:

"Sachems, Warriors of the Six United Nations, Shannoahs, and Delawares, our friends and brethren. I received your speech by the Buck's brother [Mr. Ward], who came to us with the two young men five sleeps after leaving you. We return you thanks from hearts glowing with affection for your steadfast adherence to us, for your kind speech, and for your wise counsels and directions to the Buck's brother.

"The young man will inform you where he met a small part of our army advancing towards you, clearing the road for a great number of our warriors, who are immediately to follow with our great guns, our ammunition, and our provisions.

"I could not delay to let you know our hearts, and have sent back one of the young men with this speech to acquaint you with them. I have sent the other, according to your desire, to the governor of Virginia, with the Buck's brother, to deliver your speech and wampum, and to be an eyewitness of the preparations we are making to come in haste to support you, whose interest is as dear to us as our lives. We resent the usage of the treacherous French, and our conduct will henceforth plainly show you how much we have it at heart.

"I cannot be easy without seeing you before our forces meet at the fork of the roads, and therefore I have the greatest desire that you and Escuniate, or one of you, should meet me on the road as soon as possible to assist us in council.

"To assure you of the good will we bear you, and to confirm the truth of what has been said, I herewith present to you a string of wampum, that you may thereby remember how much I am your brother and friend."

I hope my proceedings in these affairs will be satisfactory to your Honor, as I have, to the utmost of my knowledge, consulted the interest of the expedition and good of my country, whose rights, while they are asserted in so just a cause, I will defend to the last remains of life.

Hitherto the difficulties I have met with in marching have been greater than I expect to encounter on the Ohio, when possibly I may be surrounded by the enemy; and these difficulties have been occasioned by those who, had they acted as becomes every good subject, would have exerted their utmost abilities to forward our just designs. Out of seventy-four wagons impressed at Winchester, we got but ten after waiting a week; and some of those so badly provided with teams, that the soldiers were obliged to assist them up the hills, although it was known they had better teams at home. I doubt not that in some points I may have strained the law; but I hope, as my sole motive was to expedite the march, I shall be supported in it, should my authority be questioned, which at present I do not apprehend, unless some busybody intermeddles.

Your Honor will see by the resolves in council that I am destined to the Monongahela with all the diligent dispatch in my power. We will endeavour to make the road sufficiently good for the heaviest artillery to pass; and, when we arrive at Red-stone Creek, fortify ourselves as strongly as the short time will allow. I doubt not that we can maintain a possession there, till we are reinforced, unless the rising of the waters shall admit the enemy's cannon to be conveyed up in canoes; and then I flatter myself we shall not be so destitute of intelligence, as not to get timely notice of it, and make a good retreat.

I hope you will see the absolute necessity for our having, as soon as our forces are collected, a number of cannon, some of heavy metal, with mortars and grenadoes to attack the French, and put us on an equal footing with them.

Perhaps it may also be thought advisable to invite the Cherokees, Catawbas, and Chickasaws to march to our assistance, as we are informed that six hundred Chippewas and Ottawas are marching down Scioto Creek to join the French, who are coming up the Ohio. In that case, I would beg leave to recommend their being ordered to this place first, that a peace may be concluded between them and the Six Nations; for I am informed by several persons, that, as no good harmony subsists between them, their coming first to the Ohio may create great disorders, and turn out much to our disadvantage. . . .

By the best information I can get, I much doubt whether any of the Indians will be in to treat in May. Are the Indian women and children, if they settle amongst us, to be maintained at our expense? They will expect it. I have the honor to be.

George Washington.

From *The Writings of George Washington*, Volume II, by Jared Sparks, 1847.

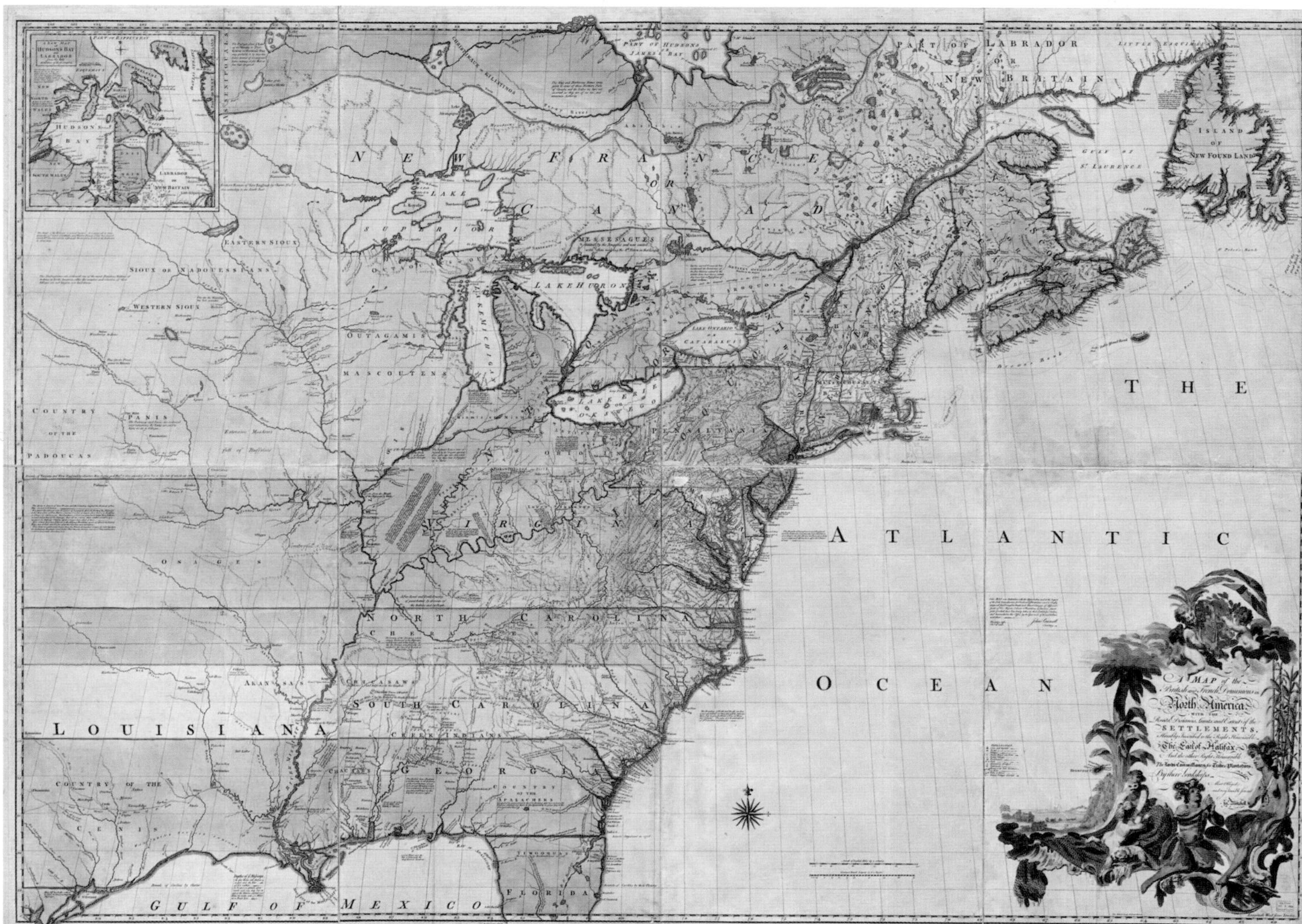

A 1755 map of the British and French dominions in North America, including the roads, distances, limits, and extent of the settlements.

ever wary of Indian attack, they reached the Monongahela in two days.

Civilization lay across the wide river, but they saw to their dismay that no continuous paving of ice awaited their feet. Instead, huge chunks (such as those Washington was to meet again during his advance on Trenton) rushed by in the rapid current. With the "one poor hatchet" they possessed, Washington and Gist built a raft. The minute it was launched, it became caught in the flow of ice. As Washington used a pole to fend off a mighty chunk, he was thrown into the freezing water. Somehow, he managed to climb back. Eventually, Washington and Gist quit their raft and struggled onto an island; their wet clothes froze as hard as armor. It was the frontiersman who had to sit up all night rubbing snow on his frostbitten toes and fingers. Washington slept, if fitfully. At dawn, he saw a lovely sight: the river was now a solid sheet of ice. The opposite shore and civilization were in reach.

Here were wings for ambition, but the diffidence that always accompanied Washington's push for power took over. He wrote that he believed he could with "diligent study" prepare himself for the second rank, but admitted that the first was beyond his knowledge and experience.

Dinwiddie was all eagerness to persuade Virginia that, to forestall French attack, the colony should pay for building the fort at the Forks of the Ohio that would also serve the interests of the Virginia Company. Despite Washington's desire to revise his journal of the expedition into better literary form, the lieutenant governor rushed it to the press because it revealed French intentions and would thus help his cause. This effort to persuade the citizenry failed for reasons that Washington undoubtedly took to heart. Since he was closely connected with the promoters of the Virginia Company, the charge of bias made it impossible for him to secure credence for what he had seen and sincerely believed. Most Virginians were, in any case, not anxious to take action; they considered the land over the Alleghenies so distant as to be of concern only to land speculators and the global ambitions of kings.

Through political bargains, Dinwiddie managed to secure from the Virginia legislature authorization for an army of three hundred men. The twenty-one-year-old major was mentioned as the commander. Here were wings for ambition, but the diffidence that always accompanied Washington's push for power took over. He wrote that he believed he could with "diligent study" prepare himself for the second rank, but admitted that the first was beyond his knowledge and experience. Dinwiddie accepted this disclaimer; circumstances (tragically, as it turned out) did not. The man appointed to the top command never caught up with his second, leaving Washington, now promoted to lieutenant colonel, as actual commander in situations that proved both politically and militarily far beyond his depth.

Dinwiddie had sent a task force of thirty-three men to build a fort at the Forks. When they reported rumors of a large French invasion, Washington was ordered over the mountains with what troops had so far been raised. The 159 men he led westward in April 1754 built for their few cannon the road that, for the first time since the creation of the world, carried wheels into the Ohio Valley.

Washington soon saw approaching him the little garrison from the fort. They reported excitedly that they had found themselves surrounded by a thousand

Frenchmen and Indians, who had come down the waterways with cannon. What was their relief not to be attacked, merely to be courteously ushered onto the trail back to settled Virginia! Washington was impressed by the news that the Half-King (who claimed that the French had boiled and eaten his father) had cursed out the invaders, expressing continued support for the English armies. In order not to let such Indian allies down, Washington decided to continue his advance, even though his force was now so greatly outnumbered.

The Half-King soon notified Washington that a French party was skulking in the nearby woods. Overlooking the fact that England and France were not officially at war, forgetting that the French had not attacked the party at the Forks and that Dinwiddie had ordered him to warn all Frenchmen away before he engaged in hostilities, Washington allowed himself to be persuaded to use the Indian tactic of a surprise attack.

Advancing through the darkest of rainy nights with forty soldiers and a posse of Indians, Washington surrounded in the morning light of dawn thirty-two Frenchmen who were lounging by their campfires. In the engagement that ensued, the Frenchmen had difficulty getting to their arms, but there was some return fire. "I heard the bullets whistle," enthused the fledging colonel, "and, believe me, there is something charming in the sound."

The victory Washington quickly won seemed total—ten Frenchmen killed and the rest taken prisoner. However, the survivors did not cower in humiliation. Waving documents, they shouted in outrage. Interpreters finally explained their claim that one of the men killed, Joseph Coulon, Sieur de Jumonville, had been leading the group on a mission similar to Washington's of a few months before: to warn the British off what the French claimed was their land. Washington, the prisoners insisted, had attacked a peaceful diplomatic mission, and murdered an ambassador.

The seriousness of the situation did not come over to Washington. Insisting that, whatever papers they carried, the French obviously had hostile intentions, he shrugged off charges that were greatly to excite the chancelleries of the two great European rivals.

Forest intelligence reported that the French, who were erecting a strong point (Fort Duquesne) at the Forks, had enough manpower left over to send eight hundred soldiers and four hundred Indians to annihilate Washington's little army. Washington wrote Dinwiddie, "I have a constitution hardy enough to encounter and undergo the most severe trials, and, I flatter myself, the resolution to face what any man durst." But he still "ardently wished" to have some experienced officer sent to command him.

> As Washington awaited, half confidently, this promotion, he was notified that the Virginia Regiment was not to be incorporated but broken up. No provincial would be allowed a commission higher than captain.

He was soon deserted by his Indian allies. The Half-King was to explain that, although "a good-natured man," Washington would not listen to advice and kept the Indians as if they were "slaves," forever on the scout. The braves foresaw a British defeat and wanted no part in it.

Before departing, the Half-King warned that the defensive fort Washington had decided to build—the Indian warrior referred to it contemptuously as "that little thing in the meadow"—was useless. "Fort Necessity" was, indeed, an exercise in pure inexperience. The stockade was not large enough to hold even Washington's tiny force. Most were protected only by an earthen parapet with a ditch before it.

This lithograph, c. 1854, part of Junius Brutus Stearns's Life of George Washington *series, shows the lieutenant colonel on horseback during the Battle of the Monongahela. Although he had demurred from accepting the rank of commander, Washington found himself in the role—and greatly over his head.*

Expecting, it seems, that the enemy would charge his works across the surrounding open fields, he was unconcerned by the bushy heights that looked down into the fort.

The battle developed on July 3, 1754. The French and Indians took cover on the raised places whence they could angle their fire into the battlements. Had the firearms of those days been accurate, Washington's army would have been annihilated within the hour. As it was, the battle dragged on, each side firing at opposing musket flashes, but with the French always having the advantage. As Washington ran around giving commands, he stepped over dead and wounded bodies, slipped on blood.

When the skies opened in midafternoon, Washington was thankful—the driving rain slowed all fire—but not for long. Fort Necessity had been so ineptly placed that it became a catch basin. From one trench after another, the men were displaced by bloody water. Since the roof of the magazine leaked, the stored powder was being ruined. But Washington was unwilling to surrender. He heartened his men by breaking open some kegs of rum. There was a renewed burst of fire from Fort Necessity, even if the musket barrels reeled.

Darkness gathered when, to Washington's amazement, the triumphing French offered to parley. Van Braam, still Washington's interpreter, went out to meet the enemy. The ceasefire enabled Washington to assess more clearly his hopeless situation. A third of his force—more than a hundred men—were dead or wounded. There was hardly any food or usable powder. The harshest surrender terms seemed in order, yet van Braam returned all smiles.

The commander of the French force, Coulon de Villiers, proved to be a brother of the dead Jumonville. In the engagement when Jumonville had fallen, Washington had taken the surrendered Frenchmen prisoner; yet de Villiers now offered to agree that Washington's troops could go home. The Virginia stripling was too pleased to puzzle for an explanation. Either because of relief, exhaustion, or a bad translation by van Braam, Washington signed, on July 4, a document which stated that the French, averse to troubling "the peace and harmony which reigns between two friendly princes," had acted solely from the need to avenge the "assassination" of their diplomat, Jumonville.

If only Dinwiddie had paid heed to Washington's protestations of inexperience! If only the youthful colonel had refused to accept responsibilities he knew were beyond him—or had been cautious once thrust into power! In a short three months, he had sown havoc. The Indians, realizing that the conflict between European encroachers was not theirs, saw their advantage in being allied to whichever side was going to win. They were persuaded by Washington's ridiculous defeat at Fort Necessity to go over in a body to the French.

And the repercussions in Europe were disastrous. On the verge of a war with France, the British Crown had been branded not only as the aggressor but as a murderer of diplomats. A French poet wrote, "The assassination of Jumonville is a monument of perfidy that ought to enrage eternity," and an English pamphleteer said that the surrender Washington had signed was "the most infamous a British subject ever put his hand to." In the eyes of the British command, Washington had demonstrated himself the very nadir of an animal they commonly laughed at and distrusted: the incompetent provincial officer.

However—so sharp was the separation of attitudes—Washington's own Virginia hailed him as hero: had he not won a victory and then, with great bravery, induced his little force to stand up to a superior enemy? In his innocence, Washington hoped to be rewarded with a commission in the regular army that would enable him to make a lifetime career as a professional British officer.

Washington's few soldiers had been designated "the Virginia Regiment." It seemed to him that nothing could be more natural than for the British, on the verge of a declaration of war with France, to incorporate the regiment in the regular establishment. This would make Washington a regular colonel at the age of twenty-two. He did not realize that such a commission was worth thousands of pounds and was, in any case, open to so young a man only under the circumstance of the highest aristocratic birth.

As Washington awaited, half confidently, this promotion, he was notified that the Virginia Regiment was not to be incorporated but broken up. No provincial would be allowed a commission higher than captain.

George Washington resigned from the army.

Three

LOVE AND MASSACRE

(1754–1755)

During December 1754, for an annual rent of fifteen thousand pounds of tobacco, Washington rented Mount Vernon and the eighteen resident slaves from the widow of his half brother Lawrence. He had determined to become a planter. Although, as he put it, "my inclinations are [still] strongly bent to arms," he spurned the suggestion of the new British commander, Governor Horatio Sharpe of Maryland, that he serve as adviser on conditions over the mountains. The title of colonel offered him was to be purely honorary. He wrote, "You must entertain a very contemptible opinion of my weakness."

Washington's existence at Mount Vernon was being troubled and made fascinating by the woman to whom he wrote, when he was old and celebrated, that none of the subsequent events of his career "nor all of them together have been able to eradicate from my mind those happy moments, the happiest of my life, which I have enjoyed in your company." What surely was the most passionate love of Washington's life had dark overtones: Sally was married, married to his neighbor and close friend George William Fairfax.

Washington's love was no flash fire that burns away quickly. He had first met Sally when she was eighteen and he was sixteen, and she had come to Belvoir as a bride. Her two years' seniority must then have created a significant gap, but the sixteen-year-old grew into the impressive giant whose physical and military adventures electrified all Virginia. The exact nature of their relationship cannot be defined. Washington was to write Sally that he recollected "a thousand tender passages"; and a mutual female friend admonished Washington, just before his defeat at Fort Necessity, to seek "some unknown she that may recompense you for all your trials" and make him abandon "pleasing reflections on the hours past." Whatever transpired did not break Washington's friendship with Sally's husband; the suitor remained welcome at Belvoir.

Unlike the Fairfax family into which she married, Sally Cary (as she had been) was an American product. She was descended from one of the richest and most cultivated families in Virginia. The only picture of her that remains is a primitive daub, yet it indicates a high forehead; dark brows that arch out over large and deep-set dark eyes; a nose that in the classic manner continues the line of her brow; a long neck, and sloping shoulders. She had, as Washington wrote her, "mirth, good humor . . . and what else?" She seems to have been driven by her overpowering admirer into a somewhat desperate coquetry. Washington's surviving communications to her are those of a complaining lover who is being taught by experience how impossible it is for him to revive what he has once known. She forbids him to write her letters, but if he withdraws, she comes forward, writing him a saucy letter of her own, keeping him forever off balance.

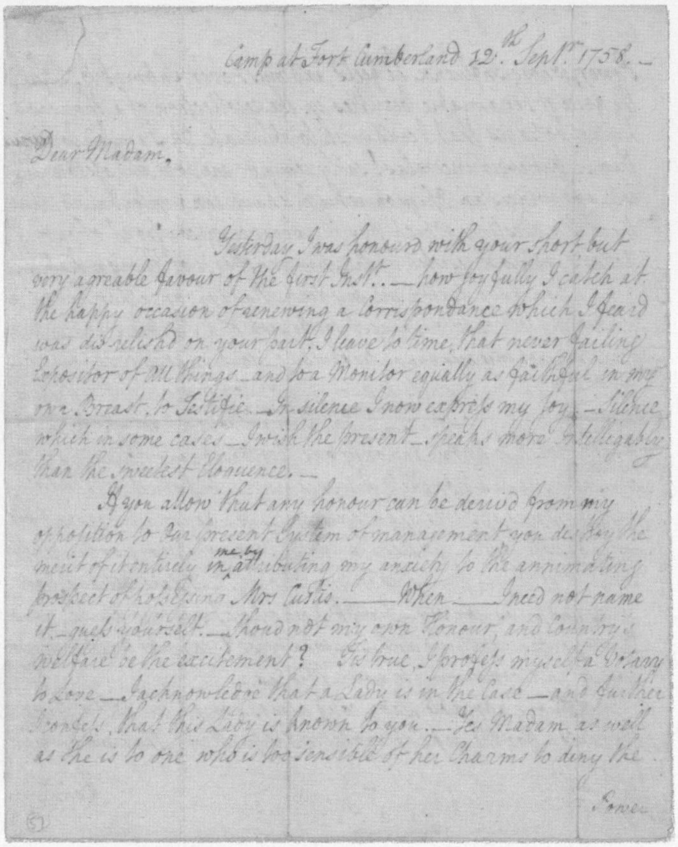

Camp at Fort Cumberland 12th. Sept. 1758.—

Dear Madam,

Yesterday I was honourd with your short but very agreable favour of the first Inst.— how joyfully I catch at the happy occasion of renewing a Corrispondance which I feard was disrelishd on your part, I leave to time, that never failing Expositor of All things—and to a Monitor equally as faithful in my own Breast, to Testifie.—In silence I now express my Joy.—Silence which in some cases—I wish the present—speaks more Intelligably than the sweetest Eloquence.—

If you allow that any honour can be deriv'd from my opposition to Our present System of management you destroy the merit of it entirely in me by attributing my anxiety to the annimating prospect of possessing Mrs Custis.——When——I need not name it—guess yourself.—Should not my own Honour, and Country's welfare be the excitement? Tis true, I profess myself a Votary to Love—I acknowledge that a Lady is in the Case—and further I confess, that this Lady is known to you.—Yes Madam, as well as she is to one who is too sensible of her Charms to deny the

Power

Above: Sally Cary Fairfax *by Duncan Smith, detail, oil on canvas, early twentieth century.*

Left: *The first page of a letter Washington wrote to Sally Fairfax less than four months before his marriage to Martha Custis.*

Although war had not yet been officially declared, France and Britain were getting more and more embroiled. Up the Potomac that flowed past Washington's lawn there sailed a British armada. In March 1755, Major General Edward Braddock arrived at Alexandria with two British regiments. When he invited the neighborhood to a review, Sally and George each had an ambition. Sally wished to persuade the British regular that she was the most dashing of all the ladies. George wished to attach himself to the general in a way that would unblock his military career and enable him to gain more "knowledge of the military art."

The review revealed how deeply he needed that knowledge. He had his first sight of the precision with which regular soldiers drilled, of how the crowded ranks could wheel and move, like an unrippling stream, in any direction. He had the chance to be overwhelmed by the multitudinous equipment, so much more complicated and efficient than anything he had imagined, of a well-supplied professional army.

With the commanding general, he did better than Sally. She was cut out by a Mrs. Wardrope, but Braddock had been informed that Washington knew more than anyone else about the wilderness through which the army would have to march on its objective to capture Fort Duquesne at the Forks of the Ohio. Impressed (as almost everybody always was) by the fiery and grave Colonial, Braddock set up a meeting to determine Washington's part in the campaign.

On the appointed day, just as Washington was about to set out for Alexandria, there was a sound of hooves on the Mount Vernon driveway and in dashed his mother. She had heard of her son's intentions. She mourned that he would go into danger while neglecting his duty to her. As Washington listened to her voice and responded as soothingly as he could, he saw the clock hand advance, revealing him ever more grievously late for the appointment on which he believed his whole future might hang. However, he could not bring himself to turn his back on his mother. Finally, she herself stamped angrily out. Then he got in touch again with Braddock, who proved not to have been offended. Since the general could not offer Washington any rank he considered suitable, Washington agreed to serve at headquarters with no rank, as a volunteer aide.

> What surely was the most passionate love of Washington's life had dark overtones: Sally was married, married to his neighbor and close friend George William Fairfax.

Braddock was having the greatest difficulty procuring the supplies and horses that were necessary to get his army across the mountains. Although Washington himself complained that you could as easily raise the dead as raise the force of Virginia, he became angry when Braddock cursed out the Colonials. "We have," he wrote, "frequent disputes on this head, which are maintained with warmth on both sides, especially on his, who is incapable of arguing without it, or giving up any point he asserts, let it be ever so incompatible with reason."

Braddock enjoyed arguing. On closer acquaintance, more than ever taken with Washington, he promised that once the campaign was successfully concluded, he would secure for the young Colonial "preferment" in the regular army "agreeable to my wishes." But the regular did not listen to Washington's warnings that "the *Canadian* French" would not fight like the French in Europe, and that the Indians had their own ways. Braddock felt only disdain for irregular forces, white or red. The possible Indian allies which the English agents painfully scratched up for him were rebuffed.

Washington, who had cut his own wheel track across the mountains, could not help being impressed with the smooth, elegantly graded, elaborately bridged boulevard which the British engineers were creating—but he knew that their slow advance could not possibly carry the army to Fort Duquesne before winter. The Colonial's protests were cut short by his becoming so "excessively ill" (probably with dysentery) that he had to be altogether left behind. His physical suffering and fear that he would miss the capture of Fort Duquesne were heightened by Sally's refusal to keep in touch.

Although far from recovered, Washington finally undertook a painful trip forward in a wagon. He rocked queasily past the site of Fort Necessity; the place of the Jumonville affair; and beyond into territory his little force had not reached. The British were now—he later claimed they followed a suggestion he had made—traveling more lightly, speeding the engineers. Washington caught up with the army two miles from the Monongahela and twelve from Fort Duquesne.

The next day, July 9, 1755, was to be the most catastrophic in all Anglo-American history. But Washington's concern at dawn was only over finding a way by which he could, without too much pain, ride a horse so that he could be present at what he foresaw as the investiture of Fort Duquesne. By tying pillows to his saddle, he managed to join the aides around Braddock. The most dangerous maneuver the officers anticipated was a double crossing of the Monongahela. This was achieved against no opposition with professional snap and skill.

WASHINGTON

A STRONG CONSTITUTION

THERE IS NO FIGURE IN AMERICAN HISTORY more clearly defined in the imagination than George Washington. We recall his iconic image instantly when we hear his name: uncommonly tall, unusually powerful, composed even in the heat of battle. Even the image of his famous silhouette, taken at the Constitutional Convention, brings to mind the awe-inspiring characteristics we associate with the leader of the American Revolution. Yet during his young adulthood he cut a very different figure than the stoic symbol portrayed by John Quincy Adams Ward on the steps of Wall Street's Federal Hall. His legendary frame, ravaged by illness, more resembled that of Ichabod Crane from W. Irving's famous tale than that of the marble and bronze hero of the American imagination. "Tall and lanky" is a clearer description of his physical stature before the Revolution.

It was a miracle that Washington survived his early twenties to lead America to freedom in the American Revolution later in life. Washington contracted smallpox in 1751 at the age of nineteen, while he was in Barbados with his half brother Lawrence, who was dying of tuberculosis. Thanks to his powerful constitution, he fought off the disease and survived, strengthening his immune system against it later on. (Although this more than likely saved his life during the Revolution, it is the most probable reason he could not have children.)

George Washington on his white horse, artist unknown, watercolor, c. 1830.

Washington not only survived smallpox, but a year earlier caught malaria, from which he often suffered feverish outbreaks throughout his life. He treated these outbreaks by consuming large amounts of quinine, which is believed to have permanently damaged his hearing and which worsened with age until he was nearly deaf at the end of his life. Dysentery almost killed him on the Braddock Expedition as a result of poor food supplies due to the British command's policy to pay minimal prices to the Colonials for meat. This policy ensured that quality meat would be sold to higher bidders, leaving nothing but tainted meat for the Continental army. He also suffered from typhoid, influenza, staphylococcus, and pneumonia. Rickets left a clear mark on the young man, withering his body and leaving him with a concave chest. It is unlikely he would have survived the Revolution without these experiences.

Disease was rampant among the Continental army. More American soldiers died from disease during the Revolutionary War than from gunfire. On the British prison ships that were located on New York's East River alone, an estimated 11,500 Colonial soldiers died from disease, famine, and exposure. This is approximately three times the number of colonial soldiers killed in every battle of the war combined. Smallpox followed armies like the plague it was—and with deadly accuracy—unlike the weaponry of the day. Both the Continental and British armies lost more men through illness than through military action.

While no one has ever questioned that Washington suffered greatly during the war, it was mostly due to undisciplined soldiers and to Congress's inability to act. Physically, aside from the frequent nagging toothaches, he experienced the healthiest and most robust period of his life during the war. Immune to many of the diseases that killed many of his soldiers and officers alike, Washington showed almost superhuman strength and fortitude throughout the campaign. As he said, "Tho' I was blessed with a good constitution, I was of a short-lived family."

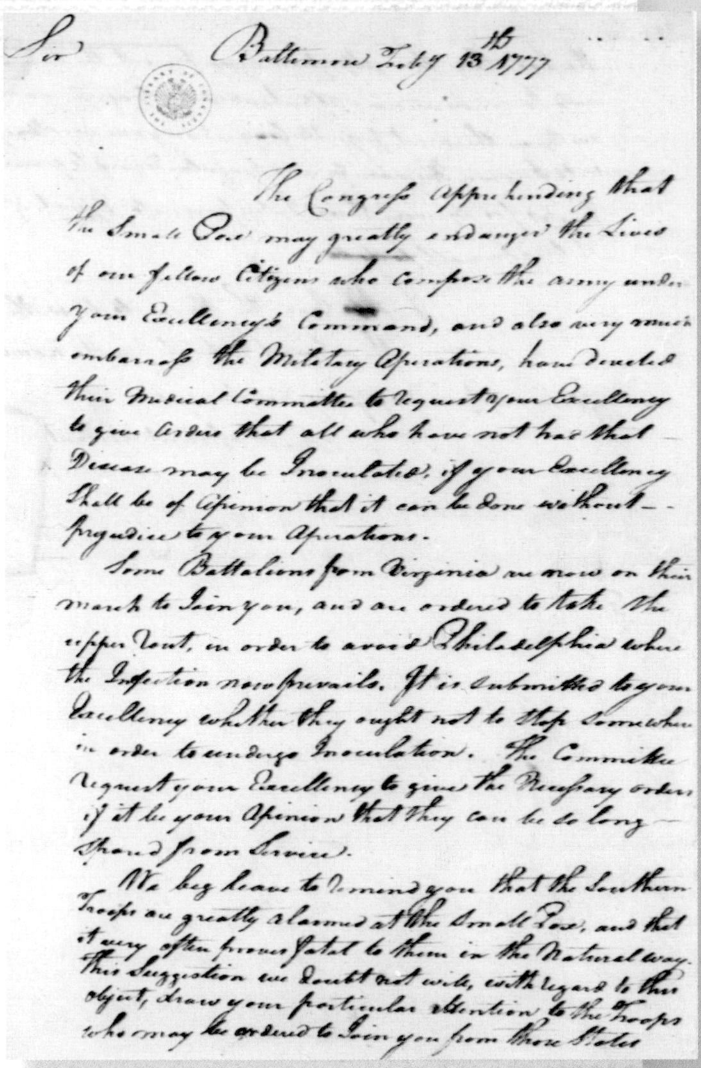

Sir Baltimore Feby 13th 1777

The Congress apprehending that the Small Pox may greatly endanger the Lives of our fellow Citizens who compose the army under your Excellency's Command, and also very much embarrass the Military Operations, have directed their Medical Committee to request your Excellency to give Orders that all who have not had that Disease may be Inoculated, if your Excellency Shall be of Opinion that it can be done without prejudice to your Operations.

Some Battalions from Virginia are now on their march to Join you, and are ordered to take the upper Rout, in order to avoid Philadelphia where the Infection now prevails. It is Submitted to your Excellency whether they ought not to Stop Somewhere in order to undergo Inoculation. The Committee request your Excellency to give the Necessary orders, if it be your Opinion that they can be So long Spared from Service.

We beg leave to remind you that the Southern Troops are greatly alarmed at the Small Pox, and that it very often proves fatal to them in the Natural way. This Suggestion we doubt not will, with regard to this object, draw your particular Attention to the Troops who may be ordered to Join you from those States

This letter from the Continental Congress Medical Committee to George Washington, dated February 13, 1777, urges inoculation of the troops against smallpox.

From an early age, Washington was convinced he was not long for this world. His grandfather lived to the age of thirty-seven, his father passed at forty-nine, and his brother Lawrence died at thirty-four. His mother, Mary Ball Washington, however, lived to be eighty-one years old, and her son inherited his mother's strong physical attributes. Both Washington and his mother were as exceptional on horseback as they were on the dance floor. Presidential balls would not end until every lady in the room had had two dances with the graceful George Washington.

The army now proceeded over relatively level ground in a twelve-foot-wide clearing cut by the engineers through thick forest. A shot that rang out ahead was followed by Indian whooping and then the sounds of much firing, which indicated that the advance guard was heavily engaged. Braddock, with Washington beside him, led the main column quickly forward. They had not gone far before the clearing filled with red-coated soldiers rushing towards them in terrified flight. The fugitives dashed headlong into the advancing reinforcements, shattering all order; and at the same time the sound of firing came running down the woods on both flanks. No enemy was visible, but the men in the road began to fall in bloody heaps. Panic now took over completely.

The British regulars were entirely untrained in fighting out of formation, as individual men. Now haphazardly huddled together in the middle of the long, thin, exposed clearing that was the road, they hysterically shot down their companions in anguished efforts to protect themselves from an unseen and deadly foe. The officers could think of nothing but to try to get the men into an orderly parade-ground formation. Braddock indignantly denied Washington's request that he be allowed to lead the provincial troops into the woods "and engage the enemy in their own way."

The officers on their horses were perfect targets. One after another they went down. Washington's horse was shot from under him. He leapt on another. Bullets tore his coat. Braddock toppled over. Washington's second horse crumpled; his hat was shot off. However, as he later wrote, "the miraculous care of Providence . . . protected me beyond all human expectation." He was now "the only person then left to distribute the [wounded] general's orders." This he was hardly able to do because his sickness was rising upon him. The dead and dying lay in piles. The survivors, no officers being left to stop them, were at long last saving themselves by running away. Having loaded Braddock into "a small covered cart," Washington led into retreat those men who could move and had remained to be led.

Since the general could not offer Washington any rank he considered suitable, Washington agreed to serve at headquarters with no rank, as a volunteer aide.

The wounded Braddock ordered Washington to ride back forty miles through the night to summon reinforcements. Washington's amazing body summoned up the necessary strength, although he recalled that illness, fatigue, and anxiety had left him "in a manner wholly unfit for the execution of the duty. . . . The shocking scenes which presented themselves in this night march are not to be described. The dead, the dying, the groans, lamentations, and cries along the road of the wounded for help . . . were enough to pierce a heart of adamant, the gloom and horror of which was not a little increased by the imperious darkness occasioned by the close shade of thick woods." At times, he had to crawl on hands and knees to find the road. Washington reached his objective, but the reinforcements he had been ordered to call forward were too terrified to march.

Braddock died. What was left of the British army fled to Philadelphia. Washington staggered to Mount Vernon, too "weak and feeble" even to call at Belvoir. From Sally, a note: "I must accuse you of great unkindness in refusing us the pleasure of seeing you this night." If he did not appear on the morrow, she and the other ladies would try to see "if our legs would not carry us to Mount Vernon."

Four

DESPERATION AND DISILLUSIONMENT

(1755–1759)

By his compatriots, Washington was regarded as the hero of Braddock's defeat. Had he not urged the regular general to adopt a different method of warfare? When finally permitted, had he not led the survivors out of the Indian ambush? His reputation now passed beyond the borders of Virginia, becoming continental. Benjamin Franklin was reported to have praised him, and a preacher intoned that God had surely preserved the youth during the holocaust for some great service to his country. The British regular officers who had served with him endorsed his "courage and resolution." But the official British inquiry into the causes of the defeat reached a conclusion opposite to that of Washington's admirers: the army's disastrous panic was attributed to Colonials, men like Washington, who had persuaded the common soldiers that if they fought Indians in the only way that it was correct to fight, they would be annihilated.

The British command had had their fill of the Ohio wilderness. Moving their American operations further north, they abandoned the area west of Virginia to the French and France's Indian allies. This left completely unprotected Virginia's settled frontier: the Shenandoah Valley between the Alleghenies and the Blue Ridge, where Washington had, as a surveyor, started his career.

The valley now boasted one town, Winchester, whose sixty or so houses (mostly log cabins) were close to passes that led through the Blue Ridge to well-settled Virginia. More than fifty miles northwest and at the mouth of passes through the Alleghenies from the French-held wilderness was Fort Cumberland. The rest of the valley was dotted with isolated homesteads which it became Washington's task, during two desperate years, to defend from hit-and-run Indian raids.

The Virginia Assembly created their own army, variously authorized between twelve hundred and two thousand men. Washington, now twenty-two, was elected "Colonel of the Virginia Regiment and Commander in Chief of all Virginia forces." Although he still expressed doubts as to his competence, he felt that, since his reputation was at stake, he should hold all the reins in his own hands. He should not be forced to rely on others. He wished to appoint his own officers and procure his own supplies. Delighted to pass the buck, the Assembly handed the whole war effort over to Washington. He was thus enrolled in a school of experience that would in many ways prepare him for the world-shaking task he was to undertake almost twenty years later.

In a major particular, Washington was worse off than he was subsequently to be. During the Revolution, most of the troops believed in what they were fighting for. This was not now the case. Virginia's draft laws were so unfairly slanted against the poor that those men who were caught felt active resentment. Desertion was always to be a problem during Washington's military years. Now he learned in the

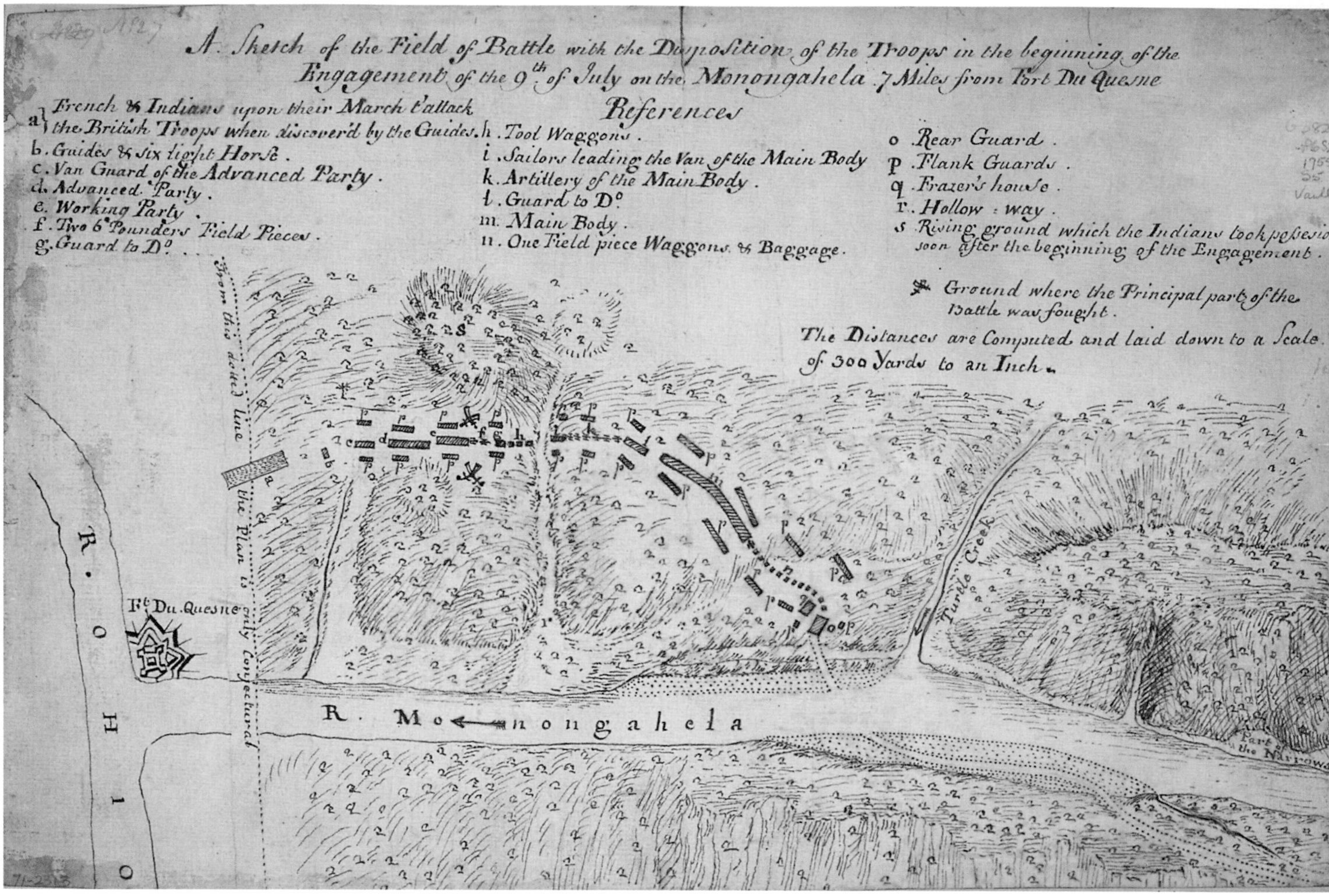

A sketch of the field of battle showing the disposition of the troops at the beginning of the July 9, 1755, engagement on the Monongahela, seven miles from Fort Duquesne.

most difficult of possible schools how to hold men by a combination of authority, violence, threats, persuasion, and inspiring leadership.

In the area of supply, Washington met many problems he was to meet again. Laws existed which he could theoretically use, but they were in practice almost useless. He was always short of money. Efforts to requisition wagons resulted only in carts and horses vanishing into the woods. To further complicate matters, Virginia produced no manufactured goods. Many necessities had to be gotten from Pennsylvania, and the Pennsylvanians would not accept the money Virginia printed. To keep Washington's cantonments populated, fed, and armed required eternal labor, eternal attention to even the smallest detail.

During the shank of the fighting season that followed Braddock's defeat, there were some Indian raids—about seventy settlers were killed or reported missing—but the frontier was not really aflame. Washington's bitterest problem was grounded on the pretensions of the English in relation to the Colonials, and on rivalries between the colonies themselves.

Although Fort Cumberland was for Virginia the necessary advance post, it was over the border in Maryland. There lurked in the fort a middle-aged Marylander, John Dagworthy. He was only a captain, but he insisted that, since his commission was in the British regular army, he outranked even the commander in chief of all Virginia. Supported by Governor Sharpe of Maryland, he gave orders to Washington's troops and commandeered the supplies Washington had so painfully raised.

Washington was too outraged to stay with his troops at Fort Cumberland. And his indignation was so strongly echoed by Virginia's political leaders that Dinwiddie became worried lest the pretensions of the low-ranked regular from Maryland might bring Virginia's war effort to a halt. He wrote the temporary British commander in chief in America, Governor William Shirley of Massachusetts, that Dagworthy would have to be curbed. Undoubtedly at the urging of Washington, whose energetic services he had come to consider indispensable, Dinwiddie added that future such contretemps could be avoided by enrolling the Virginia Regiment (if only for the duration of this conflict) in the regular army.

During February 1756, after winter had stilled all forest warfare, Washington rode for Massachusetts to persuade Shirley. The youthful colonel advanced in a style suited to his rank and the prestige of Virginia. His two servants were dressed in livery colored to go with the Washington coat of arms, and he and a companion wore the uniform he had himself designed for his regiment: scarlet and blue decorated with gold and silver lace. Yet when he reached Philadelphia, he stared in amazement. He had never before seen a city. Like any other newly arrived countryman, he went on a shopping spree.

In Boston, Shirley condescended to take some of Washington's money at cards. He did squash Dagworthy's pretensions, but in a way—by declaring him not really a regular—that created no precedent. Thus, since the governor ignored the suggestion that the Virginia Regiment be taken into the British service, Washington was still in the position where any authentic regular officer—even a mere lieutenant—could order him around. Furthermore, Shirley notified the man whom Virginia had commissioned commander in chief that his old enemy, Governor Sharpe of Maryland, was to be given a command that included the Virginia forces.

Even the British regulars with whom Washington had served agreed that he would be justified in resigning and returning to private life. An American view was that Washington had received from Shirley such unfair treatment as was always to be expected from "persons conversant at the courts of princes."

> Washington, now twenty-two, was elected "Colonel of the Virginia Regiment and Commander in Chief of all Virginia forces."

Virginia was as annoyed as Washington. The Assembly repudiated Sharpe's pretensions by voting that their tiny force had been raised for local defense exclusively and had no connection with any other army. Washington was again in the saddle, a situation he soon had great cause to regret.

When spring reopened the fighting season, his method of defense—garrisoning little forts a day's march apart—proved absolutely useless. The Indians passed invisibly between the forts to fall on isolated homesteads. Survivors of burnings and scalpings flooded into Washington's headquarters at Winchester.

"The supplicating tears of the women and moving petitions of the men," Washington cried out, "melt me into such deadly sorrow that I solemnly declare, if I know my own mind, I could offer myself a willing sacrifice to the butchering enemy provided that would contribute to the peoples' ease. . . . If bleeding, dying! would glut their insatiate revenge, I would be a willing offering to savage fury, and die by inches to save a people!"

J. DeMare
WASHINGTON AT THE AGE OF TWENTY-FIVE
From a miniature on ivory presented by Washington to his niece Harriet,
and now belonging to her daughters family.
I am Sir Yr Most Obedt Hble Servt
Fort Loudoun 10th Septr 1757
Go Washington

A portrait of Washington at age twenty-five, in 1757, by Thomas Addis Emmet.

Washington called for reinforcement from low-country militia and then, having had his first experience with this amateur military arm, wished he had not sent out the call. Militiamen arrived by the hundreds, ate up his long-hoarded provisions, refused discipline and undermined the discipline of his own troops, and then in response to rumors that the Indians were again on the warpath, fled in disarray back across the Blue Ridge. Washington penned the first of hundreds of letters in which he was to beg authorities—now Dinwiddie, later the Continental Congress—to forget about militia and strengthen the regular forces—now the Virginia Regiment, eventually the Continental Army.

The reaction in Virginia's capital to Washington's diatribe against the militia was not what he expected. Since the militia companies were in essence political clubs, the officers had the ears of legislators. Solid yeomen with a high opinion of themselves, they had resented being ordered around by Washington's officers, whom they considered pretentious whippersnappers wallowing in vice. The spirited young warriors were indeed not living according to respectable bourgeois canons. Their colonel drank with them even if he did not drink to excess; he thoroughly enjoyed gambling; and when he returned to Winchester after an absence, he received the following message from one of his lieutenants: "I imagine you by this time plunged in the midst of delight heaven can afford, and enchanted by charms even stranger than the Cyprian dame (+ M's Nel)."

The colonel came vigorously to the defense of his regiment, mourning (with his tongue in his cheek) that the Assembly had not supplied them with a minister.

Washington and his regiment were highly vulnerable to criticism because they had been assigned an impossible task. A force many times larger could not have defended so wide a frontier from the endlessly mobile Indians. As was again to be the case during much of the Revolution, the amazing thing was not that Washington failed to do better, but that he managed to keep from being discharged as a failure, that he managed to keep an army in the field at all.

Washington's greatest strength was the passionate allegiance of his officers. Despite his training by the Fairfaxes, he had repudiated the British system that based military rank on family influence. Although he believed that men with position in their neighborhoods would be the more likely to procure recruits and then be obeyed, he tried to find among them the most able. And he was determined to base subsequent promotion entirely on merit. A captain wrote the juvenile colonel, "I have altogether depended on you for protection and am sensible that, as far as justice is on my side, I may depend on your favor."

> "The supplicating tears of the women and moving petitions of the men," Washington cried out, "melt me into such deadly sorrow that I solemnly declare, if I know my own mind, I could offer myself a willing sacrifice to the butchering enemy provided that would contribute to the peoples' ease. . . ."

But Washington had not yet learned the unwisdom of attacking his civilian superiors for deficiencies beyond anyone's power to remedy. After having ridden dangerously through all the Indian-infested forests of his Shenandoah command, he wrote a horrifying report of the complete collapse of the defenses. Having thus made shockingly clear the failure of his efforts, he assigned the blame to the governor and the Assembly for not having come up with the men and supplies they had promised. His superiors, of course, tossed the blame back on him. They accused him of spending too much time away from the front lines amusing himself—he insisted he was attending to supply—and revised his strategy in a series of peremptory, humiliating (and useless) orders.

Hearing that another British professional general, Lord Loudoun, was crossing the ocean to assume the American command, Washington decided to appeal to him against the civilian authorities of the colony which the angry colonel commonly referred to as "my country." Surely this representative of the Crown would accord him justice! He sent to the Scottish peer a long letter criticizing, among others, Dinwiddie, who was also a Crown official. He then urged that an army of Colonials (presumably with him in the command) be entrusted with doing what Braddock's professional force had failed to achieve: save the frontier by driving the French from Fort Duquesne.

Supposing Loudoun had listened, would this have cemented Washington's allegiance to the Crown, thus changing the course of history? But it was, of course, impossible for the nobleman to listen to what he considered an insolent plea, in opposition to established authority, from a dubious Colonial. After Washington had journeyed to Philadelphia to see Loudoun, the peer kept him cooling his heels for weeks, and then accorded him a brief, cold interview. The local hero was not allowed to open his mouth, while the imported regular slashed his authority and dictated tactics and strategy for the Virginia Regiment. After this disillusioning interview, Washington complained, "We can't conceive that being Americans should deprive us of the benefits of being British subjects."

The Virginia draft law of 1757 was the most disastrous yet. Washington's regiment did not come within several hundred of the 1,272 authorized, and of these, four hundred were marched off by Loudoun to South Carolina. French Indians were soon burning and scalping within ten miles of Winchester. The helpless colonel tried to find comfort in "the highest consolation I am capable of feeling": his conviction that "no man that ever was employed in a public capacity has endeavored to discharge the trust reposed in him with greater honesty and more zeal for the country's interest."

With autumn, Washington became deathly ill. The dysentery he had suffered during Braddock's campaign returned with ferocity, but it did not come alone. After the death of the brother he had so passionately nursed, Washington had come down with what seemed to be Lawrence's tuberculosis. He had then recovered, but now he was seized with "violent pleuritic pains."

The army doctor, James Craik, believed that "the fate of your friends and country are in a manner dependent on your recovery." Yet he did not know what to do. What might help one malady would harm the other, and the "whole mass of blood" was "corrupted." Craik, who was to bleed Washington on his deathbed, did so now. The colonel remained so weak that he could hardly walk. He was transported to Mount Vernon, whence he piteously called for help from his neighbor Sally Fairfax.

Washington sank into the deepest dejection. Sally did not visit him as often as he wished. His hopes of making a military career in the regular army were over. In any case, he was surely dying. In January 1758, he tried to get to Williamsburg and better medical attention, but had to turn back on the road. It was March before he could reach the Virginia capital and by then his majestic physique had regained control. When a doctor told him he had nothing to fear, he suddenly discovered he was well.

Having finally planned another attack on Fort Duquesne, the British sent to the middle colonies Brigadier General John Forbes. He was to lead between six and seven thousand men, three times

Brigadier General John Forbes, artist and date unknown, oil on canvas.

Braddock's force. Since it had finally been ruled that provincial officers would no longer be commanded by regulars of inferior rank, Washington could at last serve in a royal expedition as a Virginia colonel without feeling demeaned. But he had abandoned all hope of being himself accepted as a regular, and he soon entered into a controversy with the British high command that rose in his mind to an obsession.

The route over the Alleghenies to the Ohio that Washington had pioneered and Braddock had followed started from the Potomac Valley. If further improved by Forbes's engineers, it would with peace lead the produce of the expanding West through Virginia and make Alexandria, that center nearest to Mount Vernon, the metropolis where goods brought overland would be reloaded onto oceangoing vessels. But Forbes, who had to buy his supplies in Philadelphia, saw no reason to take a sidestep in order to profit Virginia. He envisioned cutting a new road that would enter directly into Pennsylvania.

Although Washington had never explored the area involved, he was convinced that the new road would meet such insuperable geographic difficulties as would wreck the expedition. The whole scheme was a trick of the Pennsylvanians and an insult to Virginia; that Forbes would even consider it proved him a dupe "or something worse." The Virginia authorities were equally outraged. In letters to them, Washington envisioned himself as being sent across the ocean to complain to the royal government against their commander in chief.

Anxious to placate Virginia, Forbes sent an expert mediator to reason with Washington. When that failed, the British general gave the troublemaker a round scolding. But Washington remained incensed, protesting loudly concerning matters he did not understand. Although Forbes, whose principal gifts were as a supply officer, was holding the army back to complete elaborate preparations, Washington blamed the delay on the change of roads. He criticized Forbes's Indian policies in entire ignorance of major developments in the forests.

After several years of unofficial hostilities, war had finally been declared between England and France. This had unloosed the British navy, which established control of the Atlantic Ocean. One result was that the French had been unable to send to Canada the ammunition and trade goods needed to keep their Indian irregulars active and satisfied. British representatives were trying to persuade the Ohio tribes to desert an ally now so unsatisfactory. Another reason for Forbes's delay was that he was waiting for the negotiations to mature.

So little, indeed, did the Virginia colonel understand matters outside his own area that he did not even mention in his letters the British capture, hundreds of miles northward, of Fort Niagara, which cut the

French supply line to Fort Duquesne. Washington wrote passionately from one of Forbes's encampments, "All is lost! All is lost, by Heavens!" not conscious that constellations were grouping towards victory.

Forbes had every reason to dislike Washington. Yet he could not deny that the Virginian was the army's greatest expert on the wilderness and its warfare. Temporarily raised to the rank of brigadier general, Washington was given command of the advanced brigade. When two Virginia contingents, as they blundered through the wilderness, mistook each other for the enemy and started a battle, Washington rode between them, knocking up flashing guns with his sword. Fourteen were killed and twenty-six wounded, but Washington, although infinitely the most exposed, was not touched.

As winter descended, Forbes was still deep in the forest. He had just decided to wait until spring for the final attack when word came that the Indians had deserted the sheds around Fort Duquesne. Forbes decided to advance rapidly with twenty-five hundred lightly equipped men. Far ahead of the army, Washington laid out and cut part of the rough road that was now all that was needed.

On November 24, 1758, Washington camped with Forbes's reunited army, very close to Fort Duquesne. Every precaution was being taken to avoid a repetition of Braddock's disaster, when some Indians appeared making gestures of peace. They reported that they had seen "a very thick smoke . . . extending in the bottom along the Ohio." Four hours later, more news: knowing they could not defend themselves with their supply line cut and without Indian aid, the enemy had burned the fort and had disappeared down the Ohio. Thus, to what Washington admitted was his "great surprise," the seemingly unattainable objective for which he had labored so desperately during four years was achieved without the firing of a shot.

Washington wrote passionately from one of Forbes's encampments, "All is lost! All is lost, by Heavens!" not conscious that constellations were grouping towards victory.

Although part of the Virginia Regiment was assigned to garrisoning the Forks, Washington felt he could resign. The Virginia frontier was, for the foreseeable future, safe. His duty was done. Returning to Mount Vernon, he turned his back, he believed forever, on the military life. He had experienced "much that I must strive to forget."

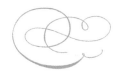

Five

GEORGE WASHINGTON'S FIRST WAR

(1753–1759)

Washington was active in the French and Indian War from the age of twenty-one to almost twenty-six. He was from the first never a follower, always a leader, even if sometimes subject to greater authority than his own. At twenty-two he became Virginia's most celebrated hero. Although often envisioned by moderns as a stuffy old man with ill-fitting false teeth, he was among the most precocious of all great Americans.

The most significant aspect of Washington's early career was that it took place at all. Every responsibility he assumed required public selection and support. When he was hardly beyond his teens, many of his associates were already convinced that his destiny was importantly linked with the destiny of America.

That his perfidious Indian guide should, even at point-blank range, have missed Washington in the wilderness seems reasonable, but it is strange that during the Braddock massacre, when every other mounted officer was struck, he remained uninjured. And then there was the time he rode between the two firing columns, striking up the guns with his sword. In subsequent years, during the Revolution, Washington was again and again to take the most foolhardy risks, but the bullets, although they tore his clothes and killed his horses, never touched his body.

Washington's seeming invulnerability to gunfire, more suited to mythology than factual history, was observed—he commented on it wonderingly himself—but it was only the most exotic aspect of that charisma which brought him so early the confidence and respect of his fellow men. Too early, indeed, for he was entrusted with responsibilities beyond his ability to handle. Not only did his inexperience make him sometimes militarily inept, but he never understood the wider implications of the situations in which he was involved. Although in moments of reflection conscious of his inadequacies, in action he could be rash, brash, impolitic, over-self-confident. He made dreadful mistakes.

Washington's seeming invulnerability to gunfire, more suited to mythology than factual history, was observed—he commented on it wonderingly himself—but it was only the most exotic aspect of that charisma which brought him so early the confidence and respect of his fellow men.

Among the reasons why, when he tripped so often, Washington was never allowed truly to fall, was that Virginia's war effort, even the British war effort in the Ohio Valley, needed his tremendous energy. Despite

INVENTING WASHINGTON

MASON LOCKE'S FAMOUS BIOGRAPHY

MASON LOCKE ("PARSON") WEEMS WAS an American book agent and author who is best known as the source of some apocryphal stories about George Washington, including the famous tale of the cherry tree. Nowadays, any biographer taking such liberties with the facts about a subject's life might be excoriated as a fraud—but in the nineteenth century, when *A History of the Life and Death, Virtues and Exploits of General George Washington* became an instant bestseller, such a book was looked upon as entertaining as well as morally instructive to the country's youth. In his book *Inventing George Washington* (New York: HarperCollins, 2011), the historian and critic Edward G. Lengel refers to Weems as "the father of popular history . . . a superb storyteller," and describes his tone as that of "an amiable grandfather with children at his knee." Weems's cherry tree story follows, along with another tale he very likely invented, involving Washington discovered on his knees in prayer at Valley Forge.

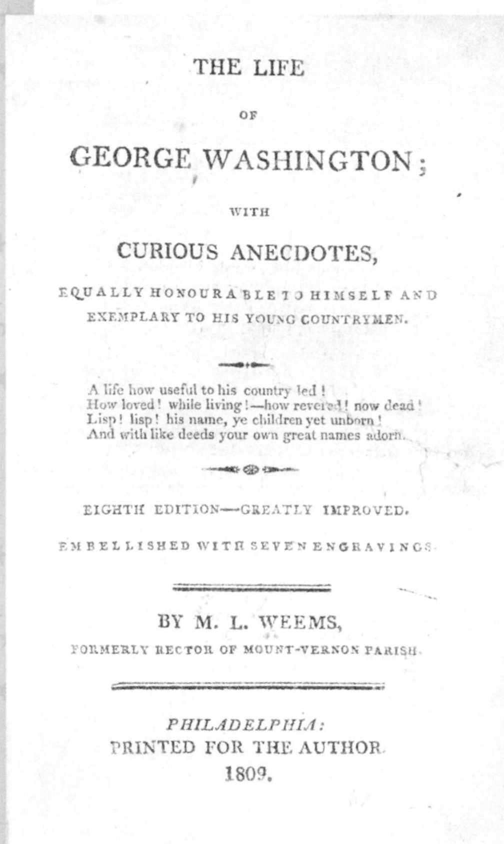
THE LIFE

OF

GEORGE WASHINGTON;

WITH

CURIOUS ANECDOTES,

EQUALLY HONOURABLE TO HIMSELF AND EXEMPLARY TO HIS YOUNG COUNTRYMEN.

A life how useful to his country led!
How loved! while living!—how revered! now dead!
Lisp! lisp! his name, ye children yet unborn!
And with like deeds your own great names adorn.

EIGHTH EDITION—GREATLY IMPROVED.

EMBELLISHED WITH SEVEN ENGRAVINGS.

BY M. L. WEEMS,

FORMERLY RECTOR OF MOUNT-VERNON PARISH.

PHILADELPHIA:
PRINTED FOR THE AUTHOR.
1809.

The title page of Mason Locke ("Parson") Weems's adulatory, often fanciful biography of Washington, published in 1809.

Some, when they look up to the oak, whose giant arms throw a darkening shade over distant acres, or whose single trunk lays the keel of a man of war, cannot bear to hear of the time when this mighty plant was but an acorn, which a pig could have demolished. But others, who know their value, like to learn the soil and situation which best produces such noble trees. Thus, parents that are wise, will listen, well pleased, while I relate how moved the steps of the youthful Washington, whose single worth far outweighs all the oaks of Bashan and the red spicy cedars of Lebanon. Yes, they will listen delighted while I tell of their Washington in the days of his youth, when his little feet were swift towards the nests of birds; or when, wearied in the chase of the butterfly, he laid him down on his grassy couch and slept, while ministering spirits, with their roseate wings, fanned his glowing cheeks, and kissed his lips of innocence with that fervent love which makes the Heaven!

Never did the wise Ulysses take more pains with his beloved Telemachus, than did Mr. Washington with George, to inspire him with an early love of truth. "Truth, George," said he, "is the loveliest quality of youth. I would ride fifty miles, my son, to see the little boy whose heart is so honest, and his lips so pure, that we may depend on every word he says. O how lovely does such a child appear in the eyes of every body! His parents dote on him. His relations glory in him. They are constantly praising him to their children, whom they beg to imitate him. They are often sending for him to visit them; and receive him, when he comes, with as much joy as if he were a little angel, come to set pretty examples to their children.

"But, Oh, how different, George, is the case with the boy who is so given to lying, that nobody can believe a word he says! He is looked at with aversion wherever he goes, and parents dread to see him come among their children. Oh, George! My son! Rather than see you come to this pass, dear as you are to my heart, gladly would I assist to nail you up in your little coffin, and follow you to your grave. Hard, indeed, would it be to me to give up my son, whose little feet are always so ready to run about with me, and whose fondly looking eyes and sweet prattle make so large a part of my happiness. But still I would give him up, rather than see him a common liar."

"Pa," said George very seriously, "do I ever tell lies?"

"No, George, I thank God you do not, my son; and I rejoice in the hope you never will. At least, you shall never, from me, have cause to be guilty of so shameful a thing. Many parents, indeed, even compel their children to this vile practice, by barbarously beating them for every little fault. Hence, on the next offense, the little terrified creature slips out a lie just to escape the rod. But as to yourself, George, you know I have always told you, and now tell you again, that, whenever by accident, you do anything wrong, which must often be the case, as you are but a poor little boy yet, without experience or knowledge, you must never tell a falsehood to conceal it; but come bravely up, my son, like a little man, and tell me of it: and, instead of beating you, George, I will but the more honor and love you for it, my dear."

Mason Locke Weems, *artist unknown, oil on canvas attached to plywood, c. 1810.*

This, you'll say, was sowing good seed! Yes, it was. And the crop, thank God, was, as I believe it ever will be, where a man acts the true parent, that is, the Guardian Angel, by his child.

The following anecdote is a case in point. It is too valuable to be lost, and too true to be doubted; for it was communicated to me by the same excellent lady to whom I am indebted for the last.

"When George," said she, "was about six years old, he was made the wealthy master of a hatchet, of which, like most little boys, he was immoderately fond, and was constantly going about chopping everything that came in his way. One day, in the garden, where he often amused himself hacking his mother's pea-sticks, he unluckily tried the edge of his hatchet on the body of a beautiful young English cherry tree, which he barked so terribly, that I don't believe the tree ever got the better of it. The next morning the old gentleman, finding out what had befallen his tree, which, by the by, was a great favorite, came into the house; and with much warmth asked for the mischievous author, declaring at the same time, that he would not have taken five guineas for his tree. Nobody could tell him anything about it. Presently, George and his hatchet made their appearance. "George," said his father, "do you know who killed that beautiful little cherry tree yonder in the garden?" This was a tough question, and George staggered under it for a moment but quickly recovered himself. And looking at his father, with the sweet face of youth brightened with the inexpressible charm of all-conquering truth, he bravely cried out, "I can't tell a lie, Pa; you know I can't tell a lie. I did cut it with my hatchet." "Run to my arms, you dearest boy," cried his father in transports, "run to my arms; glad am I, George, that you killed my tree; for you have paid me for it a thousand fold. Such an act of heroism in my son is more worth than a thousand trees, though blossomed with silver, and their fruits of purest gold."

★ ★ ★ ★ ★

I have often been informed by Colonel B. Temple (of King William County, Virginia), who was one of his aids in the French and Indian War, that he has frequently known Washington, on the Sabbath, to read scriptures and pray with his regiment, in the absence of the chaplain; and also that on sudden and unexpected visits into his marquee he has, more than once, found him on his knees at his devotions.

The Reverend Mr. Lee Massey, long a rector of Washington's parish, and from early life his intimate, has frequently assured me that "he never knew so constant an attendant on church as Washington. And his behavior in the house of God," added my reverend friend, "was so deeply reverential that it produced the happiest effects on my congregation and greatly assisted me in my moralizing labors. No company ever withheld him from church. I have often been at Mount Vernon, on the Sabbath morning, when his breakfast table was filled with guests. But to him they furnished no pretext for neglecting his God and losing the satisfaction of setting a good example. For instead of staying at home, out of false complaisance to them, he used constantly to invite them to accompany him."

His secretary, Judge Harrison, has frequently been heard to say that "whenever the general could be spared from camp on the Sabbath, he never failed riding out to some neighboring church to join those who were publicly worshipping the Great Creator."

And while he resided in Philadelphia, as president of the United States, his constant and cheerful attendance on divine service was such as to convince every reflecting mind that he deemed no levee so honorable as that of his Almighty Maker; no pleasures equal to those of devotion; and no business a sufficient excuse for neglecting his supreme benefactor.

In the winter of '77, while Washington, with the American army, lay encamped at Valley Forge, a certain good old friend, of the respectable family and name of Potts, if I mistake not, had occasion to pass through the woods near headquarters. Treading in his way along the venerable grove, suddenly he heard the sound of a human voice, which, as he advanced, increased on his ear; and at length became like the voice of one speaking much in earnest. As he approached the spot with a cautious step, whom should he behold in a dark natural bower of ancient oaks, but the commander in chief of the American armies on his knees at prayer! Motionless with surprise, friend Potts continued on the place till the general, having ended his devotions, arose; and, with a countenance of angelic serenity, retired to headquarters. Friend Potts then went home, and on entering his parlor called out to his wife, "Sarah! My dear Sarah! All's well! All's well! George Washington will yet prevail!"

"What's the matter, Isaac?" replied she, "thee seems moved."

"Well, if I seem moved, 'tis no more than what I really am. I have this day seen what I never expected. Thee knows that I always thought that the sword and the gospel were utterly inconsistent, and that no man could be a soldier and a Christian at the same time; but George Washington has this day convinced me of my mistake."

He then related what he had seen, and concluded with this prophetical remark: "If George Washington be not a man of God, I am greatly deceived—and still more shall I be deceived, if God do not, through him, work out a great salvation for America."

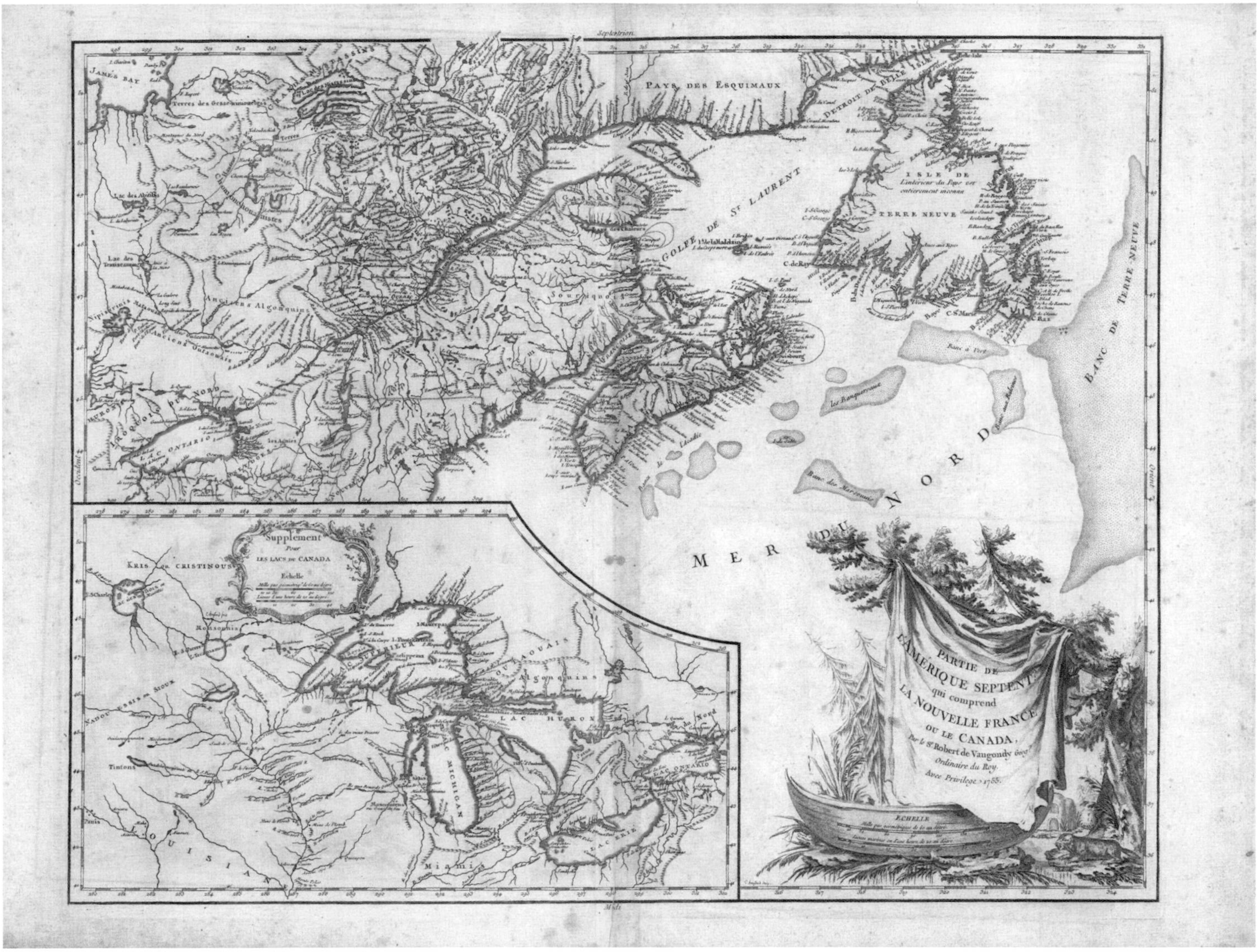

This 1755 map of Canada, or "La Nouvelle France," drawn by Sr. Robert de Vaugondy was owned by Washington.

the several extremely severe illnesses he suffered, his body and his drive remained those of a giant. Even if they found him upon occasion enraging, the Virginia authorities could not get on without him; nor, once they entered the wilderness, could the toplofty British professional command. Although his efforts to protect the inhabitants of the Shenandoah Valley succeeded so inadequately, the survivors elected him, in the middle of the war, their representative to the Virginia Assembly.

Washington was already showing abilities that seemed inconsistent with his rashness and fierce energy. One of his fellow veterans wrote, "Method and exactness are the *forte* of his character." Acting as his own supply officer, he took infinite pains to collect every obtainable shred of food or ammunition, and to see that it was used where it would serve best. Although he drank and gambled and (we gather) wenched as did his officers, he was known as a stern disciplinarian in military matters. It seems amazing to

The Course of the Ohio or Alliganey River and its Branches are laid down from Surveys and Draughts made on the Spot by Mr. Gist and others in the Years 1751. 2. 3 & 4.
From Williamsburg to York 12 E. Hampton 24 S.E. Norfolk cross at H. 42 S.E. Delawar 30 NW. Newcastle 50 NW. Hobbs Hole 67 N. Port Royal 93 NW. Fredericksburg 107 N. Alexandria 168 N.
The Road from Williamsburg Contd. to Lord Fairfax 186 NW. Winchester 194 NW. Wills's Creek 281 NW. Fort Necessity in The Great Meadow 346 NW. Fort du Quesne at the Conflux of the Monongahela and Ohio Rivers 392 NW
From Fredericksburg to Port Royal 20 S.E. Hobbs Hole 51 S.E. Alexandria 60 N. Lord Fairfax 76 NW. Winchester 84 NW. Wills's Creek 171 NW. Fort Necessity 238 NW. Fort du Quesne on the Ohio 261 NW.
From Alexandria to Lord Fairfax 78 E. Winchester 86 E. Wills's Creek 173 E.N. Fort Necessity in the Great Meadows 238 E.N. Fort du Quesne at the Conflux of the Monongahela and Ohio Rivers 283 E.N.
These Distances with the Course of the Roads on the Map I carefully collected on the Spot and entered them in my Journal, from whence they are now inserted
J. Dalrymple
London Jany. ye 1st. 1755
The Longitude from London added in this Impression is deduced from that of New York in 74. 04
P E N S Y
V I R G I N
N O R T H C A R O L
AUGUSTA
ALBEMARLE
LUNENBURG COUNTY
GRANVILLE COUNTY
ANSON COUNTY
CULPEPPER COUNTY
ORANGE
CUMBERLAND COUNTY
AMELIA COUNTY
FREDERICK
BRUNSWICK
The Ohio or Fair River
Great Konhaway
Woods River and New River
Green Briar River
Monongahela River
THE ALLEGANY RIDGE OF MOUNTAINS
THE NORTH RIDGE
THE BLUE RIDGE
JACKSONS MOUNTAINS
Laurel Thickets
Meadow Mountain
The Yadkin or Deep River
Staunton River
Dan River
Cole River
Louisa River
Clinch River
The Line between VIRGINIA and NORTH CAROLINA, from Peters Creek to Steep Rock Creek being 90 Miles and 280 Poles, was Survey'd in 1749.
By William Churton, and Daniel Weldon of NORTH CAROLINA, Joshua Fry, and Peter Jefferson of VIRGINIA.
Scale of Miles

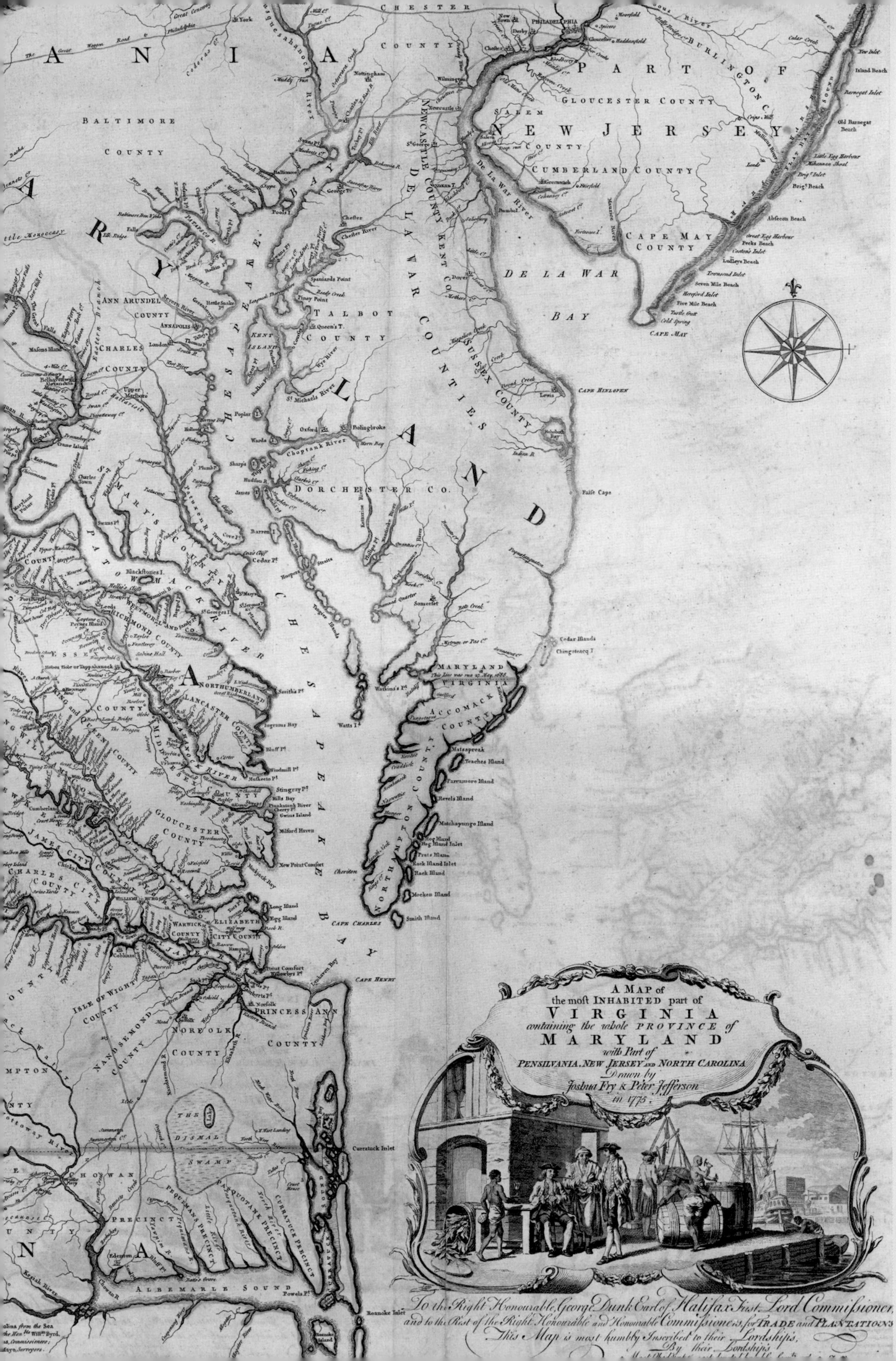

This map of the most populous part of Virginia, drawn by Joshua Fry and Peter Jefferson, 1775, was owned by Washington.

find an officer corps of frontier fighters saying farewell to a commander not yet twenty-six as follows: "In our earliest infancy, you took us under your tuition, trained us in the practice of that discipline which alone can constitute good troops. . . . Your steady adherence to impartial justice, your quick discernment and invariable regard to merit—wisely intended to inculcate those genuine sentiments of true honor and passion for glory, from which the greatest military achievements have been derived—first heightened our natural emulation, and our desire to excel." The statement went on to mourn for "our unhappy country [Virginia]" which would, through Washington's resignation, receive an irreparable loss. There was no one else so able to support "the military character of Virginia."

After Washington's resignation, the Virginia legislature passed an enthusiastic resolution in his praise. It would seem natural for the young man who had so quickly gone so far to retire in a glow of self-satisfaction, hang his sword over his fireplace, and play the triumphant hero. The temptation was the greater because so many of the directions in which Washington had behaved stupidly were still outside the scope of his comprehension. Yet he felt that he had not done as well as he should. On the private level, he had not achieved the commission in the British regular army he so desired, and on the public level, his achievement had obviously been full of flaws. He had been defeated at Fort Necessity; his defense of the frontier had been more active than effective; and his ultimate objective—driving the French from Fort Duquesne and the Ohio Valley—had been achieved over his protests in a way he found puzzling.

As a planter at Mount Vernon, Washington turned his mind away from the adventures that had made him celebrated. The remaining campaigns of the French and Indian War, which triumphantly expelled the French from Canada, are hardly mentioned in his correspondence. His old regiment regarded him as their voice in the Assembly, but he could not bear to act in that role for long.

Yet subsequent actions reveal that down the years, Washington mulled over his experiences in the French and Indian War. As his character and his world view expanded, more meanings became clear to him. He accurately defined his failures and worked out the reasons why he had failed. The results of this protracted self-education were to prove of the greatest importance to the creation of the United States.

Six

A VIRGINIA BUSINESSMAN

(1759–1775)

For sixteen years, Washington was a private man, amassing an estate according to overall patterns long conventional in Virginia: a prosperous marriage, large-scale farming, the purchase of western land.

After his recovery from his seemingly mortal illness and before he marched with Forbes, Washington became engaged to Martha Dandridge Custis, a widow slightly his senior and with two small children, who had inherited from her first husband a rich estate. The future Mrs. Washington, being about five feet tall, came up only to her suitor's chest. She was plump, with small hands and feet. Her large eyes, wide brows, and strong, curved nose would have created bold beauty had not timidity imposed a gentle charm. Despite her grand first marriage, her own family background had been modest; she preserved simple manners, uninsistent dignity. She was not given to startling ideas or brilliant talk; her intelligence and imagination ran to relations with other people. Down the long years, when her husband was so often embattled, no man or woman ever wrote of her with enmity. She proffered appreciative friendship to all. Washington was to find her such a companion as he had dreamed of when a boy under the whiplash of his termagant mother: "A quiet wife, a quiet soul."

The young soldier, who in 1758 offered her his hand, was thus described by a fellow officer: "Straight as an Indian, measuring six feet two inches in his stockings and weighing 175 pounds. . . . His frame is padded with well-developed muscles, indicating great strength. His bones and joints are large, as are his hands and feet. He is wide shouldered but has not a deep or round chest; is neat waisted, but is broad across the hips and has rather long legs and arms. His head is well-shaped, though not large, but is gracefully poised on a superb neck. A large and straight rather than a prominent nose; blue gray penetrating eyes which are widely separated and overhung by a heavy brow. His face is long rather than broad, with high round cheekbones, and terminates in a good firm chin. He has a clear though rather colorless pale skin which burns with the sun. A pleasing and benevolent though a commanding countenance, dark brown hair [actually, it was reddish] which he wears in a cue. His mouth is large and generally firmly closed, but which from time to time discloses some defective teeth. [He had one pulled the summer before in Winchester.] His features are regular and placid with all the muscles of his face under perfect control, though flexible and expressive of deep feeling when moved by emotions. In conversation, he looks you full in the face, is deliberate, deferential, and engaging. His demeanor at all times [is] composed and dignified. His movements and gestures are graceful, his walk majestic, and he is a splendid horseman."

After Martha had accepted George, Sally Fairfax could not resist teasing her longtime admirer about his "anxiety" at "the animating prospect of possessing

This inscribed English songbook was a gift from George to Martha in 1759, the year they were married.

Mrs. Custis." This elicited from the young soldier, away on Forbes's campaign, a passionate avowal that he loved only Sally: "You have drawn me, my dear Madam, or rather have I drawn myself, into an honest confession of a simple fact. Misconstrue not my meaning . . . nor expose it. The world has no business to know the object of love declared in this manner to you, when I want to conceal it." He tried to elicit from Sally a similar avowal. Although she kept Washington's letter by her for all her life, she did not give him the assurance he desired.

It is impossible to doubt that Washington's love for Sally brought him not only frustration but guilt. His marriage to Martha on January 6, 1759, brought him a grateful escape from traumatic entanglement. Although there are indications that the match did not start out smoothly, the husband soon concluded that his marriage had been the event of his life "most conducive to happiness."

Years later, Washington advised a stepgranddaughter not to "look for perfect felicity before you consent to wed. Nor conceive, from the fine tales the poets and lovers of old have told us of the transports of mutual love, that heaven has taken its abode on earth. Nor do not deceive yourself in supposing that the only means by which these are to be obtained is to drink deep of the cup and revel in an ocean of love. Love is a mighty pretty thing, but, like all other delicious things, it is cloying; and when the first transports of the passion begin to subside, which it assuredly will do, and yield, oftentimes too late, to more sober reflections, it serves to evince that love is too dainty a food to live on *alone*, and ought not to be considered further than as a necessary ingredient for that matrimonial happiness which results from a combination of causes: none of which are of greater importance than that the object on whom it is placed should possess good sense, a good disposition, and the means of supporting you in the way you have been brought up. Such qualifications cannot fail to attract (after marriage) your esteem and regard into which or into disgust, sooner or later love naturally resolves itself. . . . Be assured, and experience will convince you that there is no truth more certain than that all our enjoyments fall short of our expectations, and to none does it apply with more force than to the gratification of the passions."

His marriage to Martha taught the rash and impetuous young husband a lesson that was deeply to influence the rest of his career. It taught him that in action, judgment was preferable to passion. He must have been a receptive pupil even as she was an able teacher because, in one important particular, the marriage failed irrevocably. Year after year, Martha remained childless.

Since she was a young woman and had, during her brief previous marriage, quickened in rapid succession with four children (two died in infancy), it could well be concluded that the difficulty was not in her but in her husband. However, the magnificent athlete, who possessed in abundance every other physical prowess, could not altogether admit to himself that he was sterile. He believed, even when approaching old age, that if Martha died and he became remarried to "a girl," he might father an heir. In the meanwhile, his lack was a grievous one. Not only did it seem in the eyes of the world (to what extent in his own fears?) a conspicuous flaw in his physical manhood: according to Virginian tradition, the ultimate objective of such an estate as Washington amassed was to establish a prosperous and influential dynasty. Yet there is no indication that the childlessness of their marriage caused between the Washingtons any major strains.

After Martha had accepted George, Sally Fairfax could not resist teasing her longtime admirer about his "anxiety" at "the animating prospect of possessing Mrs. Custis."

This 1863 mezzotint of Martha Washington was drawn by W. Oliver Stone and made by John Folwell, after an original by John Woolastan.

The Wedding of George Washington and Martha Custis *from the* Life of George Washington *series by Junius Brutus Stearns, lithograph, c. 1854.*

There were, of course, the stepchildren. When he had proposed to Martha, John Parke Custis (Jackie), had been almost four, Martha Parke Custis (Patsy), two. Concerning her offspring, Martha was highly possessive. George felt for the children less a parent's concern than a stepfather's sense of responsibility. "I conceive," as he explained, "there is much greater circumspection to [be observed] by a guardian than a natural parent, who is only accountable to his own conscience." In addition to handling the property of his wards, a stepfather's duties were to be "generous and attentive."

The annual orders Washington sent to his London factor always included much for the children. Jackie, for instance, received at the age of five "handsome silver shoe and knee buckles," at eight, a silver-laced hat. At seven, Patsy received "a stiffened coat made of fashionable silk" and "one pair of pack thread stays." There were also toys: every year Patsy had to have a new fashionably dressed "doll baby."

Washington's marriage to the widow of the rich Daniel Parke Custis raised him financially from a run-of-the-mill planter to a man of substance: one-third of the large Custis estate had come to him (with certain restrictions) as Martha's husband, and he controlled the other two-thirds as guardian of the children. Perhaps it was a sense of this obligation which made him always respectful of his stepchildren's social rank, clearly much higher than his own. In trying to get the boy educated, Washington consistently pointed out to his teachers that improving his mind was of the greatest importance, as he was destined for exalted station.

Spoiled by his mother, who had at all times protected him, and possessed of the strange inheritance that came with the Custis blood, the boy proved uneducatable. As for Patsy, at the age of twelve she had a fall that was more than a fall: she was found to be an epileptic. Every effort was made to cure her and assuage her: a companion of her own age was brought in; she had a parrot and a spinet and the finest clothes that could be imported from London. A peripatetic dancing master was often in attendance and a doctor fitted her with an iron ring that was supposed to cure fits.

During 1773, Washington wrote his brother-in-law that Patsy "rose from dinner about four o'clock in better health and spirits than she had appeared to have been in for some time; soon after which she was seized with one of her usual fits and expired in it in less than two minutes without uttering a word, a groan, or scarce a sigh. This sudden and unexpected blow . . . has almost reduced my poor wife to the lowest ebb of misery." He tried to find comfort for Martha by having his mother-in-law make Mount Vernon her "entire and absolute home," but Mrs. Dandridge did not come.

Martha became all the more protective of her final remaining child. Almost uninterfered with by his stepfather, Jackie ripened into the monster he was to become.

Washington's marriage to the widow of the rich Daniel Parke Custis raised him financially from a run-of-the-mill planter to a man of substance: one-third of the large Custis estate had come to him (with certain restrictions) as Martha's husband, and he controlled the other two-thirds as guardian of the children.

Washington was to comment, in relation to the political excesses which followed the triumph in the American Revolution, that it was natural for heirs who had received a large legacy to "riot for a while." His activities during the French and Indian War had been profitable: he had received not only his salary but a commission on everything which, as his own supply officer, he bought. The death of Lawrence's widow had raised him from renter to owner of Mount Vernon. And then had come the large infusion of Custis cash. In preparation for his marriage, Washington had used a good part of his wartime earnings to raise Mount Vernon from one and a half to two and a half stories. The Custis windfall then encouraged him to enlarge the plantation with extremely extensive purchases of adjoining acres: to buy slaves to work the new land (he had not yet been assaulted with qualms about slavery) and to make his style of living comparable with that of the leading planters whose luxury he had as an impoverished boy so envied. This paroxysm of expense "swallowed before I knew where I was, all the money I got by my marriage. Nay more, brought me into debt."

According to usages almost universal in tidewater Virginia and dating back for generations, the economy of the colony had only one foot in America; the other was in England. The rivers on which the plantations bordered were also estuaries of the Atlantic Ocean. Ships dispatched by English merchants came annually to the planters' own wharves. They loaded Virginia's sole cash crop, tobacco, and unloaded what the merchant (known as a factor) had bought in London, presumably with the earnings from the previous crops. This system, which circulated Virginia's cash abroad, had been responsible for that lack of Virginia manufactures or even fine handicrafts which had forced Washington and Forbes to supply their armies in Pennsylvania, where the economy was more self-contained.

In the relationship between factor and planter, the factor had every advantage. Taking his profit on every transaction, he determined the prices at which he sold the Virginian's tobacco, and also the prices at which he bought objects for the Virginian's account. The only alley of escape open to a planter who concluded that he was being cheated—changing to another factor—was usually closed because the planter had been maneuvered heavily into his current factor's debt.

Before his marriage, Washington had done his business with one Richard Washington, who he assumed might be his cousin and might therefore treat him fairly. When he came into the Custis money, he gladly changed to the Custis' factor, Robert Cary and Company, but his letters across the ocean continued to be an unbroken series of angry charges. His tobacco was being sold for a fraction of its value, he was sent inferior goods at superior prices, and his orders were handled with inexcusable incompetence. Farm machinery would arrive with parts missing, which meant that the necessary and expensive objects would have to lie idle for a year, since there was only one shipment annually. There was the time that Patsy followed him around in tears through the hold of a ship searching for a trunk of adornments and toys that were listed on the invoice but had been left behind. Washington bought all his best clothes abroad; he sent careful measurements, but the clothes never fitted. Since this was the typical situation, we have a vision of grand parties where all the Virginians were handsomely dressed in costumes either too small or too large.

Washington so accepted the system that, as he ordered lavishly, he paid little attention to what the Cary bookkeepers were scratching down in their ledgers. When the factor decided that the time had come to notify him of debt and needle him for payment, he responded with outrage: "I must confess that I did not expect that a correspondent so steady and constant as I have proved, and was willing to have continued to your house while the advantages were in any way reciprocal, would be reminded in the instant it was discovered how necessary it was for him to be expeditious in his payments. Reason and prudence naturally dictate to every man of common sense the thing that is right, and you might have rested assured that so fast as I could make remittances without distressing myself too much,

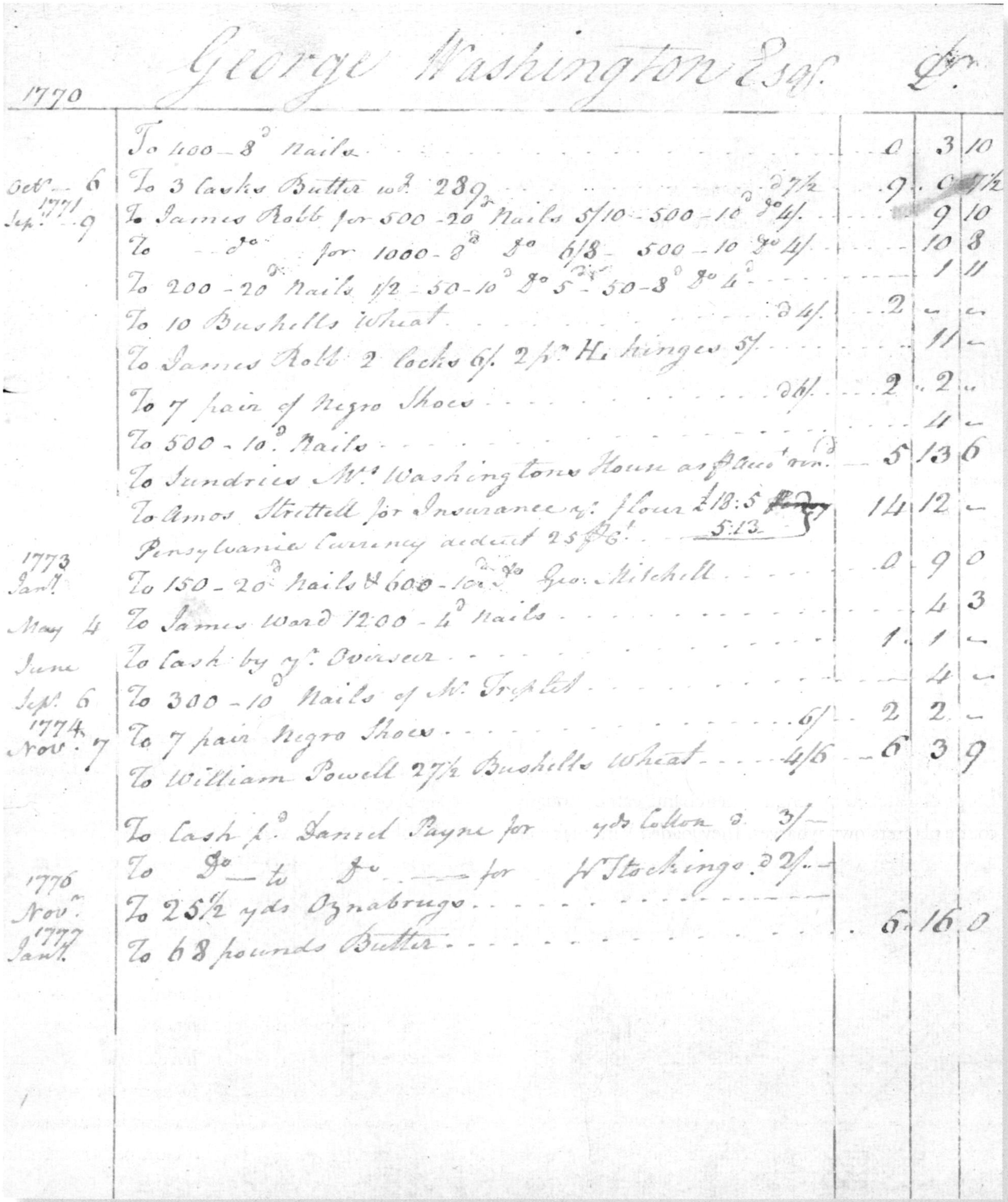

George Washington Esqr. Dr

		£	s	d
1770	To 400 – 8d Nails	0	3	10
Octr. 6	To 3 Casks Butter wt. 289 @ 7½	9	0	7½
1771 Sep. 9	To James Robb for 500 – 20d Nails 5/10 – 500 – 10d do 4/		9	10
	To do for 1000 – 8d do 6/8 – 500 – 10 do 4/		10	8
	To 200 – 20d Nails 1/2 – 50 – 10d do 5 – 50 – 8d do 4		1	11
	To 10 Bushells Wheat @ 4/	2	–	–
	To James Robb 2 Locks 6/. 2 pr. H. hinges 5/		11	–
	To 7 pair of Negro Shoes @ 6/	2	2	–
	To 500 – 10d Nails		4	–
	To Sundries Mr. Washingtons House as pr. Acct. rend.	5	13	6
	To Amos Strettell for Insurance of Flour £18:5 / 5:13 Pensylvania Currency deduct 25 pCt.	14	12	–
1773 Jany.	To 150 – 20d Nails & 600 – 10d do Geo. Mitchell	0	9	0
May 4	To James Ward 1200 – 4d Nails		4	3
June	To Cash by yr. Overseer	1	1	–
Sepr. 6	To 300 – 10d Nails of Mr. Triplet		4	–
1774 Nov. 7	To 7 pair Negro Shoes 6/	2	2	–
	To William Powell 27½ Bushells Wheat 4/6	6	3	9
	To Cash pd. Daniel Payne for yds Cotton @ 3/			
	To do to do for pr Stockings @ 2/.			
1776 Novr.	To 25½ yds Oznabrugs			
1777 Jany.	To 68 pounds Butter	6	16	0

A record of money received and expended for the purchase of goods on behalf of George Washington from 1770 to 1777.

HOW MOUNT VERNON GREW

1. The house as it was when Washington was a boy.

2. After the 1759 enlargement in preparation for his marriage to Martha.

3. The completed mansion.

my inclinations would have prompted me to it." Why did not Cary and Company put their minds on getting decent prices for his tobacco? Having appended a large order for luxuries and farm machinery that would increase the debt, he wrote grandly that he would not wish anyone to "suffer in the most trivial instances in my account." He would agree to pay interest on what he owed.

Washington might write loftily, but he knew that debts forever swelling with interest were a sure progression to bankruptcy.

Although Washington now reduced his capital investments in more lands and slaves, this did not by itself solve his problem. At a later date, he was to write a little parable explaining why an extravagant planter found it impossible to practice economy. "'How can I?' says he. . . . I am ashamed to do it; and besides, such an alteration in the system of my living will create suspicions of a decay in my fortune, and such a thought the world must not harbor.'" Whether or not Washington expressed ideas that had been his own, he failed to apply to his day-by-day expenses that virtue he found hateful: frugality. He would have to find another way out.

The trouble was not laziness. He could hardly have paid more attention to his affairs. Many a Virginia plantation was lost through the sloth of the owner, but it was natural for the proprietor of Mount Vernon to be forever on the go. If he was prevented from being active, he fell ill and was haunted by premonitions of death (his father and his beloved brother Lawrence had both died in their primes). In all aspects of life he was, as Jefferson wrote, "inclined to gloomy apprehensions." The bustle of plantation management exactly suited him. It gave his body the extensive exercise which that powerful machine craved, and, without putting his nerves on the stretch as they had been during the French and Indian War, kept his attention so filled with a succession of little problems that his innate melancholy had no opportunity to cloud over his mental skies.

Washington was up in midsummer with the dawn and at other seasons in the dark, riding his estates in a circle that had expanded as he secured more land. There was always much to ameliorate: slave labor was inefficient; overseers were sottish and brutish and stupid; the Mount Vernon fields were far from fertile. The soil had been depleted by long cultivation of Virginia's extremely demanding staple crop, tobacco. Furthermore, as Washington came gradually to realize, there existed "an understratum of clay impervious to water." During heavy rains, excess water ran off, washing topsoil into the Potomac and creating unsightly gullies, while what moisture did sink in remained near the surface causing sogginess. Washington was perpetually seeking some natural fertilizer that would generate a miracle or at least help things along, his most elaborate expedient being to scoop up and spread mud from the bottom of the Potomac. He had his men eternally digging drainage ditches that were eternally inadequate.

A devoted reader of agricultural manuals, Washington copied out long passages, probably to fix them in his memory. However, even as a beginning farmer (which he now actually was), he was unwilling to accept anything on authority. One reason was that his books were all imported from England, and he had already concluded that what would work across the ocean was not necessarily suited to America. Seeking not only to improve his own crops, to enlighten and amuse himself, but perhaps to find guidance for all Virginia farmers, Washington undertook experiments.

In each of ten compartments of a huge box, Washington placed soils from different parts of his estate, planting various grains at the same depth but with different fertilizers. "I watered them all equally alike with water that had been standing in a tub about two hours exposed to the sun." All were to be cultivated in an identical manner. Thus, at the very dawn of modern science, Washington tried to set up a controlled experiment. But there were conditions he could not control: the weather, and the cultivation while he was away on a trip to Williamsburg. It is perhaps a further indication of his potentialities as a scientist that he realized that his results were inconclusive.

Washington was eager to initiate wine culture, but he did not import European grapes. Reasoning that what was indigenous to Virginia soil grew best there, he collected about two thousand cuttings from local vines, selecting those on which the wild grapes did not ripen until late autumn. Fermentation followed, and tasting. But Washington rode off to the Revolutionary War without having hit on a delicious potation.

His curiosity carried him into widespread investigations. He determined that there were 13,411,000 grains in a bushel of timothy. As his carpenters hewed poplar boards, he made a work-time study more suited to the twentieth century, noting their motions and deciding which could be eliminated. He invented a plow which automatically dropped seeds in the furrows, and with which he continued to tinker at various times for the rest of his career. But all this activity contributed more to his interest and amusement than to any important agricultural discovery, or to paying off his English debt.

Washington was the completely responsible manager of a medium-size town which, to escape utter bankruptcy, had to be as far as possible self-contained. His "family" (as he called it) included nephews and nieces, white artisans, overseers, and a force of slaves that mounted with the years to several hundred. Pork had to be produced by the thousands of pounds (6,632 in 1762); Indian corn and cereal grains grown to feed man and beast; fish seined from the Potomac by the tens of thousands to be eaten fresh or salted down; liquor (that invaluable work incentive) distilled, cider from Washington's apple trees being stepped up to applejack. Washington's blacksmiths shoed horses and made tools from plows to axes; his coopers ran up hundreds of barrels; his carpenters built new structures and kept the old ones in repair; his weavers and shoemakers and seamstresses made the work clothes of the community. Livestock had to be bred, fed, milked, broken to harness or the saddle. Carts drawn by oxen or horses moved—Washington hoped not aimlessly or with half loads—across his thousands of acres. He had his own freight sloop on the Potomac and his own mill, even if it was superannuated and forever ailing. For many years, he accommodated with a ferry travelers who wished to cross the river.

Washington might write loftily, but he knew that debts forever swelling with interest were a sure progression to bankruptcy.

Washington handled these complications with organization that singularly resembled that of an army. There was a chain of command from the leader of a work gang up to the manager of an individual farm, on to various staff officers, and finally to the proprietor. At one side were special services—ditchers, carters, millers, fishermen, artisans—whose activities had to be keyed in at the right place and time to the general effort. With his unbounded energy and his gift for detail, Washington was at Mount Vernon an efficient commander in chief.

Yet his debt to his English factors grew.

After five years as a conventional planter, Washington came to a decision that included a declaration of independence from England. He decided that, although hallowed by tradition, the economic system of the Virginia tidewater, to which he had been raised, was in its essence "disastrous." The cultivation of tobacco ruined the land. It required a disproportionate quantity of labor. As the only cash crop, it left the planter at

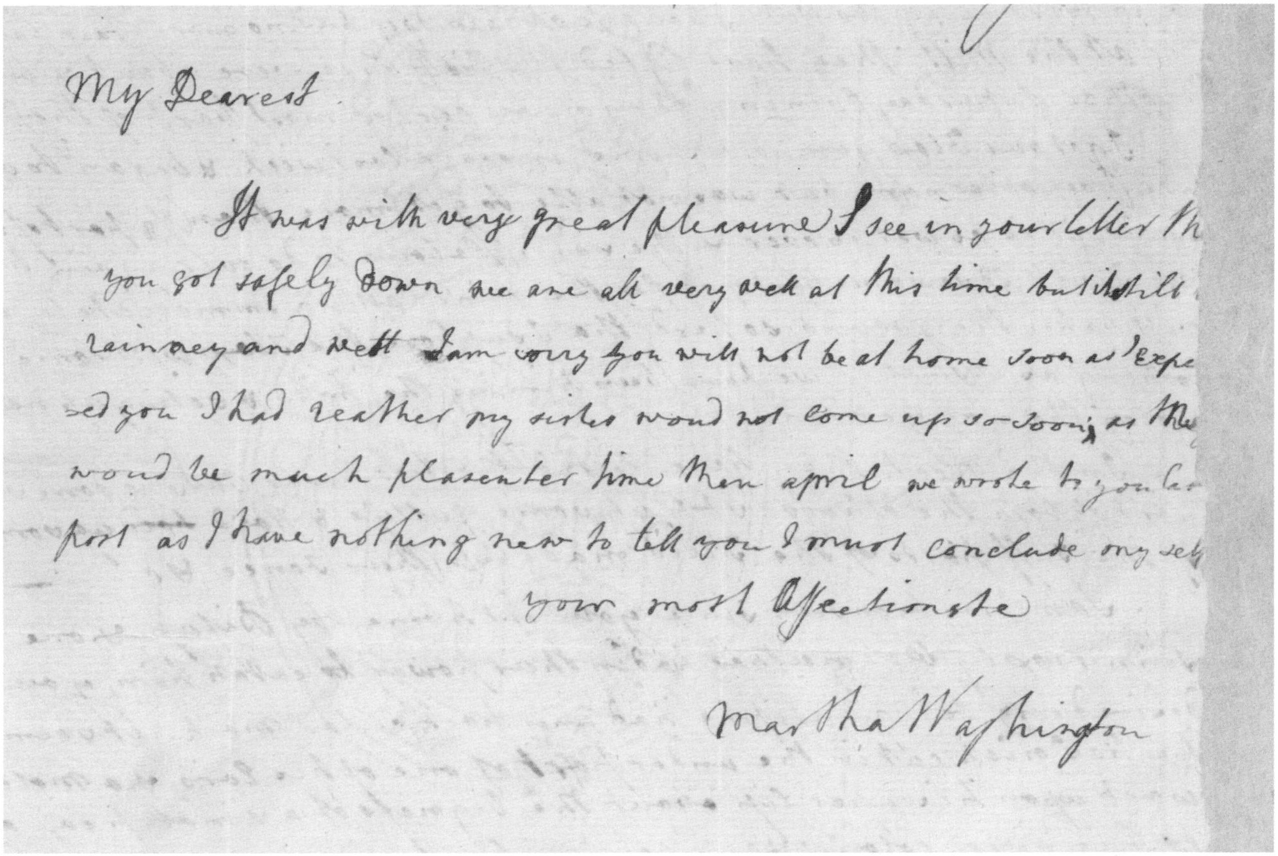

My Dearest

It was with very great pleasure I see in your letter th
you got safely down we are all very well at this time but it still
rainey and wett I am sorry you will not be at home soon as I expe
-ted you I had reather my sister would not come up so soon, as they
would be much plasenter time then april we wrote to you last
post as I have nothing new to tell you I must conclude my sel
your most Affectionate

Martha Washington

In one of only two extant examples of correspondence from Martha to George, she penned a six-line postscript with news and greetings on the second page of a letter from Lund Washington (George's cousin and business manager) on March 30, 1767. While brief, Martha's note reveals their warm, respectful relationship. She affectionately addresses him "My Dearest" just as he addresses her in a June 23, 1775 letter. At George's request, Martha burned nearly all of their correspondence before her death, so the survival of this postscript is remarkable.

the mercy of a single sequence of weather. And because tobacco had to be sold abroad, the planters were delivered into the hands of foreigners who pushed them into debt and kept them there while supplying them with expensive, out-of-date, and inferior goods.

Washington decided to apply on a large scale the economic practices of the lowly farmers who lived in the piedmont beyond the falls of the various rivers. To their farms, British boats could not penetrate; they lacked the extensive and flat acreage, and also the large work force to grow tobacco. They grew cereal grains, not only for their own use, but as cash crops, selling to local merchants who distributed produce in America as well as abroad.

During 1765, Washington grew little tobacco and during 1766, none. The output of his farm became wheat and particularly corn. Since this required much less labor, he was able to diversify further. He increased his number of weavers so that they could work for the neighbors, and he built a new commercial mill, which could grind for the entire countryside, and which he eventually had automated by the Philadelphia inventor Oliver Evans.

George Washington the Farmer *from the* Life of George Washington *series by Junius Brutus Stearns. Lithograph by Régnier, Paris, c. 1853.*

The excess produce of his estate he sold to merchants in Alexandria, who paid him in money or at least in statements of indebtedness that circulated in the middle colonies. When he wanted European goods, he could buy them from local importers susceptible to his wrath if he felt himself put upon. Or he could buy the achievements of Philadelphia artisans, who regarded the American market as the basis of their prosperity that must be pleased.

Washington's principal contact with his London factors was now paying off in installments what he owed them. How he looked forward to being quit of them altogether! Again, as when he had abandoned his ambition to join the British regular army, Washington moved psychologically away from the England that as a youth he had unquestionably considered the center and capital of his world.

Seven

WASHINGTON IN HIS LANDSCAPES

(1759–1775)

The passionate soldier had changed into a planter commonly characterized by his friends with the adjective "amiable." Here is a passage from his letter to a brother-in-law who had just fathered a male baby: "But harkee! I am told you have recently introduced into your family a certain production which you are lost in admiration of, and spend so much time in contemplating the just proportions of its parts, the ease and conveniences with which it abounds, that it is thought you will have little time to animadvert upon the prospects of your crops.

"I say how will this be reconciled to that anguished care and vigilance which is so essentially necessary at a time when our growing prosperity—meaning the tobacco—is assailed by every villainous worm that has had an existence since the days of Noah (how unkind it was of Noah, now I have mentioned his name, to suffer such a brood of vermin to get a berth in the ark), but perhaps you may be as well off as we are—that is have no tobacco for them to eat, and there, I think, we nicked the dogs, as I think to do you if you expect any more."

In 1768, Washington went to church on fifteen days, mostly when away from home, and hunted foxes on forty-nine. He made innumerable visits, often staying several nights. He attended three balls, two plays, and one horse race. Unable to resist any kind of spectacle, Washington enjoyed cockfights and puppet shows. He visited a lioness and a tiger, and gave nine shillings to a showman who brought an elk up the long driveway to Mount Vernon. Temperamentally a gambler—now at cards, later in war—he received a rebuke from a Scotch Presbyterian friend for wasting so much of his time at the gaming table. The stakes were occasionally high, but down the years he lost only a little more than he won.

Sometimes he took his hounds along when he rode around his farms, gleefully abandoning business if they started a fox. The breeding of horses and hounds was a perpetual concern. Several times he noted ruefully in one of his diaries that he had been outwitted by some household pet who, realizing before he did that one of the hound bitches was "proud," had "covered" her before she had been locked up with a suitable hunting mate.

Washington's agricultural activities were by no means limited to utility. Although he never painted a picture and wrote no more poems after he emerged from adolescence, he was always passionately concerned with aesthetic effect. This could manifest itself in the spacing on the page of a letter or of a survey. It found its greatest expression in the design of Mount Vernon (he was his own architect) and the embellishment of the grounds. He arranged not only his flower garden, but also his vegetable garden, with decorative paths and hedges that encouraged strolling; he transplanted

In the spring of 1772, Charles Willson Peale visited Mount Vernon to paint miniatures of Martha Washington (top) *and her children, John "Jackie" Parke Custis* (left) *and Martha "Patsy" Parke Custis* (right). *Peale captured them all at the height of their youth and vitality. Just over a year later, Patsy died of an epileptic seizure at age seventeen. In a letter to Burwell Basset, Washington described his devastated wife as being in the "lowest ebb of misery." The miniatures, which she wore as bracelets, perhaps afforded her some comfort.*

George Washington in his French and Indian War uniform, as painted at Mount Vernon in 1772 by Charles Willson Peale, detail, oil on canvas.

onto his lawns and into his artificial "wildernesses" decorative shrubs he had happened on in his rambles; he tried to grow exotics imported from Europe or sent to him by friends in the West.

In the seven years between 1768 and 1775, the Washingtons entertained about two thousand guests, who ranged from relations and intimate friends to passersby put up at nightfall. Hospitality was warm and food plentiful, even if the bedrooms were crowded. George found an unfilled dining room "lonesome" and Martha considered an empty house "dull," yet they liked to alternate gregariousness with privacy. In 1773 and 1774, Washington doubled the length of Mount Vernon westward by adding a domestic wing

PORTRAYING HISTORY

CHARLES PEALE AND GILBERT STUART

Charles Willson Peale Self-portrait, detail, 1822.

Gilbert Charles Stuart Self-portrait at age 24, detail, c.1778.

THE FACES AND ATTITUDES OF THE FOUNDING FATHERS ARE familiar to us thanks in large part to the two most prominent American portrait painters of their day, Charles Willson Peale (1741–1827) and Gilbert Charles Stuart (1755–1828).

As a young man, Peale worked as a saddler, watchmaker, and silversmith. His artistic career began when he exchanged a saddle for a few painting lessons and found his gift. After a period of study in England with Benjamin West, Peale returned to America and became the most fashionable portrait painter of the middle colonies.

Peale served enthusiastically in the Revolutionary War, and, in 1782, opened a portrait gallery of "Revolutionary heroes" in Philadelphia. In 1786, he founded Peale's Museum, dedicated to the study and display of objects from the natural world (though it also housed many of his own works). This institution soon became known as the Philadelphia Museum, and was the first major museum in the United States.

Over the course of his long life, Peale painted some 1,100 portraits (many of which are reproduced in this volume), including well-known images of George Washington (who sat for him seven times), Benjamin Franklin, Thomas Jefferson, and John Adams.

Peale's brother, James, and his sons Raphaelle, Rembrandt, Rubens, and Titian were also painters, copying many of his works for commercial purposes as well as creating their own portraits and other paintings.

★ ★ ★ ★ ★

Like Peale, Gilbert Charles Stuart grew up in America, but left for art school in London in 1775, where he, too, studied with Benjamin West. In 1782, he opened his own London studio, where he painted many prominent Londoners. A better artist than businessman, Stuart fled after a few years to Ireland to escape his creditors, ultimately returning to the States and attaining preeminence as a portrait painter first in New York, then Philadelphia, and, finally, Boston.

Stuart's work was admired by his contemporaries and is still valued for its fine brushwork, luminous color palette, and psychological complexity. In his lifetime, he completed nearly a thousand portraits, the most famous of which is the 1796 head of Washington that now appears on the one-dollar bill. (He himself completed some sixty copies of it.) Other significant Stuart works include portraits of Major General Henry Dearborn and John Adams.

As carried on by his less talented daughter, Jane, and other imitators, Stuart's style is reflected in much of the portraiture of the succeeding generation. His best work has been compared to that of Thomas Gainsborough and Sir Joshua Reynolds.

the same height and width as the existing house. This left the structure lopsided; he planned—it was not completed as he rode away to a new war—a matching extension to the east that would contain a two-story ballroom.

Washington sold the Custis house in the colonial capital, Williamsburg, and bought a house in his county seat, Alexandria. As a member of the House of Burgesses, he only bothered to ride to the sessions if matters of local import were to be decided.

Neighborhood offices came to him: vestryman, justice of the county court, trustee of Alexandria. He was lax about attending the boring sessions, but he was never lax if anyone knocked on his door to request charity or a loan or advice or actual intervention in tangled affairs. He wrote that no suppliant should ever be turned away from Mount Vernon, "lest the deserving suffer." In principle he was less sympathetic to the undeserving, but in fact they usually found him generous. He could not, he complained, refuse any appeal "without feeling inexpressible uneasiness."

Washington, who had had almost no experience of any way of life not grounded on slavery, had not yet questioned the institution in its fundamentals. He merely felt it his duty to be kind to his slaves. Most important to their feelings, he believed, was that they should not be separated from their families and companions, sent to strange places where they were not at home. This meant that he was unwilling to move a slave from Mount Vernon unless the slave agreed, which almost never happened. It also meant that he became unwilling to sell slaves, although natural increase, building on his earlier purchases, gave him a larger work force to feed and clothe than he needed, particularly since he had abandoned the cultivation of tobacco.

One of the causes in which Washington often found himself engaged was trying to circumvent avaricious husbands who, taking advantage of the unfair Virginia laws, tried to defraud women of their property. Concerning one such legal campaign that went on for years, an observer wrote Washington, "Charity with us is common, but steady friendship founded on that principle almost without a precedent."

Despite his complaints and his attempts at refusal, Washington was entrusted with managing the estates—and often becoming guardian to the children—of many a dying neighbor.

> Temperamentally a gambler—now at cards, later in war—he received a rebuke from a Scotch Presbyterian friend for wasting so much of his time at the gaming table.

Within his own area, Washington followed his ideal of "cultivating the affections of good men" and practicing "domestic virtues." The fiercely aggressive part of his nature found outlet in his efforts to amass wilderness acres. There was a strangeness about this obsession. Since much of what he sought and sometimes did acquire would be made valuable only by advances in settlement which he could hardly expect in his lifetime, this was of all his pursuits the one with the greatest dynastic implications. Yet he was not discouraged in his efforts by his continuing lack of an heir. Perhaps his passion was motivated (at least in

Opposite: The Artist in His Museum, *a self-portrait by Charles Willson Peale, oil on canvas, 1822, was commissioned by the trustees of the Peale Museum and was painted "in the 81st year of his age without the aid of spectacles." In it, Peale draws aside a curtain to welcome visitors to his center of "rational entertainment." The piece was meant to promote the museum and celebrate Peale's varied career as artist, naturalist, educator, and showman.*

part) by a possessive worship of the continent across which his dreams spread.

The type of real estate speculation Washington most enjoyed was not for the faint in heart. The laws dealing with land grants in the wilderness were self-contradictory, endlessly complicated, and subject to change without notice. Finding and marking out the best land beyond the reaches of settlement—flat and fertile acres accessible to rivers, potential mill sites, and the like—required geographically arduous exploration. And there was no lack of human hazards. Indians were not gentle to encroachers on land they considered their own; the employees of rival speculators carried both legal documents and rifles; squatters were devoid of documents but often forceful in numbers. And in the end, no title could be considered final until it was approved by a governmental body often open to influence and bribery. Washington referred to the whole operation as a "lottery," explaining, "No man can lay off a foot of land and be sure of holding it."

He accepted as part of the process the unscrupulousness that was created by a combination of great potential rewards with utter confusion in areas almost beyond the law. He ordered secret surveys on land reserved by royal proclamation to the Indians was not adverse to engrossing a larger percentage of river front than the law allowed. He was, on the whole, successful. No other man in all Virginia combined considerable influence with public bodies and considerable financial assets with personal prowess as a backwoodsman that made it unnecessary to rely on agents for even the most dangerous explorations. While others tried to reach out from their manors or countinghouses, he tramped wild places himself.

His most extensive adventure grew out of his personal efforts as a lobbyist. He secured confirmation of a confused promise of land made by Dinwiddie to those who had early enlisted in the Virginia Regiment. The area involved was so large it could only be found in the outer wilderness. Washington traveled in the autumn of 1770 again to the Forks of the Ohio—where he had previously seen emptiness, there was now a settlement of some twenty cabins, called Pittsburgh—and then drifted down the river for eleven days. His objective was the confluence of the Ohio with the Great Kanawha, where he had heard that the land was fine. This journey deep into the almost unexplored wilderness was in some ways a replay of the embassy northward which had opened his public career. There was danger—reports of Indian hostilities and ticklish meetings with braves in war or perhaps hunting dress; there was hardship—snow fell—but this time the impediments were not truly lethal. They added spice to lyricism.

Keeping notes of the appearance of the shores along which they passed, Washington saw an identity of beauty and utility: the taller the trees and the fairer the meadows, the more fertile the land. Deer, buffalo, and wild turkeys abounded. Eventually Washington found and marked out a paradise of rich meadows, towering vegetation, mill sites, vast reaches, boundless skies, where he eventually secured title to thirty thousand acres, most of the tracts "beautifully bordered" by the rivers.

Eight

A NEW CALL TO ARMS

(1765–1775)

Washington, who in his youth called England "home," had moved to the conclusion that the Americans could not remain forever under the domination of the British. Having become a different people, they would have to find their own destiny in their own way. Yet he hoped that the issue could be postponed "for posterity to determine." However, there rose in the mid-1760s an argument over taxation. The resulting controversy summoned up all the misunderstandings and profound differences of attitude that had been developing during the more than two centuries when Americans had been forced to serve their own needs in a land so different from the British Isles.

Because the colonists had profited from various Crown expenditures, including the winning of the French and Indian War, Parliament decided that they should be subject to taxation voted in London. The colonists responded that since they were not represented in Parliament they would not be taxed from there. This incited Parliament to repressive legislation, which excited stronger American opposition, which incited England to increase her military force in America.

Washington's reactions in the early stages of this buildup were moderate. When, trying to strike at British pocketbooks, Americans agreed not to import British goods, Washington welcomed this development only partly as a method of retaliation. He hoped that the experience of selling and buying at home would persuade his fellow planters of what he had individually worked out: that they would be better off if they were not economically dependent on England. He stepped up the household manufactures at Mount Vernon so that he could sell more goods and services to his neighbors.

By April 1769, Washington had become so worried about the suppression of American liberties that he visualized the possibility of an armed rebellion—but only as the very last resort. He still hoped that some rational line could be drawn between the rights of the mother country and the rights of the colonies. "For my own part," he added, "I shall not undertake to say where."

Washington was glad to admit he was not a political expert. He had concluded, he was to explain, that the British measures were "repugnant to every principle of natural justice" before "abler heads than my own" had convinced him that the measures were also contrary to the legal rights Americans had inherited as Britons. His modesty was undoubtedly due in part to his memory of how he had made a fool of himself during Forbes's campaign by pontificating from a local view on matters of international import.

In the current situation, Washington's desire to move only on sure ground was strengthened by his realization of extreme danger. He gave it as his "opinion that more blood will be spilt on this occasion, if the [British]

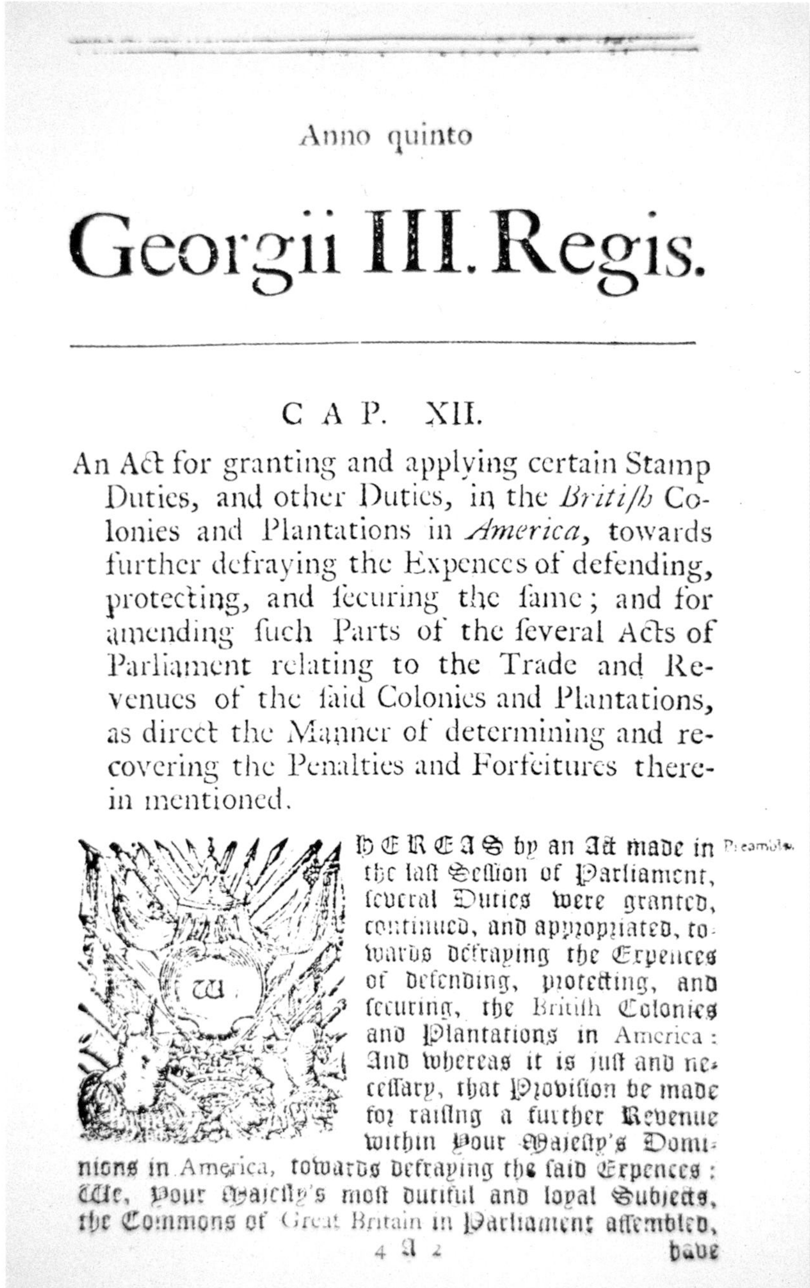

Anno quinto

Georgii III. Regis.

C A P. XII.

An Act for granting and applying certain Stamp Duties, and other Duties, in the *Britiſh* Colonies and Plantations in *America*, towards further defraying the Expences of defending, protecting, and ſecuring the ſame; and for amending ſuch Parts of the ſeveral Acts of Parliament relating to the Trade and Revenues of the ſaid Colonies and Plantations, as direct the Manner of determining and recovering the Penalties and Forfeitures therein mentioned.

WHEREAS by an Act made in the laſt Seſſion of Parliament, ſeveral Duties were granted, continued, and appropriated, towards defraying the Expences of defending, protecting, and ſecuring, the British Colonies and Plantations in America: And whereas it is juſt and neceſſary, that Proviſion be made for raiſing a further Revenue within Your Majeſty's Dominions in America, towards defraying the ſaid Expences: We, Your Majeſty's moſt dutiful and loyal Subjects, the Commons of Great Britain in Parliament aſſembled, Preamble.

4 A 2 have

The Stamp Act of 1765 constituted a tax imposed by the British onto the American colonies, requiring many printed materials to be produced on stamped paper manufactured in London. Colonists considered it a violation of their rights, as they had no say in how the tax was levied or how it would be used.

ministry are determined to push matters to the extremity, than history has yet furnished in the annals of North America."

Washington saw as the fundamental issue the question whether the British acts were random results of stupid misadministration or whether they were proofs "of a fixed and uniform plan to tax us." He was shocked to read of the Boston Tea Party because he believed it would encourage the British to further excesses. It was the extremity of those excesses that finally forced him to make up his mind. The "intolerable acts" which closed the port of Boston and abrogated the charter of Massachusetts "exhibited," he believed, "an unexampled testimony of the most despotic system of tyranny that was ever practiced in a free government." Opposition had become an absolute duty.

Although Washington, as a member of the House of Burgesses and a neighborhood leader in Fairfax County, had played his role in Virginia's various acts of protest and commercial retaliation, he had not been one of the firebrands of the revolutionary movement. Yet when the Burgesses elected seven delegates to the First Continental Congress, he received the third largest vote. Patrick Henry was far behind him and the young Thomas Jefferson failed of election.

At the official sessions held in Philadelphia during September and October 1774, Washington was mostly silent. However, his endless conviviality kept him so much on the go that he dined in his lodgings only seven times in fifty-three days, and usually had a second engagement during the evening. In the meeting room

Americans throwing the Cargoes of the Tea Ships into the River,
at Boston

An illustration of the Boston Tea Party published in The History of North America *by Rev. Mr. Cooper, 1789.*

A line of Minute Men is fired upon by British troops during the Battle of Lexington in this 1903 print by John H. Daniels & Son.

THOMAS PAINE

THE CRISIS NO. 1

IN LATE 1776, THOMAS PAINE, the revolutionary writer and intellectual, published a pamphlet series he called *The Crisis,* to bolster Americans' resolve in their fight against the British. To inspire his soldiers, General Washington had the following first pamphlet in the series read aloud to them.

Thomas Paine as depicted by George Romney (1734–1802).

These are the times that try men's souls. The summer soldier and the sunshine patriot will, in this crisis, shrink from the service of their country; but he that stands it now, deserves the love and thanks of man and woman. Tyranny, like hell, is not easily conquered; yet we have this consolation with us, that the harder the conflict, the more glorious the triumph. What we obtain too cheap, we esteem too lightly: it is dearness only that gives every thing its value. Heaven knows how to put a proper price upon its goods; and it would be strange indeed if so celestial an article as freedom should not be highly rated. Britain, with an army to enforce her tyranny, has declared that she has a right (not only to tax) but "to bind us in all cases whatsoever," and if being bound in that manner is not slavery, then is there not such a thing as slavery upon earth. Even the expression is impious, for so unlimited a power can belong only to God.

Whether the independence of the continent was declared too soon, or delayed too long, I will not now enter into as an argument; my own simple opinion is that had it been eight months earlier it would have been much better. We did not make a proper use of last winter, neither could we, while we were in a dependent state. However, the fault, if it were one, was all our own; we have none to blame but ourselves. But no great deal is lost yet. All that Howe has been doing for this month past is rather a ravage than a conquest, which the spirit of the Jerseys, a year ago, would have quickly repulsed, and which time and a little resolution will soon recover.*

* The present winter is worth an age, if rightly employed; but, if lost or neglected, the whole continent will partake of the evil; and there is no punishment that man does not deserve, be he who, or what, or where he will, that may be the means of sacrificing a season so precious and useful.

I have as little superstition in me as any man living, but my secret opinion has ever been, and still is, that God Almighty will not give up a people to military destruction, or leave them unsupportedly to perish, who have so earnestly and so repeatedly sought to avoid the calamities of war by every decent method which wisdom could invent. Neither have I so much of the infidel in me as to suppose that He has relinquished the government of the world, and given us up to the care of devils; and as I do not, I cannot see on what grounds the king of Britain can look up to heaven for help against us: a common murderer, a highwayman, or a house-breaker has as good a pretense as he.

'Tis surprising to see how rapidly a panic will sometimes run through a country. All nations and ages have been subject to them. Britain has trembled like an ague at the report of a French fleet of flat-bottomed boats; and in the fourteenth [fifteenth] century the whole English army, after ravaging the kingdom of France, was driven back like men petrified with fear; and this brave exploit was performed by a few broken forces collected and headed by a woman, Joan of Arc. Would that heaven might inspire some Jersey maid to spirit up her countrymen and save her fair fellow sufferers from ravage and ravishment! Yet panics, in some cases, have their uses; they produce as much good as hurt. Their duration is always short; the mind soon grows through them, and acquires a firmer habit than before. But their peculiar advantage is that they are the touchstones of sincerity and hypocrisy, and bring things and men to light, which might otherwise have lain forever undiscovered. In fact, they have the same effect on secret traitors, which an imaginary apparition would have upon a private murderer. They sift out the hidden thoughts of man and hold them up in public to the world. Many a disguised Tory has lately shown his head, that shall penitentially solemnize with curses the day on which Howe arrived upon the Delaware.

As I was with the troops at Fort Lee and marched with them to the edge of Pennsylvania, I am well acquainted with many circumstances, which those who live at a distance know but little or nothing of. Our situation there was exceedingly cramped, the place being a narrow neck of land between the North River and the Hackensack. Our force was inconsiderable, being not one-fourth so great as Howe could bring against us. We had no army at hand to have relieved the garrison, had we shut ourselves up and stood on our defense. Our ammunition, light artillery, and the best part of our stores, had been removed on the apprehension that Howe would endeavor to penetrate the Jerseys, in which case Fort Lee could be of no use to us; for it must occur to every thinking man, whether in the army or not, that these kind of field forts are only for temporary purposes, and last in use no longer than the enemy directs his force against the particular object which such forts are raised to defend. Such was our situation and condition at Fort Lee on the morning of the 20th of November, when an officer arrived with information that the enemy with 200 boats had landed about seven miles above. Major General [Nathaneael] Green, who commanded the garrison, immediately ordered them under arms and sent express to General Washington at the town of Hackensack, distant by the way of the ferry. Our first object was to secure the bridge over the Hackensack, which laid up the river between the enemy and us, about six miles from us, and three from them. General Washington arrived in about three-quarters of an hour, and marched at the head of the troops towards the bridge, which place I expected we should have a brush for. However, they did not choose to dispute it with us, and the greatest part of our troops went over the bridge, the rest over the ferry, except some which passed at a mill on a small creek between the bridge and the ferry, and made their way through some marshy grounds up to the town of Hackensack, and there passed the river. We brought off as much baggage as the wagons could contain, the rest was lost. The simple object was to bring off the garrison and march them on till they could be strengthened by the

Jersey or Pennsylvania militia, so as to be enabled to make a stand. We stayed four days at Newark, collected our outposts with some of the Jersey militia, and marched out twice to meet the enemy, on being informed that they were advancing, though our numbers were greatly inferior to theirs. Howe, in my little opinion, committed a great error in generalship in not throwing a body of forces off from Staten Island through Amboy, by which means he might have seized all our stores at Brunswick and intercepted our march into Pennsylvania; but if we believe the power of hell to be limited, we must likewise believe that their agents are under some providential control. I shall not now attempt to give all the particulars of our retreat to the Delaware; suffice it for the present to say that both officers and men, though greatly harassed and fatigued, frequently without rest, covering, or provision, the inevitable consequences of a long retreat, [and] bore it with a manly and martial spirit. All their wishes centered in one, which was that the country would turn out and help them to drive the enemy back. Voltaire has remarked that King William never appeared to full advantage but in difficulties and in action; the same remark may be made on General Washington, for the character fits him. There is a natural firmness in some minds which cannot be unlocked by trifles, but which, when unlocked, discovers a cabinet of fortitude; and I reckon it among those kind of public blessings, which we do not immediately see, that God hath blessed him with uninterrupted health and given him a mind that can even flourish upon care.

I shall conclude this paper with some miscellaneous remarks on the state of our affairs; and shall begin with asking the following question: Why is it that the enemy have left the New England provinces and made these middle ones the seat of war? The answer is easy: New England is not infested with Tories, and we are. I have been tender in raising the cry against these men, and used numberless arguments to show them their danger, but it will not do to sacrifice a world either to their folly or their baseness. The period is now arrived, in which either they, or we, must change our sentiments, or one or both must fall. And what is a Tory? Good God! What is he? I should not be afraid to go with a hundred Whigs against a thousand Tories, were they to attempt to get into arms. Every Tory is a coward; for servile, slavish, self-interested fear is the foundation of Toryism; and a man under such influence, though he may be cruel, never can be brave. But, before the line of irrecoverable separation be drawn between us, let us reason the matter together: your conduct is an invitation to the enemy, yet not one in a thousand of you has heart enough to join him. Howe is as much deceived by you as the American cause is injured by you. He expects you will all take up arms and flock to his standard with muskets on your shoulders. Your opinions are of no use to him, unless you support him personally, for 'tis soldiers, and not Tories, that he wants.

I once felt all that kind of anger, which a man ought to feel, against the mean principles that are held by the Tories: a noted one, who kept a tavern at Amboy, was standing at his door with as pretty a child in his hand about eight or nine years old, as I ever saw, and after speaking his mind as freely as he thought was prudent, finished with this unfatherly expression, "Well! Give me peace in my day." Not a man lives on the continent but fully believes that a separation must some time or other finally take place, and a generous parent should have said, "If there must be trouble, let it be in my day, that my child may have peace"; and this single reflection, well applied, is sufficient to awaken every man to duty. Not a place upon earth might be so happy as America. Her situation is remote from all the wrangling world, and she has nothing to do but to trade with them. A man can distinguish himself between temper and principle, and I am as confident, as I am that God governs the world, that America will never be happy till she gets clear of foreign dominion. Wars, without ceasing, will break out till that period

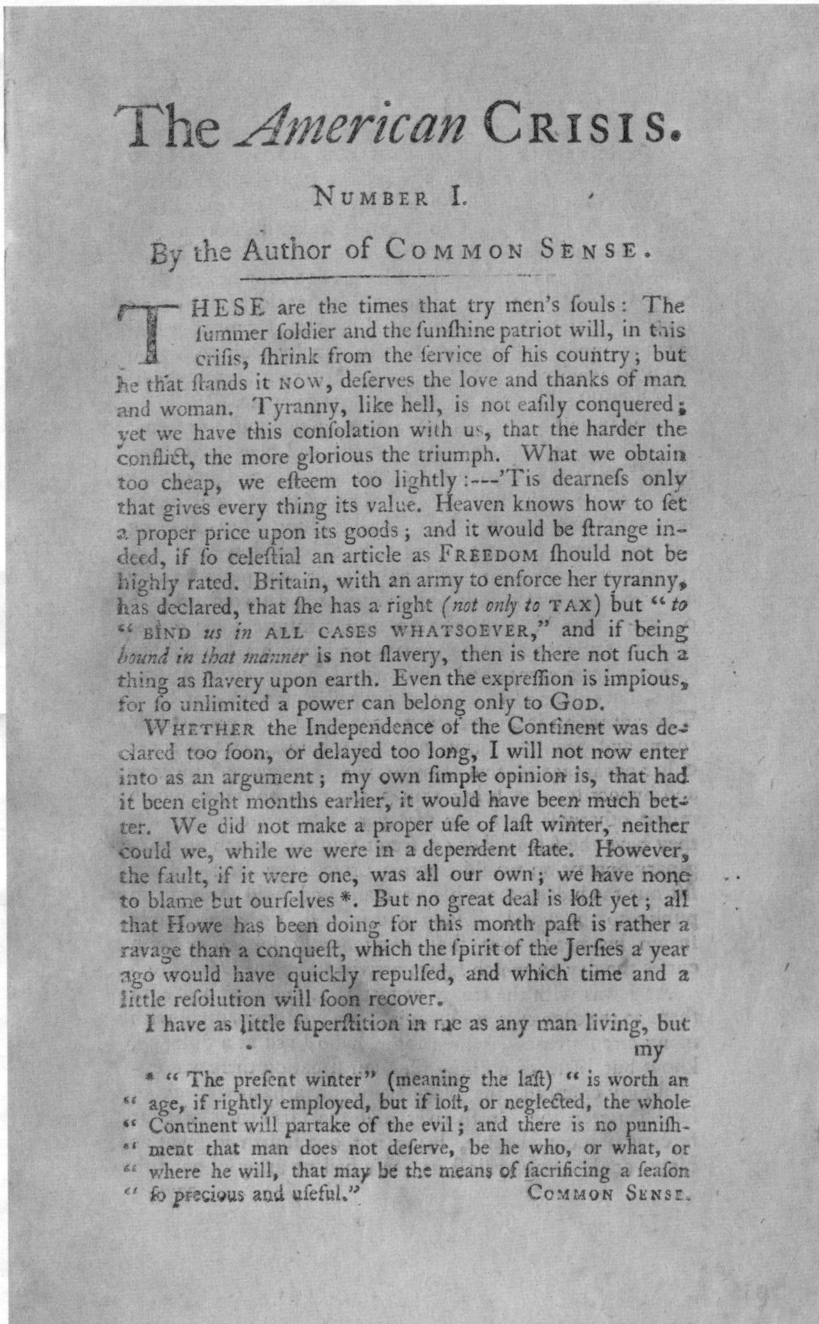

The *American* Crisis.

Number I.

By the Author of Common Sense.

THESE are the times that try men's ſouls: The ſummer ſoldier and the ſunſhine patriot will, in this criſis, ſhrink from the ſervice of his country; but he that ſtands it NOW, deſerves the love and thanks of man and woman. Tyranny, like hell, is not eaſily conquered; yet we have this conſolation with us, that the harder the conflict, the more glorious the triumph. What we obtain too cheap, we eſteem too lightly:---'Tis dearneſs only that gives every thing its value. Heaven knows how to ſet a proper price upon its goods; and it would be ſtrange indeed, if ſo celeſtial an article as FREEDOM ſhould not be highly rated. Britain, with an army to enforce her tyranny, has declared, that ſhe has a right (*not only to* TAX) but "*to* " BIND *us in* ALL CASES WHATSOEVER," and if being *bound in that manner* is not ſlavery, then is there not ſuch a thing as ſlavery upon earth. Even the expreſſion is impious, for ſo unlimited a power can belong only to God.

Whether the Independence of the Continent was declared too ſoon, or delayed too long, I will not now enter into as an argument; my own ſimple opinion is, that had it been eight months earlier, it would have been much better. We did not make a proper uſe of laſt winter, neither could we, while we were in a dependent ſtate. However, the fault, if it were one, was all our own; we have none to blame but ourſelves*. But no great deal is loſt yet; all that Howe has been doing for this month paſt is rather a ravage than a conqueſt, which the ſpirit of the Jerſies a year ago would have quickly repulſed, and which time and a little reſolution will ſoon recover.

I have as little ſuperſtition in me as any man living, but

my

* " The preſent winter" (meaning the laſt) " is worth an " age, if rightly employed, but if loſt, or neglected, the whole " Continent will partake of the evil; and there is no puniſhment that man does not deſerve, be he who, or what, or " where he will, that may be the means of ſacrificing a ſeaſon " ſo precious and uſeful." Common Sense.

The opening page of the first number in Thomas Paine's influential pamphlet series, The Crisis, *published in 1776 and printed in Philadelphia by Melchior Styner and Charles Cist.*

arrives, and the continent must in the end be conqueror; for though the flame of liberty may sometimes cease to shine, the coal can never expire.

America did not, nor does not want force; but she wanted a proper application of that force. Wisdom is not the purchase of a day, and it is no wonder that we should err at the first setting off. From an excess of tenderness, we were unwilling to raise an army, and trusted our cause to the temporary defense of a well-meaning militia. A summer's experience has now taught us better; yet with those troops, while they were collected, we were able to set bounds to the progress of the enemy, and, thank God! They are again assembling. I always considered militia as the best troops in the world for a sudden exertion, but they will not do for a long campaign. Howe, it is probable, will make an attempt on this city [Philadelphia]; should he fail on this side the Delaware, he is ruined. If he succeeds, our cause is not ruined. He stakes all on his side against a part on ours; admitting he succeeds, the consequence will be that armies from both ends of the continent will march to assist their suffering friends in the middle states; for he cannot go everywhere, it is impossible. I consider Howe as the greatest enemy the Tories have; he is bringing a war into their country, which, had it not been for him and partly for themselves, they had been clear of. Should he now be expelled; I wish with all the devotion of a Christian that the names of Whig and Tory may never more be mentioned; but should the Tories give him encouragement to come, or assistance if he come, I as sincerely wish that our next year's arms may expel them from the continent, and [that] the Congress appropriate their possessions to the relief of those who have suffered in well-doing. A single successful battle next year will settle the whole. America could carry on a two years' war by the confiscation of the property of disaffected persons, and be made happy by their expulsion. Say not that this is revenge; call it rather the soft resentment of a suffering people, who, having no object in view but the good of all, have staked their own all upon a seemingly doubtful event. Yet it is folly to argue against determined hardness; eloquence may strike the ear, and the language of sorrow draw forth the tear of compassion, but nothing can reach the heart that is steeled with prejudice.

Quitting this class of men, I turn with the warm ardor of a friend to those who have nobly stood, and are yet determined to stand the matter out. I call not upon a few, but upon all: not on this state or that state, but on every state: up and help us; lay your shoulders to the wheel; better have too much force than too little, when so great an object is at stake. Let it be told to the future world that in the depth of winter, when nothing but hope and virtue could survive, that the city and the country, alarmed at one common danger, came forth to meet and to repulse it. Say not that thousands are gone; turn out your tens of thousands; throw not the burden of the day upon Providence, but "show your faith by your works," that God may bless you. It matters not where you live or what rank of life you hold, the evil or the blessing will reach you all. The far and the near, the home counties and the back, the rich and the poor, will suffer or rejoice alike. The heart that feels not now is dead; the blood of his children will curse his cowardice, who shrinks back at a time when a little might have saved the whole, and made them happy. I love the man that can smile in trouble, that can gather strength from distress, and grow brave by reflection. 'Tis the business of little minds to shrink; but he whose heart is firm, and whose conscience approves his conduct, will pursue his principles unto death. My own line of reasoning is to myself as straight and clear as a ray of light. Not all the treasures of the world, so far as I believe, could have induced me to support an offensive war, for I think it murder; but if a thief breaks into my house, burns and destroys my property, and kills or threatens to kill me, or those that are in it, and to "bind me in all cases whatsoever" to his absolute will, am I to suffer it? What signifies it to me, whether he who does it is a king or a common man; my countryman or not my countryman; whether it be done by an individual villain, or an army of them? If we reason to the root of things we shall find no difference; neither can any just cause be assigned why we should punish in the one case and pardon in the other. Let them call me rebel and welcome. I feel no concern from it; but I should suffer the misery of devils, were I to make a whore of my soul by swearing allegiance to one whose character is that of a sottish, stupid, stubborn, worthless, brutish man. I conceive likewise a horrid idea in receiving mercy from a being, who at the last day shall be shrieking to the rocks and mountains to cover him and fleeing with terror from the orphan, the widow, and the slain of America.

There are cases which cannot be overdone by language, and this is one. There are persons, too, who see not the full extent of the evil which threatens them; they solace themselves with hopes that the enemy, if he succeed, will be merciful. It is the madness of folly to expect mercy from those who have refused to do justice; and even mercy, where conquest is the object, is only a trick of war; the cunning of the fox is as murderous as the violence of the wolf, and we ought to guard equally against both. Howe's first object is, partly by threats and partly by promises, to terrify or seduce the people to deliver up their arms and receive mercy. The ministry recommended the same plan to Gage, and this is what the Tories call making their peace, "a peace which passeth all understanding" indeed! A peace which would be the immediate forerunner of a worse ruin than any we have yet thought of. Ye men of Pennsylvania, do reason upon these things! Were the back counties to give up their arms, they would fall an easy prey to the Indians, who are all armed: this perhaps is what some Tories would not be sorry for. Were the home counties to deliver up their arms, they would be exposed to the resentment of the back counties who would then have it in their power to chastise their defection at pleasure. And were any one state to give up its arms, that state must be garrisoned by all Howe's army of Britons and Hessians to preserve it from the anger of the rest. Mutual fear is the principal link in the chain of mutual love, and woe be to that state that breaks the compact. Howe is mercifully inviting you to barbarous destruction, and men must be either rogues or fools that will not see it. I dwell not upon the vapors of imagination; I bring reason to your ears, and, in language as plain as A, B, C, hold up truth to your eyes.

I thank God that I fear not. I see no real cause for fear. I know our situation well, and can see the way out of it. While our army was collected, Howe dared not risk a battle; and it is no credit to him that he decamped from the White Plains and waited a mean opportunity to ravage the defenseless Jerseys; but it is great credit to us, that, with a handful of men, we sustained an orderly retreat for near an hundred miles, brought off our ammunition, all our field pieces, the greatest part of our stores, and had four rivers to pass. None can say that our retreat was precipitate, for we were near three weeks in performing it, that the country might have time to come in. Twice we marched back to meet the enemy and remained out till dark. The sign of fear was not seen in our camp, and had not some of the cowardly and disaffected inhabitants spread false alarms through the country, the Jerseys had never been ravaged. Once more we are again collected and collecting; our new army at both ends of the continent is recruiting fast, and we shall be able to open the next campaign with sixty thousand men, well armed and clothed. This is our situation, and who will may know it. By perseverance and fortitude we have the prospect of a glorious issue; by cowardice and submission, the sad choice of a variety of evils: a ravaged country, a depopulated city, habitations without safety, and slavery without hope; our homes turned into barracks and bawdyhouses for Hessians, and a future race to provide for, whose fathers we shall doubt of. Look on this picture and weep over it! And if there yet remains one thoughtless wretch who believes it not, let him suffer it unlamented.

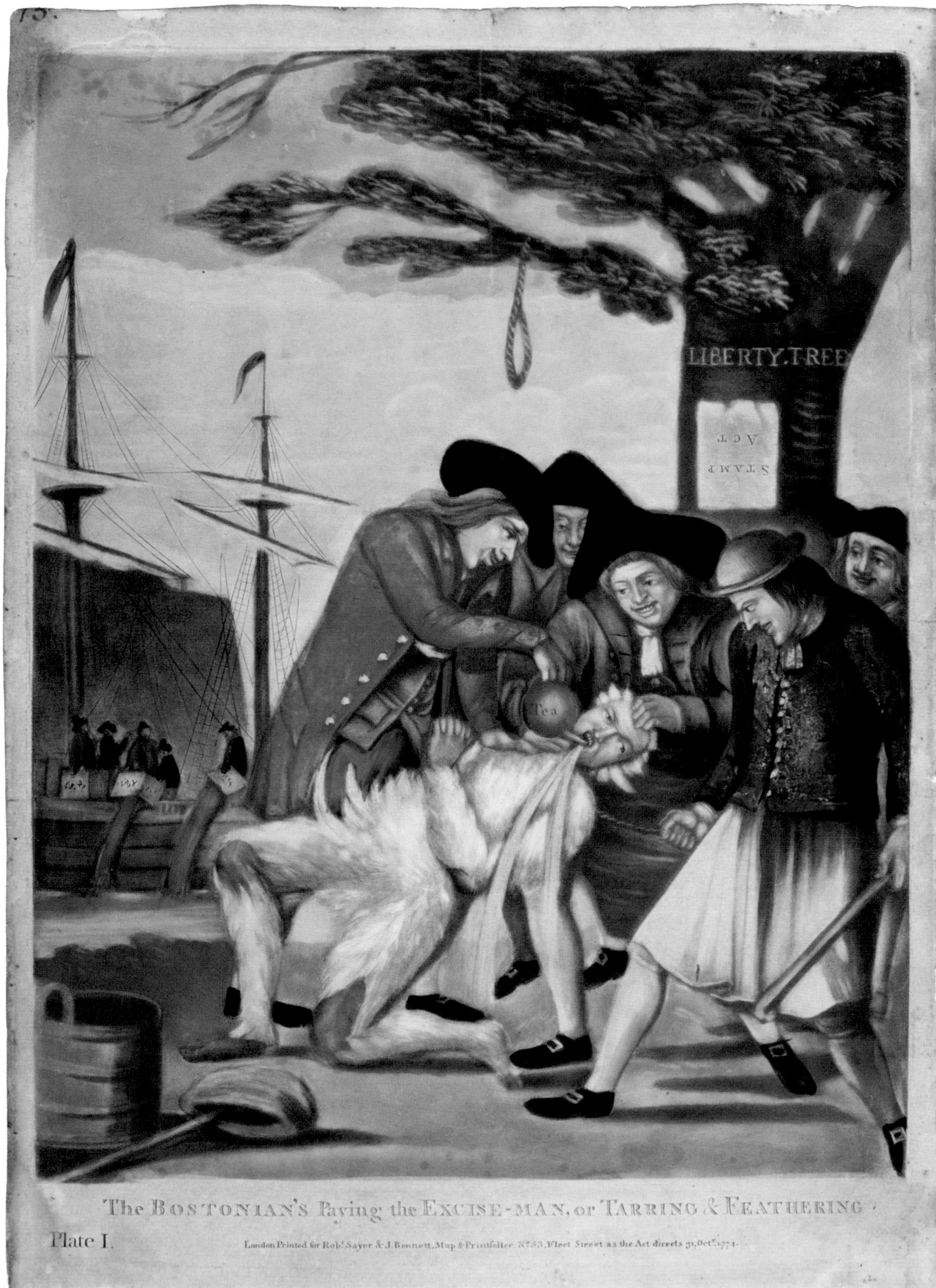
LIBERTY.TREE
STAMP ACT
Tea
The BOSTONIAN'S Paying the EXCISE-MAN, or TARRING & FEATHERING
Plate I.
London Printed for Robt. Sayer & J. Bennett, Map & Printseller, No. 53, Fleet Street as the Act directs 31, Octr. 1774.

and over tavern tables he was, whether he realized it or not, an object of anxious observation to his fellow delegates. The distant clang of arms was in the air and his reputation as a soldier had not been forgotten. Silas Deane of Connecticut was surprised to find that the hero of Braddock's defeat was still in his prime. (Washington was forty-two.)

The Congress voted, with Washington's agreement, further commercial reprisals, gave no hint of a willingness to compromise, and indicated that the colonies would unite in meeting force with force. This strong stand brought no exhilaration to the tall Virginian. He rode home sick at heart. Seventeen years before, he had turned his back on the military life. He was happy on his plantation and as a neighborhood patriarch. Now all that he had created was endangered.

By April 1769, Washington had become so worried about the suppression of American liberties that he visualized the possibility of an armed rebellion—but only as the very last resort.

There were opening up, of course, new opportunities for glory. How brightly they would have shone in his imagination when, as a younger man, he had written that his "inclinations" were "strongly bent to arms." Now, when the royal governor of Virginia seized the colony's gunpowder, Washington used all his influence to keep armed militiamen from interfering with the peaceful negotiation which finally elicited a return of the powder. But he was also drilling the militia in preparation for the worst.

By the time Washington attended the Second Continental Congress in May 1775, fighting at Lexington and Concord had released "the shot heard round the world." A numerous army of New Englanders was encamped around British-held Boston. Not being introspective, Washington undoubtedly did not probe his motives for wearing to the congressional sessions his military uniform. His conscious intention was to testify that Virginia was willing to fight. He seems to have expected that he would become, as he had been during the French and Indian War, the commander in chief of Virginia forces. When, after the Congress had convened, the rumor circulated that he might be made commander in chief of a continental army, he urged some of his fellow Virginians to try to block the move.

Washington's memories of his activities during the French and Indian War did not encourage any confidence in his military gifts, and the task ahead seemed to call for genius. At the beginning of the Revolutionary War, it was known (so he later wrote) that "the expense in comparison with our circumstances as colonists must be enormous, the struggle protracted, dubious, and severe. It was known that the resources of Britain were, in a manner, inexhaustible, that her fleets covered the ocean, and that her troops had harvested laurels in every quarter of the globe. Not then organized as a nation . . . we had no preparation. Money, the nerve of war, was wanting. The sword was to be forged on the anvil of necessity."

In this retrospective account, Washington defined the colonists' "secret resource" as "the unconquerable resolution of our citizens." However, no such "unconquerable resolution" was manifested by the debates Washington listened to in the Congress. The prevailing policy was to evince as much loyalty to the Crown as was under the circumstances possible. If the

Opposite: *This 1774 British engraving, known as* Bostonians Paying the Excise-Man, *or* Tarring & Feathering, *by Philip Dawe depicts the humiliation of the British official John Malcolm, the Boston commissioner of customs. The earlier Boston Tea Party is depicted in the background.*

colonies initiated no hostilities, if the colonies only defended themselves when attacked, surely George III, as the sovereign of America as well as England, would curb Parliament and his ministers. The Congress still hoped that the whole trouble would blow over. This teetering was far from satisfactory to Massachusetts, which had on its hands an actual war.

As John Adams, the chief of the Massachusetts delegation, puzzled over how to lead the continent into an alliance, his vision fixed on the uniformed figure of Washington. Washington was the most celebrated veteran of the French and Indian War who was still young enough to lead a new contest. He possessed charm combined with manifest physical and nervous power, a clear gift for leadership which Adams recognized, even if he resented it in a giant he considered unintellectual. And, thank heaven, Washington was from Virginia!

It was a principle as old as all efforts at American unity that leadership had to be divided between the Northeast and the South. What better way to get the Congress and through them the continent entangled in the actual hostilities than to have them elect the magnetic and experienced Virginia warrior as commander in chief of what was otherwise a purely New England army.

Adams lobbied actively for Washington's election. Washington kept away from the session at which the ballot was to be taken. His election was unanimous.

When Washington appeared before the Congress on June 16, 1775, he made no spread-eagle speech promising bloody success. He had accepted the "momentous duty" because Congress desired it, "but, lest some unlucky event should happen . . . I beg it may be remembered, by every gentleman in this room, that I, this day, declare with the utmost sincerity, I do not think myself equal to the command I am honored with." Having expressed a desire to receive no salary, being paid only for his expenses of which he would keep "an exact account," Washington sat down.

The new commander in chief was the first and only member of the Continental army. If the Congress changed mood and policy, he might be left standing alone with a sword in his hand, to triumphant British power the most conspicuous of traitors. Although the delegates were not yet ready formally to adopt the New England army, they did resolve unanimously: "This Congress doth now declare that they will maintain and assist and adhere to him, the said George Washington, with their lives and fortunes."

John Adams, who had helped engineer this vote, was worried by it. However politically necessary the move, there was grave danger in setting up a man as the symbol of a cause which might create an independent nation. Adams's reading of history had persuaded him that strong men invariably grasp all power within their reach. This George Washington was obviously a strong man. He would be a prodigy if he did not try to make himself king.

Nine

A VIRGINIAN IN YANKEE-LAND

(1775)

Once Washington had been firmly designated the leader of armed resistance against the British, anxiety took over. The congressmen who had reluctantly taken so dangerous a step needed reassurance, but the Virginian on whom they had staked their "lives and fortunes" refused to be reassuring. He remembered what he had seen during the French and Indian War of the sophistication which the British regular army brought to the type of fighting (not wilderness warfare) that now lay ahead. He continued to insist that the command he had been given was "too boundless for my abilities and far, very far beyond my experience." The congressmen had to comfort themselves with the thought that Washington's diffidence would encourage him to take advice, do nothing rash.

But where was Washington himself to find comfort? He postponed for three days notifying his wife of his election, and then begged her not to add to his perturbation with her own. She should force herself to be as content as she could. "I should enjoy more real happiness in one month with you at home than I have the most distant prospect of finding abroad, if my stay were to be seven times seven years. But, as it has been a kind of destiny that has thrown me upon this service, I shall hope that my undertaking it is designed to answer some good purpose."

Without any consciousness that he was sowing future trouble, Washington begged help from four grasping men, each of whom concluded that the new commander in chief was too incompetent to get on without the help each condescendingly promised. Two of these first advisers were soldiers, two politically important businessmen.

Charles Lee had the reputation of being a military genius. Many patriots regretted that, because he was a recent immigrant from England (and was so eccentric), he could not be commander in chief instead of Washington. After distinguished service in the British regular army, Lee had adventured to Poland, where he was a major general and accompanied a Russian army against the Turks. Having, on his return to England, written radical pamphlets and insulted George III to his face, he had settled in America. He was tall and emaciated, dirty of clothes and body, voluble, foul-mouthed, seemingly brilliant, best characterized by his Indian name, "Boiling Water." He felt that he was making perhaps too great a sacrifice in agreeing to be commanded by the amateur Washington.

Another English officer, Horatio Gates, had at Washington's request been given the major staff post of adjutant general. The son of a duke's housekeeper and presumably the duke, Gates had risen in the British regular army to the rank of major and then discovered that, despite his superior ability, his equivocal birth blocked any further advancement. Washington, who had served with him in the previous war, had persuaded him to emigrate to Virginia. Gates was stocky,

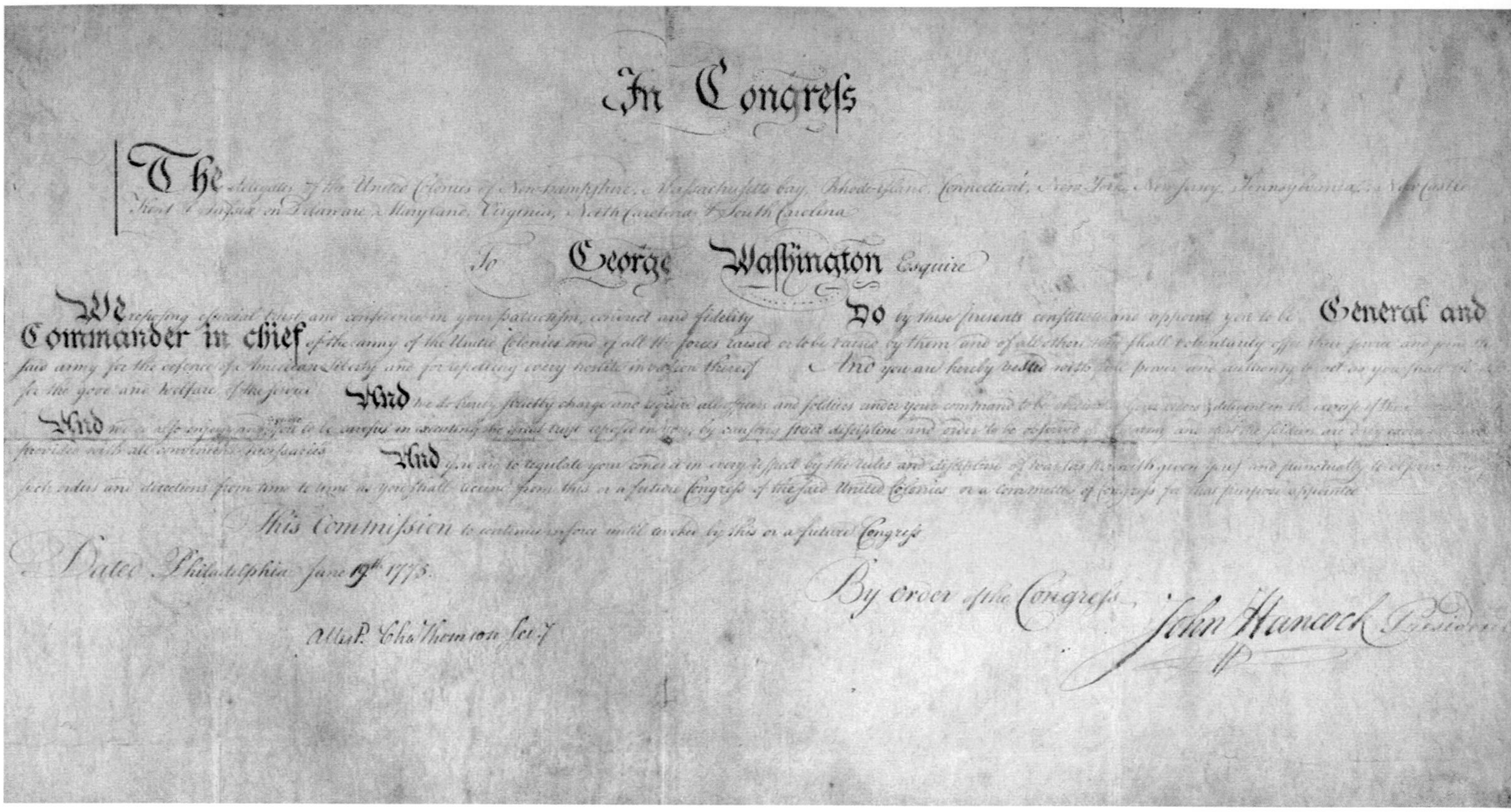

In Congress

The delegates of the United Colonies of New Hampshire, Massachusetts bay, Rhode island, Connecticut, New York, New Jersey, Pennsylvania, New Castle Kent & Sussex on Delaware, Maryland, Virginia, North Carolina & South Carolina

To George Washington Esquire

We reposing special trust and confidence in your patriotism, conduct and fidelity Do by these presents constitute and appoint you to be General and Commander in chief of the army of the United Colonies and of all the forces raised or to be raised by them and of all others who shall voluntarily offer their service and join the said army for the defence of American liberty and for repelling every hostile invasion thereof And you are hereby vested with full power and authority to act as you shall think for the good and welfare of the service

And we do hereby strictly charge and require all officers and soldiers under your command to be obedient to your orders & diligent in the exercise of their several duties

And we do also enjoin and require you to be careful in executing the great trust reposed in you, by causing strict discipline and order to be observed in the army and that the soldiers are duly exercised and provided with all convenient necessaries

And you are to regulate your conduct in every respect by the rules and discipline of war (as herewith given you) and punctually to observe and follow such orders and directions from time to time as you shall receive from this or a future Congress of the said United Colonies or a committee of Congress for that purpose appointed

This Commission to continue in force until revoked by this or a future Congress

Dated Philadelphia June 19th 1775.

By order of the Congress

John Hancock President

Attest. Chas Thomson secy

Washington's commission as commander in chief of the American army, June 19, 1775.

stubborn, extremely competent, ambitious, unsure, a little cringing.

To bring him urban know-how and political finesse, the Virginia planter recruited as aides-de-camp men prominent in the revolutionary leadership: Joseph Reed, a lawyer, and Thomas Mifflin, a merchant. Reed was a zealot with a ponderous melancholy face. Mifflin, who had handled business affairs far beyond Washington's scope, was also celebrated as an orator. His handsome features were always in facile motion.

When Washington, having found his own way, ceased to depend upon his four original advisers, all four became his extremely dangerous enemies.

On June 23, 1775, Washington's party set out to join his army in Cambridge. The commander in chief was seen off with as much military pomp as Philadelphia could muster. Fortunately, he did not know that the most influential member of Congress burned, as he watched, with jealousy. "Such," John Adams wrote, "is the pride and pomp of war. I, poor creature, worn out with scribbling for my bread and my liberty, low in spirits and weak in health, must leave others to wear the laurels which I have sown."

Washington's route passed through New York City. As coincidence would have it, on the very day he was expected to ferry across the Hudson, the royal governor, William Tryon, was expected to sail up the harbor on his return from a visit to England. Unsure of their allegiance and thus of which arrival they should celebrate, the New York Provincial Council was driven to distraction. They finally decided that one militia company should meet Washington, another Tryon, and the rest attend whoever arrived first.

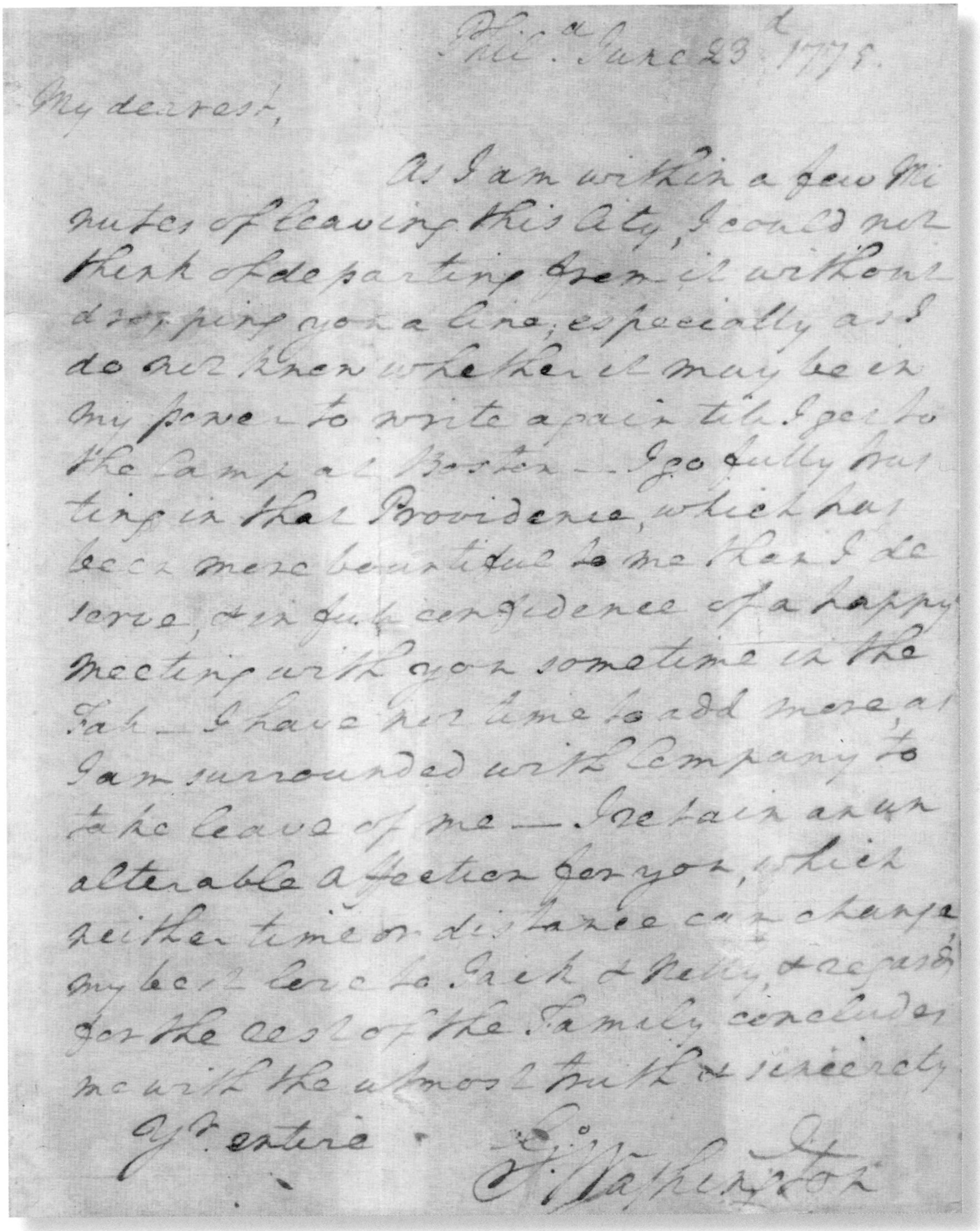

Phil.a June 23d 1775.

My dearest,

As I am within a few Minutes of leaving this City, I could not think of departing from it without dropping you a line; especially as I do not know whether it may be in my power to write again till I get to the Camp at Boston — I go fully trusting in that Providence, which has been more bountiful to me than I deserve, & in full confidence of a happy meeting with you sometime in the Fall — I have not time to add more, as I am surrounded with Company to take leave of me — I retain an unalterable affection for you, which neither time or distance can change my best love to Jack & Nelly, & regard for the rest of the Family concludes me with the utmost truth & sincerety

Yr. entire

Go: Washington

George penned this poignant note to Martha on June 23, 1775, just before departing Philadelphia for the American camp at Cambridge, Massachusetts.

Major General Charles Lee, a British soldier turned Virginia planter who became a general officer of the Continental army, is best known for his actions during the Battle of Monmouth. Washington needed a secondary commander to lead the frontal assault. He reluctantly put Lee in charge, as he was the most senior of his generals. Washington ordered him to attack the retreating enemy, but, instead, Lee ordered a retreat—and backed his men directly into Washington and his troops, who were advancing. Shortly thereafter, he was court-martialed for insubordination. Illustration from Geschichte der kriege in und ausser Europa, *Nürnberg, 1778.*

Horatio Gates *by Charles Willson Peale from life, oil on canvas, 1782. Gates took credit for the American victory at the Battle of Saratoga and was blamed for the defeat at the Battle of Camden. Historian George Bilias describes him as "one of the Revolution's most controversial military figures," due, among other reasons, to his role in a whispering campaign meant to discredit and replace Washington.*

Thomas Mifflin, *by Rembrant and Raphael Peale after Charles Willson Peale, detail, oil on canvas, c. 1795, served as Washington's aide-de-camp. On August 14, 1775, Washington appointed him the army's first quartermaster general.*

Joseph Reed, *drawn from life by Pierre Eugène du Simitière, and engraved by B. L. Prévost. Joseph Reed was the governor of Pennsylvania in 1781, when nearly half of the 2,500 men in the Pennsylvania Line of the Continental army mutinied from their camp at Morristown, New Jersey. Protesting that their three-year enlistments were up, they intended to march on the Continental Congress at Philadelphia and demand back-pay—but first, the mutineers traveled to Princeton, New Jersey, where they met with Reed, then president of the Pennsylvania Executive Council. He agreed to terms that ended the mutiny.*

Washington having arrived first, a satisfactory parade led him into the city, but in the middle of the reception in his honor many important guests slipped silently away; Tryon was receiving. The general and the governor lodged a few doors apart. As spectators tried to judge New York sentiment by comparing the amount of attention paid to each of the opposing leaders, Washington found that his first revolutionary competition was not on any battlefield but in the civilian world for popular support.

"I should enjoy more real happiness in one month with you at home than I have the most distant prospect of finding abroad, if my stay were to be seven times seven years. But, as it has been a kind of destiny that has thrown me upon this service, I shall hope that my undertaking it is designed to answer some good purpose."

In passing a resolution congratulating Washington on his arrival, the New York Assembly expressed the hope that, after "the fondest wish of every American soul, an accommodation with our mother country," had been achieved, Washington would "cheerfully" lay down his arms "and resume the character of our worthiest citizen." Washington could reply with complete sincerity that when he and his colleagues "assumed the soldier we did not lay down the civilian." They yearned for "that happy hour when the establishment of American liberty upon the most firm and solid foundations shall enable us to return to our private stations."

Washington was, indeed, so little the dedicated soldier that he never regarded fighting the enemy as the fundamental means by which the Revolutionary War would be won. He demonstrated again and again his conviction that the crucial battlefields were in the minds of individual Americans. If the majority decided that they would be better off under renewed submission to the Crown, all military efforts to defeat the British would be of as little avail as trying to stop a river that was perpetually flowing. But, if the people became such staunch supporters of American rights that they would hold steadfast through any emergency, the British might just as well march their military might into the ocean.

While in New York, Washington heard that a great battle had been fought outside Boston for the control of Bunker (or Breed) Hill. Dispatches presented the engagement as a patriot defeat because the Massachusetts army had been driven from the ground. The new commander in chief was too naïve to realize the significance of the great loss the British had suffered. The generals from overseas had been so scornful of their amateur opponents that they had sent wave after wave of professional soldiers against the seemingly ridiculous earthen redoubt that the Americans had built. When they counted their dead, the British recognized a bitter lesson: since their soldiers could only be replaced at great cost from overseas, they could not again suffer major casualties by attacking embattled American farmers who had defenses to crouch behind. When Washington became conscious of this British conclusion, it was to have a major effect on his strategy.

As Washington approached his army, he stopped off at Watertown, the seat of the Massachusetts Congress. He found there no lack of revolutionary fervor. However, what the delegates had to report was not encouraging. The army was in the greatest confusion; almost everything needed to be straightened out.

Yet, it was far from clear that the Yankee troops would willingly obey the orders of a Virginian. Washington undoubtedly remembered that his own previous visit to Massachusetts had been to protest the claims of a Marylander to give orders to the Virginia Regiment. He agreed that it would be wise for him to take advantage of the Sabbath by slipping inconspicuously into the encampment.

Washington was, indeed, so little the dedicated soldier that he never regarded fighting the enemy as the fundamental means by which the Revolutionary War would be won. He demonstrated again and again his conviction that the crucial battlefields were in the minds of individual Americans.

The review with which the new commander was said to have been greeted as he stood under "the Washington Elm" is, although enshrined in the history books, pure legend. (The army was not well enough trained to march in a review and would probably have greeted the Virginian with jeers, not cheers.) There is better reason to believe that Washington attended, on the night of his arrival, a drunken party, during which "adjutant Gibbs of Glover's was hoisted (English fashion) chair and all upon the table, and gave the company a rollicking bachelor's song."

Washington's first duty was to determine the strategic situation. The shoreline of Boston Harbor was then (much water has since been filled in) shaped like a battered half moon. The New England army was encamped along the rim of this arc and in the town of Cambridge behind it. From areas about ten miles apart, two peninsulas shaped like tennis rackets angled into the bay towards each other, their heads being separated only by a narrow channel. Boston and Charlestown necks were occupied by the enemy. Their narrow connections with the mainland were so fortified that troops could not pass either way. Out in the harbor was what looked like a forest of dead trees: masts of a British fleet that dominated all deep water.

As Washington rode through the New England encampment, the stench indicated that the troops were risking their health by not digging privies. He quickly discovered that no one gave or obeyed any orders. The militiamen, having elected their officers, expected due subservience to the sovereign voters. What entrenchments there were had been dug according to argumentative whim and indolent caprice. How true that everything needed reorganizing, replanning, enlarging, strengthening!

The grandfather of Ralph Waldo Emerson, Regimental Chaplain William Emerson, soon noted, "There is great overturning in the camp as to order and regularity. New lords, new laws. The generals Washington and Lee are upon the lines every day." Orders were read to the regiments every morning after prayers. "Great distinction is made between officers and soldiers. Everyone is made to know his place and keep it, or be tied up and receive thirty or forty lashes according to his crime. Thousands are at work every day from four till eleven o'clock in the morning. It is surprising how much work has been done."

The basic necessary reform, Washington believed, was to establish a good officer corps. "I have," he reported to a fellow Virginian in Congress, "made a pretty good grand slam among such kind of officers as the Massachusetts government abounds in . . . having broke one colonel and two captains for cowardly behavior in the action on Bunker Hill." He had discharged or was prosecuting various other officers for incompetence or peculation. "In short, I spare

This map of Boston Harbor on August 5, 1775, as depicted by J. F. W. Des Barres was owned by Washington.

none, yet fear it will not all do, as these people seem to be too inattentive to everything but their interest."

Since the enemy shipping would enable the British to concentrate their force in an attack on any spot in his defenses, Washington ordered that horses be kept saddled in every area to give the alarm. If he were to have the necessary reserves always ready, his own force would, he calculated, have to be twice the British: eighteen to twenty thousand men. He was assured that his army was at least that size, but this was only a guess. Repeated orders failed to induce his officers to send in returns of their men. "Threatening means" finally elicited imperfect reports that were frightening. The army was not more than fourteen thousand,

Currier and Ives's 1876 lithograph The Minute-men of the Revolution *shows men preparing to go off to war and the families they left behind.*

of whom twelve—hardly more than the British—were fit for duty. But at least Washington could quiet himself with the thought that he had enough powder. The storerooms, he had been assured, contained 308 barrels. But then it developed that this was the total amount that had been delivered to the army since the beginning of the campaign. Most had been expended at Bunker Hill. There were in fact only thirty-six barrels, less than nine rounds a man. The army would be helpless if the British attacked.

THE BATTLE of BUNKER HILL June 17th 1775

Inside: *A sketch of the Battle of Bunker Hill, June 17, 1775, by Sir Thomas Hyde Page.*

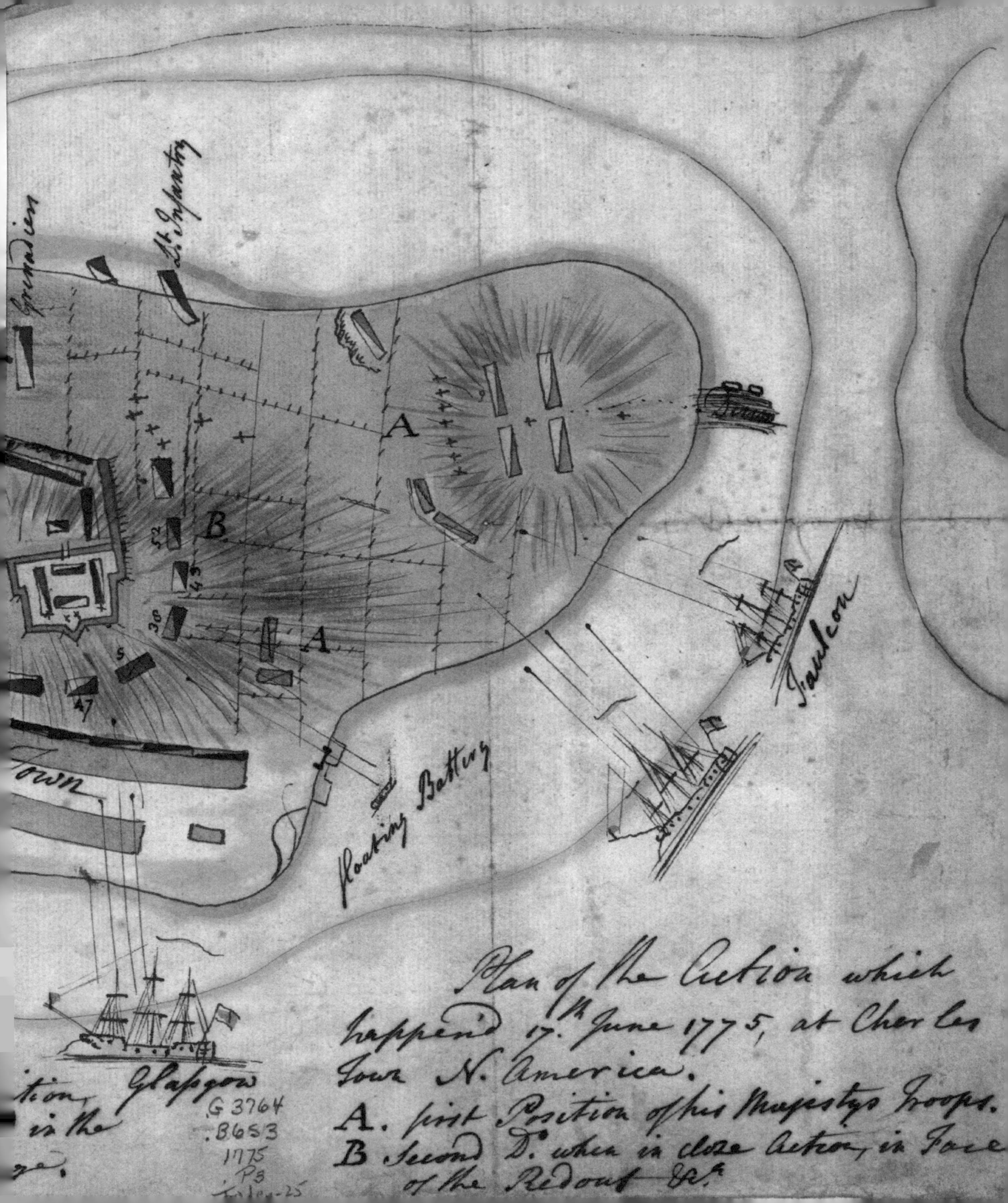
Grenadiers
Lt. Infantry
A
B
52
43
38
5
47
Town
Floating Battery
Faulcon
Glasgow
tion,
in the
ge.
Plan of the Action which happen'd 17th June 1775, at Charles Town N. America.
A. first Position of his Majestys Troops.
B Second Do. when in close Action, in Face of the Redout &c.

of the Rebels from Cambridge
C
C
C
Mistic River
Phipps's Farm
Charles
Floating Battery
Arm'd Transport
N.B. The Deep-Green shews the
and order of March, obser
Rebel-Army from Cambri

The Death of General Warren at the Battle of Bunker's Hill, 17 June 1775, *by John Trumbull, oil on canvas, after 1815–before 1831. Museum of Fine Arts, Boston. Gift of Howland S. Warren.*

CHARLES TOWN
BOSTON
View of The ATTACK on BUNKER'S HILL, with the Burning of CHARLES TOWN, June 17.1775.
Drawn by Mr. Millar
Engraved by Lodge.

This engraving, c. 1783, by Lodge after a drawing by Millar shows the attack on Bunker Hill and the burning of Charlestown.

Although Washington had no way of knowing that a leader in the Massachusetts Congress was a British spy, he cautiously kept the fact that his army was defenseless from all but two or three key men. Every conceivable spurious reason for needing powder was imagined and used in appeals broadcast across the land. As Washington spent sleepless nights listening for alarm bells, powder appeared from here and there until at last he could stretch his long form out in comparative ease.

Washington's recurring difficulties merged with his regional prejudices to fill him with such bitterness against the New Englanders that his discretion failed him. The Yankees were, the Virginian wrote, "generally speaking the most indifferent kind of people I ever saw . . . an exceedingly dirty and nasty people."

Some of these strictures were leaked to John Adams and the other New Englanders in Congress. Although—as subsequent events were to show—they did not forget, they made no attempt to remove Washington from the command.

How can one explain why the Virginian, who had come in as an unpopular appointment and had shaken up the army so violently (even making Congregationalists work on the sacrosanct Sabbath), had gained in prestige with the Yankees despite his insulting remarks?

To begin with, there was his appearance. Word traveled to London that Washington's martial dignity would set him apart among ten thousand men: "Not a king in Europe but would look like a valet de chambre by his side." And then there was his charm. On meeting him, Abigail Adams quoted to her husband what the Queen of Sheba had said on meeting Solomon, "The half was not told me."

Although the New England leaders were prevented by local equalitarianism from establishing military subordination, they realized the importance of discipline, and were glad, even if they publicly criticized Washington, to see it established. And Yankees respected frugality and labor. Washington had not only personally refused a salary, but he wasted nothing. And no one could have been more faithful. Perhaps because he had been criticized during the French and Indian War for being often away from his regiment, he never left the camp except to ride occasionally to consult the legislators at Watertown.

Washington's recurring difficulties merged with his regional prejudices to fill him with such bitterness against the New Englanders that his discretion failed him. The Yankees were, the Virginian wrote, "generally speaking the most indifferent kind of people I ever saw . . . an exceedingly dirty and nasty people."

Furthermore, the army was comfortable in its situation. The enemy remained quiescent. Food and clothing were still plentiful. Being all from a single region where immunity had been built up to the prevailing diseases, the men were healthy. The blockade at Boston was less like a military campaign than an extended mass camping trip.

It was Washington who lay awake worrying; it was Washington who suffered. James Warren, the president of the Massachusetts Congress, wrote, "I pity our poor general, who has a greater burden on his shoulders and more difficulties to struggle with than I think should fall to the share of so good a man. . . . I see he is fatigued and worried."

Ten

AN EARLY TRIUMPH

(1775–1776)

On accepting the command, Washington had written to his wife that he expected to be home by autumn. It was hard to doubt that George III, impressed by the resistance which his loyal but outraged American subjects were mounting, would curb his parliament and ministry. Furthermore, after Washington had surveyed the situation at Cambridge, he decided that a completely effective strategy was open to him. He would hold the "ministerial troops" in a tight blockade. He would successfully harass any effort they made to break out into the countryside. The army in Boston, having thus been made useless, would "sink" Great Britain "under the disgrace and weight of the expense." This would surely "overthrow the designs of the administration."

However, as the stalemate went on for month after month, Washington became increasingly concerned about the future of his own army. No preparation had been made for maintaining the blockade in midwinter—no warm clothes, no adequate shelter. And, in any case, the enlistments of almost all his troops would come to an end with the year 1775. This bothered Washington all the more because he was not temperamentally attuned to inaction. He began trying to persuade his generals that the British position in Boston was not as impregnable as it seemed. True, there were sophisticated defenses backed by expert artillery; true, any invading force would have to traverse a large expanse of water that was guarded by floating batteries. But surely brave and devoted men might face down all obstacles and smash the enemy! Washington's generals could not be convinced, and Washington was not sure enough of his conclusions to override his council of war.

And so, as the year approached its end, Washington was faced with the necessity of recruiting his army anew. Most of the common soldiers felt that they had done their stint; let others take their places. And efforts to reorganize the haphazardly raised regiments

Charles Willson Peale completed this miniature of Washington as commander in chief for Martha Washington in August of 1776.

into a force more uniform and efficient disarranged the officer corps. Although no man's commission was as old as a year, and the differences might be no more than a day—or even a few minutes—officers got into the most acrimonious hassles concerning which had the right to a higher rank because he was the senior. "Such a dearth of public spirit and want of virtue," Washington cried out, "such stock-jobbing and fertility in all the low arts to obtain advantages . . . such a dirty, mercenary spirit pervades the whole that I should not be at all surprised at any disaster that may happen." If only he could justify it "to posterity and my conscience," Washington would, he explained, abandon settled America to the British and inhabit the wilderness in a wigwam.

On New Year's Eve, so many of the troops went home that all the blockading defenses could not be manned. Although Washington did his best to cover up, the weakness was too widespread to escape the eyes of spies. It seemed certain that the British would attack. He arranged with his officers on what hills far behind the lines the fleeing remnant of his army would reassemble. But the British did not attack. They hoped the rebels would realize how ridiculous they seemed and give up. When Washington celebrated the dawn of 1776 by raising the newly designed American flag, some Britons assumed that it was a flag of surrender.

The British were annoyed rather than discouraged by their plight in Boston. The unexpected outbreak of the rebellion had found their army in a most disadvantageous position. To march into Massachusetts would serve no strategic end, and the cost in casualties of their victory at Bunker Hill did not encourage further entanglements with the determined farmers of New England. If the rebels did not before then recover their senses, the British command would, at their own good time, use their control of the ocean to move to a more advantageous base. And George III was not reacting as Washington had expected. Instead of curbing his government, he declared publicly that he intended to hire foreign mercenary troops—either Russian or German—to smash by force an insurrection which he by no means regarded as a loyal protest. The Americans, he growled, manifestly intended to establish "an independent empire."

Washington Taking Command of the Army at Cambridge 1775, *engraving by J. Rogers after Wageman, nineteenth century.*

A banner depicting Washington's Life Guard, the unit that protected him, drawn by Benson J. Lossing, 1852.

When Washington celebrated the dawn of 1776 by raising the newly designed American flag, some Britons assumed that it was a flag of surrender.

Washington, who had, up to this time, sought compromise rather than an independent empire, began to change his mind. He was deeply impressed by Thomas Paine's arguments and exhortations in *Common Sense.* On January 31, 1776, Washington first acknowledged in writing the possibility of independence. Four days later, he urged Congress to notify Great Britain that "if nothing else could satisfy a tyrant and his diabolical ministry, we are determined to shake off all connections with a state so unjust and unnatural." Washington now felt an even greater need to attack Boston and annihilate the enemy.

Several hundred miles to the northwest, an irregular force, led by Benedict Arnold and Ethan Allen, had captured the British frontier fort at Ticonderoga, and with it what Washington considered "a noble train of artillery." Colonel Henry Knox, a fat former bookseller who had studied in books the use of cannon, was Washington's commander of artillery. He supervised pulling the guns over snow and ice to Cambridge. Washington decided to use this ordnance in staging a battle that could at one stroke win (or lose) the war.

Dorchester Neck extended into the harbor southeast of Boston Neck. Neither side had occupied it, although from its heights cannon could fire into the British-held city. Washington resolved that silently, on a dark night, he would build there a fortification containing cannon. The endangered British would be forced to ferry a large detachment from Boston

Washington at Dorchester Heights *by Gilbert Stuart, oil on panel, 1806. Museum of Fine Arts, Boston. Deposited by the city of Boston.*

to clear the heights in an engagement resembling Bunker Hill. Washington hoped that his reorganized army would, in addition to inflicting heavy casualties, succeed in holding its ground.

This was only the beginning of what Washington planned to achieve. Since, in attacking Dorchester, the British would have to weaken their garrison in Boston, Washington intended to send four thousand men in small boats across the half mile of water to invade the city. Having landed at two separated beachheads, they would converge and march against the unfortified rear of the British lines on Boston Neck, smash the defenses there, and let in an additional patriot force.

During the night of March 4, 1776, three thousand of Washington's soldiers moved silently onto Dorchester Neck. The ground being frozen too hard for digging, the Americans brought their fortifications with them in wagons: bundles of sticks, three feet thick and four long, and also the heavy wooden frames into which the bundles were to be piled to make ramparts that would be held down with a little dirt scratched up from the icy soil. Moving silently among his troops on horseback, Washington listened for some unexpected sound that might warn the British, stared down towards dark Boston for some flaring of lights that would indicate the enemy was aroused. All remained silent and dark. At 3 A.M., having finished the fortifications, the three thousand builders marched back across the narrow causeway while twenty-four hundred fresh soldiers moved into the fortifications to repel attack.

While the British generals were drinking the night away, they had been notified that the Americans were active on Dorchester Neck, but they had assumed that nothing could be done there that could not be easily handled in the morning. The light of dawn revealed how much harder patriot soldiers were willing to work than the mercenaries the British officers commanded. Staring at the major works which had bloomed on Dorchester Heights, "an officer of distinction" poetically blamed "the genie belonging to Aladdin's wonderful lamp."

As Washington expected, the British embarked many regiments for a landing on Dorchester. He was about to unleash his own invasion of Boston itself, when the sky blackened with what soldiers on both sides considered the most awesome storm they had ever seen. The British commander in chief, Sir William Howe (who had recently succeeded General Thomas Gage), was glad to accept this interruption as an excuse for not undertaking what the honor of his army would otherwise have required: an attack that would have cost many soldiers who could only be replaced by reinforcements brought from across the ocean. He called back the detachment which had menaced Dorchester, thereby bringing to a halt Washington's plan to invade Boston.

Had Howe known of Washington's plan, he might well have cursed rather than blessed the storm. The American commander had yet to learn that in hand-to-hand fighting his farmboys, who considered their bayonets principally useful for roasting meat over campfires, were no match for England's professional killers. He was to be taught this lesson on terrains where the Americans could save their lives by running away. But had most of his army been trapped with the murderous British on Boston Neck, Washington might then and there have lost the war.

In Homeric times, it would have been assumed that some pro-American god had ridden the storm, procuring time for the amateur American commander to learn how to conquer.

Washington's half-completed operation achieved a victory he found surprising. Schooled in the rules of warfare, the British believed it intolerably dangerous to remain in a position that was within range of enemy cannon. Since they had abandoned any hope of removing the cannon, the deliberate move they had intended eventually to make from Boston became a hysterical flight. Too hurried to load onto their ships their heavy cannon, they spiked the guns and pushed them, along with General Howe's carriage, into the bay. On March 10, the British fleet carried the British army away over the ocean.

Many Massachusetts men were opposed to the armed protest against the British government. These "Tories" or "Loyalists" were usually prosperous citizens, sometimes the holders of British appointments, who had much to lose from civil discord. The outbreak of actual hostilities around Boston had made all but the most inconspicuous Massachusetts Loyalists flee to the city to achieve the protection of the British army. Now the army was fleeing. They were in despair. Although they scrambled to get on the ships, many were left behind. Washington wrote, "One or two of them have done what a great many of them ought to have done long ago, committed suicide." But then he added, "Unhappy wretches! Deluded mortals! Would it not be good policy to grant a generous amnesty, to conquer these people by a generous forgiveness?"

What would have been more natural than a parade of the conquering army through liberated Boston, with the commander in chief exhibiting his famous horsemanship at the head? There was no such parade. Washington slipped into the city and out again as inconspicuously as he could. However, he was proud of what had been achieved. He wrote privately to his favorite brother, John Augustine Washington, "No man perhaps since the first institution of armies ever commanded one under more difficult circumstances than I have done. . . . I have been here months together with what will scarcely be believed: not thirty rounds of musket cartridges a man. . . . We have maintained our ground against the enemy, under the above want of powder, and we have disbanded one army and recruited another within musket shot of two and twenty regiments, the flowers of the British army, and at last have beat them, in a shameful and precipitate manner, out of a place the strongest by nature on this continent."

He did not add that his triumphant army had not yet met the enemy in battle.

Eleven

THE CONTINENTAL ARMY ON TRIAL

(1776)

The British had disappeared. It eventually developed that they had gone to their base at Halifax on Nova Scotia to refit their hysterically loaded ships. But no one doubted that their eventual destination was New York, a city that could have been created by Providence as the stronghold and jumping-off place for a naval power. Manhattan Island was bordered by important rivers. The East River, connecting with Long Island Sound, led to New England. The Hudson was navigable to oceangoing vessels so far north that it could be used to cut the well-settled part of the colonies in half. And the harbor was large enough for any fleet.

Washington reached New York on April 13, 1776, to discover that every advantage the geography there offered a naval power was also a bayonet aimed at such an army as his. Manhattan Island was too long to be defended completely with the forces he had, and so narrow that an army in the little city at the tip might be trapped by a quick march to the opposite shore of soldiers landed from boats above the town. Military strategy clearly indicated that the city should be abandoned to the enemy—or better yet, burned—while a defense line was set up further north on the Hudson, where accommodating highlands dominated the river. But Washington agreed with Congress that in the current political situation, when public opinion had not coalesced in opposition to Great Britain, the effect on morale of abandoning—not to speak of burning—a major city would be disastrous. And so Washington decided to occupy New York as best he could.

The only favorable aspect of the geography was that along the Hudson River side of Manhattan there arose an easily defensible high ridge, which made blocking that river unnecessary to the defense of the city. However, on the other side of the island, a flat shore invited invasion across the East River. This meant that the East River must be made immune to British shipping. To block its mouth near where it entered the harbor, boats were sunk, creating an underwater barrier that would stop or at least slow down British warships. Guns from three forts were trained on that very spot: one from the south tip of Manhattan, one from a little island, and the third from the far shore. So far, so good. But the essential fort on the far shore could not be held unless the part of Long Island on which it was built were also held. And Long Island was much too extensive a land mass for Washington's little army completely to defend.

Week after week for more than two months, no British sails appeared. However, it was for Washington hardly a quiet time. Traveling to Philadelphia, he wrestled with Congress concerning two major problems. His own army needed strengthening. Furthermore, the northern army, under his overall command but semi-independent, was in trouble. It had almost captured Canada, but was now in flight from a combination

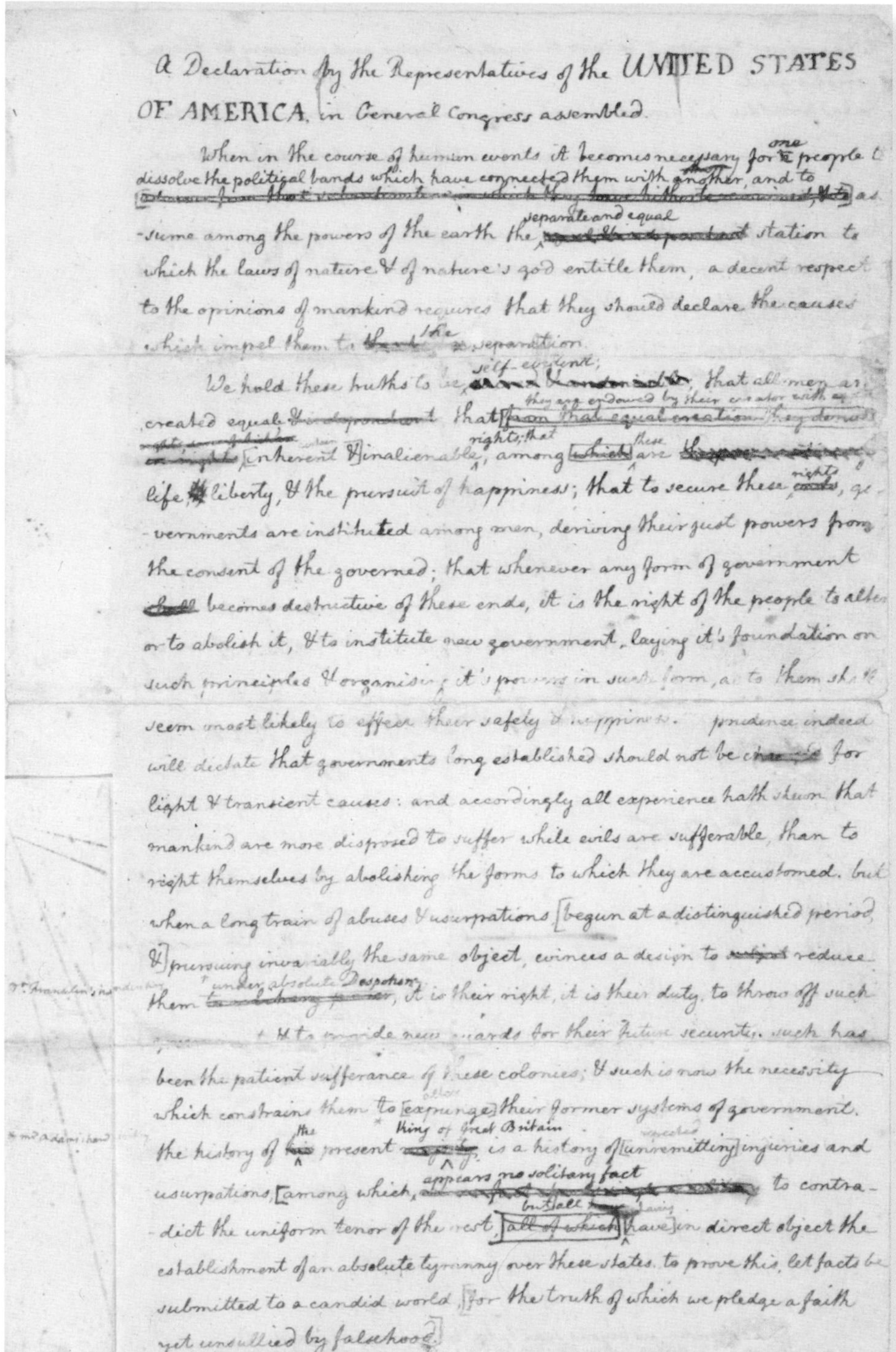

A Declaration by the Representatives of the UNITED STATES OF AMERICA, in General Congress assembled.

When in the course of human events it becomes necessary for one people to dissolve the political bands which have connected them with another, and to assume among the powers of the earth the separate and equal station to which the laws of nature & of nature's god entitle them, a decent respect to the opinions of mankind requires that they should declare the causes which impel them to the separation.

We hold these truths to be self-evident; that all men are created equal; that they are endowed by their creator with [inherent &] inalienable rights; that among these are life, liberty, & the pursuit of happiness; that to secure these rights, governments are instituted among men, deriving their just powers from the consent of the governed; that whenever any form of government becomes destructive of these ends, it is the right of the people to alter or to abolish it, & to institute new government, laying it's foundation on such principles & organising it's powers in such form, as to them shall seem most likely to effect their safety & happiness. prudence indeed will dictate that governments long established should not be changed for light & transient causes: and accordingly all experience hath shewn that mankind are more disposed to suffer while evils are sufferable, than to right themselves by abolishing the forms to which they are accustomed. but when a long train of abuses & usurpations [begun at a distinguished period, &] pursuing invariably the same object, evinces a design to reduce them under absolute Despotism, it is their right, it is their duty, to throw off such government & to provide new guards for their future security. such has been the patient sufferance of these colonies; & such is now the necessity which constrains them to [expunge] alter their former systems of government. the history of the present king of Great Britain is a history of [unremitting] repeated injuries and usurpations, [among which,] appears no solitary fact to contradict the uniform tenor of the rest, but all have in direct object the establishment of an absolute tyranny over these states. to prove this, let facts be submitted to a candid world [for the truth of which we pledge a faith yet unsullied by falsehood.]

This rough draft of the Declaration of Independence, in Thomas Jefferson's hand, shows minor emendations by John Adams and Benjamin Franklin.

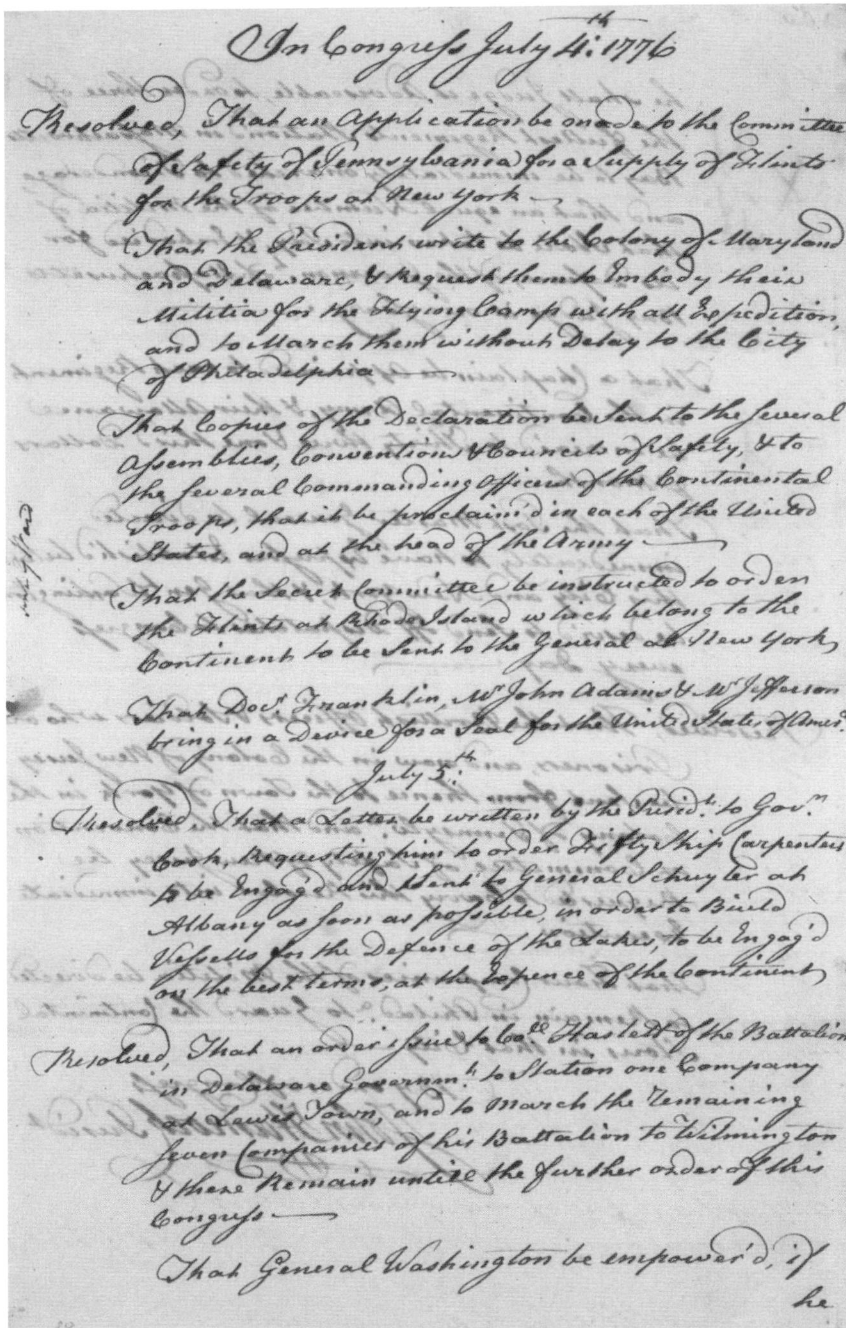
In Congress July 4th 1776

Resolved, That an Application be made to the Committee of Safety of Pennsylvania for a Supply of Flints for the Troops at New York—

That the President write to the Colony of Maryland and Delaware, & request them to Imbody their Militia for the Flying Camp with all Expedition, and to March them without Delay to the City of Philadelphia—

That Copies of the Declaration be Sent to the several Assemblies, Conventions & Councils of Safety, & to the several Commanding Officers of the Continental Troops, that it be proclaim'd in each of the United States, and at the head of the Army—

That the Secret Committee be instructed to order the Flints at Rhode Island which belong to the Continent to be Sent to the General at New York,

That Doct. Franklin, Mr John Adams & Mr Jefferson bring in a Device for a Seal for the United States of Amer.a

July 5th

Resolved, That a Letter be written by the Presid.t to Gov.r Cook, requesting him to order Fifty Ship Carpenters to be Engag'd and Sent to General Schuyler at Albany as soon as possible, in order to Build Vessells for the Defence of the Lakes, to be Engag'd on the best terms, at the Expence of the Continent,

Resolved, That an order issue to Col.o Haslett of the Battalion in Delaware Governm.t to Station one Company at Lewes Town, and to March the remaining seven Companies of his Battalion to Wilmington & there Remain untill the further order of this Congress—

That General Washington be empower'd, if he

Among the resolutions passed by the Continental Congress on July 4, 1776, was one calling for the president of the Congress, John Hancock, to send copies of the newly adopted Declaration of Independence to several commanding officers of the Continental army. Hancock sent this copy of the resolutions, along with the "Dunlap Broadside" of the Declaration, to General Washington on July 6. Washington had it read aloud to his assembled troops in New York on the 9th.

Artist William Walcutt's 1857 rendering of American soldiers tearing down the statue of George III in New York City on July 9, 1776.

of disease and British reinforcements. If the northern defenses were not reconstituted, upstate New York and New England would be open to invasion from Canada.

As Washington expostulated, the congressmen found it hard to listen, for they were struggling in their minds with the most serious possible political problem. Now that the fighting had gone so far, should the colonies abandon all efforts to compromise with the Crown? Should they make possible active support from that enemy of Great Britain, France, by declaring their independence? Would a declaration strengthen or weaken the cause at home? How many Americans who were supporting what they regarded as "a loyal protest" would go along with independence, an idea which, only a brief year before, had been given serious consideration by only a few extreme radicals? Was independence safe, was it justified, was it expedient?

Since he did not regard political decisions as the business of the military, Washington made no public statement, but he wrote privately of his regret that the delegates "of whole provinces are still feeding themselves upon the dainty food of reconciliation."

Washington was back with his army in New York when, on July 6, 1776, he received a copy of the now enacted Declaration of Independence. It was a queasy moment. Promulgation of the news would induce reactions that would indicate what percentage of the army, how many inhabitants of New York, would welcome—would indeed not rebel against—this radical change in the nature of the cause. After the brigades had been drawn up on their respective parade grounds to have the Declaration read to them, Washington heard cheers. But were they loud enough? And, once the news had spread through the civilian population with the speed of human breath, he studied the faces of people on the street, listened to the intonations of voices.

The British officials, who had still been functioning in New York, had to flee, and Tories were now liable to arrest as enemies of a new nation. Their absence would simplify defense when the British invasion came, but Washington, who left the problem to the civilian authorities, hoped that Tories would be treated with "every indulgence which . . . good judgment will permit." When a plot was discovered aiming at his own assassination, he suppressed the matter as best he could lest mobs rise and attack conservatives who might, if not molested, be persuaded to support the cause.

A few days before the Declaration reached New York, the British fleet that had disappeared from Boston reappeared in New York Harbor. The troops were landed on Staten Island. These fifty square miles of fertile farmland out in the bay were well suited to contain and support the British base that was established there. As more and more ships came in, these directly from Europe, Washington saw gathering before him what was in fact the largest expeditionary force of the eighteenth century. The total mounted to thirty thousand men, one-third of them the Hessians George III had rented from four German princes. The accompanying fleet included ten ships of the line and twenty frigates.

Washington's army was less numerous: twenty-three thousand. It had one aspect greatly pleasing to its commander in chief: it was not just from New England but truly national. However, the mixing of diseases from various regions made it very sickly.

Having delayed to determine whether the overwhelming power they manifestly wielded would not in itself make the rebels back down, the British finally advanced on August 21, 1776. A large detachment landed on the eastern tip of Long Island, too far from Washington's lines for him to make any real resistance. The key position was now Brooklyn Heights, about two square miles of cliff, across from the tip of Manhattan, on which were placed guns necessary to keep the East River shut. Beyond, in the direction of the British advance, was a rough spine of forested hills that extended from the shore of the East River some nine miles inland. In this advanced position, Washington stationed thirty-five hundred of his best men, while four thousand who were less experienced were camped in and around the protecting fortifications on the Heights.

Suspecting that the British movement on Long Island was merely a feint and that the real attack would be directly from Staten Island on the city, Washington stayed in New York. He entrusted the command in Brooklyn to the fiery and erratic Major General John Sullivan. Since Sullivan lacked the troops to guard the whole nine-mile stretch of hills, his left wing hung in the air. This did not bother him—or his commander in chief—as it would have bothered a trained regular.

Very early on the 27th, Howe created a diversion along the East River shore on Sullivan's right flank. Dawn further revealed Hessian regiments drawn up in the center under the part of the bluff Sullivan was best prepared to defend. When Washington, seeing no preparations to attack the city, dashed across the river with reinforcements, the only sound on the left flank was the singing of birds. Then suddenly there burst forth in that quiet sector musket fire and even the music of an expert military band. A powerful British column had, by making a wide sweep to the left, marched around the furthest American defenses. Now advancing to the right, it inserted itself between the fort on Brooklyn Heights and Sullivan's men along the bluff. At the same time, with another roar of gunpowder, the Hessians charged Sullivan's front.

Washington hoped that if Sullivan's men did not "flee precipitously," the battle might still be won. But, except for a Maryland regiment that made a heroic stand and was almost annihilated, the soldiers either surrendered or pelted as best they could for the fort. Washington galloped to the fort, concluding that the most vital need was to keep the four thousand rookies stationed there from reacting to panic outside with hysteria inside.

As the last fugitives dashed singly, gasping and often bloody, into the fortification, there came the sound of many feet hitting the ground in unison. In perfect formation, regiment by brightly uniformed regiment, the enemy entered the clearing outside the walls. They drew up just beyond musket range. There was a long period of suspense as the professionals stared stolidly and the quaking amateurs stared back across their ramparts, and then, to Washington's incredulous relief, the enemy wheeled and moved backwards.

Historians have long argued that Howe threw away a great opportunity by not attacking while Washington's men were, despite his best efforts, still in great fear and confusion. The British commander, however, congratulated himself on his restraint. In common with his governmental superiors overseas, Howe believed that the rebellion had been fomented by a few desperate men, who had terrorized the American majority, which still loved their sovereign. By making fools of these desperate men—as he just had done—Howe would encourage the well-disposed majority to brush them aside.

His restraint was also military prudence. Even if the Americans were not good at fighting, they were good at digging. Their earthworks were considerable and could not be stormed without considerable loss. The rebels could be more cheaply defeated for a second time by knocking down their walls with artillery. If, in the meanwhile, Washington tried to withdraw, Howe would intervene, catching the patriot army half on land and half on water.

Three days later, Howe woke up to find that the American force had disappeared—it seemed miraculously. The professional officer, whose men were trained to move only in formation, could not understand how thousands of American soldiers had slipped off in the dark so inconspicuously that no indication was given. Habituated to thinking for themselves, Washington's soldiers had flowed around obstacles and away as easily as a stream of water. And Washington had made up a convincing falsehood to explain the gathering of boats which had made the ferrying possible.

Although a London publication accorded the escape of Washington's force "a high place among military transactions," the fact was that the Continental army had, in its first pitched battle, taken a severe drubbing. Washington tried to keep up morale by referring to the Battle of Long Island (or of Brooklyn Heights) as a mere "skirmish," but he had lost some fifteen hundred men, almost half of those who had been outside his walls. He was still convinced that the British flanking maneuver would have amounted to little had the men done their "duty." He confessed to Congress that "want of confidence in the generality of the troops," made him now "despair" of holding New York City. This despair was not alleviated when thousands of soldiers, having had their first real taste of the British might which they had optimistically hoped to overcome, went home. The Connecticut militia shrank from eight thousand to two thousand.

Unwilling to follow the retreat, Washington soon loomed on horseback alone. Some fifty of the enemy dashed towards him. He watched them without moving. Had not aides galloped up and pulled him away, he would have been killed or captured. He was, General Nathanael Greene wrote, "so vexed at the infamous conduct of his troops that he sought death rather than life."

The capture of Brooklyn Heights opened the East River to British shipping, and gave the British army control of the Long Island shore opposite Manhattan's easily invaded east side. However, there remained to the patriots a defensible area known as Harlem Heights. As Manhattan narrowed towards its northern tip, the bluff along the Hudson filled the whole top of the island. Various of Washington's officers urged that the army move north to Harlem Heights. It was argued that, if the British took the middle of the island, any patriot force in the city would be trapped.

However, Congress, having refused Washington permission to burn the city, ordered him to hold it "at all costs." He decided to send nine thousand men to the

Heights, spread out five thousand to protect the miles of lowland between the Heights and the city, and leave a garrison of five thousand in New York. Historians have accused him of stupidly sentencing that garrison to capture if the British landed above them and moved across the narrow island. Manhattan was admittedly narrow, but it was, except for occasional fields, heavily wooded. Experience had taught Washington that European troops were helpless in woods. He believed that, if worse came to worse, the garrison could escape through the forest (as they were actually to do).

Having paused to see whether the rebels would not react to their drubbing by throwing themselves on the mercy of the Crown, the British struck Manhattan on September 15. Five warships anchored broadside in the East River off Kip's Bay. Although this indentation in the shoreline, which then penetrated almost to present Second Avenue, is now between Thirty-seventh and Thirty-eighth streets, it was then some miles above the northern confines of the city. Under a barrage of the great naval guns, eighty-four six-oared barges brought ashore red- or blue-clad British or Hessian troops. The defense consisted of shallow trenches filled with the least-experienced of Washington's militiamen. The farmboys took to their heels.

Galloping towards the firing, Washington, "to my great surprise and mortification," found himself surrounded with fleeing men. They only ran the faster when they saw him. Then, to his relief, two fresh brigades came marching up in good order. Washington ordered them to disperse behind some walls and in a cornfield to await the enemy. They waited bravely enough, but when a small British force—not more than sixty or seventy men—appeared, they jettisoned their guns and knapsacks and took off for the rear. Washington galloped after them, shouted, struck at them with his riding whip, but to no avail. He threw his hat on the ground, crying out, "Are these the men with whom I am to defend America?" And again, "Good God! Have I got such troops as these?"

Unwilling to follow the retreat, Washington soon loomed on horseback alone. Some fifty of the enemy dashed towards him. He watched them without moving. Had not aides galloped up and pulled him away, he would have been killed or captured. He was, General Nathanael Greene wrote, "so vexed at the infamous conduct of his troops that he sought death rather than life."

The British, satisfied that they were achieving with almost no loss their objective of capturing New York City intact, made little effort to pursue the fleeing rebels or cut off the garrison threading up from the city through the west-side forest. Almost the total army found refuge on Harlem Heights. What Washington denounced as "the dastardly behavior of the troops" had kept American casualties to a minimum, but had presented the British with an invaluable military base, and also permitted them to capture a staggering quantity of tents, baggage, wagons, cannon.

A spyglass made in London by Henry Pyefinch, c. 1774–1783. Washington depended on telescopes to monitor troop movements during the Revolution. His wartime correspondence contains frequent requests for and purchases of "[spy]glasses" and "pocket telescopes." In his will, Washington bequeathed this handsome, three-draw, mahogany and brass example to his old friend and cousin, Lawrence Washington. It was returned to Mount Vernon by Mrs. Jefferson Davis in 1899.

THE FIRE OF 1776

HOW NEW YORK CITY ALMOST *BURNED COMPLETELY*

FROM THE BRITISH PERSPECTIVE, the American Revolution was not a war at all, but an uprising of its own people. They decided to restore order swiftly, by dividing the colonies and isolating New England. The obvious strategy was to seize New York. By controlling the Hudson River, which military strategists refer to as the "Northeast Corridor," British warships could cut off New England from the wilderness to the west, and by controlling New York Harbor they could split the colonies in half. Once the southerners had seen the power of the Crown, they would become orderly—or so they thought. King George's greatest adversary was indeed a southerner.

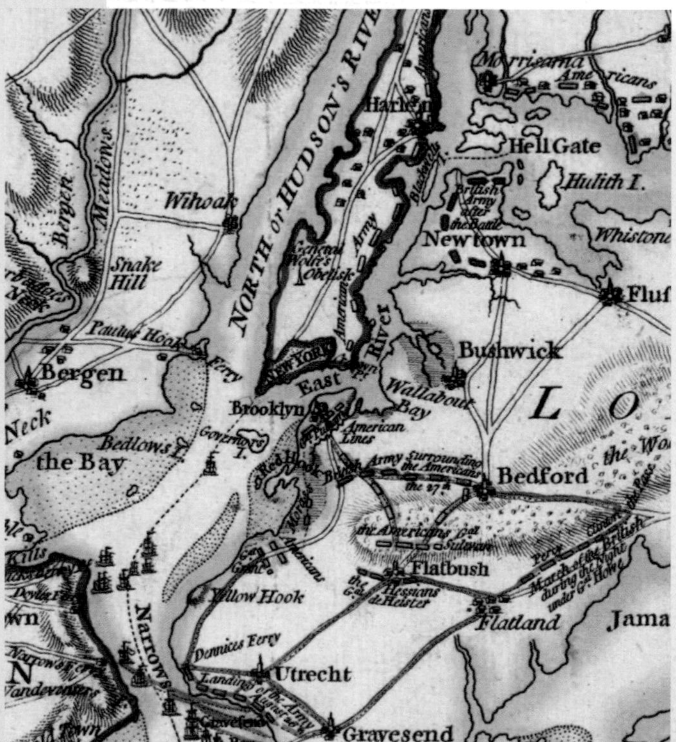

While New York Harbor presented a safe, luxurious haven for the British fleet, once captured, it presented a perplexing problem to Washington as to how to defend it. The city of New York had only developed as far north as City Hall Park, known then as the New York Common. It is only a little farther north of where the World Trade Center site is today. Manhattan being an island, warships could have surrounded the lower tip where the city stood and destroyed it in no time. The tiny colonial city presented little hope of survival against the British navy in all its splendor.

In an attempt to restore order and finish the campaign before Christmas, England attacked New York with the largest naval assault in world history until the Allied invasion of Normandy during World War II. One Staten Island farmer who saw the fleet approaching wrote, "It appeared as though all of London were afloat."

The British had sent over 400 warships and 200 frigates along with bomb ships, supply ships, and troop ships containing 30,000 of the best-trained and best-equipped soldiers in the world. On board were Scottish Black Watch soldiers and the feared German soldiers, Hessians—the paid mercenaries hired by the Crown whose reputations were well-known in the colonies. The Continental army was made up of approximately 20,000 farmers, brewers, and merchants, many using Brown Bess guns from the Seven Years' War. Even their commander in chief had never yet had a military victory in his career.

The battle that took place in Brooklyn was not only the first official battle of the war but also the largest battle of the war. Washington lost New York to the British Empire, along with a third of the forces under General Sullivan. Washington managed to save the remainder of the army trapped in Brooklyn thanks to a daring evacuation to Manhattan Island with the help of Captain John Glover and his Marblehead fisherman. What was left of his shattered army made it back to Manhattan and marched north to Harlem, leaving the city in the hands of its conquerors.

On September 2, 1776, Washington requested permission to burn New York City down, instead of allowing it to fall into British hands. Three days later, General Nathanael Greene sent the same request to Washington, not being aware he had already presented the question to congress. Congress issued a resounding refusal, reasoning that the city might be captured at a later date and that destroying the city would not endear their cause in the hearts of New Yorkers that winter.

Support for independence was not as widespread in 1776 as many might believe. Approximately a third of the colonists were Loyalists, and about another third undecided, leaving the people bitterly divided. Washington obeyed Congress, although he clearly disagreed with the decision; however, he understood and respected the chain of command. He would not usurp congress, and left New York standing as he was ordered to do.

Someone did burn the city, nonetheless. The fire was set on September 21 at the Fighting Cocks Tavern on the East River waterfront in Lower Manhattan. A northwest wind carried the flames up the west side of Manhattan, destroying a quarter of New York City, which was mostly residential space, as the East River was the industrial front where ships docked.

Fortunately, the city had been almost entirely evacuated due to the occupation of the harbor. The fire ravaged Trinity Church, leaving only a burned-out hull that the British would later use to hold prisoners of war, and narrowly missed Saint Paul's Chapel, where Washington would later pray as the nation's first president—and which in recent history served as the relief center for the rescue workers of September 11.

It is not known who actually set the fire, but there has been much speculation that it was Captain Nathan Hale, who arrived in New York on the day of the fire with a powder-flash burn on his face. He never admitted to the deed, as he was hanged for espionage the following day.

When Washington heard of the fire, he stated, "Providence or some good, honest fellow has done more for us than we were disposed to do for ourselves." He expressed disappointment that three-quarters of the city remained, leaving the British a rather comfortable winter headquarters, which the Continental army would be denied for the remainder of the war.

Right: *This depiction of a raging fire in New York was engraved by François Xavier Habermann, c. 1778.*

Opposite: *The seat of action between the British and American forces from the surveys of Major Holland, London, 1776.*

The next day, an American scouting party ran into a British advance guard in a rocky, wooded area. British reinforcements hurried up, confident that they could easily handle this part of the army they had twice so easily put to flight. But the Americans, firing from behind rocks and trees, stood. With trepidation, Washington ordered into the fight whole battalions that had fled the day before. Now it was the British who ran away. The Battle of Harlem Heights, which Washington ended by calling his troops back when sounds indicated that they were running into British artillery fire, was the first victory won in combat by Washington's army. Yet it had been no more than an enlarged skirmish. It seemed too insignificant to give Washington much comfort.

"If I were to wish the bitterest curse to an enemy on this side of the grave," Washington wrote his cousin Lund Washington, "I should put him in my stead with my feelings—and yet I do not know what plan of conduct to pursue. I see the impossibility of serving with reputation, or doing any essential service to the cause by continuing in command, and yet I am told that if I quit the command, inevitable ruin will follow from the distraction that will ensue. In confidence, I tell you that I never was in such an unhappy, divided state since I was born. To lose all comfort and happiness on the one hand, whilst I am fully persuaded that under such a system as has been adopted, I cannot have the least chance for reputation, nor those allowances made which the nature of the case requires; and to be told, on the other, that if I leave the service all will be lost, is, at the same time that I am bereft of every peaceful moment, distressing to a degree."

The "system" that was sinking the cause, so Washington explained to his masters in Congress, was the reliance on short-term troops. The militia who made up the majority of his army were perpetually in flux, appearing briefly and then disappearing, to be perhaps replaced. Having been "just dragged from the tender scenes of domestic life," they were "ready to fly from their own shadows." Themselves immune to discipline, the militia destroyed whatever discipline Washington had been able to inculcate in those more regular troops who were designated the Continental army. And the common soldiers in the Continental army, having been enlisted only for the year 1776, would soon go home.

Washington begged that the new army, which would have to be created with the new year, should be large enough so that major reliance on militia would not be necessary. The soldiers should be enlisted for three years, time enough for him to develop an efficient force. For this to be achieved, Congress would have to expend more money. Men would surely not enlist for the longer term unless they were given larger "bounties": cash sums paid common soldiers at the time of enlistment. Washington expressed worry lest the British, having a more ample war chest, should recruit Americans faster than Congress could. American liberties would then be at an end.

The long-term enlistments which Washington insisted were essential were for many congressmen a bitter pill. That the Congress lacked the necessary money was the lesser part of the problem, since the delegates had got into the habit of voting, as they now did again, funds they did not have. Members were more bothered by political implications. The leaders of the various colonies (now known as states) had by no means decided that, when the war that clearly required cooperation was won, they would agree to forming a united nation. The states, it was commonly believed, should be no more than friendly neighbors. It was thus worrisome that soldiers kept from home for three long years might lose their special allegiance to their home states. And there was always the danger, so underlined by history, that an army which became coherent within itself would become an instrument for tyranny. While accepting, because they felt they had to, three-year enlistments, the Congress made provisions for state control of officer

Forcing the Hudson River Passage, *by the British painter William Joy (1803–1857), oil on canvas, after a 1778 painting by Dominic Serres.*

WASHINGTON'S SECRET NETWORK

THE UNITED STATES' FIRST SPY RING

James Rivington

Alexander Hamilton

WHILE LITTLE IS KNOWN ABOUT the inner workings of Washington's espionage ring, it is a tribute to his skill rathen than an error in historical documentation. Invisible ink technology was available and often used, and Washington's spy network was extremely successful at not leaving a clear trail. There is much evidence, however, pointing to Alexander Hamilton as the probable mastermind of America's first spy organization.

The primary spies were New Yorkers, many of whom had a direct connection to Hamilton. Washington's confidence in Hamilton, along with his being from the very city the British occupied, were strong incentives for the general to favor him for such an assignment. Perhaps the strongest evidence is in Hamilton's corporate espionage strategies later, when he was eager to press his assault against Europe's corner concerning textile and manufacturing industries. Although he had uncanny ability at everything he set himself to do, Hamilton clearly had an inside perspective on spying.

Alexander Hamilton, although still a youth, had become rather well known in the colony after arriving from the West Indies. His oration on the New York Common, defending Bostonians who had dumped British tea into their harbor, shocked New Yorkers, who were awed at the ability of the youthful collegian. He had been published in the newspapers, and his essays "A Full Vindication of the Measures of Congress" and "The Farmer Refuted" caused quite a stir. Although his writings were anonymous, Hamilton was certainly known to James Rivington as the author. James Rivington had printed both of Alexander Hamilton's political tirades. It would have been strange indeed if he, of all people, was unaware of the identity of the radical young writer. While the *New-York Gazetteer* was a Loyalist paper, Rivington was a deeply imbedded spy for the patriots. His status as the king's official printer provided an excellent cover, and he greatly aided the war effort in 1781 by laying his hands on the British fleet's signal book, giving the French valuable intelligence at the Battle of the Virginia Capes.

Hercules Mulligan was Alexander Hamilton's college roommate. His older brother worked for Beekman and Kruger, the company that sponsored Hamilton's journey to the colonies for education. His family was Irish American and had a tailor shop on Water Street around the corner from the Tontine Coffee House. A boisterous and amusing fellow, as large in character as he was in stature, Mulligan was "better for the spleen than a ton of drugs," Aaron Burr once stated. Not only was he present at the Battle of Golden Hill, he was integral in forming the artillery company nicknamed the "Corsicans" along with Alexander Hamilton. Stealing British naval cannon from the battery, Hamilton and Mulligan managed to transport the guns on small naval chassis—not ideal for moving them more than a short distance on ship. Although guns weighed over a ton each, thanks largely to Mulligan's brawn, they managed to get them to Saint Paul's Chapel, where they would train their artillery company. Mulligan stayed behind in occupied New York as a spy after the army retreated to Harlem, reporting back to Hamilton what information he received. He was a tailor by trade, and would measure British officers while they spoke openly about military intelligence, unconcerned about the ears near their hems.

Samuel Fraunces was known as "Black Sam." He was from the West Indies, like Hamilton. His waterfront tavern had been the home of Loyalist Stephan DeLancy before angry patriots ran him out of town. Throughout the British occupation of New York, he operated his tavern, overlooking the mighty Naval fleet of the British Empire. Frequently, he would entertain naval commanders and must have received many juicy tidbits overheard by drunken officers, although much may have been overheard by gentler ears in the rooms rented upstairs.

Samuel Fraunces

When Hamilton and Mulligan stole the guns from the battery, the British responded by firing on the city. One cannonball ripped through the roof of Fraunces Tavern, a perfect metaphor for how deeply imbedded in the Revolution the tavern really was.

On December 4, 1783, Washington said farewell to his generals and officers at Fraunces Tavern. He had said goodbye to the troops earlier at Bowling Green. The following day he would leave New York for Annapolis to present himself to Congress and relinquish his sword, symbolically returning power to the people after his victory. Before leaving New York, he would have breakfast with Hercules Mulligan, where he would proclaim him a "true friend of liberty," a title earned through years of service as a trusted secret agent. He also visited the print shop of James Rivington where, speaking with him quietly in the back, Washington was seen giving Rivington a bag of gold coins. As Washington said farewell to his troops and officers, he remembered to thank the heroes of America's first spy ring. Alexander Hamilton would continue to remain by Washington's side throughout his presidency as his most trusted aide.

Opposite, top left: James Rivington *by Ezra Ames after Gilbert Stuart, detail, oil on canvas, 1792–1795.* Top right: Alexander Hamilton *by James Sharples the Elder, detail, pastel on paper, c. 1796.*

Top: Samuel Fraunces *by an unknown artist, detail, late eighteenth century.* Above: *An illustration of Liberty with the word "Spy" from the July 7, 1774 masthead of* The Massachusetts Spy, *or* Thomas's Boston Journal *by Isaiah Thomas.*

appointments that added further confusions to Washington's seemingly endless difficulties in holding the Continental army together.

Ever deliberate, the British spent a month consolidating their hold on New York City. Then, starting on October 12, they sailed up the East River and into Long Island Sound, landing troops on the mainland, well above the northern tip of Manhattan Island. If they marched westward, they might be able to draw a line from the Sound to the Hudson River that would seal Washington's army away from New England and upstate New York. Washington considered it necessary to march hurriedly north of the British beachhead. He occupied a strong position on hills near White Plains, New York. On the 28th, the enemy outflanked Washington's position by capturing with discouraging ease a nearby hill which Washington had partially fortified. Again moving silently at night, the Americans retired to higher hills near New Castle. The British thereupon wheeled to their left and disappeared in the direction of the Hudson River.

The American commanders were now faced with a series of dilemmas. If they followed the British, the enemy might, having lured them out of the way, turn back and, in a rapid countermarch, proceed into New England. If they did not follow, the enemy might continue unmolested in the direction they were going, cross New Jersey, and take the national capital, Philadelphia. The strategic situation was further confused by the fact that there was still an American presence on Harlem Heights. Washington had left a large garrison in Fort Washington, which was supposed, in cooperation with Fort Lee on the Jersey shore, to close the Hudson beyond that point to the British fleet.

Washington and his staff came up with a four-way division of their already outnumbered army. The garrisons were to remain in Forts Washington and Lee, but, since the forts might at any time have to be evacuated, three or four thousand men should be stationed in secondary forts built further up the Hudson. General Lee should stay at New Castle protecting New England with seven thousand men. With what remained, hardly two thousand men, Washington would cross the Hudson for the protection of New Jersey and Philadelphia. His hope was that he would find considerable reinforcements in New Jersey, and he assumed that, if the main British army committed itself to move towards Philadelphia, Lee would rush across the Hudson to join him.

Lee was later to claim that he had objected to the plan on the grounds that Fort Washington should be evacuated because it could now easily be surrounded (except for the riverbank) by the main British force. However, Lee may not have argued too hard, since in its entirety Washington's plan offered great opportunities to his ambitions. An experienced officer of (as he believed) great genius, he had been held down by having to serve under an amateur. Now Washington would march off, leaving him in command of the lion's share of the Continental army. Now he would be in a position to show what he could achieve! Of course, Washington might interrupt by ordering him to join in a defense of Philadelphia. If Lee had already decided that he would not obey, he gave no hint to his trusting superior.

Twelve

DEPTHS

(1776–1777)

Washington led his fraction of the army across the Hudson on November 12, 1776, and marched down the west bank to Fort Lee, the strong point opposite Fort Washington that was the headquarters of the area commander, General Nathanael Greene. Greene, a former Rhode Island ironmonger, was to develop into one of Washington's very best officers. However, he was not worried that the main British army, which had come down the east bank of the Hudson, had completely encircled Fort Washington, except for the steep cliff that rose from the river. Although Washington had hinted he might be wise to reduce the garrison, Greene had ferried across the river more men and supplies. He was convinced that the post could be held.

Nathanael Greene *by Charles Willson Peale, from life, 1783. When the war began, Nathanael Greene was a militia private, the lowest rank in the army, but by the time the war was over, he'd become a major general with a reputation as Washington's most gifted and dependable officer.*

Washington's original aide-de-camp, Joseph Reed, who was now adjutant general, argued with all the extreme fire of his nature that the men and supplies on the cliffs were a beckoning sacrifice to the enemy: bring them back across the river before it was too late! Washington, Reed remembered, "hesitated more than I had ever known him [to] on any other occasion, and more than I thought the public service permitted."

Since Greene was the high officer most familiar with the situation, Washington finally decided to accept his judgment. This was only to be for the time being, until the commander in chief had dealt with what he considered a more serious menace.

What most worried Washington was that the reinforcements he had expected to find in New Jersey had proved illusory. He concluded that Howe, when informed by spies that the blocking force was only about three thousand, would use his main army to take advantage of what seemed an open road to the American capital of Philadelphia. Washington was strengthened in this conclusion by his belief that, since Howe had refused to storm Brooklyn Heights, he would not storm Fort Washington. Surely, he would again rely on conventional siege tactics to inch his artillery slowly towards the walls. It followed that

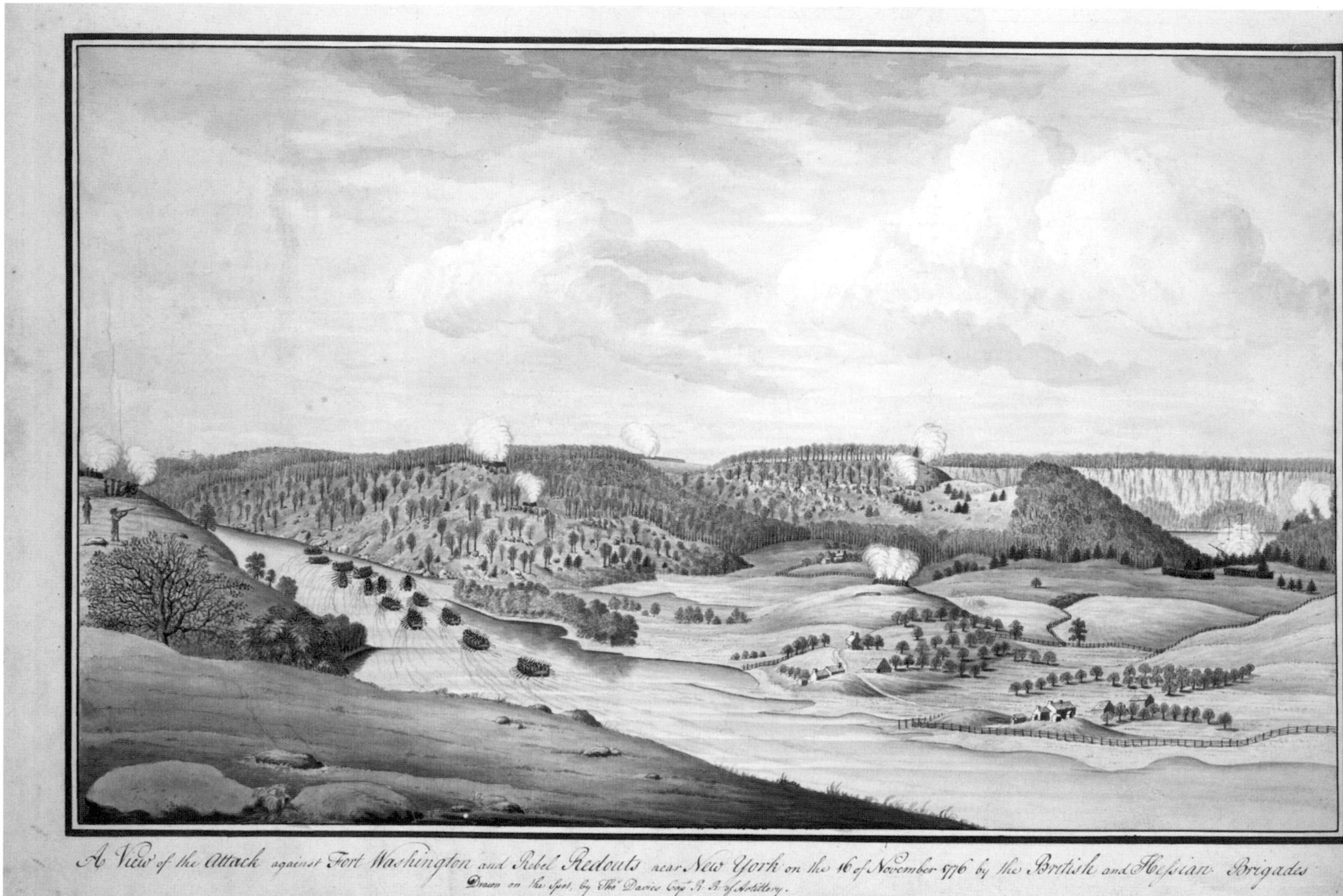

A View of the Attack against Fort Washington and Rebel Redouts near New York on the 16 of November 1776 by the British and Hessian Brigades
Drawn on the Spot, by Thos Davies Capt. R. R. of Artillery.

This watercolor by Thomas Davies offers a view of the attack against Fort Washington by the British and Hessian brigades on November 16, 1776.

there would be plenty of time to evacuate Fort Washington, but almost none to prepare the defenses in New Jersey. Washington hurried south towards the Philadelphia road.

What Washington failed to realize was that the analogy with the fort at Brooklyn Heights did not hold because that fort had been defensible against assault, while the Fort Washington post was not. This was primarily because the Americans, in their sublime ignorance of military engineering, had extended their ramparts far beyond the actual fort, in an effort to protect all of the heights, an area much too large to be adequately fortified or to be held by the existing garrison. The garrison was nonetheless too large to find protection in the fort if driven back from the other ramparts. They would be utterly vulnerable. To British professional eyes, this was a plum that cried out for picking.

Washington had not got very far towards the Philadelphia road when he was informed that the British were advancing with their full army against Fort Washington. He galloped back, but not to take the active command. He decided to leave the defense of the post to the officers who were familiar with the intricate fortifications which they had designed.

Watching from across the river at Fort Lee, Washington saw the widely spread American ramparts prove almost useless against professionally expert assault. His anguish was so poignant that he made no effort, until it was too late, to organize some way to get at least some of the troops down from the cliffs and across the river. Having absolutely no means of escape as a superior British force bore down upon them, thousands of American troops milled helplessly around the main fort, which was too small to hold them. They had only two choices: annihilation or surrender. By nightfall, they had surrendered.

The exhausted commander in chief, who had not in more than a year allowed himself a full day's rest, had presided over the worst defeat so far of the Continental army: in addition to many cannon, he had lost some three thousand men (mostly captured). This catastrophe created the greatest damage to Washington's reputation since his youthful debacle at Fort Necessity. General Lee was quick to seek advantage. He wrote a friend in Congress, "A total want of sense pervades all your military councils. . . . Had I the powers, I could do you much good." He urged the New England authorities to send reinforcements not to the commander in chief, but directly to him.

The exhausted commander in chief, who had not in more than a year allowed himself a full day's rest, had presided over the worst defeat so far of the Continental army: in addition to many cannon, he had lost some three thousand men (mostly captured). This catastrophe created the greatest damage to Washington's reputation since his youthful debacle at Fort Necessity.

Fort Lee was now indefensible. Although Washington had some time before ordered that the stores which had been kept there be removed to a safer place, they had not been. He hurried to get them out, but could not move fast enough. Three mornings after the fall of Fort Washington, a strong British column appeared on the west bank of the Hudson. As Washington led the garrison in a precipitous flight, Reed became hysterical. He commandeered a horseman to ride to General Lee. The horseman had a scrap of paper and Reed a pencil. "Dear General," he wrote. "We are flying before the British. I pray—" Here the pencil broke. He had to complete his message verbally: Lee should come at once to save the army from completely incompetent leadership. The horseman rode off to repeat what he had been told whenever he stopped for refreshment at a tavern.

His troops having successfully evaded the British, Washington wrote Lee suggesting that he bring his part of the army across the Hudson so that their combined force could make at least an appearance of a defense of New Jersey. Otherwise the citizens, seeing themselves deserted, might go over to the British, carrying many Pennsylvanians with them. Reed secretly inserted in Washington's letter one of his own, stating that the entire army felt Lee's presence was their only hope.

Washington was soon falling back through New Jersey before a British column too strong for his feeble force to oppose. Every time a dispatch rider came in, he hoped the message was from Lee. Finally a message did come. It was addressed to Reed, but the aide was absent. The commander in chief broke the seal. Lee (who had no intention of abandoning his independent command) had written that too many opportunities existed in New York for beating up the British for him to join Washington. Lee thanked Reed for his "most flattering, obliging letter. . . . To confess a truth, I really think our chief will do better with me than without me." He agreed with Reed in lamenting "that fatal indecision of mind which in war is a much greater disqualification than stupidity. . . . Eternal defeat and miscarriage must attend the man of the best parts if cursed with indecision."

The implication was unavoidable: Lee was agreeing with strictures against Washington that Reed had made. And Washington considered Reed his closest adviser. So that was what his best military friend thought of him!

Washington's first reaction was anger. He wrote Reed a cold letter that would, he knew, cause the adjutant general's resignation. But his mood soon changed. He wrote Reed a second letter, almost abjectly begging his old friend not to desert him at this desperate time.

Reed agreed to stay on. He reappeared at headquarters with a well-rehearsed explanation. When the commander in chief, not seeking an emotional reconciliation, behaved as if no unpleasantness had taken place, Reed's self-pride was hurt. He soon resigned. Elected chief executive of Pennsylvania, he used his exalted post to fight Washington's leadership.

The retreat through New Jersey continued. The troops Washington commanded remained too few for any formal resistance, and what Washington called "a level champaign country" provided no crags or even stone walls for guerrilla fighters to hide behind. The inhabitants, left without protection, lined up to swear allegiance to George III. The British were jubilant at the seeming demonstration of their belief that, when the rabid revolutionaries were driven away, the mass of Americans would give expression to a continuing love of the Crown.

Early in December, Washington's flight carried him across the broad Delaware River. Although small, frozen, sick, and starved, his army was safe; Washington had seen to it that all boats that might enable the British to follow had been moved over to the Pennsylvania shore. But the respite might be brief. The enemy could bring boats overland from New York in wagons. Then they could strike anywhere along the miles of river.

As always, Washington felt that to meet an undefinable attack, he would need twice the enemy's numbers. He had only one quarter that many. The most desperate efforts to inspire Philadelphians to

Opposite: This engraving from an 1883 edition of Harper's Weekly *shows Washington bidding farewell to New York in 1776.*

mount a last stand only increased his army to about half the British force. Congress considered it prudent to flee from Philadelphia to Baltimore.

Finally Lee, having failed in his attempts to make a splash by catching the British napping, decided to obey orders. Washington learned that his subordinate was in New Jersey, and that other reinforcements were also approaching through the hilly northern part of the state. He thereupon offered Lee everything that his second-in-command had been scheming to achieve. Lee was to try to get all the forces in New Jersey together and, then, if opportunity offered, he was to attack the enemy without waiting to consult Washington. Washington would stay on the far side of the Delaware, leaving the field open to the officer he knew was more experienced than he. This was surely one of the most magnanimous acts of Washington's whole career. He was, to further the cause, opening the possibility of a triumph to an insubordinate officer whom he could reasonably suspect of eagerness to replace him as commander in chief.

The word that came in was not that Lee had achieved a brilliant stroke, but that, while sleeping away from his army in an inn kept by a pretty widow, he had been captured by the British. Washington mourned the loss to the cause, and summoned all the troops still in New Jersey to join him in Pennsylvania. He himself would have to attack from across the Delaware.

Thirteen

HEIGHTS

(1777)

In the face of augmenting snow and cold, the British behaved in a manner that seemed to Washington as unaccountable as it was agreeable. Since regular armies do not rack themselves on winter campaigns, Howe had intended to complete his belated expedition against Philadelphia only if the capital fell comfortably into his hands. Finding himself blocked at the Delaware, he withdrew most of his army into winter quarters on three islands: Manhattan, Staten, and also Aquidneck (Newport, off the Rhode Island mainland), which the British had recently occupied.

The winter, Howe believed, would not be wasted since he would use it to demonstrate that the rebellion could be snuffed out piecemeal. As he interpreted the situation, southern New Jersey had returned to its natural allegiance. He would assist His Majesty's loyal subjects in protecting themselves from the revolutionaries by spacing, throughout the area, British military posts. If (as it seemed reasonable to assume) this method of pacifying an area proved effective, it could be extended through all the provinces, bringing the rebellion, step by step, to an end.

George Washington Before the Battle of Trenton, *by John Trumbull, oil on canvas, c. 1792–1794.*

The enemy post nearest to Washington's army was at Trenton and garrisoned by two to three thousand Hessians. Washington decided to subject it to the type of hit-and-run raid he had often seen the Indians achieve during his previous war. Only he would be more sophisticated: he would send across the Delaware three coordinated forces which, by striking at different points, would surround the enemy, making escape impossible. He would attack on Christmas Day, when

the Hessians would probably be relaxed, and before his own army went home at year's end. The result, as Washington saw it, would probably do no more than dent an edge of the British might. Yet even a small victory would be valuable in reviving patriot morale.

Washington's battle plans were almost always too complicated. As it turned out, only one of the three columns he set in motion got across the river. This was because the maneuver ran into the severest of winter weather. Yet the weather was a godsend; the commanders of the hired German troops did not believe that any army could be made to endure the hardships of a march through such a storm. The Hessians were to laugh away as ridiculous the report of the approach of a menacing column.

Under Washington's personal command, twenty-four hundred men marched up the Delaware behind concealing hills and, after darkness had hidden their

Emanuel Gottlieb Leutze's Washington Crossing the Delaware, *1851, has achieved iconic status, though it may be lacking in historical accuracy. The original hangs in New York's Metropolitan Museum of Art.*

movements, began to embark on large cargo boats that were propelled by poles pushed against the bottom of the river. The air was cold and damp with the foretaste of storm, but the wind was still moderate and the pieces of ice floating in the current were few. However, after the first contingent had been ferried over, the wind stiffened, bringing a terrible cold that froze the water on the men's clothes and also the shallows through which they had to break their way before they could embark. More and more floating ice crowded the river, threatening to smash or capsize the boats. The poles of the men trying to stave off the chunks interfered with the poles that were to be pressed against the bottom.

The artillery horses, unable to keep their footing on decks now iced over, lurched and slithered, endangering everything. Movement became slower and slower. Washington had hoped to attack with the dawn, but it became clear that the troops would have to expose themselves at Trenton in full daylight.

"My brave fellows," Washington exhorted, "you have done all I asked you to do, and more than could be reasonably expected, but your country is at stake: your wives, your houses, and all that you hold dear. You have worn yourselves out with fatigues and hardships, but we know not how to spare you. . . . The present is emphatically the crisis which is to decide our destiny."

Before the march could begin, the storm really broke: a mixture of hail, snow, and rain that soon had the men's feet slipping on the most treacherous of footing, ice covered with snow. Trenton was nine miles away, but there was no turning back. It was a desperate march. Men who lay down to rest for a moment never rose again. But Washington could comfort himself with the thought that the snow was obscuring his army as effectively as darkness would have done.

The battle at Trenton was an anticlimax to the army's difficulties in getting there. The Hessians were caught by complete surprise. Awakened from sleep, blinded by driving snow when they tried to look in the direction from which the patriot fire came, they could not get into formation—and they did not know how to fight in any other way. Surrender came quickly. Where there was a bloody hump in the snow, it invariably represented a German body; the Americans did not lose a single man.

Washington gathered together some officers and discussed the possibility of marching on and attacking the next Hessian post, some fifteen miles downriver at Burlington, New Jersey. But his men were tired and some, having broken into the Hessian storehouses, were drunk. He led his army through the still-roaring storm, back to their disembarking place, whence they again crossed the icy river. The hardships were great as before, but the men were now cheered by the presence of over nine hundred prisoners, six German brass cannon, piles of arms and supplies that had been loaded into captured wagons, and four of those regimental flags, the loss of which meant so much to European armies.

Having been asked to do what was within their possibilities and power—stand up to horrendous physical affliction—Washington's men had behaved in a manner that gave him "inexpressible pleasure."

Four days later, Washington's troops were back at the scene of their victory. A major reason for recrossing the Delaware had been to establish an emotional base for re-recruiting the men whose enlistments would expire with the new year, in two more days. "My brave fellows," Washington exhorted, "you have done all I asked you to do, and more than could be reasonably expected, but your country is at stake: your wives, your

Following page: George Washington at Princeton, *oil on canvas, Charles Willson Peale painted Washington more times from life than any other artist, and none of his works has proved more enduringly popular than this image of Washington after the Battle of Princeton. Commissioned by the Supreme Executive Council of Pennsylvania for its council chamber at Independence Hall in Philadelphia, the original now hangs in the Pennsylvania Academy of the Fine Arts. The piece was completed in early 1779, when Washington sat for Peale in Philadelphia.*

THE BATTLE of TRENTON

December 26th 1776

Inside: *A map of Trenton outlines the plan of operations of General Washington from the 26th of December 1776 to the 3rd of January 1777.*

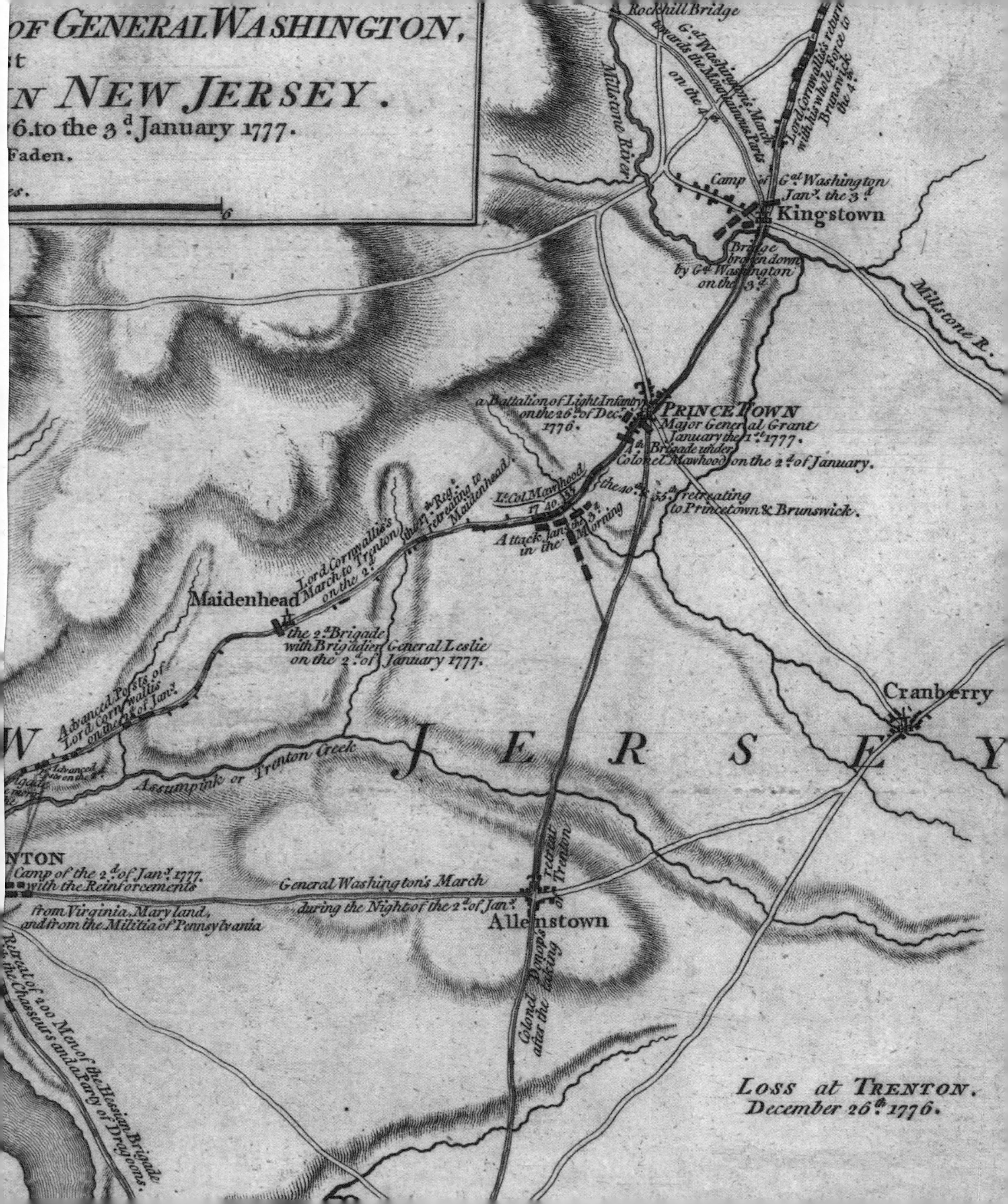
OF GENERAL WASHINGTON,
st
N NEW JERSEY.
76. to the 3d. January 1777.
Faden.
6
Rockhill Bridge
Gd. Washington's March towards the Mountainous Parts on the 4th.
Lord Cornwallis's return with his whole Force to Brunswick the 4th.
Millstone River
Camp of Gd. Washington Jany. the 3d.
Kingstown
Bridge broken down by Gd. Washington on the 3d.
Millstone R.
a Battalion of Light Infantry on the 26th. of Decr. 1776.
PRINCETOWN
Major General Grant January the 1st. 1777.
4th. Brigade under Colonel Mawhood on the 2d. of January.
Lt. Col. Mawhood
17 40 55
the 40th. & 55th. retreating to Princetown & Brunswick.
Attack Jany. the 3d. in the Morning
the 17th. Regt. retreating to Maidenhead
Lord Cornwallis's March to Trenton on the 2d.
Maidenhead
the 2d. Brigade with Brigadier General Leslie on the 2d. of January 1777.
Advanced Posts of Lord Cornwallis on the 1st. of Jany.
Cranberry
W J E R S E Y
Assumpink or Trenton Creek
NTON
Camp of the 2d. of Jany. 1777. with the Reinforcements from Virginia, Maryland, and from the Militia of Pensylvania
General Washington's March during the Night of the 2d. of Jany.
Allenstown
Colonel Donops retreat after the taking of Trenton
Retreat of 200 Men of the Hessian Brigade the Chasseurs and a Party of Dragoons.
Loss at Trenton.
December 26th. 1776.

PLAN OF THE OPERATIONS
agai
THE KINGS TROOPS
from the 26th. of December 1
by William
Six M
1
2
3
Pennington
Smith Creek
Jacobs Creek
Heath Creek
McKonkeys Ferry
The Troops in March at 4 in the Morning on the 26th.
Parade of the Troops on the evening of the 25th. of Decr. 1776.
Left Division 1200 Men and 10 Pieces of Cannon under General Washington.
Upper or Pennington Road
Lower or River Road
Right Division 1500 Men and 16 Pieces of Cannon under Major General Sullivan and General Green.
DELAWARE RIVER full of Ice
Yardley's Ferry
NEWTOWN
Head Quarters of Genl. Washington before & after the Attack of Trenton
St. John Sinclairs
Attack of the Hessian under Col. Rall at 8 in 26th.
Lower Falls
Trenton Ferry
A
N E
N S Y L V A

The Capture of the Hessians at Trenton, December 26, 1776,
by John Trumbull, oil on canvas, 1786–1828.

houses, and all that you hold dear. You have worn yourselves out with fatigues and hardships, but we know not how to spare you. . . . The present is emphatically the crisis which is to decide our destiny."

About half the men stayed on, and Washington's bold return to New Jersey was bringing out the local militia. However, a British column under Lord Cornwallis, much more powerful if hardly more numerous than Washington's force, was marching towards him from New York, determined on revenge for the defeat at Trenton. As skirmishers harassed the British advance, the patriots holed in behind Assunpink Creek, a small river that flowed along the western edge of the village of Trenton. The position was a moderately strong one, but Washington was on a narrow strip of land between the Assunpink and the Delaware. His back was towards the major river. Since his boats were elsewhere, if the British succeeded in crossing the Assunpink, they could pin the patriot army against an uncrossable torrent.

When the enemy arrived in the late afternoon, they tried at once to get over the Assunpink, but they found that the bridge was well protected by cannon. They pegged down their tents for the night, sure that they could make the kill in the morning. With complacency, they noted that the American campfires burned on through the darkness. At dawn, the British found that the bird had flown.

During the night, Washington's army had silently cohered into formation and marched down the Delaware, leaving a few men behind to feed the fires. After having moved well beyond the British left flank, the army had turned east into a back road that pointed deeper into New Jersey.

This maneuver had not been foreseen as a possibility by the British, since, for a professional army, it would have been utter madness. Washington had left a force stronger than his own between his army and all patriot-held territory. The idiot had, by God, blocked his possibility of retreat and also cut his own supply lines!

Washington was, in fact, for the first time making complete use of the advantages of his army. Men fighting for their own liberties did not need a perpetual infusion of supplies. Being devoid of heavy equipment and able to think for themselves, they could move twice as fast as a professional army. Unless actually cornered, they were as hard to catch as quicksilver.

Washington's objective was the village of Princeton, where friendly New Jersey farmers had told him there was a considerable garrison. After six or seven hours of marching, the army arrived on the outskirts in full daylight on January 3, 1777. An advance guard ran unexpectedly into two British regiments that were on their way to join Cornwallis at Trenton. The advance guard, falling back on the main American army, created confusion, while the trained Britons lined up coolly into their famous line. Washington galloped to the rescue, conspicuous on a tall white horse. He lined up his own men and then rode ahead of them as they advanced against the British. When the two forces came in range, both fired; Washington was between them. An aide, Colonel Richard Fitzgerald, covered his face with his hat to keep from seeing the commander in chief killed. When Fitzgerald lowered the hat, he saw many men dead and dying, but the general was sitting untouched on his horse.

The British were on the run. This was the first time that Washington's troops had, in open combat, made a British line break. Washington shouted, "It's a fine fox chase, my boys!" He spurred his powerful horse and dashed after the fleeing British. His horrified aides saw him disappear behind a clump of trees.

A third British regiment was in the town. Its officers, flabbergasted to see the Continental army appear where they believed it could not possibly be, surrendered without making any real resistance. But Washington's subordinates were far from happy. The commander in chief had vanished. Some time passed before Washington came charging up on his foaming horse, in the highest of spirits.

Farmers hurried in to report that a large British detachment was dashing back from Trenton "in a most infernal sweat, running, puffing, and blowing and swearing at being so outwitted." Washington's men only had time to exchange their old blankets for new British ones, and then the army set out again, leading between two and three hundred prisoners. Their direction: further into enemy-held New Jersey.

Washington yearned to march to Brunswick, the main British base in New Jersey, where so much money and equipment were stored that its capture would be a lethal blow. But his men were too tired. He moved in easy stages—the enemy was too confused to bother him—to the heights at Morristown, two-thirds of the way back from Pennsylvania to New York.

Washington's raids on Trenton and Princeton had sensational effects. For patriots everywhere, these dramatic triumphs inspired—after deep depression caused by continual catastrophe—renewed hope. And the British saw their comfortable plan for winning the war utterly shattered. It had been demonstrated as not only impractical but dangerous to try, against an army as mobile and unconventional as Washington's, to hold down a large area with a network of posts. The danger was compounded because His Majesty's presumably loving subjects, who had been counted on to rally to the defense of their "protectors" in the British service, had failed to do so.

The last part of the bitter lesson came doubly clear when the British command, not wishing to have any more outposts beaten up, withdrew their forces in New Jersey to within a few miles of their stronghold on Staten Island. The citizens who had sworn renewed allegiance to the Crown under the guns of His Majesty's mercenaries now tore up their pardons, picked up their own guns, and went hunting redcoats or Hessians. What a plaguey war! Where was the British command to find another way to win?

Fourteen

THE LOSS OF PHILADELPHIA

(1777)

The position at Morristown that Washington now occupied had originally been suggested by General Lee. That former British regular had realized, as Washington had not, how chary professional armies were of their supply lines. The high and broken country, ideally suited to American defensive skills, overlooked the New Jersey plain that connected New York with the Delaware and Philadelphia beyond. By holding these heights and descending from them on those hit-and-run raids at which they had demonstrated such ability, the Americans could keep in perpetual confusion the lifeline of any British advance. The land route to Philadelphia could thus be as effectively blocked as if Washington possessed an overwhelming army.

Having carefully forewarned his troops concerning an eclipse, lest they be frightened by the mysterious disappearance of the sun, Washington settled the men into winter quarters at Morristown. The army shrank as enlistments languished. Never able to believe that the British were as cautious as they were, Washington was in perpetual anxiety lest his ill-manned heights be, despite their defensive strength, stormed. He wrote Congress, which was still skulking at Baltimore, "I think we are now in one of the most critical periods which America ever saw!"

Congressmen, not only those who suspected that a better general could defeat the British with the troops Congress could supply, were annoyed by such perpetual complaints. Robert Morris admonished Washington that if he presented "the best side of the picture frequently," he might get more cooperation. "Heaven (no doubt for the noblest purposes) has blessed you with a firmness of mind, steadiness of countenance, and patience in sufferings that give you infinite advantages over other men. This being the case, you are not to depend on other people's exertions being equal to your own. One mind feeds and thrives on misfortunes by finding resources to get the better of them; another sinks under their weight."

Washington further annoyed Congress by the way he used the dictatorial powers they had granted him when they had fled in terror from Philadelphia to Baltimore. Their intention had been for him to take off their shoulders the weight of supplying the army by using, on his own authority, military force to requisition supplies from neighboring farmers. Washington preferred to devote his powers to advancing the general principles of tolerance and continental union.

The commander in chief ruled that citizens of New Jersey, who had, under stress, sworn allegiance to the Crown, could be uncontaminated by the single act of swearing allegiance to the United States. Those who refused to do so, or who had conspicuously cooperated with the British, should not be punished, but merely escorted to the enemy lines. The wives and children of exiles could stay in their homes "if their behavior warrants." And refugees could take

Peter Frederick Rothermel's State House on the Day of the Battle of Germantown, *oil on canvas, 1862.*

with them any personal possessions that would not strengthen the enemy.

The New Jersey radicals were furious that possible miscreants should get off so easily. However, time was to prove that Washington's lenient measures were not only kind but also the smartest possible politics. Waverers who were persecuted would glow with hate, while forgiven waverers were grateful. And the convinced Tories who were sent to New York were put in the most effective possible reformatory. Under the domination of military aristocrats who despised Colonials and equated their own desires with military necessity, the Tory refugees suffered from an oppression more extreme than any that the British had been accused of by the most violent patriot orators. Since Tories gathered there from all over the continent to be disillusioned, it could be argued that the British lost the Revolutionary War within the walls of their New York stronghold.

That the cleansing oath Washington had designated was not to the sovereign state of New Jersey but to "the United States" outraged many congressmen. The United States? That was no political entity, just an alliance. And Washington had compounded his sin by establishing "additional regiments" that were not attached to any state line, but would mingle soldiers from all parts of the continent.

The global rivalry between France and England, which had inspired Washington's first war, had been by no means abated by France's defeat. She still smarted at the loss of Canada. Thus the American rebellion was being viewed with great interest from Paris; perhaps the British could be thrown out of the North American continent after all. While waiting to see if further cooperation with the American rebels might be justified by proof that the British were really in trouble, the French sent, as discreetly as possible, munitions across the ocean. Washington was to write in April 1778, "France by her supplies has saved us from the yoke so far."

Marie Joseph Paul Yves Roch Gilbert Motier, Marquis de Lafayette *by Charles Willson Peale, after Charles Willson Peale, 1779–1780. Lafayette served as a major general under Washington. Wounded during the Battle of Brandywine, he still managed to organize a successful retreat. He also served with distinction in the Battle of Rhode Island and visited France as the war raged on to negotiate an increase in support for the colonies. On his return, he blocked troops led by Cornwallis at Yorktown.*

Another French influx was giving Washington a great deal of trouble: his headquarters were besieged with officers, come directly from France or the French Indies, who would condescend to serve in the American army if given commands suited to their pretensions. These pretensions were usually very high. Through interpreters—for Washington spoke no French and they, usually, no English—they claimed great rank and achievements abroad. Washington suspected that most were impostors, but he was sorry for those who had spent their last money in coming to him; he found it embarrassing to have to pay for the mending of a high-toned Frenchman's breeches. And there was always the possibility that some of these volatile, bragging soldiers had brought with them sophisticated military knowledge which the American army could well use. Particularly disturbing were those who arrived with such impressive auspices that French support for the American cause might be endangered if they were not given the important commissions they demanded. As Washington was led to agree to the appointment of one foreign claimant after another, his councils of war became increasingly bilingual.

Among the arrivals of 1777, three were to stand out: Colonel Louis le Bèque Duportail was to take over the leadership of the engineers with such effect that there was never again to be an asinine major fortification like the disastrous Fort Washington. Thomas Conway, an Irish officer in the French service, was to earn Washington's hatred more thoroughly than perhaps any other man ever did. And then there was the Marquis de Lafayette.

Lafayette's connections in the French court were so important that his arrival in America had induced a diplomatic protest from England. Congress eagerly made him a major general, although with the understanding that, since he had no military experience, the title was honorary. The young aristocrat—he was twenty—joined Washington's staff, delighted Washington with his modesty and eagerness to learn English, and then horrified Washington by wishing to assume at once a major general's command. The eyes of all Europe were upon him, he said, expecting great things.

Lafayette quickly calmed down. As he and Washington got to know each other better, they established an ideal father-and-son relationship which satisfied deep emotional lacks they both felt. Lafayette proved to be brilliant. With reddish hair receding up his egglike forehead, he was not handsome, but he possessed a magnetism almost equal to Washington's own. A youthful romantic, he indulged himself in daydreams of glory, some of them completely wild, which he expected his spiritual father to agree to or not as the older man's wisdom dictated. Unlike Washington's other foreign officers, who despised Washington's lack of conventional military skills, the inexperienced Lafayette became one of Washington's most rapid and apt pupils in the new type of warfare the American general was evolving. For Washington, Lafayette's arrival was a most happy chance.

The British in New York, having been reinforced from across the ocean, opened the 1777 campaign on June 17 by moving into New Jersey. They seemed to be on the way to Philadelphia, but they lingered below the Morristown Heights. Their object was double: to lure Washington into a battle on the plain, and to see whether the citizens would not welcome a return of British protection. But Washington did not budge and the citizens shouldered their guns to harass the British flanks. Howe returned to New York, made a second unsuccessful feint into New Jersey, and, then, so Washington's spies reported, began preparing his naval transports to receive his army.

Guessing out Howe's intentions was now Washington's impossible business. An important consideration was the fact that a strong force under General John Burgoyne had sailed down from Canada on Lake Champlain and had captured, without meeting any resistance, the American fort at Ticonderoga, which was supposed to hold the northern invasion route shut. If Burgoyne successfully traversed the intervening wilderness, he could either strike the unprotected rear of New England or go directly south to the upper Hudson. Howe could cooperate by sailing through Long Island Sound to New England or (as seemed more probable, considering the value of breaking the rebellion in half at the Hudson River) sailing up that river to meet Burgoyne. The third possibility was that Howe would ply through the ocean to Philadelphia.

General John Burgoyne *by Joshua Reynolds, oil on canvas, c. 1766. Often referred to as "Gentleman Johnny," Burgoyne surrendered his army of five thousand to American troops on October 17, 1777, during the Saratoga campaign, and his men were taken prisoner. Burgoyne returned to Britain under a cloud and never held another active command.*

Moving his troops back and forth through a rocky pass in the Hudson Highlands called the Clove, Washington inclined the army towards Albany and New England or towards Philadelphia as different reports came in from his spies. Then, on July 24, "one hundred and seventy topsail vessels and about fifty or sixty smaller ones" sailed from New York Harbor. Since they set out into the ocean, their objective was indicated as Philadelphia. Washington responded by marching across New Jersey. However, he went slowly, since he feared that Howe, having maneuvered him out of the way, would double back and mount the Hudson after all.

Never was there a more uncertain, nervous time. Washington breathed easier when the fleet was sighted off the Delaware River, but, then, instead of advancing up the river towards Philadelphia, the fleet disappeared again. Was Charleston their objective? Or were they now in full sail for the Hudson? Completely confused, not wishing to destroy his army by endless marching and countermarching in hot weather, Washington allowed the troops to collapse near Philadelphia. Finally, he could bear inaction no longer. He started a slow march back towards New York. It was August 22, when hard news finally came in: the British were sailing up the Chesapeake, their destination Philadelphia after all. They clearly intended to march overland from the head of the Chesapeake.

Howe, having exhausted two possibilities, was trying a third. He had first thought that by making the Continental army look ridiculous he could make the colonists reaffirm their allegiance. This had not

1.

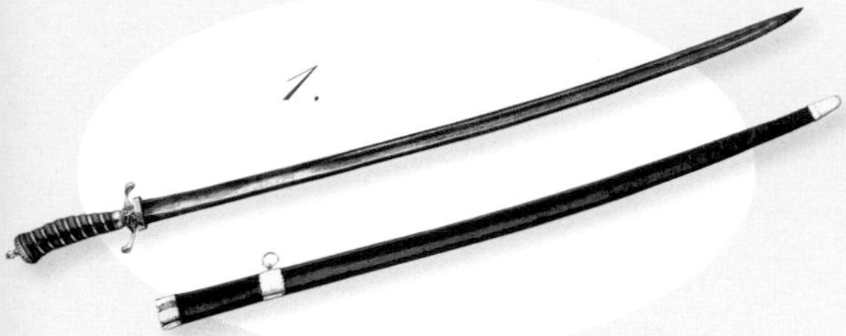

2.

3.

4.

5.

6.

7.

1. *Washington's battle sword and scabbard.*

2. *Washington's camp chest or "mess kit," which enabled him to dine in a manner reflecting his position as commander of the Continental army.*

3. *Washington's uniform from 1789 until his death in 1799. None of his uniforms from the Revolutionary War period are known to have survived.*

4. *Washington's camp cup engraved with the Washington family crest. Made by William Hollingshead, 1776.*

5. *Washington's canteen that he likely used during the French and Indian War and possibly the Revolutionary War.*

6. *Washington's folding camp cot, made of wood and canvas, was six-and-a-half-feet long.*

7. *This liquor case, probably Washington's own, was built to withstand heavy use and to safeguard its valuable contents.*

Surrender of General Burgoyne *by John Trumbull, oil on canvas, 1822.*

worked, and in the process Howe had inadvertently taught Washington that his amateur army could not stand up to the enemy professionals in formal battle. Next, Howe had tried holding down a conquered territory with scattered posts. That had backfired. Now he wished again to engage Washington's army, this time to destroy it. Washington had refused to come down from the heights near Morristown but surely he could not allow Philadelphia to fall without a fight. Furthermore, Howe believed that his possession of the American capital and largest city would do much to hamstring the rebellion, both physically and psychologically.

Howe had been right in guessing that Washington would feel it necessary to try to bar the British advance. Pausing only for a parade through Philadelphia, which he tried to make as impressive as the ragged condition of the troops allowed, Washington had set out pell-mell for the indicated British line of march. The Continental army made its stand on a seemingly strong position behind the Brandywine River. This time it was not military naïveté but misinformation—Washington's intelligence was wrong both on the geography of the region and concerning British movements—that allowed Howe to repeat the strategy of Brooklyn Heights. Making a wide sweep to the left, a British column came in behind the American defenses. However, on this day, September 11, 1777, the Continental army did not immediately disintegrate.

Successful rear-guard action, with Washington in direct command, enabled most of the army to escape. Howe had done little more than open the way to Philadelphia.

He did not immediately accept the prize, preferring to continue his efforts to lure the Continental army into a conclusive battle. Washington marched and countermarched, not willing to attempt a stand that would be to enemy advantage, forever hoping that the enemy professionals would make a mistake that would give the Continental army a chance to fight in its own way. Finally wearying of the game, the British captured Philadelphia while Washington was too far off to fire even one defensive shot.

Washington realized that he and the Continental army had been made to look foolish, all the more by contrast with the northern army. Commanded by Gates, that army had won an impressive if not conclusive victory over Burgoyne: the Battle of Freeman's Farm. Washington yearned to achieve a coup before winter set in—and at last he saw a way.

Major General Lord Cornwallis was occupying Philadelphia with three thousand men. The main British army—five thousand strong—was encamped under Howe in the suburb of Germantown, some five miles up the Schuylkill River, in the direction of Washington's own encampment. Basically, Germantown was shaped like a cross, the main road to the city being cut at right angles by a major crossroad. Spies reported that the British outposts and light infantry were stationed on the near side of the crossing, while the bulk of Howe's army was encamped just beyond it. Most invitingly, Howe indicated his disdain of the rebels by erecting no fortifications.

Why not achieve another Trenton, this time on a much larger scale? Calling in every man he dared, even weakening the forts defending the Hudson, Washington gathered eight thousand Continentals and three thousand militia. They were to spring off after dark from so great a distance—fifteen to nineteen miles—that the British would not expect an attack. They were to attack at dawn.

As usual, Washington worked out too complicated a plan: four columns converging simultaneously from four different routes. The militia regiments were to move along byroads on both wings of the advance. (As it turned out, they never succeeded in getting into the battle at all.) The main thrust was entrusted to two columns of Continentals. The column Washington led was to drive the British back along the main road, while a force under Greene, coming in from the left, was to pin them against the Schuylkill.

As Washington advanced with his men on October 3, 1777, he could only rarely consult his watch; the troops were moving as silently as possible in utter darkness. However, it was clear that they were falling heavily behind schedule. Washington anxiously scanned the sky for signs of the dawn that would frustrate catching the British by complete surprise. The sky started to pale while they were still some distance from Germantown, but the emerging sun drew up from the ground a thick fog. Washington welcomed the obscuring vapor as sent by a benign Providence, although in a few hours he was to attribute it to "some unaccountable something."

No news or sound had indicated the arrival of the other columns when Washington's advance guard engaged the British pickets. Staying with his main force, Washington could not discern through the mist the action going on ahead of him. However, the sounds of firing, by becoming less loud, indicated that the British were falling back. He ordered more regiments forward. The firing took on a deeper tone as cannon spoke, but the direction of the movement remained the same. An ever-larger British force was clearly failing to make a stand.

Finally, Washington decided to lead his reserve guard forward. In contrast to the tumult ahead, around him all was silence. Through swirls of mist, he could see on both sides of the road abandoned cannon, empty tents, all the deserted paraphernalia of a major British encampment. His heart sang—at long last the Continental army was driving a major segment of the British army!

Then he heard firing much nearer than the sound of battle. A large brick house stood like a fortress beside the road. It was occupied by British soldiers. The main American army had swept by, leaving behind many dead bodies. Flashes from the windows were now dropping Washington's men. At Washington's orders, cannonballs were fired against the house at point-blank range. The brick walls were so solid that the balls just bounced away. Finally, Washington decided that he would leave a detachment surrounding the house and take his rear guard on.

He found that the American advance had penetrated all the way to the crossroads, behind which Howe's main army was encamped. And now, although fog blotted out vision, sounds indicated that Greene was coming in from the left. Most excitingly, the new sequence of firing moved beyond the crossroads, which indicated that Greene's advance guard was entering Howe's main camp.

In his elation and eagerness, Washington rode so far to the head of his own column that he was exposed, as an aide noted with great concern, "to the hottest fire of the enemy." He saw complete victory in his grasp. Howe's encampment, he assumed, must be "in the utmost confusion." The confusion would spread, with the news of the American success, to the British garrison in Philadelphia. Fortune, he exulted, was "declaring herself in our favor."

And then, as suddenly as a coin is spun, everything changed. Greene's advance guard came bursting out of Howe's encampment at a run. Almost simultaneously, the sound of heavy firing broke out where it should not have been: on the American rear. The soldiers who were moving ahead with Washington stopped in their tracks, stood listening for a brief instant, and then joined the flight of Greene's men. Washington shouted; he flailed at the fugitives with the flat of his sword, but all to no avail. Panic had taken over.

After Washington had accepted the inevitable, he spent his energies in shepherding his troops in as orderly a manner as possible back to the encampments from which they had marched the night before. Round and round in his mind ran puzzlement as to why "the most flattering hopes of victory" had "turned into a rout."

At Washington's orders, cannonballs were fired against the house at point-blank range.

He was later to learn that the soldiers who had started the retreat had run out of ammunition. The firing at the rear, which had made the men fear they were being surrounded, had resulted when Greene's right blundered into the detachment Washington had stationed around the brick house; being unable to see through the mist, each group had thought the other the enemy.

To Europeans, it was to seem miraculous that an untrained rabble should attack a mighty regular army so effectively and so soon (twenty-three days) after their defeat at the Brandywine. Vergennes, the French foreign minister, who was wondering whether to risk an American alliance, reasoned that "to bring an army, raised within a year, to this, promised anything." Howe was impressed into withdrawing his entire force behind the fortifications he was erecting around Philadelphia. But among American patriots the event was chalked up to Washington as another defeat. This seemed the more to the discredit of his leadership when the report came in of a major victory up north: Burgoyne had surrendered at Saratoga to Gates.

Fifteen

THE CONWAY CABAL

(1777–1778)

Burgoyne's effort to invade the United States from Canada had been a conspicuous example of the inability of the British ministry and military to visualize American conditions. Because British ships could carry troops down Lake Champlain, the advance to Ticonderoga had been practicable; but from Ticonderoga to the head of Hudson River navigation near Albany, there were a hundred miles of howling wilderness to traverse. Since Burgoyne could not hope to build an effective line of fortifications before the onset of winter, he could not rationally expect to keep open the supply lines on which conventional armies depended. And, of course, regular soldiers were at a disadvantage against irregular American fighters in the forests.*

Once Burgoyne was deep in the woods, he was deep in trouble, and as soon as a British force was in trouble, American militia swarmed to the kill. Burgoyne's supply line was shattered and his advance reduced to a standstill. He could not get back to Canada, or ahead to Albany, nor could his army hope to survive a winter in the wilderness. Gates, the American commander, who had in his own time been a British regular, knew that little was required of his forces but to keep the trap closed until Burgoyne was forced to give up. It was the insubordinate combat general Benedict Arnold who staged the battles that immediately preceded Burgoyne's surrender at Saratoga (October 17, 1777). This capture of some five thousand men was the greatest victory of American arms so far.

Partly out of diffidence, partly because he was so busy elsewhere, partly because he did not believe in interfering where he did not have detailed knowledge, Washington had allowed the northern command to be semiautonomous. Gates had already taken advantage of this to be insubordinate. Now, elated by his victory, he decided to demonstrate complete autonomy from the man who had at the start of the war come to him humbly for advice. He sent his official report not to the designated commander in chief, but directly to Congress. Gates no longer needed the large force that had been gathered to oppose Burgoyne, yet he had no intention, despite orders sent him by Washington, of reinforcing his rival. He would not even return the regiments which Washington had at the moment of crisis sent up north, to the weakening of his own army.

Washington believed that if only Gates would obey orders and send troops, he could still make a strike. The forts on the Delaware below Philadelphia,

* Historians like to blame Burgoyne's debacle on Howe's failure to move to his support up the Hudson, but allover British strategy had designed Burgoyne's army to act independently. Howe was not violating the British strategic plan when he sailed for Philadelphia.

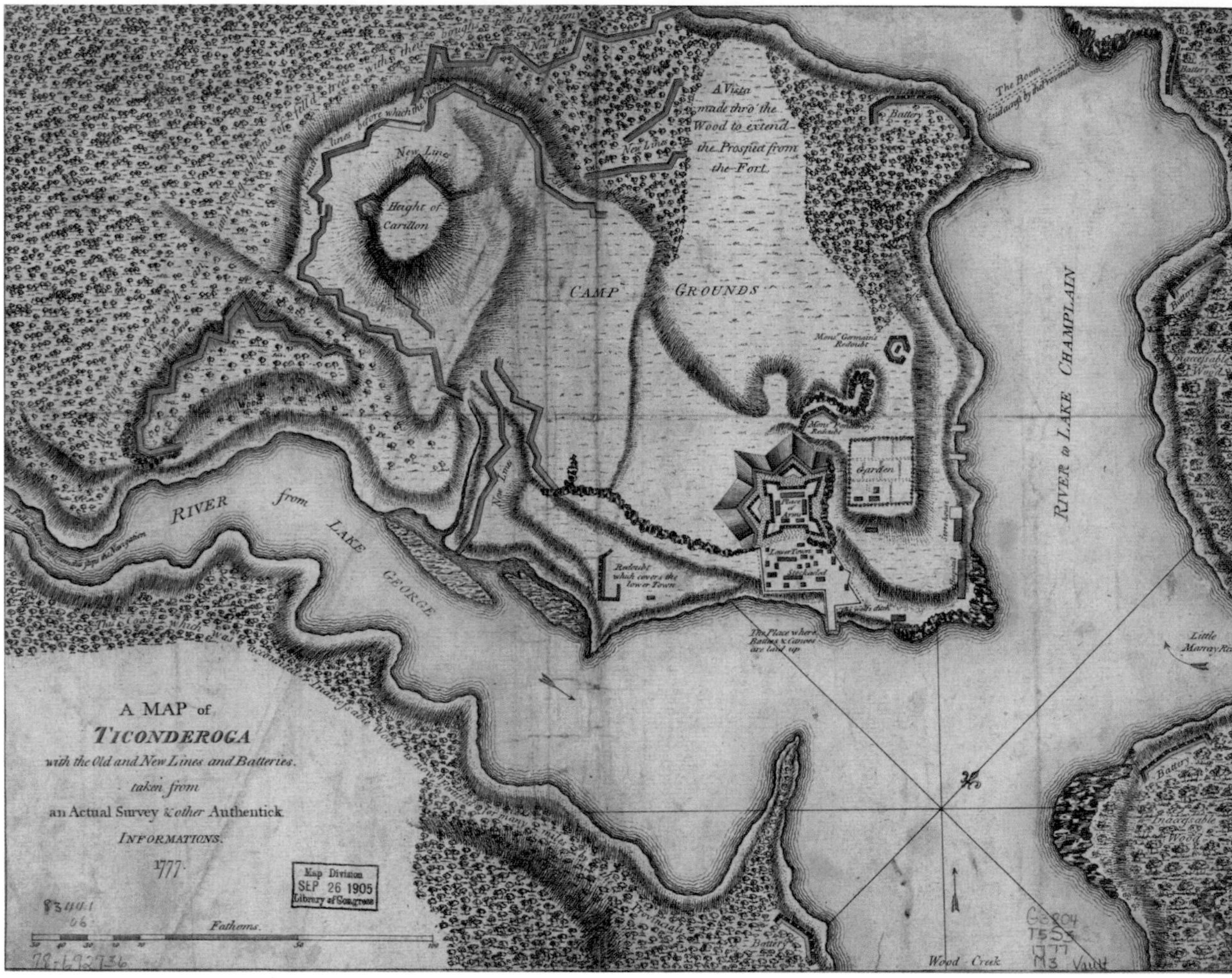

Map of Ticonderoga, 1777, with the old and new lines and batteries taken from an actual survey.

expertly planned by Duportail and other French engineers, were keeping the British navy and supply ships separated from the army. As weeks passed, it became evident that the forts could only be subdued by action on land as well as by water. This meant that British detachments would have to come out of Philadelphia. Washington intended, when adequately reinforced, to cut them off. But Gates saw to it that Washington had not been adequately reinforced and, after holding out for almost two months, the forts finally fell.

Without taking into consideration that geography had been the prime force in defeating Burgoyne, many patriots sneeringly compared Gates's victories and Washington's defeats. Washington knew that he badly needed a victory. He reconnoitered Philadelphia, trying to find some chink in the defenses. Duportail, who was with him, ruled that the city could be held against any imaginable force. Although Washington found it "distressing" to be unable to answer the expectations of the world, he led his troops into winter quarters. The address he now put on his dispatches has come in American tradition to signify hardship. It was Valley Forge.

The army was undersupplied with almost everything normally considered necessary to sustain life, shoeless feet leaving (as legend emphasizes) bloody footprints in the snow. Congress was more than ever outraged that Washington would not take what the army needed from the inhabitants at bayonet point. The commander in chief had, indeed, more respect for civilian rights than did many legislators. Charles Carroll of Carrollton wrote that Washington "is so humane and delicate that I fear the common cause will suffer." Washington himself wrote, "The misfortunes of war, and the unhappy circumstances frequently attendant thereon to individuals are more to be lamented than avoided; but it is the duty of everyone to alleviate them as much as possible."

Washington believed that what was morally most desirable was likely to be politically most valuable. Since the future liberty of the soldiers themselves would be secured by ultimate victory, let the American army earn gratitude by suffering deprivation while the British and Hessians earned hatred by stripping the countryside. To keep public opinion from being driven to the Crown, the soldiers rather than the civilians would have to accept hardship.

Washington explained to the men that to settle into any of the villages near Philadelphia would increase the difficulties of refugees from Philadelphia already crowded there. The army would have to build its own city. He had selected as the site a succession of hills eighteen miles northwest of Philadelphia.

The men were to erect huts fourteen feet wide by sixteen long and six and a half feet high. Each was to house twelve men. Fireplaces were to be made of laths covered with mud. While the huts were being built, the men lived miserably in tents. Dr. Albigence Waldo wrote, "Poor food—hard lodging—cold weather—fatigue—nasty clothes—nasty cookery—vomit half my time—smoked out of my senses—the devil's in it—I can't endure it. . . . A pox on my bad luck. There comes a bowl of beef soup—full of burnt leaves and dirt, sickish enough to make a Hector spew—away with it boys—I'll live like the chameleon upon air! . . .

"There comes a soldier, his bare feet are seen through his worn-out shoes, his legs nearly naked from the tattered remains of an only pair of stockings, his breeches not sufficient to cover his nakedness, his shirt hanging in strings; his hair disheveled; his face meager. . . . He comes and cries with an air of wretchedness and despair, 'I am sick, my feet lame, my legs are sore, my body covered with this tormenting itch . . . and all the reward I shall get will be—"Poor Will is dead!" '"

As Washington suffered with and for his troops at Valley Forge, it was made increasingly clear to him that he was menaced by what he considered an effort to "exalt" General Gates "on the ruins of my reputation."

Far from expressing sympathy, the Pennsylvania legislature protested that, by going into winter quarters at Valley Forge, the army had left the inhabitants unprotected. Washington replied, "I can assure those gentlemen that it is a much easier and less distressing thing to draw remonstrances in a comfortable room by a good fireside than to occupy a cold, bleak hill and sleep under frost and snow without clothes or blankets. However, although they seem to have little feeling for the naked, distressed soldiers, I feel superabundantly for them, and from my soul pity those miseries which it is neither in my power to relieve or prevent."

As Washington suffered with and for his troops at Valley Forge, it was made increasingly clear to him that he was menaced by what he considered an effort to "exalt" General Gates "on the ruins of my reputation."

The surprising aspect of the agitation to replace Washington as commander in chief is not that it took place, but that it had taken so long to develop. Washington had again and again been defeated, but he had never defeated the main British army. (At

Trenton and Princeton he had beaten up outposts.) If he were not losing the war—which was very open to question—he was surely failing to win it. He had started out by offending New England and, then, as he lost his provincialism, had shifted into what seemed to many leaders a worse fallacy: the belief that the United States was not an alliance but a nation, one and indivisible. Although admittedly not allied with the conservatives, he had outraged many a radical by protecting all conservatives who could be persuaded to go along with the cause. And many congressmen remained worried by his insistence on such a long-term united army, trained to obey an expert officer corps, as it weakened the soldiers' state ties and seemed a possible instrument of tyranny.

Rt. Hon. General [Thomas] Conway, published in European Magazine, *April 2, 1782. Washington hated the Irish-Frenchman Thomas Conway more than any other man. The movement Conway spearheaded to try to remove Washington from his post is known as the "Conway Cabal."*

Utopian thinking backed the political preferences of state leaders by postulating that the best fighting force would be made up of militiamen who exerted their God-given natural gifts as they took turns defending their fields. Suspicions that it was Washington's personal incompetence that made him insist that he could not win with such an army were encouraged by the fact that much of Gates's triumphant force had been militia. It was only too easy to conclude that if Gates could thus beat Burgoyne, he could thus beat Howe.

Although the foreign officers in the American service could not agree with the more radical members of Congress on the glories of militia, many of them were only too glad to testify that the American general—he did not obey the correct rules of war—was incompetent. The most vociferous such critic was that Irish-born Frenchman, Brigadier General Thomas Conway. The movement to remove Washington is called (somewhat inaccurately) the Conway Cabal.

Conway, who could never forget that he had served under Frederick the Great, announced himself as the most experienced officer in Washington's army, and made no bones about admitting that he was there because, if he became a major general in the American service, he could become a brigadier when he returned to the superior French service. The catch was that he was a junior brigadier in America, and the blockhead Washington would not agree to his being promoted over the heads of a flock of other American blockheads. Nor was his voice listened to with adequate deference at the councils of war, where he was so dictatorial that Washington found him unbearable.

To congressmen already unhappy about Washington, Conway communicated that his own services were desperately needed to counteract the deficiencies of the commander in chief. However, an officer of his merit could not accept humiliation. He would be forced to resign if not given his rightful rank as major general. Eventually, Richard Henry Lee, one of the congressmen who most distrusted Washington, informed the commander in chief that Congress intended to promote Conway.

Washington's reply reveals how tight his nerves were drawn. To raise an officer "without conspicuous merit" over the heads of many senior brigadiers would, he wrote, "give a fatal blow to the existence of the army." And then, for the first time in his Revolutionary service, Washington hinted that he might himself resign: "It will be impossible for me to be of any further service if such insuperable difficulties are thrown in my way."

Horatio Gates at Saratoga *by James Peale, oil on canvas, c. 1800.*

This letter revealed to Washington's opponents that in Conway they had a lever which might be used to pry the commander in chief loose.

The next development was a drunken indiscretion blurted out by Gates's favorite aide, Colonel James Wilkinson. Washington, on being notified by some of his own supporters of what Wilkinson had said, wrote Conway laconically:

"Sir: A letter I received last night contained the following paragraph: 'In a letter from General Conway to General Gates, he says, "Heaven has been determined to save your country, or a weak general and bad councillors would have ruined it."'

"I am, Sir, your humble servant, George Washington."

By now, an experienced politician was gathering up the various strands of opposition to Washington. Thomas Mifflin had been one of Washington's four first advisers. He had felt in himself great potentialities as a warrior, and his influence on Congress had brought him high rank, but he was a hysterical soldier, and Washington had kept him dealing with supply as quartermaster general. Finally, he had hightailed from the army, leaving Washington with no quartermaster general.

Mifflin realized that Washington's magic was still so great that Congress would not vote to discharge him. Better not to raise any definite issue, but to put Washington in a position which would force him to resign. Towards this end, Mifflin and Richard Henry Lee perverted two suggestions Washington had himself made. Washington had wished to have a semipermanent Board of War substituted for the ever-shifting congressional committees that supplied the army. And he had asked that he be empowered to appoint as inspector general an experienced foreign officer who would help him establish a uniform system of drill and maneuver.

Mifflin and Lee changed the conception of the Board of War. Far from being limited to supplying the army, it was to have the top military authority, outranking the commander in chief. And the inspector general would not be just an adviser on European technical skills. He was to supervise all Washington's commands and acts, reporting directly to the Board of War. It was now only necessary to man this structure with the right people. The president of the Board of War, who was informed unofficially that his mission was the "total reform and regulation" of Washington's army, was, of course, Gates. Mifflin put himself on the board, which he filled with other critics of Washington. But the real stroke of genius was the choice of the inspector general: Washington's enemy Conway was advanced to major general and appointed to rule over him.

Mifflin managed to get all this through Congress, not because that body was hostile to Washington, but because no one paid any attention. The watchword, until Washington's letter of resignation lay safely in hand, had to be "hush." Mifflin was thus greatly concerned when Washington's letter to Conway revealed that information was leaking. Whether by chance or by expert strategy, Washington had given his opponents no hint as to the means by which he had been informed concerning Conway's correspondence with Gates. Mifflin assumed that some agent of the commander in chief's—perhaps Hamilton—had secretly raided Gates's files. He warned Gates.

Gates took it for granted that his files had actually been tampered with. He wrote Washington, sending copies to Mifflin and officially to Congress, a letter in which he by clear implication accused Washington of instigating dishonorable acts. Washington thereupon revealed his source as the blabbering of Gates's own aide.

Conway was soon also engaged in public controversy. When he had appeared at Valley Forge, immensely pleased with himself and bearing his commissions from the Board of War, Washington used a technicality to brush him aside. Conway thereupon

BICKERSTAFF's
BOSTON
ALMANACK,
For the Year of our REDEMPTION,
1 7 7 8.
Being the Second Year of AMERICAN INDEPENDENCE.
And the Second after LEAP-YEAR,
Calculated for the Meredian of BOSTON, Lat. 42′ 25° N.
CONTAINING, beſides what is neceſſary in an Almanack, a Variety of uſeful and inſtructing Pieces.
The GLORIOUS WASHINGTON and GATES.

Bickerstaff's Boston Almanack, *printed in Danvers, Massachusetts, by Ezekiel Russell, featuring woodcut profiles of "the glorious Washington and Gates." The Washington profile, though somewhat inaccurate, was first used in 1776 by Russell and represents the earliest published image of the future first president of the United States.*

wrote Washington two insulting letters. By mocking the commander in chief as an amateur soldier—"I do not pretend, sir, to be a consummate general, but . . . an old sailor knows more about ships than an admiral who has never been to sea"—Conway in effect claimed superiority for all the European volunteers over the native American officers.

What Mifflin had hoped would be a subtle maneuver behind the scenes had now come most gaudily into the light of day. Rumor buzzed through the army camps, galloped from crossroad to crossroad, to report that Washington had been insulted, that an underhand effort was being made to force him to resign. Men who had been passionate in criticism of Washington flew to his defense with twice the passion.

Washington's opponents were soon in full flight. Conway found that those who had egged him on were refusing even to speak to him; he was forced out of the army. Gates lied to Washington about his correspondence with Conway and expressed a hope that the whole matter might be dropped. Mifflin announced publicly that Washington was the best friend he ever had in his life.

Washington was not easily appeased. In order to keep from encouraging the enemy and dispiriting his own followers, he had hidden from the world the shortages from which he had suffered, accepting criticism for what he considered not his fault. For the sake of the unity of the cause, he had bowed his head to many an insult. But the end of his control had come; his anger poured out with all the fury of a flood long restrained by a dam. He encouraged his supporters to harass his enemies with threats of duels. He expressed amusement that Mifflin had to do some fancy footwork to keep from a bloody engagement with the grim martial, General John Cadwallader. Cadwallader actually fought Conway, wounding him in the neck and mouth. Thinking he might die, Conway wrote Washington an abject letter which Washington did not answer. Conway recovered.

The Conway Cabal achieved exactly the opposite of what had been intended. Like a lightning rod, it released harmlessly fears, doubts, and resentments that might otherwise, as the long years of indecisive war rolled on, have massed until Washington was struck down. The threat that he might be eliminated made Americans visualize the leadership without him. Supposing he were replaced by the noisy controversialist Gates, who fostered and was fostered by a radical clique in Congress? That would clearly be, whatever the military result, a disaster for national unity: faction would rise to fight faction. And if not Gates, who else? The answer was that there was no one else. Washington was recognized as the indispensable man. Until the fighting was almost over, his leadership was not again seriously challenged.

The Conway Cabal achieved exactly the opposite of what had been intended. Like a lightning rod, it released harmlessly fears, doubts, and resentments that might otherwise, as the long years of indecisive war rolled on, have massed until Washington was struck down. The threat that he might be eliminated made Americans visualize the leadership without him.

Sixteen

THE ROAD TURNS UPWARD

(1778)

Valley Forge was the very image of misery only during the first two of the army's six months there. At about the time that the Conway Cabal misfired, by mid-February 1778, food became, if not delectable, adequate. The men had all moved from cold and smoky tents to cabins of their own building; leaks had been plugged and chimneys adjusted to draw efficiently. Firewood abounded. Furthermore, long enlistments had populated the "spacious city" with men mutually congenial; all were temperamentally attuned to military service. The prevailing lack—clothes—was not serious when the inhabitants of each hut could assemble one complete costume for whoever was called to duty out in the cold.

In this c. 1900 engraving, Washington visits wounded soldiers at Valley Forge.

Nakedness became a joke. A French volunteer remembered a dinner party to which no one was admitted who possessed a whole pair of trousers. By combining their rations, the guests feasted on tough steak and potatoes, with hickory nuts for dessert. With "some kind of spirits" they made a salamander, "set the liquor on fire and drank it up, flame and all. Such a ragged and at the same time merry set of fellows were never before brought together."

Washington shared the prevailing high spirits only when he did not think ahead. Although his army was outnumbered by a well-supplied and expert enemy, Congress seemed to be doing nothing. In mid-April, he exploded to his civilian masters, "I shall make no apology for the freedom of this letter. . . . My agreement with the committee entitled me to upwards of forty thousand Continental troops." In all the American army posts there were hardly fifteen thousand.

The perversion of the inspector-generalship to the ends of the Conway Cabal had blocked Washington's desire to have a foreign officer teach his men the conventional military skills that would enable them to stand up against a foreign army in open battle. That the solution had arrived was far from clear when there rode into camp a seemingly toplofty German volunteer who announced himself as Lieutenant General Friedrich Wilhelm Ludolf Gerhard Augustin, Baron von Steuben, and who claimed to have held high rank under Frederick the Great. It

soon developed that Steuben was not a baron and had held no high military rank. But the impostor proved both an able drillmaster and open-minded enough to appreciate the peculiarities of American troops. No European army, the bogus nobleman pointed out, would have held together under equivalent hardships. "The genius of this nation," he wrote a European comrade, "is not in the least to be compared with the Prussians, the Austrians, or French. You say to your soldier, 'Do this,' and he doeth it, but I am obliged to say, 'This is the reason that you ought to do that,' and then he does it."

In cooperation with American officers, Steuben worked out a simplified manual of arms pragmatically suited to American needs. He taught the soldiers how to use bayonets. He taught them how to maneuver in ranks, thus curing their tendency to advance in single file, which had forced Washington into complicated maneuvers that would permit several columns to strike at once. And Steuben made the whole thing fun by his ebullient temperament: ecstasy when maneuvers went well, and at mistakes hysterical rages, which the troops came to expect and relish.

Drilling with Steuben became the favorite sport at Valley Forge. While engaging in what could almost be a more complicated square dance, the men learned skills that had previously escaped them. Keen competition grew up between the different corps. Delinquent officers were fined quarts of brandy.

Early in May, Washington learned that France had recognized the independence of the United States, a move that seemed to dictate war between France and England. In excitement, Washington wrote, "Calmness and serenity seems likely to succeed in some measure those dark and tempestuous clouds which at times appeared ready to overwhelm us. The game, whether well or ill played hitherto, seems now to be verging fast to a favorable issue." Embroiled in Europe, the British might well abandon their American effort. Washington visualized himself back in Mount Vernon, enjoying, in peace and prosperity, American independence.

Opposite: *A preliminary sketch for* George Washington at Valley Forge *by Tompkins Harrison Matteson, 1854.*

A contemporary photo of Washington's headquarters at Valley Forge National Historic Park.

Britain's American endeavor was indeed in turmoil. The capture of the rebel capital had achieved little beyond creating a brilliant social season for the Tory girls who had remained in Philadelphia. The rebellion flowed almost unhindered around the occupied city, and the British were unable to sortie into the countryside without being surrounded by clouds of guerrilla fighters. Howe's hope of recruiting a large corps of Americans disillusioned with the rebel cause had been frustrated by Washington's gentleness to Tories and the mostly good behavior of the Continental army. When Howe was recalled to England, his officers and their girls fittingly said farewell with a grand ball.

Howe was succeeded by his second-in-command, the dour, neurotic, self-righteous Sir Henry Clinton, who was an audacious planner and a hesitant doer. As soon as Clinton arrived from New York, the word was that Philadelphia would be evacuated. Washington waited eagerly for reports that the transports were being fitted for a long ocean voyage to the Indies or to Europe. But the navy carried the army's baggage to New York. The troops were clearly going to march there through the lowlands of New Jersey.

In mid-June, the washerwomen, who were among Washington's most effective spies, reported that the British officials in Philadelphia had ordered their linen delivered at once, "finished or unfinished." It followed that the march was about to start. Sure enough, on the 18th, the enemy force crossed the Delaware. Again, as when Boston was evacuated, there was the opportunity for a triumphal parade with the commander in chief at the head. Again, there was no such parade. Washington was busy trying to decide how to react to the British move.

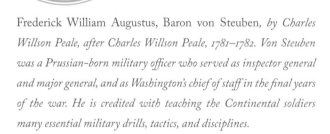

Frederick William Augustus, Baron von Steuben, *by Charles Willson Peale, after Charles Willson Peale, 1781–1782. Von Steuben was a Prussian-born military officer who served as inspector general and major general, and as Washington's chief of staff in the final years of the war. He is credited with teaching the Continental soldiers many essential military drills, tactics, and disciplines.*

Owing to the prevalent practice of exchanging prisoners, Washington had been reunited with an old colleague: General Lee had come riding back from the British lines. Washington did not know that Lee had, during his captivity, made suggestions for British action that could well be considered traitorous to the American cause. Washington, of course, remembered that Lee had been insubordinate to him personally. Yet he was glad to have the military wizard back again.

He looked forward particularly to showing Lee how, with Steuben's help, he had in a year and a half improved the discipline and the skills of the army. Lee was not impressed. Washington's efforts to develop a force that could stand up to the British in open battle seemed to Lee pure idiocy. Washington, Lee stated, was "not fit to command a sergeant's guard." Lee was so publicly critical of the weakness of the Continental army that Washington, having pointed out that much was irremediable, asked that criticisms be limited to discussions at headquarters.

Washington was on the horns of a dilemma. He had prepared his army to attack the British. The British were now available, but in open country where they fought best. And the total situation was breaking so well for the Americans that it seemed foolhardy to take a risk. Regretfully, Washington limited his active intervention with the British march to sending skirmishes against their flanks. He would lead his main army parallel with the enemy through the New Jersey uplands. When the enemy reached their bases in New York, he would reinforce the defenses on the Hudson.

As if for the purpose of tantalizing Washington (actually because they found bridges torn down and paused to rebuild them in style), the British moved across New Jersey with an excruciating slowness. On June 24, Washington called a council of war. The enemy, he reported, numbered nine to ten thousand. The Americans had 10,684, not counting twelve hundred regulars and twelve hundred militia hovering on the British flanks. Might not an attack be staged? Lee was instantly on his feet. He insisted that the inexpert Americans were

General Sir Henry Clinton in a 1778 patriotic engraving attributed to Fielding & Walker.

"I NEVER SAW THE GENERAL TO SO MUCH ADVANTAGE . . ."

ALEXANDER HAMILTON'S DESCRIPTION OF THE BATTLE OF MONMOUTH

AS THE LARGEST, OLDEST, AND WEALTHIEST of the original thirteen colonies, Virginia played a central role in the fight for independence and as a state in the new republic. This importance is reflected in the number of Virginians who filled key national leadership positions. Three remarkable Virginians stand out in their service to the new nation: George Washington as commander in chief during the Revolutionary War, Thomas Jefferson as the philosophic voice of the country, and James Madison as the chief architect of the nation's new constitutional system. In *The Great Virginia Triumvirate* (Charlottesville and London: University of Virginia Press, 2010), John Kaminski presents a series of biographical portraits that bring these three men to life for the modern reader. Below is a quote from Alexander Hamilton, Washington's aide during the war, in a vivid description of the Battle of Monmouth.

As we approached the supposed place of action we heard some flying rumors of what had happened, in consequence of which the general rode forward and found the troops retiring in the greatest disorder and the enemy pressing upon their rear. I never saw the general to so much advantage. His coolness and firmness were admirable. He instantly took measures for checking the enemy's form and made proper disposition. He then rode back and had the troops formed on a very advantageous piece of ground. . . .

The sequel is, we beat the enemy and killed and wounded at least a thousand of their best troops. America owes a great deal to General Washington for this day's work; a general rout, dismay, and disgrace would have attended the whole army in any other hands but his. By his own good sense and fortitude he turned the fate of the day. Other officers have great merit in performing their parts well; but he directed the whole with the skill of a Master workman. He did not hug himself at a distance and leave an Arnold to win laurels for him [an indirect, although not too subtle, reference to Horace Gates, whostood back while Benedict Arnold led the American attack at Saratoga]; but by his own presence, he brought order out of confusion, animated his troops and led them to success.

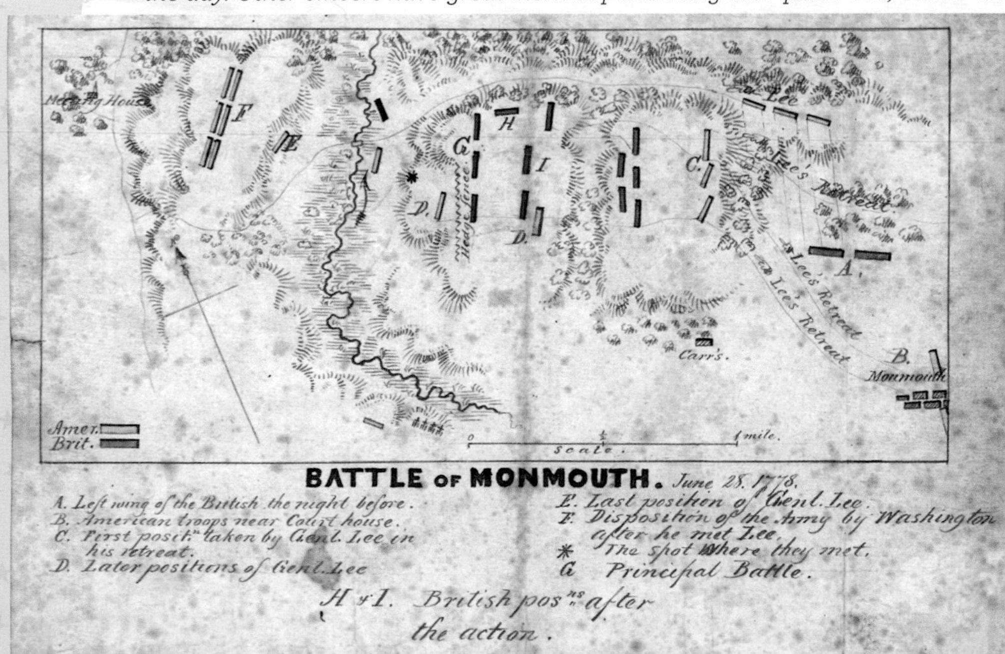

A map of the Battle of Monmouth, June 28, 1778.

merely a morsel for the British. Why, when a French alliance was impending, risk disaster? Behaving (so wrote Washington's brilliant young aide Alexander Hamilton) in a manner which "would have done honor to the most honorable society of midwives," the council voted against any major action.

> Owing to the prevalent practice of exchanging prisoners, Washington had been reunited with an old colleague: General Lee had come riding back from the British lines. Washington did not know that Lee had, during his captivity, made suggestions for British action that could well be considered traitorous to the American cause.

That night, Greene, Lafayette, and General Anthony Wayne sent protests to Washington. Greene pointed out that the enemy line stretched for miles; the baggage train itself was twelve miles long. Light troops could make "a serious impression" on the flank and rear "without suffering them to bring us into a general action." But the main army should be close enough to join in. "If it should amount to a general action, I think the chance is greatly in our favor."

Much as Washington disliked overruling a council of war, he could no longer resist. Greatly reinforcing his skirmishers, he ordered them to attack the enemy left and rear if "fair opportunity offered." Protocol required that he offer the leadership of so large a detachment to his second-in-command. But Lee, insisting that the plan was foolhardy, refused. Washington turned to Lafayette.

Clinton, informed by his spies of the growing threat, shifted his line to put his crack troops on the left and rear. Washington responded by ordering another thousand men to join Lafayette. This augmented the detachment to about half the army. In came a letter from Lee saying that, although he disapproved of Washington's strategy, his honor required that he accept the command of what had become so major a movement. Washington recognized Lee's "distress of mind," but, instead of being worried by it, was glad to "ease" the concern of an old companion while at the same time gaining such experienced leadership.

Washington's long hesitation, joined with the further delay caused by an intervening storm, had created a situation where there was only one day left to attack. On June 28, 1778, the British, if not interrupted, would traverse the twelve miles between Monmouth Court House (now Freehold) and hills that would protect the rest of their march. On the night of the 27th, Lee encamped within six miles of the enemy. With the other half of the army, Washington was within nine. He ordered Lee to attack in the early morning "unless there should be very powerful reasons to the contrary." He would advance with his own army to give any necessary support.

The morning of the 28th was so hot and muggy that, as Washington pushed ahead with maximum speed, some of his men, stripped to the waist, dropped from the heat and did not rise again. Worried lest the British should succeed in eluding Lee, Washington listened for firing. At last, distant cannon shots and the crackle of small arms! Washington was jubilant. But then the sound of battle shredded into silence.

Washington sent officers ahead to ascertain what had happened. Soon he encountered on the road a fifer from one of Lee's regiments. The fifer "appeared to be a good deal frighted." He stated that Lee's corps was in retreat. This seemed impossible, as the sounds had indicated only the brief beginning of a battle. Lest what seemed a malicious report should discourage his troops whom he intended to hurry ahead all the faster, Washington ordered the fifer be segregated under guard.

But soon Washington's advance met whole regiments in retreat. The officers were confused, sure of no more than that they were obeying orders.

Leaving Greene in command of his column, Washington charged ahead. Soon he saw, in front of more retreating regiments, a familiar scarecrow figure: Lee was chatting comfortably with his aides. Washington spurred over to him, asked, "What is all this confusion for, and retreat?"

Such was the commander in chief's angry vehemence* that Lee was for the moment stunned. Finally, he entered into a confused rigamarole: he had received contradictory intelligence; his orders had been disobeyed; people had been impertinent; he had found himself "in the most extensive plain in America," where such troops as he commanded would be helpless before the enemy horse. Furthermore, the whole maneuver had been contrary to his best judgment. Washington shouted, "All this may be very true, sir, but you ought not to have undertaken it unless you intended to go through with it."

Washington rode away from Lee and was almost instantly informed that the British rear guard had not, after brushing Lee aside, continued their retreat, but were in close pursuit. Washington reacted with dismay. Unless the confusion with which he was surrounded could be instantly overcome, the upshot might be "fatal to the whole army."

Now was the time for the army's new training to show itself, and, by God, it did! Men apparently in disarray obeyed with alacrity. "General Washington," so testified Lafayette, "seemed to arrest fortune with one glance. . . . His presence stopped the retreat. . . . His graceful bearing on horseback, his calm and deportment which still retained a trace of displeasure . . . were all calculated to inspire the highest degree of enthusiasm. . . . I thought then as now that I had never beheld so superb a man."

The ground on which Washington found himself was suited to a delaying action. The road was a narrow passage between hills and a thick hedgerow. Washington stationed troops on both sides and had two cannon aimed down the road. Then he galloped back to find a more permanent defense.

Washington came on Greene's regiments advancing in good order. Sending Lee's still-confused corps to the rear to re-form, he decided to make his stand with the fresh troops. The regiments were hardly in position before the men who had been engaged in the delaying action appeared, moving rapidly but in formation, firing over their shoulders. Then there was a tumultuous galloping of British horse. Two American regiments, although protected only by a fence, held their fire until they could annihilate the cavalrymen. Horses and men fell screaming.

Next came a ponderous advance of British infantry. Unable to dent the American front, they tried to turn the left flank and, that failing, maneuvered to the right. Then, to the utter amazement of the British command, the American yokels advanced like regular troops, driving the professionals back. It was the British who had to take refuge in a strong position, and, during the night, slip silently away.

Washington believed that at the Battle of Monmouth he had been cheated of a major victory by General Lee. Lee insisted that he had saved his force from being

* Every type of American has wished to make Washington an exemplar of his favorite activity, and thus it has been often repeated that on this occasion, Washington established a record for eloquent profane swearing. The many eyewitness accounts describe fury but no oaths.

eaten alive by the more expert British. The result was an acrimonious controversy, during which Lee revived the old charges of incompetence against Washington. Washington forgot his affection for Lee. He had never, he stated, felt more than "common civility" towards a man whose "temper and plans were too versatile and violent to attract my admiration." Lee was eventually discharged from the army and wounded in a duel by one of Washington's aides.

Masses of evidence brought forward at the time and in controversies subsequently staged by historians have obscured the truly basic issue: to what extent was Washington's new army able to stand up against European regulars? On this issue, General Clinton gave his silent testimony by preferring, during the rest of his command, to fight where the Continental army was not.

After the Battle of Monmouth, the British hurried behind their fortifications at New York. For once, Washington felt no need to follow them quickly. He gave his men time to rest on the way. Exhibiting the usual eighteenth-century fear of the danger of bathing, he ordered his sergeants to see that the troops did not swim in the heat of the day or remain long in the Raritan River.

He himself stayed in various well-appointed houses en route, enjoying the songs of pretty daughters, and watching his aides flirt with patriot belles exiled from New York. Events everywhere seemed to be moving favorably. Nine states had ratified the Articles of Confederation, which were a step towards creating a single unified nation that would match the single unified Continental army Washington had already created. And a French fleet under Count d'Estaing appeared at Philadelphia, revealing that France intended to become an active belligerent on the American side of the ocean.

The National Memorial Arch at Valley Forge.

With his army relaxed around him, looking from those high cliffs, the Palisades, across the Hudson to where the British were strengthening their New York ramparts, Washington commented, "It is not a little pleasing nor less wonderful to contemplate that after two years maneuvering and undergoing the strangest vicissitudes that perhaps ever attended one contest since the creation, both armies are brought back to the very point they set out from, and that that which was the offending [offensive] party in the beginning is now reduced to the use of the spade and pickax for defense. The hand of Providence has been so conspicuous in all this that he must be worse than an infidel that lacks faith, and more than wicked that has not gratitude enough to acknowledge his obligations—but it will be time enough for me to turn preacher when my present appointment ceases, and therefore I shall add no more on the Doctrine of Providence."

Seventeen

HOPE ABROAD AND BANKRUPTCY AT HOME

(1778–1779)

Since North American products tended to compete with England's economy rather than supplement it, the sugar islands in the West Indies were the more profitable to the British Empire; thus, many statesmen considered defense of the islands more important than regaining the North American colonies. And being near French islands, the British Indies were particularly vulnerable to amphibious attack. Clinton had abandoned Philadelphia in preparation for obeying orders to send away eight thousand men—about a third of his command—mostly to the British Indies. This reduction in his force, added to the warning of new patriot possibilities he had received at Monmouth, made him move with extreme caution. Except for an occasional raid on a carelessly guarded American post, and one major foraging expedition into New Jersey, too well planned to offer Washington any opportunities, Clinton remained, for the rest of the 1778 campaign, quiescent in New York.

Washington's principal excitement after mid-July was due to the presence of d'Estaing's fleet, which had given the American side what it had never before possessed: naval superiority in the coastal waters. This was known to be temporary. Thirteen British ships of the line under Admiral John Byron ("Foul Weather Jack," the poet's grandfather) were rushing across the ocean. But while the supremacy lasted, six thousand Hessians, who were camped at Newport a mile off the Rhode Island mainland, were in peril.

D'Estaing had brought four thousand marines. He landed them and a considerable patriot force on the island near the Hessians. Then, suspecting that Byron was in the offing, he gathered up his marines and sailed away, leaving the patriot force stranded. Only the Americans' skill at escaping from a jam saved them from a severe drubbing.

After the troops had escaped, Washington had to deal with a potentially worse danger. The American citizenry, not forgetting their long history of warfare with France, were furious at having their soldiers placed in a dangerous position and then deserted. When d'Estaing reappeared and anchored in Boston Harbor, riots culminated in the killing of a French officer as he tried to defend a French bakery. Was the new alliance to be upset before it really got started?

An eighteenth-century portrait of Charles Henri, Count of Estaing (1729–1794), by Jean Pierre Franque.

Washington was himself angry, all the more because the Frenchmen in his own army were (despite the downfall of Conway) continuing to condescend to him and his American generals. "I most devoutly wish," he could not resist writing privately, "that we had not a single foreign officer among us except the Marquis of Lafayette." However, in his official capacity, Washington sprayed out soothing letters to civilian leaders and peremptory commands that his officers conciliate their powerful ally. All had become peaceful again (at least on the surface) when d'Estaing sailed off, without condescending to confide to Washington where he was going or whether he intended to return.

Washington's admiration for Lafayette included faith in his disciple's patriotism; the Frenchman's first loyalty would, of course, not be to the United States but to France. He was thus bothered when Lafayette suggested a Franco-American attack on Canada, the French to take the ruling stronghold of Quebec. Congress was enchanted and encouraged their French major general to sail home to promote the idea. Washington, who had fought to drive the French from Canada, suspected (research reveals wrongly) that his disciple's scheme had been inspired from Paris. More cautious than the civil authorities to whom foreign affairs were entrusted, Washington warned that, whatever they might promise, the French would, if they got hold of Quebec, never let go. "Possessed of New Orleans on our right, Canada on our left, and seconded by the numerous tribes . . . whom she knows so well how to conciliate," France would, after the defeat of England, "have it in her power to give law to these states." In December 1778, he posted to Philadelphia to block the move, as he successfully did. But his affection for Lafayette was not diminished.

Although the winter of 1778–1779 would surely see no military action, Washington wished to make his stay in the capital as brief as possible. "Were I to give in to private conveniency and amusement, I should not be able to resist the invitation of my friends to make Philadelphia (instead of a squeezed up room or two) my quarters for the winter, but the affairs of the army require my constant attention and presence . . . to keep it from crumbling. As peace and retirement are my ultimate aim, and the most pleasing and flattering hope of my soul, everything advancive of this end contributes to my satisfaction, however difficult and inconvenient in the attainment, and will reconcile any place and all circumstances to my feelings whilst I continue in service."

However, efforts to work out with Congress practical expedients held him in Philadelphia for almost two months. This period was among the most educational of his life, although much of what he learned was not to be applied until he became president. Had Jefferson been a pupil beside him, Washington's presidency would surely have been less tempestuous.

While the British lay still, a new enemy was on the move, more insidious because it struck everywhere, invading the very huts of the soldiers. That enemy was inflation. Washington asked, "When a rat in the shape of a horse" could not be bought for less than two hundred pounds, "what funds can stand the present expenses of the army?"

Since it was hard to procure food with any currency the seller would accept, or to hire wagons that would transport supplies any distance, Washington had not dared to quarter his army, even shrunken as it was, in a single camp. The troops were hutted for the winter on both sides of the Hudson in a zigzag line stretching some seventy miles through New York and New Jersey. But this dangerous decision helped only a little. The soldiers remained miserably supplied, and what pay they could send home would not buy enough to support their families. Add that the bounties offered for enlistment had too little real value to attract recruits.

Washington was himself in danger of bankruptcy. He felt it his duty, as the most conspicuous leader of the cause, to put his prestige behind the currency by accepting the almost worthless stuff at face value in payment of what was owed him, even old debts contracted before the Revolution. But those from whom Washington had to buy had no such scruples: they demanded vastly enlarged payments which reflected the actual value of the paper. The squeeze finally became so great that Washington irritably instructed his estate manager not to consult him about accepting paper currency. He should do whatever the most patriotic neighbors did.

Philadelphia was the capital and the grinding mill of the inflation. On his arrival there, Washington's reaction was a farmer's and soldier's outrage at the luxury engaged in by the moneymen—often suppliers of the army—who knew how to turn the fluctuations of the currency to their own advantage. While the value of money was sinking five percent a day until it might cease to circulate altogether, dances, concerts, and dinners, displaying the greatest expense and elegance, were, so Washington complained, absorbing attention to the exclusion of the problems of the nation. Washington could not help enjoying a good party, but, as General Greene wrote, the "luxury and profusion" gave him "infinitely more pain than pleasure." Revisualizing the death agonies he had seen on battlefields, remembering his starving men shivering in nakedness, Washington thundered, "Speculation, peculation, and an insatiable thirst for riches seem to have got the better of every other consideration and almost of every order of men."

Then, as was natural for him, Washington put his mind on analyzing the problem. For some time (since March 1777) the future brilliant financier Alexander Hamilton had been on his staff. However, there is conclusive evidence that Washington had not discussed national financial problems with the youth, then still in his early twenties and somewhat naïve on the subject. In Philadelphia, Washington turned to Robert and Gouverneur Morris, the men who were later to educate Hamilton. The two Morrises (who were not related) became Washington's intimate friends.

Washington was himself in danger of bankruptcy. He felt it his duty, as the most conspicuous leader of the cause, to put his prestige behind the currency by accepting the almost worthless stuff at face value in payment of what was owed him, even old debts contracted before the Revolution.

Under the Morrises' tutelage, the planter-warrior began to learn about currency. As an acceptable expedient, governments printed money on the understanding that it would be brought back for cancellation by tax revenues. This was, in effect, a method for anticipating taxes. The Continental Congress had printed money because it had no other way of paying for anything. But the states, unwilling to diminish their own power, had refused the central body the right to tax. It was agreed that the tax revenues needed to bolster or retire the Continental paper were to be supplied by the states, but once state officials got their hands on any cash, they were unlikely to let it go. Thus Congress was left, as time passed, with no resource except to create more and more paper behind which there were no assets whatsoever. Again, as in the necessary strengthening and reorganizing of the army, state jealousy of national power stood strongly in the way of victory.

Another difficulty was the fundamental nature of the American economy. A nation devoted almost exclusively to agriculture, handicrafts being on a small scale and scattered, could not produce the goods necessary to carry on the war. Not only were heavy

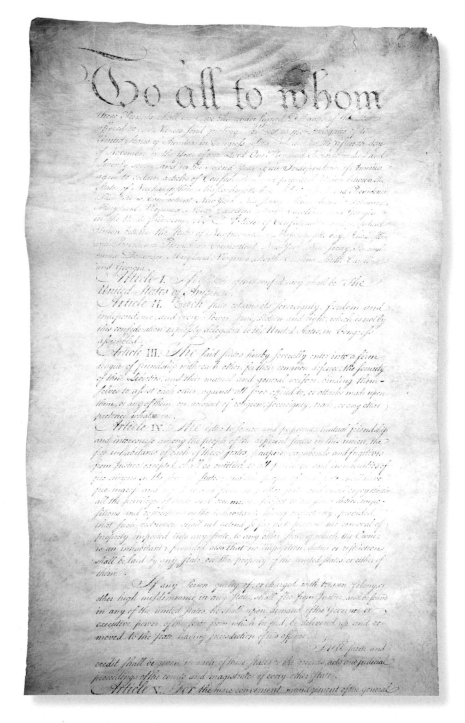
To all to whom

and Georgia.

Article I. The Stile of this confederacy shall be "The United States of America."

Article II. Each state retains its sovereignty, freedom and independence, and every Power, Jurisdiction and right, which is not by this confederation expressly delegated to the United States, in Congress assembled.

Article III. The said states hereby severally enter into a firm league of friendship with each other, for their common defence, the security of their Liberties, and their mutual and general welfare, binding themselves to assist each other, against all force offered to, or attacks made upon them, or any of them, on account of religion, sovereignty, trade, or any other pretence whatever.

Article IV. The better to secure and perpetuate mutual friendship and intercourse among the people of the different states in this union, the free inhabitants of each of these states, paupers, vagabonds and fugitives from Justice excepted, shall be entitled to all privileges and immunities of free citizens in the several states;

all the privileges of trade and commerce, subject to the same duties, impositions and restrictions as the inhabitants thereof respectively, provided that such restriction shall not extend so far as to prevent the removal of property imported into any state, to any other state of which the Owner is an inhabitant; provided also that no imposition, duties or restriction shall be laid by any state, on the property of the united states, or either of them.

If any Person guilty of, or charged with treason, felony, or other high misdemeanor in any state, shall flee from Justice, and be found in any of the united states, he shall upon demand of the Governor or executive power of the state from which he fled, be delivered up and removed to the state having jurisdiction of his offence.

Full faith and credit shall be given in each of these states to the records, acts and judicial proceedings of the courts and magistrates of every other state.

Article V. For the more convenient management of the general

The Articles of Confederation, 1781, which served as the Constitution of the United States until March 4, 1789, when the present Constitution went into effect.

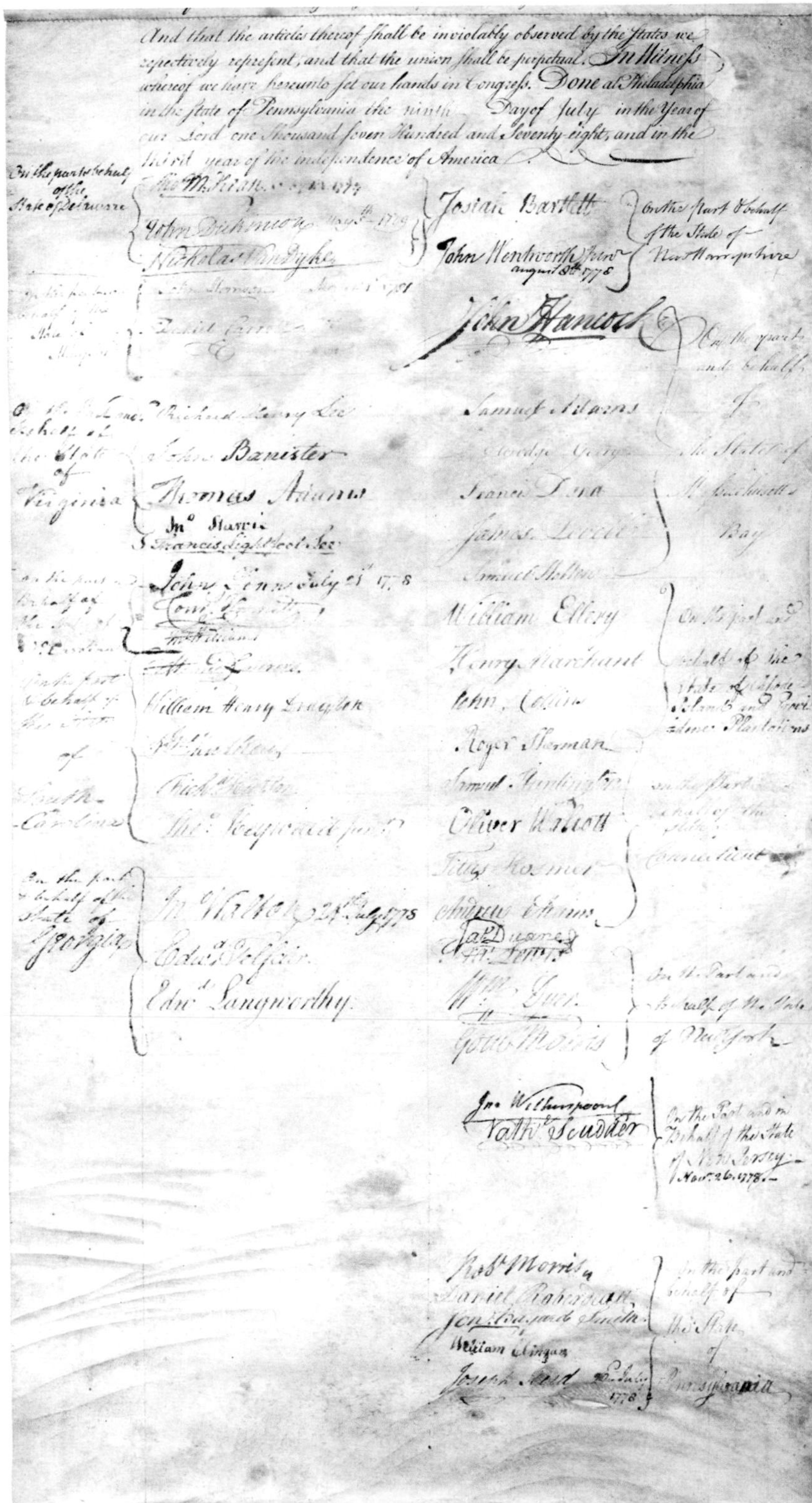
And that the articles thereof shall be inviolably observed by the states we respectively represent, and that the union shall be perpetual. In Witness whereof we have hereunto set our hands in Congress. Done at Philadelphia in the state of Pennsylvania the ninth Day of July in the Year of our Lord one Thousand seven Hundred and Seventy-eight, and in the third year of the independence of America.

On the part & behalf of the State of Delaware
John Dickinson
Nicholas Vandyke

Josiah Bartlett
John Wentworth Junr August 8th 1778
On the part & behalf of the State of New Hampshire

John Hancock
On the part and behalf of the State of Massachusetts Bay
Samuel Adams
Elbridge Gerry
Francis Dana
James Lovell
Samuel Holten

On the part and behalf of the State of Virginia
Richard Henry Lee
John Banister
Thomas Adams
Jno Harvie
Francis Lightfoot Lee

John Penn July 21st 1778

William Ellery
Henry Marchant
John Collins
On the part and behalf of the State of Rhode Island and Providence Plantations

On the part & behalf of the State of South Carolina
William Henry Drayton
Thos Heyward Junr

Roger Sherman
Samuel Huntington
Oliver Wolcott
Titus Hosmer
Andrew Adams
On the part and behalf of the State of Connecticut

On the part & behalf of the State of Georgia
Jno Walton 24th July 1778
Edwd Telfair
Edwd Langworthy

Jas Duane
Fra Lewis
Wm Duer
Gouv Morris
On the Part and behalf of the State of New York

Jno Witherspoon
Nathl Scudder
On the Part and in Behalf of the State of New Jersey. Novr 26, 1778.

Robt Morris
Daniel Roberdeau
Jona Bayard Smith
William Clingan
Joseph Reed 22d July 1778
On the part and behalf of the State of Pennsylvania

Washington's confidants and mentors in matters of finance, Gouverneur Morris and Robert Morris, *by Charles Willson Peale, oil on canvas, 1783.*

manufactures like cannon impossible, but it was extremely difficult to concentrate in one place enough of such ordinary supplies as shoes and clothes to supply an army. Equally serious was the fact that agrarianism—assets being in land and slaves and a basic means of exchange being barter—failed to produce fluid capital. The government might offer bonds for sale, but where was the cash to buy them? Washington was so impressed with this situation that he became worried by his own passionate, ancestral dedication to agriculture. He admitted to his favorite brother that his continuing desire "to have my property as much as possible in lands . . . is not consistent with national policy."

During the summer of 1780, Washington's business friends were to achieve a most impressive demonstration. The Continental currency being by then even more worthless than in 1779, the merchants of Philadelphia decided to establish a new and separate system of paper money that would not depreciate because it would be guaranteed by actual funds. Their means was to establish such an institution as had not formerly existed in America: a bank. They subscribed as capital over a million pounds in Continental currency. The existence of a large capital fund meant that certificates of indebtedness—more or less the equivalent of modern checks—drawn on the Bank of Philadelphia could at any time be cashed. Thus, there was no pressure on the holder to change his draft into currency. It was more convenient for him to pass the draft on to another man in payment of a debt. That creditor, having equal faith in its value, was glad to receive the draft, which he handed on to a creditor of his own. The paper of the Bank of Philadelphia was circulating as sound currency. And, since there was no reason to suppose that every holder of a draft would want cash at the same moment, the bank did not need to keep all its capital in its vaults. A part could be applied to bolstering the general economy and supplying the army.

Enchanted with this development, Washington urged that similar banks be started in other cities, but the idea was too novel. The certificates of the Bank of Philadelphia remained a tiny island in the boundless sea of depreciating paper. The memory of what it had achieved was to come back to Washington during his presidency, when Jefferson was feuding with Hamilton over the Bank of the United States.

As Washington conferred with Congress about the 1779 campaign, it became clear that the only way to keep the cause afloat was to pare the expenses for the army down to the smallest amount possible without losing the war. Washington considered it essential to replace the 4,380 regulars whose enlistments were expiring, but he did not request a force large enough to take any initiative. Unless d'Estaing—from whom nothing had been heard—should reappear with his marines, in the main military theater only defensive operations would be feasible.

Washington was preparing to apply the strategy which, when reminiscing as an old man, he defined thus succinctly: "Time, caution, and worrying the enemy until we could be better provided with arms and other means, and had better disciplined troops to carry on, was the plan for us."

Washington relied for his immediate defenses on the twin conceptions that the British would not risk their scarce manpower by attacking patriots fortified on strong ground, and would not endanger vital supply lines by skirting around American strong points. There were three directions in which the enemy could march from New York. The route up the coast to New England was blocked by an American encampment on the heights around White Plains and New Castle. On the Hudson, the patriots were ever strengthening their major fortification, West Point. And the road through New Jersey to Philadelphia was blocked, as of old, by American forces on the heights at Morristown. This bought time but would not, alas, bring victory.

Washington was now visualizing his army in three categories, each suited to a different kind of warfare. The militia, deployed across the countryside, were prepared to harass those "foraging parties" which were forced to emerge from the enemy fortifications to procure food for man and especially for beast (one horse needed twenty-four pounds of fodder every day). Not only did such service keep the militia out of the main encampments, thus preventing them from undermining the discipline of the regulars, but it gave them tasks to which they were ideally suited. Since they were usually inhabitants of the countrysides they defended, they were familiar with every path, cliff, and stone wall. Their natural skills enabled them to take cover, fighting in detachments as small as one man. And, if British action proved too strong, they could, by merely hiding their guns, turn into farmers wandering, it seemed, innocently around their fields. Should the British, unable to determine who was a soldier and who was not, be incited to random violence against men grasping plows, this too served the patriot cause by engendering hate against oppressing invaders.

Washington's second arm consisted of elite corps, sometimes riflemen (although he found these frontiersmen dangerously unwilling to obey orders), more often the light infantry companies that were attached to every regiment, but could be assembled for a specific mission. Their function was to beat up in sudden raids any considerable group of the enemy who became exposed. During 1779, the light troops, under General Anthony Wayne, surprised a British-held fortification at Stony Point on the Hudson, carrying off prisoners and cannon. Although they had to abandon the post almost instantly after taking it, this exploit gave, in the middle of the long doldrums, something to boast about.

Neither the militia nor the elite corps was capable of any military action that would in itself end the war. Washington was trying to develop the main Continental army into a force that could deliver a sledgehammer blow. Although his numbers were vastly insufficient, he did have a nucleus. His regulars were tough, disciplined veterans, immune to camp diseases. Trying to build for the future, he insisted that, however much the arrival of desperately needed recruits might be slowed, none might join the army until—the process then took several weeks—they had been inoculated against smallpox.

As the spring, summer, and autumn of 1779 wore slowly away, patience was the virtue Washington most needed. He tempered it with the hope that something would turn up to dispel his frustration. How his heart leaped at reports that d'Estaing, who had won a naval battle in West Indian waters, was on his way back to the North American coast! Sick of half measures, Washington revealed, as he made feverish plans, the strategic conception which was to remain dominant in his thinking. If the war were to be brought to a quick end, the key British base in New York City must be captured.

Officers waiting with fast boats on the Jersey coast were to streak out to the French fleet as soon as it appeared. They were to urge d'Estaing not to pause lest his arrival warn the British, but to sail directly up New York Harbor. At the sound of their cannon, Washington would move. A few triumphant hours, and the homesick planter could turn his back on war!

But d'Estaing never appeared. After an abortive attempt on some minor British fortifications on the Georgia coast, the French admiral returned to a winter anchorage in the Indies. The campaign of 1779 was over. Victory was not one inch closer.

Eighteen

ENTER A FRENCH ARMY

(1779–1780)

During the winter, Washington encamped his main army—it was small—all together on Morristown Heights. A new method of procuring supplies had been inaugurated for which Washington at first had hopes, however faint.

Congress, despairing of being allowed adequate revenue by the states, had requested that every state supply its own regiments. Most of the states were far away. All proved lax. And when some local government did in fact move, there developed an emotionally difficult situation: one regiment was eating while its neighbor was not. What hope Washington had that the system might possibly work slid away. He was spurred into formulating, years before the Constitution was drafted, its basic principle: "Unless the states will content themselves with a full and well-chosen representation in Congress, and vest that body with absolute powers in all matters relative to the great purposes of war and of general concern by which the states unitedly are affected, reserving to themselves all matters of local and internal polity . . . we are attempting an impossibility and very soon shall become (if it is not already the case) a many-headed monster, a heterogeneous mass, that never will or can steer to the same point."

The soldiers too were seething. Greene pointed out that "a country overflowing with plenty are now suffering an army employed for the defense of everything that is dear and valuable to perish for lack of food." One colonel stated, "I damn my country as void of gratitude!" and another expressed a wish to bathe his hands in the blood of the villains who were starving the army.

Washington lived in daily fear of mutiny. The Connecticut line did emerge from their huts and threaten to go home. They were dissuaded. Had they not been dissuaded, Washington warned Congress, the whole army might have followed. "The prospect, my dear Baron," he wrote Steuben, "is gloomy and the storm thickens." However, he was inured to difficulties. He refused to despair.

Since the very start of her husband's military service, Martha Washington had journeyed from Virginia to spend with "the General" the months during which there was no fighting. Every year, she dreaded the journey and half hoped that she would not be summoned, but, when called, she went, and in whatever encampment the tides of war had designated, she labored, with all her charm and social skill, to lighten the grimness. "The poor General," she summarized, "was so unhappy that it distressed me exceedingly."

When Martha had made her first hegira—this time to Cambridge—that terrifying Boston bluestocking, Mercy Warren, had been charmed into writing, "The complacency of her manners speaks at once the benevolence of her heart, and her affability, candor, and gentleness qualify her to soften the hours

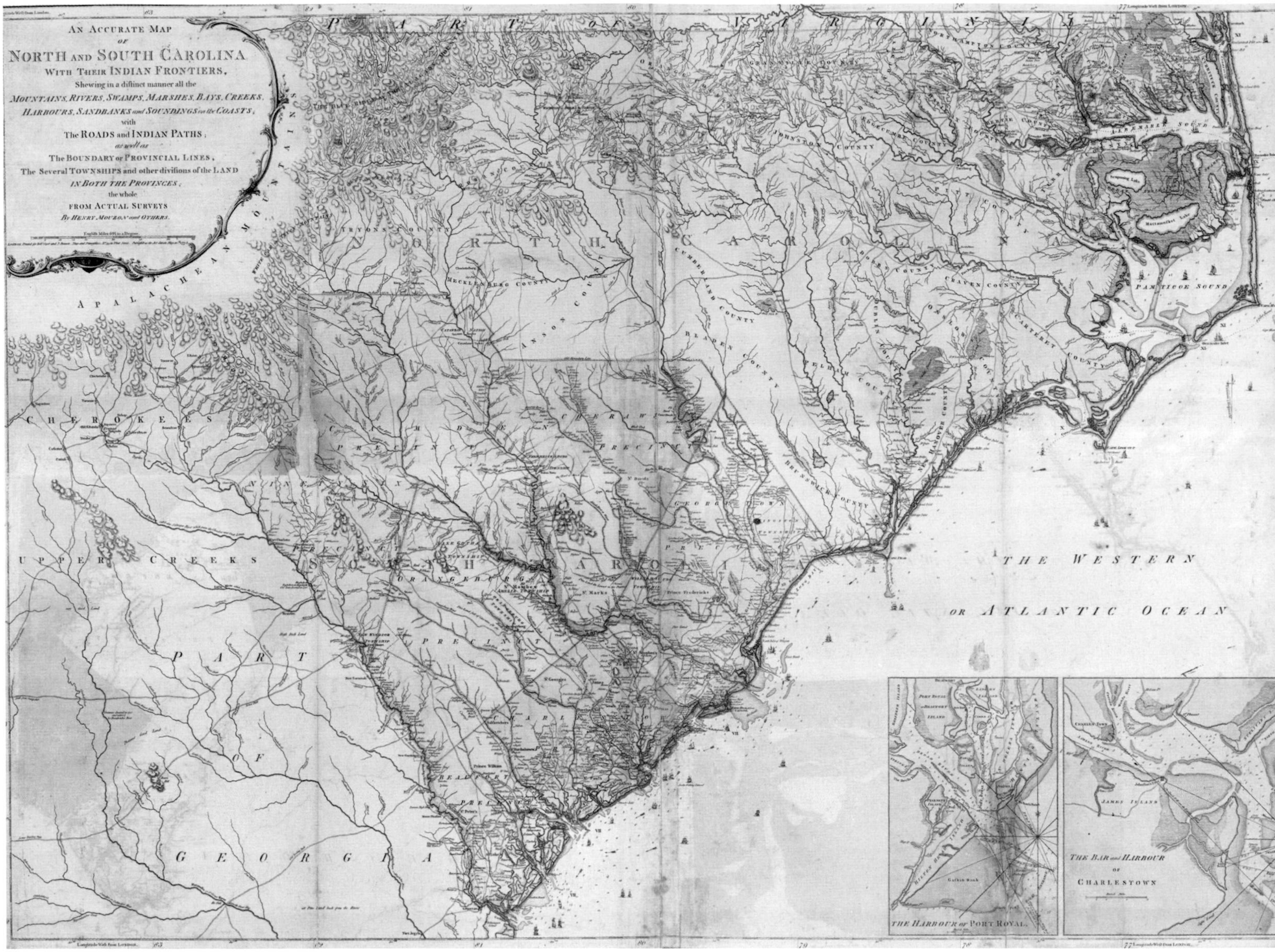

This map of North and South Carolina designating their Indian frontiers, drawn by Henri Mouzon, May 30, 1775, was owned by Washington.

of private life, or to sweeten the cares of a hero, and smooth the rugged pains of war."

For Washington, his wife's visits had an almost magical significance. Mount Vernon had become what seemed an inaccessible dream. Mrs. Washington brought with her, in addition to intimate companionship, a feeling of his hearth, a sense that he was breathing the air of home. With the shades drawn, the fire burning, and his wife working quietly on the fine needlework she enjoyed, he could almost forget the war. Almost.

One of the pleasures of Martha's visits was that she attracted to headquarters a circle of ladies whose soft complexions, gentle words, and frivolous costumes cheered the general. He enjoyed flirtatious banter. During the previous winter, the wife of a Virginia colonel had written a female confidante, "Now let me speak of our noble and agreeable commander, for he commands both sexes, one by his excellent skill in military matters, the other by his ability, politeness, and attention." Although usually busy in the morning, "from dinner till night he is free for all company. His worthy lady seems to be in perfect felicity when she is by the side of her Old Man as she calls him. We often make parties on horseback." Then General Washington "throws off the hero and takes on the chatty, agreeable companion. He can be downright impudent sometimes—such impudence, Fanny, as you and I like."

> "Now let me speak of our noble and agreeable commander, for he commands both sexes, one by his excellent skill in military matters, the other by his ability, politeness, and attention."

An example of Washington's "impudence" is supplied by a note written—as it happened in Martha's absence—to a handsome widow, Annis Boudinot Stockton, who had sent him an ode in his praise with the coy request that he give her absolution for writing poetry. Washington replied that if she would dine with him "and go through the proper course of penitence, which shall be prescribed, I will strive hard to assist you in expiating these poetical trespasses on this side of purgatory." He might even prescribe that she write more poetry. "You see, Madam, when once the Woman has tempted us and we have tasted the forbidden fruit, there is no such thing as checking our appetites, whatever the consequences may be." On thinking this passage over, Washington clearly considered it a little fresh—but he liked it too much not to send it. To tone things down, he added that he deserved nothing more from Mrs. Stockton than "the most disinterested friendship has a right to claim."

The extent of the strain that filled the air at Morristown during the winter of 1779–1780 is indicated by the fact that on this occasion Martha's arrival proved an additional cause of tension. The commander in chief had been able to procure for his wife, aides, and servants only some rooms in a not commodious house. He promised Martha to make the situation bearable by having a separate kitchen erected. He gave the order, but was told that the necessary boards could not be procured. Then, as he rode through the camp, he saw other officers' quarters being made comfortable with boards. He wrote the commissary general that "to share a common lot and participate in the inconveniences has with me been a fundamental principle"—but this was too much. At about the same time, he got into a roaring rage with the commander of the headquarters guard over a trivial matter concerning a tent.

A dinner party given by Colonel Clement Biddle, the deputy quartermaster general, started out convivially enough. Trouble began only after the ladies had withdrawn, leaving the gentlemen sitting over their wine. The officers observed that George Olney, a civilian commissary who could be considered one of those who were starving the army, wore a look of disapproval while he watched the officers drink. As Olney's wife later put it, the officers retaliated with an "unpolite and irrational attempt to sink him below the brute creation by getting him drunk." Olney fled to the ladies.

Then, so testified Washington's aide Tench Tilghman, "It was proposed that a party should be sent to demand him, and, if the ladies refused to give him up, that he should be brought by force." Washington volunteered to lead the invasion. The officers advanced "with great formality to the adjoining room, and sent in a summons which the ladies refused. Such a scuffle then ensued as any good natured person might suppose."

But good nature was shattered when Mrs. Olney shouted to Washington "in a violent rage" that, if he did not let go of her hand, "I will tear out your eyes and the hair from your head." At this, General Greene's plump and handsome wife came to Washington's defense in a fury which she later admitted had been "unbecoming." Greene separated the ladies, led both Olneys into another room, and told the commissary that he should "adopt a less positive and blunt way of refusing to drink."

The Olneys seem to have been spirited away since there, for the moment, the controversy ended. But Mrs. Greene told everyone that Mrs. Olney had insulted the general; Mrs. Olney thereupon insulted Mrs. Greene; Mr. Olney appealed to Washington to come to the rescue of his wife's reputation. Washington refused to get into the controversy, handing the matter over to Tilghman. The aide's reply treated the incident as a joke. Washington, he wrote, remembered only "good humor and gaiety."

As Washington stagnated at Morristown, the main action of the war moved, for the first time, southward. Some eight thousand soldiers and most of the British fleet had sailed from New York and were besieging Charleston. Remembering the lesson taught him at the fort that had borne his name, Washington warned General Benjamin Lincoln, who commanded in South Carolina, to beware lest his army be trapped in the fortified city.

Washington cursed the national laxness which had allowed his own army to become so weak that he could not take advantage of the absence of so considerable a British force by taking New York City. Then, in May 1780, he received electrifying news: a French expeditionary force, accompanied by a fleet, was on its way to North America. Again Washington prepared plans for the French to sail, without pause, against now-weakened New York. He was all alertness when a fleet was sighted actually on its way there. But the ships sailed into the harbor without being fired on. Alas, it was the British expeditionary force coming home.

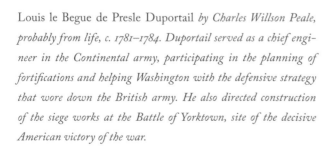

Louis le Begue de Presle Duportail *by Charles Willson Peale, probably from life, c. 1781–1784. Duportail served as a chief engineer in the Continental army, participating in the planning of fortifications and helping Washington with the defensive strategy that wore down the British army. He also directed construction of the siege works at the Battle of Yorktown, site of the decisive American victory of the war.*

Lincoln having ignored Washington's advice, the British had captured not only Charleston but twenty-five hundred Continentals and two thousand militia. This now ranked as the patriot army's worst defeat. But Washington saw a bright side in the fact that the British second-in-command, Lord Cornwallis, had been left in South Carolina with a force considered large enough to subdue the South. Dimly foreseeing Cornwallis's eventual surrender at Yorktown, Washington wrote, "The enemy, by attempting to hold conquests so remote, must dissipate their force, and, of course, afford opportunities for striking one or the other extremity."

For the time being, Cornwallis raged through South Carolina like an invincible lion. Gates, whom Congress rushed off to the rescue, only succeeded in demonstrating the impossibility of fighting British regulars on open ground with militia. His helter-skelter army was trounced by a smaller British force at Camden, with a loss of two thousand men. Organized resistance in the Carolinas was now at an end. As Gates followed Conway and Charles Lee into involuntary retirement, Congress threw the whole mess into Washington's lap. He sent General Greene, his ablest disciple, to command in the South.

On July 10, four French regiments, complete with cavalry and artillery—five thousand men—appeared in American waters. There was no possibility of their joining Washington in a surprise attack on New York, since they were convoyed directly to the island off the Rhode Island mainland which the Hessians had recently evacuated. After the accompanying fleet anchored in Newport Harbor, the army made themselves comfortable in the town.

Washington, who had suffered so during the French and Indian War from British determination that their regular officers, of however low rank, should automatically command American officers, however exalted, was pleased to learn that the French had leaned over backwards on this issue: Americans were not only to command Frenchmen inferior to them but even of the same rank. The French commander in chief, the Count de Rochambeau, was to obey Washington.

That there were also secret orders Washington did not know. Although the French ministry, not wishing to encourage the conflict between allies which d'Estaing had incited, had put forward a conciliatory front, they had no intention of really risking their army by entangling it with provincial amateurs. Rochambeau was instructed not to allow a pretense of subservience to make him follow Washington into any strategy of which he disapproved. Having established his encampment on an island, Rochambeau was to stay there, keeping the two armies entirely separate until the need for active cooperation was overpowering. As it turned out, the French regular was not, during the entire war, to bolster the inexperienced Americans by assigning to their service a single expert: artilleryman, engineer, or whatever. Washington's French experts were all, like the engineer Duportail, volunteers who had enrolled, entirely independently of the French expeditionary force, in the American army.

The commanding general from well-organized France was horrified by what he saw of the ally with whom he was supposed to fight. The American government, Rochambeau reported home, was "in

Jean Baptiste Donatien de Vimeur, Comte de Rochambeau *by Charles Willson Peale, from life, c. 1782. The commander in chief of the French expeditionary force, Rochambeau distrusted Washington.*

consternation." Washington had only three thousand men (this was roughly accurate) and paper money had fallen sixty to one. "Send us troops, ships, and money, but do not depend on these people nor upon their means: they have neither money nor credit; their means of resistance are only momentary and called forth when they are attacked in their own homes."

Washington was still in a frenzy to attack New York. Admittedly, Rochambeau's army plus his own did not add up, now that a surprise appearance was no longer possible, to a strong enough force, but something might turn up. Rochambeau hoped for reinforcements—perhaps they would come. Perhaps the British would further weaken their main base by sending more troops south. Perhaps a French armada would pop in, like a *deus ex machina*, from the Indies. And, in any case, dangling as bait the possibility of capturing New York was most likely to inspire Congress and the state governments to find recruits. Maybe his own army would grow to adequate size. In the meanwhile, so Washington urged, Rochambeau's army should join his army to the patriot army outside New York City. The combined force would then be ready to pounce if ever an opportunity offered.

Used to calculating existing opportunities rather than tossing up bubbles of hope, Rochambeau found it most bothersome to have the American he was supposed to pretend to obey perpetually babbling about an assault for which no true possibility existed. The elderly veteran of innumerable European campaigns concluded that Washington was a fool. With the overelaborate courtesy of an experienced courtier—which Washington found irritating—Rochambeau expressed extreme regret that he could not leave Newport. He explained that the fleet which had brought him there, being weaker than the British fleet in American waters, would be safe only if protected by the presence of his army.

Members of Rochambeau's staff described Washington as impressive, majestic, with a mildness that indicated moral qualities and a shade of sadness that gave him an interesting air.

For two months the allied commanders communicated through delegates and dispatches. Then Washington asked for a personal interview. He had a strategy to sell.

The two commanders finally met at Hartford, Connecticut, on September 20, 1780. Members of Rochambeau's staff described Washington as impressive, majestic, with a mildness that indicated moral qualities and a shade of sadness that gave him an interesting air. Baron Ludwig von Closen, who served as interpreter, noted that the American gave striking evidence of military talents and knowledge: "I could not find strong enough words," to communicate what Washington said, "as vividly and forcefully as I should."

Washington urged that the French fleet dash for Boston Harbor, where it would be protected by the Massachusetts patriots. Although Washington was willing to admit that he did not actually foresee an attack on New York, he argued that the presence of the combined armies should keep Clinton from sending any more troops south. Or, if Clinton took the risk, perhaps, after all, the attack could be made.

Such importuning only made Rochambeau regard Washington as even more of a problem: the primitive soldier, who was actually staring him in the face, had to be disobeyed while seemingly obeyed. To his relief, the Frenchman found a way to put Washington off balance. They would discuss next year's campaign: how many troops would the United States raise, what supplies? Washington had to admit that confusion in the government and the currency made it impossible to guess. In relation to Washington's immediate strategy, Rochambeau was evasive, but indicated no inclination to budge from his island. Washington was too polite to put his presumed authority to any test. "My command of the F— T— [French troops]," he concluded, "stands upon a very limited scale."

As he rode off with a heavy heart, Washington did not realize that, before he got back to his headquarters, he would receive what was perhaps the greatest emotional shock of his entire career.

Nineteen

TREASON

(1775–1780)

When, during the dark hours of the long, inconclusive war, Washington counted his assets, high on his list was a former scapegrace apothecary who had demonstrated genius at leading men and at fighting. Benedict Arnold was, in fact, the greatest combat general in the war on either side. He had taken a major part in capturing Ticonderoga and the cannon with which Washington had driven the British from Boston. The commander in chief had then commissioned him to lead an army up wild rivers and through mountainous passes in the hope that he could surprise the fortress city of Quebec by appearing where it was believed no army could penetrate. Although his army was assailed in the wilderness by blizzards and a hurricane that created floods, Arnold got most of his men through. It was not his fault that while he was delayed by storms, Quebec had been reinforced.

Benedict Arnold, *detail, engraved in Paris by Benoît Louis Prévost, 1780, after a drawing by Pierre Eugène du Simitière.*

In a desperate assault on the now well-defended city, Arnold was wounded; yet, despite his own suffering and the failure of the attack, he managed to inspire his freezing, starving men to spend the winter in a blockading circle around Quebec. Spring brought British reinforcements and murderous epidemics. All American forces fled from Canada. To keep the enemy from following into northern New York and onwards, Arnold turned admiral. He supervised the building of a fleet from green wood, and then so battered a stronger British armada on Lake Champlain that the enemy abandoned, for that fighting season, their effort to invade. The next fighting season, Burgoyne came down with his great army from Canada. It was Arnold who led, to Gates's disapproval, the battles that preceded Burgoyne's surrender. Arnold was so seriously wounded in the leg that he seemed to have been permanently crippled.

An obbligato to Arnold's military genius was his inability to get on with civilian authorities. Congress denied him the promotions he had earned. While he was still in mid-career, Washington admitted that the slights he had received would have justified him in resigning. But Arnold resolutely continued in uniform to be at last prostrated by British fire.

Born into a prominent Philadelphia family with Loyalist tendencies, Peggy Shippen met Benedict Arnold during his tenure as military commander of the city following the British withdrawal in 1778, and became his second wife in April 1779. Not long after, Arnold began conspiring with the British, and Shippen was very likely his accomplice. This drawing of her was made by Major John André, another co-conspirator, in 1778.

When, after months of anguish, Arnold appeared at Valley Forge, he was unable to stand unless an attendant held him upright. Washington yearned to find a post suited to the crippled patriot. Applying perhaps more sentiment than judgment, in May 1768, he made Arnold, after the British had evacuated Philadelphia, military commandant there.

Arnold became fascinated with a young lady Washington had known since she was a child: the handsome, high-born Peggy Shippen. Peggy had stayed in the city during the British occupation and flirted with the British adjutant general, John André. She was generally considered a Tory. But Arnold was reveling in a society higher than any he had ever known. To impress his new love and keep up with the rich families who belonged to the extreme right of the patriot party, the unpropertied Arnold lived on a scale which seemed inexplicable if he were not taking graft.

Arnold's behavior enraged the president of the Supreme Executive Council of Pennsylvania, who published whacking charges that the military commander encouraged Tories and was engaged in peculation. There can be little doubt that Washington's emotions were with the wounded hero. Washington wished conservatives to be included in the cause. And the Pennsylvania president was none other than Joseph Reed, who had betrayed Washington's friendship during the retreat through New Jersey. Reed made it clear that one purpose of his campaign against Arnold was to assert the power of the state governments over the Continental army. Furthermore, the charges that Arnold had used his office to encourage and profit by illegal deals were (although historical researches have demonstrated them gravely true) substantiated only on the most trivial scale in the court-martial Washington ordered. The court sentenced Arnold to be reprimanded. Washington carefully phrased the reprimand: "The commander in chief would have been much happier in an occasion of bestowing commendations on an officer who has rendered such distinguished services to his country."

He was glad when Arnold married his Peggy; pleased to see Arnold so recovered that he could move energetically in a high-heeled boot; delighted that the verdict of the court-martial had freed the great

COLONEL ARNOLD.
Who Commanded the Provincial Troops sent against QUEBEC, through the Wilderneſs of
and was Wounded in Storming that City, under General Montgomery.
London Published as the Act directs 26 March 1776 by Thos Hart

Colonel Benedict Arnold (1741–1801)
as portrayed by Thomas Hart, 1776.

soldier for further military duty. That some of Arnold's communications to him during the controversy had revealed extreme hysteria touched Washington's sympathies rather than inspiring any serious doubts.

Washington had no way of knowing that Peggy's old flirtation with André had borne new fruit. Angry and disillusioned, egged on by his avaricious and ambitious pro-British young wife, Arnold had secretly offered his services to Peggy's old friend and Clinton's adjutant general. André had at first expressed doubt that Arnold had anything of value to sell, but had finally agreed to pay handsomely if Arnold could secure the command of West Point.

It was, of course, not by chance that Washington had built his army's major fortification on the Hudson River. Extending from north to south, the Hudson was navigable for oceangoing ships all the way from the sea to the wilderness. If Arnold would, by arranging the capture of West Point, open the Hudson to the British navy, the river could become, so it was reasoned, a watery wall cutting the rebellion in half.

Washington did not envision putting a great fighter in so static a post. Knowing that Arnold had been happiest in the most active service, Washington resolved to give him command of the right wing of the Continental army. Rumors to this effect frightened Arnold: a command under the eyes of Washington and the whole corps of generals gave him nothing easily deliverable to betray.

When Arnold and Washington met on horseback during a maneuver, Washington smilingly informed his subordinate of "the post of honor" to which he had been appointed. Arnold's reaction amazed the commander in chief: "His countenance changed and he appeared to be quite fallen, and, instead of thanking me or expressing any pleasure at the appointment, never opened his mouth."

Arnold mooned around headquarters and finally stated that he was not well enough for active service. He wished the stationary command at West Point. Washington's reaction was pity; he believed that all of Arnold's misfortunes had broken his spirit. Like an affectionate father, Washington tried to inspire Arnold. But Arnold would not be inspired; he just talked about West Point. Finally, on August 3, 1780, Washington gave Arnold what he desired.

Arnold had commanded West Point for two months when Washington, on his way back from his depressing conference with Rochambeau, intended to inspect the fortress. He looked forward to spending a day and a night with the valiant officer and his very pretty wife. After a considerable ride, he arrived at their headquarters, some miles upriver from West Point, on September 24 for a late breakfast. He was dashed to be received only by an aide. Mrs. Arnold, he was told, had not yet arisen, and General Arnold had embarked in his barge on the river. The general had left word that he had gone to the fortress to prepare a reception for "His Excellency."

Washington ate his breakfast with no emotions deeper than disappointment, and then himself set out on the river. Concern first appeared in his mind when, as the fortress that rose high on the right bank of the river loomed ever closer, he could see on the landing place only somnolently pacing sentries. There was no sign of the reception which Arnold had said he was going to prepare.

As soon as Washington landed, he asked for Arnold. None of the officers had seen him that day. As Washington proceeded with his inspection of the various redoubts, he kept hoping that Arnold would appear. "My mind misgave me," he later remembered, but "I had not the least idea of the real cause."

Washington was back at Arnold's headquarters in time to spruce up for a four o'clock dinner. Hamilton, who had been left behind to receive any dispatches that might come in, reported that nothing had been heard of Arnold. Peggy had sent word down that she was indisposed.

The party dispersed to their rooms. As Lafayette was dressing, Hamilton dashed in with the request that he attend at once on the commander. He found Washington trembling with emotion, a packet of papers in his hands. "Arnold," Washington cried out, "has betrayed us! Whom can we trust now?"

"In no instance since the commencement of the war has the interposition of Providence been more conspicuous than in the rescue of the post and garrison of West Point from Arnold's villainous perfidy."

The papers revealed that "John Anderson" had been stopped on his way from the American to the enemy lines, dressed as a civilian and hiding in his shoes papers in Arnold's handwriting giving information which would assist the British in capturing West Point. There was also a meticulously written letter from "Anderson" which revealed that he was no common spy but a high officer. It stated, "What I have as yet said concerning myself was in the justifiable attempt to be extricated. I am too little accustomed to duplicity to have succeeded. . . . The person in your possession is Major John André, adjutant general to the British army."

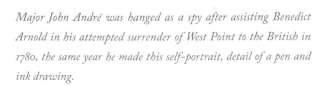

Major John André was hanged as a spy after assisting Benedict Arnold in his attempted surrender of West Point to the British in 1780, the same year he made this self-portrait, detail of a pen and ink drawing.

It was not clear how wide was the plot or how great the immediate danger to West Point. Although André had been apprehended, other messages might have got through. And the wind, blowing upriver, was perfectly angled to hurry British warships from New York Bay to the fortress, which might be secretly prepared for surrender. The obvious necessity was to take the precaution of changing commanders at key posts while at the same time putting West Point on the alert for attack. These things Washington failed to do. So great was the shock of discovering the perfidy of a man he had so deeply trusted that only one thing seemed important to him: capturing the traitor.

Two of Washington's aides, who had arrived at Arnold's headquarters in the early morning, remembered that he had received a message obviously disturbing to him. He had taken to the river. Enough time had passed since then for Arnold to have reached the anchored British warship from which André had previously disembarked. Yet Washington held on to the hope that Arnold had not been notified of the discovery of his treason and was somewhere in American territory where he could be captured. To keep the villain in ignorance, Washington resolved to make no move that would indicate that the plot had been revealed. He did nothing more than send Hamilton and a companion thundering on horseback down to King's Ferry, the last outpost that could stop Arnold's barge.

One of Arnold's aides came up to Washington and reported that Mrs. Arnold seemed to have gone mad. She had been running through the upstairs halls almost naked, shouting that "there was a hot iron on her head, and no one but General Washington could take it off."

Washington mounted the stairs. The beautiful young woman was now in bed, dandling her baby, raving, weeping, revealing, as her bedclothes parted, charms usually hidden. She paid no attention to the tall figure standing in the door. Arnold's aide spoke to her: "There is General Washington."

Finally Washington went downstairs. He felt all the more bitter against a traitor who had caused so lovely a lady such anguish.

"No!" she cried, and denied that he was Washington.

Leaning over her with the greatest concern, he gently assured her that he was. "No!" she shrieked, gesturing to shield her infant. "No! That is not General Washington! That is the man who was agoing to assist Colonel Varick in killing my child."

When Washington finally persuaded her of his identity, she accused him of "being in a plot to murder her child." Her husband, she moaned, could not protect her. "General Arnold will never return. He is gone. He is gone forever, *there, there, there:* the spirits have carried him up there!" She pointed at the ceiling. "They have put hot irons on his head."

Finally Washington went downstairs. He felt all the more bitter against a traitor who had caused so lovely a lady such anguish.

Washington wandered around like a man in a nightmare. It was after six in the evening when a message came in from Hamilton reporting that Arnold had escaped to a British warship, from which he had sent two letters that were enclosed. The one to Peggy, Washington sent upstairs unopened with the message that, although it had been his duty to try to capture Arnold, he was happy to relieve her anxiety by telling her that her husband was safe. The other letter was addressed to Washington. He read it with rage, since Arnold contended that it was true patriotism which had carried him to the British.

Now, at long last, Washington took the steps which he should have taken hours before. In dispatches headed sometimes "seven o'clock," sometimes "seven and a half o'clock," and sometimes merely "o'clock," he prepared the army for a British assault. During the night, the wind changed, and the immediate danger was over.

The next day, Washington had to face the painful problems of what to do about Peggy and what to do with André. The young wife (who had been in the plot from the start) need not have used such heavy artillery on Washington; he always labored to shield women from the rigors of war. The next morning, she admitted to no memory of her hysteria and stated quietly that she was utterly innocent. Washington accepted the statement without question. He sent her back to her father in Philadelphia.

To make the problem of André the more heartrending, the young officer behaved in his mortal danger with the utmost courage and the utmost charm. Washington was deeply touched, all the more because of André's temperamental resemblance to Lafayette. Washington's young aides, including Hamilton, were almost aswoon with sympathy for the prisoner. But a court-martial could not avoid the verdict that André had acted as a spy and must be sentenced to death.

Washington longed for some way to escape the inevitable. He could not pardon André out of hand without making it seem to American public opinion that the army was soft on treason. But supposing he could substitute on the gibbet the right man? Knowing that André was Clinton's intimate friend, Washington sent unofficial (they could be no more) messages to his British opposite that he would be happy to release André if Arnold were made available for capture. But Clinton could not agree without torpedoing the whole British effort to win over American officers.

The most exquisitely painful issue then arose. Accepting his death as unavoidable, André asked to be shot (which was considered a gentleman's death), not hanged like a varlet. But hanging was prescribed for

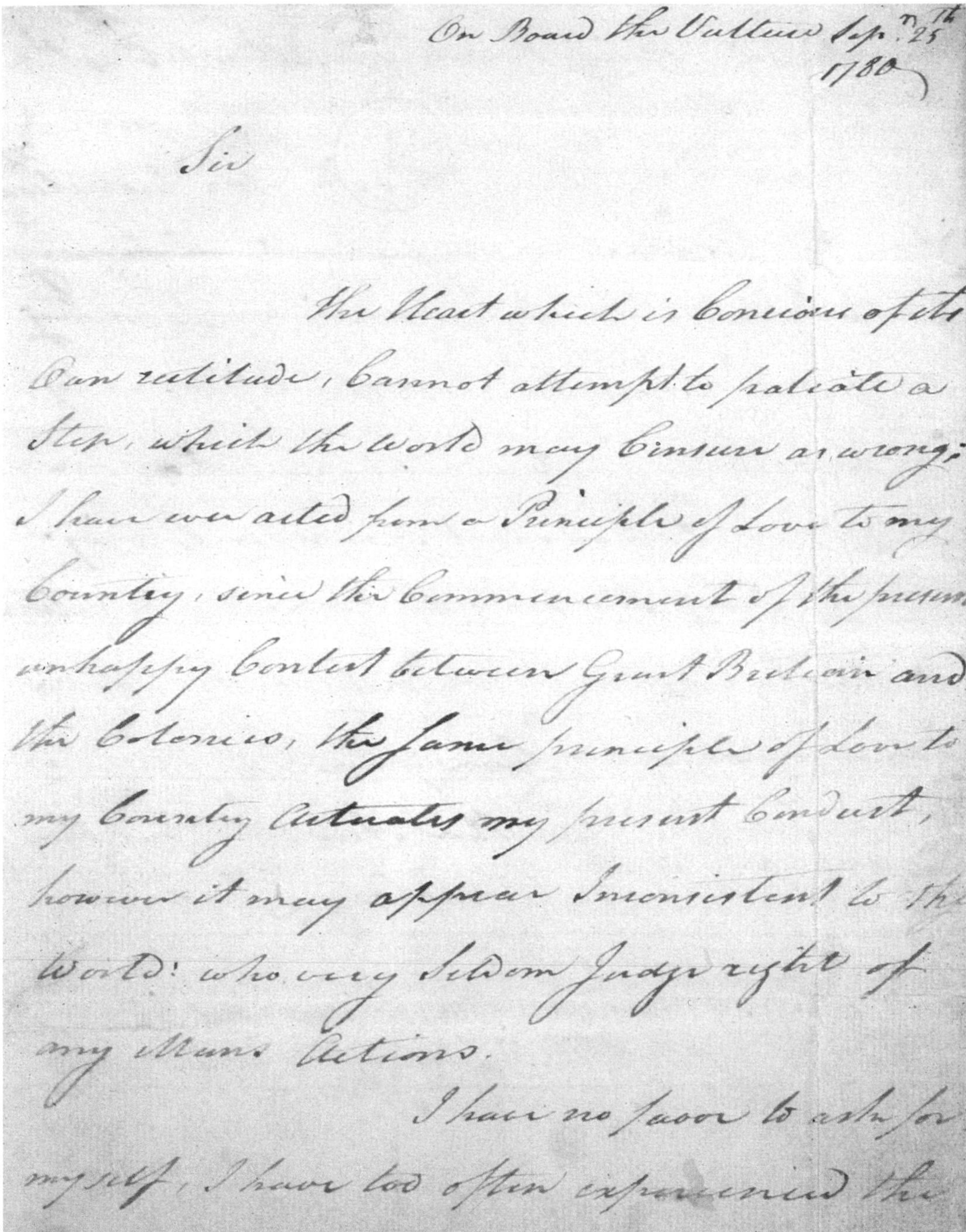

On Board the Vulture Sep.r 25th 1780

Sir

The Heart which is Conscious of its Own rectitude, Cannot attempt to paliate a Step, which the World may Censure as wrong; I have ever acted from a Principle of Love to my Country, since the Commencement of the present unhappy Contest between Great Britain and the Colonies, the same principle of Love to my Country Actuates my present Conduct, however it may appear Inconsistent to the World: who very Seldom Judge right of any Mans Actions.

I have no favor to ask for myself, I have too often experienced the

The September 25, 1780 letter from Benedict Arnold to George Washington begging Washington to help his wife Peggy. After his attempt to surrender the stronghold to the British, Arnold's name became synonymous with "traitor." In spite of attempts to bring him to justice, he spent the rest of the war serving as a brigadier general in the British army, leading raids on Virginia and Connecticut. After the war, he and his family moved to England, where he died in 1801.

spies, and Washington feared that changing the manner of death would give further ammunition to the British propaganda machine, which was already crying out that he intended to murder a legitimate prisoner of war. Although Hamilton growled angrily, "Some people are only sensitive to motives of policy," Washington saw no way that he could interfere with the legally established penalty. It was for him a dreadful moment when the clock struck the hour of the hanging.

As Washington concocted an elaborate scheme—which misfired—to have Arnold kidnapped from New York City, the British tried to make every use of Arnold's defection to disrupt patriot morale. The British propaganda machine ground out statements for Arnold which described his acts as true patriotism and tried, by opening up every sore that rankled in patriot minds, to induce others to imitate him. But hatred for the traitor swept the nation.

Washington's investigations indicated (as was the fact) that there had been no widespread plot. Except for mean go-betweens, Arnold (and Peggy) had operated alone. Yet there remained a most dangerous issue. While in Philadelphia, Arnold had been supported by the conservatives, and he had long been a protégé of Washington's. If guilt by association were accepted, the right wing of the patriot cause and the commander in chief would be tainted. It is terrifying to think what use a modern "super-patriot" rabble-rouser could have made of this issue. The radical Reed did take some initial steps, but, then, frightened it seems by the possible consequences, stepped back.

Washington warned that witch hunts would serve the enemy "by sowing jealousies, and, if we swallow the bait, no character will be safe. There will be nothing but mutual distrust." He labored to turn the popular emotion to gratitude that the plot had been foiled: "In no instance since the commencement of the war has the interposition of Providence been more conspicuous than in the rescue of the post and garrison of West Point from Arnold's villainous perfidy."

Twenty

VIRGINIA ENDANGERED

(1780–1781)

As Rochambeau's army, richly possessed of hard money with which to buy supplies, cozied themselves down on their island for the winter of 1780–1781, Washington could not keep in touch with his allies because he could not procure feed for his couriers' horses. Occupying at New Windsor on the Hudson Highlands, "very confined quarters" at a "dreary station," Washington had to use his own pocketbook to put food on the headquarters table. Formerly he had tried to keep as many Continentals in service as possible, but now he reduced the number of mouths to feed by inconspicuously leaking away the men whose enlistment would not outlast 1780. He warned Congress that to expect the unpaid, unfed, and naked army to "rub through" another campaign like the last "would be as unreasonable as to suppose that because a man had rolled a snowball till it acquired the size of a horse that he might do so till it was as large as a house."

For the first time, Washington envisioned peace without victory. England, Spain,* and France, he heard, were getting tired of the war. Rumor reported that the mediation of neutral powers would establish peace in Europe. The American settlement would secure to England any colonies that she controlled at the time of the treaty. This possibility made the upcoming campaigns extremely crucial since their results might be perpetuated. And Washington could not, for the moment at least, see any way that such a European settlement could be overturned. The situation in the United States, he admitted, called for peace even at this price—or else a large loan from France.

Congress took another step towards using Washington as if he were president. Ordinary diplomatic channels having failed to procure enough help from France, Washington was to send a personal envoy. He instructed Colonel John Laurens to ask in Paris not for reinforcement to Rochambeau's army, but rather for the money which such reinforcements would cost. If financially aided, "we shall be in a condition to continue the war as long as the obstinacy of the enemy may require." Without financial support, the next campaign would be "feeble and expiring" and would put "in all probability, the period to our opposition."

At about noon on January 3, 1781, Washington received such news as he had long dreaded. The Pennsylvania troops, who were stationed at Morristown, had mutinied, killed one officer, and mortally wounded another. Under the command of

* As an ally of France, Spain had entered the war against England. However, she remained hostile to the American Revolution. She had colonies of her own in the Western Hemisphere which she feared would get ideas and slip the leash.

John Laurens *by Charles Willson Peale, from a miniature after Charles Willson Peale, c. 1784.*

sergeants and armed with cannon, they were marching on Philadelphia. They intended to present Congress with a series of demands. The most important of these: since bounties were being paid in cash for new enlistments while the soldiers already in service were not being paid, the mutineers wished to be allowed to resign and then, if they pleased, reenlist.

Washington rushed off a warning to the legislators not to flee from the mutineers. If the angry soldiers found Congress gone, they might join with the town rabble and sack the city. This was not necessarily the worst of the dangers. British agents were among the mutineers, offering them substantial pay in hard money if they would shift over to the British service. And the rest of the Continental army was in the same financial plight as the protesting Pennsylvanians.

Although Washington did his best to keep the news from the troops in his own camp, they were sure to hear sooner or later. Discreet inquiries revealed that the situation on the Hudson was so explosive that his officers feared a revolt there should Washington ride off to deal with the existing mutiny. Furthermore, if he tried to lead a march on the mutinous troops, the soldiers might, instead of putting the insurrection down, join it. However, Washington decided to "hazard everything." A thousand picked men should be prepared for the expedition by being—as far as was possible—clothed and shod and amply fed.

Before it became necessary to hazard all, word came in that the mutineers had been satisfied—but at what a price! Not only had the men won financial concessions, but half were to be given an absolute discharge and the other half a furlough until April. The Pennsylvania line had, for all practical purposes, ceased to exist. What was to keep other state lines from seeking to achieve the same thing in the same way?

Washington could only wait for the next blow. When it came, he was not altogether regretful, for this mutiny was so small that it could be put down as a lesson to the whole army. Only some two hundred New Jersey soldiers were marching on the state capital at Trenton. Washington had some six hundred well-fed and well-armed men at West Point. They were sent in pursuit. The mutineers threw down their arms. Three were sentenced to death. Washington pardoned one, and the others were shot by their weeping companions.

This brought to an end (at least temporarily) the wave of mutinies. But the financial situation that underlay all difficulties was subject to no firing squad. "We are," Washington mourned, "at the end of our tether."

Even into Washington's darkest moments a little light had filtered from his dream that, when the war was over, he would return in peace to Mount Vernon. But now the possibility of ever realizing that dream was menaced—and by whom? By the traitor Benedict Arnold.

Anxious to encourage defections among other American generals, Clinton had given Arnold a command in the British army. With fifteen hundred men, he was sent raiding in Virginia. Greene's army was far away in the Carolinas facing Cornwallis.

Neither Washington nor Rochambeau could send any troops against Arnold since the distance was too great for a march, and the French transports did not dare appear in a British-dominated ocean. Arnold, who was not averse to burning the property of rebels, had an almost free hand in Virginia.

At about noon on January 3, 1781, Washington received such news as he had long dreaded. The Pennsylvania troops, who were stationed at Morristown, had mutinied, killed one officer, and mortally wounded another.

Then, in February 1781, a storm shifted the local naval balance. The British anchorage in Gardiners Bay, at the northern tip of Long Island, was less well protected than the French anchorage in Newport Harbor. Enough British ships were damaged to give the French a numerical advantage until the British shipwrights, who were instantly at work, could repair their vessels. And Arnold was ending up the winter in a base vulnerable to amphibious attack: at Portsmouth, Virginia, where the James River flowed into the Chesapeake.

Washington reasoned that the French should wake from their long somnolence, sail in full force for Portsmouth, annihilate Arnold's detachment, hurry back to Newport before the British navy had adequately repaired their ships—and deliver Arnold up to him for hanging. But, before Washington's plan could reach Rochambeau, the French sent out a small naval detachment, which reduced their main fleet into renewed immobility, but was itself too weak to do anything except conquer a few of Arnold's ships. Washington's disappointment was extreme. Then he heard that the French detachment had, after achieving nothing much, returned. His original plan was again feasible, but, as the British passionately refitted, the time was now shorter. Washington gathered the best-fed horses he could find and took off with his staff for Newport.

He did not pause when the horse he rode fell through Bull's Bridge into the Housatonic River. Leaping free, he shouted that the horse be attended to, leapt on another mount, and was gone. But when he reached the French encampment at Newport, the tempo changed. Far from showing any urgency to sail and attack, the French received him with leisurely ceremony. He had to smile appreciatively as he was informed over and over that the seemingly endless honors paid him were ordinarily accorded to no one lower than a marshal of France or a prince of the blood. Remembering his own hungry and tattered troops, he observed with wonder the elaborate French uniforms, which looked as if they had just come from a tailor's shop, and the faces of the soldiers, lineless with rest and rubicund with plentiful food.

That evening there was a great ball. Washington opened it with the reigning belle of Newport, but his thoughts were absorbed by the fact that, despite a perfect wind, the French warships and transports showed no signs of preparing to sail. As he returned bows and tried to match compliments, the titular commander in chief yearned to urge action but recognized that he could not in fact attempt an order or even ask for an explanation.

The French eventually did sail—but they had waited too long. Having repaired enough ships, the British followed them. There was an inconclusive skirmish, and then the French slipped back into Newport Harbor, the opportunity lost.

Washington was inspired to a series of the most indiscreet letters he had written since he had been a fledgling commander in Cambridge. Marking his most violent attacks on the strategy of his French allies "private," he forgot that the army's inability to feed couriers' horses made his letters travel in ordinary mailbags that were periodically captured by the British. And, sure enough, one of his letters surfaced in the British Tory press. This was the more embarrassing because in his rage and disappointment, Washington had misstated the facts. He had implied that the first small French expedition, which had been dispatched before his suggestions arrived, had been sent contrary to his orders.

In came a courteously phrased protest from Rochambeau in which he gave Washington an out—perhaps the letter was a forgery—and fatuously repeated that his king had placed him under Washington's orders.

Perhaps it was annoyance at the repetition of the fiction that gave him seeming responsibility without actual power that made Washington refuse to accept the evasion Rochambeau had proffered. He did not agree that the letter was a forgery. He expressed "extreme pain" that an "accident" had made public a letter "disagreeable" to Rochambeau. It had been a private letter to a friend totally unconnected with public affairs. It had been "written in haste and might have been inaccurately expressed."

Although Washington's disciple Greene made much trouble for Cornwallis in the Carolinas, he had been unable to dam the tide of British regulars and had been forced to flee into Virginia. Then the two armies switched positions. Cornwallis having decided to operate in Virginia, Greene returned to the Carolinas. This left Washington's native state almost completely in the British power.

During April 1781, the British sloop *Savage* sailed up the Potomac and trained her guns on Mount Vernon. Washington was horrified to hear that his estate manager had gone on board and bought immunity by supplying provisions. This, Washington wrote the manager angrily, "will be a precedent for others." He would rather "they had burnt my house and laid the plantation in ruins."

British raiders descended on the Virginia legislature, capturing several members and sending Governor Thomas Jefferson fleeing into the mountains. If, as seemed possible, the war would soon end with an agreement to preserve the then–status quo, Virginia would, unless previously recaptured by the patriots, return to British rule. Washington might never be able to go home again.

In this situation, so harrowing to his emotions, temptations were laid before Washington. Governor Jefferson begged that he return to his native state. Jefferson feared that the inhabitants, seeing no other way out, might lie down under British rule. However, if Washington appeared, "the difficulty would then be how to keep men out of the field."

Not so very long before, Washington would hardly have cared what happened to the rest of North America as long as Virginia was safe. Now he wrote, "Nobody, I persuade myself, can doubt my inclination to be immediately employed in the defense of that country where all my property and connections are." However, he saw "powerful objections to my leaving this army," and even more powerful objections to trying to march the army southward several hundred miles.

The government of Virginia being scattered and inoperative, Washington received anguished pleas from powerful leaders that he become political as well as military dictator over his native commonwealth. He brushed these suggestions aside.

Twenty-One

YORKTOWN

(1781)

Since Washington's favorite strategy (like the Indians') was to catch the enemy by surprise, he took great precautions to prevent any leakage of his plans. Even major generals were, until the very moment of action, kept in ignorance. This had contributed to the charge, disseminated during the Conway Cabal, that the army was run by a small clique of Washington's confidants and aides. When the French finally served beside the Americans, Rochambeau's staff officers expressed amazement at how much less gossip about movements circulated in the American than in the French camp. But, all the more because of Washington's indiscreet letter that had got into the Tory press, the French command did not trust Washington's discretion.

When, in May 1781, Washington met with Rochambeau at Wethersfield, Connecticut, to discuss the coming campaign, the French general withheld from his ally (and titular commander) the truly essential piece of information. Although Washington was informed that a large French fleet under the Count de Grasse was to operate during that summer in the Indies, he was given no hint that the fleet had been ordered to sail to North America during July or August. Rochambeau was, indeed, so obviously evasive that Washington complained to the French diplomatic representative in Philadelphia, "It is not for me to know in what manner the fleet of His Most Christian Majesty is to be employed in the West Indies this summer, or to inquire at what epocha it may be expected on this coast."

The information Rochambeau did confide was not encouraging. He expected few reinforcements and little money. Then he initiated what he said was speculation: Supposing a French fleet did appear, how should it be employed? Washington plumped as always for killing off the war by capturing New York City. Only if this proved impossible should some objective be sought in the South. Keeping up the formal fiction of Washington's command, Rochambeau signed a paper agreeing with this strategy.

Francois Joseph Paul, Comte de Grasse (1723–1788), Lieutenant General of the Navy, by Jean Baptiste Mauzaisse, 1842.

In a secret dispatch, Rochambeau urged de Grasse to ignore the official document. The admiral was to sail directly for the Chesapeake. Rochambeau would see that he would be met there by the combined American and French armies. The objective of this strategy was not (despite what many histories tell us) Yorktown or even specifically Cornwallis's army. Cornwallis was now inland and there was no reason to suppose that he

George Washington and His Generals at Yorktown
by Charles Willson Peale, oil on canvas, c. 1781.

would settle on the coast, making himself vulnerable to amphibious action. Rochambeau hoped to pick off the shipping associated with Cornwallis's expedition, and also the minor British post that was still being maintained at Portsmouth.

Although, during their conference, Rochambeau had behaved to Washington (according to another French general) with "all the ungraciousness and all the unpleasantness possible," he had finally given in to Washington's request that his army join the Continental army on the banks of the Hudson. He was so obliging because the march would, without giving away his secret objective, carry his troops that much closer to the Chesapeake.

Rochambeau returned to Newport and Washington to the Hudson. There he heard from his own representative in Paris, Laurens, that the French West Indian fleet had been ordered to the North American coast. Laurens also stated that he had secured from the court at Versailles a gift of six million livres. The delegate attributed this success "to the exalted opinion which the Ministers have of your Excellency and everything which comes from you."

Washington, now that he knew that a French fleet was expected, was anxious to open all alternatives.

He began drawing up plans for an attack on the South, should New York City not prove vulnerable. However, he continued to broadcast word that New York City was menaced. This was regarded by the French (and subsequently by many historians) as an indiscretion. Actually it served two purposes: it encouraged American enlistment and frightened Clinton into ordering Cornwallis to send two thousand men back to New York. Abandoning his effort to subdue Virginia, Cornwallis fortified, as a base for what army he had left, a besiegable position on the Virginia coast at Yorktown. Thus Washington's strategy set the trap which Rochambeau's secret plans were to close.

It was July 6, 1781, when Rochambeau's army moved in beside Washington's, some twelve miles north of Manhattan in the neighborhood of Dobbs Ferry. Social problems excruciating to the Americans instantly arose. Officers in faded and torn uniforms or no uniforms at all had to hold up their heads in the presence of officers spotless, gold-braided, brightly colored, bemedaled, beplumed. Using their hard money to buy plentiful supplies, the French entertained sumptuously, but when the Americans entertained back, they could hardly scratch up enough food to postpone hunger.

Herculean efforts of procurement enabled Washington to give dinner to thirty Frenchmen a day. They complained that the coffee he served was weak and the salad dressing merely vinegar. Furthermore, since each guest was given only one plate, everything had to be sloshed together. They were amazed by the informality of the American headquarters, at how long everyone sat at the table, and at how much Washington enjoyed the dinners. He and his fellow American officers cracked hickory nuts by the hour, the conversation "free and agreeable," the toasts jocose and often ribald. Since Washington did not himself drink heavily, a French nobleman concluded that this conviviality was an emotional release from the problems that forever assailed him.

Trying to find some European conception which would fit the ragged American army, various officers compared them with the picturesque brigands who were then swashbuckling around in preromantic literature. Von Closen wrote more seriously, "It is incredible that soldiers composed of men of every age, even of children of fifteen, of whites and blacks, almost naked, unpaid, and rather poorly fed, can march so well and stand fire so steadfastly."

Trying to find some European conception which would fit the ragged American army, various officers compared them with the picturesque brigands who were then swashbuckling around in preromantic literature. Von Closen wrote more seriously, "It is incredible that soldiers composed of men of every age, even of children of fifteen, of whites and blacks, almost naked, unpaid, and rather poorly fed, can march so well and stand fire so steadfastly." He credited "the calm and calculated measures of General Washington, in whom I daily discover some new and

Following page: *Bicentennial commemorative memento of the Battle of Yorktown, based on a 1782 original.*

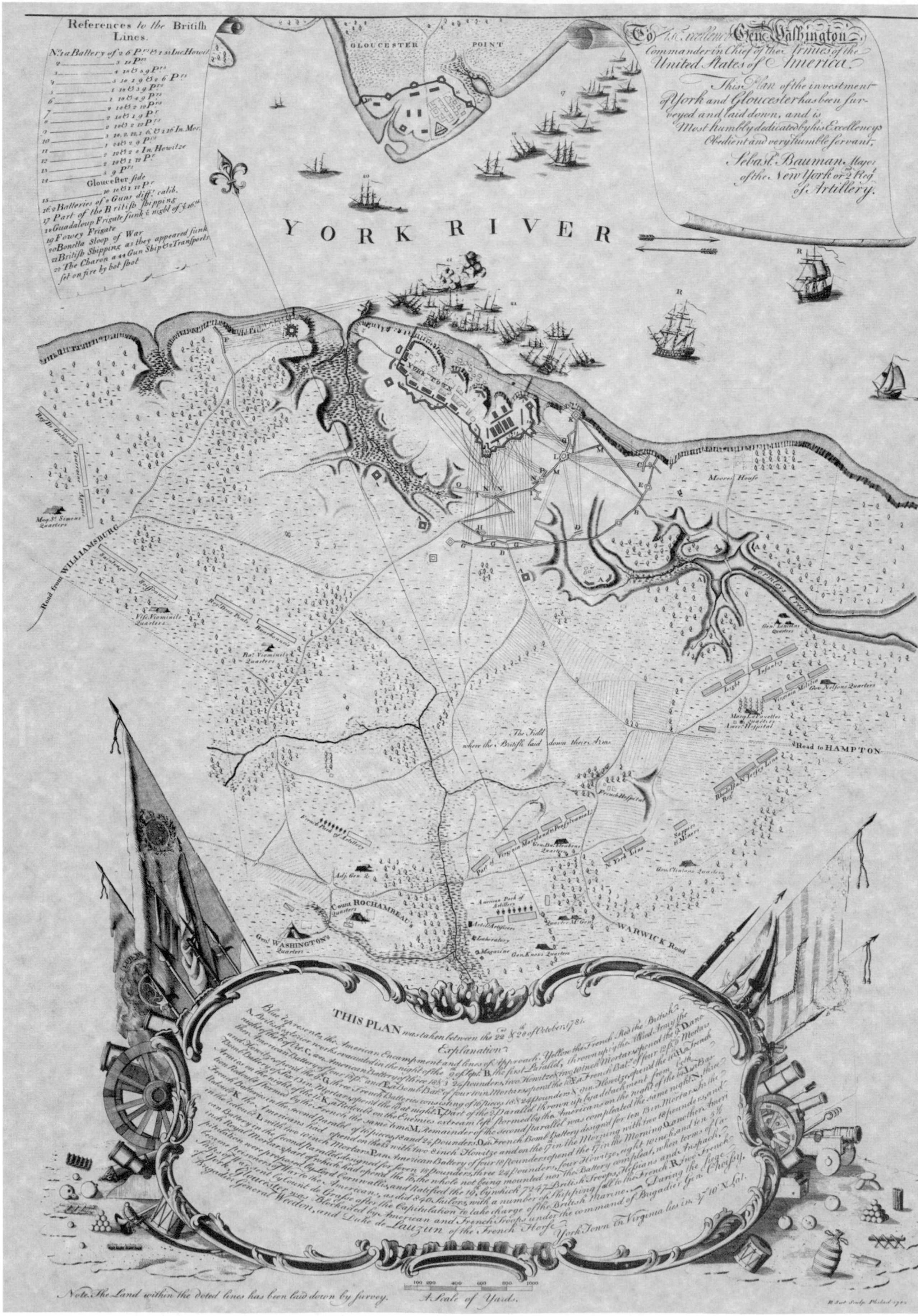

To His Excellency Gen. Washington
Commander in Chief of the Armies of the United States of America.
This Plan of the investment of York and Gloucester has been surveyed and laid down, and is Most humbly dedicated by his Excellency's Obedient and very humble servant,
Sebast. Bauman Major of the New York or 2d Regt. of Artillery.
References to the British Lines.
Gloucester side
16 2 Batteries of 8 Guns diff. calib.
17 Part of the British shipping
18 Guadaloup Frigate sunk the night of the 16th
19 Fowey Frigate
20 Bonetta Sloop of War
21 British Shipping as they appeared sunk
22 The Charon a 44 Gun Ship & 2 Transports set on fire by hot shot
GLOUCESTER
POINT
YORK RIVER
YORK TOWN
Moores House
Wormleys Creek
Road from WILLIAMSBURG
Road to HAMPTON
The Field where the British laid down their Arms
French Hospital
Light Infantry
Virginia Militia
Gen. Nelsons Quarters
French Park of Artillery
Count ROCHAMBEAU
Genl. WASHINGTON's Quarters
American Park of Artillery
Laboratory
Magazine
Gen. Knoxs Quarters
WARWICK Road
THIS PLAN was taken between the 22d & 28th of October, 1781.
Explanation
York Town in Virginia lies in 37° 10' N. Lat.
Note. The Land within the doted lines has been laid down by survey.
A Scale of Yards.
100 200 400 600 800 1000

THE BATTLE of YORKTOWN

October 19th 1781

Inside: *A map of Yorktown and Gloucester shows the area of Virginia where the American and French armies defeated Cornwallis on October 19, 1781.*

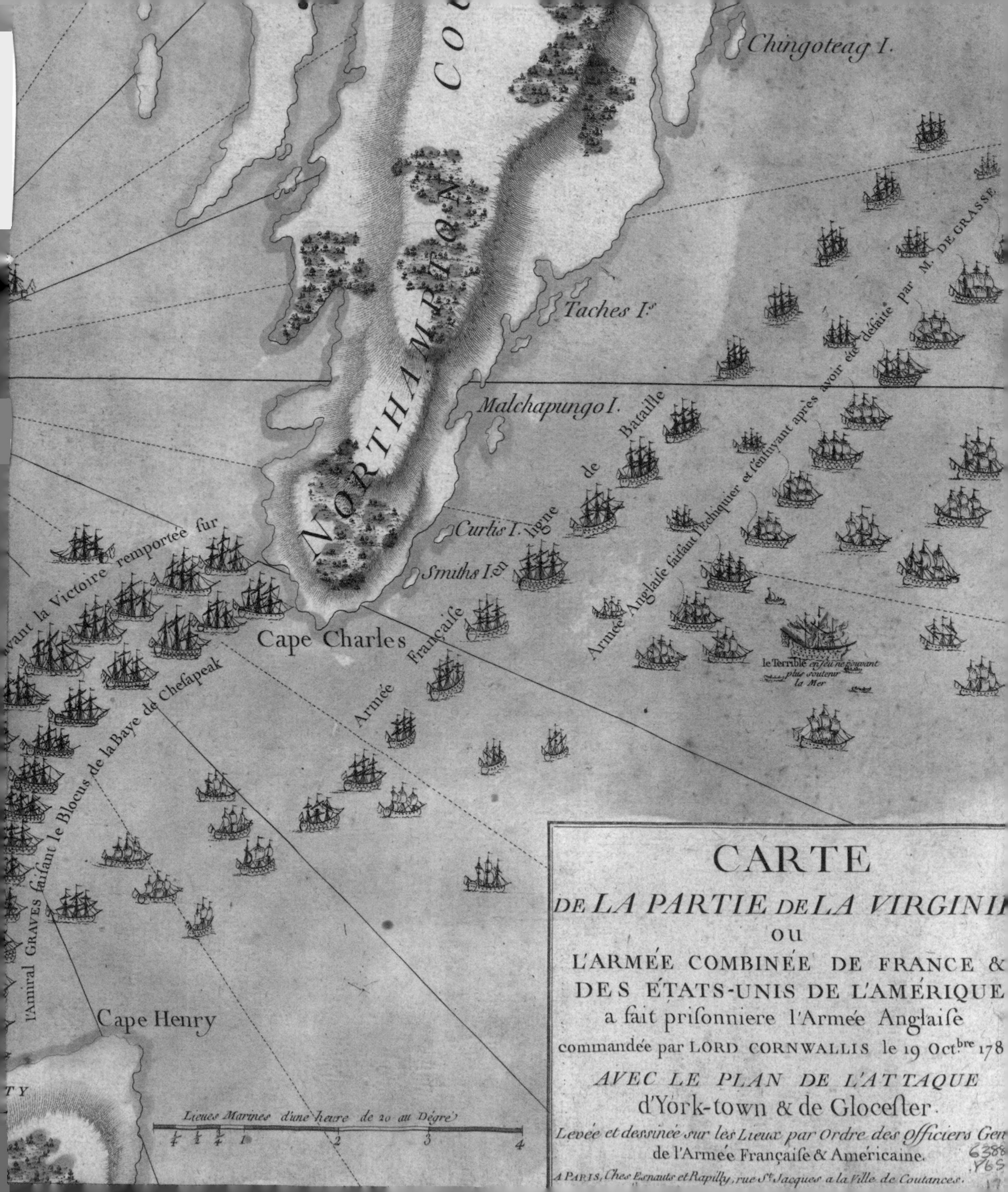
Chingoteag I.
COU
NORTHAMPTON
Taches Ies
Malchapungo I.
Curtis I.
Smiths I.en
Cape Charles
Armée Françaife
Armée Angloise faisant l'échiquier et s'enfuyant après avoir été défaite par M. DE GRASSE
ligne de Bataille
le Terrible en feu ne pouvant plus soutenir la Mer
…vant la Victoire remportée sur l'Amiral GRAVES faisant le Blocus de la Baye de Chesapeak
Cape Henry
Lieues Marines d'une heure de 20 au Dégré
¼ ½ ¾ 1 2 3 4
CARTE
DE LA PARTIE DE LA VIRGINI…
OU
L'ARMÉE COMBINÉE DE FRANCE &
DES ÉTATS-UNIS DE L'AMÉRIQUE
a fait prisonniere l'Armée Anglaise
commandée par LORD CORNWALLIS le 19 Oct.bre 178…
AVEC LE PLAN DE L'ATTAQUE
d'York-town & de Glocester.
Levée et dessinée sur les Lieux par Ordre des Officiers Gen…
de l'Armée Française & Américaine.
A PARIS, Ches Esnauts et Rapilly, rue St. Jacques a la Ville de Coutances.
6388
Y65

River
B A
Lewis
Fairfield
Rosewel
Mockjack Bay
Corps d'Hussards
Corps Americaine et Française
Légion de Lauzun
Postes de Mr. de Choisy
YORK
RIVER
Toes Point
Glocester
Fort
LAMSBURG
Digges
Redoutes
Corps du Marquis de St. Simon
YORK-TOWN
Fort
Redoute
Volontaires de la Fayette
Batteries de Canons et Mortiers
Parc d'Artillerie
Corps du Cte. de Rochambeau
Corps d'Armée du Général Washington
COUNTY
Long Island
Egg I.
Back Bay
Halfway House
Bray
Burwell
YORK
ELIZABETH CTY
Seldon
Rascow
Hampton
JAMES RIVER
Warrasqueak
CHESAPEAK
Armée Navale de France aux Ordres du Cte. DE GRASSE
Fort George
Comfort Pt.
Sowels Pt.
Graney I.
Willowbys Pt.
OF WIGHT CTY
Sack Pt.
Smithfield
NORFOLK CTY
Lamberts Pt.
PRINCESS ANN
Norfolk

Surrender of Lord Cornwallis *by John Trumbull, oil on canvas, 1820.*

eminent qualities. . . . He is certainly admirable as the leader of his army, in which everyone regards him as his father and friend."

On August 14, Washington received from his French "subordinates" news that was a command. De Grasse was expected to arrive with a major fleet and thirty-two hundred soldiers on September 3, but he would not come anywhere near New York, either to menace that base or to carry the American and French armies southward in his ships. He would steer directly for the Chesapeake. He could not stay beyond the middle of October. The armies on the Hudson would have to march four hundred and fifty miles to meet him.

Washington was deeply disturbed. Since patriot affairs were "in the most ruinous train imaginable," he believed it extremely dangerous "to embark in any enterprise wherein, from the most rational plan and accurate calculations, the favorable issue should not have appeared as clear to my view as a ray of light." If the arduous march ended in disaster or even just frustration, patriot morale might collapse irrevocably.

The strategy which Rochambeau had forced upon him was packed with uncertainties, any one of which could overturn the whole. Most serious, de Grasse might not arrive. He might change his mind, be stopped by contrary orders, be blocked by one of those storms that were so destructive to fleets of sailing vessels, be driven into cautious withdrawal or even defeated by the stronger British fleet which, so rumor reported, was being ordered up from the Indies to counteract the French move. The French cannon were in Newport and too heavy to be transported overland; they could only be carried south if the little fleet attached to Rochambeau, which had never yet dared challenge British superiority in the local waters, were able to slip secretly by the vessels watching them. To get the Continental army—to say nothing of the French—from the Hudson to the mouth of the Chesapeake would strain the vanishing patriot resources to the breaking point or beyond. And even if everything else worked, if the two armies and de Grasse's fleet did converge, the bird might have flown.

Washington now knew that Cornwallis was fortifying Yorktown as the base for his army, but Washington also knew there was no force available in Virginia to hold Cornwallis in these fortifications. If warned of his danger, he could escape from the trap merely by marching inland. How was he to be kept from being warned? The allied armies could not march off under (so to speak) Clinton's nose without Clinton noticing it, and if Clinton realized they were going south, he would guess that they were to meet de Grasse there. A dispatch boat sent from New York would, ocean travel being so much the quicker, reach Cornwallis before the trudging armies could. The only hope was to get well on the way before the British had any inkling of the allies' destination.

This was possible since an attack on the British position in New York from the rear, via Staten Island, could involve marching two-thirds of the distance across New Jersey. Allowing spies laboriously to achieve glimpses of presumably secret papers, Washington persuaded Clinton that de Grasse was coming north to cooperate in an operation against Staten Island. Washington sent out engineers to prepare in New Jersey what looked like a major camp, even building ovens capable of baking thousands of loaves of bread. The ruse was successful. The two armies got to the Delaware before Clinton guessed.

The plan was to travel by water down the Delaware to a point from which it was only a twelve-mile march to the head of the Chesapeake, where more boats would be waiting. But there was a shortage of boats and of everything else. As Washington sped around to procure necessities, his nerves were harassed by conflicting reports concerning the different operations which would have to key together if the result were not to be catastrophe.

On September 5, Rochambeau and his staff were drifting down the Delaware when they saw on the waterfront at Chester, Pennsylvania, a tall man in blue and buff regimentals dancing up and down, waving a hat and a handkerchief. It looked from a distance as if this jumping jack were His Excellency, George Washington. Indeed it was. He was yelling that de Grasse's fleet had actually arrived. According to the duc de Lauzun, "I never saw a man overcome with more great and sincere joy." The Duc de Deux-Ponts recorded that Washington behaved like "a child whose every wish had been gratified." Washington even went so far as to embrace Rochambeau "warmly."

Now, as if miraculously, everything fell in place. Cornwallis, unwarned until he was actually menaced by the approaching allied armies, chose not to march out of his fortifications but to strengthen them. The weak French fleet from Newport, having escaped British observation, sailed in, bringing not only the cannon but ships of shallow enough draft to ferry the troops down the Chesapeake. The British naval reinforcement proved, on its appearance, not as strong as had been expected or as ably commanded: the famous Admiral Rodney had been taken ill. After an inconclusive skirmish with de Grasse, the British navy retired, leaving de Grasse in control of the water and Cornwallis immured at Yorktown.

As always when the British were in trouble, patriots came flocking: Washington soon had ninety-five hundred effectives. The French troops, those commanded by Rochambeau plus those de Grasse had brought, numbered eighty-eight hundred. The safety of Cornwallis's men, estimated at five to six thousand, depended altogether on their fortifications. These had been expertly designed by British engineers—but there was counterexpertise. Rochambeau, who boasted that he had been present at fourteen sieges, told Washington that, from here on, the sequence of moves was dictated by military science, and unless an unexpected British reinforcement turned the tables, the result was inevitable: the Yorktown defenses would fall and Cornwallis would surrender.

The initial step was to start a trench so far beyond British cannon range that troops could enter it unscathed. The trench was extended towards the fortifications at an angle that prevented it from being enfiladed by enemy cannon fire. After this "first parallel" had advanced the intended distance, sunken bases were built for the reception of heavy cannon. Gangs of crouching men pulled in the heavy guns. These would then batter the Yorktown walls until the British cannon were silenced.

The softening-up process being completed, a "second parallel" would be advanced so close to the walls that cannon in new positions could lob their shells over the fortifications into the enemy encampment itself. Two British redoubts had been placed to bar the way of a second parallel. These would have to be stormed, but, since they were separated from the main fortification and could not hold many men, they would surely be taken.

At some point, the honor of the British army would require a sortie from behind the walls into the Franco-American trenches, but the balance of power was such that this maneuver, like the defense of the redoubts, could yield nothing but piles of dead and wounded men. And once the British encampment and the town behind the walls were open to cannon fire, the time of surrender depended only on how many casualties Cornwallis was willing to accept.

Washington was impressed by this scenario as it was described to him, but he was also puzzled. Cornwallis surely understood the sequence as well as did the French. Since Washington himself could not possibly await without action almost inevitable disaster, he could not conceive that Cornwallis would do so. Surely Cornwallis would make an effort, however dangerous, to break away, and it seemed to Washington that he had an available route.

The York River, which flowed by the back of the Yorktown fortifications, penetrated westward into Virginia. A little British fleet was huddled against

The British and Continental Armies at Yorktown, Virginia, *detail of etching, October 19, 1781.*

the walls. Although many of the ships drew too much water to go upriver, enough were usable so that Cornwallis could evacuate his men with a favorable wind on a dark night. He would, of course, have to leave behind most of his artillery and supplies, but that did not seem to the commander of the Continental army an insuperable difficulty. If Cornwallis could get free in Virginia, he might, proceeding in the manner of Washington's own army, find his way to safety.

Washington described this possibility to de Grasse, and urged that several French frigates, taking their own advantage of darkness and wind, slip by the Yorktown defenses and block the river. The French admiral laughed at the whole idea. The risk to his own frigates would be too great and Cornwallis would not be that crazy.

De Grasse's worries (which also became Washington's and were, in fact, Cornwallis's hopes) were that the British fleet would be, as some reports indicated, reinforced, and would return again to challenge French control of that part of the ocean. Or that unforeseen difficulties would so slow the siege that the admiral's other commitments would force him to return to the Indies before Yorktown was reduced.

As it turned out, no British fleet appeared, and the siege proceeded according to schedule. Every morning, Washington attended a conference during which he was instructed by the French experts on what the American army should do that day. When the first parallel was completed, he was invited, as the titular commander in chief, to fire the first gun. It was a French gun, brand new, containing perfectly fitted ammunition, manned by trained artillerymen. Washington was amazed to see the ball strike the exact spot on the British walls that had previously been pointed out to him. The American ragtag and bobtail artillery was utterly outclassed.

After the first parallel had served its deadly purpose, the redoubts in the way of the second parallel were effectively stormed. The expected British sortie passed ineffectually with the expected number of casualties. The guns placed in the second parallel set fire to the little British fleet in the York River and pounded the town. Deserters reported that Cornwallis was cowering in a "grotto" with the hopeless despair of a rabbit while the ferrets dug ever closer. Finally, as the blood and destruction above his shelter became completely unbearable, Cornwallis gave a convulsive twitch: he made and then abandoned an effort to ferry his army across the York River. On October 17, he sent a messenger to Washington proposing a twenty-four-hour truce "to settle terms for the surrender."

During the surrender negotiations, Washington, not wishing victory to be marred by persecution, agreed to a subterfuge which enabled the British to spirit away American Tories, who would otherwise be arrested, and American deserters, who would otherwise be hanged, to the British army. Captured slaves were to be returned to their owners, and the British army would become, without reservations, prisoners of war. But one grievous issue did arise: Washington's insistence that "the same honors shall be granted to the surrendering army as were granted to the garrison of Charleston."

When Charleston had fallen, Clinton had expressed his disdain for the rebels by refusing them "the honors of war" traditionally accorded a defeated army which had fought well. In addition to other humiliations, the American army had not been allowed to march to the surrender ceremony with their flags flying. If the same strictures were applied to Cornwallis, his army would be disgraced before all Europe. But Washington was adamant.

Cornwallis thereupon decided that he was personally too sick to attend the surrender ceremony. His representative, Brigadier General Charles O'Hara, did his best to hand his sword not to Washington but to some French officer. Washington then refused to accept the sword. If Cornwallis was to be represented by a deputy, so would he be. O'Hara was forced to surrender to General Lincoln, who was the officer Clinton had insulted at Charleston.

Popular history equates Cornwallis's surrender with American victory in the Revolution. But Washington, who still mourned that de Grasse's cooperation had not resulted in smashing the British bastion at New York, wrote that the capture of Yorktown was "an interesting event that may be productive of much good if properly improved, but if it should be the means of relaxation and sink us into supineness and [false] security, it had better not have happened."

True, the bag at Yorktown was larger than Washington had expected: 7,241 soldiers and 840 seamen, 244 pieces of artillery and thousands of small arms. But the British had lost only a quarter of their might on American soil. The enemy forces in various bases from Halifax to Charleston still outnumbered by several times the Continental army. And de Grasse hoisted his sails and returned to the Indies, restoring to the British the control of the American ocean.

Twenty-Two

A GULF OF CIVIL HORROR

(1781–1783)

Although the war would go on, no further major action was indicated for the rest of 1781—and Washington was in Virginia, not far from Mount Vernon. During almost seven years, his mind had been perpetually "on the stretch." He looked forward to at least several weeks of a relaxing vacation. But it was not to be.

His stepson, John Parke Custis, had sat out most of the war, an indolent, self-indulgent, rich young man who had not scrupled to take advantage of his stepfather's absence to cheat him in little ways. But the possibility of associating outside Yorktown with aristocratic French officers had filled Custis with sudden martial ardor. He attached himself to Washington as a volunteer aide. This would have caused no more than irritation had not the soft young man, who had not been exposed to any of the camp diseases, sickened. On the very day that Washington intended to start his vacation, John Parke Custis died. Washington was unable to express any personal grief. However, his beloved wife was completely desolated.

Mount Vernon, where he had hoped to find some quiet, was turned, as he expressed it, into "the House of Mourning." Washington became glad to take Martha to Philadelphia, away from the place where every object reminded her of her loss.

He intended soon to join his army beside the Hudson, but he was held in the capital for four months. The basic military problems were now more than ever grounded in the civilian sphere. Despite the still powerful British presence, there was a general feeling that the Revolution was as good as won. This portended so much more neglect of the already extremely neglected army that, should Clinton or his government decide to undertake another serious military effort, the Continental force might be helpless. And there was also the possibility that the American soldiers, embittered by indifference to their needs, would themselves destroy, in one way or another, the freedom for which they had fought.

The financial difficulties—no money available to give bounties to or to support and pay the existing army—were symptoms of a more serious rot. The thirteen colonies had been driven into close cooperation by a crisis which gave them the alternatives Benjamin Franklin had so aptly described: if they did not hang together, they would hang separately. But even on the heights of the crisis, the states had argued for years before they could agree on the Articles of Confederation, which did little more than create a loose alliance. Now that the crisis seemed to be fading, the states were becoming increasingly indifferent to the Continental Congress and the combined effort it fostered.

Under Washington's urging, the Congress appropriated for the next campaign eight million dollars. Although this was barely enough to keep the core of an army in the field and although Washington wrote

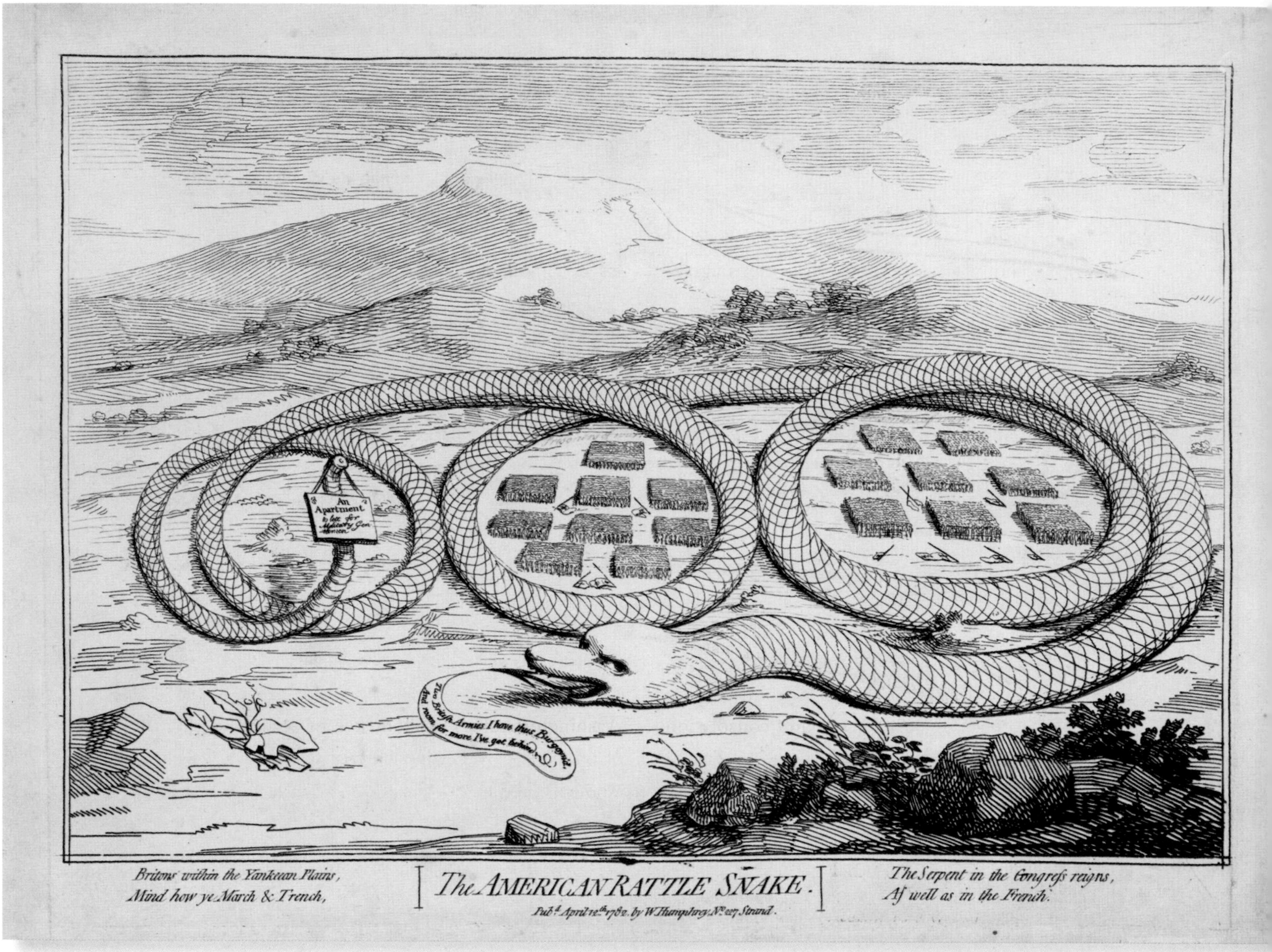

The American Rattle Snake, *an editorial drawingby James Gillray published in London in April 1782, when peace negotiations had begun. This etching suggests the futility of further British efforts to forcibly suppress the Americans.*

hortatory letters to the various governors, the states did not supply Congress with money enough to pay even the interest on already outstanding debts.

The obvious and necessary solution was that the central body be allowed to raise money in its own right. Washington's hopes and the anticipations of the troops came to depend on the proposition that Congress be empowered to collect customs duties. However, the Articles of Confederation had so rigorously preserved local sovereignty that federal taxation could only be authorized through unanimous agreement of all the states. As winter dragged into the spring of 1782 and on towards autumn, the matter was considered by the various state legislatures. Favorable votes were reported, but the fact remained that if any laggard voted no or refused to act, the army would surely not receive its past and present dues.

In Philadelphia, with his mourning wife beside him, Washington found dull and depressing a social season that was generally considered brilliant. Back with his army on the Hudson in April, he was lonely for the officers away on the southern campaign. He wrote General Greene, "To participate and divide our feelings, hopes, fears, and expectations with a friend is almost the only source of pleasure and consolation left us in the present languid and unpromising state of our affairs."

Washington must have got some grim satisfaction when Clinton was replaced by Sir Guy Carleton; he had now outlasted his third British commander in chief. But his hopes of French assistance that would enable him to drive the enemy from New York were knocked down by the news that in a naval action off the West Indies, de Grasse had been decisively defeated by Admiral Rodney. Rochambeau and the French army remained inactive until, in the autumn, they sailed back to France.

By that time, Washington had been notified by Carleton that peace negotiations had been commenced in Paris at which George III intended not only to accept but to propose the independence of the United States. Washington was less exhilarated than frightened. The news, which would probably remove what bit of backbone was left in the support of the army, might well have been fabricated for that purpose: "From the former infatuation, duplicity, and perverse system of British policy, I confess I am induced to doubt everything, to suspect everything."

Washington did his best to think of ways of amusing his troops in idleness. He sent his officers home on long furloughs, urged the men to vie with each other in decorating their huts and their hats. Encouraging one of New England's favorite sports, he wrote that religious discourses "must afford the most pure and rational entertainment for any serious and well-disposed mind." But he noted that the dissatisfaction was taking on a new and ominous note. Formerly, the officers had tried to quiet the men. Now they were leading the protests.

The situation was already dangerous enough when Congress decided to cut expenses by reducing the number of regiments in a way that would demobilize many officers. However, no provision was made for giving them any pay, although some were owed (as Washington noted) for "four, five, or perhaps six years." A promise of pensions previously made at a dark moment in the war showed no likelihood of being honored. To officials in Philadelphia, Washington wrote bitterly that the demobilized officers would depart "goaded by a thousand stings of reflection on the past and of anticipation on the future . . . soured by penury and what they call the ingratitude of the public, involved in debts, without one farthing of money to carry them home, after having spent the flowers of their days, and many of them their patrimonies, in establishing the freedom and independence of their country, and suffered everything human nature is capable of enduring on this side of death. . . . I cannot avoid apprehending that a train of evils will follow of a very serious and distressing nature."

A map showing the United States after the 1783 Treaty of Paris, with the British possessions of Canada, Nova Scotia, and Newfoundland divided with the French and the Spanish territories of Louisiana and Florida.

The summer of 1782 passed in frustrating doldrums. Washington hoped to spend the following winter at Mount Vernon, recruiting his strength and attending to his neglected private concerns. But when the time for departure came, he felt that the temper of the army was such that he could not leave.

The plight of the officers who had already been demobilized could not help seeming frighteningly prophetic: when no longer needed to protect the civilian population, every soldier, all obligations forgotten, would also be sent home in penury. It seemed to follow that while the troops were still together, they should take the steps necessary to make sure that the civilian authorities would give them the pay that was owed and secure to them the pensions that had been voted them. The Massachusetts regiments sent a delegation to their own government, only to be shunted on to the Congress. But Massachusetts was delinquent (as were all the other states) in meeting her part of the quota that would help make Congress solvent enough to pay the army.

Almost every revolution in the history of the world, however idealistically begun, had ended in tyranny. The American Revolution had now reached its moment of major political crisis.

Over campfires in the chill autumn, warmed sometimes with rum, the officers fingered the hilts of their swords and talked of taking the law in their own hands. Only by the most intense persuasion did Washington channel the discontent into a petition to Congress. There had been petitions before, but this one was accompanied by a not-too-subtle threat. It was to be presented by a committee of three high officers who were to stay in Philadelphia until it became clear whether justice would be done or not. If not, the army would consider more decisive action.

Since Congress's requisitions to the states were continuing to fall on deaf ears, everything depended on the fate of the amendment to the Articles that would allow Congress to collect its own taxes. Hardly had the military committee reached the capital when adverse votes of both Rhode Island and Virginia carried the amendment to defeat. The committee angrily warned Congress that the soldiers "were verging on a state which we are told will drive wise men mad." But Congress, being bankrupt, could do nothing.

Almost every revolution in the history of the world, however idealistically begun, had ended in tyranny. The American Revolution had now reached its moment of major political crisis.

Now that independence seemed at hand, the state leaders felt their own urgency: it should be made clear, for the impending future, that the United States was not one nation but thirteen. But state autonomy was not the basis on which the war had been fought. It had been necessary to create a Continental Congress and a Continental army, and also to incur Continental debts. These debts were not only to the soldiers. Congress also owed much to civilians. There was the currency it had printed, which should be honored, even if at less than face value. There were certificates of indebtedness: bonds and various acknowledgments of loans; paper Washington had, when deprived of more specific means of payment, given to farmers and wagoners; the multitudinous other kinds of paper emitted by a bankrupt government scrambling for existence. Since the poor had been unable to wait, they had usually sold their certificate of indebtedness to speculators for a fraction of the true value. The paper had thus found its way into the hands of large operators. The financial community was as deeply involved as were the soldiers in the national obligations which the states were trying, as they delicately looked the other way, to sweep under the rug.

The fact that the army and the ablest, most prosperous businessmen were being similarly defrauded opened a promising field for common action. The members of the military committee that had been sent to Philadelphia conferred with the leading financiers, particularly Robert and Gouverneur Morris. It was agreed that the only protection for the creditors, whether civilians or soldiers, was the military strength of the army. The army should, even if peace were declared, refuse to go home until the states agreed to a system by which all federal debts could be paid. If necessary, violence should be threatened to achieve what was basically required: a strong central government that could protect the rights of its creditors. Should military force be used to reform the state legislatures, that would, it was said (and probably often believed), be only a temporary expedient until the necessary changes were achieved. Then the government would be returned to the people. So it was argued. The modern reader will see being groomed and saddled the horses of fascism.

The road ahead seemed clear except for one serious potential barrier: George Washington. Would the national hero be willing to countenance a movement to use the army as a political force? And if he refused to go along, could he be pushed aside?

The conspirators agreed that the ground should be prepared for getting rid of Washington and finding another leader. However, it would be infinitely better to persuade Washington. Washington's former aide, Alexander Hamilton, now a congressman from New York, announced that he knew how to handle the general. He would undertake the mission.

Washington's role in the Revolution had always been more than military. After electing him commander in chief, the members of Congress had committed themselves to the cause by committing themselves to support him. And their need for his help had proved to be great. As a legislative body entrusted with all executive functions, the Congress had tried to administer the war and the army by setting up committees of its members. There were soon more committees than the members had time for, and the method was at best cumbersome. Because the committees so often failed to act, Washington was continually forced, in order to keep his army alive, into himself making decisions with much wider implications than the purely military. And on several occasions when Congress became frightened by British successes, the legislators officially dumped in the commander in chief's lap powers to determine civilian concerns. Although he fought off rather than sought these extensions of responsibility and made as little use of them as was feasible, Washington became, while still commander in chief, as much of a chief executive as the United States then had.

This did not escape observation, and many influential patriots considered that the possibility of making Washington a one-man government was an asset which could be fallen back on in a severe emergency. As we have seen, he had been begged by major political leaders to take over the government of Virginia. In May 1782, he had received from one of his colonels, Lewis Nicola, a letter urging him to accept the responsibility of becoming king of the United States.

The road ahead seemed clear except for one serious potential barrier: George Washington. Would the national hero be willing to countenance a movement to use the army as a political force? And if he refused to go along, could he be pushed aside?

The suggestion seemed to Nicola highly reasonable. Every major nation in the world was then ruled by a king, and royalty had been throughout history almost exclusively the accepted form of government. But Washington replied, "No occurrence in the course of the war has given me more painful sensations than your information of there being such ideas existing in the army. . . . I must view with abhorrence and reprehend with severity" a conception that was "big with the greatest mischiefs that can befall my country."

However, Washington had taken this stand before it was known that the states would not of their own volition make possible a central government strong enough even to pay its just debts to the

Join, or Die, *by Benjamin Franklin, published in the* Pennsylvania Gazette, *May 9, 1754. The cartoon accompanied Franklin's editorial about the "disunited state" of the colonies and the increasingly oppressive British Royal government.*

national creditors and to the soldiers who had fought under his leadership for so many years.

Washington was at his headquarters on the banks of the Hudson at Newburgh, New York, when, during mid-February of 1783, Hamilton's effort to inveigle him arrived in the form of a subtly composed letter. As a congressman, Hamilton reported that there were no further possibilities of supplying the army; by June, the troops would have to take everything they needed at bayonet point. As a colonel (he was still a member of the army), Hamilton informed Washington that, should peace come, the army intended to use its bayonets "to procure justice to itself."

Washington's own command, so Hamilton warned, was in danger. The army felt that his "delicacy carried to an extreme" had made him stand in the way of their achieving their just dues. They might very well act without him. Then "the difficulty will be to keep a complaining and suffering army within the bounds of moderation." But if Washington took the lead, the result could be salutary rather than destructive. By cooperating with "all men of sense," the army could, under Washington's benign control, operate on "weak minds" to establish the federal taxation "which alone can do justice to the creditors of the United States . . . and supply the future wants of government."

Washington's headquarters at Newburgh on the Hudson, c. 1775, as rendered in oil by James William Fosdick in the nineteenth century.

Washington as commander in chief, engraved in Paris by Benoit Louis Prévost, detail, 1780, after a drawing by Pierre Eugène du Simitière.

In came a letter from one of Washington's confidential correspondents, Congressman Joseph Jones of Virginia. Jones warned that "dangerous combinations in the army" were using "sinister practices" to tear down Washington's reputation so that "the weight of your opposition will prove no obstacle to their ambitious designs." Jones believed that the plot was likely to succeed. "Whether to temporize or oppose with steady, unremitting firmness," he continued, ". . . must be left to your own sense of propriety and better judgment."

During "many contemplative hours," Washington, as he put it, puzzled over "the predicament in which I stand as a citizen and soldier." In that year of 1783, the efforts of the United States to establish a republican government were unique in the world. Modern history presented no evidence that people could rule themselves. Even political philosophers who thought that the people might under some circumstances be able to do so commonly believed that republican forms could only survive on a small scale—and was this not being demonstrated by the behavior of the states? Even worse, it was generally believed in Europe that efforts at popular rule could only eventuate in anarchy and chaos. As Washington paced in perplexity, anarchy and chaos seemed about to overwhelm America. Was it not his patriotic duty, as Hamilton said, to accept the inevitable, as he had so often done on physical battlefields? And what of his ambitions? In a world of kings, why should not George Washington also be a king? He was later to thank the Ruler of the Universe—"the Greatest and Best of Beings"—for having led him "to detest the folly and madness of unbounded ambition."

Yet, when he placed ambition behind him, that only made the situation more "difficult and delicate." The injustices being visited on the army were obvious and no peaceful remedies were in sight. His own investigations revealed that the army was more rebellious than he had realized, and that his leadership was in fact under severe attack. He suspected his old enemy General Gates, who was finally back in active service, of being deep in the intrigue.

It was early March before Washington answered Hamilton's letter. He could not, he wrote, countenance a movement which would be "productive of civil commotions and end in blood." Despite the menace to his own leadership and reputation, "I shall pursue the same steady line of conduct which has governed me hitherto; fully convinced that the sensible and discerning part of the army cannot be unacquainted (although I never took pains to inform them) of the services I have rendered it on more occasions than one."

Washington's letter made it clear that the conspirators would have to proceed independently, either catching him up in the tempest they raised or blowing him aside.

Through the camp at Newburgh, unsigned papers began circulating. One ignored Washington's authority by calling a mass meeting of officers. Another stated that the author had lost faith "in the justice of his country." He urged his fellow soldiers to "suspect the man who would advise to more moderation and further forbearance." If peace should be declared, nothing should separate the army "from your arms but death." If the war continued, "courting the auspices and inviting the direction of your illustrious leader, you will retire to some unsettled country, smile in your turn, and 'mock when their fear cometh on.'"

In a world of kings, why should not George Washington also be a king? He was later to thank the Ruler of the Universe—"the Greatest and Best of Beings"—for having led him "to detest the folly and madness of unbounded ambition."

Washington was himself deeply moved by the anonymous author's emotional description of the soldier's plight—he felt that the "force of expression has rarely been equaled in the English language"—but he believed it his duty "to arrest on the spot the foot that stood wavering on a tremendous precipice, to prevent the officers from being taken by surprise while the passions were all inflamed, and to rescue them from plunging themselves into a gulf of civil horror from which there might be no receding."

The commander in chief expressed "disapprobation of such disorderly proceedings" as the illegally called meeting. He summoned a meeting of his own for the following Saturday, March 15, 1783. This was probably the most important single gathering ever held in the United States. Supposing, as seemed only too possible, Washington should fail to prevent military intervention in civil government?

Just a few hours after the Declaration of Independence was adopted by the Continental Congress on July 4, 1776, the first committee to design a seal for the United States was appointed. After undergoing numerous changes, on June 20, 1782, the seal, as it appears here, was officially adopted.

The commander in chief hinted that he would not appear personally, and thus when he strode on the stage, it was a surprise. And the faces of his gathered officers made it clear that the surprise was not a pleasant one. For the first time since he had won the love of the army, he saw facing him resentment and anger.

As Washington began to speak, he was "sensibly agitated." He talked first of his own early and devoted service, of his love for his soldiers. The faces before him did not soften. He pointed out that the country which the anonymous exhorter wished them to tyrannize over or abandon was their own: "our wives, our children, our farms and other property." As for the exhorter's advice that they should refuse to listen to words of moderation, this would mean that "reason is of no use to us. The freedom of speech may be taken away, and, dumb and silent, we may be led, like sheep, to the slaughter." By now, the audience seemed perturbed, but the anger and resentment had not been dispelled.

Washington then stated that he believed the government would, "despite the slowness inherent in deliberative bodies," in the end act justly. He urged the officers not "to open the floodgates of civil discord, and deluge our rising empire in blood." They should "afford occasion for posterity to say, when speaking of the glorious example you have exhibited to mankind, 'had this day been wanting, the world had never seen the last stage of perfection to which human nature is capable of attaining.'"

Washington had come to the end of his prepared speech, but his audience did not seem truly moved. He clearly had not achieved his end. He remembered he had brought with him a reassuring letter from a congressman. He would read it. He pulled the paper from his pocket, and then something seemed to go wrong. The general seemed confused; he stared at the paper helplessly. The officers leaned forward, their hearts contracting with anxiety. Washington pulled from his pocket something only his intimates had seen him wear: a pair of eyeglasses. "Gentlemen," he said, "you will permit me to put on my spectacles, for I have not only grown gray but almost blind in the service of my country."

This homely act and simple statement did what all Washington's arguments had failed to do. The hardened soldiers wept. Washington had saved the United States from tyranny and civil discord. As Jefferson was later to comment, "The moderation and virtue of a single character probably prevented this Revolution from being closed, as most others have been, by a subversion of that liberty it was intended to establish."

Twenty-Three

GOODBYE TO WAR

(1775–1783)

On April 18, 1783, Washington's general orders announced "the cessation of hostilities between the United States of America and the King of Great Britain." Although the peace treaty had not been signed, the armistice, so Washington continued, "opens the prospect to a more splendid scene, and, like another morning star, promises the approach of a brighter day than hath hitherto illuminated the Western Hemisphere." He congratulated the troops on "the dignified part they have been called to act (under the smiles of Providence) on the stage of human affairs; for happy, thrice happy, shall they be pronounced hereafter who have contributed anything, who have performed the meanest office in erecting this stupendous fabric of Freedom and Empire on the broad basis of Independency; who have assisted in protecting the rights of human nature and establish an asylum for the poor and oppressed of all nations and religions."

Although Washington's praises comprised civilians as well as soldiers, he did not feel warmly towards the financiers who had, as he came increasingly to realize, played a major part in the efforts to induce the army to dictate to the civilian governments. He wrote Hamilton, angrily, "The army . . . is a dangerous instrument to play with." In his appeals to Congress, and through Congress to the nation, that what was owed to the army should be paid, he made no reference to the debts owed the financiers. But concerning his fellow soldiers he was emotional. If they were forced "to wade through the vile mire of despondency and owe 'the miserable remnant of that life to charity which has hitherto been spent in honor,' then I shall have learned what ingratitude is; then I shall have realized a tale which will embitter every moment of my future life."

As lesser verbal artillery gave no indication of ameliorating the situation, Washington decided to send to the states a circular letter which would dig deep into the political fundamentals of the problem. He justified thus stepping out of his military role, and also endowed his words with a special solemnity, by announcing that this was his farewell to public life. Once the final peace permitted him to return to Mount Vernon, he would never again "take any share in public business."

Privately, Washington was already urging such a constitutional convention as would not be convened until five years and much history had passed by. He yearned for a new "federal constitution" which would cut the power of the states down to dealing with primarily local problems. But he realized that this was too radical a suggestion to be included in the circular letter that came to be known as "Washington's Legacy." In this document, he only urged that the Articles of Confederation be interpreted and extended to create a central government adequate to obvious needs. Unless this were achieved, the Americans might "find by our own unhappy experience that there is a natural and necessary progression from the extreme of anarchy to the extreme of tyranny."

Until the armistice was followed by a final treaty, peace was not official. However, Congress decided to send home all of the army except a small force to watch the British troops who were awaiting in New York the final peace. Congress passed resolutions directed at keeping the released soldiers from departing penniless, but resolutions buy nothing and there was no money available. As they prepared to depart with empty pockets, the officers expressed great bitterness at having allowed themselves to be bamboozled by Washington; they canceled a farewell dinner at which he was to be guest of honor. "The sensibility," Washington wrote, "occasioned by a parting scene under such peculiar circumstances will not admit of description."

Despite his yearning to get back to Mount Vernon, Washington decided that his duty would not permit him to abandon the remnant of his army who remained encamped on the Hudson. He had to "wear away," as he wrote, seven months of "this distressing tedium." Some relaxation was supplied by a trip around the northern frontier, where he examined the sites of battles he had not commanded, and a period of attending on Congress, during which he made recommendations for a peacetime military

Called "the most famous map in the history of American diplomacy," this document is variously known as "Mitchell's Map," "the Red-lined Map," and "King George's Map." It was used by British and American peace negotiators in Paris in the fall of 1782 to delineate the boundaries of the original territory that became the United States.

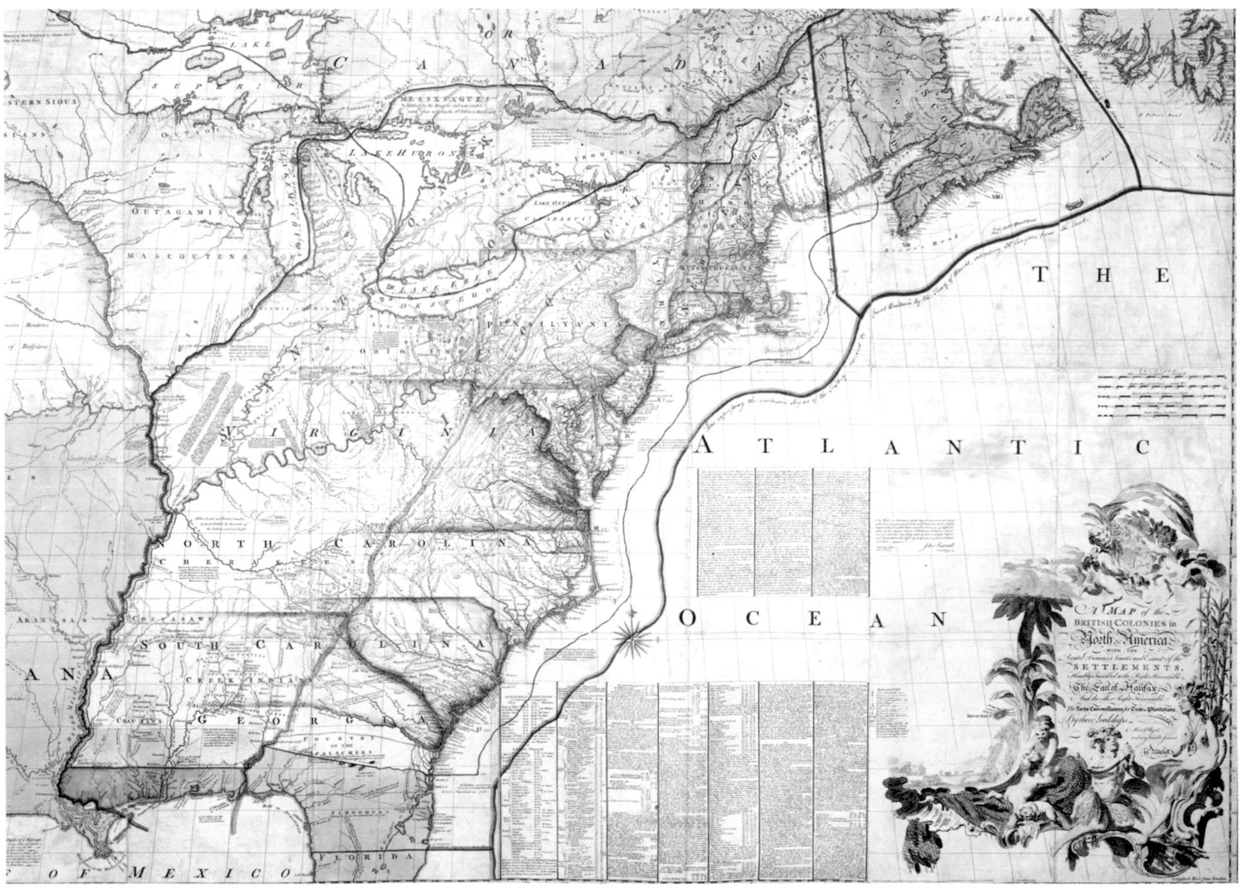

NEW-YORK, November 26.

Last Sunday night arrived the Lord Hyde Packet, in 47 days from Falmouth. From the English papers brought we have extracted the following important ADVICES:

LONDON, September 30.

THE

Definitive Treaty,

Between GREAT-BRITAIN and the UNITED STATES of America, signed at Paris the 3d day of September, 1783.

In the Name of the most holy and undivided Trinity.

IT having pleased the Divine Providence to dispose the hearts of the most serene and most potent prince George the third, by the grace of God, king of Great-Britain, France and Ireland, defender of the faith, duke of Brunswick and Lunenburgh, arch-treasurer and prince elector of the holy Roman empire, &c. and of the United-States of America, to forget all past misunderstandings and differences that have unhappily interrupted the good correspondence and friendship which they mutually wish to restore, and to establish such a beneficial and satisfactory intercourse between the two countries, upon the ground of reciprocal advantages and mutual convenience, as may promote and secure to both perpetual peace and harmony; and having for this desirable end already laid the foundation of peace and reconciliation, by the provisional articles signed at Paris on the 30th of November, 1782, by the commissioners empowered on each part, which articles were agreed to be inserted in, and to constitute the treaty of peace proposed to be concluded between the crown of Great-Britain and the said United States, but which treaty was not to be concluded until terms of peace should be agreed upon between Great-Britain and France, and his Britannic majesty should be ready to conclude such treaty accordingly; and the treaty between Great-Britain and France having since been concluded, his Britannic majesty and the United States of America, in order to carry into full effect the provisional articles above-mentioned, according to the tenor thereof, have constituted and appointed, that is to say, his Britannic majesty on his part, David Hartley, esq. member of the parliament of Great-Britain, and the said United States on their part, John Adams, esq. late a commissioner of the United States of America at the court of Versailles, late delegate in Congress from the state of Massachusetts, and chief justice of the said state, and minister plenipotentiary of the said United States to their high mightinesses the states-general of the United Netherlands; Benjamin Franklin, esq. late delegate in Congress from the state of Pennsylvania, president of the convention of the said state, and minister plenipotentiary from the United States of America at the court of Versailles; and John Jay, esq. late president of Congress, and chief justice of the state of New York, and minister plenipotentiary from the said United States at the court of Madrid, to be the plenipotentiaries for the concluding and signing the present definitive treaty; who, after having reciprocally communicated their respective full powers, have agreed upon and confirmed the following articles:

Art. 1. His Britannic majesty acknowledges the said United States, viz. New-Hampshire, Massachusetts-Bay, Rhode-Island and Providence Plantations, Connecticut, New-York, New-Jersey, Pennsylvania, Delaware, Maryland, Virginia, North Carolina, South Carolina, and Georgia, to be free, sovereign, and independent states; that he treats with them as such, and for himself, his heirs and successors, relinquishes all claims to the government, property, and territorial rights of the same, and every part thereof.

Art. 2. And that all disputes which might arise in future, on the subject of the boundaries of the said United States, may be prevented, it is hereby agreed and declared, that the following are and shall be their boundaries, viz. From the north-west angle of Nova Scotia, viz. that angle which is formed by a line drawn due north from the source of St. Croix river to the Highlands, along the said Highlands, which divide those rivers that empty themselves into the river St. Lawrence, from those which fall into the Atlantic Ocean, to the north-westernmost head of Connecticut-River; thence down along the middle of that river to the forty-fifth degree of north latitude; from thence by a line due west on said latitude, until it strikes the river Irriquois or Cataraqui; thence along the middle of the said river into Lake Ontario; through the middle of the said lake until it strikes the communication by water between that lake and Lake Erie; thence along the middle of said communication into Lake Erie, through the middle of said lake, until it arrives at the water communication between that lake and Lake Huron, thence through the middle of said lake to the water communication between that lake and Lake Superior; thence through Lake Superior, northward of the isles Royal and Phelipeaux to the Long Lake; thence through the middle of said Long Lake and the water communication between it and the Lake of the Woods, to the said lake of the Woods, thence through the said lake to the most north-western point thereof, and from thence on a due west course to the river Mississippi; thence by a line to be drawn along the middle of the said river Mississippi; thence by a line to be drawn along the middle of the said river Mississippi until it shall intersect the northernmost part of the thirty first degree of north latitude. South, by a line to be drawn due east from the determination of the line last mentioned in the latitude of thirty-one degrees north of the equator, to the middle of the river Apalachicola or Catahouche; thence along the middle thereof to its junction with the Flint River; thence strait to the head of St. Mary's River; and thence down along the middle of St. Mary's River to the Atlantic Ocean; east, by a line to be drawn along the middle of the River St. Croix from its mouth in the Bay of Fundy to its source, and from its source directly north to the aforesaid Highlands which divide the rivers that fall into the Atlantic Ocean from those which fall into the River St. Lawrence, comprehending all islands within twenty leagues of any part of the shores of the United States, and lying between lines to be drawn due east from the points where the aforesaid boundaries between Nova Scotia on the one part, and East Florida on the other, shall respectively touch the Bay of Fundy and the Atlantic Ocean, excepting such islands as now are or heretofore have been within the limits of the said province of Nova Scotia.

Art. 3. It is agreed that the people of the United States shall continue to enjoy unmolested the right to take fish of every kind on the Grand Bank, and on all the other banks of Newfoundland, also in the gulph of St. Lawrence, and all other places in the sea, where the inhabitants of both countries used at any time heretofore to fish. And also that the inhabitants of the United States shall have liberty to take fish of every kind on such part of the coast of Newfoundland as British fishermen shall use, (but not to dry or cure the same on that island) and also on the coasts, bays and creeks of all others of his Britannic majesty's dominions in America; and that the American fishermen shall have liberty to dry and cure fish in any of the unsettled bays, harbours and creeks of Nova-Scotia, Magdalen Islands and Labrador, so long as the same shall remain unsettled; but so soon as the same or either of them shall be settled, it shall not be lawful for the said fishermen to dry or cure fish at such settlement, without a previous agreement for that purpose with the inhabitants, proprietors or possessors of the ground.

Art. 4. It is agreed that the creditors on either side shall meet with no lawful impediment to the recovery of the full value, in sterling money, of all bona fide debts heretofore contracted.

Art. 5. It is agreed that Congress shall earnestly recommend it to the legislatures of the respective states, to provide for the restitution of all estates, rights and properties, which have been confiscated, belonging to real British subjects; and also of the estates, rights and properties of persons resident in districts in the possession of his majesty's arms, and who have not borne arms against the said United States: and that persons of any other description shall have free liberty to go to any part or parts of any of the Thirteen United States, and therein to remain twelve months unmolested in their endeavors to obtain the restitution of such of their estates, rights and properties, as may have been confiscated; and that Congress shall also earnestly recommend to the several states a reconsideration and revision of all acts or laws regarding the premises, so as to render the said laws or acts perfectly consistent, not only with justice and equity, but with that spirit of conciliation, which, on the return of the blessings of peace, should universally prevail: and that Congress shall also earnestly recommend to the several states, that the estates, rights and properties of such last mentioned persons shall be restored to them, they refunding to any persons who may be now in possession the bona fide price (where any has been given) which such persons may have paid on purchasing any of the said lands, rights or properties since the confiscation.

And it is agreed, that all persons who have any interest in confiscated lands, either by debts, marriage settlements, or otherwise, shall meet with no lawful impediment in the prosecution of their just rights.

Art. 6. That there shall be no future confiscations made, nor any prosecutions commenced against any person or persons for, or by reason of the part which he or they may have taken in the present war; and that no person shall, on that account, suffer any future loss or damage, either in his person, liberty, or property; and that those who may be in confinement on such charges, at the time of the ratification of the treaty in America, shall be immediately set at liberty, and the prosecutions so commenced be discontinued.

Art. 7. There shall be a firm and perpetual peace between his Britannic majesty and the said states, and between the subjects of the one and the citizens of the other; wherefore all hostilities, both by sea and land, shall from henceforth cease; all prisoners on both sides shall be set at liberty, and his Britannic majesty shall, with all convenient speed, and without causing any destruction, or carrying away any negroes, or other property of the American inhabitants, withdraw all his armies, garrisons and fleets, from the said United States, and from every post, place and harbour, within the same, leaving in all fortifications the American artillery that may be therein; and shall also order and cause all archives, records, deeds and papers belonging to any of the said States, or their citizens, which in the course of the war may have fallen into the hands of his officers, to be forthwith restored, and delivered to the proper state and persons to whom they belong.

Art. 8. The navigation of the river Mississippi, from its source to the ocean, shall for ever remain free and open to the subjects of Great-Britain, and the citizens of the United States.

Art. 9. In case it should so happen that any place or territory belonging to Great Britain, or to the United States, should have been conquered by the arms of either from the other, before the arrival of the said provisional articles in America, it is agreed, that the same shall be restored without difficulty, and without requiring any compensation.

Art. 10. The solemn ratifications of the present treaty, expedited in good and due form, shall be exchanged between the Contracting Parties in the space of six months, or sooner, if possible, to be computed from the day of the signature of the present treaty. In Witness whereof, we the undersigned, their ministers plenipotentiary, have in their name, and in virtue of our full powers, signed with our hands the present Definitive Treaty, and caused the seals of our arms to be affixed thereto.

Done at Paris, this 3d day of September, in the year of our Lord one thousand seven hundred and eighty-three.

(L. S.) JOHN ADAMS,
(L. S.) DAVID HARTLEY,
(L. S.) B. FRANKLIN,
(L. S.) JOHN JAY.

PHILADELPHIA: Printed by David C. Claypoole, in Market-street.

The Treaty of Paris that ended the Revolutionary War between the United States and Great Britain, 1783.

establishment which that powerless legislature was too debilitated to enact.

After the definitive peace had been signed, the British announced that they would evacuate New York on November 25, 1783. For once, Washington was willing to take part in a triumphal procession. However, the parade was ridiculously delayed because the British had, in a final mocking gesture, left their flag flying over Fort George with the halyards cut and the pole greased. Not until an ingenious sailor had mounted the pole and substituted an American flag could Washington consummate victory by advancing down the streets. It was as sad an occasion as a joyful one, for the city was desolate and battered; the few inhabitants who came out to cheer were thin and strained. There was a further wait until the British fleet finally sailed out of the harbor. Then Washington ordered a boat to take him across the Hudson to New Jersey. But first he would say farewell to the few officers still in service and to any others residing in the vicinity.

Congress passed resolutions directed at keeping the released soldiers from departing penniless, but resolutions buy nothing and there was no money available. As they prepared to depart with empty pockets, the officers expressed great bitterness at having allowed themselves to be bamboozled by Washington; they canceled a farewell dinner at which he was to be guest of honor. "

The assurances Washington had given his officers, during that stormy meeting at Newburgh, that they would receive what was due them had, despite his own best efforts, come to nothing. He approached this last parting with a sad and anxious heart. The small group of men who turned as he came in the door of the room at Fraunces Tavern saw that their general's face was working with strong emotion. He walked over to the table where a collation was laid, tried to eat, but failed. He filled a glass of wine and motioned for the decanters to go around. As the officers saw his hand shake and his lip tremble, the bitterness in their hearts was drowned by love. The men who had fought so hard with Washington and suffered so deeply found tears in their eyes. With tears streaming down his own face, Washington embraced each separately, and, then, the height of emotion having become unbearable, walked out of the room.

Washington left New York on December 4. His trip to Annapolis, where Congress was meeting, was clogged by crowds who wished to do him honor. The ceremony before Congress during which he returned his commission was again wet with tears. Then, after almost nine years of service, he was free. As he rode up the circular drive to Mount Vernon, there were candles in the windows. Martha stood in the doorway. It was Christmas Eve.

Debates have raged concerning Washington's ability as a soldier. Writers have contended that he was so incompetent that he would have been defeated

American Commissioners of the Preliminary Peace Negotiations with Great Britain, *unfinished painting by Benjamin West, oil on canvas, sometime between 1783–1819.*

Evacuation Day, an 1879 chromolithograph by Edmund P. and Ludwig Restein, depicts Washington's triumphal entry into New York City on November 25, 1783.

by any other human beings except the dullards the British sent against him. He has been described as an equal of Caesar, Hannibal, Napoleon. The debate has overlooked the fact that Washington was never really a soldier. He was a civilian in arms.

Civilians had always seemed more important to him than soldiers. However, since there was a war, an army was an essential instrument. It should guard and preserve the population to the greatest extent it could. To repel that civilian discouragement which could foster a wavering of loyalty to the cause, the soldiers should seek an impressive record. (Washington often helped the record along with inaccurate dispatches.) Washington further realized that a war won primarily by the force of public opinion would of necessity be a war of attrition, a very long war. He yearned for military victories that would cut the process short. But he knew that victories involving brutality against civilians and thus achieved at the expense of public opinion would, in fact, be defeats.

Washington's belief that the war was more basically a civilian than a military conflict was underlined by chronology. From his assumption of the command to the last battle he led against the main British army was almost exactly three years. From the Battle of Monmouth to the final departure of the British army was four and a half. The second period contained, of course, the largely French-engineered victory at Yorktown. Yet Cornwallis's surrender was not in essence a much more serious defeat than Burgoyne's, and the conditions that had made it possible evaporated with the departure of the French fleet so completely that there was no reason for the British to believe that this enemy triumph could ever be repeated. They would have regarded Yorktown as no more than an unfortunate check were they not being gravely defeated on more

General George Washington Resigning His Commission, *detail, by John Trumbull, oil on canvas, 1824.*

important battlefields. They came to realize the utter hopelessness of conquering a people who had become united against them. Washington's role in fostering this unity had been great.

Washington entered the contest almost as entirely untrained in sophisticated warfare as were his troops. The British and Hessians were very well trained. Until Washington got over fighting European regulars in the conventional manner, the Continental army went down to defeat after defeat. The break came with Trenton and Princeton, when Washington made use of the particular qualities of dedicated soldiers who would march quickly in the face of any hardship; would fight with brilliance individually if not so well in formation; and would exist on nonexistent supplies. These qualities were particularly suited to American economic and political disorganization, which made the loss of even the national capital not crippling, and to the American terrain, which encouraged guerrilla warfare and made formal battles easy to avoid.

Being practically without schooling, Washington had always taught himself from experience. He learned the lessons of the American war all the more readily because he had no conventional lessons to unlearn. The British and the Hessians, on the other hand, suffered the confusion common to acknowledged experts when their expertise ceases to function. Instead of seeking new solutions, they felt they were up against something inexplicable and became increasingly timid. Back in London, another foreseeable reaction took place: if an expert does not deliver as he should, you replace him with another who is expected to apply the accepted rules more effectively. Washington survived four British commanders in chief.

Long before the end of the war, Washington had become much more effective than any of his military opponents. But this did not mean that what he had taught himself would have made him a great general on the battlefields of Europe. Evolved not from theory but from dealing with specific problems, his preeminence was achieved through a Darwinian adaptation to environment. It was the triumph of a man who knows how to learn, not in the narrow sense of studying other people's conceptions, but in the transcendent sense of making a synthesis from the totality of experience.

Among the legacies of the Revolution to the new nation, the most widely recognized and admired was a man: George Washington. He had no rivals. When the war ended, not a single officer was really powerful in the army who had not been elevated and trained by the commander in chief—and who was not loyal to him. In the civilian sphere, no individual had national stature comparable with Washington's. The general had, more than any political figure, served as the nation's chief executive. Yet no continuation of leadership figured in his happy imaginings.

"At length, my dear Marquis," Washington wrote Lafayette, "I am become a private citizen on the banks of the Potomac, and under the shadow of my own vine and my own fig tree. Free from the bustle of a camp and the busy scenes of public life, I am solacing myself with those tranquil enjoyments which the soldier who is ever in pursuit of fame; the statesman whose watchful days and sleepless nights are spent in devising schemes to promote the welfare of his own, perhaps the ruin of other countries (as if this globe was insufficient for all); and the courtier who is always watching the countenance of his prince, in hopes of catching a gracious smile, can have very little conception. I am not only retired from all public employments, but I am retiring within myself, and shall be able to view the solitary walk and tread the paths of private life with heartfelt satisfaction. Envious of none, I am determined to be pleased with all, and this, my dear friend, being the order of my march, I will move gently down the stream of life until I sleep with my fathers."

Twenty-Four

PLEASURES AT HOME

(1783–1787)

After his return to Mount Vernon, Washington wrote that he felt "as I conceive a wearied traveler must do, who after treading many a painful step with a heavy burden on his shoulders is eased . . . and from his housetop is looking back and tracing with a grateful eye the meanders by which he escaped the quicksands and mires which lay in his way, and into which none but the all-powerful guide and disposer of human events could have prevented his falling."

Washington had long visualized that on his retirement, his public career would sink to a source of happy meditation, which would include the knowledge that his countrymen were grateful to him and recognized that he had served them well. Otherwise, everything would be as it had been before the Revolution, when he had been content as a successful planter and neighborhood patriarch.

Yet the man who had for so long been concerned with mighty affairs could not at first relax into the stillness with which he was surrounded. Through the plantation air there came to the physical giant such premonitions of death as he had never felt on the battlefields. "Those trees," George Washington wrote in a vein of poetry not usually accorded to his legend, "which my hands have planted . . . by their rapid growth, at once indicate a knowledge of my declination and their disposition to spread their mantles over me before I go hence to return no more. For this, their gratitude, I will nurture them while I stay." To Lafayette he added that he came from "a short-lived family, and might soon expect to be entombed in the dreary mansions of my fathers. . . . But I will not repine: I have had my day."

Often, when he looked downriver at nighttime and saw darkness where there had been lights, he felt a particularly poignant sense of loss. Belvoir, the mansion of his former friends and patrons, the Fairfaxes, and particularly of his youthful love Sally, had been burned. Although he yearned to have Sally and her husband, who were residing in England, come back, more than a year passed before he could find the fortitude to ride the short, familiar distance to determine the actual condition of their deserted property. Some walls and a chimney still

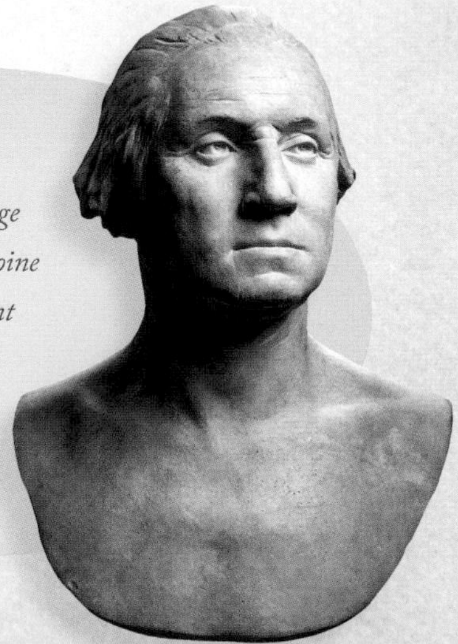

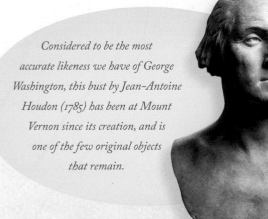

Considered to be the most accurate likeness we have of George Washington, this bust by Jean-Antoine Houdon (1785) has been at Mount Vernon since its creation, and is one of the few original objects that remain.

stood, but "the whole are, or very soon will be, a heap of ruins. . . . When I viewed them, when I considered that the happiest moments of my life had been spent there; when I could not trace a room in the house (now all rubbish) that did not bring to my mind the recollection of pleasing scenes, I was obliged to fly from them with painful sensations, and sorrowing for the contrast."

Washington's defense against melancholy remained movement. As soon as the initial exhaustion of war passed from him, he burst into multitudinous action. He assumed simultaneously the roles of expansive host, family and neighborhood patriarch, farmer, agricultural experimenter, landscape architect, interior decorator, merchandiser, landlord, exploiter of western lands, builder of roads and canals.

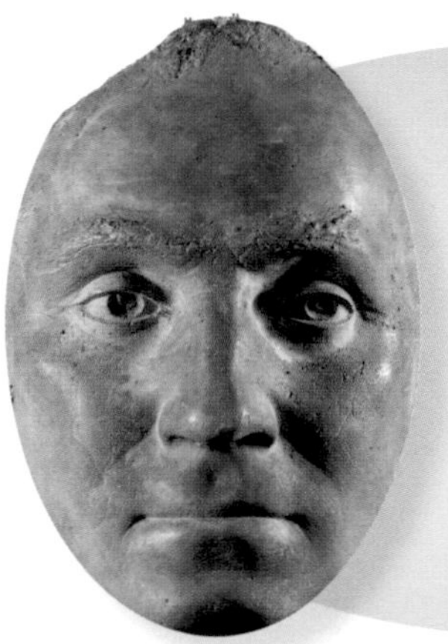

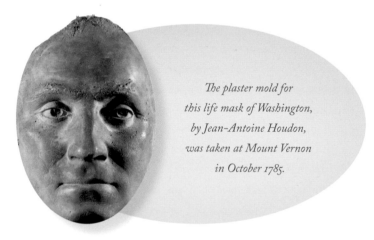

The plaster mold for this life mask of Washington, by Jean-Antoine Houdon, was taken at Mount Vernon in October 1785.

Mount Vernon had irrevocably become with his return more than a private house. Not only was it the habitat of the most conspicuous actor in the most conspicuous contemporary event of the Western world, but, since Congress was now altogether secondary to the state governments, the United States had no national capitol to vie with Washington's home as the most prestigious building in the nation. People flowed up the driveway in a flood, and, the nearest inn being several hours' ride away, Washington felt obliged to house many visitors over at least one night.

He rarely wrote any of his old military companions without including an invitation to Mount Vernon. Strangers appeared with letters, those from Europe often gimlet-eyed with a desire to describe Washington and his way of life in travel books. There were unexpected visitors of obvious importance, and others who had no auspices, but whom Washington considered it inhospitable to turn away. When a military-appearing Frenchman marched in with high claims and no papers, Washington suspected (history reveals correctly) that the visitor was an impostor, but he nonetheless entertained him for two nights.

Artists came, eager to take likenesses of the world's most famous man; they could make and sell innumerable copies. Since Washington hated to sit still and was embarrassed at being stared at, serving the painters was unpleasant enough. The sculptors were worse; part of their technique was to make "life masks" by smearing plaster over Washington's features and allowing it to harden as the hero lay flat on his back and breathed through tubes placed in his nostrils. Believing that "to encourage literature and the arts is a duty which every good citizen owes to his country," Washington was docile.

Washington, indeed, felt a responsibility towards anyone who came to him. This was well exemplified when a ragged New Englander with a wild face appeared and announced himself as "John Fitch, Inventor of Steamboats." As Fitch contended that he alone knew how to make boats move against wind and current, he saw on Washington's face "some agitations of mind that was not expressed." He stopped in mid-speech to ask whether his plans competed with the schemes of a Virginia boatbuilder named James Rumsey. Washington knew that Rumsey was also speculating on the possibilities of using steam—but he had promised to keep Rumsey's confidences secret.

Fitch had no claim on Washington and was clearly not a gentleman. The obvious move was to be evasive and then see the uninvited caller to the door. But

Tobias Lear, private secretary to Washington. After some initial misgivings about his employer, Lear wrote that he had had "occasions to be with him in every situation in which a man is placed in his family . . . and I declare that I have never found a single thing that could lessen my respect for him."

this Washington could not do. He went into another room and puzzled to work out some way that he could satisfy Fitch without betraying Rumsey. When he finally concluded that there was no way, he loaded the intruder with invitations to stay for dinner, to spend the night. But Fitch departed in a fury and for the rest of his life expressed hatred for Washington.

Mount Vernon had a large resident population. The Washingtons had taken in, on John Parke Custis's death, Martha's two youngest grandchildren: George Washington Parke Custis (Little Washington) and Eleanor Parke Custis (Nelly). Martha absorbed herself in their activities and welfare with an intensity which made her husband all the more painfully conscious that he had no children of his own. Relations of both Martha's and George's stayed for months or years because it was convenient, because they were sick or poor. Extending into Washington's presidency was his concern that his niece Harriot (whose father, Samuel Washington, had died bankrupt) would ruin her best clothes either by wearing them perpetually or by wadding them up in a pile on the floor.

After several false starts, Washington found an efficient secretary. A self-reliant Yankee, Tobias Lear was at first afraid that his famous employer would try to dominate him into "servility," and was then hurt by what he considered Washington's "reserve and coldness." However, when Washington got over what Lear now decided had only been caution and prudence, he "drew me towards him by every tender and endearing tie." After two years, Lear wrote that he had had "occasions to be with him in every situation in which a man is placed in his family—have ate and drank with him constantly, and almost every evening played at cards with him, and I declare that I have never found a single thing that could lessen my respect for him. A complete knowledge of his honesty, uprightness, and candor in all his private transactions have sometime led one to think him more than a man."

Visitors, family, secretary—all these left Washington, the endlessly gregarious, lonely for an intimate friend. He invited his former military aide David Humphreys for an indefinite visit: "The only stipulations I shall contend for are that in all things you shall do as you please—I will do the same—and that no ceremony may be used or any restraint be imposed on anyone." Washington added, "My manner of living is plain. I do not mean to be put out of it. A glass of wine and a bit of mutton are always ready, and such as will be content to partake of them are welcome. Those who expect more will be disappointed, but no change will be affected by it."

Although Mount Vernon could have been contained more than twenty times in a great English country house, and guests had to sleep three or four to what we would today consider a small room, Washington's "manner of living" was not, according to American standards, "plain." The mansion house was finely furnished, if more simply than its English counterparts. Humphreys noted, "Whether there be company or not, the table is always prepared by its elegance and exuberance for their reception."

Dinner was served at two in the afternoon. Washington commonly ate only a single dish but drank half

a pint of Madeira. If the company was agreeable, he would sit "an hour after dinner in familiar conversation and convivial hilarity." Towards evening, he drank "one small glass of punch, a draught of beer, and two dishes of tea." Although a "very elegant" supper was served to his guests, he did not usually appear, and went to bed at nine. However, if intimate friends or men with interesting news arrived towards evening, Washington would come to the supper table. Then he would drink several glasses of champagne, get "quite merry," and "laugh and talk . . . a great deal."

The high point of grandeur at Mount Vernon was the two-story banquet hall, which Washington, always his own architect, had designed before he rode off to the Revolution. Finishing the interior was now one of his many concerns. His desire to have the walls decorated, according to the latest taste, with designs worked in stucco, inspired a long-frustrating search for suitably accomplished workmen, but in the end he achieved much of the result he desired. Although the banquet hall is not one of America's great rooms, it has delicacy and lightness, and blends high spirits with decorum.

Many more strangers impinged on Washington through the mails than through actual visits. He complained that he was bothered concerning a thousand "matters with which I ought not to be troubled more than the Great Mogul," but he believed that every correspondent had a right to a courteous answer.

Washington was amused when one of his Philadelphia friends, Francis Hopkinson, dedicated to him *Seven Songs for the Harpsichord,* although he could "neither sing one of the songs nor raise a single note on any instrument." Washington philosophized to Hopkinson, "We are told of the amazing powers of music in ancient times. . . . The poets of old (whatever they may do in these days) were strangely addicted to the marvelous; and if I before *doubted* the truth of their relations with respect to the power of music, I am now fully convinced of their falsity, because I would not, for the honor of my country, allow that we are left by the ancients at an immeasurable distance in everything; and if they could soothe the ferocity of wild beasts, could draw the trees and stones after them, and could even charm the powers of Hell by their music, I am sure that your productions would have had at least virtue enough in them (without the aid of voice or instrument) to melt the ice of the Delaware and Potomac, and in that case you should have had an earlier acknowledgment of your favor of the first of December."

Since Washington had never missed an opportunity to buy or rent land contiguous to Mount Vernon, the property was now huge: it stretched for some ten miles along the Potomac and penetrated inland at its widest point for about four. There were now five distinct farms, each with its own overseer and work force. These were separated by extensive areas of scrub growth, which testified to the poorness of the soil by producing little wood substantial enough for fencing. Almost every morning except Sunday, Washington rode the circuit of these farms.

As he had in the army, he arose early, with dawn in midsummer, in other seasons, by candlelight. He shaved himself, but his valet, Will, brushed his long hair, pulling it back tightly in a "military manner" (no curls at the side) and tying the queue with a ribbon. Washington kept busy around the house until seven o'clock, when he finally had breakfast: "three small Indian hoecakes (buttered) and as many dishes of tea (without cream)." Then he was off on his horse, moving at a canter, for he liked to ride quickly.

Opposite: The East Front of Mount Vernon *(top) and* The West Front of Mount Vernon *(bottom) by Edward Savage, oil on canvas, c. 1787–1792. These works are the earliest known eyewitness views of the house and grounds.* The East Front *portrays the bucolic setting of the mansion, while* The West Front, *with the circular driveway in the foreground, captures the bustle of everyday life.*

He seems never to have tired of the innumerable small details of farming. Not only did he supervise what every work gang was doing in every field, but he later relived each happening by recording it extensively in one of his journals. Jefferson was to comment that these notations occupied the leisure time that a more bookish man would devote to reading.

Washington wrote that of all occupations, he found "agricultural pursuits and rural amusements . . . most congenial with my temper."

As before, Washington was concerned with agricultural experimentation. He copied out long passages from English agricultural journals, but when asked to contribute to one, refused on the grounds that for such an amateur as he that would be "ostentation." The major reforms he tried to work out for his neighbors were the growing of grass specifically for grazing (cows were then normally let loose to forage in the woods, which meant that they could not be milked nor could their manure be collected as fertilizer); the establishment of economic wool production through a superior line of sheep; the development of fertilizers indigenous to Virginia (that fertilizers might be manufactured chemically was a revolutionary idea that came to Washington as a bizarre surprise); the invention of a method of rotating crops that would replenish the fertility of the fields; and the founding of a line of supermules.

Washington's adventures with the mules have, despite their comic side, been taken with great seriousness by equine historians, who state that the jackasses he imported underpinned the whole race of mules still prevalent in the South. (A mule, itself sterile, is the offspring of an ass and a mare.)

The origins of the drama were, on the one hand, Washington's desire to secure from Spain, although such export was forbidden, a highborn jackass; and, on the other hand, the desire of the king of Spain to keep, through his possession of Louisiana, American frontiersmen from using the Mississippi as a trading outlet to the world. The Spanish foreign office decided that it would be advantageous to sweeten the disposition of the most influential American, and the king personally made Washington a present of two otherwise unprocurable jackasses.

Only one jack survived the ocean crossing. Washington was greatly excited by the news that he had landed in Boston. The former commander in chief planned the donkey's march overland to Mount Vernon as carefully as he had ever planned a military campaign. In order to have waiting a large harem of mares, he deprived his Arabian stallion, Magnolio.

On his arrival, Royal Gift (as Washington named the jackass) revealed a most impressive physique. But when a mare was placed in his paddock, he sniffed her and turned disdainfully away. After he had proved no more stimulated by a succession of equine charmers, Washington was torn between the suspicion that the Spanish king had played a trick on him by sending an impotent beast and amusement at the ridiculous denouement of his expectations. He wondered whether the jackass was, as a king's former favorite, too great a snob to have anything to do with plebeian American horses; or whether, like a true courtier, he based his behavior on that of his former master, who was too old to respond with alacrity to "female allurements." Washington commented that His Most Catholic Majesty surely could not "proceed with more deliberation and majestic solemnity to the act of procreation."

That Royal Gift proceeded at all was due to a ruse that Washington finally worked out. He would tantalize the jackass with a female of his own species, and when the royal beast was excited, quickly remove

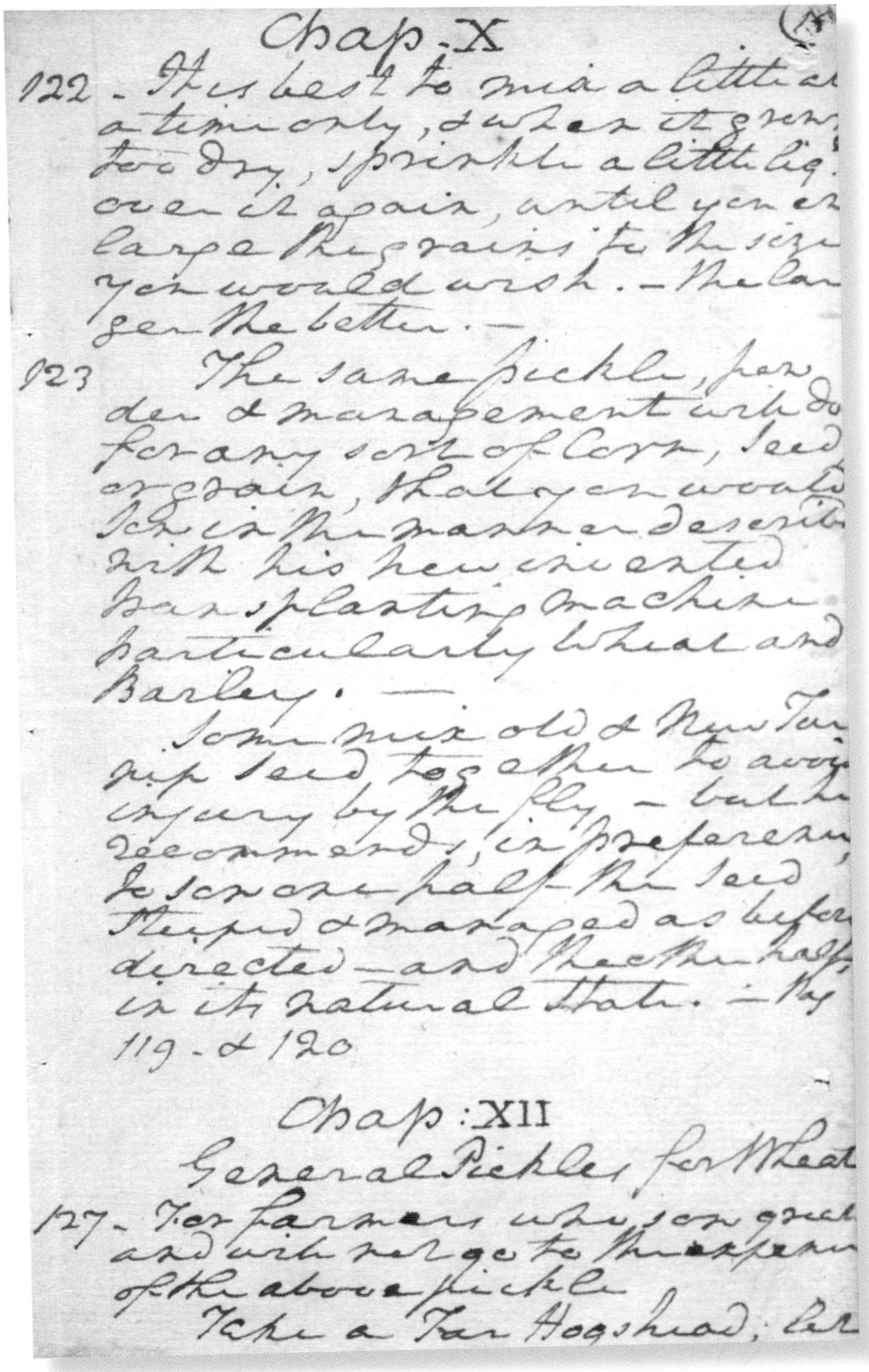

Chap. X

122 - It is best to mix a little at a time only, & when it grows too dry, sprinkle a little liq[uor] over it again, until you enlarge the grains to the size you would wish. — The larger the better. —

123 The same pickle, powder & management will do for any sort of Corn, Seed or grain, that you would sow in the manner describ[ed] with his new invented transplanting machine particularly Wheat and Barley. —

Some mix old & New Turnip seed together to avoid injury by the fly — but he recommends, in preference, to sow one half the seed steeped & managed as before directed — and the other half in its natural state. — Pag 119 - & 120

Chap: XII

General Pickles for Wheat

127 - For farmers who sow great and wish not go to the expense of the above pickle

Take a Tar Hogshead; ...

Washington had some revolutionary ideas about agriculture. This page features his handwritten notes on Charles Varlo's A New System of Husbandry, *published in 1785.*

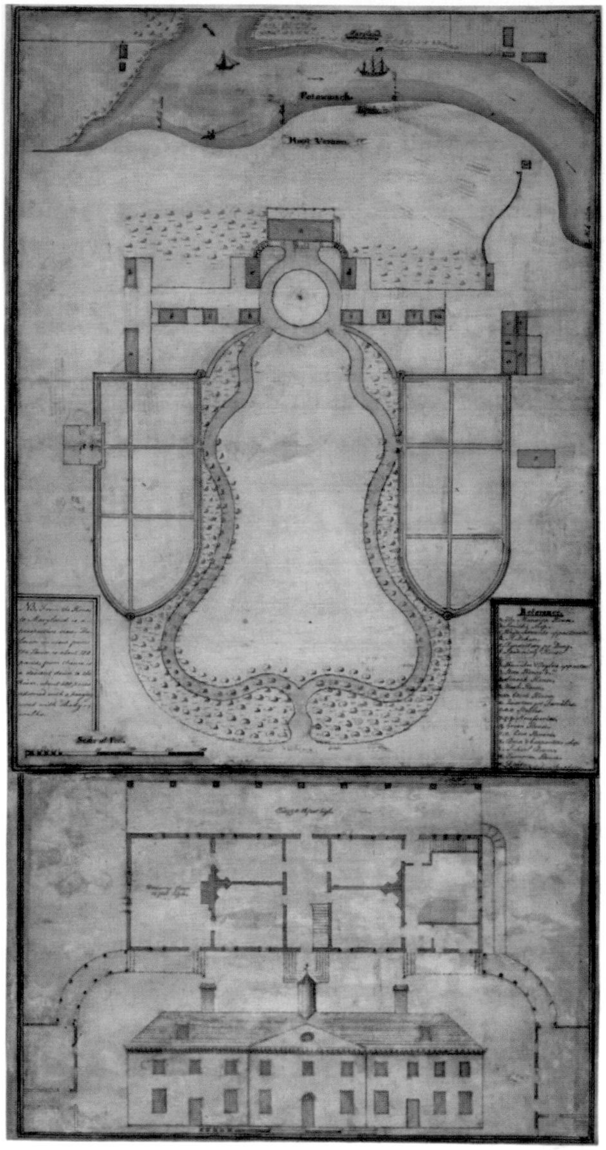

Plan of Mount Vernon *by Samuel Vaughan, ink and watercolor on laid paper, 1787.*

the donkey and substitute a mare. Upon occasion, the jackass was allowed to finish with the donkey, which produced younger jackasses whom Washington sent touring the countryside to his own profit and the great improvement of the mules in each region. He intended, he announced, to hitch only mules to the elegant coach which had been given Martha by the government of Pennsylvania. Mrs. Washington seems quietly to have warded off this enthusiasm.

Washington wrote that of all occupations, he found "agricultural pursuits and rural amusements . . . most congenial with my temper." As in the case of the mules, it was hard to determine where serious pursuits ended and play began. He was still much concerned with breeding horses and hounds, with races and hunts, with landscaping and with gardening for aesthetic as well as practical ends. It is indeed surprising how various and extensive were the hobbies Washington engaged in at times like this, when the pressure of great events allowed him leisure. Guests noted how much more cheerful he seemed than in the military camps, how much more relaxed. His stepgrandson was to write that his retirement after the Revolution was the happiest period of Washington's life.

Twenty-Five

CANALS AND CONVENTIONS

(1783–1787)

On Washington's return from the Revolution, he found his business records in utter disorder. They had been scrambled by being hastily moved on the several occasions when Mount Vernon had been in danger of being burned by the British. Washington was now full of good resolutions to determine, by sorting the papers, his overall financial situation. During the summers, he stated he would do it in the winter when his farms were less demanding. In the winters, he preferred doing other things.

Finally, his new secretary, Lear, discovered that during the war Washington had lost at least ten thousand pounds sterling. This was in part because he had felt it his duty to back the prestige of the Continental currency by accepting payment of old debts in new paper that actually represented only a fraction of the value; in part, because he had been reimbursed in an unsatisfactory manner for many of his military expenditures. He had himself paid not only his own expenses but often those of the whole headquarters operation. At moments of crisis, he had advanced money for various other military needs from his own pocket. After he had presented his expense account, Congress, being as always short of cash, had met much of what they owed with certificates of indebtedness. Subsequently, like many another government creditor, Washington had raised cash by selling certificates, at a great discount, to speculators.

Washington's current finances were in a serious situation because the Mount Vernon plantation was losing money. Births in his slave quarters, combined with his unwillingness to sell any slaves, had resulted in an uneconomically large labor force. The official entertaining forced on him, combined with his private entertaining and his unwillingness to do anything in a haphazardly manner, ran him into great expense. Finding himself chivied by bill collectors, he complained that his previous experience had never taught him how "to parry a dun."

Various governmental bodies expressed eagerness to come to Washington's assistance. However, he remained determined to receive no reward for his military service except gratitude. He would not even accept public help towards his official entertaining. When Virginia forced a gift on him, he announced that he would devote it to a public charity.

The relinquishment that undoubtedly came hardest to Washington was of the bounties in western lands which were voted to veterans; his share, as commander in chief, would have been tremendous. And he had by no means lost his lust for western lands.

Those he had amassed before the Revolution were now his best hope for meeting his annual deficit. He offered his acres for rent or for sale, making in September 1784 a trip across the mountains to see what he could achieve by being himself on the ground. The area around the Forks of the Ohio (now Pittsburgh), which he had first known as a howling wilderness, was filling up with settlers. This created economic possibilities, but what he saw also inspired political fears. The new inhabitants were to a considerable extent immigrants who had "no particular predilection" towards the United States.

Beyond the Alleghenies, the Ohio-Mississippi river system offered the only method, according to the transportation possibilities of those days, by which bulky farm products could be moved away for sale. Rising in British Canada and disgorging through French Louisiana, the liquid highways bypassed the existing states. If, in their search for commercial outlets, the settlers allied themselves with England or Spain, they might, Washington wrote, become extremely dangerous neighbors to the United States. And they stood, "as it were on a pivot. The touch of a feather would turn them any way."

Fortunately (in Washington's opinion) both European powers were keeping their ends of the waterway closed out of a desire to stifle migration across the Alleghenies which they felt would change the western balance of power to the advantage of the United States. An opportunity was thus presented which Washington felt ought not to be lost. To cement relations between the frontier and the older settlements, the trade of the West should be quickly—before either England or Spain became wiser and changed her policy—drawn eastward over the mountains and through the older United States.

This new vision overlapped a plan Washington had formerly developed for his own economic advantage and that of his neighborhood. During his young manhood, in peace and in war, Washington had wandered the Potomac to its headwaters and had gone on over the mountains to where other waterways flowed downward to the Ohio River system. If the rivers were to be made navigable to high points that could be joined by a short wagon road, the trade of the West would be induced to move along the Potomac. At the fall line, where ocean navigation ceased, all goods would be transshipped from canal boats to larger vessels. The community at the fall line was Alexandria, Mount Vernon's near neighbor, for which Washington as a youthful surveyor had made the first town plan. Alexandria would become (as New York was actually to do with the opening of the Erie Canal) the metropolis of the United States.

Before the Revolution, Washington had secured approval from the Virginia legislature for a stock company that would improve the navigation of the river and then charge tolls. But, since Maryland was on the Potomac's north bank, the approval of that state was also necessary. The opposition of the Baltimore merchants, who saw their city bypassed, had then proved invincible.

Washington was hardly back from the Revolution when he received a letter from Jefferson warning that unless Virginia got moving at once, New York might engross the western trade with her own canal. If Washington would put his prestige behind a revival of the Potomac plan, "what a monument to your retirement it would become!" Washington did not have to be urged twice. He undertook the leadership of the Potomac Canal project in a manner that made Madison comment, "The earnestness with which he espouses the undertaking is hardly to be described, and shows that a mind like his, capable of great views and which has long been occupied with them, cannot bear a vacancy."

Washington's prestige was now so great that it overran the opposition of the Baltimore merchants: the Potomac Canal Company was chartered by both Maryland and Virginia. When in 1784 Washington went west to attend to his landholdings, he spent many happy days exploring to find the shortest and most practical connection between the eastward- and the westward-flowing rivers. However, final determi-

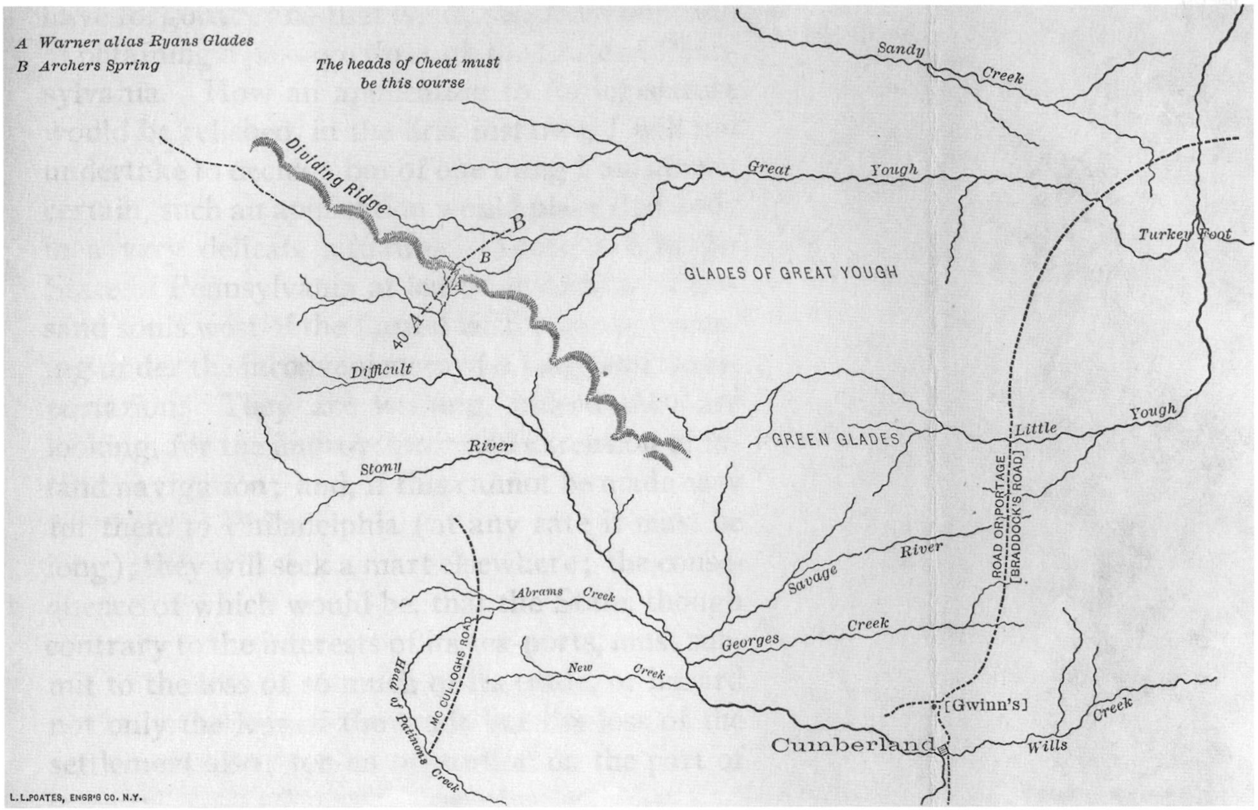

A map of the area between the Potomac and Youghiogheny rivers created by Washington in September 1784, as published in 1905 in Washington and the West.

nation of that matter could wait; the immediate needs were to raise the necessary capital and then open the Potomac to navigation.

Although free capital was extremely scarce in the United States, Washington's name lured so many investors that twice the required shares of stock were sold. But the physical river presented very serious problems.

Conventional canal engineering created on one bank of a natural waterway what was in effect an aquatic flight of stairs. The steps were level ditches, each extending as far as the lay of the land allowed, and flanked by paths for the horses that towed the boats along. The boats were carried from step to step by locks, walled pits in which the water level was raised or lowered. Such engineering was well suited to the short distances and not-too-precipitous terrain of well-settled Europe, but the Potomac was a mountain river that would have to be opened for two hundred miles. In its craggy banks, ditches could be dug only at great expense, and the ground dropped so sharply that the proliferation of locks would be murderously expensive. Furthermore, the river was subject to tumultuous floods inclined to lick any works down off the banks. The problem was, indeed, as new to canal building as the American terrain had been to conventional warfare. Washington had won the war by improvising and he intended to build his canal the same way.

Washington admitted that locks would be needed to get around the Great Falls and that a European engineer would probably have to be imported to design them. For the rest, he intended merely to clear the best channel of all impediments. This meant that the often tremendously swift current would not be conquered. Some novel way would have to be found to propel boats upstream.

Washington was wringing his brains when he met that inventor of mechanical boats, James Rumsey. In a burst of wild enthusiasm, Washington concluded that Rumsey would solve his problem by one scheme or another, perhaps through his projected use of steam. Should Rumsey's propellants all fail, capstans set in rocks at suitable intervals could be turned by horses to pull boats against the current.

A tackle box, 1760–1800, probably made in England. Washington enjoyed fishing both as a gentleman's contemplative recreation and as a practical means of securing provisions while on the frontier. His diary records successful catches of a dolphin and shark in Barbados, a legendary catfish in the Ohio Country, and trout and perch during the recess of the Constitutional Convention in the hot summer of 1787. The contents of this tackle box—including handwrought hooks, horsehair and silk fishing lines, and wax for preparing the lines—provide a rare glimpse of the tackle typically used by fishermen in colonial America.

As Rumsey pottered with his inventions and labored, on being appointed the official engineer, to clear the roaring channel, Washington labored to clear away various governmental problems. In so doing, he did much to set the stage for the Constitutional Convention.

Washington's promise to his officers that he would do all in his power to procure what was owed them was in effect a promise that he would labor to promote a national government powerful enough to pay its debts. That the advice he had given in his so-called "legacy" concerning the strengthening of the Union was not immediately heeded did not immediately worry him. He considered it only natural that the states, like heirs just come into an inheritance, would (as he himself had done with the money that had come to him from his marriage) squander for a while. Yet surely the American people would soon reform themselves since "there is virtue at the bottom." In the meanwhile, conspicuous abuses were to be welcomed as well as deplored; they would clearly demonstrate the need for better governmental organization. "The people," Washington believed, "must feel before they will see; consequently, are brought slowly into measures of public utility."

This attitude allowed Washington to relax into the joys of retirement. But he became increasingly disturbed. The movement he had confidently expected towards sound government and national unity was failing to develop. The Continental Congress was so neglected by the states that there were rarely enough delegates present to make a quorum. New York violated the Articles of Confederation by making a private treaty, to her own advantage, with the Indians. Various states, rather than compel voters to pay prewar debts to British merchants, violated the peace treaty in a way which the British used to justify their own refusal to evacuate frontier forts that had been surrendered to the United States. When the British passed customs laws discriminatory against American shipping, the United States could not retaliate since the states would permit no central customs authority; New York, for instance, wanted no interference with her own laws that milked Connecticut and New Jersey. And the state governments tended to remain rudimentary, following

Europe was fascinated with the much-lauded American general, and this portrait by Michel Bounieu, after a Charles Willson Peale painting owned by Lafayette, was one of the first likenesses of Washington to circulate there. Later printings corrected the spelling of his name.

This iconic image of Benjamin Franklin by Joseph Siffred Duplessis, detail, c. 1785, is still featured on the American 100-dollar bill.

the whims of the majority to a neglect of minority rights. Minorities, sometimes frontiersmen, sometimes the urban prosperous, were so displeased that the gates seemed to be opening to what Washington had long dreaded: class conflict.

Writing privately, Washington mourned, "We have probably had too good an opinion of human nature in forming our confederation. Experience has taught us that men will not adopt and carry into execution measures the best calculated for their own good, without the intervention of a coercive power. I do not conceive we can exist long as a nation without having lodged somewhere a power which will pervade the whole Union."

However, he had no conscious intention of intervening.

The development of inland navigation necessarily violated state boundaries. Washington's passionate predilection for the Potomac project—he bored visitors to Mount Vernon with statistics to prove its superiority to all other possible canal routes—did not keep him from foreseeing a centrally planned system of canals and improved rivers that would go everywhere, bringing "navigation almost to every man's door." In the meanwhile, Pennsylvania's cooperation had to be secured if the Potomac Canal were to have connections with the Ohio. And the innumerable issues involved in administering waters on which both states abutted brought Maryland and Virginia together in what came to be known as the Mount Vernon Conference. The delegates agreed that their states should meet annually "for keeping up harmony in the commercial relations."

When ratifying the decisions that Washington had presided over at Mount Vernon (although he was not officially a delegate), Maryland decided to invite Pennsylvania and Delaware to the annual conferences. Virginia thereupon proposed a conference of all thirteen states "to consider how far a uniform system in their commercial regulations may be necessary to their common interest and their permanent harmony." This resulted in the Annapolis Convention, which met in that Maryland city during September 1786. Preserving his private role, Washington did not attend the convention, but he expressed a wish that more than commercial relations be considered. Only five of the thirteen states sent delegates, yet they took the bold step of calling another convention to meet in Philadelphia and "render the Constitution of the federal government adequate to the exigencies of the Union."

The meeting thus summoned has gone down in history as the Constitutional Convention. But no one could then have called it that, since no one knew that it would write a new constitution. It was, indeed, not authorized to do so. In agreeing to the call, the

Continental Congress had provided that the convention was merely to revise the Articles of Confederation.

There was much reason to foresee that the new convention would only be one more abortive move in the long vain effort to find national unity. Washington feared that the maneuver might actually do harm by chalking up another failure. "We are certainly in a delicate situation," he wrote, "but my fear is that the people have not yet been sufficiently *misled* to retract from error."

Washington's promise to his officers that he would do all in his power to procure what was owed them was in effect a promise that he would labor to promote a national government powerful enough to pay its debts.

Late in 1786, a crisis developed which seemed so menacing that Washington wondered whether all efforts to strengthen the government might not be, in fact, too late. Dislocations in the currency of Massachusetts (each state had its own financial system) had created a situation where many western settlers could not, however hard and effectively they worked, secure cash with which to pay their debts. Farms were seized and the owners sometimes thrown into debtor's prison. In what came to be known (after its leader, Daniel Shays) as Shays's Rebellion, mobs arose, terrified courts that might foreclose on their property, and, as they milled around, threatened to capture the Continental arsenal at Springfield, where there were "ten to fifteen thousand stands of arms in excellent condition." Reports came in to Washington that, if the insurgents joined with people of similar sentiment in the western counties of adjoining states, they would constitute a body of twelve to fifteen thousand men well suited to fighting, a larger force than Washington had commanded during much of the Revolution. Secretary of War Knox, who had been sent by the Continental Congress to investigate, wrote Washington that the object of the uprising was to drown all debts in a flood of paper money. The argument was that all property had been saved from British domination by all the people and it thus belonged to all. According to Knox, the insurgents insisted that anyone who opposed this doctrine "ought to be swept from off the face of the earth."

To historical hindsight, the most amazing thing about this still-minor insurrection (which was to prove little more than an anguished protest) was the terror into which it threw almost all responsible leaders, including those whom modern historians classify as being on the political left. The explanation was that Americans had long been worried by the reiterated prophecy, standard in Europe, that government by the people could have only one outcome: anarchy. And it was a too-obvious fact that, if Shays's Rebellion really spread, there was no power in the United States capable of putting it down. The Continental Congress could not hope to raise an army since it had no way of paying the troops.

Washington was in despair. Had someone warned him, when he retired from the army, "that at this day, I should see such a formidable rebellion against the laws and constitutions of our own making . . . I should have thought him a bedlamite, a fit subject for a madhouse." He had believed that the British and the Tories judged the republican institutions "from the depravity of their own hearts," but now he feared that perhaps they were "wiser than others." He cried out, "What, gracious God, is man that there should be such inconsistency and perfidiousness in his conduct?"

An institution from the days of the Newburgh Addresses, when Washington had risked his command to stop the potentially "fascist" alliance of army officers and financiers, had remained active into the time of Shays's Rebellion. As the officers had prepared angrily to go home unpaid, they had organized the Society of the Cincinnati. Washington, assured that the society was a charitable organization aimed at ameliorating the hardships into which the deprived officers might fall, had gratefully accepted the post of president-general. But no sooner was he back at Mount Vernon that it was charged that the Cincinnati was actually an effort to graft a hereditary aristocracy on the United States.

When Washington reread the charter, now suspiciously, he saw there were dangerous provisions: membership was to pass, like titles in Europe, by primogeniture, and there were clauses that would permit the expansion of the society by the election of nonmilitary citizens. To make this seem all the more ominous, the Cincinnati was the only important organization in addition to the Continental Congress that extended across all the thirteen states.

At the first convention of the Cincinnati, in 1784, Washington had fought hard to have the provisions that had any political bearing removed. When it seemed that he had succeeded, he accepted reelection as president-general. But the state societies managed to veto what had been passed by the national meeting. And now, in 1786, Shays's Rebellion coincided with the appointed time for the next national meeting. Here was an opportunity to fight fire from the left with at least the threat of fire from the right. But Washington refused to countenance the meeting of the organization which had refused to become apolitical. He announced that he would not go. As a result, the Cincinnati's meeting was poorly attended and came to little.

Shays's Rebellion also petered out. The insurgents, when faced with a small, privately financed Massachusetts force, decided to have recourse to the ballot box (which was to serve them well). But, since national vulnerability had been demonstrated, national fright went on. Madison, for instance, foresaw the development of a more "awful crisis." Support for the convention to strengthen the government sprang up all over the land.

When it had seemed probable that the convention would not amount to much, there had been little pressure on Washington to take part. Regarding the weight of his influence as perhaps their greatest asset, the supporters of strong federal government did not want to squander that asset on what might be an inconclusive move. But as a result of the new developments, Washington was strongly urged to abandon his retirement and head the Virginia delegation. This put Washington into such a quandary that his health, which had been perfect since his return to Mount Vernon, broke down. The "fever and ague" (malaria?) from which he had suffered as a young man returned in a "violent attack," and he was afflicted with such rheumatism that he could hardly turn over in bed.

Washington was assured that his attendance at the convention could be an isolated act from which he would return unperturbed to his retirement. But he had little doubt that his desire "to view the solitary walk" would be for years frustrated. His only rival as the most conspicuous man at the convention would be Benjamin Franklin. Since Franklin was eighty-one years old, the leadership would surely fall on Washington. If (as still seemed very possible) the convention failed, the reputation for which he had so painfully labored would be grievously damaged. (He stated frankly that he felt he had more to lose than delegates who were less famous.) And if the convention did, under his leadership, establish a stronger government, he would be committed to doing everything in his power to help that government succeed.

SHAYS'S REBELLION

A PEOPLE'S INSURRECTION

Daniel Shays

Job Shattuck

IN 1786, DESPERATE AND DEBT-RIDDEN FARMERS in western Massachusetts, crippled by the economic depression that followed the Revolution, petitioned the state senate to issue paper money and to halt foreclosure of mortgages on their properties. They knew that they faced imprisonment if they couldn't come up with the money to pay the sky-high land taxes.

Sentiment was particularly high against the commercial interests that controlled the state senate in Boston, and the lawyers who hastened the farmers' bankruptcy by their exorbitant fees for litigation. When the senate failed to undertake reform, armed insurgents in the Berkshire Hills and the Connecticut Valley under the leadership of Daniel Shays and others, like Job Shattuck, began to barricade the county courts, preventing them from deciding cases against the debtors. In September, they forced the state supreme court at Springfield to adjourn.

Early in 1787, Governor James Bowdoin appointed General Benjamin Lincoln to lead a brigade of 4,400 men against the rebels—but before the troops could arrive at Springfield, soldiers already stationed there repelled an attack on the federal arsenal. Losing several men, the rebels dispersed and Lincoln's troops pursued them to Petersham, where they were finally routed.

Shays escaped to Vermont. Most of the rebels were pardoned almost immediately, and Shays was finally pardoned in June 1788. Still, the importance of the Shays's Rebellion must be recognized: it influenced Massachusetts's ratification of the U.S. Constitution and swept Bowdoin out of office for good.

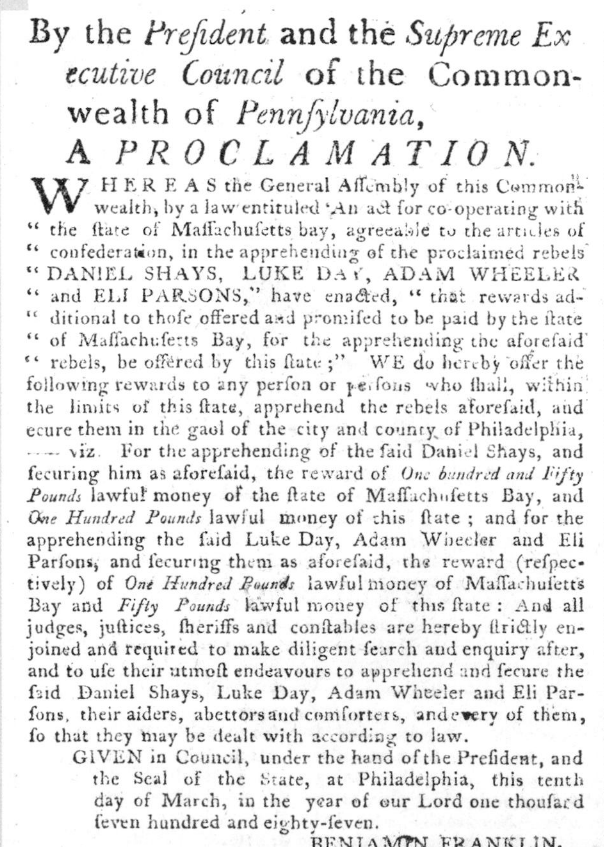

By the *Preſident* and the *Supreme Executive Council* of the Commonwealth of *Pennſylvania*,

A *PROCLAMATION.*

WHEREAS the General Aſſembly of this Commonwealth, by a law entituled "An act for co-operating with "the ſtate of Maſſachuſetts bay, agreeable to the articles of "confederation, in the apprehending of the proclaimed rebels "DANIEL SHAYS, LUKE DAY, ADAM WHEELER "and ELI PARSONS," have enacted, "that rewards ad- "ditional to thoſe offered and promiſed to be paid by the ſtate "of Maſſachuſetts Bay, for the apprehending the aforeſaid "rebels, be offered by this ſtate;" WE do hereby offer the following rewards to any perſon or perſons who ſhall, within the limits of this ſtate, apprehend the rebels aforeſaid, and ecure them in the gaol of the city and county of Philadelphia, —— viz. For the apprehending of the ſaid Daniel Shays, and ſecuring him as aforeſaid, the reward of *One hundred and Fifty Pounds* lawful money of the ſtate of Maſſachuſetts Bay, and *One Hundred Pounds* lawful money of this ſtate; and for the apprehending the ſaid Luke Day, Adam Wheeler and Eli Parſons, and ſecuring them as aforeſaid, the reward (reſpectively) of *One Hundred Pounds* lawful money of Maſſachuſetts Bay and *Fifty Pounds* lawful money of this ſtate: And all judges, juſtices, ſheriffs and conſtables are hereby ſtrictly enjoined and required to make diligent ſearch and enquiry after, and to uſe their utmoſt endeavours to apprehend and ſecure the ſaid Daniel Shays, Luke Day, Adam Wheeler and Eli Parſons, their aiders, abettors and comforters, and every of them, ſo that they may be dealt with according to law.

GIVEN in Council, under the hand of the Preſident, and the Seal of the State, at Philadelphia, this tenth day of March, in the year of our Lord one thouſand ſeven hundred and eighty-ſeven.

BENJAMIN FRANKLIN.

Above: *Details of Daniel Shays* (left) *and Job Shattuck* (right) *as they appeared in* Bickerstaff's Boston Almanack *in 1787.* Left: *A proclamation by the State of Pennsylvania, signed by Benjamin Franklin on May 19, 1787, offers a reward for Daniel Shays and three other rebellion ringleaders.*

It was surprising the variety of worries that crowded into Washington's mind. Since he had publicly stated that he would never return to public life, would he be accused of indecision, of devious ambition even? Or, if he stayed home, would he be accused of failing to put his shoulder to the wheel because he wished the American republican experiment to collapse so that he could make himself king? More serious: would the convention be defeated before it started by each state's binding its delegates with so many instructions that the men from the different regions would be prevented from agreeing on anything? And then there was the fact that his beloved wife was in a state of consternation: she had grounded her happiness, so she tearfully reiterated, on the belief that nothing could possibly happen that would destroy her tranquillity by calling her husband back to public life.

Yet, however much Washington repined and struggled, he had no choice once it became clear that the convention presented a solid hope of matching the military victory of the Revolutionary army he had led with a political victory that would not only stabilize the nation but demonstrate for all the world to see that a people's government was not synonymous with anarchy.

It was surprising the variety of worries that crowded into Washington's mind. Since he had publicly stated that he would never return to public life, would he be accused of indecision, of devious ambition even?

Washington's ultimate agreement to attend had a tremendous effect on American public opinion, all the more because his hesitations and reluctance were well known. In a statement involving three future presidents, Madison wrote Jefferson about Washington: "To forsake the honorable retreat to which he had retired and risk the reputation he had so deservedly acquired, manifested a zeal for the public interest that could, after so many and illustrious services, scarcely have been expected of him."

Twenty-Six

THE CONSTITUTION OF THE UNITED STATES

(1787–1788)

Washington, who had been consistently ill as the time for his departure from retirement approached, was sick on the road, but as soon as he reached Philadelphia, in May 1787, purposeful activity cured him overnight. The delegates were, it is true, slow in assembling—eleven days passed before there was a quorum—but as they came in one by one, Washington made two hopeful discoveries. However much they disagreed on specifics, they all agreed that "something is necessary" because the existing government "is at an end, and unless a remedy is soon applied, anarchy and confusion will inevitably ensue." And they were not tied down, as Washington had feared they might be, by instructions that would make eventual unity impossible.

During the 1930s, it became fashionable to argue that the Constitutional Convention was a right-wing plot to put shackles on the people. Actually, the convention gave no countenance to the conception, almost universal in those days, that only men possessed of a certain amount of property could vote; decisions on this matter were left to the states. Since the delegates came from areas as widely separated as England was from the tip of Italy, their regional predilections were too various for them to share any single economic outlook. Furthermore, in those days before business specialization, most delegates had, as had Washington, widely diversified interests that urged contradictory financial measures. The only economic conviction all shared was that personal property should not be expropriated by governmental action.

Everyone saw as a major danger the tendency of legislative majorities to dictate by moving from enthusiasm in a zigzag course, and in the process trampling on minority rights. Fortunately, such political theorists as England's Blackstone and France's Montesquieu had worked out on paper a solution. The government should consist of branches, chosen in different manners at different times for different terms of office, which would check and balance each other and would all have to agree before a proposition became law. Foreign theory and also American experience as it came down from the colonial era urged an executive, a legislature made up of two houses, and a judiciary. Washington, who had brought this conception with him to the convention, found that most of the other delegates agreed. In order to establish such a government, the convention would have to go beyond its instructions by jettisoning the Articles of Confederation, but should the delegates do so, they had a blueprint on which to proceed.

Washington urged audacity. According to a fellow delegate, he stated, "It is too probable that no plan we propose will be adopted. Perhaps another dreadful conflict is to be sustained. If, to please the people, we offer what we ourselves disapprove, how can we

We the People of the United States, in Order to form a more perfect Union, establish Justice, insure domestic Tranquility, provide for the common defence, promote the general Welfare, and secure the Blessings of Liberty to ourselves and our Posterity, do ordain and establish this Constitution for the United States of America.

Article. I.

Section. 1. All legislative Powers herein granted shall be vested in a Congress of the United States, which shall consist of a Senate and House of Representatives.

Section. 2. The House of Representatives shall be composed of Members chosen every second Year by the People of the several States, and the Electors in each State shall have the Qualifications requisite for Electors of the most numerous Branch of the State Legislature.

No Person shall be a Representative who shall not have attained to the Age of twenty five Years, and been seven Years a Citizen of the United States, and who shall not, when elected, be an Inhabitant of that State in which he shall be chosen.

Representatives and direct Taxes shall be apportioned among the several States which may be included within this Union, according to their respective Numbers, which shall be determined by adding to the whole Number of free Persons, including those bound to Service for a Term of Years, and excluding Indians not taxed, three fifths of all other Persons. The actual Enumeration shall be made within three Years after the first Meeting of the Congress of the United States, and within every subsequent Term of ten Years, in such Manner as they shall by Law direct. The Number of Representatives shall not exceed one for every thirty Thousand, but each State shall have at Least one Representative; and until such enumeration shall be made, the State of New Hampshire shall be entitled to chuse three, Massachusetts eight, Rhode Island and Providence Plantations one, Connecticut five, New York six, New Jersey four, Pennsylvania eight, Delaware one, Maryland six, Virginia ten, North Carolina five, South Carolina five, and Georgia three.

When vacancies happen in the Representation from any State, the Executive Authority thereof shall issue Writs of Election to fill such Vacancies.

The House of Representatives shall chuse their Speaker and other Officers; and shall have the sole Power of Impeachment.

Section. 3. The Senate of the United States shall be composed of two Senators from each State, chosen by the Legislature thereof, for six Years; and each Senator shall have one Vote.

Immediately after they shall be assembled in Consequence of the first Election, they shall be divided as equally as may be into three Classes. The Seats of the Senators of the first Class shall be vacated at the Expiration of the second Year, of the second Class at the Expiration of the fourth Year, and of the third Class at the Expiration of the sixth Year, so that one third may be chosen every second Year; and if Vacancies happen by Resignation, or otherwise, during the Recess of the Legislature of any State, the Executive thereof may make temporary Appointments until the next Meeting of the Legislature, which shall then fill such Vacancies.

No Person shall be a Senator who shall not have attained to the Age of thirty Years, and been nine Years a Citizen of the United States, and who shall not, when elected, be an Inhabitant of that State for which he shall be chosen.

The Vice President of the United States shall be President of the Senate, but shall have no Vote, unless they be equally divided.

The Senate shall chuse their other Officers, and also a President pro tempore, in the Absence of the Vice President, or when he shall exercise the Office of President of the United States.

The Senate shall have the sole Power to try all Impeachments. When sitting for that Purpose, they shall be on Oath or Affirmation. When the President of the United States the Chief Justice shall preside: And no Person shall be convicted without the Concurrence of two thirds of the Members present.

Judgment in Cases of Impeachment shall not extend further than to removal from Office, and disqualification to hold and enjoy any Office of honor, Trust or Profit under the United States: but the Party convicted shall nevertheless be liable and subject to Indictment, Trial, Judgment and Punishment, according to Law.

Section. 4. The Times, Places and Manner of holding Elections for Senators and Representatives, shall be prescribed in each State by the Legislature thereof; but the Congress may at any time by Law make or alter such Regulations, except as to the Places of chusing Senators.

The Congress shall assemble at least once in every Year, and such Meeting shall be on the first Monday in December, unless they shall by Law appoint a different Day.

Section. 5. Each House shall be the Judge of the Elections, Returns and Qualifications of its own Members, and a Majority of each shall constitute a Quorum to do Business; but a smaller Number may adjourn from day to day, and may be authorized to compel the Attendance of absent Members, in such Manner, and under such Penalties as each House may provide.

Each House may determine the Rules of its Proceedings, punish its Members for disorderly Behaviour, and, with the Concurrence of two thirds, expel a Member.

Each House shall keep a Journal of its Proceedings, and from time to time publish the same, excepting such Parts as may in their Judgment require Secrecy; and the Yeas and Nays of the Members of either House on any question shall, at the Desire of one fifth of those Present, be entered on the Journal.

Neither House, during the Session of Congress, shall, without the Consent of the other, adjourn for more than three days, nor to any other Place than that in which the two Houses shall be sitting.

Section. 6. The Senators and Representatives shall receive a Compensation for their Services, to be ascertained by Law, and paid out of the Treasury of the United States. They shall in all Cases, except Treason, Felony and Breach of the Peace, be privileged from Arrest during their Attendance at the Session of their respective Houses, and in going to and returning from the same; and for any Speech or Debate in either House, they shall not be questioned in any other Place.

No Senator or Representative shall, during the Time for which he was elected, be appointed to any civil Office under the Authority of the United States, which shall have been created, or the Emoluments whereof shall have been encreased during such time; and no Person holding any Office under the United States, shall be a Member of either House during his Continuance in Office.

Section. 7. All Bills for raising Revenue shall originate in the House of Representatives; but the Senate may propose or concur with Amendments as on other Bills.

Every Bill which shall have passed the House of Representatives and the Senate, shall, before it become a Law, be presented to the President of the

Drafted in secret by delegates to the Constitutional Convention during the summer of 1787, the four-page Constitution, signed on September 17, 1787, established the government of the United States.

afterwards defend our work? Let us raise a standard to which the wise and the honest can repair. The event is in the hand of God."

While they were waiting for a quorum, the Virginia delegates, including Washington, drew up a plan for a powerful central government entrusted with all broad national affairs. It would be based on a separation of powers and designed to create a system of checks and balances. Since the state legislatures would presumably not thus weaken themselves, it was suggested that special conventions be elected in each state to decide whether to ratify. After only five days of discussion, the whole convention took the giant step of scrapping the Articles of Confederation. It voted to establish "a national government . . . consisting of a supreme legislative, executive, and judiciary."

The problem then was to determine what weight to assign on the checks and balances to the various political bodies, interests, and forces.

George Washington *by Charles Willson Peale, oil on canvas, 1787. Washington at the time of the Constitutional Convention.*

As Washington well realized, in this convention a mere majority vote was as useless as it had been in the wartime Continental Congress. What would be gained by having seven states sign the document eventually drafted while six went off in a rage? Even one state permanently lost would violate national unity. And, although Washington recognized that the work of the convention might be repudiated by the people, he wished to make this as unlikely as possible. Clearly, any upsurge of opposition in the convention that was not satisfied presaged a similar upsurge in some part of the nation.

Unity could only be hoped for if there were mutual understanding between delegates from the different regions. At the start of the convention, this understanding was conspicuously absent. Washington, who was more traveled in the United States than almost any other delegate, had not penetrated into New England north of the Boston area and had never been south of Virginia. Madison admitted that he knew no more of Georgia than Kamchatka. Furthermore, ignorance was fortified by mutual suspicions and hostilities that often dated back to the earliest years of settlement.

Washington had seen colonial distrusts and rivalries fade away as men from various regions were thrown together in the army camps during eight years of war. Now the process had to be repeated, but much more quickly—during a few months of stifling summer weather. The delegates were rubbed against each other in two ways: in formal debate and over tavern tables. It may well be that the tavern meetings

THE ROAD TO THE CONSTITUTION

THE FEDERALIST PAPERS

THE FEDERALIST PAPERS COMPRISE A SERIES of eighty-five essays promoting the ratification of the United States Constitution. Seventy-seven of the essays were published serially in the *Independent Journal* and the *New York Packet* between October 1787 and August 1788. A compilation of these and eight others was published in two volumes in 1788.

At the time of publication, the authorship of the articles was a closely guarded secret, though astute observers guessed that Alexander Hamilton, James Madison, and John Jay were the likely authors. Following Hamilton's death in 1804, a list that he drew up became public, claiming fully two-thirds of the essays for himself (including some that seem more likely the work of Madison). The authors used the pseudonym "Publius" in honor of Roman consul Publius Valerius Publicola.

There are many highlights among the essays. In *Federalist No. 10*, Madison discusses the means of preventing rule by majority faction and advocates a large, commercial republic. It is generally regarded as the most important of the eighty-five articles from a philosophical perspective.

Federalist No. 10

To the People of the State of New York:

Among the numerous advantages promised by a well-constructed Union, none deserves to be more accurately developed than its tendency to break and control the violence of faction. The friend of popular governments never finds himself so much alarmed for their character and fate as when he contemplates their propensity to this dangerous vice. He will not fail, therefore, to set a due value on any plan which, without violating the principles to which he is attached, provides a proper cure for it. The instability, injustice, and confusion introduced into the public councils, have, in truth, been the mortal diseases under which popular governments have everywhere perished, as they continue to be the favorite and fruitful topics from which the adversaries to liberty derive their most specious declamations. The valuable improvements made by the American constitutions on the popular models, both ancient and modern, cannot certainly be too much admired; but it would be an unwarrantable partiality to contend that they have as effectually obviated the danger on this side, as was wished and expected.

Complaints are everywhere heard from our most considerate and virtuous citizens, equally the friends of public and private faith, and of public and personal liberty, that our governments are too unstable, that the public good is disregarded in the conflicts of rival parties, and that measures are too often decided, not according to the rules of justice and the rights of the minor party, but by the superior force of an interested and overbearing majority.

However anxiously we may wish that these complaints had no foundation, the evidence of known facts will not permit us to deny that they are in some degree true. It will be found, indeed, on a candid review of our situation, that some of the distresses under which we labor have been erroneously charged on the operation of our governments; but it will be found, at the same time, that other causes will not alone account for many of our heaviest misfortunes; and, particularly, for that prevailing and increasing distrust of public engagements and alarm for private rights, which are echoed from one end of the continent to the other. These must be chiefly, if not wholly, effects of the unsteadiness and injustice with which a factious spirit has tainted our public administrations.

By a faction, I understand a number of citizens, whether amounting to a majority or a minority of the whole, who are united and actuated by some common impulse of passion, or of interest, adverse to the rights of other citizens, or to the permanent and aggregate interests of the community.

There are two methods of curing the mischiefs of faction: the one, by removing its causes; the other, by controlling its effects. There are again two methods of removing the causes of faction: the one, by destroying the liberty which is essential to its existence; the other, by giving to every citizen the same opinions, the same passions, and the same interests. It could never be more truly said than of the first remedy, that it was worse than the disease. Liberty is to faction what air is to fire, an ailment without which it instantly expires. But it could not be less folly to abolish liberty, which is essential to political life, because it nourishes faction, than it would be to wish the annihilation of air, which is essential to animal life, because it imparts to fire its destructive agency.

The second expedient is as impracticable as the first would be unwise. As long as the reason of man continues fallible, and he is at liberty to exercise it, different opinions will be formed. As long as the connection subsists between his reason and his self-love, his opinions and his passions will have a reciprocal influence on each other; and the former will be objects to which the latter will attach themselves. The diversity in the faculties of men, from which the rights of property originate, is not less an insuperable obstacle to a uniformity of interests. The protection of these faculties is the first object of government. From the protection of different and unequal faculties of acquiring property, the possession of different degrees and kinds of property immediately results; and from the influence of these on the sentiments and views of the respective proprietors, ensues a division of the society into different interests and parties.

The latent causes of faction are thus sown in the nature of man; and we see them everywhere brought into different degrees of activity, according to the different circumstances of civil society. A zeal for different opinions concerning religion, concerning government, and many other points, as well of speculation as of practice; an attachment to different leaders ambitiously contending for preeminence and power; or to persons of other descriptions whose fortunes have been interesting to the human passions, have, in turn, divided mankind into parties, inflamed them with mutual animosity, and rendered them much more disposed to vex and oppress each other than to cooperate for their common good. So strong is this propensity of mankind to fall into mutual animosities, that where no substantial occasion presents itself, the most frivolous and fanciful distinctions have been sufficient to kindle their unfriendly passions and excite their most violent conflicts. But the most common and durable source of factions has been the various and unequal distribution of property. Those who hold and those who are without property have ever formed distinct interests in society. Those who are creditors, and those who are debtors, fall under a like discrimination. A landed interest, a manufacturing interest, a mercantile interest, a moneyed interest, with many lesser interests, grow up of necessity in civilized nations, and divide them into different classes, actuated by different sentiments and views. The regulation of these various and interfering interests forms the principal task of modern legislation, and involves the spirit of party and faction in the necessary and ordinary operations of the government.

No man is allowed to be a judge in his own cause, because his interest would certainly bias his judgment, and, not improbably, corrupt his integrity. With equal, nay with greater reason, a body of men are unfit to be both judges and parties at the same time; yet what are many of the most important acts of legislation, but so many judicial determinations, not indeed concerning the rights of single persons, but concerning the rights of large bodies of citizens? And what are the different classes of legislators but advocates and parties to the causes which they determine? Is a law proposed concerning private debts? It is a question to which the creditors are parties on one side and the debtors on the other. Justice ought to hold the balance between them. Yet the parties are, and must be, themselves the judges; and the most numerous party, or, in other words, the most powerful faction must be expected to prevail. Shall domestic manufactures be encouraged, and in what degree, by restrictions on foreign manufactures? Are questions which would be differently decided by the landed and the manufacturing classes, and probably by neither with a sole regard to justice and the public good. The apportionment of taxes on the various descriptions of property is an act which seems to require the most exact impartiality; yet there is, perhaps, no legislative act in which greater opportunity and temptation are given to a predominant party to trample on the rules of justice. Every shilling with which they overburden the inferior number is a shilling saved to their own pockets.

It is in vain to say that enlightened statesmen will be able to adjust these clashing interests and render them all subservient to the public good. Enlightened statesmen will not always be at the helm. Nor, in many cases, can such an adjustment be made at all without taking into view indirect and remote considerations, which will rarely prevail over the immediate interest which one party may find in disregarding the rights of another or the good of the whole. The inference to which we are brought is that the causes of faction cannot be removed, and that relief is only to be sought in the means of controlling its effects. If a faction consists of less than a majority, relief is supplied by the Republican principle, which enables the majority to defeat its sinister views by regular vote. It may clog the administration, it may convulse the society; but it will be unable to execute and mask its violence under the forms of the Constitution. When a majority is included in a faction, the form of popular government, on the other hand, enables it to sacrifice to its ruling passion or interest both the public good and the rights of other citizens. To secure the public good and private rights against the danger of such a faction, and at the same time to preserve the spirit and the form of popular government, is then the great object to which our inquiries are directed. Let me add that it is the great desideratum by which this form of government can be rescued from the opprobrium under which it has so long labored, and be recommended to the esteem and adoption of mankind.

By what means is this object attainable? Evidently by one of two only. Either the existence of the same passion or interest in a majority at the same time must be prevented, or the majority, having such coexistent passion or interest, must be rendered, by their number and local situation, unable to concert and carry into effect schemes of oppression. If the impulse and the opportunity be suffered to coincide, we well know that neither moral nor religious motives can be relied on as an adequate control. They are not found to be such on the injustice and violence of individuals, and lose their efficacy in proportion to the number combined together, that is, in proportion as their efficacy becomes needful. From this view of the subject it may be concluded that a pure democracy, by which I mean a society consisting of a small number of citizens, who assemble and administer the government in person, can admit of no cure for the mischiefs of faction. A common passion or interest will, in almost every case, be felt by a majority of the whole; a communication and concert result from the form of government itself; and there is nothing to check the inducements to sacrifice the weaker party or an obnoxious individual. Hence, it is that such democracies have ever been spectacles of turbulence and contention; have ever been found

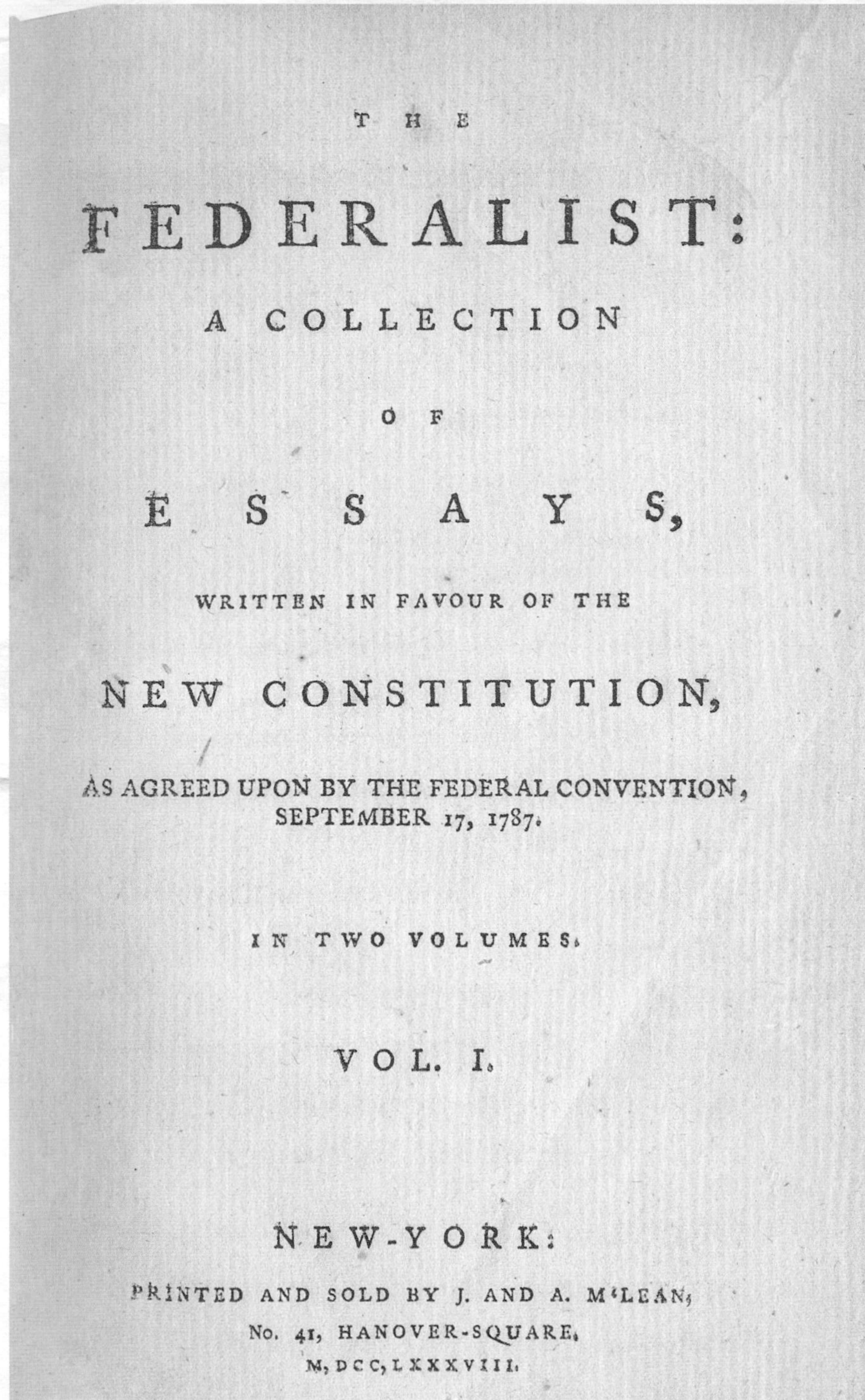

THE

FEDERALIST:

A COLLECTION

OF

ESSAYS,

WRITTEN IN FAVOUR OF THE

NEW CONSTITUTION,

AS AGREED UPON BY THE FEDERAL CONVENTION, SEPTEMBER 17, 1787.

IN TWO VOLUMES.

VOL. I.

NEW-YORK:

PRINTED AND SOLD BY J. AND A. M'LEAN,

No. 41, HANOVER-SQUARE,

M,DCC,LXXXVIII.

Madison campaigned for the ratification of the Constitution by co-authoring a series of essays with John Jay and Alexander Hamilton called The Federalist *(1788), known today as* The Federalist Papers.

incompatible with personal security or the rights of property; and have in general been as short in their lives as they have been violent in their deaths.

Theoretic politicians, who have patronized this species of government, have erroneously supposed that by reducing mankind to a perfect equality in their political rights, they would, at the same time, be perfectly equalized and assimilated in their possessions, their opinions, and their passions.

A republic, by which I mean a government in which the scheme of representation takes place, opens a different prospect and promises the cure for which we are seeking. Let us examine the points in which it varies from pure democracy, and we shall comprehend both the nature of the cure and the efficacy which it must derive from the Union.

The two great points of difference between a democracy and a republic are first, the delegation of the government, in the latter, to a small number of citizens elected by the rest; secondly, the greater number of citizens, and greater sphere of country, over which the latter may be extended. The effect of the first difference is, on the one hand, to refine and enlarge the public views by passing them through the medium of a chosen body of citizens whose wisdom may best discern the true interest of their country, and whose patriotism and love of justice will be least likely to sacrifice it to temporary or partial considerations. Under such a regulation, it may well happen that the public voice, pronounced by the representatives of the people, will be more consonant to the public good than if pronounced by the people themselves, convened for the purpose.

On the other hand, the effect may be inverted. Men of factious tempers, of local prejudices, or of sinister designs, may, by intrigue, by corruption, or by other means, first obtain the suffrages, and then betray the interests of the people. The question resulting is whether small or extensive republics are more favorable to the election of proper guardians of the public weal; and it is clearly decided in favor of the latter by two obvious considerations:

In the first place, it is to be remarked that however small the republic may be, the representatives must be raised to a certain number in order to guard against the cabals of a few; and that however large it may be, they must be limited to a certain number in order to guard against the confusion of a multitude. Hence, the number of representatives in the two cases not being in proportion to that of the two constituents, and being proportionally greater in the small republic, it follows that if the proportion of fit characters be not less in the large than in the small republic, the former will present a greater option, and consequently a greater probability of a fit choice.

In the next place, as each representative will be chosen by a greater number of citizens in the large than in the small republic, it will be more difficult for unworthy candidates to practice with success the vicious arts by which elections are too often carried; and the suffrages of the people being more free, will be more likely to center in men who possess the most attractive merit and the most diffusive and established characters. It must be confessed that in this, as in most other cases, there is a mean, on both sides of which inconveniences will be found to lie. By enlarging too much the number of electors, you render the representatives too little acquainted with all their local circumstances and lesser interests; as by reducing it too much, you render him unduly attached to these, and too little fit to comprehend and pursue great and national objects.

The federal Constitution forms a happy combination in this respect; the great and aggregate interests being referred to the national, the local and particular to the state legislatures. The other point of difference is the greater number of citizens and extent of territory which may be brought within the compass of republican than of democratic government; and it is this circumstance principally which renders factious combinations less to be dreaded in the former than in the latter. The smaller the society, the fewer probably will be the distinct parties and interests composing it; the fewer the distinct parties and interests, the more frequently will a majority be found of the same party; and the smaller the number of individuals composing a majority, and the smaller the compass within which they are placed, the more easily will they concert and execute their plans of oppression. Extend the sphere, and you take in a greater variety of parties and interests; you make it less probable that a majority of the whole will have a common motive to invade the rights of other citizens; or if such a common motive exists, it will be more difficult for all who feel it to discover their own strength, and to act in unison with each other. Besides other impediments, it may be remarked that where there is a consciousness of unjust or dishonorable purposes, communication is always checked by distrust in proportion to the number whose concurrence is necessary.

Hence, it clearly appears that the same advantage which a republic has over a democracy, in controlling the effects of faction, is enjoyed by a large over a small republic, is enjoyed by the Union over the states composing it. Does the advantage consist in the substitution of representatives whose enlightened views and virtuous sentiments render them superior to local prejudices and schemes of injustice? It will not be denied that the representation of the Union will be most likely to possess these requisite endowments. Does it consist in the greater security afforded by a greater variety of parties, against the event of any one party being able to outnumber and oppress the rest? In an equal degree does the increased variety of parties comprised within the Union increase this security. Does it, in fine, consist in the greater obstacles opposed to the concert and accomplishment of the secret wishes of an unjust and interested majority? Here, again, the extent of the Union gives it the most palpable advantage. The influence of factious leaders may kindle a flame within their particular states, but will be unable to spread a general conflagration through the other states. A religious sect may degenerate into a political faction in a part of the Confederacy, but the variety of sects dispersed over the entire face of it must secure the national councils against any danger from that source. A rage for paper money, for an abolition of debts, for an equal division of property, or for any other improper or wicked project will be less apt to pervade the whole body of the Union than a particular member of it; in the same proportion as such a malady is more likely to taint a particular county or district than an entire state.

In the extent and proper structure of the Union, therefore, we behold a republican remedy for the diseases most incident to republican government. And according to the degree of pleasure and pride we feel in being republicans, ought to be our zeal in cherishing the spirit and supporting the character of Federalists.

PUBLIUS

were more important towards creating the Constitution than the formal debates.

At the convivial gatherings, Washington was endlessly present, dining at one place, having supper at another, chatting between the acts of plays. He sought always to bring diverse points of view into the open and then together. History will never be able to assess the extent of the contribution Washington made through such personal contacts, but it was surely great. His years of military service and his hospitality at Mount Vernon had made many of the delegates already his friends or acquaintances; his personal prestige was awesome even with those who had not previously met him; and he had, to a superlative degree, the gift of finding beneath controversy common ground.

His years of military service and his hospitality at Mount Vernon had made many of the delegates already his friends or acquaintances; his personal prestige was awesome even with those who had not previously met him; and he had, to a superlative degree, the gift of finding beneath controversy common ground.

The convention having unanimously elected Washington president, he was prevented by his office from taking part in the discussions. However, all remarks were titularly addressed to him, and the room was small. (There were rarely as many as thirty delegates present.) His face was clearly visible to everyone. Often he listened torpidly. His wartime aide John Laurens wrote, "When the muscles are in a state of repose, his eye certainly wants animation." But "his countenance, when affected either by joy or anger, is full of expression." Many delegates were to remember how the proceedings of the convention were influenced by his "anxious solicitude" at angry disagreement, his pleasure at fruitful compromise.

Since the convention was trying to establish a government altogether new under the sun, there were no precedents to violate—but also none to steer by. All the issues involved in government stalked the hall at one time or another. Among the troublesome problems were drawing lines between state and federal power, decisions concerning slavery (the more defensively protected in the South because disapproved of in the North), southern suspicions that federal trade regulations would make them serfs to New England shippers, taxation, fear of tyranny at one extreme or anarchy at the other. The level of agreement reached was phenomenal, and, when agreement proved too difficult, many a decision was left vague, to be worked out in actual practice.

As Washington had five years before suggested, the new Constitution, leaving local jurisdiction to the states, gave the federal government control over matters affecting the entire Union. Bypassing the state legislatures, which had previously chosen all elected national officials, the Constitution gave federal ballots to individual voters everywhere. But the state pretensions, which had made Washington so much trouble during the Revolution and had torn the subsequent government apart, survived to create the one issue that threatened to wreck the Constitutional Convention.

Opposite: The Earl of Chesterfield's Letters to His Son *contain eighteenth-century guidelines for gentlemanly behavior and proper manners. Washington purchased this four-volume set, the first American edition, while presiding over the Constitutional Convention in Philadelphia on September 5, 1787.*

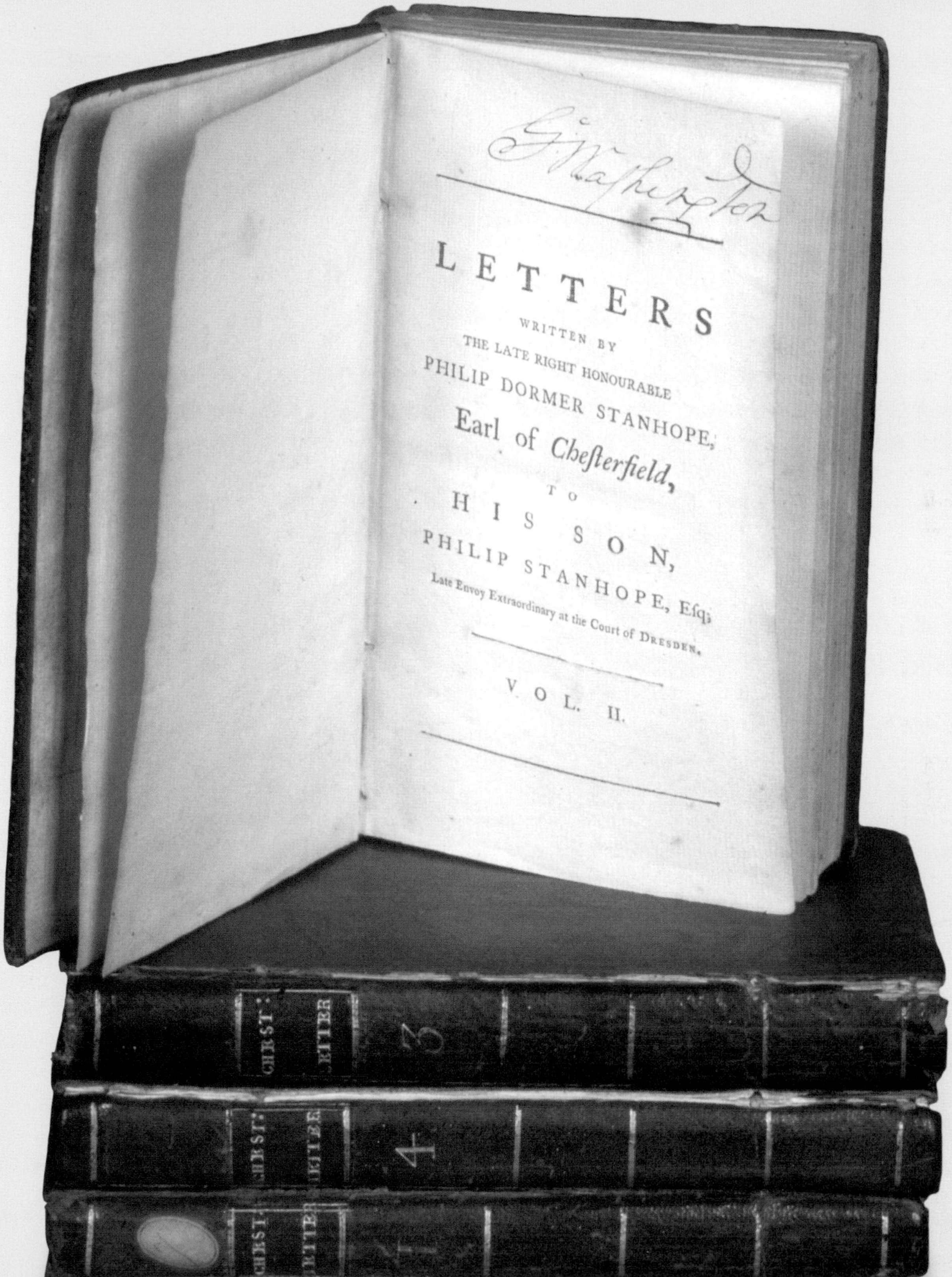
LETTERS
WRITTEN BY
THE LATE RIGHT HONOURABLE
PHILIP DORMER STANHOPE,
Earl of Chesterfield,
TO
HIS SON,
PHILIP STANHOPE, Esq;
Late Envoy Extraordinary at the Court of DRESDEN.
VOL. II.
CHEST:
LETTER
3
4

The states differed vastly in size (Virginia, for instance, being about fifteen times as populous as Delaware). If, as Washington believed, in a true people's government every vote should carry the same weight, the inhabitants of the larger states would automatically outvote those of the smaller. But the smaller states, which had historically considered themselves equivalent to the mammoths, were determined not to lose their consequence. They wished each state to have, as was the case in the Continental Congress, an equal vote.

When, led by Madison, the larger states revealed determination to have representation be not by states but by population, spokesmen for the smaller went so far as to threaten that they would make alliances with foreign powers to protect themselves. Washington wrote, "I almost despair . . . and do therefore repent having had any agency in the business." But no one really wanted to give up. Finally, all delegations accepted a compromise by which, after special powers in relation to treasury bills were given to the popularly elected House of Representatives, the representation in the Senate was established not by population but by states.

Washington was personally most involved in decisions concerning the executive. If it were to be a committee of three men, each representing a major section of the country, he could return undisturbed to Mount Vernon. But once the president was set up as a single individual, no one could doubt who that individual would be. In a world frightened by a long history of kings, the convention decided on one president and allowed him an amazing amount of power. He was to be elected independently of the other branches and to be indefinitely reelectable. He could carry out the many important functions assigned to him uncontrolled by any statutory advisers. He was to be commander in chief of the armed forces and, while the Congress could not interfere in his province, he could interfere with the Congress through a veto. He could only be removed from office because of treason or criminal behavior. A delegate explained, "Many of the members . . . shaped their ideas of the powers to be given to a president by their opinions of his [Washington's] virtues." The impress of Washington's prestige remains in the strength allowed the president of the United States.

Rhode Island had boycotted the convention. On September 17, the delegations of the other twelve states unanimously (although three individual delegates voted no) accepted the completed draft. Wearily, Washington wrote Lafayette that the Constitution "is now a child of fortune, to be fostered by some and buffeted by others. What will be the general opinion on, or the reception of it, is not for me to decide, nor shall I say anything for or against it. If it be good, I suppose it will work its way good. If bad, it will recoil on the framers."

The task that lay ahead—to secure adoption of the Constitution by the nine states necessary to make it operative, by the thirteen necessary for peace and harmony on the continent—was in many ways a more difficult, if less creative, task than drawing up the document. It was agreed that no delegate would aid the opposition by specifying which points he had, in the spirit of compromise, agreed to reluctantly. Since Washington abided by this rule, it is not clear why he was not at first enthusiastic about the Constitution, but it is clear that he was not. He wrote three Virginia leaders identical letters stating, "Your own judgment will at once discover the good and the exceptionable parts of it, and your experience of the difficulties which have ever arisen when attempts have been made to reconcile such variety of interests and local prejudices as pervade the several states will render explanation unnecessary. I wish the Constitution which is offered had been made more perfect, but I sincerely believe it is the best that could be obtained at this time; and, as a constitutional door is open to amendment hereafter, the adoption of it under the present circumstances of the Union is, in my opinion, desirable." He believed that if nothing had been agreed upon, "anarchy would soon have ensued, the seeds being richly sown in every soil."

In a world familiar with the tyranny of kings, popular fears clustered around executive power. That everyone expected Washington to be the first president was reassuring, but would it have comforted so much had he actively labored to persuade the people to give him the opportunity to exert such power?

The debate over ratification elicited a flood of pamphlets on both sides. Washington read them all. He became convinced that the arguments of the opponents, based mostly on regionalism and an identification of strong government with tyranny, were hysterical when they were not self-serving. The pamphlets supporting the Constitution, particularly *The Federalist* written by Hamilton, Madison, and John Jay, persuaded Washington that "this Constitution is really in its formation a government of the people; that is to say, a government in which all power is derived from and, at stated periods, reverts to them; and that, in its operation, it is purely a government of laws, made and executed by the fair substitutes of the people alone. . . . It is clear to my conception that no government before introduced among mankind ever contained so many checks and such efficacious restraints to prevent it from degenerating into any species of oppression."

Washington became passionately eager to have the Constitution ratified. The various state conventions followed a recurring pattern that was harrowing to the nerves. The majority of the delegates arrived opposed to the Constitution. But, as the debates went on, one delegate after another became convinced, and finally the majority voted "yea." As Washington watched, he again and again strained as on a leash to interfere. However, he had resolved to take no active part in the debate.

At one particularly dangerous turn on the road to ratification, Washington wondered if he had not "meddled . . . in this political dispute less perhaps than a man so thoroughly persuaded as I am of the evils and confusions which will result from the rejection of the proposed Constitution ought to have done." Yet, whether because of political acumen or because of some deep identification between what came naturally to him and what most appealed to the collective mind of the American people, his continued refusal to take part was surely the most effective role he could have played.

In a world familiar with the tyranny of kings, popular fears clustered around executive power. That everyone expected Washington to be the first president was reassuring, but would it have comforted so much had he actively labored to persuade the people to give him the opportunity to exert such power?

Furthermore, if Washington had entered the debate, the thrust of his influence might have been dissipated in arguments over specifics. As it was, all voters knew that he had presided over the creation of the Constitution and had been the first to sign. In his physical absence, his prestige hovered over every state convention. How carefully the opposition had to tack around this invisible presence was revealed by Luther Martin of Maryland, who intoned, "The

Following page: Washington Addressing the Constitutional Convention *by Junius Brutus Stearns.*

The delegates to the Constitutional Convention with Washington at the podium.

name of Washington is far above my praise! I would to Heaven that on this occasion one more wreath had been added to the number of those which are twined around his amiable brow—that those with which it is already surrounded may flourish with immortal verdure, not wither or fade till time shall be no more, is my fervent prayer!" But—

In writing Jefferson, James Monroe thus assessed Washington's role: "Be assured, his influence carried this government."

Late in June 1788, more than ten months after Washington had put his signature on the proposed Constitution, almost simultaneous word came to Mount Vernon of two more ratifications. The total of assenting states was thus raised to one more than the nine needed to make the Constitution operative. As Washington, to the booming of celebrative cannon, stood on his piazza looking down over a Potomac aglow with the lights of boats coming to offer him congratulations, he hailed in his own mind what he later described as "a new phenomenon in the political and moral world, and an astonishing victory gained by enlightened reason over brute force."

Twenty-Seven

HYSTERIA AND RESPONSIBILITY

(1788–1789)

Washington had truly dreaded going to the Constitutional Convention, but once he had taken that step, his feet were irrevocably on the public road. He had feared that the road would carry him into the darkest ravines, but it had mounted to what he believed were shining heights. Using one of the theatrical metaphors of which he was so fond, he wrote the Irish patriot Sir Edward Newenham, "You will permit me to say that a greater drama is now acting on this theater than has heretofore been brought on the American stage, or any other in the world. We exhibit at present the novel and astonishing spectacle of a whole people deliberating calmly on what form of government will be most conducive to their happiness." America was approaching "nearer to perfection than any government hitherto instituted among men."

Hazards remained. Three states had not ratified. Although the absence of Rhode Island and North Carolina could be temporarily accepted, if the huge, central state of New York stayed outside, that would be grave. As Washington watched from Mount Vernon, there was another struggle against odds, but in the end New York did ratify.

Next came the congressional elections. If Congress were not to be filled with men opposed to the Constitution who might sabotage the new government, the educative process which had persuaded the Constitutional Convention and then the eleven state conventions would have to be extended to the people at large. Washington protested angrily a new post office regulation that would impede the distribution of newspapers. "The friends of the Constitution," he wrote, wanted "the public to be possessed

Augustus Weidenbach made this chromolithograph (1876) after a painting by Gilbert Stuart.

of everything that might be printed on both sides of the question." He was convinced that, if informed, the people would be won over. And enough were won over to enable him to exult concerning the first Congress that "the self-created respectability [worthiness of respect] and various talents of the members will not be inferior to any assembly in the world."

During the Constitutional Convention, a listing of the rights reserved to the people had been proposed but considered unnecessary since "natural law" dictated that the people retained all rights that they did not specifically delegate to their government. However, when the debates at the state ratifying conventions made clear that a "bill of rights" would give, as Washington put it, "extreme satisfaction," he urged that the indicated amendments—freedom of religion, of speech, of the press, and so on—be immediately enacted.

As the months passed, during which the Continental Congress laboriously presided over setting the new government in motion, Washington made no comment concerning the universal expectation that the electoral college would unanimously select him as the first president. He made not the slightest gesture that could be considered campaigning. He stayed closer to his front lawn than he had ever done for an equivalent period of time, but his mind was no longer on his acres. Privately, he spoke of great "sacrifice," but the truth seems to have been that he was looking forward to the office with eagerness.

On a purely practical level, the presidency would rescue Washington from the dilemma caused by his continually living beyond his income: although he intended to refuse a salary, his living and entertaining expenses for most of each year would be paid. Furthermore, he would find a delicious excitement in leading so glorious an experiment—and he did not envision the task as extremely difficult. The most important labor would be to solidify the government by cementing to it the allegiance of the people. This would be done by visible virtue, a spirit within the government not of contention but compromise, by soothing regional prejudices, by improving the prosperity of the nation.

At long last, on April 14, Washington received formal notification of his election. He set out in his coach "with more anxious and painful sensations than I have words to express."

Already, before he had reestablished connections with his former military aide and future financial adviser, Alexander Hamilton, Washington considered it as a primary necessity "to extricate my country" from the great shortage of financial credit. But he foresaw no elaborate schemes. Since the country was rich in resources, he felt it only necessary to remove impediments that blocked free enterprise. Prosperity would be "the natural harvest of good government."

Although Washington agreed with Jefferson that the United States should and would remain an agricultural country, he demonstrated, as the presidency loomed, a sudden interest in manufacturing. Why should America allow her staples to be processed abroad? In his eagerness to encourage a native textile industry, he was to wear at his inauguration a great rarity: a suit made from cloth woven in the United States.

Himself hating tax collectors, Washington resolved that a sure way to the hearts of the people was to make the government as cheap as possible. The former commander in chief wanted only a minimal standing army, and saw no need for a navy as long as American merchants kept on the seas vessels that could

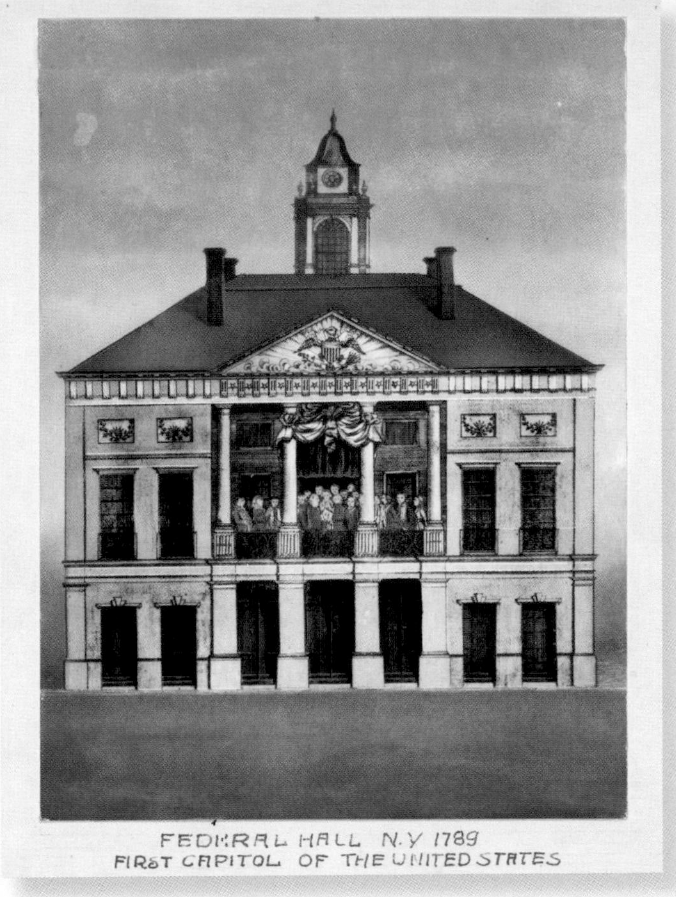

Above: *Washington taking his oath of office as president, April 30, 1789, by Amos Doolittle after a drawing by Peter Lacour, 1790.*

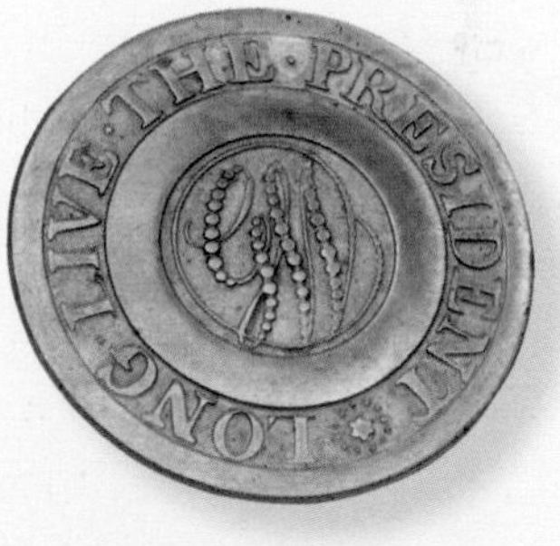

Left: *A commemorative inaugural button from 1789.*

Right: *This coat button features Washington's cipher surrounded by the salute "Long Live the President," the phrase pronounced by Robert Livingston after administering the oath of office to Washington on April 30, 1789, at Federal Hall in New York.*

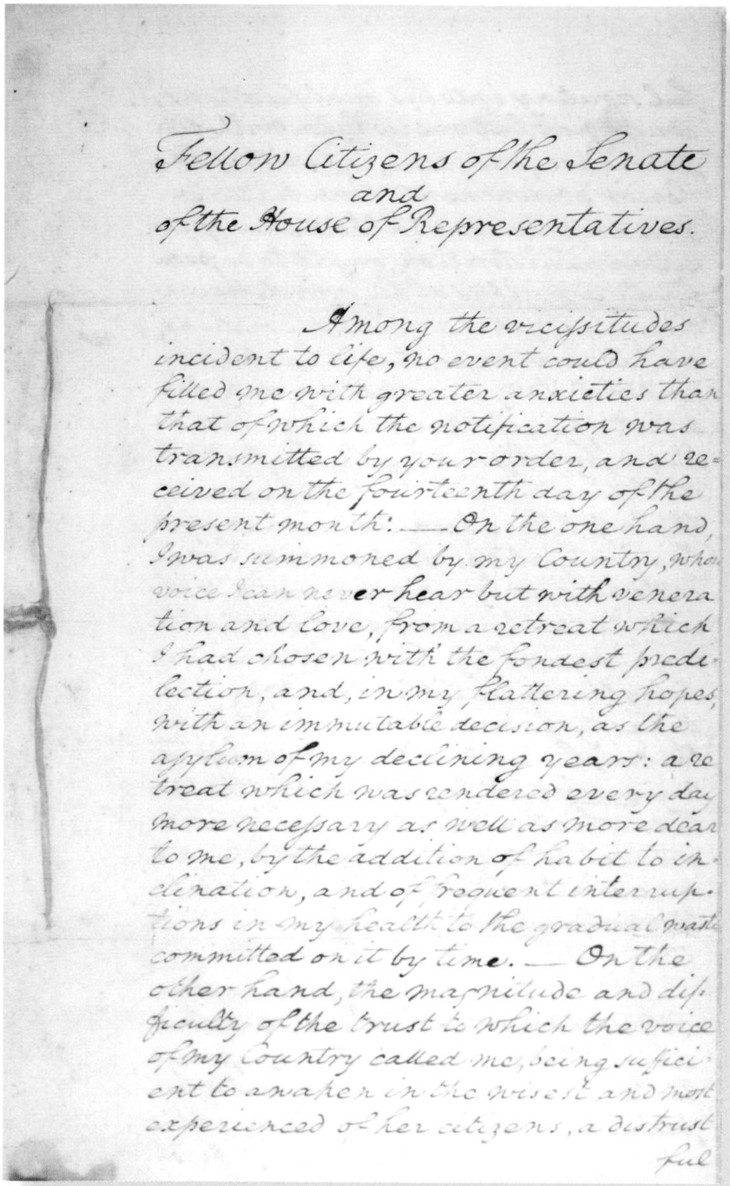

Fellow Citizens of the Senate
and
of the House of Representatives.

Among the vicissitudes incident to life, no event could have filled me with greater anxieties than that of which the notification was transmitted by your order, and received on the fourteenth day of the present month: — On the one hand, I was summoned by my Country, whose voice I can never hear but with veneration and love, from a retreat which I had chosen with the fondest predilection, and, in my flattering hopes, with an immutable decision, as the asylum of my declining years: a retreat which was rendered every day more necessary as well as more dear to me, by the addition of habit to inclination, and of frequent interruptions in my health to the gradual waste committed on it by time. — On the other hand, the magnitude and difficulty of the trust to which the voice of my Country called me, being sufficient to awaken in the wisest and most experienced of her citizens, a distrustful

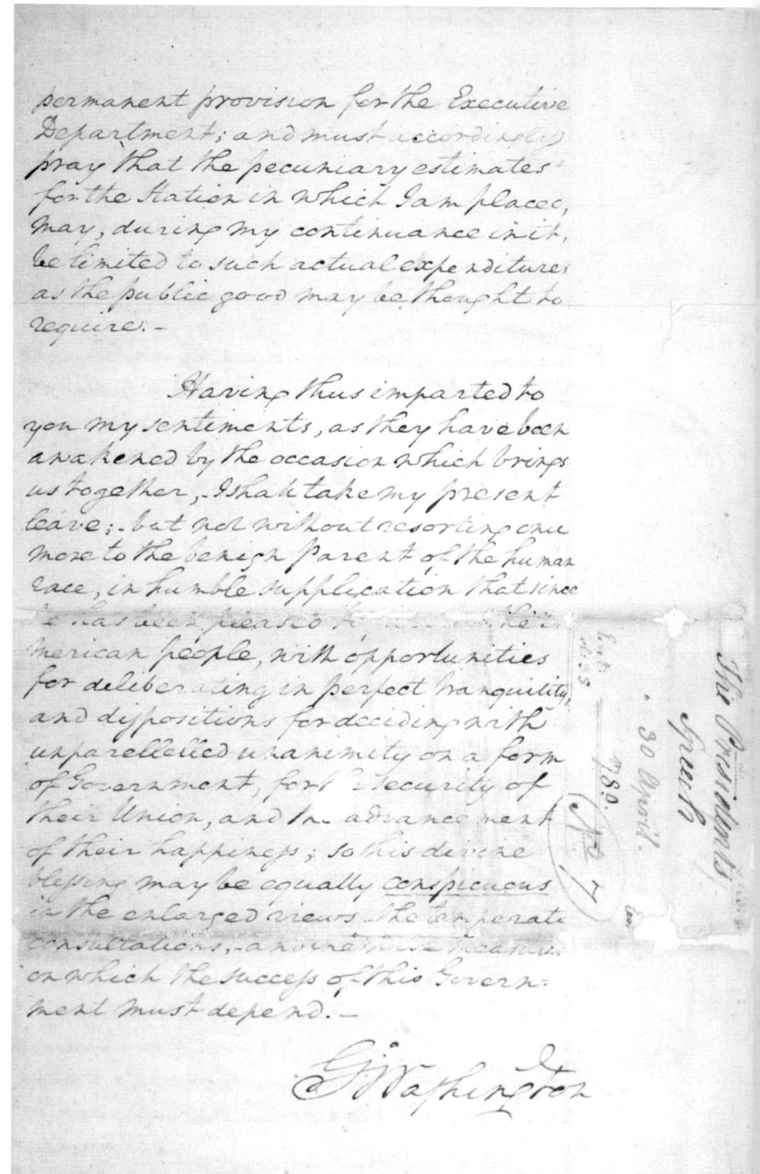

permanent provision for the Executive Department; and must accordingly pray that the pecuniary estimates for the station in which I am placed, may, during my continuance in it, be limited to such actual expenditures as the public good may be thought to require. —

Having thus imparted to you my sentiments, as they have been awakened by the occasion which brings us together, I shall take my present leave; but not without resorting once more to the benign Parent of the human race, in humble supplication that since he has been pleased [illegible] the American people, with opportunities for deliberating in perfect tranquility, and dispositions for deciding with unparallelled unanimity on a form of Government, for the security of their Union, and the advancement of their happiness; so his divine blessing may be equally conspicuous in the enlarged views, the temperate consultations, and the wise measures on which the success of this Government must depend. —

G^o Washington

In delivering an inaugural address, Washington went beyond the constitutional requirement of taking an oath of office, and so he established a precedent that has been followed by every elected president since. The newly elected president delivered his speech in a deep, low voice that betrayed what one observer called "manifest embarrassment." Aside from recommending constitutional amendments to satisfy citizens demanding a bill of rights, Washington confined himself to generalities. He closed by asking for a "divine blessing" on the American people and their elected representatives.

in an emergency be armed. Behind her ocean moat, the nation was not likely to be attacked, and she should not herself reach out to meddle abroad. In international affairs, the people should "guard against ambition as their greatest enemy."

On February 4, 1789, Washington became the unanimous choice of the electoral college. His election was not only inevitable but absolutely necessary. As Madison observed, his leadership was the only aspect of the new government that really appealed to the people.

What happened next was frightening. The vote could not be official until the electors' ballots had been counted in the presence of both legislative houses. However, the senators and representatives gathered so slowly that, while the nation drifted rudderless for more than a month, there was no quorum. Washington's worry over the "stupor and listlessness" being displayed was not lightened by the news that the delay in getting going had cost the government in tax revenues the then huge sum of £300,000.

However much he was himself kept waiting, Washington was opposed in principle to holding up anyone else. Most of his baggage was packed. Week after week he paced his long piazza or stared disconsolately down his curving driveway. His eager expectations shredded into dismay. "My movements to the chair of government," he now wrote, "will be accompanied by feelings not unlike those of a culprit who is going to the place of his execution." The situation was darkened by Martha's gloom. She was too unhappy to accompany her husband to the official world in which they were again to move. He could summon her later.

Added to everything was the fact that Washington possessed hardly any cash. Wishing to pay off his debts in Virginia before he left the state, he tried to borrow over a thousand pounds. His credit was not considered good enough. Finally, he managed to secure five hundred from a citizen of Alexandria. This went so fast that he had to beg another hundred so that he could pay the expenses of his trip to the temporary capital, New York City.

At long last, on April 14, Washington received formal notification of his election. He set out in his coach "with more anxious and painful sensations than I have words to express."

Among the worries that now bothered him was a fear that the people might resent his return to public office after his promise that he would never do so. The enthusiasm with which he was greeted on the road not only extinguished this fear but raised its opposite. As he moved, he could not see the countryside because of the dust churned up by the horsemen who in relays surrounded his carriage. At every hamlet there were speeches; at every city he had to lead a parade and be toasted at a sumptuous dinner; everywhere and always, people were jostling him, shaking his hand, cheering and cheering until his ears ached. Throughout the jubilations that stretched down the long days and late into the nights, Washington sensed a hysteria which he found "painful." How easily and with what frenzy could this irrational emotion turn, if the government did not immediately please, "into equally extravagant (though I will fondly hope unmerited) censures. So much is expected, so many untoward circumstances may intervene, in such a new and critical situation that I feel an insuperable diffidence in my own abilities."

The task which he was now approaching was both more uncertain and infinitely more important than that which had lain before him when in 1775 he had ridden north to take command of the Continental army. His duty then had been to win military victory. Since such victories had been won ten thousand times, there was no philosophical reason to doubt that success was possible. And, if he did fail, the result would be sad for America, catastrophic perhaps for himself and his companions, but no more than a tiny footnote in the history of mankind.

Washington's present mission might change all history. As he himself put it, "the preservation of the sacred fire of liberty and the destiny of the republican model of government are justly considered as *deeply*, perhaps as *finally*, staked on the experiment entrusted to the hands of the American people." He was on his way to lead an enterprise which, if it succeeded, would prove to all the world, and for the future to time immemorial, the falsity of the contention that men were "unequal to the task of governing themselves and therefore made for a master." That contention had, down the ages, been accepted by many of the greatest thinkers. Supposing the failure of the American experiment should seem to prove them right? How long would it be before this "awful monument" to the death of liberty would be forgotten, before the experiment was tried again? And if, through inability or misunderstanding, Washington contributed to the catastrophe, how deep and eternal would be his personal guilt?

Washington subscribed to the religious faith of the Enlightenment: like Franklin and Jefferson, he was a deist. Although not believing in the doctrines of the churches, he was convinced that a divine force, impossible to define, ruled the universe, and that this "Providence" was good. With what passion he now turned for reassurance and guidance to this force is revealed by the inaugural address he delivered with trembling voice and trembling hands on April 30, 1789, to a joint meeting of the houses of Congress. The religious passages took up almost a third of the address.

Speaking not for conventional effect but from his own heart, he avoided, as was his deist custom, the word "God." He expressed "my fervent supplication to that Almighty Being who rules over the universe, who presides in the Councils of Nations, and whose providential aids can supply every human defect" for assistance in the effort of the American people to find "liberties and happiness" under "a government instituted by themselves." Every step which the United States had taken towards becoming "an independent nation," so he continued, "seems to have been distinguished by some token of providential agency." The recent creation of a united government through "the tranquil deliberations and voluntary consent of so many distinct communities . . . cannot be compared with the means by which most governments have been established without some return of pious gratitude along with an humble anticipation of the future blessing which the past seems to presage."

In responding to the constitutional provision that the president recommend measures he judged "necessary and expedient," Washington hardly went beyond urging a spirit of compromise and the pursuit in public matters of "private morality. . . . There exists in the economy and course of nature an indissoluble union between virtue and happiness, between duty and advantage, between the genuine maxims of an honest and magnanimous policy and the solid rewards of public prosperity and felicity."

Various witnesses to the occasion tell us that "time had made havoc" on Washington's face and that his aspect as he spoke was "grave almost to sadness." As he proceeded, he moved his manuscript from his left to his right hand and put several fingers of his left hand into his breeches pocket. Then he extracted his right hand and made with it "an ungainly gesture." The famous orator, Fisher Ames, was amazed by the effect of Washington's simple delivery: "It seemed to me an allegory in which virtue was personified, and addressing those whom she would make her votaries. Her power over the heart was never greater." The whole audience, even Vice President John Adams, who was passionately jealous of Washington, was greatly moved.

Twenty-Eight

A SECOND CONSTITUTIONAL CONVENTION

(1789)

At the Constitutional Convention, many a problem had been compromised by not being solved at all, but left to be worked out in practice. The first active period of the new government, the more than five months that comprised the first session of Congress, was, in effect, a second Constitutional Convention. The task was made easier because there were now general guidelines to follow. It was made more difficult because postponement was no longer possible. Fortunately, a summer of peace and prosperity inserted few outside distractions into the task of government-building. The only major crisis came near the very start. Washington was stricken with a deathly illness.

He had developed a tumor of the thigh that was diagnosed as anthrax. So that no noise would disturb the stricken hero, straw was placed on the sidewalk outside his house to deaden footsteps, while ropes banned carriages. Surgery was considered necessary. When the tumor was laid open, it proved to have spread much further than had been foreseen. In those days before any anesthesia deadened pain, the younger surgeon quailed at the task before him. "Cut away," the older surgeon cried. "Deep—deeper—deeper still. Don't be afraid. You see how well he bears it!" The operation was a success. The time soon came when Washington could be laid full-length in his carriage to profit from what exercise jogging over rough streets gave him. Yet it was forty days before he could return to his desk. His own comment was, "The want of regular exercise with the cares of office will, I have no doubt, hasten my departure for that country from whence no traveler returns."

"Few who are not philosophical spectators," Washington wrote concerning his presidential duties, "can realize the difficult and delicate part which a man in my situation has to act. . . . I walk on untrodden ground. There is scarcely any part of my conduct which may not hereafter be drawn into precedent."

Washington's most obvious plight did not particularly bother him. Having once been the only soldier in the Continental army, he was not dismayed to find that, at the opening of the government, he and the vice president were the only members of the new executive. Their solitary eminence did not draw the two men together. In his fear of tyranny (and perhaps his jealousy of Washington), Adams had fought in the Continental Congress against Washington's desire to build a professional, long-term army. Adams's selection as vice president had been dictated by the old need to balance a Virginia leader with a leader from Massachusetts. Recognizing the political wisdom of the choice, Washington had agreed to it, but he had no intention of working closely with his old opponent, nor did Adams want to work closely with Washington. It lay within the bounds of the Constitution that the vice president could become the president's prime minister, but the Washington–Adams hostility placed the vice presidency in the shadow from whence it has never emerged.

The Constitution made no specific provisions for a cabinet.* Whether what were defined as "the heads of the great departments" were to be under the jurisdiction of the president was not stated; the president was merely empowered to require their opinions relating to their duties. Clearly, however, they were among the major nonelective officers (including the justices of the Supreme Court) who were to be appointed by the president with the approval of the Senate.

When Congress acted to establish the great departments, it was argued that the provision that the senators must approve the appointments implied that they should also insist on the power to veto dismissal. Such a provision would, by allowing the senators to keep in office cabinet ministers with whom they agreed but who opposed the policies of the president, reduce the president to a figurehead similar to a constitutional monarch. Thus the issue became a rallying ground for all who distrusted a strong executive.

John Adams *by John Trumbull, detail, oil on canvas, 1793.*

Washington remained silent, but his intimate collaborator, Madison, persuaded the House to vote against empowering the Senate to veto dismissals. The Senate was not so easily persuaded. There was a tie vote there, which the presiding officer, Vice President Adams, broke to preserve the authority of the executive. Who can doubt that, had the president been less popular and trusted than Washington, the decision would have gone the other way, changing the whole direction of the American government?

The Constitution provided that the president should negotiate treaties with the advice and consent of the Senate. Was the Senate's concurrence to be secured by distant communication or face to face? Washington tried the latter method by going to the Senate chamber to be present at the debate concerning a proposed treaty with the Creek Indians. So much time was wasted, despite the frowns that increasingly darkened Washington's face, by what he considered inconsequential bickering that, as he left the chamber, he was overheard to say that he would "be damned if he ever went there again!" Thus was forever ended the possibility that the American executive might, like the British, present and defend its acts at legislative sessions.

Taking literally the separation of powers, Washington did not mobilize congressional support for programs he favored. It was his constitutional duty to make recommendations to Congress in his annual address, and this he did, although charily and always in terms of general principles rather than specifics. But once the legislative debates began, he meticulously kept hands off. He considered that legislative action had ceased to be his concern until, according to constitutional provision, a bill that had been enacted was placed on his desk for approval or veto.

Only one bill that passed during the first session really outraged him. He had regarded as a major argument for a centralized government the possibility of imposing on a national scale customs duties that would apply to British shipping the restrictions that the British applied to the American. Due to opposition in the Senate that could not be overcome, the customs bill submitted to Washington contained no such clauses. He considered a veto, but his principles forbade.

* The term "cabinet," although too useful not to be used here, was not current during most of Washington's presidency.

Washington believed that the presidential veto was not primarily intended to be used because of disagreement over policy. Its true object was to enable the president to protect the Constitution. This assumed that the president would be an impartial judge, unmoved by the pressures of partisan conflict—such a man as Washington in fact was. When later presidents became the leaders of political parties, they could no longer be expected to be impartial. Then the necessary task was assumed, with no constitutional authority, by the Supreme Court. Here was a fundamental change in the governmental structure, all the more because a presidential veto can be overcome by a two-thirds vote of Congress, while a Supreme Court ruling can be negated only by the infinitely complicated task of amending the Constitution.

Another use of the veto, foreseen by Hamilton in The Federalist, was to protect the presidency from congressional encroachment. For this Washington had no need, perhaps because his own hands-off policy in relation to the legislature reassured the Congress. Once Congress had abandoned its effort to control the tenure of the department heads, it enhanced the power of the presidency by showering responsibilities on Washington.

The initiation of even the most minor appointments was entrusted to him. He took the task with deep seriousness. Since many appointees would be the only aspects of the federal government visible in their neighborhoods, it seemed essential to the ever deepening unity he sought that they both please and impress the inhabitants. His youthful experience with the British system of preferment through family connection made him seek, as few of his successors have done, to avoid all favoritism, to judge altogether on the qualifications of the individual. These qualifications did include influence in the community, which would bring prestige to the government rather than take it away, but Washington wanted no incompetent representatives of leading clans. The usually critical John Adams noted, "He seeks information from all quarters and judges more independently than any man I ever knew."

While Washington made do with holdovers from the Confederation—Knox as secretary of war and Jay as secretary of foreign affairs—Congress set up the great departments. They entrusted Indian affairs (revealingly) to the secretary of war, who had little else to do as there was hardly any standing army. Europe, being on the far side of a broad ocean, seemed to impinge so little that the new post of secretary of state combined foreign affairs with various domestic responsibilities. Regarding (as the eighteenth century typically did) the power to tax as the power to govern, a direct line that bypassed the president was drawn between the House of Representatives and the secretary of the Treasury. The attorney general, thought of as a lawyer advising the president, was given a retainer rather than complete employment.

Knox continued as secretary of war. Washington offered to Jay the expansion of his former office, but he expressed a preference, to which Washington agreed, for the chief-justiceship of the Supreme Court. Washington thereupon wrote Jefferson, who was minister to France and on his way home for a visit, offering him the secretaryship of state. Since neither of the Morrises was available, everyone whom Washington consulted agreed that the obvious man for the Treasury was Hamilton. The attorney-generalship being so minor a post, Washington felt justified in appointing a young friend who would be an agreeable companion: Edmund Randolph of Virginia.

Surveying the team, which would be completed if Jefferson

A lithograph of James Madison by John Vanderlyn.

MARY BALL WASHINGTON AT THE AGE OF ABOUT FOUR-SCORE

Washington's mother, Mary Ball Washington, in a printed copy of a painting by Roger Edge Pine shortly before she died of breast cancer at age eighty-one.

agreed, Washington was sanguine. The men were able and he saw no conceivable reason why they should not all pull together in harmony.

As the congressional session was drawing to a close, news arrived that cut to the very roots of Washington's existence. His mother, who had for some time suffered from cancer of the breast, had died at the age of eighty-one.

Their relationship had always been stormy. Mary Ball Washington's attitudes towards her son's activities in the French and Indian War and in the Revolution had been the same: he was meddling in matters that should not concern him, to the neglect of his duty to her. Although he had set her up in a small and elegant house at Fredericksburg and seen that she was well supplied with money and goods, she had embarrassed him, when he was away as commander in chief, by complaining "upon all occasions and in all companies" that she was neglected, left "in great want." She even initiated a movement in the Virginia legislature whereby the state would come to the financial rescue of the mother of the commander in chief. Washington found her action extremely humiliating and squashed it.

After the war, her demands for money became so oppressive and annoying that Washington suggested that she sell her house and live with one of her children. He quickly added that this was not an invitation to Mount Vernon. Since Mount Vernon was always crowded with strangers, she would be forced to do one of three things: be always dressed for company, appear in deshabille, or be a prisoner in her own chamber. The first, her son assumed, would be too fatiguing at her age. The second would be unsuitable as his guests were often "people of the first distinction." Nor would it do for her to stay in her room: "for what with the sitting up of company, the noise and bustle of servants, and many other things, you would not be able to enjoy that calmness and serenity of mind which, in my opinion, you ought now to prefer to every other consideration in life." But Mary Washington had no more desire to become a conventional fireside figure than her son had to be the most obedient of sons. The old lady had died in her own house, putting up to the last a daily "small battle" against taking her medicine.

Although the mother and son had been for so long at odds, her death revealed deep emotion on both sides. She left George her most personal possessions and, ignoring the fact that among her offspring he least needed a legacy, the lion's share of her estate. And Washington, who usually saw no light on the other side of the grave, was moved into one of his very few references to the possibility of heaven: "awful and affecting as the death of a parent is," there was consolation in "a hope that she is translated to a happier place."

After Congress had adjourned on September 30, 1789, Washington could look back on a period of great creativity achieved with a minimum of conflict. The constitutional skeleton had been fleshed out and a healthy government was striding across the land, "to the satisfaction," Washington wrote, "of all parties." When Jefferson reached the capital, he was amazed to find that "the opposition to our new Constitution has almost totally disappeared." He credited primarily the behavior and influence of the president.

Twenty-Nine

THE SOCIAL MAN

(1789)

The aspect of the presidency that Washington came most quickly to dislike was that it forced his natural conviviality into unnatural channels. He had hardly been inaugurated before he discovered that it was impossible for him relaxedly to keep open house as he had in Virginia. He could not get his work done because people called all day long to mouth rotund compliments and put forward their pretensions to be employed in the government or further entertained. Although conscious that he might be accused of snobbery and worried lest he separate himself from personal contacts that would keep him informed concerning public opinion, he felt it necessary to establish a rigid schedule of whom he would receive, and when, and what kind of invitations he would accept.

On her belated arrival from Virginia, Martha was outraged: "I live a very dull life here and know nothing of what passes in the town. I never go to any public place. Indeed, I think I am more like a state prisoner than anything else. There is certain bounds set for me which I must not depart from. And, as I cannot do what I like, I am obstinate and stay home a great deal."

Washington's official schedule of entertaining specified three kinds of affairs: his "levees" for men only, every Tuesday from three to four; Martha's tea parties, for men and women, held on Friday evenings; and official dinners staged on Thursdays at four in the afternoon.

The levees were open without invitation to any respectably dressed male. (In the eighteenth century, none other presumed to come.) As aristocracies had learned by long experience, only ceremony can give satisfactory content to altogether formal entertaining. Washington's aide, David Humphreys, did his best to supply the need. On one occasion, he arranged for the guests to gather in what he called the "presence chamber." He accompanied Washington to the door,

This wine cooler was one of four that Washington purchased during his presidency for use by men who remained at the dinner table after the ladies had departed. Made of English Sheffield silver, each cooler held on a bed of ice four quart-size decanters that were filled with four different wines.

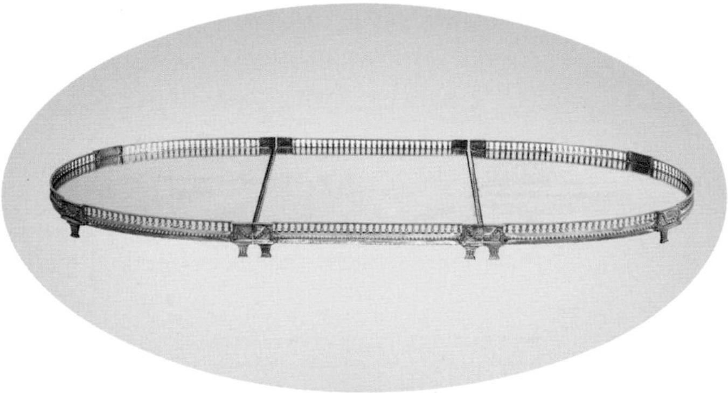

Top: *Down the middle of the presidential table stretched a glass plateau purchased by Gouverneur Morris in Paris at Washington's request, and designed in pieces that could be combined to form various lengths and shapes.* Bottom: *To decorate and reflect in the plateau, he added twelve figurines of French bisque. The group here was the centerpiece.*

threw it open, entered first, and shouted, "the President of the United States."

Washington, so Jefferson's account continues, was so disconcerted that he did not recover his composure during the whole time of the levee. When it was finally over, he told Humphreys angrily, "Well, you have taken me in once, but by God, you will never take me in a second time!" Thereafter, Washington was discovered standing uneasily in his most formal dress with a hat (designed to be thus carried) under his arm and his dress sword peeping out from under his black coat, when, on the dot of three, the servants threw open the doors to whatever was that day's hustle of visitors.

This situation brought to the fore that shyness which also made Washington so embarrassed under the scrutiny of portrait painters. When notified that rumor in Virginia accused him of snubbing good republicans, he answered that he could not imagine "what pomp there is in all this. . . . Perhaps it consists in not sitting"—but there was no room large enough in the house Congress had rented for the president to hold a third of the chairs that would be required. "Gentlemen, often in great numbers, come and go, chat with each other, and act as they please. A porter shows them into the room, and they retire from it when they please and without ceremony. At their *first* entrance, they salute me and I them, and as many as I can talk to I do." As for the criticism that his bows were awkward, would it not be more charitable to ascribe this to old age or the unskillfulness of his teachers rather than to pride of office?

The president was much more at ease at his wife's tea parties. The ladies, having no more elegant presidential receptions to attend, did not spare the hairdressers and costumers. Washington, who enjoyed the company of the fair, circulated gaily without sword or hat. Martha remained seated. Perhaps the more because he did not get on well with the vice president, Washington was careful to see that the seat to Martha's right was assigned to the vice president's wife. If another lady happened to be sitting there when Abigail Adams arrived, he got the interloper to move with a tact that made Mrs. Adams comment, "This same president has so happy a faculty of appearing to accommodate and yet carrying his point, that, if he was not really one of the best-intentioned men in the world, he might be a very dangerous one." She continued in a manner that would have irritated her husband: "He is polite with dignity, affable without familiarity, distant without haughtiness, grave without austerity, modest, wise, and good."

To prevent any contest for invitations, Washington devoted his dinners to entertaining in orderly rotation government officials and foreign representatives. Since such of his best friends as Knox and Senator Robert Morris were in the government, the occasions could be gay, but there were also monumental failures like the party which William Maclay recorded for posterity.

A hypochondriacal and puritanical senator from rural Pennsylvania, Maclay distrusted Washington and was highly suspicious of Philadelphia society. As he dressed in preparation for the presidential dinner, the senator warned himself not to let his pure republicanism be undermined by the seductions of Washington's entertaining. He was happy to see that the women all sat on one side of the table flanking Martha, with men on the other flanking Washington, but he gleefully suspected that a couple who had arrived together were not married.

Seduction then approached in a form that endangered Maclay's resolutions: food. "Soup, fish, roasted and boiled meats, gammon, fowls, etc. . . . The dessert was first apple pies, pudding, etc., then iced creams, jellies, etc., then watermelons, muskmelons, apples, peaches, nuts." Unable to deny that the meal was the best he had ever experienced, Maclay nonetheless found soothing dissatisfactions: the room was "disagreeably warm," and the food was eaten in solemn silence: "not a health drunk."

After the cloth had been removed, there were too many toasts. To Maclay's disgust, the president "drank to the health of every individual by name around the table." The guests imitated him, "and such a buzz of 'Health, sir' and 'Health, madam' never had I heard before."

Silence sank again until the ladies withdrew. Then Washington told an anecdote—about "a New England clergyman who had lost a hat and wig in passing a river called the Brunks"—which Maclay did not consider funny. Another guest delighted and horrified Maclay by referring to Homer when he meant Virgil.

"The president kept a fork in his hand," but instead of using it to open nuts, he "played with the fork, striking on the edge of the table with it." Maclay assumed that the president was being pompous and dull, but perhaps Washington was hearing yearningly in his mind's ear laughter on the banks of the Potomac.

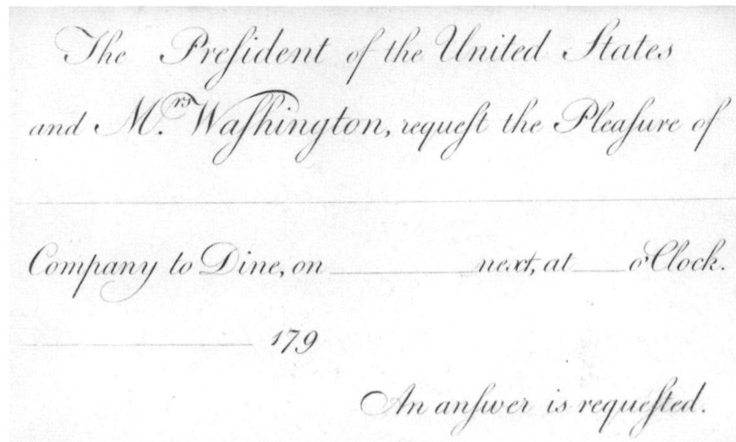
The Preſident of the United States and Mrs. Waſhington, requeſt the Pleaſure of

Company to Dine, on ______ next, at ____ o'Clock.

______ 179

An anſwer is requeſted.

As the first president, Washington set many social standards that would be followed by later administrations. He and Martha maintained a full schedule of public visits and more formal affairs.

Washington was eager to get back, for as long vacations as possible, to Mount Vernon, but during the break between sessions of the first Congress, in the fall and winter of 1789, he felt that his duty prevented any extended departure from the capital; his cabinet was brand new and also incomplete, as Jefferson hesitated and dawdled. Washington had to be satisfied with a month's trip through New England. His object, he wrote his sister, was "relaxation from business and reestablishment of my health." Policy was also involved. He wished to become familiar anew with an area he had known only in wartime, and to make, in this powerful part of the nation, the federal government visibly felt.

In previous travel diaries, Washington had primarily jotted down agricultural observations. Now he concerned himself with nonagricultural economics. He noted the nature of exports and the number of ships which had sailed from various ports. He sought out and described the infant factories along his route. Most impressive was a sail factory in Boston where twenty-eight water-powered looms were tended by young women. Washington commented on the advantages of offering such respectable employment to "daughters of decayed families," and observed the employees with admiration, "telling the overseer he believed he had collected the prettiest girls in Boston."

> Washington's official schedule of entertaining specified three kinds of affairs: his "levees" for men only, every Tuesday from three to four; Martha's tea parties, for men and women, held on Friday evenings; and official dinners staged on Thursdays at four in the afternoon.

Skirting Rhode Island (the one state still delinquent, since North Carolina had by now joined the Union), he traveled according to a prearranged schedule through Connecticut (Fairfield, New Haven, Hartford) and Massachusetts (Springfield, Worcester, Boston, Newburyport). He was received with cheers and ceremonies everywhere, but his sensitive ear did not perceive in the greetings that hysterical note which had so bothered him on his trip from Mount Vernon to his inauguration. He concluded that the people were no longer on edge. They had settled down comfortably with a satisfactory government.

After he had reached the northernmost point of his trip, Washington decided that he could abandon his official progress and on his way back travel in the more agreeable role of a private gentleman. Yet he was too tensed up to relax. Rolling unannounced through the countryside, he found the inconveniences "intolerable." The Massachusetts roads, he complained, "are amazingly crooked to suit the convenience of every man's fields; and the directions you receive from the people equally blind and ignorant." In Connecticut, he was annoyed at being trapped in the little village of Ashford because it was "contrary to law and disagreeable to the people of this state to travel on the Sabbath." The tavern in which he was becalmed was "not a good one." No diversions being offered except the morning and evening services in the local meetinghouse, Washington suffered through two "very lame" discourses "from a Mr. Pond."

On November 13, Washington "arrived at my house at New York, where I found Mrs. Washington and the rest of the family all well."

Thirty

INFIGHTING FORESHADOWED

(1790)

During the first session of Congress, solid foundations had been laid for the government of the United States. The second session presaged fissures that were to widen until they tore Washington's administration apart.

The main actors in the future controversy now met each other for the first time. Hamilton had been at work since the moment of his appointment as secretary of the Treasury, but for three months, Jefferson had hesitated, unable to decide whether to accept as secretary of state, and then he had spent another month on private business. The congressional session was some five weeks old when, on March 21, 1790, Jefferson appeared in New York to undertake his duties and incidentally meet Hamilton.

Washington had known both men well, although in different contexts. Hamilton had come to him at the age of about twenty as a military aide so brilliant that he rapidly became, in effect, chief of staff. All the more defiantly proud because of his illegitimate birth, this immigrant from the West Indies had rebuffed Washington's advances of friendship, preferring, as he wrote, "to stand rather on a footing of military confidence than of private attachment." After Washington had repeatedly demonstrated his unwillingness to lose his invaluable aide by giving him some more conspicuous assignment, Hamilton picked a quarrel and resigned his staff post in anger. Washington forgave, and belatedly rewarded, the fiery youth with a glamorous opportunity at Yorktown. Yet the two men remained on no more than distantly friendly terms until brought again into close collaboration by the cabinet appointment.

With Jefferson, Washington had not previously worked closely. Yet the fellow Virginians shared deep hereditary and environmental interests that were far out of Hamilton's range. Between the Revolution and the presidency, they corresponded on what were then Washington's two major concerns: agriculture and the Potomac Canal. When the retired commander in chief became, despite his wishes, reinvolved in public matters, he turned naturally to Jefferson for advice.

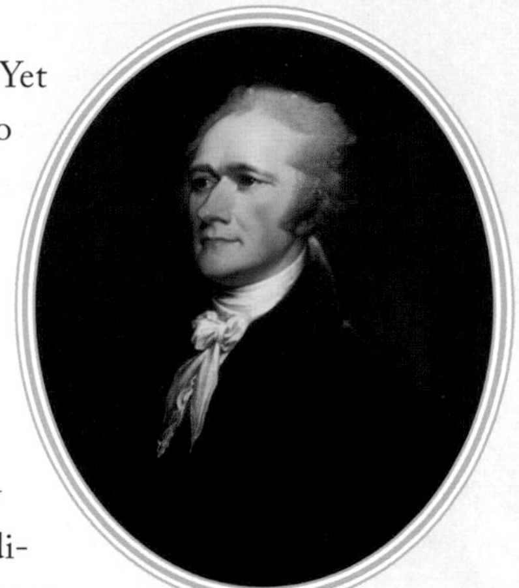

Alexander Hamilton *by John Trumbull, detail, oil on canvas, 1806.*

Although no one had yet recognized the fact, Hamilton and Jefferson were born to hate each other. Alike in having dominant personalities, they were opposite in manners and temperament. A shorter man than Jefferson, Hamilton moved with military crispness; Jefferson slouched. Hamilton dressed meticulously; even Jefferson's admirers felt he overdid the sloppiness of a philosopher. Hamilton's mind moved in the straight line of a doer; Jefferson's with the discursiveness of a thinker.

The rivalry that was to arise between them was not only doctrinal and for political power. They competed for the admiration and countenance of Washington. Jefferson's father had died when he was a child; Hamilton's father was a ne'er-do-well who had soon drifted away. Both younger men found in the president a substitute father, whom neither was willing, as they came to hate each other, to share.

All controversy, however, lay in the future. Madison was their mutual friend and brought them smilingly together. They felt the same anxiety when Washington was so stricken with pneumonia that on the fifth day of his illness he was, as Jefferson wrote, "pronounced by two of the three physicians present to be in the act of death. . . . You cannot conceive of the public alarm on this occasion. It proves how much depends on his life."

That same afternoon, while Jefferson was expressing "total despair," Washington took a turn for the better. Soon he could ride out prone in his coach. When he was still too weak to attend to public business, the president comforted himself with the thought that "by having Mr. Jefferson at the head of the Department of State, Mr. Jay of the Judiciary, Hamilton of the Treasury, and Knox of that of War, I feel myself supported by able coadjutors who harmonize extremely well together."

At the time of Jefferson's arrival and for some time after Washington's recovery, governmental attention was focused on Hamilton's plans for meeting the debts which had been incurred during the Revolution. Despite the agitations of the financiers and Washington's assurances to his soldiers when he had sent them home unpaid, these debts had for the most part been allowed to fester during the Confederation. Washington, who must have suffered from a sense of guilt that he had not been more successful in his efforts to procure recompense for his army, could only be pleased that his efficient secretary of the Treasury was now purposefully grappling with the problem.

Hamilton's recommendations had, of course, been shown to Washington before they were sent to the House of Representatives, but the direct communication which Congress had established between the Treasury and the House absolved the president of specific responsibility. He would have no duty for decision until such bills as Congress passed came to him for signature or veto.

Although no one had yet recognized the fact, Hamilton and Jefferson were born to hate each other. Alike in having dominant personalities, they were opposite in manners and temperament.

After it had been decided that the federal government should meet the obligations incurred by the Continental Congress that were still outstanding, there remained three major issues: "discrimination," "funding," and "assumption."

Most of the original recipients had, in order to get some usable money in hand, sold their Continental paper to speculators. Arguing that it was unjust for those who had themselves bled or otherwise suffered to be excluded from the government's belated act of justice, Madison proposed "discrimination." He moved in the House that present possession of a certificate should only entitle the holder to part payment. The rest should go to the original holder.

Although highly popular with everyone except the moneymen, discrimination proved on examination to be unworkable: it was illegal since the certificates had printed on them that the value be paid to the bearer;

The earliest known likeness of Thomas Jefferson, painted by Mather Brown in 1786.

the cost of seeking out the original owners would be astronomical and most of them could probably not be found; and, since some of the paper had gone abroad to European capitalists, refusing completely to honor what had been bought in good faith would destroy the foreign credit of the United States.

Hamilton had another secret reason for opposing discrimination. If the money were dribbled out across the country, it would disappear in small purchases. If, on the other hand, it enriched a small group of urban financiers, it would become capital available for initiating and bolstering enterprises that would strengthen the economy. The general prosperity thus created, so Hamilton's reasoning ran, would elevate the economic standard of the theoretically defrauded veterans more than would the fragmentary purchase of a new cow or a new carpet or a few additional acres.

By the time Jefferson appeared in New York, discrimination had already been voted down. He could not have supported it, in any case. While in Europe, he had assured bankers that it was safe for them to invest in the American paper, which would be paid in full.

Washington undoubtedly wished that discrimination could be made practical. That would be to the advantage of the soldiers who had fought beside him and also to his own advantage, since he too had sold paper to speculators. Publicly, he adhered to his principles by making no comment. Privately, he expressed unhappiness about the controversy, stating that, although discrimination had been urged for "the purest motives . . . the subject was delicate and perhaps had better never been stirred." Not only might a defeat of the proposal make poor people regard the government as their enemy, but the debate tended to exacerbate regional divisions. Most of the paper originally held in the South had been sold to northeasterners, who thus stood almost alone to profit.

Discrimination was defeated by a large majority.

The most fundamental of Hamilton's schemes was "funding," and this paradoxically made it the least divisive: the implications were really understood only by the financial community, who were unanimously for the plan. Hamilton proposed that the old paper be exchanged for new securities. To meet interest payments and pay off some holders, specific sums of tax money would be sequestered. However—and this was the nub of the scheme—only two percent of the bonds could be bought back by the government in one year. Being semipermanent and altogether secure, the bonds would circulate as if they were money, and the interest payments would also add to the nation's fluid capital.

Not conscious that Hamilton was engrafting onto a farming society the self-reproducing cells of capitalism, the agrarian opposition did not go beyond a feeling that there was something immoral about not

"A FREE PEOPLE OUGHT NOT ONLY TO BE ARMED, BUT DISCIPLINED..."

WASHINGTON'S FIRST STATE OF THE UNION ADDRESS

On January 8, 1790, George Washington gave this country's first State of the Union Address, a wide-ranging speech in which he addressed the need for a regular army, better roads, improved communication, and a national census. A key point was his belief in the importance of establishing a good system of education, thereby insuring that all would come of age understanding, among other things, their rights under the Constitution.

State of the Union Address
George Washington
January 8, 1790
Fellow Citizens of the Senate and House of Representatives:

I embrace with great satisfaction the opportunity which now presents itself of congratulating you on the present favorable prospects of our public affairs. The recent accession of the important state of North Carolina to the Constitution of the United States (of which official information has been received), the rising credit and respectability of our country, the general and increasing good will toward the government of the Union, and the concord, peace, and plenty with which we are blessed are circumstances auspicious in an eminent degree to our national prosperity.

In resuming your consultations for the general good, you cannot but derive encouragement from the reflection that the measures of the last session have been as satisfactory to your constituents as the novelty and difficulty of the work allowed you to hope. Still further to realize their expectations and to secure the blessings which a gracious Providence has placed within our reach will in the course of the present important session call for the cool and deliberate exertion of your patriotism, firmness, and wisdom.

Among the many interesting objects which will engage your attention, that of providing for the common defense will merit particular regard. To be prepared for war is one of the most effectual means of preserving peace.

A free people ought not only to be armed, but disciplined; to which end a uniform and well-digested plan is requisite; and their safety and interest require that they should promote such manufactories as tend to render them independent of others for essential, particularly military, supplies.

The proper establishment of the troops which may be deemed indispensable will be entitled to mature consideration. In the arrangements which may be made respecting it, it will be of importance to conciliate the comfortable support of the officers and soldiers with a due regard to economy.

There was reason to hope that the pacific measures adopted with regard to certain hostile tribes of Indians would have relieved the inhabitants of our southern and western frontiers from their depredations, but you will perceive from the information contained in the papers which I shall direct to be laid before you (comprehending a communication from the Commonwealth of Virginia) that we ought to be prepared to afford protection to those parts of the Union, and, if necessary, to punish aggressors.

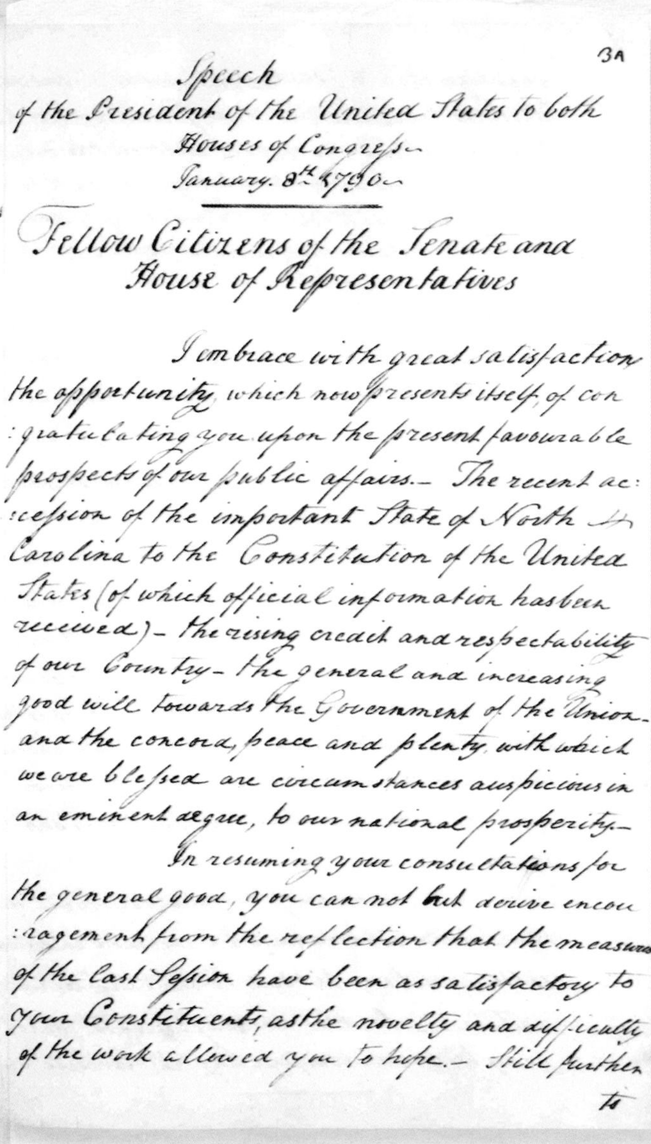
3A

Speech
of the President of the United States to both
Houses of Congress—
January. 8th 1790—

Fellow Citizens of the Senate and
House of Representatives

I embrace with great satisfaction the opportunity, which now presents itself, of congratulating you upon the present favourable prospects of our public affairs.— The recent accession of the important State of North Carolina to the Constitution of the United States (of which official information has been received)— the rising credit and respectability of our Country— the general and increasing good will towards the Government of the Union— and the concord, peace and plenty, with which we are blessed are circumstances auspicious in an eminent degree, to our national prosperity—

In resuming your consultations for the general good, you can not but derive encouragement from the reflection that the measures of the last Session have been as satisfactory to your Constituents, as the novelty and difficulty of the work allowed you to hope.— Still further

to

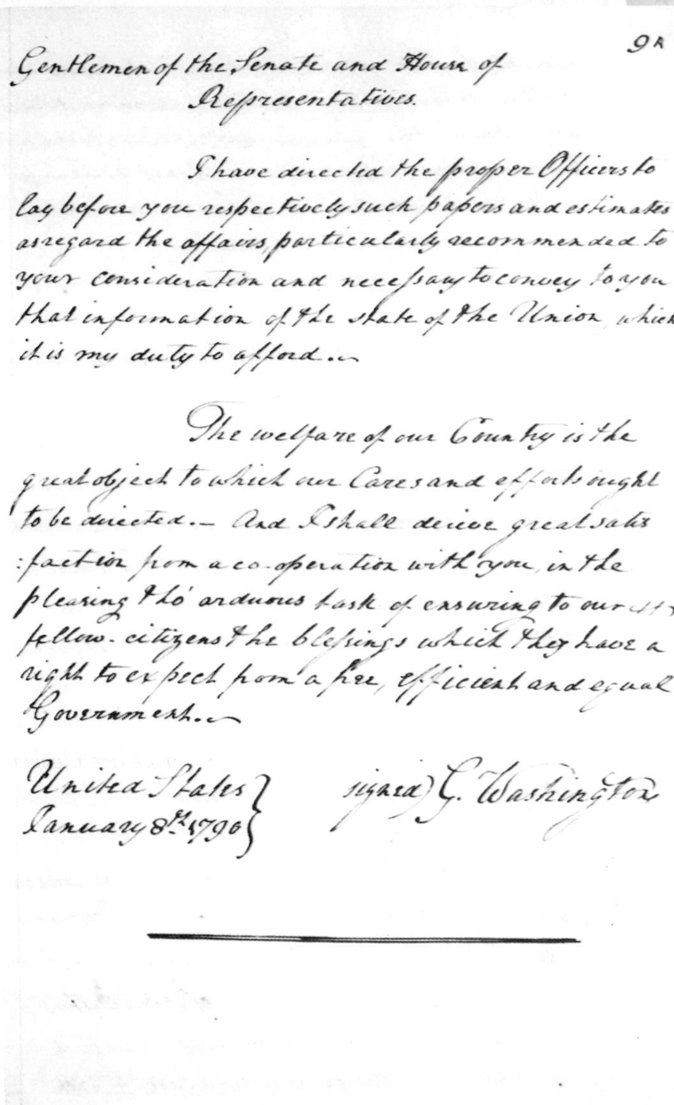
9A

Gentlemen of the Senate and House of
Representatives.

I have directed the proper Officers to lay before you respectively such papers and estimates as regard the affairs particularly recommended to your consideration and necessary to convey to you that information of the state of the Union which it is my duty to afford.—

The welfare of our Country is the great object to which our Cares and efforts ought to be directed.— And I shall derive great satisfaction from a co-operation with you, in the pleasing tho' arduous task of ensuring to our fellow-citizens the blessings which they have a right to expect from a free, efficient and equal Government.—

United States }
January 8th 1790 }   signed G. Washington

The first and last pages of George Washington's annual address to Congress, January 8, 1790.

The interests of the United States require that our intercourse with other nations should be facilitated by such provisions as will enable me to fulfill my duty in that respect in the manner which circumstances may render most conducive to the public good; and to this end that the compensation to be made to the persons who may be employed should, according to the nature of their appointments, be defined by law, and a competent fund designated for defraying the expenses incident to the conduct of foreign affairs.

Various considerations also render it expedient that the terms on which foreigners may be admitted to the rights of citizens should be speedily ascertained by a uniform rule of naturalization.

Uniformity in the currency, weights, and measures of the United States is an object of great importance, and will, I am persuaded, be duly attended to.

The advancement of agriculture, commerce, and manufactures by all proper means will not, I trust, need recommendation; but I cannot forbear intimating to you the expediency of giving effectual encouragement as well to the introduction of new and useful inventions from abroad as to the exertions of skill and genius in producing them at home, and of facilitating the intercourse between the distant parts of our country by a due attention to the post office and post roads.

Nor am I less persuaded that you will agree with me in opinion that there is nothing which can better deserve your patronage than the promotion of science and literature. Knowledge is in every country the surest basis of public happiness. In one in which the measures of government receive their impressions so immediately from the sense of the community as in ours it is proportionably essential.

To the security of a free constitution it contributes in various ways—by convincing those who are intrusted with the public administration that every valuable end of government is best answered by the enlightened confidence of the people, and by teaching the people themselves to know and to value their own rights; to discern and provide against invasions of them; to distinguish between oppression and the necessary exercise of lawful authority; between burthens proceeding from a disregard to their convenience and those resulting from the inevitable exigencies of society; to discriminate the spirit of liberty from that of licentiousness—cherishing the first, avoiding the last—and uniting a speedy but temperate vigilance against encroachments, with an inviolable respect to the laws.

Whether this desirable object will be best promoted by affording aids to seminaries of learning already established, by the institution of a national university, or by any other expedients will be well worthy of a place in the deliberations of the legislature.

Gentlemen of the House of Representatives:

I saw with peculiar pleasure at the close of the last session the resolution entered into by you expressive of your opinion that an adequate provision for the support of the public credit is a matter of high importance to the national honor and prosperity. In this sentiment I entirely concur; and to a perfect confidence in your best endeavors to devise such a provision as will be truly with the end I add an equal reliance on the cheerful cooperation of the other branch of the legislature.

It would be superfluous to specify inducements to a measure in which the character and interests of the United States are so obviously so deeply concerned, and which has received so explicit a sanction from your declaration.

Gentlemen of the Senate and House of Representatives:

I have directed the proper officers to lay before you, respectively, such papers and estimates as regard the affairs particularly recommended to your consideration, and necessary to convey to you that information of the state of the Union which it is my duty to afford.

The welfare of our country is the great object to which our cares and efforts ought to be directed, and I shall derive great satisfaction from a cooperation with you in the pleasing though arduous task of insuring to our fellow citizens the blessings which they have a right to expect from a free, efficient, and equal government.

paying off the national debt as quickly as possible. But they were soothed by the thought that the immediate tax burden would be lighter.

Washington made no comment. He was himself no financial expert. However, his experiences during the Revolution, when the lack of fluid capital had done so much to starve the army and prolong the war, made him sympathetic to the broad conception of enlarging financial credit.

Hamilton's funding plan moved comfortably through Congress.

The hullabaloo rose over "assumption," which was the name given to Hamilton's proposal that the federal government take over the still-unpaid war debts of the various states. This action, he explained, would strengthen the nation by "doing away with the necessity of thirteen complicated and different systems of [state] finance." The lion's share of taxes would be carried into the federal system, and it would become the interest of all public creditors to support the central authority.

As he was a passionate believer in a strong centralized government, these objectives were for Hamilton a series of pluses. But those who did not wish the Union to override the states saw minuses. And the states that had already paid off their debts were outraged at the suggestion that they should be taxed to bail out the delinquent states. Unfortunately, the largest states of the two great regions were on opposite sides: Virginia had paid most of her debts; Massachusetts was waiting on the federal government. And the whole matter was made more irritating to the South by the fact that most of the state paper had, like the federal paper, ended up in northern strongboxes. Again, it was the business community that would profit.

The legislative battle over assumption rose to Herculean proportions. As the debate went on for month after month, the holders of state paper were thrown into consternation. Hopeful or discouraging rumors made speculators buy or sell in an erratic manner that wracked the economy. Hamilton prophesied that the nation would topple into a bottomless financial crash if assumption failed, while the debtor states that hoped to be gotten off the hook—Massachusetts was joined by South Carolina—threatened to secede from the Union if the other states left them dangling.

Washington favored assumption. He had, while preparing for the presidency, drawn up a "Plan of American Finance" in which all taxes were collected by the Union. And he argued privately that the expenses of the war had been incurred in a common cause. "Had the invaded and hard-pressed states believed the case would have been otherwise," they might well have surrendered "and given a different determination to the war." However, the president had no intention of intervening publicly. It remained for Jefferson to tip—in a way which he later regarded as the greatest mistake of his life—the scale in Hamilton's direction.

Still unsuspicious of the secretary of the Treasury, Jefferson was worried at the way the Union seemed to be pulling apart—and he saw the basis for a deal. Another major issue was the location of the permanent national capital. In those days of poor communication and slow transportation, each region saw great advantages in having the government, so to speak, in its hands. Meeting with Madison and Hamilton, Jefferson presided over a swap: in exchange for enough northern votes to put the capital in the South, enough southern votes would be recruited to pass assumption. On this basis, the issue was settled.

Although Washington took no part in this deal, he was pleased with both halves of the compromise, all the more because Congress provided that the permanent capital should be on the Potomac. Washington was himself empowered to pick the exact spot. His was now the opportunity to create near Mount Vernon, whether the Potomac Canal succeeded or not, the great city he had for so long envisioned. Yet he did not hurry to approve the twin bills that grew out of the compromise. Before doing so, he carefully investigated a constitutional objection raised by a pamphleteer.

Even as he sighed with relief that the controversy had been brought to a seemingly peaceful end, he was worried. He feared that that "warmth and intemperance, with prolixity and threats," which had characterized the debate in the House, would decrease national respect for the Congress. He considered it outrageous that congressmen, by imputing the worst motives to each other, should have spread far and wide "jealousies and distrusts."

Washington himself had not been spared. For the first time since he had become president, he heard an undertone of personal attacks: he had, it was charged, sold out his troops by not insisting on discrimination; he had sold out the entire nation to get the national capital at his door.

Rhode Island had at last made the Union complete by coming in. This gave Washington, after the second congressional session had ended, excuse for a junket. At Newport, he "completely fatigued the company" by walking, fortified by the wine and punch served in four different houses along the route, briskly from nine in the morning until one in the afternoon. Yet, energetic as he seemed, he was worried about his health.

In providing for the permanent capital on the Potomac, Congress had thrown a sop to Pennsylvania. During the ten years it would take for the permanent capital to be exactly located and then built, Philadelphia should be the capital. As he contemplated moving from New York, Washington wrote a Philadelphia land agent expressing his wish to acquire a small farm near that city. "I shall candidly declare that to pay money is out of the question with me. I have *none* and would not, if it was to be had, run in debt to borrow." He wished to exchange "valuable lands, improved" that he owned in western Pennsylvania.

Washington explained that he needed the acres near Philadelphia "for the amusement of farming and for the benefit arising from exercise." Both he and his physicians believed "that my late change from active scenes, to which I have been accustomed and in which the mind has been agreeably amused, to the one of inactivity which I now lead and where the thoughts are continually on the stretch, has been the cause of more illness and severe attacks of my constitution within the last twelve months than I had undergone in thirty years preceding put together. A deviation therefore is necessary."

The agent, Washington added, should burn his letter "as soon as you have read it." He did not wish the government or some patriotic individuals to supply what he considered necessary to his health. Since even three thousand acres within sixteen miles of Pittsburgh were not considered a fair exchange for sixty acres near Philadelphia, the survival of the keystone of the national government remained endangered.

Thirty-One

THE GREAT SCHISM OPENS

(1790–1792)

When Congress reconvened in December 1790, no one expected anything but harmony. Even after Hamilton had proposed the next step in his master financial plan, it was only belatedly realized that a Pandora's box of discord had been opened.

Hamilton urged that Congress charter "the Bank of the United States." It would be "a great engine of state" but not actively controlled by the government. He argued—and so experience during the Revolution seemed loudly to testify—that the national currency should not be at the mercy of governmental action. When pinched, governments always pursued expedients that resulted in inflation. But to ensure their own prosperity, so Hamilton contended, private interests would keep the economy healthy.

The government would hold only a fifth part of the capital of the bank and would select only a fifth of the directors. However, long-range control would be assured: the records would always be open to the secretary of the Treasury, and the bank would have to act in a way that would induce Congress to renew its charter after a period of years.

Hamilton did not envisage such an ordinary bank as stands on city street corners. The Bank of the United States would deal only in large-scale operations: service the national debt; make loans to the government and for major private projects. The bank's bills of indebtedness (Congress had failed to authorize a mint) would circulate as the basic currency of the United States. Using its powers to create and control credit, the bank would ward off excessive inflation or deflation, would force its policies on local banks.

It should have been clear at a glance that Hamilton's scheme would enrich an inner group of private businessmen and give them great national power, but, at first, no objection was raised. The bank bill passed the Senate casually, with a voice vote, and in a preliminary vote the House backed the scheme without opposition. It was only as the House approached a final vote that Madison arose to argue that the Constitution did not give the federal government the power to incorporate a bank. Although Madison talked for a whole day, the House passed the bill thirty-nine to twenty. The problem was thus moved onto Washington's desk. As he believed that the principal function of the presidential veto was to protect the Constitution, he found himself "greatly perplexed."

Washington called in Madison for a long conference, and asked the advice of members of his cabinet. Jefferson and Randolph backed the argument of their fellow Virginian. The Constitution did not specifically authorize Congress to incorporate institutions. Therefore Congress could not do so unless the act were absolutely necessary to keep functions specifically granted Congress in the Constitution from being (to use Jefferson's word) "nugatory." Madison scoffed at the idea that a bank could be authorized

Congress of the United States,
begun and held at the City of New-York, on
Wednesday the fourth of March, one thousand seven hundred and eighty nine.

THE Conventions of a number of the States, having at the time of their adopting the Constitution, expressed a desire, in order to prevent misconstruction or abuse of its powers, that further declaratory and restrictive clauses should be added: And as extending the ground of public confidence in the Government, will best ensure the beneficent ends of its institution.

RESOLVED by the Senate and House of Representatives of the United States of America, in Congress assembled, two thirds of both Houses concurring, that the following Articles be proposed to the Legislatures of the several States, as amendments to the Constitution of the United States, all, or any of which Articles, when ratified by three fourths of the said Legislatures, to be valid to all intents and purposes, as part of the said Constitution; viz.

ARTICLES in addition to, and Amendment of the Constitution of the United States of America, proposed by Congress, and ratified by the Legislatures of the several States, pursuant to the fifth Article of the original Constitution.

Article the first.... After the first enumeration required by the first article of the Constitution, there shall be one Representative for every thirty thousand, until the number shall amount to one hundred, after which, the proportion shall be so regulated by Congress, that there shall be not less than one hundred Representatives, nor less than one Representative for every forty thousand persons, until the number of Representatives shall amount to two hundred, after which the proportion shall be so regulated by Congress, that there shall not be less than two hundred Representatives, nor more than one Representative for every fifty thousand persons.

Article the second.... No law, varying the compensation for the services of the Senators and Representatives, shall take effect, until an election of Representatives shall have intervened.

Article the third.... Congress shall make no law respecting an establishment of religion, or prohibiting the free exercise thereof; or abridging the freedom of speech, or of the press, or the right of the people peaceably to assemble, and to petition the Government for a redress of grievances.

Article the fourth.... A well regulated militia, being necessary to the security of a free State, the right of the people to keep and bear Arms, shall not be infringed.

Article the fifth.... No Soldier shall, in time of peace be quartered in any house, without the consent of the Owner, nor in time of war, but in a manner to be prescribed by law.

Article the sixth.... The right of the people to be secure in their persons, houses, papers, and effects, against unreasonable searches and seizures, shall not be violated, and no Warrants shall issue, but upon probable cause, supported by oath or affirmation, and particularly describing the place to be searched, and the persons or things to be seized.

Article the seventh.... No person shall be held to answer for a capital, or otherwise infamous crime, unless on a presentment or indictment of a Grand Jury, except in cases arising in the land or naval forces, or in the Militia, when in actual service in time of War or public danger; nor shall any person be subject for the same offence to be twice put in jeopardy of life or limb, nor shall be compelled in any Criminal case to be a witness against himself, nor be deprived of life, liberty, or property, without due process of law; nor shall private property be taken for public use without just compensation.

Article the eighth.... In all criminal prosecutions, the accused shall enjoy the right to a speedy and public trial, by an impartial jury of the State and district wherein the crime shall have been committed, which district shall have been previously ascertained by law, and to be informed of the nature and cause of the accusation; to be confronted with the witnesses against him; to have compulsory process for obtaining Witnesses in his favor, and to have the assistance of counsel for his defence.

Article the ninth.... In suits at common law, where the value in controversy shall exceed twenty dollars, the right of trial by jury shall be preserved, and no fact tried by a jury shall be otherwise re-examined in any Court of the United States, than according to the rules of the common law.

Article the tenth.... Excessive bail shall not be required, nor excessive fines imposed, nor cruel and unusual punishments inflicted.

Article the eleventh.... The enumeration in the Constitution, of certain rights, shall not be construed to deny or disparage others retained by the people.

Article the twelfth.... The powers not delegated to the United States by the Constitution, nor prohibited by it to the States, are reserved to the States respectively, or to the people.

ATTEST,

Frederick Augustus Muhlenberg Speaker of the House of Representatives.

John Adams, Vice-President of the United States, and President of the Senate.

John Beckley, Clerk of the House of Representatives.

Sam. A. Otis Secretary of the Senate.

Although twelve amendments were originally proposed, the ten that were ratified became the Bill of Rights in 1791.

under the right to regulate trade. He asked, with a farmer's sublime ignorance of such matters, "Would any plain man suppose" that a bank had "*anything* to do with trade?"

The developing debate was a confrontation between two basic attitudes towards the Constitution: "strict interpretation" vs. the acceptance of "implied powers." However, the stand taken by the Virginians was actually a cover for something very different. This is evident because in their present support for "strict interpretation," Madison and Jefferson were reversing their previous positions. Madison, indeed, has been considered "the father of implied powers." He had written in *The Federalist* that "no axiom is more clearly established in law and reason that wherever the end is required, the means are authorized; wherever a general power to do a thing is given, every particular power for doing it is included."

Hamilton, caught by surprise by Madison's about-face, worked feverishly for days on the rebuttal he subsequently submitted to Washington. Strict interpretation, he pointed out, would, by banning any response to new situations, soon make the federal government obsolete. The state governments, being not similarly tied, would keep up to date and therefore take over, thus defeating the object of the federal union.

Since Hamilton's argument was—as almost all modern historians agree—unanswerable, Washington had no choice but to sign the bill. It was this act which brought to the surface the fundamental flaw in the harmony of Washington's administration—and of the nation.

The true issue that had sidled in under the cloak of an argument about constitutionality reflected a dichotomy so deep in American life that it was to explode several generations later into the great national tragedy of the Civil War. Washington recognized that the disagreements which had stirred strong controversy since he had become president were regional in application. It was not by chance that the compromise which had solved the crisis over assumption had been a swap between the South and the Northeast. Concerning the arguments over the bank, Washington mourned that "the line between the southern and the eastern interests appeared more strongly marked than could have been wished."

Oceans of ink have been spilled in describing the mounting conflict between Jefferson and Hamilton—and, in the process, the fundamentals have tended to become drowned.

Most confusing to the record has been the Marxist interpretation that arose in the 1930s, which envisions the controversy as an example of "class warfare" waged between Hamilton as a champion of privilege, and Jefferson, who desired laws that would help the underprivileged. This attributes twentieth-century issues to the eighteenth. Those who wished through government action to support the poor in opposition to the rich were in those days known as "levelers." Far from being a leveler, Jefferson boasted that the nation's "mass of weight and wealth" supported his ideas. Had a welfare state been thought of during Washington's presidency, it would surely have been less sympathetic to Jefferson than Hamilton, since it involved so great an increase in governmental power. The controversy which embroiled the two champions was not basically concerned with the haves and the have-nots. It was between rival economic systems, each of which was aimed at generating its own men of property.

The profoundest reason for the Jeffersonian–Hamiltonian controversy dates back to long before the birth pangs of the United States: it reflects one of the most basic shifts in the whole history of European man. For many centuries, society was agricultural, regions being primarily self-sustaining, wealth (and with it, temporal power) appertaining to the ownership of land. Gradually, as communications improved, merchants began to compete with the landowner, but this remained, except in a few commercial cities, an unequal battle until the industrial revolution ranged its products and its possibilities on the mercantile side. An agricultural community subsisted basically on barter—goods exchanged for other goods or for services; and money, which was hard for agriculturalists to come by, was regarded (all the more because sometimes desperately needed) as an evil force. "Usury," which meant lending money at profitable interest, was considered a sin and often a crime. But money was the lifeblood of the emerging society, and usury, redefined as "the expansion of credit," came to be deified as a major engine of "progress."

The settlement of America, being an offshoot of mobility and trade, was, of course, an aspect of the huge change that was advancing with majestic slowness down the centuries. The American Revolution, which pitted the self-reliant individual against hereditary power, was a world-shaking explosion of new points of view. Yet the eighteenth-century American experiment was by no means the final move in the great cultural shift from the medieval to the modern world. Although fought a considerable distance down the road, the battle between Jeffersonianism and Hamiltonianism was a contest between the old agrarianism and the new economics that was, for better or worse, on the rise. It was not inapposite that, when the conflict finally burst all bounds into the bloody Civil War, southern officers often thought of themselves in terms of medieval chivalry.

The nature of the land had dictated a rough four-part division of American society. New England, with its hilly, rocky fields that precluded mass cultivation, had developed no agricultural aristocracy. The yeoman farmers were individual entrepreneurs, and a drive to seek a livelihood from the ocean created a large class of merchants. Society in the middle colonies was more mixed than that of New England, but, being influenced by the rising city of New York and the great city of Philadelphia, was on the whole sympathetic to mercantilism. Along the frontier, mobility being very restricted, the economic pattern was agricultural barter. The South was also agrarian but had, unlike the frontier, fostered an agricultural aristocracy.

More than any other American group, the Virginia aristocrats resembled in their lifestyles what had for some time been the most vocal political opposition in Great Britain. The protesting Englishmen, known as the Old Whigs, were gentlemen farmers, members of country families that had led the Glorious Revolution, which had in 1688 brought the crown to William and Mary. Since then, the Old Whigs had been forced into the background by a few rich families who also called themselves Whigs. The members of this oligarchy had added to aristocratic lineage and major country estates wealth that was pouring into England as a result of her world leadership in finance and trade. Except when their course had been temporarily interrupted by the pretensions to royal power of George III, the rich Whigs had long ruled England, changes in government being a shifting of coalitions between the various dominant clans.

The political polemics of the Old Whigs had been eagerly studied by the fathers of the American Revolution, and the points of view expressed were still active in the United States. The Old Whigs were highly independent, powerful in their neighborhoods and over their tenantry, and, although short of fluid cash, economically secure. Standing upright in their fecund fields, they preached that political virtue was synonymous with agricultural virtue. They were eloquent concerning dangers involved in a government dominated by a small elite that clustered in the capital. Having political enemies who lived in splendor, dressed elegantly, gambled for high stakes, and slept with each other's wives, the Old Whigs shouted that luxury, with its attendant train of vices, enervated a nation. Gibbon's celebrated *Decline and Fall of the Roman Empire* was a multivolume historical parable to prove this point.

The Virginia Republicans saw in their own plantation society the forthright agricultural virtues claimed by the British country gentlemen. Although the slave economy on which they existed seemed regrettable to advanced planters like Jefferson, they did not regard it as the type of vice that would undermine the nation as Gibbon's Rome had been undermined. They denounced instead the lifestyle of the northeastern mercantile and business classes.

The true issue that had sidled in under the cloak of an argument about constitutionality reflected a dichotomy so deep in American life that it was to explode several generations later into the great national tragedy of the Civil War.

Republican apprehensions were given a great boost by an event largely coincidental: the shift of the national capital from New York to Philadelphia. Still recovering from long years of British military occupation, New York was not a resplendent city, but the British occupation of Philadelphia had been only for one winter. That winter, when the city had been filled with British officers, had seen the grandest social season in all American history, and fostered a covey of great belles. The dancing partners of aristocrats had subsequently intermarried with the speculators who had flocked back to Philadelphia when it became again the Revolutionary capital of the United States.

After the Continental Congress had moved away in 1782, the gaiety had gone on, but without an official center. What was the jubilation at the return after eleven years of a government now more powerful and with as its leader the world's most famous hero! "You have never seen anything like the frenzy which has seized upon the inhabitants here," a commentator wrote. "They have been half mad ever since the city became the seat of government."

A psychological transference (which had its comic side) now took place. The British ruling families, against whom the Old Whigs inveighed, were (whatever their profitable contacts with trade and colonial exploitation) inheritors of titles and of agricultural estates, where they lived in alternation with their city residences. They remained aristocrats in the traditional sense. They were thus an altogether different class from the prosperous Philadelphia bourgeois, who had often risen from humble beginnings and had no true link with the land. Yet some of the Philadelphians (and particularly their wives) dreamed of themselves as the American equivalents of the British social and political oligarchy. They lived in as much splendor as they could manage (which was piddling compared to the luxuries of London) and did their best to achieve upper-class vices. They liked to think of themselves as an American aristocracy—but, of course, they were not.

The true American aristocrats were, even if they spoke in the name of the common man, the Virginia Jeffersonians. As a Randolph of Virginia, Jefferson had as blue blood as any man on the continent, and his livelihood was based on an inherited estate. Hamilton had been born in the West Indies, the illegitimate son of a woman jailed for sexual misbehavior; he had come to the United States as a pauper. Jefferson considered Hamilton a vulgar upstart and Hamilton considered Jefferson a snob who railed about equality.

The manners of the agriculturists were hallowed by generations of tradition. Those of the businessmen were not, and the organization of the bank presented what was viewed as a horrifying portent of America's future unless Hamilton were suppressed. Not wishing to seem to favor the rich, Hamilton offered the scrip which could eventually be turned into bank stock at a very low price: twenty-five dollars a share. That this was less than the scrip was actually worth set off a frantic spiral of speculation. Philadelphia became crowded with rapacious moneymen, and the opening of the sale created a near riot. The stock was oversubscribed by four thousand shares. Many of the lucky applicants who actually received some hawked their scrip from tavern tables or even street corners. Speculators borrowed money to buy so that they could sell at a profit. In less than a month, the value of scrip rose five hundred percent.

To farmers, used to making money more tangibly and more slowly, and who visualized moneymen primarily as foreclosers of mortgages, what was taking place seemed wicked. A newspaper paragrapher, somewhat incoherent in his outrage, described how "the men who had resigned their lives in the war, or who had parted with their patrimonies or hard-earned estates to save the public liberty, stood at a distance and with astonishment beheld the singular and unexpected phenomenon."

The passage of Hamilton's first series of recommendations was specifically accompanied by a sop to the South. The South had been given the national capital. No such sop accompanied the Bank of the United States. That the bank served other interests than the agrarian became increasingly clear, as few of the bank's certificates circulated below the Mason and Dixon line, where the economy had little use for fluid capital.

The Jeffersonians felt that they had every reason to view with general alarm. They were being pushed aside like the Old Whigs by evil men entrenched in the capital. These men were busily establishing a new kind of economy hostile to the agricultural way of life. They were enervating the nation with vices and wished to establish themselves, despite their lack of family, manners, and breeding, as an American aristocracy. Some seemed eager to crown an American king. And what made the whole thing the more sinister was the fact that their leader, Alexander Hamilton, was a man of genius. Who could doubt that he was as corrupt as he was able? Certainly he was opposed to popular rule. He might well prove to be a Samson who would pull the temple of American republicanism down.

Expressing what they truly believed in, all the more because the American majority was agrarian, the Jeffersonians adopted for themselves the name "Republican."* To stress their concern with national union, the Hamiltonians preempted a term which had formerly been applied to all supporters of the Constitution: "Federalist." But Jefferson had another name for the Hamiltonians. As a bomb to hurl, he coined for them the designation (which combined the terms "monarchy" and "aristocrat") of "Monocrat." To fight the Monocrats was for the Republicans a sacred duty.

Hamilton did not hide his admiration for the British system which the Old Whigs and the Jeffersonians deplored: he had his vagaries when he talked in a manner that seemed to justify the epithet Monocrat; but basically he realized that the plans he espoused were not really aristocratic in tendency. He never

Opposite: *Thomas Jefferson's February 15, 1791 opinion on the unconstitutionality of a national bank is considered one of the key arguments for limiting the government's powers and adhering to a strict interpretation of the Constitution. Jefferson's adversary, Alexander Hamilton, advocated the broadest possible interpretation of the document, and was the leading advocate for a national bank. The two were outspoken opposition leaders.*

* Although Jefferson is now considered the father of the Democratic party, he himself avoided the appelation Democrat, which in the eighteenth century connoted, to many minds, support for mob rule.

The bill for establishing a National Bank undertakes, among other thi[ngs]

1. to form the subscribers into a Corporation.

2. to enable them, in their corporate capacities to receive grants of land; an[d] so far is against the laws of Mortmain.*

3. to make alien subscribers capable of holding lands, & so far is against the laws of Alienage.

4. to transmit these lands, on the death of a proprietor, to a certain line of successors: & so far changes the course of Descents.

5. to put the lands out of the reach of forfeiture or escheat: & so far is again[st] the laws of Forfeiture & Escheat.

6. to transmit personal chattels to successors in a certain line: & so far is against the laws of Distribution.

7. to give them the sole & exclusive right of banking under the national authority: & so far is against the laws of Monopoly.

8. to communicate to them a power to make laws paramount to the laws of the states: for so they must be construed, to protect the in-stitution from the controul of the state legislatures; & so, proba[bly] they will be construed.

I consider the foundation of the Constitution as laid on this groun[d] that "all powers not delegated to the U.S. by the Constitution, nor prohibit[ed] by it to the states, are reserved to the states or to the people" [XII. Amendm.t] to take a single step beyond the boundaries thus specially drawn around the pow[ers] of Congress is to take possession of a boundless field of power, no longer susceptible of any definition.

---

* though the constitution controuls the laws of Mortmain so far as to permit Congress it-self to hold lands for certain purposes, yet not so far as to permit them to communicate a similar right to other corporate bodies.

A N.W. View of the State House in Philadelphia, *c. 1790, engraved by James Trenchard, after Charles Willson Peale.*

envisioned an American crown. Believing, in sharp opposition to Jefferson, that the people were incapable of ruling themselves, he sought a nonroyalist road that would lead the United States safely between the twin evils of anarchy and tyranny. His solution was a prevision of modern business oligarchy. He wished to foster a powerful group of moneymen who would bolster the federal government because it was in their interest to do so, thus offering a firm financial structure on which centralized and conservative republican institutions could safely be hung. He believed that by opposing what he regarded as an essential expedient, Jefferson was revealing himself not as the supporter but as the opponent of personal freedom. Should chaos result from the collapse of the government, force would have to be employed to restore order. Might this not be what Jefferson desired? Might he not be looking forward to steering himself the juggernaut which his policies had brought into motion?

Jefferson insisted that he had been hoodwinked by Hamilton into organizing the deal which, by carrying assumption, had put over the first installment of the Treasury's program. What was more natural than for Jefferson now to assume that Washington had accepted the bank because he too had been hoodwinked, but had not yet succeeded in breaking out from under the hypnotic influence of the secretary of the Treasury? Jefferson thus began laying the foundation for the historical myth which describes Washington as a kind of sorcerer's apprentice under the spell of Hamilton. Washington was nothing of the sort.

Washington was neither a Hamiltonian nor a Jeffersonian. His point of view combined the attitudes of both men. It was his genius to reach, by recognizing the essence of a problem, the bedrock that underlay opposites.

The parallels to English developments which so exercised Jefferson and Hamilton seemed to Washington irrelevant. He knew that Hamilton's moneymen could never make themselves the equivalent of the dominant English aristocrats. Jefferson's worry lest titles of nobility, even a monarchy, grow up in the United States seemed to Washington ludicrous: the nation was too solidly republican. Nor did he believe that domination of the United States by an oligarchy of financiers was a danger. The danger was, as his Revolutionary experiences had taught him, quite the reverse.

Washington visualized a mixed economy in which agrarianism and business activity would move together. American financial forms needed strengthening because they were weak. The United States, Washington rightly believed, would remain primarily agricultural for many generations. Should at any future date the balance show signs of tipping too far the other way, the matter could be handled then. For the time being, the need was to reconcile all parts of the nation to policies which would strengthen all parts.

> To farmers, used to making money more tangibly and more slowly, and who visualized moneymen primarily as foreclosers of mortgages, what was taking place seemed wicked.

Washington's personal financial activities were altogether in the agrarian pattern, as was demonstrated by the fact that, although he lived high at Mount Vernon, he had been so lacking in free capital that he had to borrow the cash to carry him to his inauguration in New York. However useful he thought them for the nation, he did not personally take any advantage of Hamilton's financial institutions. Yet (as will be demonstrated later in this volume) he had become too unhappy about slavery to regard the Virginia way of life as sacrosanct.

When he had contemplated the presidency, Washington had visualized the American economy as a giant hobbled by unnecessary shackles. The need, he then believed, was only to cut those bonds away. Now, Hamilton tried again and again to induce him publicly to credit the rising prosperity to the Treasury's financial policies. Washington was never willing to do so. He attributed the growing strength of the United States to the freedoms established by republican government, to the virtues of the citizenry, to the benign isolation and inherent wealth of the American continent, and to the smiles of a beneficent Providence.

Far from being upset by the scenes of speculation which accompanied the sale of the bank scrip, Washington considered the phenomenon "pleasing" as it revealed that "our public credit stands on that ground which three years ago it would have been considered as a species of madness to have foretold." He admired the tools with which Hamilton had hacked at the bonds of the American financial giant, and he also admired the man who had proposed them. But he had no intention of sacrificing for either the basic values of the government. He would have vetoed the bank bill—he had indeed commissioned Madison to prepare a veto message—had not Hamilton in the end persuaded him that the principles on which the bank would have been declared unconstitutional would have gutted the entire government. And, when Hamilton came up with the third part of his master plan, Washington, although he strongly approved of the ends, could not accept the means.

During the congressional session that ran from December 1791 to May 1792, Hamilton presented his Report on Manufactures. Treating the subject with all the broadness of his far-ranging financial intellect, Hamilton summarized the existing state of American manufactures; showed that industrialization was the magic wand that would change economic colonialism to world power; argued that northern processing of southern staples would help unite the nation; demonstrated that the United States could not safely depend on imports in case of war; and deduced that Congress should encourage native manufactures through tariffs, bounties, subsidies, and premiums. As Hamilton's biographer John C. Miller wrote, the "Report on Manufactures contained the embryo of modern America."

Remembering his bitter experiences with wartime shortages, Washington had, from the moment he had visualized himself as president, concerned himself with the investigation and encouragement of manufactures. Yet he did not back Hamilton's scheme. No public ruling proved necessary, because the plan was too revolutionary to come before the president through congressional vote. However, Washington communicated privately to Hamilton that he considered the recommendations both beyond "the powers of the general government" and "the temper of the times."

In the controversies between the agrarian and urban way of life, Washington found himself naturally on both sides. He had sought to secure, in order to further both amusement and health, a farm outside Philadelphia; while trapped in the urban capital, he yearned for Mount Vernon; yet when he set out of an evening (he was now giving himself more social leeway than he had in New York) it was usually not to visit, in a boardinghouse, some out-of-town agrarian official. An admirer of good food, elegant rooms, fine gardens, and stylish ladies, he found them in Philadelphia, as he had in Virginia, where they were naturally rooted.

The pretensions to aristocracy of the flashing Philadelphia women (and some of the men) seemed to him a harmless aberration; having himself been a passionate gambler and being no prude about sex, he was more amused than disturbed (there being no soldiers shivering unfed on snowbound hillsides) by extravagant gaieties; having fought the Revolution with self-made officers, he was untouched by plantation snobbery towards self-made financiers. Many, he found, were extremely intelligent and well informed about the world into which their ships and goods penetrated.

Washington had long since decided to forget, as an ill-judged, passionate reaction to immediate crisis, the effort of the financiers to use the army at the time of the Newburgh Addresses. He had made Hamilton his secretary of the Treasury and Gouverneur Morris his personal diplomatic representative in England. The Washingtons' closest family friends became those leaders of financial activity and Philadelphia high society, the Robert Morrises. To the dismay of Jeffersonians, Washington relaxed contentedly in the drawing rooms which the agrarians viewed as sinks of vice and centers of monarchial plots.

Periods of rapid transition in the history of man often produce extremely great men because the simultaneous existence of two systems of thought and behavior opens twice as many alternatives as are available to individuals living in a static time when only one system prevails. All the American Founding Fathers looked, Janus-like, to some extent both forward and backward. Yet, on the issue of agrarian versus business society, the Jeffersonians and the Hamiltonians ranged themselves in battle array on the two sides of the gap. Only Washington transcended the dichotomy, wishing to gather equally from both systems what he considered most useful to the United States. He was, indeed, so far above the battle that, although he was bothered by symptoms of national disunity, he was not conscious that his most intimate collaborators, Madison and Jefferson on one hand and Hamilton on the other, were beginning to hate and profoundly distrust one another. He still interpreted their disagreements as being no greater than those which naturally appear, in all human affairs, as way stations on the road to eventual agreement. He was to be greatly shocked when he came to realize how deep the schism actually was.

Thirty-Two

EUROPEANS AND INDIANS

(1783–1791)

The foreign relations that gave Washington active concern were limited to dealing with the Indian tribes, Great Britain, and Spain. The stirring events that were taking place as France moved towards her world-shaking revolution had on the president only an emotional impact. They required no practical handling.

The Indians, stretched along the entire western frontier, were potentially the most powerful military menace to the United States. Their manpower combined with their genius at guerrilla warfare should have made them invincible in the forests, but tribes had for each other traditional hatreds which made unified action impossible. Furthermore, they had allowed themselves to become completely dependent on their white enemies. Having lost their skill with bows and arrows, they needed for hunting, and also for self-defense, guns and gunpowder. Yet their taboos prevented them from learning how to concoct gunpowder or even mend a broken gun. Each tribe was thus reduced to trying to play the three white powers on the continent against each other for its particular advantage.

George Washington by Jean-Antoine Houdon, c. 1786.

Of the three powers, the Indians most disliked the United States. Since British Canada and Spanish Louisiana had no excess population pressing on the frontiers, their interest was the same as the Indians': to keep the forests wild as harvesting grounds for the furs which the Indians sold the white men to their mutual profit. But the instant the Revolution ended, the various American states staged powwows at which they bought, for trinkets, quantities of Indian land. These "treaties" were often suspect: the Indians were kept drunk, and tribal organization was so loose that it was extremely difficult to determine which "chiefs," if any, had authority to sell what hunting grounds. The tribes often refused to accept the treaties, attacking the settlers who appeared.

When supplied by England or Spain with munitions, the Indians could devastate a frontier. Each European power was glad to use the tribes in ways that would enhance its own interests.

Spain had received Louisiana from France in the settlement which closed the American Revolution.

She had few nationals in the colony, which was in any case underpopulated and weak. Her North American policy was defensive, her weapons two: her Indian allies and her ability to keep closed to trade the mouth of the Mississippi, which she controlled.

The Indians were to keep American settlements as far upriver as possible and to prevent any expedi-

This medal is believed to have been awarded on March 13, 1792, at a conference in Philadelphia attended by a Native American delegation (the Seneca, Cayuga, Onondaga, Oneida, Tuscarora, and Stockbridge tribes), President Washington, the secretary of war, the governor of Pennsylvania, and others.

tions from floating down (either as freebooters or with the approval of a state or the federal government) to capture Louisiana and open the Mississippi by force. The tribes also contributed to Spanish prosperity by selling their furs to traders from Louisiana.

Holding the Mississippi closed reduced, by making settlement less profitable, the flow of frontiersmen above. It could also be used in an effort to pry the settlers who did appear away from the United States. The "Spanish Conspiracy," which Washington inherited when he became president, involved offering trading concessions (and also bribes) to those individuals or groups who would move from American territory on the east bank of the Mississippi onto Spanish territory on the west bank, or else would seek to form independent nations allied with Spain.

Although during the Confederation, Washington had been frightened of such intrigue, writing that the settlers were as on a pivot that could turn any way, he was now convinced that the matter could be handled by effective administration. A strong, united, and prosperous United States would hold loyalty like a magnet. The Spanish Conspiracy did indeed fade, all the more because Congress extended governmental bodies across the mountains, establishing the Southwest Territory and admitting Kentucky into the Union.*

Not Spanish intrigue but the state of Georgia created the greatest danger in the southern forests. Taking advantage of a fraudulent purchase, negotiated before the federal government had been established, Georgia authorized a vast land grab between the Mississippi and Yazoo rivers. The tribes, whose hunting grounds would be preempted, threatened a war, which might well bring the United States into conflict with Spain, the Indians' ally. Washington leapt into the breach: he issued a proclamation forbidding settlement in the Yazoo tract, and negotiated with the Creek Indians the Treaty of New York (August 1790) which returned to the tribes a quantity of land that Georgia claimed. Since Spain wanted war no more than did Washington, all parties except Georgia were pleased.

The southern frontier remained quiescent throughout Washington's first term. Not so the northern, where Great Britain supported and incited Indian warfare.

The treaty which had ended the Revolutionary War had not ended British hostility. England had not only enacted trade regulations that were greatly to the disadvantage of American shipping, but had refused to establish diplomatic relations with the United States. Early in 1791, Washington departed from his usual hands-off policy with Congress. He backed Jefferson in a renewed attempt to secure laws that applied to British ships the same restrictions that Britain applied to American ships.

* A balance between North and South was kept by simultaneously admitting Vermont, raising the number of states to fifteen.

Hamilton greatly admired the British. He believed that upsetting the existing pattern of commerce—the lion's share was with Britain—would damage American prosperity, and also bankrupt the federal government, whose customs revenues depended on a flourishing trade. In a manner which would have horrified Washington (had he known of it), Hamilton conferred secretly with an undercover British representative in Philadelphia. He warned George Beckwith that the situation was dangerous, but added that it could be handled if the British soothed public opinion by finally opening formal diplomatic relations. A British announcement that they would send a minister worked as Hamilton had foreseen. Despite Washington and Jefferson, Congress defeated trade retaliation.

Although Washington was disappointed, the issue was by no means as grievous as those on the northern frontier.

At the post-Revolutionary peace conference, the British negotiators had revealed ignorance of American geography by ceding to the United States the forts on the Great Lakes, from Oswego to Niagara, which controlled the route along which the fur harvest from the Northwest reached Canada. Another colossal error was granting to the new nation the fur-bearing forests south of the Great Lakes and north of the Ohio. These two mistakes threatened to destroy the Canadian fur trade, which was the most profitable single industry in North America.

When the British realized what had been sacrificed, they began taking steps to redress the blunder. They noted that the American negotiators had agreed that the prerevolutionary debts owed British merchants would be paid. The states, mostly southern, where the debtors lived, had refused to enact laws that would enforce compliance. The British used this American breach of the treaty as a justification for not surrendering their forts. Washington protested endlessly to the British, but the federal government lacked the power to clear up the situation by forcing payment on the delinquent states.

Hamilton greatly admired the British. He believed that upsetting the existing pattern of commerce—the lion's share was with Britain—would damage American prosperity, and also bankrupt the federal government, whose customs revenues depended on a flourishing trade.

To hold the Ohio region, the British had a different strategy. Everyone agreed that the treaty provision concerning this land did not extinguish the Indian titles; it only gave the United States an exclusive right to buy. The British encouraged the tribes to insist that all purchases made by the Americans were fraudulent, and they saw to it that the warriors were armed. Americans who insisted on settling west of the Ohio were slaughtered.

Arthur St. Clair *by Charles Willson Peale, from life, 1782–1784.*

It took Washington some time to realize the extent of British participation and the resulting seriousness of the menace. Thus, in the fall of 1790, he blamed "a small refugee banditti of Cherokees and Shawnees, who can be easily chastized."

Having recognized the British role, Washington secured from Congress the enlargement of the tiny regular army by one regiment. In 1791, a force under General Arthur St. Clair advanced from Fort Washington (Cincinnati) into present-day Indiana to chastise the warring tribes. Washington warned St. Clair to beware of ambush. During November, St. Clair was ambushed in a replay of the defeat of Braddock that was perhaps Washington's most dreadful memory.

A leading Revolutionary commander, General Anthony Wayne, was now empowered to raise a larger army. As his force gradually accreted during the summer of 1792, Indian terror spread to settlements east of the Ohio, and Washington undertook the most extensive effort in American history to find some better solution to the Indian problem than continual fighting.

He tried to impress on Congress and the state governments the importance of justice in Indian relations. The frontier would always be aflame if the murder of an Indian were not considered the same as the murder of a white man. The courts should protect Indian property, and he took it upon himself to order new negotiations with the tribes at which old treaties would be examined. If the treaties were found to have been unjustly negotiated, the Indians would be indemnified with new purchase money or given back their land.

Jefferson encouraged political alliance between the southern agrarians and those on the frontiers by protesting. He insisted that to return any land ever annexed by the United States was contrary to the Constitution. He demanded that military action against the Indians be not sacrificed to negotiation. Washington tried vainly to win Jefferson around, but was not deflected from his own course.

The Indians, whom he had denounced during the French and Indian War as "butchering" monsters, he now regarded as "poor wretches." Anxious to prevent the inevitable western expansion from driving them ever deeper into exile, he wished to undertake "such rational experiments . . . as may from time to time suit their condition" to prepare the Indians to be absorbed, as so many other groups were being, into white American life. They would have to abandon their hunting economy, which required huge tracts of forest that would certainly be destroyed by settlement, but if they would learn farming and handicrafts, they could remain on their most fertile tracts as settlement came in around them.

Since this would involve not only a total revolution in Indian culture, but also a revolutionary reversal of the attitudes towards each other of frontiersmen and Indians, it may well have been the most impractical idea that Washington ever seriously espoused. In any case, no time could have been less ripe. Having defeated two military forces sent against them by the United States, the Indians felt confident that they could defeat any successors. And the British continued to egg them on.

Washington's unofficial representative in London, Gouverneur Morris, reported that British policy was to make her control of the northern Indians so clear that the United States would be driven to call her in as mediator. Britain would then establish an extensive permanent Indian territory north of the Ohio which would supply her fur trade, and, under her protection, act as a buffer for the defense of Canada.

Washington spluttered to Morris, "The United States will never have occasion, I hope, to ask for the interposition of that power or any other to establish peace within their own territory." But the British continued to sabotage all efforts towards a peaceful settlement. Wayne's army would probably have to march.

Washington was still trying to negotiate with the Indians when his first term ended.

The storming of the Bastille by a Parisian mob on July 14, 1789, marked the beginning of the French Revolution. As commander of the Paris National Guard in 1789, the Marquis de Lafayette received the keys to the loathsome political prison and symbol of absolute monarchy. In 1790, he sent this key and a drawing of the prison in ruins to George Washington.

The American diplomatic corps in Europe, which had in fact almost ceased to exist, had to be reorganized in response to the British recognition of the United States. Washington appointed as minister to Great Britain, Thomas Pinckney, a South Carolinian satisfactory to Jefferson. Jefferson was gratified by having his former secretary, William Short, appointed to Holland. Finally filling the vacancy left when Jefferson had accepted State, Washington appointed to France his own intimate friend Gouverneur Morris.

Morris was brilliant: the actual wording of the Constitution came from his pen. But Morris was sarcastic to those he considered more stupid than he and possessed of such a reputation for licentiousness that the leg he had lost in a carriage accident was generally considered to have come off as a result of his jumping out of a lady's window as her husband came in at the door. He was an inveterate prankster. Those who believed Washington was always proper and grave could not understand why he was intimate with such a man. They did know that Washington relished scapegraces who kept him amused.

As a financier intimately associated with the Hamiltonian circle, Morris belonged to the pro-British faction. Yet, as Washington's unofficial representative in London, he had followed without deviation the interests of the United States, making reports Washington had used in his efforts to persuade Congress into commercial retaliation. Now, although Washington's prestige carried the confirmation through, Morris was strongly opposed in the Senate.

Washington, usually so determined to keep personal affection from influencing his political acts, felt called on to write a remarkable letter. He had, he told Morris, appointed him "with *all my heart.*" But Morris should know that he had been charged in Congress with "imprudence of conversation and conduct. It was urged that your habits of expression indicated a *hauteur* disgusting to those who happen to differ from you. . . . That in France you were considered as a favorer of aristocracy. . . . That under this impression, you could not be an acceptable public character." His critics believed that Morris lacked the "circumspection" that "should be observed by our representatives abroad."

Washington blamed Morris's reputation on "the promptitude with which your lively and brilliant imagination is displayed," which allowed "too little time for deliberation and correction. . . . In this statement you have the pros and cons. By reciting them, I give you a proof of my friendship if I give none of my policy or judgment." He was sure that Morris would use his own good judgment to reform.

The first major violent act of the French Revolution, the storming of the Bastille, resulted in Washington's receiving a package from France. It contained the "main key" of the "fortress of despotism." Lafayette had sent it as "a tribute which I owe as a son to my adoptive father, as an aide-de-camp to my general, and as a missionary of liberty to its patriarch." Washington hung the key in the presidential mansion, but added, so as not to prejudice the foreign policy of the United States, an engraved portrait of Louis XVI.

Lafayette was leading the French revolt in an effort to reform the French monarchy peacefully rather than to overthrow it with violence. He was, in fact, trying to achieve such a benign social change as had eventuated from the American Revolution. Washington was, of course, extremely sympathetic, yet he was far from sanguine.

"I assure you," he wrote his spiritual son, " I have often contemplated with great anxiety the danger to which you are personally exposed. . . . The tumultuous populace of large cities are ever to be dreaded. Their indiscriminate violence prostrates for the time all public authority and its consequences are sometimes extensive and terrible. In Paris, we may suppose these tumults are peculiarly disastrous at this time, when the public mind is in a ferment and when (as is always the case on such occasions) there are not wanting wicked and designing men whose element is confusion and who will not hesitate in destroying public tranquillity to gain a favorite point."

Washington could only hope, so he wrote Gouverneur Morris, that the "disorders, oppressions, and incertitude . . . will terminate very much in favor of the rights of man."

In mid-August 1791, Washington was bowing repeatedly to the circle of gentlemen at one of his levees when he was notified that Louis XVI and Marie Antoinette had shattered Lafayette's effort towards reform. The royal couple had been apprehended as they tried to flee from Paris to join a loyal military force that would protect them until the aristocratic armies of Prussia and Austria could come to their aid. Jefferson noted with disapproval that he had never seen Washington "so dejected by any circumstance."

> Washington spluttered to Morris, "the United States will never have occasion, I hope, to ask for the interposition of that power or any other to establish peace within their own territory." But the British continued to sabotage all efforts towards a peaceful settlement.

Jefferson continued to be concerned by Washington's "forebodings." Early in 1792, when the Terror was hardly more than a year away, the secretary of state still believed that France was hurrying towards a political utopia. Why had Washington so little faith that he was worried lest France go ever deeper "into confusion"? The fault could lie with the dispatches of Morris, "a high-flying monarchy man" who, in Jefferson's opinion, was "shutting his eyes and his faith to every fact against his wishes." But why had Washington appointed Morris?

A dreadful thought which he could not repel formed in Jefferson's mind. Perhaps the president was in fact at heart a monarchist!

Thirty-Three

DESIRE TO ESCAPE

(1791–1792)

In April 1791, Washington set out on a tour of the southern states similar to his New England tour of the previous summer. In these days of redundant communication, it is hard to credit that, owing to a confusion of roads and mails, the president was completely out of touch with his government for two months. He had provided for decisions to be made in his absence, and, as it turned out, none of importance were called for.

Jefferson's expressed concern about the president's safety was not because he was taking along no secret service men, no guards—his companions were only his valet and hostlers—but because the roads would be perilously bad. Jefferson urged Washington to "lower the hang of your carriage" and to employ not a coachman but two postilions who would ride ahead, one for each pair of the four horses. Washington shrugged off precautions.

Washington had never before visited North Carolina, South Carolina, or Georgia. Traveling south along the coast—Halifax, Newbern, Wilmington, Charleston, Savannah—and back along the fall line—Augusta, Camden, Salisbury, Winston-Salem—he was surprised by the prevailing barrenness of the land and the wretchedness of the taverns. Populations were indeed so sparse that word of his advance did not travel before him. Far from being bothered, as in New England, by endless ceremonial greetings and dust-raising militiamen on horseback, he moved often through complete emptiness. Innkeepers were amazed when a little cavalcade that had turned into their dooryards—a coach, a baggage wagon, and some led extra horses—proved to contain "the greatest man in the world."

Innkeepers were amazed when a little cavalcade that had turned into their dooryards—a coach, a baggage wagon, and some led extra horses—proved to contain "the greatest man in the world."

As an agriculturalist and a student of manufactures, Washington found little to record, but he was fascinated by the belles who crowded to meet him in every considerable settlement. He recorded in his diary that there were "about seventy" in Newbern, "sixty-two" in Wilmington, and in Charleston, a city where he much admired the "beauty" of the streets, "at least four hundred ladies, the number and appearance of which exceeded anything of the kind I had ever seen." He was later to send his "grateful respect" to the "fair compatriots" of Charleston who had so "flattered" him.

Having found amusement in keeping careful track, Washington noted that while away from Philadelphia

NEWSPAPER WARS

THE NATIONAL GAZETTE

THOUGH IT LASTED ONLY A FEW YEARS in the early 1790s, the semiweekly newspaper known as the *National Gazette* remains unique in the annals of American journalism. Founded by the poet and printer Philip Freneau at the urging of Republican leaders James Madison (who had been Freneau's close friend at Princeton University) and Thomas Jefferson, its purpose was frankly partisan—to counter the influence of the Federalist newspaper known as the *Gazette of the United States.*

Philip Freneau
by T. Halpin.

Many prominent Republicans contributed articles to the *National Gazette*—including Madison and Jefferson—though usually under pseudonyms. To understand how singular this publication was, imagine a similar situation today: a national publication receives significant support from major players within a sitting administration, all the while attacking that administration's own policies. Prominent Federalists, including Alexander Hamilton, attacked this as a conflict of interest—though Hamilton was among the significant supporters of the rival partisan newspaper, the *Gazette of the United States*, which was devoted to the effusive praise of Washington and his policies.

A typical *National Gazette* article described Hamilton's financial policies as "pregnant with every mischief"; another called Washington's sixty-first birthday party "a forerunner of other monarchical vices." Naturally, Washington loathed the paper, describing its editor as "that rascal, Freneau."

The polemical paper was to be short-lived. It ceased publishing in 1793 as its subscriptions dwindled, in part as a result of the outbreak of yellow fever in Philadelphia. Jefferson, of course, would soon resign as secretary of state. Ultimately, Freneau retired to a more rural life, continuing to write occasional political pieces along with poetry and other works.

National Gazette.

Vol. I. MONDAY, April 16, 1792. Numb. 49.

With Jefferson and Madison's encouragement and backing, Philip Freneau's National Gazette, *published in Philadelphia, became the first official Republican newspaper and a leading critic of Hamilton's Federalist political programs during its two-year existence (1791–1793).*

he had traveled 1,887 miles. He was proud that "the same horses performed the whole tour and, although much reduced in flesh, kept up their full spirits to the last day." He himself had "rather gained flesh."

Washington diagnosed general satisfaction with the federal government, although he found anger in Georgia at the reversal of the Yazoo land grab. "Little was said of the banking act." He was worried enough by rumors of frontier opposition to a tax which had been voted on whiskey that, on his way back to Philadelphia, he made a special trip to western Pennsylvania—Reading and Lancaster. He decided that nothing more was required to make the law palatable than certain minor changes. He concluded that the pockets of opposition to the government that he encountered were to be blamed on "some demagogue" or speculator in western land.

During that summer, Jefferson and Madison also made a trip. They had it well in mind that a new House of Representatives was to be elected in 1792. Although they asserted that their journey through New York State was no more than a vacation, historians have reasoned that they were seeking political allies. This was to be done by reviving an old issue.

At the time of the ratification of the Constitution, opposition in New York had been particularly strong. States' rights sentiment had by no means died away there. The perennial governor, George Clinton, distrusted federal power. Although Madison had been at the Constitutional Convention a passionate advocate of federal power, he now shared with Jefferson the belief that the federal government was becoming malign under the control of Hamilton. However inconsistently, he further agreed that, since opposition in the states (and particularly Virginia) was the most available antidote, the Republicans should advocate states' rights. Why then should there not be a coalition between the Virginians and the powerful faction in New York which was ambivalent about the whole conception of federal government?

Whether or not Jefferson and Madison began at this time building their political alliance with Clinton, it is certain that they did take the fateful step of recruiting Philip Freneau. They wished to create, by appealing to the people, a popular surge that would bring into the House of Representatives a majority following their principles. Freneau, a former classmate of Madison's at Princeton, was not only a poet but a journalist brilliant at vituperative controversy. He was induced to move from New Jersey to Philadelphia. Jefferson appointed him translator to the Department of State, a salaried post that left him plenty of time for other pursuits. The Republicans then backed Freneau in founding the *National Gazette.* A journal not merely local but intended to be distributed all over the nation, the *National Gazette* would grapple with the only other comparable periodical, the *Gazette of the United States,* which was partly supported by Treasury advertising and was Hamiltonian.

In February 1792, Freneau opened a sustained attack on Hamilton's measures: they would load the nation with unnecessary debt, encourage speculation, and lead to monarchy. "Artifice and deception," Freneau charged, were fostering a "revolution in favor of the few. Another revolution must and will be brought about in favor of the people."

Hamilton did not need to hire a propagandist. He leapt into the newspapers himself under a series of aliases. Jefferson, he stated, was using the government payroll to mount a treacherous attack on the government and should resign. Jefferson's objective was to undermine the national government by destroying financial credit. A bankrupt nation would slip into disunion and anarchy, opening the way for Jefferson to lead the United States down the bloody road of the French Revolution.

"The newspapers," Washington commented, "are *sur*charged and *some of them* indecently communicative of *charges* that stand in need of evidence for their support." He feared for the unity or at least the harmony of the nation.

The election of 1792 was not only for members of Congress. It was also a presidential year. Washington informed his cabinet and his old friend Madison that he did not intend to run again.

Washington wished by stepping down to encourage such a "rotation in the elective officers" as would bring "liberty and safety" to the government.

This decision was partly due to his belief that his voluntary retirement—he knew that should he accept a second term he would not be opposed—was necessary to complete the republican experiment that he hoped would point to a glorious future for all mankind. Aristocratic theorists believed that the people could not peaceably engineer a turnover from one chief executive to another. If Washington were to stay on until he died in office, to be succeeded by his elected "crown prince," the vice president, the succession would resemble the practice of monarchies. Washington wished by stepping down to encourage such a "rotation in the elective officers" as would bring "liberty and safety" to the government.

Washington's personal reasons for seeking retirement were also strong. Most grievous was the fear that he was losing his mental powers. He was, it is true, only sixty, but the Washingtons were a short-lived family; he had suffered through many severe illnesses; he had been torn by decades of strain. To Madison, he stated that even at the start of his presidency, he had "found himself deficient in many of the essential qualifications, owing to his inexperience in the forms of public business, his unfitness to judge of legal questions and questions arising out of the Constitution." Now this situation had worsened.

To Jefferson, Washington explained "that he really felt himself growing old; his bodily health less firm; his memory—always bad—becoming worse; and perhaps the other faculties of his mind showing a decay to others of which he was insensible himself. That this apprehension particularly oppressed him; that he found, moreover, his activity lessened. Business, therefore, [became] more irksome, and tranquillity and retirement became an irresistible passion."

Washington was still worried at having broken his promise, made on his resignation from the army, that he would never emerge from private life. Assurances that his participation would help the people accept a government "of sufficient efficacy for their own good" had lured him to the Constitutional Convention and the first presidency. Were he to continue longer, "it might give room to say that, having tasted the sweets of office, he could not do without them."

The truth was that what sweets of office he had first enjoyed had turned sour. He told Madison that "his inclination would lead him rather to . . . take his spade in his hand and work for his bread than remain in his present situation."

The unpleasantness of that situation was being augmented by "a spirit of party" in his own government and by increasingly clear "discontents among the people." Although, as he commented to Jefferson, Freneau's *National Gazette* had refrained from attacking him personally, "he must be a fool indeed to swallow the little sugar plums here and there thrown out to him." In condemning the executive "they condemned him, for if they thought there were measures pursued contrary to his sentiment, they must conceive him too careless to attend to them or too stupid to understand them."

Opposite: *James Madison sent this draft of Washington's farewell address to him for his review on June 21, 1792.*

(copy)

{The period which will close the appointment with which my fellow-citizens have honored me, being not very distant, and the time actually arrived at which their thoughts must be designating the citizen who is to administer the Executive Government of the U.S. during the ensuing term, it may be requisite to a more distinct expression of the public voice that I should apprize such of my fellow citizens as may retain their partiality towards me, that I am not to be numbered among those out of whom a choice is to be made.

I beg them to be assured that the resolution which dictates this intimation has not been taken without the strictest regard to the relation which as a dutiful citizen I bear to my country; and that in withdrawing that tender of my service which silence in my situation might imply, I am not influenced by the smallest deficiency of zeal for its future interests, nor of grateful respect for its past kindness; but by the fullest persuasion, that such a step is compatible with both.

The impressions under which I entered on the present arduous trust were explained on the proper occasion. In discharge of this trust, I can only say, that I have contributed towards the organization & administration of the Government, the best exertions of which a very fallible judgment was capable. For any errors which may have flowed from this source, I feel all the regret which an anxiety for the public good can excite; not without the double consolation however arising from a consciousness of their being involuntary, and an experience of the candor which will interpret them. If there were any circumstances which could give value to my inferior qualifications for the trust, these circumstances must have been temporary. In this light was the

undertaking

Washington mourned that the United States had some "infamous newspapers." However, if their misrepresentations were balanced against "the infinite blessings resulting from a free press," there could be no doubt concerning the pitch of the scale. He urged on Congress postal laws that would encourage "the transmission of newspapers to distant parts of the country." His personal conclusion was that, since his presence was not fostering harmony, "his return to private life was consistent with every public consideration."

This conclusion elicited protests from everyone to whom he confided his hopes. Jefferson and Madison, as well as Hamilton, stated that he must remain until the present controversy was resolved or at least abated. Fears sometimes reached great heights. Randolph warned of a possible "civil war" if Washington stayed home. Jefferson told Washington, "North and South will hang together if they have you to hang on."

To help him draft a farewell address, Washington called in not Hamilton but his older adviser, Madison. Madison was to point out "in plain and modest terms . . . that we are *all* children of the same country. . . . That our interest, however diversified in local and smaller matters, is the same in all the great and essential concerns of the nation."

The economic proclivities of the various regions could be made to key together to "render the whole (at no distant period) one of the most independent in the world."

He also wished to point out "that the established government, being the work of our own hands, with the seeds of amendment grafted in the Constitution, may by wisdom, good dispositions, and mutual allowances, aided by experience, bring it as near to perfection as any human institution ever approximated; and therefore the only strife among us ought to be who should be foremost in facilitating and finally accomplishing such great and desirable objects by giving every possible support and cement to the Union."

Washington asked Madison to advise him on when to notify the electorate that he would not again be available. Madison insisted that he must stay on. Washington replied that his "disinclination to it was becoming every day more and more fixed."

Thirty-Four

NO EXIT

(1790–1793)

Concerning such a changeover of power as Washington's retirement would necessitate, the lessons of history were hardly reassuring. Contests over succession had proved so calamitous that monarchies consistently preferred the acceptance of a sadistic, half-witted legitimate heir to opening the Crown to the bloody rivalry of pretenders. So that the government would go on as smoothly as possible, Washington wished his own withdrawal to be the only change in the executive. He wished the entire cabinet to remain, at least until the will of the new president was known. Washington confidently believed that as he himself withdrew, Jefferson and Hamilton would go on hand in hand. He did not recognize the depth of the disagreement between his two most important ministers.

As long as men were seeking the same objective—in this case, the strengthening of the nation through republican procedures—there was no reason, as Washington saw it, why they could not argue concerning the best road, but nonetheless proceed together. As he later put it, while recognizing marked differences in "political sentiments among his advisers," he had "never suspected it had gone so far in producing a personal difference." The discovery was, when it came, a shocking one: reason could reconcile political arguments, but personal differences?—hatreds?

As he had listened to cabinet discussions, his mind had been so directed at the essence that he had discounted the fire and rancor with which arguments were presented. Preferring to comprehend each point of view in its pristine entirety, he had rarely intervened at the debates to bring the opponents into agreement. Because less time was then wasted on what he considered surface matters, he often asked each contestant to present him with a separately prepared written argument. His methods allowed every man his say, and he seriously attended to every opinion. He therefore expected all to accept his eventual conclusions.

Washington prepared, if only in his mind, the agenda of the meetings, and was so opposed to deviations that his ministers could only initiate a subject if they could somehow hook it onto some matter the president had decided to discuss. He was convivial with his cabinet ministers, but at social occasions he engaged only in light talk. No government official and no adviser, not even Jefferson or Hamilton, was encouraged to request an interview on his own. At any interview the president did grant, he discouraged personal revelation. No one was allowed to weep on his shoulder.

Washington seems never to have realized that he might seem overbearing when he failed to argue with his subordinates or to seek out their personal emotions, when he kept his own thoughts hidden until he announced his final decision. He felt that such behavior

Washington holds the proposed plan for the new capital city of Washington in this mezzotint by Edward Savage, 1793.

was essential if he were not to encourage trivialities and vitiate his own force in inconclusive palaver.

The historical legend that Washington looked pompous while others decided for him could not be more incorrect. How he rode down even as strong a man as Jefferson is exemplified by the establishment of the new national capital, now known as Washington, D.C.

Having voted in 1790 that the "Federal City" be somewhere along a sixty-seven-mile reach of the Potomac, Congress had left all other decisions up to the executive branch. As the great departments were then set up, the responsibility fell, after Washington, on the secretary of state. Jefferson had been to Europe, where he had made a study of architecture; he was, indeed, to earn a second fame as an architect. Washington had never been to Europe, and his attitude towards architecture was not informed but pragmatic. He had designed Mount Vernon, as he put it, not to satisfy rules but to please the eye.

Without consulting Jefferson, Washington chose the site for the city (as near as possible to Mount Vernon) and in March 1791, appointed as town planner a Frenchman whom he had first known as a major of engineers in the Continental army. Although the selection of Pierre Charles L'Enfant was another example of Washington's gift for recognizing genius, Jefferson soon regarded the appointment as a disaster.

In any case grandiose by temperament, L'Enfant decided to plan at once a capital that would serve for the great nation the United States would surely become. Only a tiny center would now be erected, but the design and the land acquired should spread out for miles so that the inevitable enlargement would enhance, not destroy, an artistic whole. Furthermore, advantage should be taken of the topography to create vistas and central points where legations and grand houses could be built, monuments erected. Washington, who had a surveyor's conception of developing regions, a colonizer's realization that surrounding land must be procured before improvements made values skyrocket, a taste for the grand, and an innate aesthetic sense, enthusiastically supported his appointee. L'Enfant's design is rated (although it has subsequently been debased) a masterpiece of town planning.

Suspecting (as was true) that Hamilton was egging L'Enfant on, Jefferson was outraged that the capital of the United States should be envisioned as one of those hives of aristocracy, business enterprise, and vice—a big city. Desiring an enlarged village, in scale less like Philadelphia than Virginia's capital of Williamsburg, Jefferson had drawn up a plan that, except for the very central part, was an even grill of streets. This covered a small area. He jotted down that any necessary extension could be "laid out in the future."

Without identifying the author, Washington showed Jefferson's plan to L'Enfant, who commented that it revealed "some cool imagination wanting a sense of the really grand and truly beautiful." If extended, the grill of streets would "become at last tiresome and insipid."

Without consulting Jefferson, Washington chose the site for the city (as near as possible to Mount Vernon) and in March 1791, appointed as town planner a Frenchman whom he had first known as a major of engineers in the Continental army.

Whether or not Jefferson saw this comment, he found L'Enfant and his ideas insupportable. Nor could he have been pleased by Washington's reaction when he extracted from his files, as models which he would like to distribute to the builders of houses in the capital, cherished engravings he had collected in Europe "of the handsomest fronts of private buildings." Much more concerned with original genius than traditional taste, Washington replied unenthusiastically that Jefferson's scheme "may answer a good purpose" if it could be "carried into effect at a moderate expense."

Having entered the government determined to be a right hand to a man he then greatly revered, Jefferson carried out without protest presidential orders concerning the Federal City that went against his own convictions and his trained taste. Only after L'Enfant, who was utterly without tact or subordination, had gotten into a destructive quarrel with the local landowners and then defied all intervention including that of the president, did Jefferson see an opportunity to act. In reply to a request for advice from Washington, he urged L'Enfant's dismissal. Commenting that "the feelings of such men [artists] are always alive," Washington bent way over backwards. The intractable genius spurned all concessions. Since the entire project was endangered, Washington was at last forced to let L'Enfant go. He expressed extreme regret. Jefferson did not confide to his chief his jubilation.

Washington's insistence that the cabinet stay on while he retired knocked down the wall that had long hidden from him the rancor among his ministers. The shattering blow was Jefferson's statement that nothing would induce him to stay, even if Washington himself stayed, into a second term.

During the following months, Washington held, in his efforts to dissuade his secretary of state from resigning, a series of discussions, in person or by letter, during which Jefferson at last felt free to speak. As he poured out to Washington his hatred for Hamilton and his fears of the Treasury's policies, the president found, on at least one occasion, the talks too "painful" to proceed.

Jefferson informed Washington of his belief that Hamilton's "corrupt squadron" in the Congress were stuffing their own pocketbooks while voting measures that "chained . . . about our necks for a great length of time" high taxes. Hamilton's system of paper money was no more than a "gaming table" which took the energies of the nation away from productive agriculture into destructive speculation. The Constitution was being perverted, the objective being to establish a monarchy.

For once Washington argued, but he remained reticent. At the time of an early talk, Hamilton's recommendations concerning government support for manufactures had not yet failed in Congress. Jefferson spoke of the proposal as the ultimate proof of how the government was being made into something quite different from what the people who had accepted the Constitution had intended. Here was an opportunity for Washington to soothe his secretary of state by revealing that he also opposed, as unconstitutional and untimely, Hamilton's plan. Washington remained silent.

Jefferson was later to claim that his affection for Washington had been much greater than Hamilton's, yet he could not bring himself (perhaps because his emotions were deeply hurt) to express any affection or loyalty or any regret at leaving his friend in the lurch.

Using restraint in the other direction, Washington refrained from asking, when Jefferson insisted that the moneymen in Congress should be forbidden to vote on bills that affected their interests, whether the same strictures should not apply to agrarians and slaveholders. He merely replied, "As to that interested spirit in the legislature, it was what could not be avoided in any government unless we were to exclude particular descriptions of men . . . from all office." Nor did Washington point out, when Jefferson complained of Hamilton's attempts to interfere in his department, that Jefferson had done his best to interfere in Hamilton's. Actually, Washington, who used his cabinet as a whole, was pleased to have one secretary advise him concerning the department of another.

To Washington's gratification, Jefferson agreed that funding and assumption could not be reversed without destroying the honor of the government. But Jefferson did wish the abolition of the Bank of the United States. Washington replied that a decision on the bank should be postponed until experience revealed how it would function. Although Jefferson, when himself president after 1800, decided that the bank's record justified its continuance, in 1792 he was shocked by the president's answer.

Being unable to persuade Washington that the nation was tottering dangerously on the brink of a fatal subversion of republican principles, Jefferson came to the melancholy decision that the president had revealed himself as "really approving the Treasury system." Jefferson refused to withdraw his resignation.

After Jefferson's worries and rancors had become clear to him, Washington decided that he must smoke out Hamilton. Copying from one of Jefferson's letters the strictures on the Treasury, he sent them, with a false attribution of their source, to Hamilton.

Hamilton replied that the obligations his measures had met were not of his making but inherited. The continuing national debt inherent in funding could not be paralyzing the economy since the parts of the nation where the greatest number of debt certificates were held also had the most circulating capital. Charges that the Congress had been corrupted were "malignant and false." No corruption had been demonstrated. And surely grounding the republican government on a sound financial foundation was no way to foster monarchy.

"I *know*," Hamilton continued, "that I have been the object of uniform opposition from Mr. Jefferson. . . . I have long seen a party formed in the legislature under his auspices bent on my subversion . . . which, in its consequences would subvert the government." He accused Jefferson (Washington knew this was not true) of wishing to create chaos by undoing the funding system, thereby prostrating "the credit and honor of the nation."

Washington wrote Jefferson and undoubtedly expressed the same sentiments to Hamilton. "I will frankly and solemnly declare that I believe the views of both of you are pure and well meant; and that experience alone will decide with respect to the salubrity of measures which are the subject of dispute. Why then, when some of the best citizens in the United States, men of discernment, uniform and tried patriots, who have no sinister views to promote, but are chaste in their ways of thinking and acting, are to be found some on one side and some on the other of the questions which have caused these agitations, should either of you be so tenacious of your opinions as to make no allowances for those of the other? . . . I have a great, a sincere esteem and regard for you both, and ardently wish that some line could be marked out by which both of you could walk."

Jefferson replied to such appeals by presenting himself as the innocent victim of Hamilton's attacks. He stated disingenuously that he had not hired Freneau with the intention of starting a newspaper. In any case, the *National Gazette* was a scourge for "aristocratical and monarchical writers" and not an opponent of the government. It was up to Hamilton to reform, not him.

Hamilton admitted his role in the newspapers, insisting that he had been driven to it by the necessity to protect his own reputation and also the essential financial stability of the nation. "I find myself placed in a situation not to be able to recede *for the present*." However, although he considered himself "the deeply injured party . . . I pledge you my honor, sir, that if you shall hereafter form a plan to reunite the members of your administration . . . I will fully concur." Hamilton assured Washington, "It is my most anxious wish, as far as may depend upon me, to smooth the path of your administration and to render it prosperous and happy."

Jefferson was later to claim that his affection for Washington had been much greater than Hamilton's, yet he could not bring himself (perhaps because his emotions were deeply hurt) to express any affection or loyalty or any regret at leaving his friend in the lurch. Jefferson's own records of their conversations show him taunting the substitute father he felt had betrayed him. He knew that Washington was just as eager to get home as he was, and in just as much need of paying personal attention to his estate. Yet, as he insisted that the president was trapped in office, he expatiated on the pleasures and the profit he anticipated from being able to return to Monticello. That Jefferson is described by his biographers as being himself "thin-skinned," supersensitive, makes his behavior to Washington seem all the more extraordinary.

Mrs. Samuel (Eliza) Powel *by Matthew Pratt, oil on canvas, c. 1793. Shown here in a portrait by Matthew Pratt, Mrs. Powel was Washington's favorite female companion. Married to one of Philadelphia's wealthiest and most sophisticated gentlemen, Mrs. Powel wrote Washington a heartfelt letter begging him not to give up the presidency.*

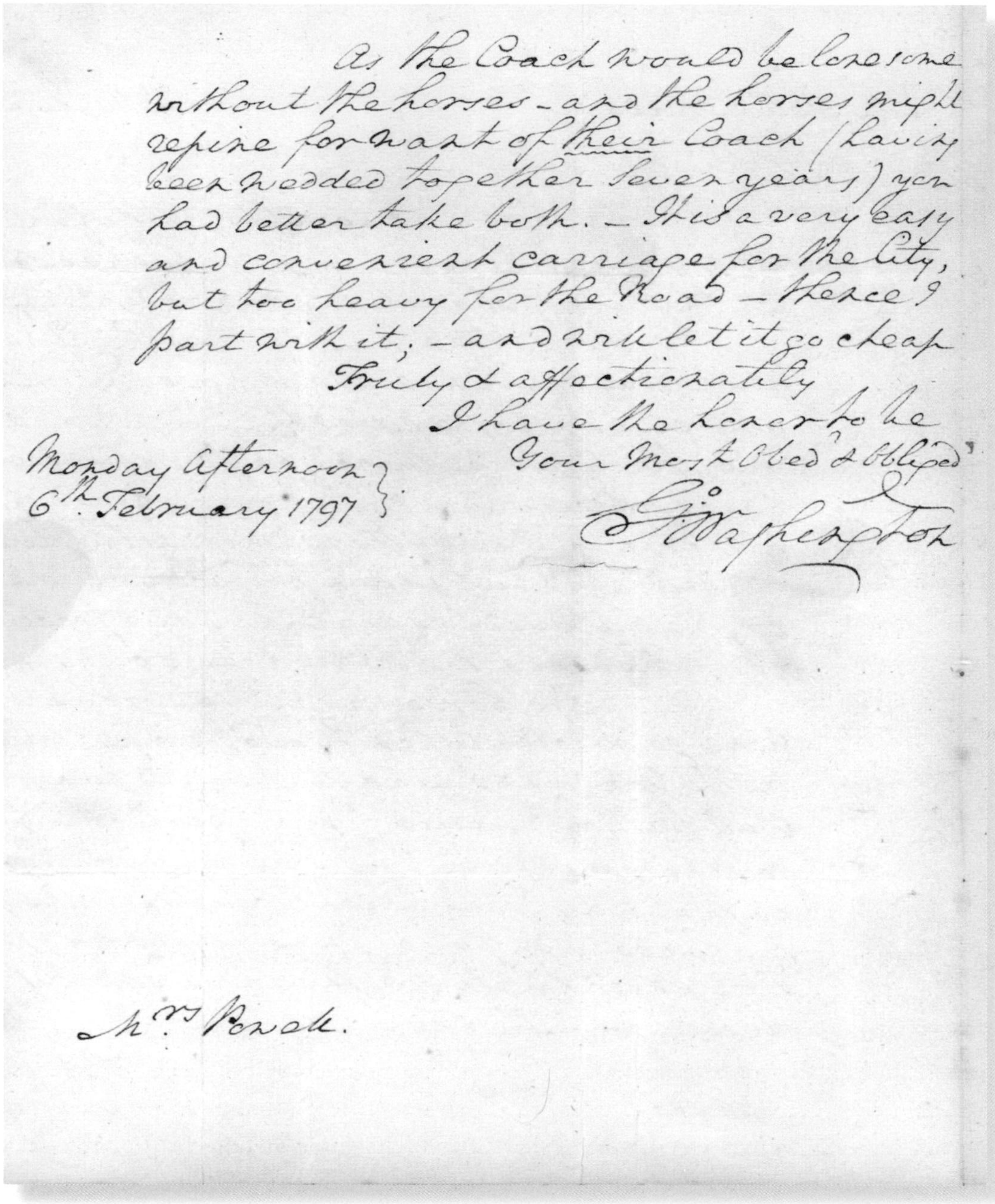

As the Coach would be lonesome without the horses—and the horses might repine for want of their Coach (having been wedded together seven years) you had better take both.—It is a very easy and convenient carriage for the City, but too heavy for the Road—hence I part with it;—and will let it go cheap

Truly & affectionately
I have the honor to be
Your Most Obed. & obliged
G.o Washington

Monday Afternoon
6th February 1797

Mrs Powel.

In this letter from Washington to Eliza Powel, dated February 6, 1797, he attempts to convince her to buy his coach and horse. It offers a rare glimpse of his sense of humor.

During the summer of 1792, Washington spent as much time at Mount Vernon as his conscience would permit. Yet it was hardly a restful period. His estate manager had for some time been his favorite nephew, George Augustine Washington, who was married to Martha's favorite niece, Fanny Bassett. Now George Augustine was replaying the greatest tragedy of Washington's young manhood. As the president's half brother Lawrence had done, George Augustine was dying of tuberculosis. And Fanny appeared to be coming down with her husband's disease. "Intermittent fevers" (malaria) were striking down Washington's servants and slaves more severely, so it seemed to him at that strained season, than ever before. And, since the president had lacked the heart to keep his two secretaries from going off "on visits to their friends . . . all my business, public and private, is on my own shoulders."

Washington now found tiring the long rides to inspect his extensive farms which he had once found relaxing, and which were now doubly necessary since his manager was completely incapacitated. A change to sedentary interests was revealed by Washington's decision concerning the pack of foxhounds who had for so many years been his delight and pride.

During his absence, the fence of his deer park had broken, allowing "about a dozen" half-tame deer to "range in all my woods. . . . It is true, I have scarcely a hope of preserving them long, although they come up almost every day, but I am unwilling by any act of my own to facilitate their destruction." Since they were "as much afraid of hounds . . . as the wild deer are," Washington got rid of his hounds. Instead of leaning eagerly forward as he rode shouting to the chase, he sat quietly on his porch awaiting the shy appearance of the gentlest of forest creatures.

It must have been with mixed feelings that Washington undertook inquiries to discover whether the people would prefer to him some other man as president. He valued almost above anything else the love and confidence of his fellow citizens, but on the other hand—. The other hand showed no signs of existing. Requested to ask around Philadelphia, his secretary Lear replied that everyone viewed the possibility of his retirement with "apprehension." This might be true in the capital, but what about the South? Jefferson, dropping in at Mount Vernon on September 31, told Washington, "As far as I knew there was but one voice" in the South. It was "for his continuance."

On November 8, after most of the offices open to direct election had been filled, Washington was still uncertain whether he would allow his name to go before the electoral college. This indecision prompted a letter written to him by a remarkable woman.

Martha Washington's favorite niece, Fanny Bassett. Detail of a family portrait by Robert Edge Pine, oil on canvas, 1785.

Eliza Powel had for some time now been Washington's favorite female companion. She belonged to Philadelphia's leading mercantile family: her father, Thomas Willing, had been the financial mentor of Robert Morris. Her husband, Samuel, was among Philadelphia's richest and most sophisticated citizens. The family lived in the Willing family enclave in the middle of the city, an extensive formal garden containing four mansions. Compared to the elegance here, Mount Vernon was simple, rural. The decorative walks were bordered by statuary. Washington admired Samuel Powel's "profusion of lemon, orange, and citron trees, and many aloes and other exotics."

Eliza was twenty times as sophisticated as Martha Washington; clever and neurotic where Martha was homey and placid; talkative and, unlike Martha, political. Ten years Washington's junior, Eliza had a round, firm, handsome face from which blue eyes shone. Always fashionably dressed, she was gay when she was not passionately melancholy. As is made clear by a letter in which she teased the president on his continence, she was not his mistress, but he found her extremely amusing. She would argue with him on government policy intelligently if banteringly; she made playful fun of him as no one else dared to do.

The letter she now wrote begging Washington not to resign reveals how an able woman, intimately familiar with Washington's character, felt she could most effectively reach his emotions. She urged him to overcome his "diffidence of your abilities." She made no mention of Jefferson or Hamilton or any specific issues. In stating that his departure would be a disaster, she did not refer to the effect on any class or group or area, but on "the repose of millions."

Eliza gave particular emphasis to an argument so personal that others seem to have been afraid to use it. Knowing "your sensibility with respect to public opinion," she felt obliged, as Washington's friend, to point out that much of his popularity "will be torn from you by the envious and malignant should you follow the bent of your inclinations." It would be said "that a concurrence of unparalleled circumstances had attended you," and that since "ambition has been the moving spring of all your acts," when the going became hard, "you would take no further risks" for the people. It would be said that, foreseeing collapse of the government, he was fleeing to escape the crash.

On an even more personal note, Eliza asked whether, even if he could retire with "the benediction of mankind," his happiness would truly be enhanced. She hoped that "until the extremest of old age" Washington would "enjoy the pure felicity of employing your whole faculties" in "those duties which elevate and fortify the soul." His pleasure as well as his duty lay in laboring "for the prosperity of the people for whose happiness you are responsible, for to you their happiness is entrusted."

Eliza was twenty times as sophisticated as Martha Washington; clever and neurotic where Martha was homey and placid; talkative and, unlike Martha, political.

Among the papers Washington's beloved friend so carefully kept, there is no reply from Washington. He must have answered verbally. How he responded to her affectionate pleading is thus hidden, but we do know that ever stronger arguments reverberated, like a battery of cannon, in his ears. These arguments were the inescapable facts of the situation. Washington's presence was desperately needed to keep the already festering wounds in the body politic from opening wider. He had no choice.

Since Washington had made no announcement to the contrary, on February 13, 1793, the electoral college unanimously elected him to a second term. The aging leader was thus sentenced to a continuance of what he had described to Jefferson as "the extreme wretchedness of his existence."

Thirty-Five

BAD OMENS

(1792–1793)

Before the unanimous decision of the electoral college had blocked Washington from possible escape, the French boiler had exploded. The attempted flight of Louis XVI and Marie Antoinette had been followed by war between revolutionary France and aristocratic Austria and Prussia. Since the fighting was altogether landlocked, there was, to Washington's relief, no way that the United States could become physically involved. But ideas know no physical limitations.

The defeat of French armies, one of them commanded by Lafayette, touched off in Paris mass Jacobin demonstrations. The Tuileries were stormed, the king thrown into prison, the constitution suspended, and a revolutionary government set up. Accused of treasonable collusion with the king, Washington's spiritual son fled to Austria, where he was imprisoned.

When in December 1792 news reached Philadelphia that the radical changes in the French government had been followed by military victories, cheering crowds poured into the streets. The citizenry assumed that the French happenings reflected the example of the American Revolution: "The Spirit of '76," advancing in Europe, would pull all aristocracies down! To revel in support of France became an American passion. Cannonades were fired by all who could get their hands on cannon; oceans of liquor were consumed in toasts; and the marching song, *"Ah Ça Ira! Ça Ira!,"* seemed an exciting replacement for the old anthem, set to the tune of "God Save the King," which began, "God Save Great Washington."

The information which soon reached America of the Terror—the rise and fall of the guillotine to the seemingly endless plop of severed heads—did not dampen the enthusiasm of the American republicans. Jefferson wrote that the tree of liberty had to be watered by human blood. He was willing to see "half the earth desolated. Were there but an Adam and Eve left in every country, and left free, it would be better than as it now is."

Washington, who had seen men die in bloody anguish as Jefferson had not, was neither enthused nor encouraged. He believed that "cool reason, which alone can establish a permanent and equal government, is as little to be expected in the tumults of popular commotion as an attention to the liberties of the people is to be expected in the dark divan of a despotic tyrant."

Washington was worried lest pro-French sentiment so overwhelm the American public that, for the first time since the Revolution, the nation would lose control of her own destiny by entanglement in European affairs. However, Jefferson was enchanted that the American reactions to French events "kindled and brought forth the two [political] parties with an ardor which our own interests merely could never incite."

The Jeffersonian warnings against Hamiltonian policies had not disturbed the broad public: the Republican party had hardly extended beyond

Virginia, and the Federalists had found no reason to expand beyond a small pressure group. Party lines had, indeed, remained so vague that, although it was generally felt that the Jeffersonian strength had been increased, no one knew for sure what was the political complexion of the recently elected new House of Representatives.

Washington was worried lest pro-French sentiment so overwhelm the American public that, for the first time since the Revolution, the nation would lose control of her own destiny by entanglement in European affairs.

But now there seemed a clear issue. Conservative in philosophy and desiring to duplicate the British economic system, the Federalists viewed with horror the excesses in France and charged what they to some extent feared: the Jeffersonians were eager to import the Terror. The Republicans shouted that this Federalist attitude indicated a taste for monarchy. At last, the abusive name of Monocrat showed signs of sticking, since the majority of the people were enthusiastically pro-French. The resulting surge of popularity for his views and his own person delighted Jefferson into a move that delighted Washington. He decided not to resign after all. For the time being at least, he would stay in the cabinet.

Deprived by geography of any way to influence the European fighting, the pro-French leaders attacked conservative American symbolism and behavior. A movement was started to melt down as a disgraceful bauble the House of Representatives' silver mace. The salutations "sir" and "madam" were considered disgraceful when one could say "citizen" and "citess." The *National Gazette*, which had hitherto refrained from direct attacks on Washington, felt emboldened to call his formal entertainments and "fastidious" behavior the "legitimate offspring of inequality, begotten by aristocracy and monarchy upon corruption." The freemen of America, so the writer continued, understood their rights and dignities "too well to surrender them for the gratifications of the ambition of any man, however well he may have deserved of his country." This marked the first public effort to discredit Washington since the far-off days of the Conway Cabal.

Washington told Jefferson that he would be glad to behave in any way that pleased the people if their pleasure could be ascertained. In the immediate future, his second inauguration loomed. He asked his cabinet to determine, at conferences which he pointedly did not attend, whether the swearing-in should be conducted in private or in public, and with what ceremony if any. The decision was for a simple occasion in the Senate chamber to which he should travel through the streets "without form, attended by such gentlemen as he choose."

He chose to ride, on March 4, 1793, alone in his coach. That his thoughts were bitter was revealed by his second inaugural address. Here it is in its entirety:

Fellow Citizens: I am again called upon by the voice of my country to execute the functions of its chief magistrate. When the proper occasion for it shall arise, I shall endeavor to express the high sense I entertain of the distinguished honor, and of the confidence which has been reposed in me by the people of the United States.

Previous to the execution of any official act of the president, the Constitution requires an oath of office. This oath I am now about to take and in your presence, that if it shall be found during my administration of

Left: *An eighteenth-century anonymous portrait of King Louis XVI.*
Right: *A 1783 portrait of Queen Marie-Antoinette by Louise Elizabeth Vigee-LeBrun (1755–1842).*

the government I have in any instance violated willingly or knowingly the injunction thereof, I may (besides incurring Constitutional punishment) be subject to the upbraidings of all who now witness the present solemn ceremony.

Having talked thus darkly of duty and punishment, Washington took the oath, and returned, as quickly and unobtrusively as possible, to the presidential mansion.

On March 17, word came in that Louis XVI had been guillotined and France declared a republic. As long as the monarchy had been titularly intact, relations with France had involved no new policy decision. But now Washington was forced to an official step which involved taking sides.

For the United States to recognize the new French regime would outrage the aristocratic powers of Europe and the American Federalists. Not to recognize would outrage the French revolutionaries and the American Republicans. Washington empowered Secretary of State Jefferson to recognize: "We surely cannot deny to any nation the right whereon our own government is founded, that every nation may govern itself according to whatever form it pleases." Washington also agreed to pay the new French government, even before the due date, an installment on the Revolutionary War debt, which reflected borrowings from the now-assassinated French monarch.

The new situation in France created for Washington personal problems. He took down his engraving of Louis XVI, leaving the key to the Bastille to dominate the European symbolism in the presidential mansion.

When a plea came from Madame Lafayette that he use his official influence to free his spiritual son from the Austrian prison, he could only decide, however sharp his heartache, that he could not act effectively without prejudicing the foreign policy of the United States. And at home in Philadelphia, foreign policy again forced him to behave in a manner he found painful towards a Revolutionary veteran: Lafayette's brother-in-law, the Count de Noailles. Since Noailles was an aristocratic exile said to be on a secret mission to influence the foreign policy of the United States, any cordiality that Washington showed him would be considered a political act. And yet Washington, had he achieved his desire to return to private life, would have ridden many miles to greet on the road to Mount Vernon his old friend.

Mount Vernon itself sometimes seemed to be fading away. Not only had Washington's estate manager and nephew died of tuberculosis, but the replacement Washington had laboriously found was almost instantly incapacitated by the same disease. In April 1793, the president took time off for a quick trip home to try to straighten out his affairs. He had hardly arrived when he learned that the European storm had crossed the ocean to break with frightening force over the United States.

George Washington *after Charles Willson Peale (1741–1827), oil on canvas.*

Thirty-Six

EARTHQUAKE FAULTS

(1793 and thereafter)

France and England were fighting. Thus were created the underlying situations that, whatever the surface developments at home or abroad, caused the political earthquakes which rocked Washington's second term as president.

The conflict between American adherents of the rival powers now moved from purely emotional expression to very painfully practical considerations. Involved were not only American prosperity and unity, but also whether the United States, which had during its colonial past been drawn into every general European war, could and should keep from becoming a belligerent on one side or the other.

Washington was convinced that the nation should stay neutral at almost any cost. As he put it, "If we are permitted to improve without interruption the great advantages which nature and circumstances have placed within our reach, many years will not revolve before we may be ranked not only among the most respectable [worthy of respect] but among the happiest people on this globe. Our advances on these points are more rapid than the most sanguine among us ever predicted. A spirit of improvement displays itself in every quarter, and principally in objects of the greatest public utility, such as opening the inland navigation . . . improving the old roads and making new ones, building bridges and houses, and in short pursuing those things which seem most eminently calculated to promote the advantage and accommodation of the people at large. Besides these, the enterprises of individuals show at once what are the happy effects of personal exertions in a country where equal laws and equal rights prevail."

Most Americans agreed, at least in abstract terms, that the United States would be better off if she kept out of the war. This conclusion carried with it a fundamental straining paradox. Secretary of State Jefferson and the majority of the people were pro-French, but pacifism on the part of the United States was irrevocably to the advantage of Britain. Since Britain possessed the greater sea power, it was France that needed reinforcing on the ocean. And England had in Canada a North American base, with many strong harbors, which France could not rival unless she could induce the United States to serve as her naval base.

Both Britain and France depended on seaborne commerce for food and war materials at home and also in their colonies. The United States possessed a large merchant marine, which in peacetime traded primarily with England, the variously owned West Indian islands, and also directly with France. Since it was to the advantage of each combatant to force this commerce into channels that nation found

Following page: *This detail of an anonymous eighteenth-century oil painting depicts the taking of the Bastille on July 14, 1789.*

WASHINGTON'S LETTER TO GOUVERNEUR MORRIS

GOUVERNEUR MORRIS, ONE OF WASHINGTON'S strongest allies and intimate friends, agreed with Washington and favored both a strong central government and that the United States should stay neutral among European affairs. In the letter below, Washington advises Morris, who served as minister plenipotentiary to France from 1792 to 1794, that the States should maintain neutrality at all costs.

Philadelphia, March 25th, 1793

My Dear Sir,

It was not till the middle of February that I had the pleasure to receive your letter of the 23rd of October. If you, who are at the fountain head of those great and important transactions which have lately engrossed the attention of Europe and America, cannot pretend to say what will be their event, surely we, in this distant quarter, should be presumptuous indeed in venturing to predict it. And unwise should we be in the extreme to involve ourselves in the contests of European nations, where our weight could be but small, though the loss to ourselves would be certain. Lean, however, with truth ever that this country is not guided by such a narrow and mistaken policy, as will lead it to wish the destruction of any nation under an idea that our importance will be increased in proportion as that of others is lessened. We should rejoice to see every nation enjoying all the advantages that nature and its circumstances would admit, consistent with civil liberty and the rights of other nations. Upon this ground, the prosperity of this country would unfold itself every day, and every day it would be growing in political importance.

Mr. Jefferson will communicate to you such official information as we have to give, and will transmit the laws, public papers, etc.

I have thought it best, my dear Sir, not to let slip this opportunity of acknowledging the receipt of your letter, lest no other should occur to me very soon, as I am called to Mount Vernon by the death of my nephew, Major Washington, and am on the point of setting out for that place tomorrow. I need not tell you that this is, of course, a very busy moment with me. It will therefore account for the conciseness of this letter, by which, however, you must not measure my regard.

You see me again entering upon the arduous duties of an important office. It is done so contrary to my intention that it would require more time than I have allowed myself to as sign the reasons; and, therefore, I shall leave them to your own suggestion, aided by the publications which you will find in the gazettes. I am your sincere friend and affectionate servant.

George Washington.

From *The Life of Gouverneur Morris with Selections from His Correspondence and Miscellaneous Papers*, Volume II, by Jared Sparks, 1832.

most satisfactory, American skippers had reason to quail when they saw armed vessels on the horizon. Unless the American vessels were also to be armed and permitted by national policy to fight, their only protection from violent interference (apart from superior speed in escape) lay in rights granted to neutrals by specific treaties or generally by international law.

During the passionate years of Washington's second term, two definitions of neutral rights had major currency. One, known as "free ships make free goods" provided that, except for objects like cannon directly intended for making war, and also except when a port was tightly sealed by an effective blockade, neutral shipping could carry anything unimpeded anywhere. However, the maritime code known as *Consolato del Mare* defined as contraband—cargo which might legally be removed from neutral ships—any goods that could be construed by one belligerent as the property of the other. Beyond these conventions lay the possibility that, when a neutral merchantman was overhauled, more would be done, on one pretext or another, than merely removing contraband; the ship would be confiscated and its sailors made captive. Of course, vessels flying the flag of any active belligerent were fair game, with no reservations, for vessels commissioned by the enemy.

This type of warfare was entirely apart from the movements of fleets and all formal naval battles. Encounters were (long before the days of radio) solitary meetings on the vast ocean under no eyes but the sun and the moon and the stars. Activity and severity were encouraged by the fact that making captures greatly enriched the captors. Any contraband removed or any ship impounded was regarded as a "prize." If a "prize court" set up by the side that had made the capture ruled that the capture was legal under whatever rules that belligerent was then observing, the prize was considered "condemned" and the captured property (often including the very clothes the sailors wore) was sold at auction. The proceeds were divided

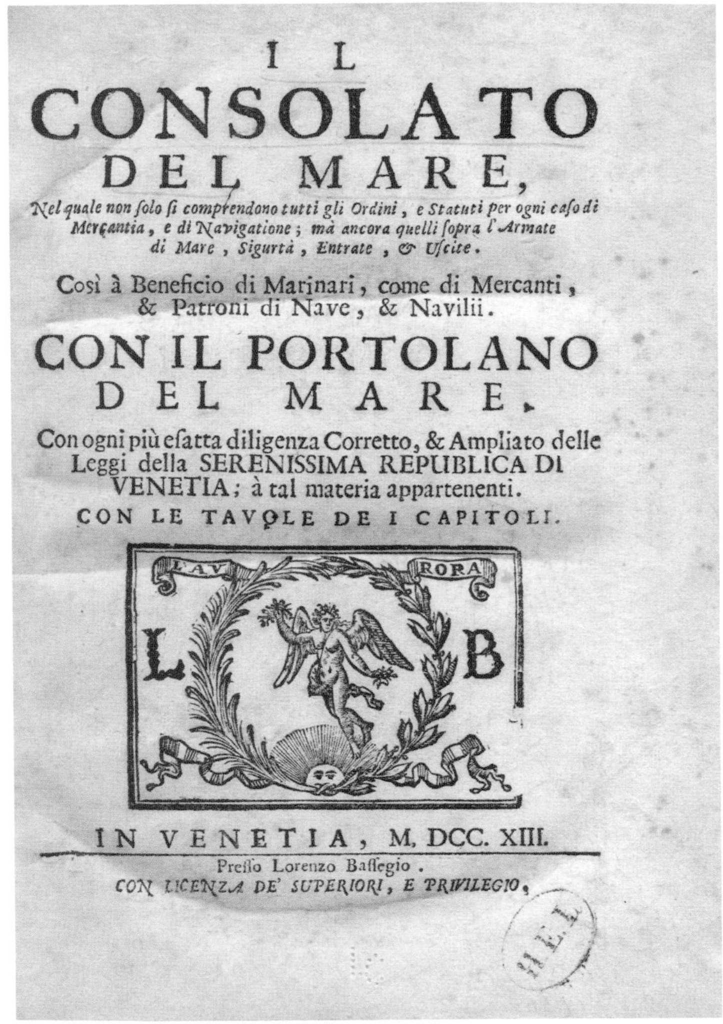
IL
CONSOLATO
DEL MARE,
Nel quale non solo si comprendono tutti gli Ordini, e Statuti per ogni caso di Mercantia, e di Navigatione; mà ancora quelli sopra l'Armate di Mare, Sigurtà, Entrate, & Uscite.
Così à Beneficio di Marinari, come di Mercanti, & Patroni di Nave, & Navilii.
CON IL PORTOLANO
DEL MARE.
Con ogni più esatta diligenza Corretto, & Ampliato delle Leggi della SERENISSIMA REPUBLICA DI VENETIA; à tal materia appartenenti.
CON LE TAVOLE DE I CAPITOLI.

IN VENETIA, M. DCC. XIII.
Presso Lorenzo Basegio.
CON LICENZA DE' SUPERIORI, E PRIVILEGIO.

The title page of Il Consolato del Mare *published in Venice in 1713.*

between the owners and the crew of the vessel that had made the capture.

Should the captor be a naval vessel, the owner's share went to the government. But most of the raiders were "privateers." Privateering was legalized piracy. Any ship which could secure an official commission—known as a "letter of marque"—from a representative of a belligerent government could go a-raiding. No quicker way of making money existed than to have a privateer in which you were concerned bring in a rich prize that was satisfactorily condemned by a friendly prize court.

"If we are permitted to improve without interruption the great advantages which nature and circumstances have placed within our reach, many years will not revolve before we may be ranked not only among the most respectable [worthy of respect] but among the happiest people on this globe."

Since France, the weaker sea power, could not keep the sea-lanes open by force, she was eager to keep them open by interpretations of international law favorable to her. She was all for the doctrine that free ships made free goods. But England had no intention of sacrificing the rewards for her greater maritime strength. She insisted on that narrower interpretation of neutral rights, the *Consolato del Mare,* and found excuses for going further, seizing, when her interests seemed to make this imperative, all American ships bound for French possessions.

Pro-French sentiment in the United States was strongly in favor of the doctrine that free ships made free goods. The Francophiles argued that for American vessels to be able to trade almost as they pleased was greatly to America's economic advantage. Jefferson, as secretary of state, with the support of the president, tried to make the free doctrine stick. Yet no one should have been surprised that Great Britain merely shrugged.

Apart from what American trade the British should permit with French possessions, an extremely sore point was British impressment of American seamen. Most of the common sailors in the Royal Navy had been brutally forced into service and were brutally treated. At foreign ports, they scurried across wharves at midnight and enlisted on American merchantmen

A hand-colored aquatint lithograph published by John Fairburn, 1800, of the July 10, 1799 battle between the American merchant ship Planter *and a French national privateer.*

where, because of the similarity of language, they were indistinguishable from native sailors. No one denied that when an American ship was stopped on the high seas, the British had the right to take their own deserters back. The difficulty was that British captains, who admittedly suffered from the confusion, took advantage of it and impressed at gunpoint squads of American citizens.

As it exacerbated Anglo-American relations, the situation eluded solution. The Anglophobe Jefferson considered that giving American seamen certificates of citizenship would only make matters worse since the certificates would be lost or stolen, and their absence would be considered *ipso facto* proof that the seamen were British deserters. Jefferson's suggestion was that, unless an American ship was found carrying an obviously inflated crew, all should be assumed to be Americans. This meant, in effect, that free ships made free sailors. To this the British could not agree, as it would soon have left their naval vessels unmanned.

Significantly, it was the agrarians who got most excited about the rights of American merchants and their crews. The merchants themselves wanted to help England, and they accepted the fact that American trade was at the British mercy. Better to take advantage of what practices Britain would encourage and accept than to incite that naval power into wielding with greater violence a whip which the United States, possessing no warships, could not take from her hands. If that proved the only available way, the merchants could prosper from trading, under British protection, with British possessions alone.

The strongest partiality for the French and their revolution could not blunt the hard fact that, should the United States be drawn into the war, she would be much safer on the side of Britain than on the side of France. Francophiles might argue that France would eventually conquer Europe and then be a valuable friend or a dangerous enemy, but in any situation immediately foreseeable, her friendship could do little to help the United States, and her enmity could find little way to express itself across a British-dominated ocean. Since the United States possessed no navy, throwing what sea power she could raise—refitted merchantmen—into the French scale would not change the British domination of the ocean. Against the British, the American seacoast would be as painfully vulnerable as it had been during the Revolution. And the British bastion of Canada had recently become doubly menacing.

Up until the French Revolution, Spain had been on the opposite side from England in the European balance of power; there had thus been no danger of cooperative action between Canada and Louisiana. But mutual hatred for the French regicides had brought the kings of England and Spain into alliance. Washington now had to fear a pincer movement up and down the Mississippi and Ohio river systems. The armies of England and Spain would be strengthened by clouds of Indian allies.

That the United States did possess weapons against Britain in some ways further complicated the situation, since it raised the question of how far these weapons could be used without bringing on war. To begin with, trade with the United States was of great importance to England's beleaguered isle. This trade could be impeded or stopped in American ports by such tariff legislation as Washington and Jefferson had long vainly supported, or, in extreme instances, by an actual embargo on vessels owned by England or intending trips to British possessions. Furthermore, although the United States could not change the balance of navies, her privateers could harass the British sea-lanes. A continuing pro-French argument ran that war with the United States would be so disadvantageous to Britain that in helping France, the United States could go very far. How far?

Britain desired no more from the United States than passive acceptance of the rulings her government made. France desired active help, and she had trump cards to play.

The strongest partiality for the French and their revolution could not blunt the hard fact that, should the United States be drawn into the war, she would be much safer on the side of Britain than on the side of France.

There were hangovers from the treaties negotiated during the American Revolution in return for French aid. The Treaty of Alliance committed the United States—this was known as "the guarantee"—to protect the French West Indies should the French call for such assistance. The Commercial Treaty provided that French privateers could bring their prizes to American ports and that powers hostile to France were forbidden to fit out privateers in the United States.

The guarantee had continuing value for pro-French propaganda, but invoking it was not, at least for the time being, to the French advantage. Without a navy, the United States could do little as an active belligerent towards protecting the French West Indies. Better to have America supply the islands (which were cut off from the homeland) as a neutral. British sea power could then be counteracted by having American diplomacy extend neutral rights to the ultimate possibility.

The second French advantage was the popularity of their cause in the United States. The revolutionaries in Paris, insisting that they were fighting for the rights of all men, considered one of their most valuable weapons the ability to appeal to the people of other nations in opposition to rulers who were in opposition to France. No population seemed more promisingly pro-French than the American.

The French liked the idea of inspiring American frontiersmen to attack Spanish Louisiana, but the truly magic word in their American policy was "privateering." Under a broad interpretation of the Commercial Treaty, the United States could give invaluable assistance to French privateers. France had her diplomatic representatives in the United States. They could set up prize courts on American soil, removing any necessity for French privateers operating in the western Atlantic to brave the British navy by carrying their prizes across the ocean to French soil. French privateers could be fitted out in the United States and manned by American seamen eager for prize money and anxious to serve what they considered the cause of freedom. Best of all, the diplomatic representatives could give French letters of marque to American shipowners, creating a legal fiction that would allow American boats to go raiding on the ocean in the French service.

That such action would greatly endanger the neutrality of the United States, the French realized, but they considered the advantages to their war effort so great that they were willing to jeopardize the lesser advantages they would achieve by having American shipping able to claim neutral rights in the face of British naval power. If Washington's priorities were otherwise, if he were to consider American neutrality more important than filling the western Atlantic with pro-French privateers, why, they would have to use their popularity with the American Republicans to brush Washington aside.

Thirty-Seven

A FRENCH BOMBSHELL

(1793)

During Washington's presidency, news of European happenings reached the government and the people simultaneously and in the identical manner: through intelligence brought into seaports by the casual arrival of merchantmen. First there would be rumors, often the result of gossip exchanged when ships out of various foreign ports met in mid-ocean, and then there would be solid accounts, usually copies of foreign newspapers which skippers waved excitedly as their vessels tied up to American wharves. Newspaper editors began setting up type even as government officials began exchanging dispatches.

At the very moment when Washington learned of the outbreak of war between England and France, the maritime community reacted to the same news. This was followed by a further thundering of hooves in the Mount Vernon driveway. At the very first glance, the president recognized the information brought him as extremely grave. French consuls were giving American shipowners letters of marque and American vessels were fitting out with cannon so that they could seize British merchantmen plying the nearby waters.

It was impossible to believe that the British would accept the veneer of legality that made these American ships seem French ships or would sit quiet while their vessels and sailors were brought as captives into American ports. Motivated by a combination of greed for prize money and pro-French idealism, a small group of private citizens were preparing, in effect, to bring the United States into the war with England. They would have to be stopped—but how?

Congress was not in session, yet the Constitution provided that the president could act in foreign policy matters only with the "advice and consent" of the Senate. Wide geography and slow transportation dictated that a special session could not be convened in less than six weeks or perhaps two months. By then, the ocean would be aflame.

Washington decided that, whatever the legal niceties, the executive would have to strike fast and hard. As horses were prepared for the dash of his carriage to Philadelphia, he wrote Jefferson and Hamilton to draw up plans for measures that would prevent American citizens from embroiling the United States with either England or France. War with France was included in the request in order to keep a neutral balance. The actual need was to keep the United States from being drawn by France into war with England. That this was the case filled Washington with concern as he rumbled northward through the tender green of early spring. What would be the reaction of the strongly pro-French secretary of state?

Jefferson was thrown into the quandary that was for the rest of his service in the cabinet to tear at his nerves—and his candor. It was contrary to his principles to help the British; it was contrary to his principles for the executive to override a constitutional prerogative of the Senate. But he could not deny it was to the interest of the United States not to fight England. When the cabinet met, he voted with the other ministers for an executive proclamation. His face-saving proviso (tactfully prepared for him by Hamilton) was to insist that the statement should not define American policy towards the European conflict as "neutrality." This proved so flimsy a cover that the presidential fiat was known, then and ever after, as the Neutrality Proclamation.

The proclamation, published on April 22, 1793 (ten days after firm news had reached Washington of war between England and France), warned that citizens who contributed to hostilities on the ocean would receive no protection from the United States and would be prosecuted whenever their acts were within the jurisdiction of American courts. "The duty and interest of the United States," the president stated, "require that they should with sincerity and good faith adopt and pursue a conduct friendly and impartial towards the belligerent powers." Washington was to assert that throughout the rest of his presidency, he pursued without deviation the policy thus laid down.

As soon as the proclamation was published, the Republican press howled that France and freedom had been betrayed. The executive had finally revealed its itch for monarchy. These attacks deeply disturbed Washington. Jefferson's reactions were confused. He could not resist writing ecstatically to Senator Monroe, "All the old spirit of '76 is kindling." Yet the fact remained that he had voted for the proclamation.

Madison, who was vacationing in Virginia during the recess of the House, sent Jefferson angry blasts. Since Madison wanted no more than did Jefferson an all-out war with England, Jefferson could have replied that if it had been his friend who was secretary of state, saddled with unavoidable responsibility, Madison would have been forced to vote as Jefferson had. Instead, Jefferson inaugurated his continuing practice of pretending to his correspondents that he behaved at the cabinet sessions as he would actually have done had he been free to respond to his emotions rather than to practical necessity. In writing to Madison, Monroe, and others, he denounced the proclamation as a pro-British plot fomented by Hamilton, and explained away his own support under a web of various pretexts.

Freneau, flying ever higher on the wings of vituperation, published that Washington had signed the Neutrality Proclamation because the Anglophiles had threatened otherwise to cut off his head. Jefferson noted that this made Washington "sore and warm. . . . I took his intention to be that I should interpose in some way with Freneau, perhaps withdraw his appointment of translating clerk in my office. But I will not do it! His paper has saved our Constitution which was galloping fast into monarchy."

Believing a rumor that "an old militia general up the North [Hudson] River" possessed a plan in Hamilton's handwriting for crowning an American king, Jefferson felt all the more strongly that the safety of the American republic depended on a French victory. He was far from reassured to have Washington pooh-pooh the possibility of monarchy at home and express worry for the future of the French rather than the American republic. France, Washington stated, seemed "in the highest paroxysm of disorder, not so much from the pressure of foreign enemies . . . but because those in whose hands the [governmen]t is entrusted are ready to tear each other to pieces and will, more than probably, prove the worst foes the government has." As Jefferson dreamed of a Gallic utopia, Washington dimly prophesied Napoleon. He foresaw "a crisis of sad confusion" leading possibly to an "entire change in the French system."

The revolutionary government in France, recalling the minister who had represented Louis XVI, was sending its own minister to the United States. At a cabinet meeting, Hamilton insisted that in receiving Edmond Charles Genêt, the president should state

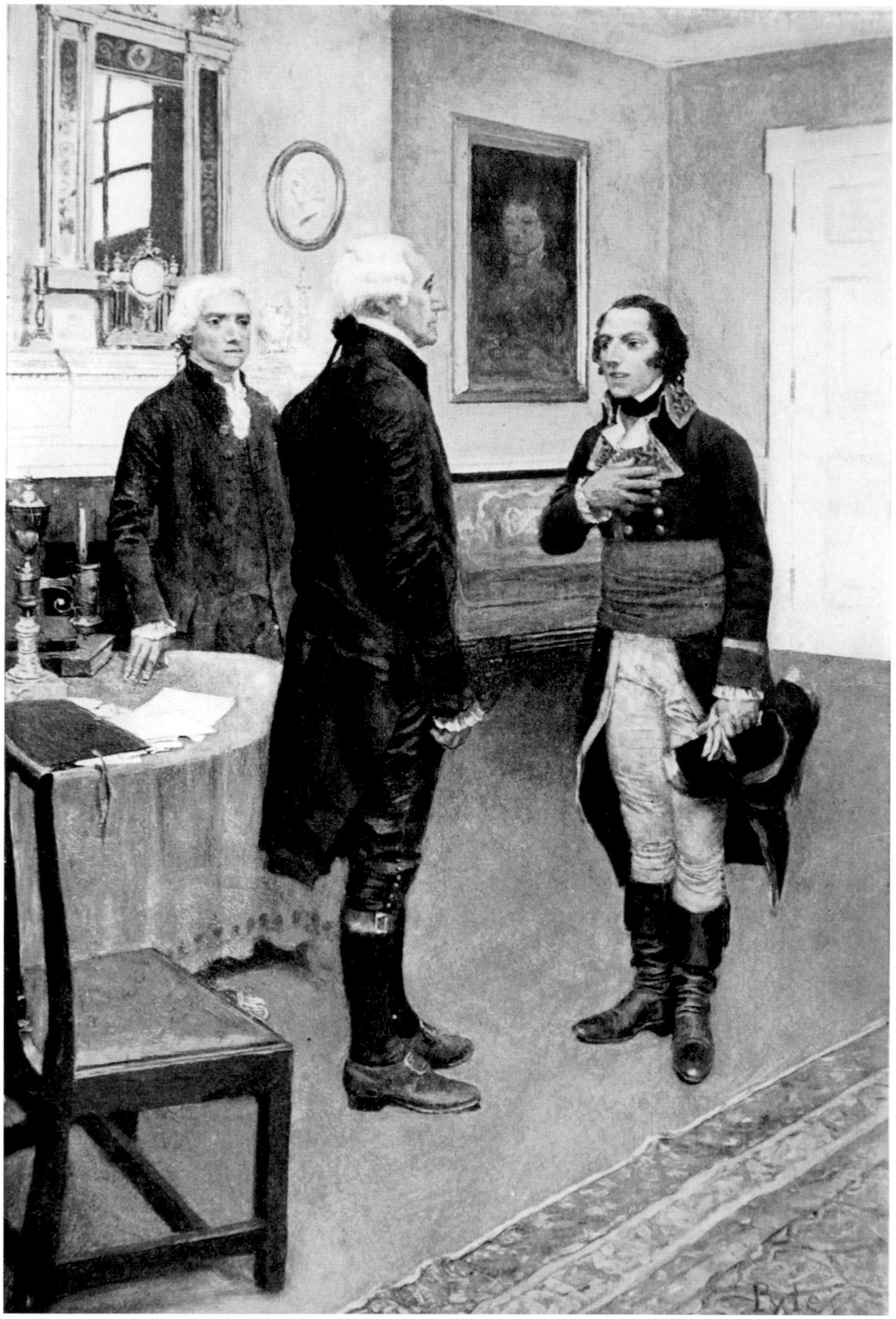

French envoy Edmond Charles Genêt by Howard Pyle, as reproduced in Harper's New Monthly *magazine in April 1897. Genêt spoke perfect English and was soon the toast of the South, while ignoring proper protocols and dismissing Washington's Neutrality Proclamation. Even Jefferson fell under his spell. Genêt's scheme—in direct opposition to Washington—was to raise an army of American citizens that would liberate Louisiana from Spain and create an independent nation under French aegis.*

that the various dangerous clauses in the French treaties—"the guarantee," etc.—were no longer in force. Since the government with which the treaties had been negotiated had been overthrown, this would be in conformity with international law. But, so Hamilton continued, if Genêt were received without reservations, the dangerous clauses would be in effect reaffirmed, to be picked up at will by the bloody hands of the French revolutionaries.

Jefferson reacted with such fury that he could hardly enunciate. Later, he sent Washington a memorandum in which he contended that denouncing the treaties would in international law be a ticklish business and that receiving the minister would, in any case, commit the United States to nothing. While agreeing that the "law of self-preservation" overrode all others, Jefferson contended that the clauses should only be denounced if the danger became "great, inevitable, and imminent."

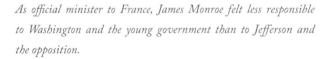

As official minister to France, James Monroe felt less responsible to Washington and the young government than to Jefferson and the opposition.

Washington, who (as he later admitted) considered Hamilton's contentions silly, also believed in never crossing bridges until you came to them. He was the more pleased with Jefferson's memorandum because the secretary of state, now the practical statesman, not the Francophile, saw a way to get around the most immediately troublesome problem the treaties raised. It had been provided that the enemies of France could not fit out privateers or sell prizes in the United States. But, so Jefferson pointed out, it was not specifically stated that the French could. Washington agreed that the same rule might be applied to both belligerents, leaving the French with no important exclusive privileges in relation to privateers.

This policy was to become the basis for a rending fight with the new French minister.

Genêt's head had remained on his shoulders rather than dropping from the guillotine blade because he was so indiscreet. Brought up, although a commoner, in the court of Louis XVI, he had been assigned to various diplomatic missions. That he always fought with his superiors, forcing his recall, gave him, when the monarchy fell, credentials as an opponent of the royal government. He now threw all the ebullience of his nature into the revolutionary cause. The inexperienced government, being desperately in need of diplomats with experience, gave the man who referred to himself as "Citizen Genêt" his choice of missions. He chose the United States.

Genêt should have landed in Philadelphia to present his credentials to the president. His warship landed him in Charleston, South Carolina, where he was instantly busy enlisting an army to attack Louisiana and seeing to the commissioning and fitting out of American ships as privateers.

The endlessly vital envoy, who spoke perfect English and was an ecstatic orator, was acclaimed in the streets and toasted at banquets until he concluded that the American people were so overwhelmingly pro-French that he did not need to worry about their silly little government in Philadelphia. He was sure that his superiors in Paris, who had warned him to proceed cautiously, would, if they heard the plaudits he received, agree that there was no need for guile. Should the American government oppose him, he would undertake and win a popularity contest with that friend of the counterrevolutionary Lafayette who was said to be pro-British, with *le vieillard* (the old man) Washington.

Having finally completed his business in Charleston, he did not sail in his waiting frigate to Philadelphia, but moved slowly overland, haranguing the people at every crossroads. He was at Richmond, Virginia, when he learned of the Neutrality Proclamation. He considered the proclamation clearly ridiculous, but realized that the situation needed looking into. He now advanced as rapidly as he could to Philadelphia.

Not only did the Philadelphia crowds surge and roar French revolutionary slogans, but the secretary of state fell most satisfactorily under the magnetic Frenchman's sway. As Genêt's reports to his government reveal, Jefferson disassociated himself to the French minister, as he was in the habit of doing to his Virginia supporters, from acts which at cabinet meetings he had in fact approved. In

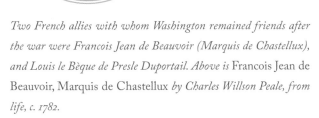

Two French allies with whom Washington remained friends after the war were Francois Jean de Beauvoir (Marquis de Chastellux), and Louis le Bèque de Presle Duportail. Above is Francois Jean de Beauvoir, Marquis de Chastellux *by Charles Willson Peale, from life, c. 1782.*

officially communicating cabinet decisions in his role as secretary of state, Jefferson would explain that he was acting only as "the passive instrument of the president." Jefferson, Genêt wrote, "did not conceal from me that Senator [Robert] Morris and Secretary of the Treasury Hamilton, attached to the British interest, exerted the greatest influence on the mind of the president, and it was only with the greatest difficulty that he counteracted their efforts." Genêt concluded that the least he could do for France and freedom and indeed American republicanism was to use his own obvious popularity to work (as he viewed it) side by side with the secretary of state against the president.

Under Genêt's spell, Jefferson committed his greatest indiscretion while in the cabinet. To officials in Kentucky he backed, subtly but yet clearly, Genêt's scheme for raising an army of American citizens that would liberate Louisiana from Spain and create an independent nation under the French aegis. Jefferson must have known that this was exactly opposite to the policies of his president. Washington was doing all in his power to reduce the possibility of war with Spain. Such a conflict would surely involve the British, who were further demonstrating their ability to prevent the United States from even conferring with the most belligerent northwestern tribes. And Washington was violently opposed to establishing in the West new nations with foreign connections. They would, Washington foresaw, break up the American continent into another bickering Europe.

When word came back to Philadelphia of the Kentucky plots, Jefferson obediently relayed Washington's orders that any freebooting expeditions against Spain should be suppressed, but he continued to hide from the president what he had previously done.

Jefferson watched with "affectionate" eyes when Genêt finally and belatedly presented his credentials to Washington. The Frenchman delivered a speech in which he dwelt on his nation's magnanimity in not evoking "the guarantee," her generosity in offering trade concessions in her West Indian islands (that Washington knew was to the French advantage). "We wish you," Genêt intoned, "to do nothing but what is for your own good." "Cherish," he admonished, "your own peace and prosperity!"

Washington was courteous while saying little, a combination which allowed Genêt to depart in a flood of self-satisfaction concerning the effect of his performance. Only later did he realize that Washington had

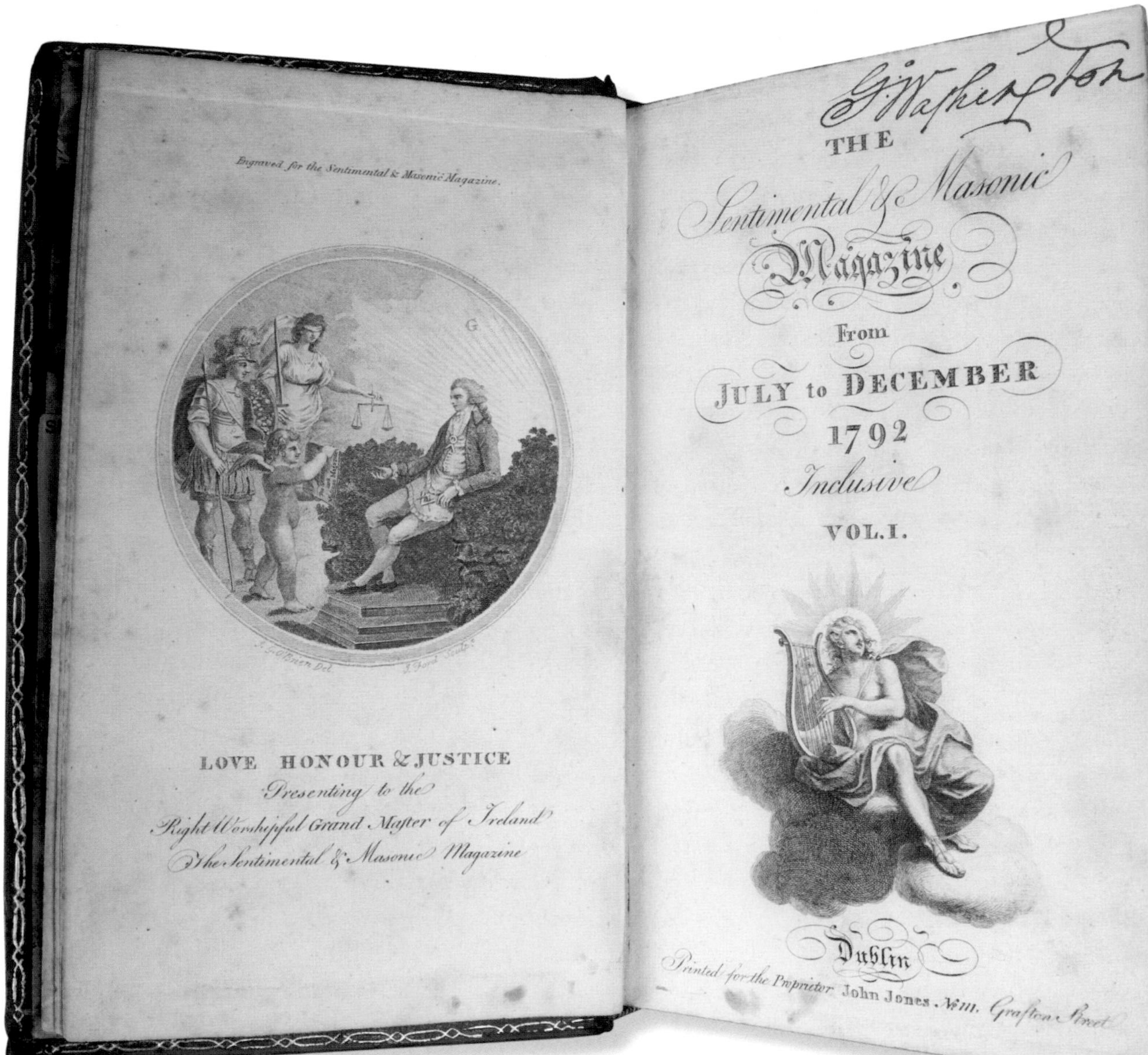

In 1752, at the age of twenty, Washington was initiated into the fraternal organization of Freemasons, and in 1788 he was appointed master of the Alexandria Lodge. In 1795, John Jones of Dublin, Ireland, the proprietor of the Sentimental and Masonic Magazine, *sent Washington this set of five volumes with a letter requesting permission to dedicate a sixth to Washington and to include an elegant portrait of "His Excellency."*

expressed no desire to assist what Genêt considered a sacred crusade for liberty; Washington had not gone beyond speaking of the desire of the United States "to live in peace and harmony with all the powers and particularly France."

On June 9, 1793, Jefferson wrote Madison, "The president is not well. Little lingering fevers have been hanging about him for a week or ten days, and have affected his looks most remarkably. He is also extremely affected by the attacks made and kept on him in the public papers. I think he feels those things more than any person I ever yet met with. I am extremely sorry to see them." But, so Jefferson continued, Washington had brought the attacks on himself. "Naked he would have been sanctimoniously reverenced, but enveloped in the rags of royalty, they can hardly be torn off without laceration. It is the more unfortunate that this attack is planted on popular ground, on the love of the people to France and its cause, which is universal."

As a matter of fact, Washington's emotional sympathies were more with France than England. He had in his two wars fought both nations, but the Revolution had been fratricidal and thus more bitter. Traveling through New England during his first presidential term, he had commented on "the destructive evidences of British cruelty" yet visible in Connecticut. After the Revolution, he did not have a single English friend, but he remained close, if only by letter, to Frenchmen who had fought in his army and as his allies: not only his beloved Lafayette, but the Marquis de Chastellux and others. The French, furthermore, were seeking freedom from aristocratic domination, even if their road took strange turns.

Washington's cabinet was now engaged in endless discussion of specific interpretations of the Neutrality Proclamation. Although Jefferson continued to present himself to his followers as a solitary champion fighting a solid block of pro-British monarchists, Washington agreed, when there was a difference, more often with Jefferson than with the pro-British Hamilton. This was made possible by the fact that, applying to his official acts the practical and balanced side of his nature, Jefferson rarely allowed his bias to carry him beyond the confines of judicious behavior. And Washington was glad to lean as far towards the French side as he thought was compatible with the fundamental principle enunciated in the Neutrality Proclamation.

Since Hamilton very rarely put his emotions on paper, we do not know how he reacted, from issue to issue, on being so often overridden. But in late June 1793, he sent Washington an angry letter: "Considerations relative both to the public interest and to my own delicacy" had made him resolve to resign his office towards the end of the present session of Congress. Washington commented that Hamilton "had often before intimated dispositions to resign, but never as decisively before." Washington must have tried to change his secretary's mind, but for the moment, at least, Hamilton adhered to his intention.

Jefferson was coming to realize that by his early confidences to Genêt, he had encouraged a menace to American peace and a wild force who might by extreme behavior damage in American public opinion the French cause. Genêt had his own interpretation of America's treaty obligations. In his opinion, the French clearly had a right to create and man privateers in the United States, and to set up their own courts that would award to the captors prizes brought into American harbors. If the executive continued to try to enforce the Neutrality Proclamation, which Genêt had ruled illegal, the French minister would arrange to have Congress called in a special session. Or by writing in the newspapers, he would undermine the superannuated and reactionary president, who was jealous, Genêt believed, because Genêt was closer to the American people than he.

Jefferson now tried to tone the Frenchman down, but it was like arguing with a tornado. "He renders my position immensely difficult," Jefferson complained. ". . . I am on a footing to advise him freely, and he respects it, but he breaks out again on the very first occasion." (Genêt was later to claim that Jefferson had double-crossed him.)

Washington's new estate manager had become incapacitated with tuberculosis, leaving no one at the helm—and just at the time of the June harvest. The president felt required to make a flying trip home. Although the manager died before he arrived and everything proved to be in dismal confusion, Washington felt he could stay at Mount Vernon for only ten days. He posted back to Philadelphia, arriving on July 11, 1793, to find on his desk a pile of papers marked in Jefferson's handwriting, "instant attention."

The documents revealed that Genêt was publicly challenging the government. He was mounting cannon and enlisting an American crew on a former British brigantine, the *Little Sarah,* which the French had captured before the Neutrality Proclamation and renamed *La Petite Démocrate*. When the Pennsylvania authorities, who had jurisdiction because the bustle was going on in Philadelphia's harbor, warned him that he was breaking the law, Genêt defied them. He had also defied the intervention of Jefferson.

Washington read with horror Genêt's statement that the crew of the ship, most of whom were American citizens, were such "high-spirited" French patriots that they would resist by force any efforts to stop their sailing. Genêt had furthermore warned a Pennsylvania mediator that "he would appeal from the president to the people." In a fury that a foreign representative should "threaten the executive," Washington called for Jefferson to come to him at once. Jefferson, who wanted to take as little responsibility as possible, pleaded illness (he was well the next day) and did not come.

Further papers sent by Jefferson reported a debate that had taken place in the cabinet. Hamilton and Knox had argued that if the United States allowed the *Little Sarah* to sail, the prestige of the government would be wounded and England would have a cause for war. Jefferson had argued that attacking the ship would exaggerate a minor infraction and give France a cause for war. While the ministers bickered, Genêt sailed the ship to a point where the United States, having no naval frigate, could not stop her. She was soon out in the ocean, where she proved a very effective raider.

Genêt was convinced of the rectitude of his acts. "When treaties speak," he explained, "the agents of nations have but to obey." And he could not doubt that he could mitigate Washington's anger with his persuasive charm. Ignoring Jefferson's warnings, he made a surprise call on the president. He explained that his own popularity in the United States was not due to any scheming on his part; it reflected "the honesty and integrity" of the American people. Washington would of course realize that Genêt could not, unless he were to be a traitor, submit to the Neutrality Proclamation, which "annulled the most sacred treaties." France was emerging triumphant from the war and would, Genêt assured the president, treat the United States with magnanimity.

Having listened in silence, Washington replied only to Genêt's comments on popularity: "He did not read the gazettes, and it was of very slight importance to him whether his administration was talked about."

Genêt departed with "flattering thoughts" that he had mollified Washington. The next day, he hurried to Jefferson's office to boast of his triumph. He had hardly begun when a door opened and in walked a stony-faced Washington. Genêt made one of his best bows, and then saw that Jefferson was now equally stony faced. He looked from one to the other for "an invitation to remain for which I would willingly have given part of my life." Jefferson made "an imperative sign." Hurt and amazed at such behavior by a man he considered his friend and supporter, Genêt felt forced to retire.

Thirty-Eight

TROUBLE ALL AROUND

(1793)

It was a summer of riots. As a very old man, John Adams reminisced about "the terrorism excited by Genêt in 1793, when ten thousand people in the streets of Philadelphia day after day threatened to drag Washington from his house," start a revolution, and declare war on England. This is a senile exaggeration, yet it is a fact that discontents were widespread in Virginia and mobs did roam city streets, hooting at any visible elegance and threatening the Federalists.

"That there are in this as well as in all other countries," Washington wrote, "discontented characters, I well knew, and also that these characters are actuated by very different views: some good, from an opinion that the measures of the general government are impure; some bad, and (if I might be allowed to use so harsh an expression) diabolical, inasmuch as they are not meant to impede the measures of that government generally, but more especially (as a great means towards the accomplishment of it) to destroy the confidence which it is necessary for the people to place (until they have unequivocal proof of dismerit) in their public servants." Washington could not resist adding that he could better be called a slave than a servant.

Washington was eyeing with great uneasiness the Pennsylvania Democratic Society, organized by friends of Genêt with the avowed object of sponsoring a network of clubs across the nation to rouse pro-French and anti-administration sentiment. The movement is variously said to have been based on the Committees of Safety which had helped foment the American Revolution or on the Jacobin Clubs that had brought the French Revolution to its bloodiest phase. Neither alternative could be reassuring to those who did not believe that the United States needed a second revolution. "I early gave it as my opinion to the confidential characters around me," Washington was to remember, "that if these societies were not counteracted (not by prosecutions, the ready way to make them grow stronger), or did not fall into disesteem" through knowledge of the purposes for which they were instituted "by their father, Genêt, . . . they would shake the government to its foundations."

Hamilton insisted that Genêt was applying to the United States France's general policy of subverting all governments. Jefferson argued that Genêt was no more than an unfortunate appointment. Washington, with his eyes focused on the domestic scene, believed that the fault lay with the Americans (he was not well enough informed to include Jefferson) who had egged Genêt on.

Since Jefferson now regarded the French minister as a liability, the executive leadership was unanimous that Genêt's recall should be requested. Cabinet debates turned on how the request should be worded and whether the record of Genêt's misbehavior should be published. Hamilton was, of course, for a stern protest to Paris and complete disclosure. Jefferson

Rufus King, a signer of the Constitution, as portrayed by Gilbert Stuart in 1820.

wanted the request to be as between friends, and, in opposing disclosure, he found himself arguing against his professed principles. He believed in obeisance to the legislature, but he knew that informing Congress would be to inform the people. One of his favorite contentions was that the people should be completely trusted, yet he feared that, if Genêt's desire to interfere in the American government were known, "universal indignation" would wound pro-French sentiment and the emerging Republican party.

Washington again agreed with Jefferson. He wished the dispatch to state that the United States did not blame France for what they regarded as Genêt's personal misbehavior. The president's desire for national unity so overrode his hope that the Democratic Societies be discredited that he decided not to publish, at least for the time being, even the fact that Genêt's recall had been requested. The government would have to do its best to put up with the intransigent minister until word came back from France.

Washington's decisions elicited violent opposition from Hamilton and Knox. They warned that, unless the public were notified of their danger, sedition would sweep the country. Knox made two attempts to rouse Washington's anger at the personal insults being offered him. On the second attempt, when he referred to a satire which described Washington being guillotined for his aristocratic crimes, Knox succeeded.

Washington liked to say that, since "neither ambitious or interested motives have influenced my conduct, the arrows of malevolence . . . never can reach the vulnerable part of me." But now, so Jefferson noted, he "got into one of those passions when he cannot command himself, ran on much on the personal abuse which had been bestowed on him, defied any man on earth to produce one single act of his since he had been in the government which was not done on the purest motives." He stated "that he had never repented but once having slipped the moment of resigning his office, and that was every moment since, and that *by God* he had rather be in his grave than in his present situation. That he had rather be on his farm than to be made *emperor of the world,* and yet that they were charging him with wanting to be a king. That that *rascal Freneau* sent him three of his papers every day, as if he thought he would become the distributor of his papers, and that he could see in this nothing but an impudent design to insult him. He ended in this high tone."

Washington's burst of rage did not make him change his decision not to publish the Genêt record. However, Hamilton could not bear to lose what Jefferson called "the advantage they have got." Under the nom de plume "No Jacobin," he stated in the press that Genêt was attempting to subvert the government in order to drag the United States, a French prisoner, into war with England.

When fifteen warships of the French West Indian fleet appeared in New York Harbor, Genêt, ignorant that his recall had been requested, rushed there jubilantly. Washington warned Jefferson that he claimed he now had fifteen thousand seamen at his command. He might use them to fit out privateers "*in our ports.*"

Sensing a grave crisis, the Federalists undertook a bold move. A letter appeared in the press, remarkable in that it was signed, not by a nom de plume as was then the almost universal practice, but by two high officials of the government in their true names: Rufus King, senator from New York, and John Jay, chief justice of the Supreme Court. They stated succinctly: "Mr. Genêt, the French minister, had said he would appeal to the people from certain decisions of the president."

Genêt responded with a public letter ostensibly addressed to the president. He recalled that he had "demonstrated" to Washington that official American policy sacrificed the French interest and seemed contrary to "the views of the people of America." Was Genêt to infer that "the slightest hint of an appeal, which a magistrate deserving of his high office would ardently desire, was to you the greatest offense I could offer?" Having thus publicly attacked Washington and tried to go over his head to the people, Genêt demanded Washington's "explicit declaration" that he had never done either of these things.

The immediate reaction induced a replay of what had happened during the Revolution when the public, on learning that Washington had been insulted by that other Frenchman, General Conway, had felt a surge of renewed affection for their national leader. Washington was of course pleased to hear the previously augmenting pro-French explosions begin to muffle, but in relation to Jay and King, he did not deviate from what he considered impartial propriety. Having been officially so requested by the French minister, the president set on foot an inquiry to determine whether the foreign diplomat had been libeled.

Jay and King were furious at what they considered Washington's lack of gratitude. They wrote him an immoderate protest at which he was deeply offended. Knox sprang into the breach. Through his mediation, the conflict was patched up. As King watched, Washington threw all the angry correspondence into the fire. However, Jay, who could not bear even the tiniest slight to his self-importance, seems not to have forgiven the president. This was to have calamitous repercussions later in Washington's second term.

The role of noncombatant in a political and ideological fight is not a happy one. While Jay and King were still fuming, Washington received a letter, dated July 31, 1793, in which Jefferson renewed his resignation.

Washington responded by riding to Jefferson's country retreat on the outskirts of Philadelphia. His appeal to the loyalty of his old friend fell on deaf ears. Jefferson stated that not only did he have "an excessive repugnance to public life," but he found especially repulsive the social life in Philadelphia. And his private affairs at home needed attending to.

Washington then "expressed great apprehension at the fermentation which seemed to be working in the mind of the public, that many descriptions of persons, actuated by different causes, appeared to be uniting. What it would end in, he knew not."

Jefferson assured Washington that the Republicans were not opposed to the government; they merely wished to reestablish the independence of Congress. The danger, Jefferson reiterated, was an American monarchy. As before, Washington scoffed at the possibility of such a danger.

Jefferson's ears must have pricked forward when Washington confided that Hamilton had asked to retire towards the close of the next congressional session. If Jefferson would postpone his departure to the same date, Washington could fill both vacancies simultaneously. This would enable him to reshuffle the geographic distribution, putting perhaps a southerner in the Treasury and a northerner in State. The conferees then discussed, without coming up with any impressive possibilities, who could fill the two vacancies. Washington again pressed Jefferson to stay. When Jefferson asked if he might postpone his final decision for three days, Washington replied, "Like a man going to the gallows, he was willing to put it off as long as he could."

Jefferson took advantage of a traveler going south to send Madison and through him the other Virginian political leaders a packet which, he explained, "could never have been hazarded by post." The papers included a complete transcript of his private conversation with Washington, "which may enable you to shape your plan for the state of things which is actually to take place," and also a long letter outlining a new Republican strategy.

Washington liked to say that, since "neither ambitious or interested motives have influenced my conduct, the arrows of malevolence . . . never can reach the vulnerable part of me."

Hamilton's power should be undermined by breaking the Treasury Department in half. There should be two secretaries: one to collect customs duties and the other, internal taxes. The House should declare the bank unconstitutional, which would have a popular impact even if the Senate were too "unsound" to concur. Then Jefferson, who had condoned, if regretfully, the attacks on Washington, urged that they be stilled. But not because of any affection or admiration for the president.

The Federalists, Jefferson confided, were trying to persuade Washington that they were "the only friends to the government." If the president were convinced that "the people" were supporting Genêt against him, he would probably publish the record of Genêt's behavior. This would be disastrous. Thus the Republicans should praise Washington, abate their attack on the Neutrality Proclamation, and withdraw their support from Genêt.

Madison, and to a greater extent Monroe, expressed unwillingness to abandon Genêt. In separate letters, they urged Jefferson not to resign. Their arguments were based on their acceptance of Jefferson's statements that he alone in the executive was unsympathetic to monarchy and not pro-British. Having been told that Washington never paid any attention to anything Jefferson advised, they concluded that Washington's motive in wishing to keep Jefferson in the cabinet was only "self-love," the desire to use the presence of the Republican leader as a "shield" to protect him from even more violent newspaper attacks. Jefferson should take advantage of Washington's need to hide behind him. He should stay on and make "as few concessions as possible."

Jefferson had to reach his decision long before he received these replies. He concluded that he could stay on if he could avoid the responsibility that forced him to support necessary decisions that were counter to his emotions and his politics. Towards this end, he worked out a scheme which would enable him to remain painlessly in office until the end of 1793. He would insist on going home for six weeks, and he knew that Washington intended to get off for three weeks. It being obvious that the president and the secretary of state should not be away at the same time, this would get him, as far as policymaking was concerned, "rid of nine weeks." During the remaining four of his service, Congress

This political cartoon depicts Jefferson attempting to slow Washington's move toward the Federalist Party.

would be in session and the executive presumably not making decisions but awaiting them. "My view in this," Jefferson explained to Madison, "was precisely to avoid being at any more councils as much as possible, that I might not be committed in anything further."

After Jefferson had suggested (without stating his motives) this schedule to Washington, he worried lest the president had not understood him. He sent a letter expressing "in writing more exactly what I meant to have said yesterday."

Washington replied, "I clearly understood you on Saturday, and of what I conceive to be two evils, must prefer the least: that is to dispense with your temporary absence in autumn (in order to retain you in office till January) rather than part with you altogether at the close of September."

The more extreme Republicans were continuing to support the French minister against the American president. Genêt himself was perpetually in the press, denouncing Washington, urging warlike preparations against England. As Jefferson had feared, this clamor swelled the revulsion of popular sentiment which had been started by the revelation of Jay and King. Mass meetings held across the land had previously adopted resolutions denouncing the executive and the Neutrality Proclamation. Now, even those which expressed sympathy for the French cause praised Washington and agreed that it should be national policy to treat both belligerents equally.

The Republicans who had so libeled Washington were out on a limb that could be sawed off behind them. An easy opportunity to do this was given the president by his long-standing practice of publicly answering every resolution sent him. But when Washington asked Hamilton's help in answering a resolution, he made it clear that he was not calling on that propagandist's controversial gifts. He wished "such alterations in the expression of the draft . . . as will, in your opinion, make it palatable to all sides, or unexceptional."

Thirty-Nine

A TRAGIC DEPARTURE

(1793)

No one then understood how yellow fever was transmitted. Unsuspected by science, mosquitoes took over Philadelphia. In August 1793, the disease moved on insect wings down the streets from the waterfront, creating the most murderous epidemic in all American history. Hamilton was soon believed to be dying. Those still-living inhabitants who had not fled the city cowered indoors, the principal movement on the streets being of open carts driven by African Americans, who were considered immune, on which sprawled corpses being hurried to the pits, which had taken over from the glutted graveyards.

The presidential office, Washington wrote, was "in a manner blockaded by the disorder," yet word came to him that his presence in the city was one of the few things that gave inhabitants hope. Although he had announced a date for his departure for a Mount Vernon holiday, he decided to remain. However, Martha could not be persuaded to leave without him. Unwilling to expose her and the children to the contagion, he agreed to leave, but not one day sooner than he had previously intended.

Whatever hopes Washington had harbored for a restful vacation proved utterly vain. Since that distant date when he had undertaken the Revolutionary command, whenever other authorities had failed to function, the responsibility had devolved on him. Now the capital was sealed off from the rest of the United States by disease, and most members of the government had scattered, even disappeared. All federal business flowed into Mount Vernon. This was the more vexing because Washington, having not foreseen the situation, had not brought with him any of the relevant records. From the windows of the mansion house, he could see his managerless plantation deteriorating, but he hardly had time to step out of doors.

With autumn, the disease began to abate, and Washington called such members of his cabinet as he could locate to join him in Germantown, six miles northwest of the stricken city. Jefferson met him on the road in a very bad humor. The secretary of state's plan for escaping responsibility had been destroyed because the yellow fever had made him journey to Monticello when Washington was also away. He was being forced to return to duty at exactly the moment he had most wished to avoid: when, in preparation for the upcoming congressional session, the executive would have to make crucial decisions.

Germantown was crowded with refugees from Philadelphia. Setting up his headquarters in the elegant mansion of Colonel David Franks, Washington stayed in the same house—and perhaps slept in the same bed—where the British commander in chief, Sir William Howe, had, fifteen years before, received the shocking news that the Continental army was advancing amazingly down Germantown's streets.

Edmund Jennings Randolph (1753–1813) (far right) was the seventh governor of Virginia, the second secretary of state—appointed by Washington upon Jefferson's resignation in 1793—and the first U.S. attorney general. Randolph managed to maintain a precarious neutrality in the feud between Jefferson (his second cousin) and Alexander Hamilton, though Jefferson came to loathe him for what he considered his insufficient loyalty.

Now Washington's appearance again created a sensation. It was taken as a demonstration that the calamity had passed. His advisers feared that his "indifference about danger" might make him risk his own life, and those of the inhabitants who would "crowd" after him, by riding into the city while contagion still lurked. Washington was not to be dissuaded. The mosquitoes having been killed by the chilly weather, neither he nor the "multitudes" who followed his example were harmed.

The main business before the cabinet was determining what to report to Congress about the Neutrality Proclamation and about Genêt. Concerning the proclamation, there had long been a constitutional debate between Hamilton and Jefferson. The Hamiltonian view was that the president had exerted a right to lead foreign policy, it being only required that he consult the Senate after the event. Jefferson asserted that the president would have encroached had he in fact promulgated a new foreign policy; he had merely declared the existing situation when the country was actually at peace. Washington agreed with Jefferson, stating that "he had never had an idea that he could bind Congress against declaring war."

The long-postponed question of whether the Genêt record should be made public by presenting the documents to Congress could, now that Congress was convening, no longer be postponed. This was the issue Jefferson had most wished to avoid, all the more because the refusal of his own followers to accept his advice to abandon Genêt had clearly made it necessary for the government to defend itself by justifying the request for his recall. It was with a feeling of being unfairly trapped that Jefferson made unanimous the cabinet decision to present Congress with the record of Genêt's behavior.

Debate then turned on whether the revelations unfavorable to France should be balanced by revelations unfavorable to England. Not only were the British ignoring American protests concerning the northwestern posts, but they were illegally damaging American trade with the French West Indies. Jefferson urged full publication. Hamilton, Knox, and Randolph stated that important information should be held back as negotiations were pending. "I began to tremble now for the whole," Jefferson remembered, "lest all should be kept secret." But Washington intervened "with more vehemence than I have seen him show" and decided that without reserve "the British acts be revealed." He commissioned Jefferson to prepare the report to Congress.

Since Genêt was still engaged in trying to undermine the government, Washington asked his cabinet whether the minister should not be dismissed without waiting to hear from the French government. This created such a cat-and-dog fight that the president postponed a decision. He was relieved when, early in the new year, he heard that Paris was indeed acting.

On Washington's sixty-third birthday, a new envoy, Jean Antoine Joseph, Baron Fauchet, presented his credentials. He seemed, Martha wrote, "a plain, grave, and good man." Fauchet wished to arrest Genêt and send him back to France, where the diplomat would undoubtedly have paid for his indiscretions on the guillotine. Desiring no such revenge, Washington gave Genêt asylum in the United States. After marrying the daughter of Governor Clinton of New York, Genêt for the rest of his life devoted the boiling of his brain to impractical inventions.

Hamilton's bout with yellow fever had left him weak. He felt "chagrin" at the "weakness or wickedness" of those he had to contend with in the government. Yet he withdrew his resignation. It was Jefferson who remained determined to depart. He turned down Washington's continuing appeals so "decidedly" that the president concluded, "I can no longer hint this to him."

> Jefferson's retirement was undoubtedly the greatest catastrophe Washington suffered during his presidency. It was not only that the powerful political leader, now no longer held down by an executive responsibility, went over completely into the opposition. The very essence of Washington's decision-making process was set awry.

Washington's search for a successor was not a happy one. The two other Americans most conversant with foreign affairs, Jay and Robert R. Livingston, were both New Yorkers, and thus could not serve beside the New Yorker, Hamilton. Governor Thomas Johnson of Maryland, at best a lame choice, refused because of ill health. And so Washington turned to a man who had no foreign experience but had been present at all cabinet discussions, the attorney general, Edmund Randolph.

Carriages rumble through the streets to pick up the dying and the dead during the Yellow Fever epidemic of 1793. This woodcut shows Stephen Girard on an errand of mercy in Philadelphia.

Dynastically, Randolph (who was Jefferson's cousin) had been born to rule in Virginia. Having served briefly as Washington's military aide, he had become governor of the state at thirty-three. Because of his mellifluous oratory, he had been chosen to present, at the Constitutional Convention, "the Virginia plan" on which the Constitution had been built. He had been Washington's personal lawyer and was Washington's close friend. In cabinet discussions, he had been particularly valuable since he was not a zealot on either side. He had often presented the compromise which Washington accepted.

Jefferson felt that, as a fellow Virginian and a relation, Randolph should always have taken his side. He hated and despised Randolph, whom he regarded as a "mere chameleon" always changing color. He considered that no more "unfortunate appointment could be made." Yet his own determination to retire was not shaken. On the last day of 1793, his courteously phrased but firm letter of resignation was on Washington's desk.

Washington's reply expressed "sincere regret. . . . Since it has been impossible to prevail upon you to forgo any longer the indulgence of your desire for private life, the event, however anxious I am to avert it, must be submitted to. But I cannot suffer you to leave your station without assuring you that the opinion that I had formed of your integrity and talents . . . has been confirmed by the fullest experience. . . . My earnest prayers for your happiness accompany you in your retirement."

Jefferson's retirement was undoubtedly the greatest catastrophe Washington suffered during his presidency. It was not only that the powerful political leader, now no longer held down by an executive responsibility, went over completely into the opposition. The very essence of Washington's decision-making process was set awry. Since he endeavored, before he reached a conclusion, to balance all points of view, he found it immensely valuable to have laid before him the arguments of the ablest members of both principal factions. Now, when Hamilton spoke, there was no equally strong voice to answer.

This imbalance in Washington's cabinet was made the more dangerous—as he seems himself to have realized, if not altogether in his conscious mind—by the fact that the infirmities of age, which he had feared as he accepted his second term, were indeed rising slowly in him. The departing Jefferson noted of Washington, "The firm tone of his mind, for which he had been remarkable, was beginning to relax; its energy was abated; a listlessness of labor, a desire for tranquillity had crept on him, and a willingness to let others act or even think for him."

Hamilton was eager to act and think for him. Hamilton was young, brilliant, efficient, energetic. How and to what extent would the aging president be able to resist?

Forty

OPPOSITE HANDS ACROSS THE OCEAN

(1794)

No sooner had the crisis with France abated than an even more dangerous crisis exploded with England. A British governmental decree, known as the Provision Order, had gone far beyond the *Consolato del Mare,* which permitted the removal of a belligerent's goods from neutral bottoms. With no legal justification whatsoever, the British empowered their vessels to capture any American ship containing any French goods or sailing for any French port. After communicating the order to their own commanders, the British kept it secret from the Americans for almost three months, during which their warships and privateers had fallen on the unsuspecting American shipping that crowded the sea-lanes to the French West Indies. Hundreds of ships were soon anchored in English West Indian harbors awaiting formal confiscation, while the sailors were given the choice of joining the British navy or dying in prison hulks alive with tropical fevers.

Northwest of the Ohio River, the British had so successfully frustrated Washington's efforts to make peace with the Indians that he had finally given in to frontier sentiment by ordering Wayne's army to advance in preparation for attacking the tribes in the spring. Word now came that the governor-general of Canada had announced at an Indian parley that his king would soon be at war with the United States; the British and the Indians would then divide up the forests at their own pleasure. Washington ordered investigations concerning how many British regulars there were in Canada and what would be the loyalties of the French Canadians "if matters should come to extremities."

Writing the British philanthropist Lord Buchan, Washington mourned, "If, instead of the provocations to war, bloodshed, and desolation (oftentimes unjustly given) the strife of nations and of individuals was to excel each other in acts of philanthropy, industry, and economy, in encouraging useful arts and manufactures, promoting thereby the comfort and happiness of our fellow men; and in exchanging on liberal terms the products of one country and clime for those of another, how much happier would mankind be! But providence, for purposes beyond the reach of mortal scan, has suffered the restless and malignant passions of man, the ambitious and sordid views of those who direct them, to keep the affairs of this world in a con-tinual state of disquietude; and will, it is to be feared, place the prospects of peace far off, and the promised millennium at an awful distance from our day."

News of the Provision Order and its harsh, unfair enforcement reached the United States during February and March 1794. Inflammatory anti-British bills were soon before Congress. One would sequester all debts owed by Americans to Britons as a guarantee that American shippers and sailors be indemnified. Another would halt all commercial intercourse with Great Britain until every English soldier was out of the northwestern forts and an illegal maritime damage paid for.

These proposals horrified the Federalists. Expropriating private property was blasphemy to businessmen. They knew that a long break in commerce with that prime American market and supplier, England, would destroy American trade and the customs revenues essential to the federal government. And if war with England ensued, would that not, by discrediting the pro-British conservatives, throw the United States into the bloody hands of the American Jacobins? Senator King diagnosed "the most alarming irritation" against Britain in regions usually anti-French. The Massachusetts Federalist Fisher Ames mourned, "The English are absolutely madmen. Order in this country is endangered by their hostility."

Congress passed and Washington signed a month's embargo not only on British but on all transatlantic trade. This was agreed on by both parties: the Republicans because intercourse with French possessions had in any case been stopped, and the Federalists because keeping American ships out of the ocean would prevent further depredations that might topple the peace. But the Federalists could only accept this as a most temporary expedient. And they feared that by passing violent anti-British laws, Congress would incite even greater violence in the British.

Led by Hamilton, the Federalists put pressure on Washington to employ his prestige in soothing Congress down. Following his constitutional principles, the president refused to intervene with the legislature. But there was a constitutional way for the executive to step into the breach. Needing only to secure the consent of the pro-Federalist Senate, Washington could appoint a special envoy to iron out the troubles with Britain. Congress would then be impelled to postpone all anti-British measures until the envoy achieved the slow voyage across the ocean and, having negotiated, reported as slowly back.

Washington was to explain to the Senate, "A mission like this, while it corresponds with the solemnity of the occasion, will announce to the world a solicitude for friendly adjustment. . . . Going immediately from the United States, such an envoy will carry with him knowledge of the existing temper and sensibility of the country, and will thus be taught to vindicate our rights with firmness, and to cultivate peace with sincerity."

James Monroe, *c. 1817, by Gilbert Stuart. Monroe resigned his Senate seat when he was appointed minister to France in 1794. As ambassador, he secured the release of all American prisoners including Thomas Paine, who was being held in a French prison for his opposition to the execution of Louis XVI. Eventually becoming the nation's fifth president, Monroe was the last Founding Father to ascend to the position.*

Since Washington had taken similar steps in previous crises, there is every reason to believe that the conception occurred to him spontaneously.* The recommendation also came in from various advisers. A group of Federalist senators urged that the envoy be Hamilton.

At first, the Republicans opposed the idea of an executive mission that would take the initiative away from Congress. But when it became clear that Congress could achieve no action that did not point to war, the argument moved on to whom should be appointed. The Republicans were as afraid of Hamilton as the Federalists were for him; they feared that the demon would either sell out the United States or be so effective at securing concessions from his British friends that he would succeed Washington as president.

Hamilton did not hide from Washington that he was all eagerness. Realizing that his secretary of the Treasury did not possess "the general confidence of the country," Washington hesitated to appoint him. Yet the pressure from his most valuable aide prevented the aging president from settling on anyone else. The Federalists, worried lest the whole proposition be allowed to lapse, finally persuaded Hamilton to withdraw. Hamilton then suggested Chief Justice Jay. Washington appointed Jay. It was not an ideal appointment, but where was Washington to find better?

The two men had worked together for years but had never been intimate. (Washington's friendliest gesture had been to offer that his jackass should serve Jay's mares at no charge.) Jay could bear no insult to his importance: he had taken violent umbrage at Washington's reaction to his and King's publication on Genêt. He was cold, grave, and withdrawn, self-righteous with the consciousness of belonging to one of the great leading families of New York. Lacking the tact that grew out of respect for public opinion, he had been led by his conscience into various extremely unpopular moves. But he was a potent leader in New York, and no other man in the United States had had more experience in foreign affairs. During the Revolution, he had been minister to Spain. He had been one of the commissioners who had negotiated the peace treaty with England. Under the Confederation, he had been secretary of foreign affairs.

John Jay, *the first chief justice of the United States, by Joseph Wright, oil on canvas, 1786. Jay's diplomatic mission to England helped create some of the thorniest problems Washington would face as president. In July 1782, the earl of Shelburne offered the Americans independence, but Jay rejected the offer on the grounds that it did not recognize American independence during the negotiations. His aggressive stance slowed negotiations, and the final treaty left many regions in dispute.*

* He had been instrumental in sending Colonel John Laurens to France during the Revolution; he had sent Gouverneur Morris to Britain.

Jay's appointment might seem to tip the government towards the Federalists, but Washington saw a way to right the balance. In recalling Genêt, the French had requested the recall of Gouverneur Morris, who was suspected of royalist leanings. Washington resolved to send a Republican whom the French would be glad to receive. Robert R. Livingston, the secretary of foreign affairs during the Revolution, refused. Madison refused. Washington refused (with his flair for diagnosing character) to appoint Aaron Burr. And so the offer descended to James Monroe.

That Monroe had been considerably more violent than his cronies Madison and Jefferson in his distrust of Washington's policies, Washington did not know.

Washington saw Monroe primarily as a young man who had been a brilliant officer during the Revolution and who later, as a senator from Virginia, had always been suave, gracious, mild-seeming, even if often in the opposition. That Monroe had been considerably more violent than his cronies Madison and Jefferson in his distrust of Washington's policies, Washington did not know.

Monroe was amazed to have the appointment offered him: "I really thought I was the last man to whom it would be made." He consulted his political collaborators, who persuaded him that "I should accept upon the necessity of cultivating France."

Having been unable to keep balance in his cabinet between Federalists and Republicans, Washington thus applied it to his foreign missions. Furthermore, he saw an advantage in sending to each of the belligerent powers a man whose personal attitudes would be agreeable to the governmental officials with whom he would have to deal. Washington assumed that both envoys, being American patriots, would put American interests first.

He seems not to have been worried by the fact that the envoys would escape, by months of sailing across the ocean, from his dominating scrutiny. Always opposed to tying the hands of individuals dealing with problems at such a distance that he himself could not follow immediate developments—it was thus that he had allowed General Gates to consider himself so important and become so insubordinate—Washington agreed to give Jay the greatest possible latitude towards negotiating a new treaty with Great Britain. He assumed that both his appointees would, as they entered the government service, lay aside their party ties and become loyal members of the administration. They would, of course, conscientiously apply the impartial neutrality which was the government policy and also, Washington was convinced, the only intelligent option for a patriotic citizen of the United States.

Before he sailed, Jay consulted at length with the Federalist leaders on what terms he should seek, and, after he had reached London, he reported more fully to Hamilton than to the president and the secretary of state. Monroe worked out with Jefferson a code that would enable him to communicate secretly with the leaders of the opposition.

Forty-One

THE WHISKEY REBELLION

(1790–1794)

The British marched over the Canadian border into the United States and built a fort at the Forks of the Miami. To discredit at a single stroke both the president and the Jay mission, a Republican newspaper stated that Washington, having committed "an atrocious crime," had sent Chief Justice Jay out of the United States so that, as president, he could not be constitutionally tried. From retirement on his rural hilltop, Jefferson recommended such violent pro-French intervention in the war as he had, when secretary of state, labored to avoid.

Yet, however much the Republicans fumed, practical reality dictated that, in its official acts in relation to Great Britain, the United States await the outcome of the Jay mission. Congress was stymied. The embargo, after being extended for a second month, was voted down. The aggressive anti-British reprisals were voted down. Ruefully, Madison and Monroe agreed that the strength of the executive, based on the people's faith in Washington, had ended in frustration what should have been a triumphant session for the pro-French Republicans.

But Hamilton had no cause for rejoicing. His official acts were for the second time investigated by the Republican-oriented House of Representatives. They could unearth no evidence that he had (as was widely charged) engaged in graft, but they did discover that he had on one occasion applied to domestic purposes funds appropriated for the foreign debt. Hamilton's defense was that he had been authorized by Washington. Learning of the defense, Washington expressed "surprise and passion." He refused to admit, despite Hamilton's reminder that his memory was unreliable, that he might have given sanction verbally. Nor would Washington accept Hamilton's claim that his allover trust in the Treasury secretary's probity made him almost automatically accept the financial measures Hamilton recommended.

Madison crowed that the Hamiltonians found Washington's behavior "inexpressibly mortifying." Hamilton himself, unable to believe that Washington would of his own volition treat him thus, blamed the malign influence of Randolph. However, he decided it was prudent to take a step he had not previously considered necessary: he wrote Washington, withdrawing his several-months-old statement that he wished to resign towards the end of the present congressional session.

The pleasure Washington expressed at Hamilton's willingness to stay "until the clouds over our affairs, which have come on so fast of late, shall be dispersed" would surely have changed to dismay had he overheard conversations between Hamilton and the British minister, George Hammond. Hammond reported to his government Hamilton's assurances that the United States would settle for very watered-down neutral rights and would, despite threats included in Jay's instruction, never entangle herself by joining Russia, Sweden, and Denmark in an alliance to protect neutral shipping from British aggression. Many historians contend that this had a major effect on the outcome of Jay's negotiation.

It was June 1794 when Washington, en route to a short Mount Vernon vacation, inspected from horseback some locks being erected for the Potomac Canal. On the rough terrain, his horse "blundered and continued blundering until by violent exertions on my part to save him and myself from falling among the rocks, I got such a wrench in my back" that he subsequently found it impossible to ride and difficult to sit upright. This was the first physical injury the great athlete had suffered in all his long life. His aging bones had betrayed him.

Again—it seemed an inexorable fate—he was prevented from attending to plantation affairs. As he lay half-prone, Washington received a packet from the Democratic Society of Lexington, Kentucky. In it there was a letter to the society from a French inhabitant of Louisiana, regretting that an American frontier army had not returned Louisiana to France. And there was an answering resolution demanding that the president and Congress give the king of Spain the choice of opening the Mississippi to navigation or fighting the United States.

Washington expressed anxiety lest Kentucky "force us either to support them in their hostilities against Spain or disavow and denounce them. War at this moment with Spain would not be war with Spain alone. The lopping off of Kentucky from the Union is dreadful to contemplate, even if it should not attach itself to some other power."

Washington Reviewing the Western Army at Fort Cumberland, Maryland, *attributed to Frederick Kemmelmeyer, oil on canvas, after 1795.*

No man stood higher in the estimation of the Kentucky Democrats than Jefferson. The ideal solution would be to send Jefferson to Spain as Jay had been sent to England. Although he had been informed—he did not believe it—that Jefferson was maligning him at the Monticello dinner table, Washington empowered Randolph to offer the appointment.

Jefferson replied that he was suffering from rheumatism and, in any case, "no circumstances . . . will ever tempt me to engage in anything public." Washington thereupon delegated Thomas Pinckney, who could, while Jay was in London, temporarily leave his post as American minister to Great Britain.

With no major storms to be expected until word came back from the various missions, foreign problems were now quiescent. But at home, trouble broke loose.

The ostensible cause was an excise tax on whiskey, to be collected from the distiller. The law had been enacted during 1790 to help pay the costs of Hamilton's financial measures. Excises (levies on the manufacture, sale, or consumption of commodities) were among the few taxes other than customs duties permitted by the Constitution to the federal government. The United States failed to possess many industries extensive enough to be worth taxing. Liquor (always a prime target for tax collectors) was selected, along with snuff, loaf sugar, and that luxury, carriages. The legislation was accepted everywhere but on the frontier.

The backwoodsmen had their own particular relationship with whiskey. Many had their own stills and, since they consumed much of their product themselves, they could not pass that much of the tax on to purchasers. Extreme individualists, they objected to strangers—particularly revenuers—snooping on their property. The grain they grew was too bulky to be moved by the means of transportation available to them unless it was distilled into whiskey. Then jugs could be used locally as currency and exported over the mountains for sale. Furthermore, federal courts were so scarce that if a backwoodsman was arrested for moonshining, he had to travel for many days in order to stand trial.

Backwoods opposition to the whiskey tax arose almost instantly after the bill had been passed and, at Washington's recommendation, successive congressional sessions modified the law to make it less objectionable. However, no move was made, even by the frontier representatives, to repeal the law. Opposition gradually quieted down. But during 1794, the issue erupted into violence in the four western counties of Pennsylvania. Informed historians generally agree that this renewed and more extreme opposition was based on the spread of the Democratic Societies across the Alleghenies.

The whiskey grievance was only the foremost among many. The frontier had many interests—one was passionate concern with the opening of the Mississippi—which were not taken with equal seriousness by the various legislatures, state and federal, whose membership was so largely from more settled areas. In addition, there existed in western Pennsylvania what rarely developed in the United States of that time—active class warfare.

Settlement of the backwoods normally proceeded in two phases. There were the pioneers who broke into the virgin forests, often misfits, sometimes psychopaths, but always self-reliant, warlike, physically active. The pioneers were followed by the consolidators, who farmed conventionally, built clapboard houses, set up stores and law offices, began the creation of cities. During the Whiskey Rebellion, the little town of Pittsburgh—some two hundred houses—was in active fear of being sacked by the wild men of the further forests.

The extreme frontiersmen distrusted law coming in from over the mountains and were unable to cope with it. But the consolidators welcomed the laws and used them to oppress the pioneers. On the whiskey

Citizens are enraged by Hamilton's excise tax on liquor, and a government inspector is tarred and feathered during the insurrection of 1794 known as the Whiskey Rebellion.

excise, there was a specific difference. The better-organized inhabitants, who owned large commercial stills, could afford to pay the tax and were not altogether sorry to foresee that it would put backyard stills out of competition.

An armed band of small distillers attacked the house of the prosperous citizen who had agreed to become tax collector. An army platoon that rushed to the rescue was forced to surrender, and a man was killed.

As the insurrection developed, the still of any man who paid the excise was wrecked; government representatives were seared with hot irons; mailbags were taken at gunpoint and citizens persecuted for what was found in the seized correspondence. Not only did all government come to an end in western Pennsylvania, but the local Democratic Societies appealed to their mates down the mountain line—including the Kentucky Society, which had recently threatened its own aggression against Spain—to join in a general rebellion. There was talk of establishing a separate trans-Alleghenian nation, or of marching on Philadelphia to force on the federal government measures dictated by the frontier.

Washington could not foresee that Abraham Lincoln was to face, although on a much larger scale, a similar problem in 1863. But the first president, always conscious that he was establishing precedents, realized that the situation would rise again. Some other section of the United States would surely arm and threaten to secede because of opposition to laws passed by the general government. Should such acts be accepted, the Union could not long stand. Apart from the danger of secession, Washington contended that if a minority—in this case it was "a small one"—were permitted to dictate to the majority, "there is an end put at one stroke to republican government, and nothing but anarchy and confusion is to be expected thereafter: for some other man or society may dislike another law and oppose it with equal propriety until all laws are prostrate and everyone (the strongest, I presume) will carve for himself."

Washington's formula, expressed at the time of Shays's Rebellion, was to define legitimate grievances, right these grievances, and, then, if the disturbances continued, "employ the force of the government." In the case of the Whiskey Rebellion, the first two steps had, in Washington's opinion, been taken. Force therefore seemed required, and there were strong arguments for moving quickly. If given time, the insurrection might well spread southward down the long frontier. And Washington, having during the French and Indian

War fought over the same mountain passes, realized how difficult the approach of winter would make any invasion of the rebellious counties. Yet he decided that at all hazards another effort at mediation should be made. It might succeed. If it failed, the attempt should persuade the nation that the government had done everything in its power to achieve a peaceful solution.

Washington sent three federal commissioners into western Pennsylvania. He reinforced their hands with a proclamation commanding that all insurgents "disperse and retire peaceably to their homes" by September 1. And he ordered that 12,950 militiamen prepare to march if the proclamation were not obeyed.

The risks that would be involved if military action proved necessary were, Washington well knew, frightening. If the frontiersmen mobilized to protect their territory, they would be formidable in the mountain passes. States' rights sentiments offered another hazard. Since Pennsylvania was unwilling to take on the rebels by herself, Washington was forced to call also on the New Jersey, Maryland, and Virginia militia. There might well be outrage at the "invasion" of one state by another. And the extreme Republican press was shouting that an aristocratic executive was planning to fall without adequate justification on simple farmers in their fields. Did this mean that the militiamen who answered Washington's call would all be (as Hamilton secretly hoped) Federalists? Such a partisan army would distort the national precedent Washington wished to establish, and perhaps incite general civil war.

Alarming reports came in from the rebellious counties. The efforts of Washington's commissioners to stage a referendum were frustrated by terrorism. At one polling place, for instance, the attendant mob shouted down a motion that those who supported the government should not have their barns burned—and then everyone was invited to vote in public. But other news was enchantingly good. The old fear that the inherent danger of republicanism was anarchy motivated the vast majority of the American population, even as it had at the time of Shays's Rebellion. Whatever their private emotions, the leaders of the opposition did not dare accept the onus of encouraging armed resistance to the law. The parent Democratic Society, that of Pennsylvania, having denounced the excise in highly colored terms, nonetheless voted that, since it had been constitutionally enacted, the law must be enforced. Five times as many men offered to enlist as could be accepted.

"It has been," Washington exulted, "a spectacle displaying to the highest advantage the value of republican government to behold the most and least wealthy of our citizens standing in the same ranks as private soldiers." This would show the Britons, who had asserted "we should be unable to govern ourselves . . . that republicanism is not the phantom of a deluded imagination; on the contrary, that under no form of government will the laws be better supported, liberty and property better secured, or happiness more effectually dispensed to mankind."

Washington sent three federal commissioners into western Pennsylvania. He reinforced their hands with a proclamation commanding that all insurgents "disperse and retire peaceably to their homes" by September 1. And he ordered that 12,950 militiamen prepare to march if the proclamation were not obeyed.

The time Washington had set for the insurrection to cease having passed with the law still prostrate, he called for the army to come together, under the shadow of the Alleghenies, in the Shenandoah Valley. He decided that he would himself take command. Perhaps because he no longer felt competent to handle the necessary masses of detail, he agreed to take Hamilton along. Hamilton had been his chief of staff during the Revolution, but he was now known as the father of the excise, the man most accused of wishing to suppress government by the people and to establish rule by force. By riding off side by side with the hated Federalist, Washington committed what was to date his worst political indiscretion.

En route to join the army, Washington received gratifying news of another campaign. General Wayne had decisively defeated the northwestern Indians at the Battle of Fallen Timbers, and had furthermore obeyed orders by avoiding any engagement with nearby British troops, who had encroached on American territory and were completely in his power.

After Washington had established his headquarters at Reading, Pennsylvania, he received a two-man delegation from over the mountains. Both prosperous landholders who had infiltrated the radical movement, they stated that "the people of consequence" were in favor of submission. The simpler people were not. They had been convinced that their cause was so popular that Washington could not raise an army against them. Now they were thoroughly frightened. Being "men of little or no property" who "cared but little where they resided," the leaders of the revolt would, if given time, flee the threat against them, allowing quiet to return. Since the situation would thus eventually right itself, the delegates begged that no army be sent into the western counties. If, as seemed probable from the unruly behavior of the troops at Carlisle, the army wreaked havoc, the inhabitants would have to unite against them.

Washington answered that, since the object of the whole expensive maneuver was "the support of the laws," the army would march unless there were proof of total submission.

Although it seemed highly improbable that any military effort would be made to defend the rebel area, no proof could be offered that the laws could be enforced there without the presence of the army. Washington's concern thereupon came to be the psychological state of his own troops. It was essential that they function not as "executioners." They should do no more than bring offenders before civil authorities for fair trial. But some of the soldiers had turned out with the intention of punishing the rabble; one man had already been killed. Washington, as a Pennsylvania politician recorded, "labored incessantly" to impress on the soldiers "a conduct scrupulously regardful of the rights of their fellow citizens, and exemplary for decorum, regularity, and moderation."

Leaving Governor Henry Lee of Virginia in the military command and Hamilton to represent the federal government, Washington rode back to Philadelphia, where Congress was about to convene. The army that advanced across the mountains met no opposition and obeyed orders so scrupulously that not a single citizen was hurt, no property damaged. Washington, who was eventually to pardon the two insurrectionists sentenced to death, boasted to Jay that the whiskey rebels had been brought to "a *perfect* sense of their misconduct without spilling a drop of blood."

One reason that the whole situation had been viewed with such anxiety by the Republicans was the fear that the Hamiltonians would succeed in presenting it as proof that a standing army was needed to keep the peace at home. Madison commented that this would surely have happened had not the expedition been so managed that there was no fighting. Even as it was, Madison continued, the dread conclusion might have been drawn if "the president could have been embarked in it." The president would not embark on it. He ordered that the army be disbanded.

However, Washington had been so worried by the Whiskey Rebellion that he committed the most indiscreet act of his entire presidential career.

Forty-Two

THE DEMOCRATIC SOCIETIES

(1794)

Washington reached Philadelphia from a campaign exhausting to an elderly man only eighteen days before he was to deliver his Sixth Annual Address to Congress. In the bustle of the army camps, he had wondered whether he ought not to warn the people against the Democratic Societies, on which he blamed the insurrection. Randolph, the most Republican of his advisers, spontaneously urged that he do so. In dark moments, Washington "felt perfectly convinced" that if the societies "cannot be discountenanced, they will destroy the government of this country."

In his address, delivered on November 19, 1794, Washington spoke disparagingly of "certain self-created societies" and asked the people to "determine" whether the insurrections "had not been fomented by combinations of men who, careless of consequences and disregarding the unerring truth that those who rouse cannot always appease civil convulsions, have disseminated, from ignorance or perversion of facts, suspicions, jealousies, and accusations of the whole government?"

Compared with what was daily published in pamphlets and the press, Washington's strictures were milk and water. He denounced nothing and nobody by name; connected what he attacked with no faction at home or (although he believed French machinations were involved) no influence from abroad; opposed no political conception except inciting and misleading the people; urged no penalties legal or social, no political reprisals. Yet his few sentences caused a sensation. They were remarkable as the first criticism of any aspect of the opposition that the national hero had ever publicly uttered.

The Democratic Society movement, which had up till that moment been burgeoning, wilted as if sprinkled with weed killer. The Republicans, who had been encouraging the societies as a political weapon, did not dare come to their defense. It was only in private they fumed, accusing Washington of things he had never said. Thus Jefferson wrote angrily, "It is wonderful, indeed, that the president should have permitted himself to be the organ of such an attack on the freedom of discussion, the freedom of writing, printing, and publishing."

The Democratic Societies were, of course, an initial step towards the organization of the political parties which have become an integral part of American democracy. This has induced historians to state that Washington was attacking the democratic process itself. But organized "factions" (as they were then called) had not yet received broad popular acceptance. Washington was not alone in fearing the effect of bodies that were considered extraneous—"self-created" since not provided for in the Constitution—which nonetheless sought to insert themselves between the people and their government. He had on the same principle opposed political activity by that organization of the

WASHINGTON'S LETTER TO JOHN JAY

WASHINGTON WAS A STAUNCH OPPONENT to the Democratic Societies, as he felt they were a direct threat to both the government and republican system in that they did not allow people to decide matters on their own but, instead, through "demagogues," who advocated their own self-benefiting beliefs. In the letter below to John Jay, Washington both elucidates his disapproval of the Societies and explains how he will speak strongly against them in his upcoming speech to Congress.

Philadelphia, November 1st, 1794
My Dear Sir,

On Tuesday last, I returned from my tour to the westward. On Monday, Congress by adjournment are to meet; and on the day following, Mr. Bayard, according to his present expectation, is to leave this city for London. Thus circumstanced (having so little time between my return and the opening of the session to examine papers and to prepare my communications for the legislature), you will readily perceive that my present address to you must be hurried. At the same time, my friendship and regard for you would not let an opportunity so good as the one afforded by Mr. Bayard pass without some testimony of my remembrance, and an acknowledgment of the receipt of your private letters to me dated the 23rd of June, 21st of July, and 5th and 11th of August. These comprehend all the letters I have received from you since your arrival in England to the present date.

That of the 5th of August dawns more favorably upon the success of your mission than any that had preceded it, and for the honor, dignity, and interest of this country—for your own reputation and glory—and for the peculiar satisfaction I should derive from it, as well on private as on public considerations, no man more ardently wishes you complete success than I do. But, as you have observed in some of your letters, that it is hardly possible in the early stages of a negotiation to foresee all the results, so much depending upon fortuitous circumstances and incidents which are not within our control, so to deserve success by employing the means with which we are possessed to the best advantage, and trusting the event to the all-wise Disposer, is all that an enlightened public and the virtuous and well-disposed part of the community can reasonably expect; nor in this, will they, I am sure, be disappointed. Against the malignancy of the discontented, the turbulent, and the vicious, no abilities, no exertions, nor the most unshaken integrity are any safeguard.

As far as depends upon the executive, measures preparatory for the worst, while it hopes for the best, will be pursued; and I shall endeavor to keep things in status quo until your negotiation assumes a more decisive form, which I hope will soon be the case, as there are many hot heads and impetuous spirits among us who with difficulty can be kept within bounds. This, however, ought not to precipitate your conduct; for, as it has been observed, "there is a tide in human affairs," which ought to be watched; and because I believe all who are acquainted with you will readily concede that considerations both public and private combine to urge you to bring your mission to a close, with as much celerity as the nature of it will admit.

As you have been, and will continue to be fully informed by the secretary of state of all transactions of a public nature which relate to or may have an influence on the points of your mission, it would be unnecessary for me to touch upon any of them in this letter was it not for the presumption that the insurrection in the western counties of this state has excited much speculation and a variety of opinions abroad; and will be represented differently according to the wishes of some, and the prejudices of others, who may exhibit it as an evidence of what has been predicted "that we are unable to govern ourselves." Under this view of the subject, I am happy in giving it to you as the general opinion that this event having happened at the time it did was fortunate, although it will be attended with considerable expense.

That the self-created Societies, which have spread themselves over this country, have been laboring incessantly to sow the seeds of distrust, jealousy, and of course discontent, thereby hoping to effect some revolution in the government, is not unknown to you. That they have been the fomenters of the western disturbances admits of no doubt in the mind of anyone who will examine their conduct; but, fortunately, they precipitated a crisis for which they were not prepared, and thereby have unfolded views which will, I trust, effectuate their annihilation sooner than it might otherwise have happened. At the same time, it has afforded an occasion for the people of this country to show their abhorrence of the result and their attachment to the Constitution and the laws; for I believe that five times the number of militia that was required would have come forward, if it had been necessary, in support of them.

The spirit which blazed out on this occasion, as soon as the object was fully understood and the lenient measures of the government were made known to the people, deserve to be communicated. For there are instances of general officers going at the head of a single troop and light companies; of field officers, when they came to the places of rendezvous and found no command for them in that grade, turning into the ranks and proceeding as private soldiers under their own captains; and of numbers, possessing the first fortunes in the country, standing in the ranks as private men and marching day by day with their knapsacks and haversacks at their backs, sleeping on straw with a single blanket in a soldier's tent during the frosty nights we have had, by way of example to others. Nay, more, of many young Quakers (not discouraged by the elders) of the first characters, families, and properties, having turned into the ranks and marching with the troops.

These things have terrified the insurgents, who had no conception that such a spirit prevailed; but while the thunder only rumbled at a distance, were boasting of their strength, and wishing for and threatening the militia by turns, intimating that the arms they should take from them would soon become a magazine in their hands. Their language is much changed, indeed, but their principles want correction.

I shall be more prolix in my speech to Congress on the commencement and progress of this insurrection than is usual in such an instrument, or than I should have been on any other occasion; but as numbers (at home and abroad) will hear of the insurrection and will read the speech that may know nothing of the documents to which it might refer, I conceived it would be better to encounter the charge of prolixity by giving a cursory detail of facts (that would show the prominent features of the thing), than to let it go naked into the world, to be dressed up according to the fancy or inclination of the readers or the policy of our enemies.

I write nothing in answer to the letter of Mr. Wangenheim (enclosed by you to me). Were I to enter into correspondences of that sort (admitting there was no impropriety in the measure), I should be unable to attend to my ordinary duties. I have established it as a maxim neither to invite nor to discourage emigrants. My opinion is that they will come hither as fast as the true interest and policy of the United States will be benefited by foreign population. I believe many of these, as Mr. Wangenheim relates, have been, and I fear will continue to be, imposed upon by speculators in land and other things. But I know of no prevention but caution, nor any remedy except the laws . . . military, or other employment, so easy to obtain as foreigners conceive, in a country where offices and the seekers of them bear no proportion to each other. With sincere esteem and great regard, I am, dear Sir, your affectionate servant.

George Washington.

From *The Life of John Jay with Selections from His Correspondence and Miscellaneous Papers by His Son in Two Volumes*, Volume II, by William Jay, 1833.

opposite complexion from the Democratic Societies, the Society of the Cincinnati.

Washington believed that the government should have the most direct possible connection with each citizen as an individual. He was in favor of everything that would enable the individual citizen to act intelligently: education was his favorite charity, and he urged again and again that the government should give every encouragement to the dissemination of newspapers and political pamphlets through the mails.

Realizing that it was hard for one simple citizen to make his voice heard, Washington saw as the natural grouping the neighborhood. It was not by chance that his one formal intervention in the Constitutional Convention had been to reduce the size of the districts that would elect a member of the House of Representatives. These representatives should carry their constituents' wishes to Congress; should work out with representatives from other regions what was best for all; and should then report back to their constituents.

The people had two methods of expressing dis-pleasure: one was the ballot box, the other, the calling of a mass meeting that would in a resolution express their views to the government. Washington visualized these meetings as arising from the neighborhood, rather than being engineered, as the

Be it known that
is a Member of the Society of the Cincinnati, instituted by the Officers of the American Army, at the Period of its Dissolution, as well to commemorate the great Event which gave Independence to North America, as for the laudable Purpose of inculcating the Duty of laying down in Peace Arms assumed for public Defence, and of uniting in Acts of brotherly Affection, and Bonds of perpetual Friendship the Members constituting the same.

IN TESTIMONY whereof I, the President of the said Society, have hereunto set my Hand at in the State of this Day of Year of our Lord One Thousand Eight Hundred and and in the Year of the Independence of the United States.

By order
Secretary.
President.

On Stone by C. Parsons.
G. & W. Endicott Lith. New York.

A Society of Cincinnati membership certificate, c. 1845–1848.

Democratic Societies were, from some political center. As president, he paid attention to every such resolution, himself answering each message in an individual reply. Thus the neighborhood could, when it felt strongly enough, establish direct contact with the president.

Everything that intervened between the people in their neighborhoods and the federal government, Washington regarded as an impediment to the true functioning of the republican system. This went for the state governments with their attendant flocks of politicians serving local views. And it went for "demagogues," whose object was not, he contended, to give the people the materials from which they could make up their own minds but rather to sell them predigested opinions, make them not thinkers but followers. Washington regarded the Democratic Societies as the creation and stamping grounds of demagogues. He deplored the adversary theory which sees government as a tug-of-war between the holders of opposite views, one side eventually vanquishing the other. Washington saw the national capital as a place where men came together not to tussle but to reconcile disagreements. This attitude grew out of his entire experience and also from the nature of his own genius. The Revolution had been won only by gathering as many people as possible into the cause. His greatest fear for the Constitutional Convention was that the delegates would arrive with their hands so tied by regional instructions that they could not learn from one another, working out by mutual understanding and compromise a government satisfactory to the whole far-flung nation. And Washington's own greatest mental gift was to be able to bore down through partial arguments to the fundamental principles on which everyone could agree.

Thus, Washington's disapproval of the Democratic Societies grew out of his basic conviction. However, his public denunciation was contrary to his convictions, since it was divisive. When still a member of the cabinet, Jefferson had warned him that speaking out against the societies would be "calculated to make the president assume the station of the head of a party instead of the head of the nation." Had Jefferson still been by his side, Washington would undoubtedly have again listened and been stopped. As it was, raddled and hurried after a strenuous campaign, no longer thinking with the clarity that he had once possessed, he slipped into what was for him—however typical it might have been of many presidents who succeeded him—a major misstep.

Washington was not one to confess mistakes or take back anything he had said. Yet he gave the most convincing proof of his realization that he had veered onto the wrong road. He never again as president denounced publicly any aspect of the opposition. Nor did he ever again make any public statement capable of rational interpretation as limiting the basic freedoms of the people.

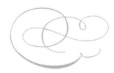

Forty-Three

A DISASTROUS DOCUMENT

(1795)

The opening of 1795 brought major changes in Washington's cabinet. Knox, needing to attend to unwise land speculations he had made in Maine, resigned as secretary of war. Hamilton also resigned. He was angry and disgusted at the attacks to which public office subjected him. The charges that he had taken graft being untrue, he required a greater income to support his family. He had carried through as much of his scheme for revolutionizing the economy as Congress would accommodate, and did not consider it worth his energies merely to administer laws already passed. He surely recognized that conciliating Britain was so essential to the United States that his daily presence in the pilot house was not necessary. And he intended to remain, as he practiced law in New York, Washington's principal adviser.

Washington had scraped the bottom of the barrel of truly able Founding Fathers. As replacements, he brought in two men who proved to be malign, not only in his administration but in that of his successor, John Adams. Recognizing that (there being hardly any army) the functions of secretary of war were mostly Indian affairs, he appointed Timothy Pickering, a stony-faced Puritan with hawk eyes. Pickering had opposed Washington at the time of the Conway Cabal, but he was an able administrator who agreed with Washington's desire not to drive and isolate the tribes, but rather to embrace them in the life of the United States. To administer the Treasury, Washington accepted Hamilton's first assistant: fat, plausible, scheming Oliver Wolcott Jr.

Although Washington could not know that his new cabinet ministers had a low opinion of his abilities as compared to Hamilton's, he did not trust them. Unlike their predecessors, they were not consulted concerning executive decisions; they were limited to the routine of their departments. And Hamilton himself waited in vain for appeals for advice. Perhaps Washington was annoyed that his aide had left his side. In any case, the president enforced a distinction between members of the government, who had a right to certain authority, and civilians, who had none. Hamilton was now a civilian. Much water was to flow under the bridge before Washington was forced by desperation to turn again to his former right-hand man.

However, the passage of every month made Washington more in need of someone to lean on. Randolph was the only remaining original member of his cabinet. Randolph was Washington's longtime disciple and affectionate friend. If he depended more on charm than genius, was too light a weight to be capable of himself taking over, this may have reassured the aging president, who knew that his own powers were failing. In any case, he came (as it turned out, tragically) to depend on the mellifluous-voiced Randolph more than he had ever before depended on any one man.

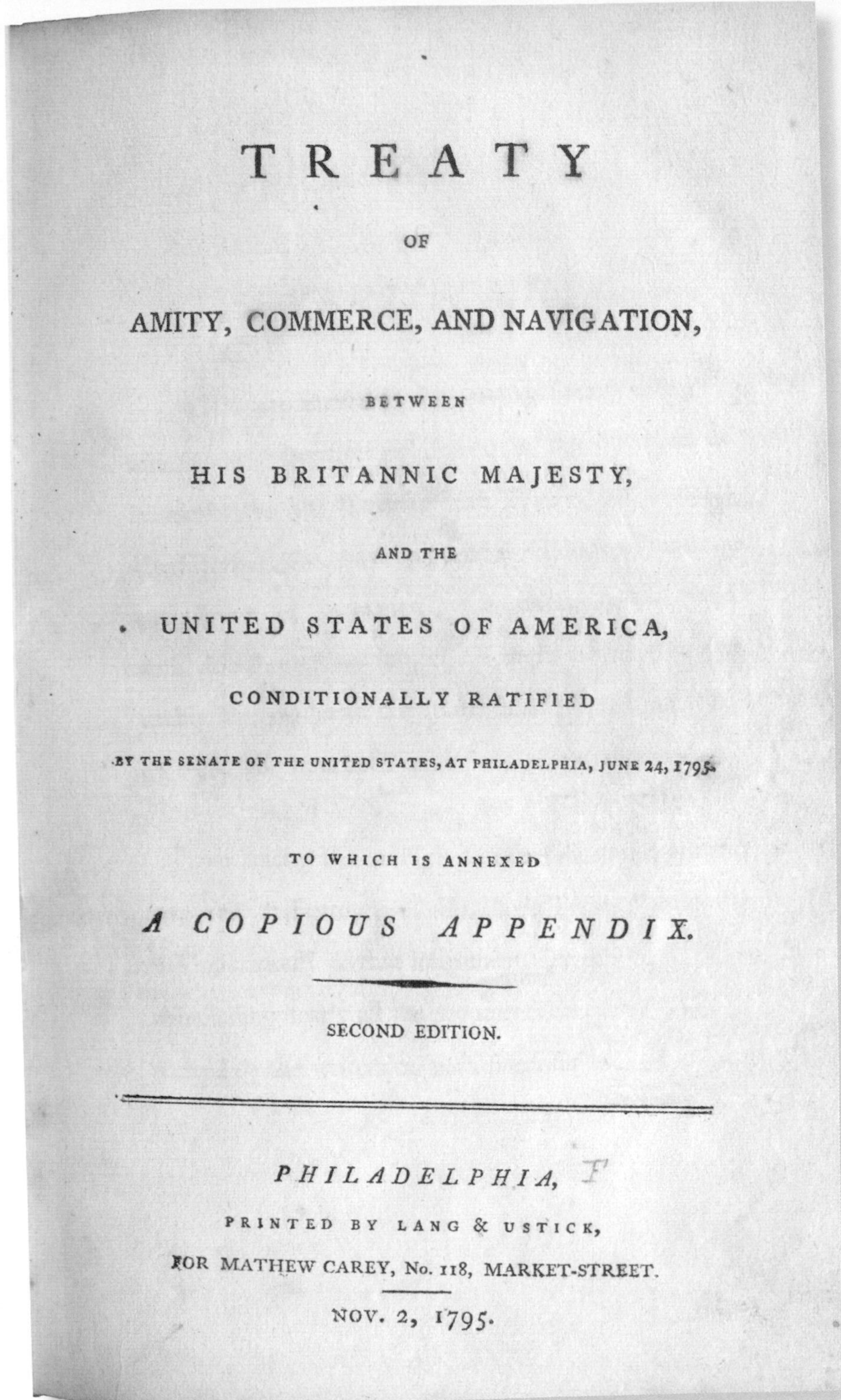

TREATY

OF

AMITY, COMMERCE, AND NAVIGATION,

BETWEEN

HIS BRITANNIC MAJESTY,

AND THE

UNITED STATES OF AMERICA,

CONDITIONALLY RATIFIED

BY THE SENATE OF THE UNITED STATES, AT PHILADELPHIA, JUNE 24, 1795.

TO WHICH IS ANNEXED

A COPIOUS APPENDIX.

SECOND EDITION.

PHILADELPHIA,

PRINTED BY LANG & USTICK,

FOR MATHEW CAREY, No. 118, MARKET-STREET.

NOV. 2, 1795.

The Treaty of Amity.

Congress dawdled through its session, waiting to hear from Jay. On January 31, 1795, an excited sea captain reported the rumor that a treaty had been signed, but for week after week thereafter there was no confirming word. As Congress prepared to adjourn on March 3, Washington, convinced that a treaty must soon arrive, prepared by calling a special session for June 8. The congressmen were on their way home when the Jay Treaty did appear. One can imagine the anxiety with which Washington and Randolph opened the dispatch box. They quickly discovered that they had every reason to be perturbed.

The best thing about the treaty was that the British were willing to sign. Here were rules, however unsatisfactory to the United States, which would, if followed, prevent a disastrous war. But had Jay really been unable to escape making so many concessions? As Washington commented sadly, he was "not favorable to it."

On the long-disputed issue of the Canadian border, the British contracted to evacuate the western posts even if at an irritatingly distant date, June 1, 1796. But Jay had agreed to perpetuate the Canadian fur interest by allowing the British to trade freely with the Indians in American territory.

The treaty included the stipulation that nothing therein would be binding which was contrary to the previous international obligations of the United States. The old treaties with France could therefore, at least in principle, not be violated. However, there were many provisions to which the French and their partisans would object. Jay had not only abandoned all claims that free ships made free goods and bowed (as he could not avoid doing) to the *Consolato del Mare.* He had agreed that almost everything that could be of any use to France was contraband, which could legally be removed by British raiders from American vessels. And he had thrown away what the Jeffersonians regarded as their best method of retaliation against the British: the possibility that private British funds in the United States might be sequestered.

Washington had interpreted the Senate's consent to the Jay mission as authorization to negotiate all difficulties with the British, long-standing ones in addition to those specifically caused by the war. Jay had thus been empowered to regulate commercial relations as long as he observed one unalterable proviso: the British must open their West Indian islands to American shipping. This proviso Jay had honored only pro forma: the British had agreed to admit only tiny American ships—seventy tons or less. In return for this minuscule concession, Jay had conceded, to vast potential damage to the southern states, that no American ships would carry to Europe a variety of American goods—including the cotton which the South was just beginning to grow—which were also produced in the West Indies. That the commercial part of the Jay Treaty was to be in effect for only fifteen years would do little to diminish what Washington realized would be the screams of outrage. It would be shouted that Jay had not only sold out the cause of France and freedom, but the prosperity of the United States as well.

Washington admitted that he needed more "intimate" knowledge of American trade fully to understand the commercial sections of the treaty, and the man most fully informed would have been enchanted to step into the situation and inform him. But Washington made no effort to get in touch with Hamilton. He agreed with Randolph that they two would keep the contents of the treaty completely secret for the three months until the special session of Congress would convene. The Senate would then, under whatever rules concerning publication it would itself establish, undertake its constitutional role of "advice and consent." Washington wished the Senate's decision not to be set awry by what would certainly be, if the provisions were now made public, three months of violent controversy.

The elderly president hoped that he would be able to follow the Senate's decision. He himself saw only

John Jay Burned in Effigy, *engravng, c. 1794, by Felix Octavius Carr Darley.*

the horns of a dilemma. If the treaty were denied, war with England would be more than probable. If the treaty, with all its obvious imperfections, were ratified, national discord would rise to terrifying heights.

When the special session finally convened, Washington presented the treaty to the Senate with no recommendation. The Senate resolved continued secrecy and, then, after eighteen days of stormy debate, reached its conclusion by exactly the required two-thirds vote: twenty to ten. They advised ratification of all of the articles except the one that dealt with trade to the British West Indies. This should be the subject of "further friendly negotiations."

The need to renegotiate one section of the treaty put Washington into a constitutional quandary. If the consent of the Senate had to be procured concerning the new provisions, how could this be done without keeping the whole treaty issue dangling? And when a revised clause finally came back from England, it would become the subject of renewed debate at a time when passions might well have risen extremely high. Washington considered preparing immediately a text for submission to the Senate, but was dissuaded by Randolph, who pointed out that doing so would imply that he had made up his mind to sign the rest of the treaty. Finally, Washington decided that he might as well, for once, consult his cabinet. After his Hamiltonian ministers, who wished to accelerate the accommodation with England, urged unanimously that new senatorial consent did not have to be secured, Washington accepted this view.

Although the Senate had advised him to keep the full text of the treaty secret until he had himself acted, Washington concluded that the time had come to publish. However, he was anticipated by a Virginia senator who leaked the text to an opposition editor. The pamphlet that was soon flying around the nation stated that the people were being given what their government had tried to hide from them.

Washington had scraped the bottom of the barrel of truly able Founding Fathers. As replacements, he brought in two men who proved to be malign, not only in his administration but in that of his successor, John Adams.

Now that the responsibility of ultimate decision had come to him, neither Washington's conscience nor his temperament would allow him to follow his original intention of passing the buck by automatically following the Senate. After a month had gone by, Randolph noted that he was still undecided.

Since the treaty was now known to all and was under public discussion, Washington felt that he could with propriety consult Hamilton. But he knew Hamilton well enough to write a letter that would prevent the former secretary of the Treasury from considering himself the final authority. Washington, so he stated, believed that Hamilton had paid as much attention to commercial matters "as most men." He therefore wished "to have the favorable and unfavorable side of each article stated and compared together that I may see the tendency and bearing of them, and, ultimately on which side the balance is to be found."

Despite Washington's lukewarm wording, Hamilton leapt at the opportunity with such hunger that his letter, to which he was to add two supplementary mailings, occupies, in his collected works, forty-one printed pages. His final conclusion was the Senate's: the West Indian article was unacceptable but the rest of the treaty should be signed.

With this conclusion, Randolph and indeed all Washington's advisers agreed. Then a new blow struck. The British, who had of their own volition relaxed the Provision Order that was so destructive to American commerce, suddenly revived it. That such action could perhaps be justified under the Jay Treaty's vague definition of contraband made the situation the more frightening, since it seemed an indication that the British intended to interpret the treaty in the harshest possible manner. If this revelation had been known to the Senate, the Senate might have acted differently. Their decision therefore ceased to be a staff on which Washington could lean. The executive was now off on its own.

Washington asked the advice of Hamilton and also his cabinet ministers. Hamilton recommended that Washington ratify, but instruct his representative in London not to deliver the document until the Provision Order was rescinded. The three lesser cabinet ministers urged that, having signed the treaty, the president should have it delivered with an accompanying memorandum of protest. Washington decided, without notifying Hamilton or the lesser cabinet ministers, to follow Randolph's advice on a course less favorable to Britain. He would hold off ratification until the Provision Order was actually withdrawn.

Randolph then suggested that the reopening of the negotiation could be used to clarify other points to the American advantage. The president empowered the secretary of state to prepare a memorial to this effect. Then, finding "the intense heat of the city" almost unbearable, Washington did what he had never done before. Leaving the government in the hands of a favorite minister, he went off to Mount Vernon for a long stay in the midst of crisis.

It seemed an inexorable fate that the relaxation Washington needed desperately and hoped to achieve when at Mount Vernon should prove utterly elusive. A persistent small matter during that summer of 1795 was that he had allowed his personal staff so to deteriorate that he had to write all his correspondence, official as well as private, in his own hand. The major matter was the storm of indignation over the Jay Treaty, which passed beyond all previous bounds of controversy. Even Federalists were up in arms; the mercantile community felt that they were better off with no treaty than they would be under Jay's provisions. And the national majority interpreted the treaty as an about-face in American foreign policy. It had been assumed that, since the United States had never denounced her treaty of alliance with France, she was, even if cautious of her neutrality, in the pro-French orbit. The Jay Treaty was interpreted as an alliance with Britain. No one seemed to give credence to Washington's belief that the Jay Treaty would be a continuation (if an unfortunate one) of the effort to keep the United States unentangled with either belligerent—as neutral as the facts of the war permitted.

Jefferson exulted that the treaty "has, in my opinion, completely demolished the monarchical party here.... Those who understand the particular articles of it, condemn these articles. Those who do not understand them minutely, condemn it as wearing a hostile face to France. The last is the most numerous class, comprehending the whole body of the people."

Everyone was after Washington to turn the treaty down out of hand. He still believed that to do so meant war with England. But now, all other courses seemed also to point to the same war. Once the French received news of the American reaction, they would surely use it to lead American public opinion by the nose to their own ends. "I have never," he mourned, "since I have been the administration of the government, seen a crisis which, in my judgment, has been so pregnant of interesting events; nor one from which more is to be apprehended."

The major matter was the storm of indignation over the Jay Treaty, which passed beyond all previous bounds of controversy.

Washington, who had down the years found his way out of so many crises, was in an utter quandary. He considered dashing for Philadelphia, but feared that his mainstay, Randolph, was on the road to Mount Vernon and they would miss each other. Then a strange letter appeared in his postbag. It was signed by Pickering:

"For a *special reason* which can be communicated to you only in person, I entreat therefore that you will return." Washington should in the meantime "decide on no important political measure.... Mr. Wolcott and I (Mr. Bradford concurring) waited on Mr. Randolph and urged his writing to request your return. He wrote in our presence.... This letter is for your own eye alone."

In great puzzlement and perturbation, Washington commanded the hitching up of his horses.

Forty-Four

TRAGEDY WITH A FRIEND

(1795)

Kept in ignorance of what the executive was doing—they were not shown the Jay Treaty before it went to the Senate and subsequently did not now know what the president was deciding—Pickering, Wolcott, and Bradford resented Randolph's perpetual close contact with the president. They suspected that the insinuating Virginian was urging Washington to repudiate the treaty in order to foment a war with England that would throw the United States into the hands of such Jacobins as they suspected Randolph secretly was.

When finally, at Washington's order sent from Mount Vernon, Randolph revealed to his colleagues what was planned, Wolcott wrote Hamilton: "What must the British government think of the United States, when they find the treaty clogged with one condition by the Senate, with another by the president, with no answer given in precise form after forty days, no minister to that country to take up negotiations proposed by ourselves,* the country rising into flame, their minister's house insulted by a mob, their flag dragged through the streets as in Charleston and burnt before the doors of their consul, a driveler and a fool appointed chief justice?† Can they believe that we desire peace? I shall take immediate measures with two of my colleagues this very day. . . . We will, if possible . . . save our country."

The disgruntled cabinet ministers possessed a document. It was a dispatch to his government from Fauchet, the French minister in Philadelphia, which had been captured in mid-ocean. The British government had sent it to their minister in Philadelphia with the comment that it "might be made useful to the king's service." The minister handed it on to Wolcott. Wolcott, in consultation with Pickering and Bradford, decided that it could be used to ruin Randolph.

On the evening of Washington's arrival in Philadelphia—August 11, 1795—he was relaxing with Randolph in the president's house when Wolcott and Pickering appeared. "After taking a glass of wine," Pickering remembered, "the president rose, giving me the wink. I rose and followed him into another room.

"'What,' said he, 'is the cause of your writing me such a letter?'"

---

* Jay was home and Pinckney not yet back from Spain.

† Jay had resigned as chief justice to become governor of New York, and Washington had eagerly grasped the opportunity to give more representation to the South by accepting a request for the post from the elderly South Carolina patriot John Rutledge. The Federalists charged that Rutledge, an ardent Republican, was senile.

"'That man,' said I, 'in the other room'—pointing to the room in which we had left Randolph—'is a traitor!'"

Pickering spent two or three minutes summarizing the situation and, then, so his account continues, handed Washington the dispatch. The president then said, "Let us return to the other room to prevent any suspicion of the cause of our withdrawing."

Eventually, the guests went off and left Washington alone with the fateful document. Once before he had been faced with a similar crisis. He had been handed papers which pointed to the treason of a general he had deeply trusted. The revelation concerning Benedict Arnold had been one of the blackest moments of his life. Then he had been surrounded with friends: Lafayette, Hamilton, and many another. Now, except for servants, he was alone in the silent presidential mansion. Martha and the children, his secretary who was his entire staff, were all away. In the dark city that stretched outside his window, the only intimate he might have consulted was the man accused. Who knows how long he hesitated before he unfolded the sheets and began to read?

The seemingly endless dispatch had clearly been written at the time of the Whiskey Rebellion. There were glints here and there which indicated that Randolph had given political information to Fauchet, who considered him pro-French. Another passage dealt with the time when the Philadelphia Democratic Society was wavering as to whether it should support or oppose the use of force against the whiskey insurgents. Fauchet believed that Randolph, being "at the head," had the power to determine the society's decision. He "came to me with an air of great eagerness and made to me the overtures of which I have given you an account in my number six." Fauchet's sixth dispatch was not present, but the paper Washington was reading continued, "Thus, with some thousands of dollars, the [French] republic could have decided on civil war or on peace! Thus the consciences of the pretended patriots of America already have their prices." However, the French republic was too noble to sink to bribery.

Washington (who did not know that Hamilton and Jefferson and Wolcott had done the same thing) was worried that Randolph had discussed American politics with a foreign diplomat. But the real horror was the strong implication that he had requested a bribe. That he was always short of money, Washington knew. Was he now in the French pay? Had Randolph been the mastermind behind the wave of protests against the Jay Treaty? Had he advised Washington to postpone ratification and himself dawdled in preparing documents in order to allow a conspiracy enough time to force the United States into war with Britain?

Having tossed all night in his bed, Washington concluded that national suspense concerning the Jay Treaty was too dangerous to be allowed to continue. If, with all his accumulated prestige behind him, he presented the people with an irrevocable decision, the pro-French thrust—whether or not Randolph was actually among its instigators—would be blunted. It followed that, to avoid the most immediate danger—war with England—Washington would have to accept the treaty in the most positive manner open to him. Without further pause, he would follow the advice of the Senate exactly as it was given: not trying to reopen negotiations concerning other matters, he would ratify everything except the provisions concerning West Indian trade. He would make a separate protest against the Provision Order.

This conclusion involved another, from a personal point of view, very painful. So that the secretary of state would not be encouraged to fly into the opposition before he had carried through his essential part in the ratification of the treaty, Washington would

Opposite: George Washington *by Charles Willson Peale, detail, oil on canvas, c. 1795–1800.*

Oliver Wolcott Jr. *by Gilbert Stuart after John Vanderlyn, oil on canvas, c. 1820.*

Timothy Pickering *by Charles Willson Peale, from life, 1792–1793.*

have to dissemble with his old friend, pretending that everything was as before. Only later could Randolph be given an opportunity to defend (and, Washington hoped, exonerate) himself.

The next morning, August 12, 1795, Washington, to Randolph's utter amazement, announced his firm intention of ratifying the Jay Treaty.

How was Washington to discover whether or not Randolph was actually guilty of treason? He had no secret service to put on the job. He could not request the courts to subpoena Randolph's records or any witnesses from the Democratic Societies without publicly accusing his friend—who might be innocent—and creating vast internal turmoil. To ask the French for the missing, clarifying dispatches would be pointless, since, if a conspiracy existed, the French would surely supply a doctored text. Washington saw no expedient but confrontation. The incriminating document would, in the presence of the accusing Wolcott and Pickering, be sprung on Randolph without warning. Whether he was guilty or innocent would be revealed by the way he reacted.

As he prepared this trap, Washington, his heart sore, loaded Randolph with civilities. Then the awful day came 'round.

Randolph was amazed, when he came to confer with the president, to find that Wolcott and Pickering, who were so rarely consulted, had been asked to be there before him. After attempting some small talk, Washington said, "Mr. Randolph! Here is a letter which I desire you to read and make such explanations as you choose."

Washington (who did not know that Hamilton and Jefferson and Wolcott had done the same thing) was worried that Randolph had discussed American politics with a foreign diplomat. But the real horror was the strong implication that he had requested a bribe.

It must have taken Randolph at least half an hour to read the long dispatch. Washington, Pickering remembered, had "desired us to watch Randolph's countenance while he perused it. The president fixed his own eye upon him, and I . . . never saw it look so animated." Finally Randolph looked up. He commented that, since this was all new to him, the implications were not clear in his mind. He could state little more than that he had never made a communication to Fauchet which he considered improper, and that he had never sought or received French money.

Washington then asked him to withdraw and wait in an anteroom while his three observers conferred. To Washington's vast relief, Wolcott and Pickering were forced to agree that the accused had behaved "with composure" that indicated innocence. The president gleefully went to the door to call his exonerated friend back.

But it was a different man who returned. Randolph's face was alive with agitation. He shouted that he "could not continue in the office one second after such treatment." He ran from the room, down the stairs, and out of the presidential mansion.

According to the principles by which Randolph's ordeal had been planned, he had demonstrated guilt. It was now Wolcott's and Pickering's time to be gleeful. They pushed the conclusion home to the president, who sat there in the dismay of an old man whose formerly clear judgment of his associates seemed to have clouded, a man of warm emotions whose close friend appeared to have revealed himself a traitor.

Washington had written that, if Randolph's behavior proved him guilty, the government would have to protect itself by publishing the accusing dispatch. He would merit "*no* favor," and if explanation were not given, "*he* and his friends" would use his separation from the government as a proof that the administration was pro-British.

Now Randolph turned on his former patron with all the fury of the spurned. To Madison, he wrote, "I feel happy at my emancipation from attachment to a man who has practiced on me the profound hypocrisy of a Tiberius and the injustice of an assassin." He informed the newspapers that he would explain and justify his resignation in an "appeal to the people of the United States." When Pickering, who had become acting secretary of state, refused to deliver up some private presidential dispatches, Randolph announced the matter in the press.

Faced with the actual issue, Washington found that he did not have the heart to fight back. Holding Pickering and Wolcott on as tight a leash as he could (they certainly leaked some information), he kept secret the incriminating French dispatch. He allowed his former friend to monopolize the public stage. And he decided that any effort on his part to suppress information would be more damaging than complete exposure. Although so doing would allow Randolph to show how the president had vacillated and then changed his mind concerning the Jay Treaty, the president gave Randolph permission to secure and "publish without reserve any and every private and confidential letter I ever wrote you: nay more, every word I have ever uttered in your presence." Washington's one request was that his permission be quoted in whatever vindication Randolph published. The public would, Washington hoped, "appreciate my motives even if it would condemn my prudence in allowing you the unlimited license herein contained."

Washington, who hated suspense, had to wait a long time for the blow to fall. Two months passed before Randolph's *Vindication* appeared on December 18.

Randolph's defense concerning the implication that he had asked for a bribe was backed up by a purported transcript, which he had procured from the French, of the missing dispatch. The story was that he had wished to demonstrate that it was the British who were fomenting the Whiskey Rebellion. He believed that proof was in the hands of four New York flour merchants, but the mouths of these witnesses were sealed by debts which the British could use to ruin them. Randolph had suggested that the French make the evidence available by paying these debts.

Randolph further claimed that his behavior at the confrontation had been no demonstration of guilt, but had rather been made inevitable by Washington's treating him, under the eyes of his enemies, in a manner insufferable to a man of honor.

The long and confused pamphlet Randolph published bristled with anger against Washington. Although intended to wound, the description of the president's vacillations and final about-face concerning the Jay Treaty was not altogether damaging, since it revealed his unhappiness concerning the document. Yet the picture of Washington that emerged from the 103 closely printed pages carried strong implications of weakness and indecision. This was partly because Randolph, in revealing the great influence he himself had had over the president, involuntarily revealed himself, as he wallowed in self-praise and self-pity, as a fool. He also stated nastily, for the whole nation to see, what Washington himself suspected and feared: that the president was losing his mental powers.

Forty-Five

DOWNHILL

(1795–1796)

On returning to public life after the Revolution, Washington had mourned that he was placing again in the hands of fate the greatest reward he had earned during eight anguished military years: his fame, the love of his fellow citizens. Now his worst fears seemed to have come true. Rather than stilling public controversy as he had hoped, his ratification of the Jay Treaty had turned the anger on himself. The broad public, which had previously resented attacks on their hero, now accepted them with avidity. Every aspect of his career was insultingly discussed in the newspapers. He had been made commander in chief because he was such a nonentity that Congress was convinced that he could not become a tyrant—but how wrong Congress had been! Even the infirmities of old age were used to blast at him. Why did he not walk around or ride horseback as he used to do? That he only passed through the streets in his well-appointed carriage surely expressed anti-Republican disdain.

George Washington *by Gilbert Stuart, detail, oil on canvas, c. 1798. Martha Washington commissioned Stuart to create portraits of herself and her husband in 1796. Although George's jaw and mouth look stiff and uncomfortable due to a new set of ill-fitting dentures, Stuart was so satisfied with the resulting likeness that he made and sold at least seventy-five replicas. Washington thought Stuart presumptuous, and found the process of sitting for him—which he did on numerous occasions—unpleasant, to say the least.*

At this dark moment, the opposition revealed—the facts seem to have been let out by Randolph—that Washington had consistently overdrawn his salary. Wolcott attempted a rebuttal: despite the overdrafts, Washington had been forced to dig into his personal funds to help pay presidential expenses. This did not impress those who believed that Washington was living too extravagantly, in a monarchical manner. The bad odor was increased by the memory that, at the time of his inauguration, Washington had seemed self-sacrificing when he had vainly tried to persuade Congress to pay him no salary, only expenses. Since Washington's secretaries kept his accounts and the Treasury had not objected to the drafts they had submitted in his name, it is quite possible that Washington had been ignorant of the situation—yet he could not doubt that his image had been tarnished.

In another way, which Washington could not foresee, his image was much more grievously damaged. A painful physical disability was being grafted onto his legend so that in the minds of future Americans, his attribute—like Saint Catherine's wheel or Saint Sebastian's arrows—became ill-fitting false teeth.

Washington did wear clumsy dentures. Only one of his own teeth was in his mouth in 1789 when he presided over the capital in New York. That tooth soon vanished. Washington wore terrifying-looking contraptions, made of substances like hippopotamus ivory. The upper and lower jaws, that were hinged together at the back of the mouth, opened and closed with the assistance of springs. He himself complained that they distorted his lips. However, as he could command the best dentists, he was probably no more disfigured than was then common among the elderly and prosperous.

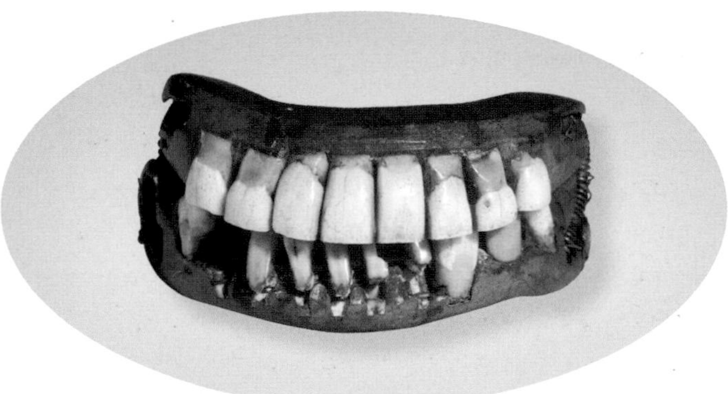

Stories of Washington's "wooden teeth" are apocryphal, but he did wear dentures, fitted with a combination of human teeth, cow teeth, and elephant ivory, hinged together at the back of the mouth with springs to help them open and close. This set is c. 1790. He complained that they distorted his appearance, though they were probably no more disfiguring than was common at the time.

Washington's false teeth were propelled into legend by the ablest and most sophisticated portraitist who ever painted him. Born in Rhode Island, Gilbert Stuart had trained himself so well in that world capital of portraiture, London, that he was often considered there the younger painter most likely to succeed to the mantle of the great Sir Joshua Reynolds. But he was extravagant and intemperate. Having fled from debts, he appeared in Philadelphia during 1795, one of his projects being to pay for the floods of liquor that flowed down his throat, by creating and selling a multitude of portraits of the world's greatest man. Washington sat for him for three separate portraits, and Stuart expanded the number of images with copies running to several hundreds.

Alas, Washington and Stuart did not get on. The painter was in the habit of keeping his sitters amused and their faces alive by a flood of showy and outrageous talk. Washington, who always felt uneasy at remaining still and being stared at, was put out rather than amused. And Stuart, who believed that artists were fundamentally superior to all other men, including presidents, resented Washington's formality. He could not forget what had resulted when, in trying to unstiffen the hero, he had gone to the length of saying, "Now, sir, you must let me forget that you are General Washington and I am Stuart the painter."

Washington replied (as it seemed to him, politely), "Mr. Stuart need never feel the need for forgetting who he is and who General Washington is."

Stuart emphasized, as no other portraitist did, the distortions of Washington's mouth, and none of the other artists who painted Washington had Stuart's vast skill in creating a convincing likeness. The artist's justification for dwelling on the deformity was that the effigy of so major a historical figure should be more a factual document than the likeness of an ordinary citizen. But it may well be that Stuart, who angrily used General Knox's portrait as the door of his pigsty, was motivated in his relation with Washington also by rage. No other man's rage did Washington's historical image more harm.

Randolph's resignation and the death of Attorney General Bradford left two vacancies in the cabinet, and soon there were also two in the Supreme Court: the Senate refused to confirm Rutledge as chief justice, and another justice resigned. To his dismay, Washington found a universal unwillingness to accept the odium of joining his government. He offered State, for instance, to William Paterson of New Jersey, former Governor Thomas Johnson of Maryland, Charles Cotesworth Pinckney of South Carolina, and the old Virginia patriot Patrick Henry. Washington had selected these men as satisfactory to the Republicans. Since they had all declined, he decided that if the office were to be filled, he would have to accept a Federalist.

For the ten months since Hamilton's resignation, Washington had kept his former adviser at arm's length. Now, deserted by all others, Washington turned to Hamilton. Among his requests was that Hamilton discover whether New York's Federalist senator, Rufus King, would accept State.

Hamilton replied that "the disgust which a virtuous and independent mind" feels at making itself a target for "foul and venomous shafts of calumny" induced King to refuse the office. "I wish, sir," Hamilton continued, "I could present to you any useful ideas as a substitute, but the embarrassment is extreme as to secretary of state.... In fact, a first-rate character is not attainable. A second-rate must be taken with good dispositions and barely decent qualifications. I wish I could throw more light. 'Tis a sad omen for the government."

All this time, the dour Pickering, who was acting secretary, was waiting angrily in the wings. When Washington was finally reduced to offering the post to him, Pickering made the president plead before he condescendingly agreed.

Still accepting the second-rate, Washington bagged three southerners: his former aide and drinking companion, James McHenry, as secretary of war; Charles Lee, who practiced law near Mount Vernon, as attorney general; and Thomas Chase of Maryland for the Supreme Court. This achieved, Washington felt he could appoint as chief justice a Massachusetts Federalist, Oliver Ellsworth.

"The offices are once more filled," John Adams noted, "but how differently than when Jefferson, Hamilton, Jay, etc., were here!"

With anticipations often sadistic, politically minded Americans awaited Washington's Seventh Annual Address. How would the president defend himself? How would he defend the Jay Treaty? Would he attack the independent mass meetings that had blasted his policies as he had attacked the centrally organized Democratic Societies? Would he express personal bitterness as he had in his second inaugural? There was tenseness in the Senate chamber when Washington walked in on December 8, 1795. It soon changed to amazement.

"Fellow citizens of the Senate and the House of Representatives," Washington began. "I trust I do not deceive myself when I indulge the persuasion that I have never met you at any period when more than at the present the situation of our public affairs has afforded just cause for mutual congratulation; and for inviting you to join me in profound gratitude to the Author of all good for the numerous and extraordinary blessings we enjoy."

Then Washington began enumerating blessings: Wayne's victory plus the entente with England promised peace on the northwest frontier; an accommodation was being reached with the Barbary pirates who had molested American shipping; Pinckney reported progress on a treaty with Spain. Washington then mentioned the Jay Treaty—everyone was agog—but he merely said that applying "the best judgment I was able to form of the public interest" he had followed the advice of the Senate. "The result on the part of his Britannic Majesty is unknown. When received, the subject will, without delay, be put before Congress." Washington's summary was that "prudence and moderation on every side" could now extinguish all causes of discord "which have heretofore menaced our tranquillity."

Pro-French legislators, who insisted that the Jay Treaty was anti-French, could hardly believe their ears as Washington moved on from foreign affairs without mentioning France. But even in their incredulity they realized that the president had outflanked them. The discussion having been of nations that menaced American tranquillity, the omission could be taken as a recognition of common interest.

The pendulum, which had swung so far against Washington, was swinging back. But, as Washington wrote, "the restless mind of man cannot be at peace."

Turning to domestic affairs, Washington made no mention of his critics. He contrasted the peaceful and prosperous state of the United States with the desperation in Europe. "The molestations of our trade" were overbalanced by the benefits the nation derived from her neutral position. Population was growing; internal improvements were rushing forward accompanied with tax burdens so light as to be scarcely felt. "Is it too much to say that our country exhibits a spectacle of national happiness never before surpassed if ever before equaled?" And should not Americans "unite our efforts to preserve, prolong, and improve our immense advantages?"

The Republicans were so devoted to controversy that their first reaction was that Washington had raised the white flag of surrender. Some, indeed, believed that this was a prelude to his resignation. But it quickly became clear that Washington (with an assist from Hamilton, who had helped him draft the speech) had made a master stroke. To the simplistic argument that the Jay Treaty was anti-French, he had opposed an equally simplistic argument, which was much closer to the experience of every citizen. He had cut as of old through layers of controversy down to the basic, unassailable truth. The nation was still free and, despite irritations on the ocean and at the conference tables, more prosperous than it had ever been. The nation was a growing colossus whose security rested not on which belligerent won the European victory but on the continuation of conditions that would allow it to achieve unhampered its maturity. If this were the case—and every American who looked around him dispassionately saw that it was indeed the case—why all this howling of faction, all these accusations that the government was selling out the country? Why all this hysteria about the details of a treaty that was serving the major end of allowing the nation to grow undisturbed?

The pendulum, which had swung so far against Washington, was swinging back. But, as Washington wrote, "the restless mind of man cannot be at peace." A grave constitutional crisis loomed.

According to the Constitution, only the Senate had to acquiesce in a treaty. Senators were then elected indirectly, by state legislatures. There was a Federalist majority. The House was elected directly by the people and was considered the "popular," the democratic branch of the government. It had a Republican majority which was still infuriated by the Jay Treaty, and it also resented the domination which exclusive legislative concern with foreign affairs gave the Senate. There was the further fact that in his commercial treaty with

George Washington *by James Sharples, pastel on paper, c. 1795–1796.*

Great Britain, Jay had regulated trade matters which had formerly been subject to action by the entire Congress. This could be interpreted as usurpation by the Senate and the executive of matters that correctly belonged to "the people" gathered in the House.

The House had a weapon which its Republican majority intended to use the instant the Jay Treaty came back, duly signed, from England. Money bills originated in the House. Various appropriations would be necessary to implement the treaty. The House intended to reopen the whole question of the treaty and refuse to vote the money if, as seemed most probable, they did not approve it.

This issue was hanging over Washington's head when he celebrated his sixty-fifth birthday. The House showed its teeth by voting, fifty to thirty-eight, not to recess for half an hour so that the members could call on the president. Nonetheless, bells rang, cannon boomed, and the presidential mansion was besieged by visitors. Towards nightfall, Washington received the best possible birthday present: a copy of the treaty Pinckney had negotiated with Spain.

Having withdrawn from her alliance with England against France, Spain was afraid that the Jay Treaty would be followed by an alliance between England and the United States that would overwhelm her North American possessions. Conciliation seemed called for. Spain had opened the Mississippi to American shipping and cleared away in a satisfactory manner all the other controversies that had for so long embroiled the southwest frontier.

No one, of course, could object to this treaty or to another in which, by not exorbitant sums, the navyless United States bought off the Barbary pirates.

Late in February, a certified copy of the ratified Jay Treaty appeared. The leaders of the House expected Washington to take no action until they had been consulted, but on leap-year day, 1796, Washington declared the treaty the law of the land. The House instantly struck back, voting sixty-two to thirty-seven that their body had the right to reconsider treaties and demanding that Washington turn over to them all papers, omitting only those that would embarrass current foreign negotiations, which might "throw light" on the treaty or how it had been negotiated.

Never before had Washington been subject to such vituperation. However, he adhered to his old principle of not entering into public controversy beyond the constitutional requirements of his office.

Washington's old-time constitutional adviser, Madison, believed he would give in to the request. The politically active Virginia attorney (later chief justice) John Marshall explained that "the difficulty of resisting the popular branch" was always great and "particularly so when the passions of the public have been strongly and generally excited." Marshall pointed to the wide popularity of the House's demand, the overwhelming vote, the implication that if he refused, Washington had something to hide, and the danger he faced "of separating himself from the people."

Washington wrote that this was "one of those great occasions than which none more important had occurred or probably may occur again."

Washington believed that "the *real* question" was not the Jay Treaty, but whether the House could increase its power. This guess was corroborated in Jefferson's private correspondence with Monroe: "On the precedent now to be set will depend the future construction of our Constitution. . . . It is fortunate that the first decision is to be in a case so palpably atrocious as to have been predetermined by all America." Jefferson admitted that the challenge would "bring on an embarrassing and critical state in our government," but he considered the risk worth taking.

If the House were permitted to sabotage the Jay Treaty after it had constitutionally become the law of the land, the wound with England would be reopened without there being any constitutional way of closing it—or, indeed, of making any treaty that the executive could in good conscience ratify or a foreign power accept. How would Washington steer a rudderless ship of state between the Scylla of war with England and the Charybdis of war with France?

A forewarning of what would happen was given by the fact that every time an American vessel had reached home, its anchor was permanently dropped; no one wanted to risk the reprisal of British cruisers. And since farm prices depended on export, prosperity was skidding into general depression.

The Republicans argued that war was not a danger since it was only necessary to twist the British lion's tail to make him back down. But so far the lion had shown no tendency to cower. And a war with England, so obviously fomented by the Republicans, might well, the geographic distribution of political views being what it was, create civil war within the United States. The Union might well be destroyed.

Washington's personal feelings were also much involved. The House was not only encroaching on the Senate, but had demanded presidential papers as a right. Washington had been careful not to encroach on the other branches, and he had no intention of letting any other branch encroach on the executive. This was not only a constitutional matter: he had never in his life willingly allowed anyone to push him around.

Another consideration was Washington's strong desire to escape from the presidency at the next major election, which would mark the end of his second term. If potentially catastrophic internal turmoil raged, he would surely be forced to stay on. Such compulsion would be more than a personal tragedy; it might well frustrate his desire to demonstrate that republican succession could be peacefully achieved by a free election. He would probably (as he realized) die during a third term, which would mean that the vice president would succeed as a crown prince succeeds in a monarchy.

As for the constitutional confusions, Washington recognized that they existed, but he felt that each branch should be recessive, except when the nation was clearly endangered. The House could veto a foreign policy decision if it had been achieved by fraud or presented "such striking evidence of national injury . . . as to make war or any other evil preferable." Washington believed that "every unbiased mind," would agree that this was not the case with the Jay Treaty.

Whether or not it turned the people against him, Washington felt he had no choice. To the amazement and rage of the Republican leadership in and out of the House, he refused, on constitutional grounds, to turn over a single document.

Never before had Washington been subject to such vituperation. However, he adhered to his old principle of not entering into public controversy beyond the constitutional requirements of his office. Again, this served him well. As other men ranted and accused and waved their fists in the air, the extreme virulence of their attacks on the president and the Jay Treaty encouraged a backlash. So many protests flooded into the House against their intended action that the majority wavered and at last withdrew the claim. Jefferson commented bitterly, "Congress has risen. You will see by their proceedings the truth of what I have always observed to you: that one man outweighs them all in influence over the people, who have supported his judgment against their own and that of their representatives. Republicanism must lie on its oars, resign the vessel to its pilot, and themselves to the course he thinks best for them."

This did not mean that the Republicans were reconciled. According to John Marshall, Washington's unequivocal denial of the claims of the House "appeared to break the last cord of that attachment which had theretofore bound some of the active leaders of the opposition to the person of the president. Amidst all the agitations and irritations of the party, a sincere respect and real affection for the chief magistrate, the remnant of former friendship, had still lingered in the bosoms of some who had engaged with ardor in the political contests of the day. But, if the last spark of affection was not now extinguished, it was at least concealed under the more active passions of the moment."

July 1796 saw the last exchange of letters between Washington and Jefferson. For some reason, Jefferson felt called on to deny that it was he who had released an old official document to the press. He added disingenuous assertions that he was no longer engaged in politics. Washington answered angrily. He had not believed until recently "that parties would, or even could, go to the length I have been witness to, nor . . . that, while I was using my utmost exertions to establish a national character of our own, independent, as far as our obligations and justice would permit, of every nation of the earth; and wished, by steering a steady course, to preserve this country from the horrors of a desolating war, that I should be accused of being the enemy of one nation, and subject to the influence of another; and to prove it, that every act of my administration would be tortured, and the grossest and most insidious misrepresentations of them be made (by giving one side only of a subject, and that too in such exaggerated and indecent terms as could scarcely be applied to a Nero, a notorious defaulter, or a common pickpocket). But enough of this. I have already gone further in the expression of my feelings than I intended."

The inescapable fact was that Washington had suffered a major defeat. He had wished to relinquish to his successor a unified nation that would demonstrate to all the world harmony achieved under free government. He had wished to bring together all rational points of view in his person and his government. He could still, it was true, sway the people to ends he considered essential, but in so doing he had to batter away a numerous and vocal group which comprised many of his former dear companions.

John Adams confided to his wife that Washington was deeply hurt. "All the studied efforts of the Federalists to counterbalance abuse by compliment don't answer the end."

Forty-Six

WASHINGTON'S FAREWELL ADDRESS

(1796)

During May 1796, Madison wrote Monroe in cipher, "It is now generally understood that the president will retire, and Jefferson is the object on one side, Adams apparently on the other." Although the Federalists were worried—"If a storm gather," Hamilton asked Washington, "how can you retreat?"—Washington wrote firmly that he would "close my public life on March 4 [1797], after which no consideration under heaven that I can foresee shall again draw me from the walks of private life."

In that embattled springtime, Washington believed that he would have to withdraw, facing his enemies, sword in hand. Although he did not intend to make his announcement before late fall, when "it shall become indispensably necessary for the information of the [presidential] electors," he jotted down a bitter and defensive draft of a farewell address. To prove that his desire to retire four years before was known "*to one or two* of those characters" (Madison and Jefferson) who were trying to "build their own consequence" by accusing him of tyrannical ambitions, Washington quoted entirely the address which Madison had helped him prepare at that time.

Having argued for unity, for tolerance, for true neutrality, Washington launched angrily into one of those paragraphs which affirm what they deny: "As some of the gazettes of the United States have teemed with all the invective that disappointment, ignorance of facts, and malicious falsehoods could invent, to misrepresent my politics and affections—to wound my reputation and feelings—and to weaken, if not entirely destroy, the confidence you have been pleased to repose in me, it might be expected at the parting scene of my public life that I should take some notice of such virulent abuse. But, as heretofore, I shall pass them over in utter silence."

He continued in a pitiful vein quite uncharacteristic of the proud old hero: he hoped that, "as I did not seek the office with which you have honored me, that charity may throw her mantle over my want of abilities to do better; that the gray hairs of a man" who had spent "*all the prime of his life* in serving his country, be suffered to pass quietly to the grave, and that his errors, however numerous, if they are not criminal, may be consigned to the tomb of oblivion."

He denied willful error. His administration, "the infancy of the government and all other things considered," had been "as delicate, difficult, and trying as may occur again in any future period," and throughout he had, to the best of his abilities, "consulted the true and permanent interests of our country, without regard to local considerations—to individuals, to parties, or to nations." He had not served because of ambition or in any ignorance of the hazards to which he was exposing his reputation. Noting that he had refused "the bounty of several legislatures at the close of the war," he stated that his service had brought no addition to his finances, but

Washington offers a toast to his successor, President-elect John Adams, at his farewell dinner.

rather the reverse. "I leave you with undefiled hands, and uncorrupted heart, and with ardent vows to heaven of the welfare and happiness of that country in which I and my forefathers to the third and fourth progenitor drew our first breath."

Worried, as he later stated, by "the egotisms" in this draft, Washington allowed it to lie in his desk until, at Hamilton's request, he sent it to his adviser. He empowered Hamilton to prepare an altogether new speech, but wished also to have his own draft back in revised form. Hamilton did what he was asked. He removed from Washington's draft the most achingly personal passages and expanded it into an appeal to the nation concerning the problems being immediately faced. However, he realized that this document would not contribute to Washington's permanent reputation. Undoubtedly inspired by real affection and admiration for his longtime patron and also by the desire of the Federalists to have in the succeeding years a great figure to cling to, Hamilton wrote a new draft, intended to be "*importantly* and *lastingly* useful." Washington agreed with his adviser that the new version—known to history as "Hamilton's Main Draft"—was the better. It became the basis for "Washington's Farewell Address."

Washington began his own revisions by transcribing the text in his own handwriting, making innumerable verbal changes. The ideas he found expressed were with a few exceptions his own. No man was more familiar than Hamilton with Washington's sentiments, and long experience had taught him that Washington would not knowingly allow himself to be pushed. The way to influence him was to put forward ideas in a manner that made them seem an extension of his own thinking. Had Hamilton drafted the address according to his own thinking, Washington would have simply laid it aside. The experienced aide only inserted sentiments with which Washington might not agree if he thought he could do it so inconspicuously that the president would not notice. Almost all of them came out. Washington also cut out almost all the "egotisms" which Hamilton, probably in deference to Washington's draft, had inserted in the new manuscript.

The chances are very good that, had Washington been left to himself, he would never have released the defensive, angry, and almost lachrymose draft which he had written long before the need and which would have shattered his principle of avoiding partisan controversy. However, the fact remains that it was Hamilton who presented the alternative on which the final address was based. Despite Washington's many changes, much of Hamilton's style remains. This is most conspicuous in the prolixity. Washington's natural tendency was to be concise, to pack sentences until a dense but clear paragraph covered all phases of the problem. Hamilton argued things out, as in a legal brief. The Farewell Address could be considered Hamilton's had it expressed Hamilton's ideas. It expressed Washington's. It was as much Washington's as any presidential paper was likely to be that had been drafted by an intimate aide. If all such documents were attributed to the speech writers, history would read very differently and surely less accurately. Although grounded on Hamilton's Main Draft, the famous paper is correctly called Washington's Farewell Address.

The Address, as finally promulgated, passed quickly over personal considerations—Washington had not sought the presidency, had not wished a second term, was getting older, and hoped from his retirement to see the nation continuing on a virtuous path that would lead the rest of the world to liberty.

The next section stated that since union was the basis on which American liberty rested, and also the nation's protection against involvement in foreign broils, it would obviously be the focus of attack from "internal and external enemies." The Constitution was the instrument of unity. A thirst for innovation could be dangerous. Only experience should inspire changes.

The Address next attacked "the spirit of party" as fostering geographic schisms and foreign intrigues; as intervening between the people and the government; as encouraging the rule of minorities and demagogues. Political contention was "a fire not to be quenched," but "it demands a uniform vigilance lest, instead of warming, it should consume." While denouncing "demagogues" at considerable length, the address also warned against the machinations of "a small but artful, enterprising minority." Thus the text struck at what could be considered the inherent dangers of both the Republican and Federalist parties.

Passages on the need for religion to establish public morality and the need for financial credit for economic health were followed by the longest section. It dealt with foreign affairs. Those Americans who wished to serve foreign causes were described as "fools and dupes." The basis on which national policy should be built was the Neutrality Proclamation.

Now that the federal capital crawls with publicity men, it is hard to believe that the President had no regular channel for getting his address to the public. He decided to release it to one Philadelphia newspaper, David Claypoole's *American Daily Advertiser,* and let it work its way from there. Since Claypoole expressed regret at relinquishing the invaluable manuscript, Washington gave it to the printer. The president was on the road to Mount Vernon when on September 19, 1796, Claypoole, devoting his front page as usual to advertising, ran the Farewell Address under a small head on the second and third of his four pages. There ensued a great scurrying in the offices of other new papers, first in Philadelphia, then along the highroads, then down the byways, then in cities across the ocean, as the Address was set up again and again. Washington was now home, listening for what the reaction would be.

The Address quickly took the privileged position in American life which it has retained. It carried the magical significance, as old as mankind, of a patriarch's dying words. And the point of view expressed was basic to American thinking, even that of most of the opposition. Washington's attacks on those who served European policies and on faction had been made to cut both ways. Despite vocal supporters of what we today call "brinksmanship," no responsible group really wanted to get into the foreign war; and political parties were still so much in their infancy that few yearned to come to their defense, particularly in the light of the bloody results of factionalism in France. As for Washington's insistence on the importance of national union, regionalists might huff and puff, but no one really wanted to tear the nation apart.

Newspapers glowed with praises; mass meetings and legislatures passed resolutions of thanks. And all but a few among the controversialists of the opposition considered it politic to ignore the Address. They aimed their continuing darts where they considered Washington more vulnerable.

VOICE OF REASON

WASHINGTON'S FAREWELL ADDRESS

WASHINGTON CLOSED HIS HISTORIC TERM with a thoughtful farewell address, now considered a groundbreaking statement of American political values. Drafted with help from Hamilton, it touches on the importance of national unity, the value of the Constitution and the rule of law, the evils of political parties, and the proper virtues of a republican people. Washington warns against foreign influence in domestic affairs and American meddling in European affairs, as well as bitter partisanship in domestic politics. He counsels friendship and commerce with all nations, but warns against involvement in European wars and entering into long-term alliances.

Friends, and Fellow Citizens:

The period for a new election of a citizen to administer the executive government of the United States being not far distant, and the time actually arrived, when your thoughts must be employed in designating the person, who is to be clothed with that important trust, it appears to me proper, especially as it may conduce to a more distinct expression of the public voice, that I should now apprise you of the resolution I have formed to decline being considered among the number of those out of whom a choice is to be made. I beg you, at the same time, to do me the justice to be assured that this resolution has not been taken without a strict regard to all the considerations appertaining to the relation, which binds a dutiful citizen to his country, and that, in withdrawing the tender of service which silence in my situation might imply, I am influenced by no diminution of zeal for your future interest, no deficiency of grateful respect for your past kindness, but am supported by a full conviction that the step is compatible with both.

The acceptance of, and continuance hitherto, in the office to which your suffrages have twice called me, have been a uniform sacrifice of inclination to the opinion of duty, and to a deference for what appeared to be your desire. I constantly hoped that it would have been much earlier in my power, consistently with motives, which I was not at liberty to disregard, to return to that retirement, from which I had been reluctantly drawn. The strength of my inclination to do this, previous to the last election, had even led to the preparation of an address to declare it to you; but mature reflection on the then perplexed and critical posture of our affairs with foreign nations, and the unanimous advice of persons entitled to my confidence, impelled me to abandon the idea. I rejoice that the state of your concerns, external as well as internal, no longer renders the pursuit of inclination incompatible with the sentiment of duty or propriety; and am persuaded, whatever partiality may be retained for my services, that in the present circumstances of our country you will not disapprove my determination to retire.

The impressions with which I first undertook the arduous trust were explained on the proper occasion. In the discharge of this trust, I will only say that I have, with good intentions, contributed towards the organization and administration of the government the best exertions of which a very fallible judgment was capable. Not unconscious, in the outset, of the inferiority of my qualifications, experience in my own eyes, perhaps still more in the eyes of others, has strengthened the motives to diffidence of myself; and every day the increasing weight of years admonishes me more and more, that the shade of retirement is as necessary to me as it will be welcome. Satisfied that if any circumstances have given peculiar value to my services, they were temporary. I have the consolation to believe that while choice and prudence invite me to quit the political scene, patriotism does not forbid it.

In looking forward to the moment, which is intended to terminate the career of my public life, my feelings do not permit me to suspend the deep acknowledgment of that debt of gratitude which I owe to my beloved country for the many honors it has conferred upon me, still more for the steadfast confidence with which it has supported me, and for the opportunities I have thence enjoyed of manifesting my inviolable attachment, by services faithful and persevering, though in usefulness unequal to my zeal. If benefits have resulted to our country from these services, let it always be remembered to your praise and as an instructive example in our annals, that, under circumstances in which the passions agitated in every direction were liable to mislead, amidst appearances sometimes dubious, vicissitudes of fortune often discouraging, in situations in which not infrequently want of success has countenanced the spirit of criticism, the constancy of your support was the essential prop of the efforts, and a guarantee of the plans by which they were effected. Profoundly penetrated with this idea, I shall carry it with me to my grave as a strong incitement to unceasing vows that Heaven may continue to you the choicest tokens of its beneficence; that your Union and brotherly affection may be perpetual; that the free constitution, which is the work of your hands, may be sacredly maintained; that its administration in every department may be stamped with wisdom and virtue; that, in fine, the happiness of the people of these States, under the auspices of liberty, may be made complete by so careful a preservation and so prudent a use of this blessing as will acquire to them the glory of recommending it to the applause, the affection, and adoption of every nation which is yet a stranger to it.

Here, perhaps, I ought to stop. But a solicitude for your welfare which cannot end but with my life, and the apprehension of danger, natural to that solicitude, urge me on an occasion like the present, to offer to your solemn contemplation and to recommend to your frequent review, some sentiments, which are the result of much reflection, of no inconsiderable observation, and which appear to me all important to the permanency of your felicity as a People. These will be offered to you with the more freedom, as you can only see in them the disinterested warnings of a parting friend, who can possibly have no personal motive to bias his counsel. Nor can I forget, as an encouragement to it, your indulgent reception of my sentiments on a former and not dissimilar occasion. Interwoven, as is the love of liberty with every ligament of your hearts, no recommendation of mine is necessary to fortify or confirm the attachment.

The unity of government which constitutes you one People is also now dear to you. It is justly so; for it is a main pillar in the edifice of your real independence, the support of your tranquility at home, your peace abroad, of your safety, of your prosperity, of that very liberty which you so highly prize. But as it is easy to foresee, that from different causes and from different quarters much pains will be taken, many artifices employed, to weaken in your minds the conviction of this truth; as this is the point in your political fortress against which the batteries of internal and external enemies will be most constantly and actively (though often covertly and insidiously) directed. It is of infinite moment that you should properly estimate the immense value of your national union to your collective and individual happiness; that you should cherish a cordial, habitual, and immoveable attachment to it, accustoming yourselves to think and speak of it as of the palladium of your political safety and prosperity—watching for its preservation with jealous anxiety; discountenancing whatever may suggest even a suspicion that it can in any event be abandoned; and indignantly frowning upon the first dawning of every attempt to alienate any portion of our country from the rest, or to enfeeble the sacred ties which now link together the various parts.

For this you have every inducement of sympathy and interest. Citizens by birth or choice, of a common country, that country has a right to concentrate your affections. The name of American, which belongs to you in your national capacity must always exalt the just pride of patriotism more than any appellation derived from local discriminations. With slight shades of difference you have the same religion, manners, habits, and political principles. You have in a common cause fought and triumphed together. The independence and liberty you possess are the work of joint councils, and joint efforts of common dangers, sufferings, and successes. But these considerations, however powerfully they address themselves to your sensibility, are greatly outweighed by those which apply more immediately to your interest. Here, every portion of our country finds the most commanding motives for carefully guarding and preserving the Union of the whole.

The North, in an unrestrained intercourse with the South, protected by the equal laws of a common government, finds in the productions of the latter, great additional resources of maritime and commercial enterprise and precious materials of manufacturing industry. The South, in the same intercourse, benefitting by the same agency of the North, sees its agriculture grow and its commerce expand. Turning partly into its own channels the seamen of the North, it finds its particular navigation invigorated; and while it contributes, in different ways, to nourish and increase the general mass of the national navigation, it looks forward to the protection of a maritime strength, to which itself is unequally adapted. The East, in a like intercourse with the West, already finds, and in the progressive improvement of interior communications, by land and water, will more and more find a valuable vent for the commodities which it brings from abroad, or manufactures at home. The West derives from the East supplies requisite to its growth and comfort; and what is perhaps of still greater consequence, it must of necessity owe the secure enjoyment of indispensable outlets for its own productions to the weight, influence, and the future maritime strength of the Atlantic side of the Union, directed by an indissoluble community of interest as one nation. Any other tenure by which the West can hold this essential advantage, whether derived from its own separate strength, or from an apostate and unnatural connection with any foreign power, must be intrinsically precarious.

While then every part of our country thus feels an immediate and particular interest in union, all the parts combined cannot fail to find in the united mass of means and efforts greater strength, greater resource, proportionally greater security from external danger, a less frequent interruption of their peace by foreign nations; and what is of inestimable value! They must derive from union an exemption from those broils and wars between themselves, which so frequently afflict neighboring countries not tied together by the same government, which their own rival ships alone would be sufficient to produce, but which opposite foreign alliances, attachments, and intrigues would stimulate and embitter. Hence, likewise, they will avoid the necessity of those overgrown military establishments, which under any form of government are inauspicious to liberty, and which are to be regarded as particularly hostile to republican liberty. In this sense it is that your union ought to be considered as a main prop of your liberty, and that the love of the one ought to endear to you the preservation of the other. These considerations speak a persuasive language to every reflecting and virtuous mind, and exhibit the continuance of the Union as a primary object of patriotic desire. Is there a doubt, whether a common government can embrace so large a sphere? Let experience solve it. To listen to mere speculation in such a case were criminal. We are authorized to hope that a proper organization of the whole, with the auxiliary agency of governments for the respective subdivisions, will afford a happy issue to the experiment. 'Tis well worth a fair and full experiment. With such powerful and obvious motives to union, affecting all parts of our country, while experience shall not have demonstrated its impracticability, there will always be reason to distrust the patriotism of those who in any quarter may endeavor to weaken its bands.

In contemplating the causes which may disturb our Union, it occurs as matter of serious concern that any ground should have been furnished for characterizing parties by geographical discriminations: Northern and Southern; Atlantic and Western; whence designing men may endeavor to excite a belief that there is a real difference of local interests and views. One of the expedients of party to acquire influence, within particular districts, is to misrepresent the opinions and aims of other districts. You cannot shield yourselves too much against the jealousies and heart burnings which spring from these misrepresentations. They tend to render alien to each other those who ought to be bound together by fraternal affection. The inhabitants of our western country have lately had a useful lesson on this head. They have seen, in the negotiation by the executive and in the unanimous ratification by the Senate, of the treaty with Spain, and in the universal satisfaction at that event throughout the United States, a decisive proof how unfounded were the suspicions propagated among them of a policy in the general government and in the Atlantic states unfriendly to their interests in regard to the Mississippi. They have been witnesses to the formation of two treaties, that with Great Britain and that with Spain, which secure to them every thing they could desire, in respect to our foreign relations, towards confirming their prosperity. Will it not be their wisdom to rely for the preservation of these advantages on the Union by which they were procured? Will they not henceforth be deaf to those advisers, if such there are, who would sever them from their brethren and connect them with aliens?

To the efficacy and permanency of your Union, a government for the whole is indispensable. No alliances however strict between the parts can be an adequate substitute. They must inevitably experience the infractions and interruptions which all alliances in all times have experienced. Sensible of this momentous truth, you have improved upon your first essay by the adoption of a Constitution of government, better calculated than your former for an intimate Union and for the efficacious management of your common concerns. This government, the offspring of our own choice uninfluenced and unawed, adopted upon full investigation and mature deliberation, completely free in its principles, in the distribution of its powers, uniting security with energy, and containing within itself a provision for its own amendment, has a just claim to your confidence and your support. Respect for its authority, compliance with its laws, acquiescence in its measures, are duties enjoined by the fundamental maxims of true liberty. The basis of our political systems is the right of the people to make and to alter their constitutions of government. But the Constitution which at any time exists, 'till changed by an explicit and authentic act of the whole people, is sacredly obligatory upon all. The very idea of the power and the right of the people to establish government presupposes the duty of every individual to obey the established government.

All obstructions to the execution of the laws, all combinations and associations, under whatever plausible character, with the real design to direct, control counteract, or awe the regular deliberation and action of the constituted authorities, are destructive of this fundamental principle and of fatal tendency. They serve to organize faction, to give it an artificial and extraordinary force, to put in the place of the delegated will of the nation the will of a party, often a small but artful and enterprising minority of the community; and, according to the alternate triumphs of different parties, to make the public administration the mirror of the ill concerted and incongruous projects of faction, rather than the organ of consistent and wholesome plans digested by common councils and modified by mutual interests. However combinations or associations of the above description may now and then answer popular ends, they are likely, in the course of time and things to become, potent engines by which cunning, ambitious, and unprincipled men will be enabled to subvert the power of the people and to usurp for themselves the reins of government, destroying afterwards the very engines which have lifted them to unjust dominion.

Towards the preservation of your government and the permanency of your present happy state, it is requisite not only that you steadily discountenance irregular oppositions to its acknowledged authority, but also that you resist with care the spirit of innovation upon its principles, however specious the pretexts. One method of assault may be to effect, in the forms of the Constitution, alterations which will impair the energy of the system, and thus to undermine what cannot be directly overthrown. In all the changes to which you may be invited, remember that time and habit are at least as necessary to fix the true character of governments, as of other human institutions; that experience is the surest standard by which to test the real tendency of the existing Constitution of a country; that facility in changes upon the credit of mere hypotheses and opinion exposes to perpetual change from the endless variety of hypotheses and opinion. And remember, especially, that for the efficient management of your common interests, in a country so extensive as ours, a government of as much vigor as is consistent with the perfect security of liberty is indispensable. Liberty itself will find in such a government, with powers properly distributed and adjusted, its surest guardian. It is indeed little else than a name, where the government is too feeble to withstand the enterprises of faction, to confine each member of the society within the limits prescribed by the laws, and to maintain all in the secure and tranquil enjoyment of the rights of person and property.

I have already intimated to you the danger of parties in the state, with particular reference to the founding of them on geographical discriminations. Let me now take a more comprehensive view and warn you in the most solemn manner against the baneful effects of the spirit of party. Generally, this spirit, unfortunately, is inseparable from our nature, having its root in the strongest passions of the human mind. It exists under different shapes in all governments, more or less stifled, controlled, or repressed; but, in those of the popular form it is seen in its greatest rankness and is truly their worst enemy. The alternate domination of one faction over another, sharpened by the spirit of revenge natural to party dissention, which in different ages and countries has perpetrated the most horrid enormities, is itself a frightful despotism. But this leads at length to a more formal and permanent despotism. The disorders and miseries, which result, gradually incline the minds of men to seek security and repose in the absolute power of an individual; and sooner or later the chief of some prevailing faction more able or more fortunate than his competitors turns this disposition to the purposes of his own elevation, on the ruins of public liberty. Without looking forward to an extremity of this kind (which nevertheless ought not to be entirely out of sight) the common and continual mischiefs of the spirit of party are sufficient to make it the interest and duty of a wise people to discourage and restrain it. It serves always to distract the public councils and enfeeble the public administration. It agitates the community with ill-founded jealousies and false alarms, kindles the animosity of one part against another, foments occasionally riot and insurrection. It opens the door to foreign influence and corruption, which find a facilitated access to the government itself through the channels of party passions. Thus the policy and the will of one country are subjected to the policy and will of another.

There is an opinion that parties in free countries are useful checks upon the administration of the government and serve to keep alive the spirit of Liberty. This within certain limits is probably true, and in governments of a monarchical cast, patriotism may look with indulgence, if not with favor, upon the spirit of party. But in those of the popular character, in governments purely elective, it is a spirit not to be encouraged. From their natural tendency, it is certain there will always be enough of that spirit for every salutary purpose. And there being constant danger of excess, the effort ought to be, by force of public opinion, to mitigate and assuage it. A fire not to be quenched; it demands a uniform vigilance to prevent its bursting into a flame, lest instead of warming it should consume. It is important, likewise, that the habits of thinking in a free country should inspire caution in those entrusted with its administration, to confine themselves within their respective Constitutional spheres, avoiding in the exercise of the powers of one department to encroach upon another. The spirit of encroachment tends to consolidate the powers of all the departments in one, and thus to create whatever the form of government, a real despotism. A just estimate of that love of power, and proneness to abuse it, which predominates in the human heart, is sufficient to satisfy us of the truth of this position. The necessity of reciprocal checks in the exercise of political power; by dividing and distributing it into different depositories, and constituting each the guardian of the public weal against invasions by the others, has been evinced by experiments ancient and modern, some of them in our country and under our own eyes. To preserve them must be as necessary as to institute them. If in the opinion of the people the distribution or modification of the Constitutional powers be in any particular wrong, let it be corrected by an amendment in the way which the Constitution designates. But let there be no change by usurpation; for though this, in one instance, may be the instrument of good, it is the customary weapon by which free governments are destroyed. The precedent must always greatly overbalance in permanent evil any partial or transient benefit which the use can at any time yield. Of all the dispositions and habits which lead to political prosperity, religion and morality are indispensable supports. In vain would that man claim the tribute of patriotism who should labor to subvert these great pillars of human happiness, these firmest props of the duties of men and citizens. The mere politician, equally with the pious man, ought to respect and to cherish them. A volume could not trace all their connections with private and public felicity. Let it simply be asked where is the security for property, for reputation, for life, if the sense of religious obligation desert the oaths, which are the instruments of investigation in courts of justice? And let us with caution indulge the supposition that morality can be maintained without religion. Whatever may be conceded to the influence of refined education on minds of peculiar structure, reason and experience both forbid us to expect that national morality can prevail in exclusion of religious principle. 'Tis substantially true, that virtue or morality is a necessary spring of popular government. The rule indeed extends with more or less force to every species of free government. Who, that is a sincere friend to it, can look with indifference upon attempts to shake the foundation of the fabric. Promote, then, as an object of primary importance, institutions for the general diffusion of knowledge. In proportion as the structure of a government gives force to public opinion, it is essential that public opinion should be enlightened. As a very important source of strength and security, cherish public credit. One method of preserving it is to use it as sparingly as possible, avoiding occasions of expense by cultivating peace; but remembering also that timely disbursements to prepare for danger frequently prevent much greater disbursements to repel it; avoiding likewise the accumulation of debt, not only by shunning occasions of expense, but by vigorous exertions in time of peace to discharge the debts which unavoidable wars may have occasioned, not ungenerously throwing upon posterity the burthen which we ourselves ought to bear. The execution of these maxims belongs to your representatives; but it is necessary that public opinion should cooperate. To facilitate to them the performance of their duty it is essential that you should practically bear in mind, that towards the payment of debts there must be revenue; that to have revenue there must be taxes; that no taxes can be devised which are not more or less inconvenient and unpleasant; that the intrinsic embarrassment inseparable from the selection of the proper objects (which is always a choice of difficulties) ought to be a decisive motive for a candid construction of the conduct of the government in making it; and for a spirit of acquiescence in the measures for obtaining revenue which the public exigencies may at any time dictate.

Observe good faith and justice towards all nations. Cultivate peace and harmony with all. Religion and morality enjoin this conduct, and can it be that good policy does not equally enjoin it? It will be worthy of a free, enlightened, and, at no distant period, a great nation, to give to mankind the magnanimous and too novel example of a people always guided by an exalted justice and benevolence. Who can doubt that in the course of time and things the fruits of such a plan would richly repay any temporary advantages which might be lost by a steady adherence to it? Can it be that Providence has not connected the permanent felicity of a nation with its virtue? The experiment, at least, is recommended by every sentiment which ennobles human nature. Alas!, is it rendered impossible by its vices?

In the execution of such a plan nothing is more essential than that permanent, inveterate antipathies against particular nations and passionate attachments for others should be excluded; and that in place of them just and amicable feelings towards all should be cultivated. The nation, which indulges towards another an habitual hatred, or an habitual fondness, is in some degree a slave. It is a slave to its animosity or to its affection, either of which is sufficient to lead it astray from its duty and its interest. Antipathy in one nation against another disposes each more readily to offer insult and injury, to lay hold of slight causes of umbrage, and to be haughty and intractable when accidental or trifling occasions of dispute occur. Hence, frequent collisions, obstinate envenomed, and bloody contests. The nation, prompted by ill will and resentment, sometimes impels to war the government, contrary to the best calculations of policy. The government sometimes participates in the national propensity and adopts through passion what reason would reject; at other times, it makes the animosity of the nation subservient to projects of hostility instigated by pride, ambition, and other sinister and pernicious motives. The peace, often, sometimes perhaps the liberty, of nations has been the victim. So, likewise, a passionate attachment of one nation for another produces a variety of evils. Sympathy for the favorite nation, facilitating the illusion of an imaginary common interest, in cases where no real common interest exists, and infusing into one the enmities of the other betrays the former into a participation in the quarrels and wars of the latter without adequate inducement or justification. It leads also to concessions to the favorite nation of privileges denied to others, which is apt doubly to injure the nation making the concessions; by unnecessarily parting with what ought to have been retained; and by exciting jealousy, ill will, and a disposition to retaliate, in the parties from whom equal privileges are withheld. And it gives to ambitious, corrupted, or deluded citizens (who devote themselves to the favorite nation) facility to betray, or sacrifice the interests of their own country, without odium, sometimes even with popularity, gilding with the appearances of a virtuous sense of obligation a commendable deference for public opinion, or a laudable zeal for public good, the base or foolish compliances of ambition, corruption, or infatuation.

The great rule of conduct for us, in regard to foreign nations, is in extending our commercial relations to have with them as little political connection as possible. So far as we have already formed engagements, let them be fulfilled with perfect good faith. Here, let us stop. Europe has a set of primary interests, which to us have none, or a very remote relation. Hence, she must be engaged in frequent controversies, the causes of which are essentially foreign to our concerns. Hence, therefore, it must be unwise in us to implicate ourselves, by artificial ties, in the ordinary vicissitudes of her politics, or the ordinary combinations and collisions of her friendship or enmities.

Our detached and distant situation invites and enables us to pursue a different course. If we remain one people, under an efficient government, the period is not far off, when we may defy material injury from external annoyance; when we may take such an attitude as will cause the neutrality we may at any time resolve upon to be scrupulously respected; when belligerent nations, under the impossibility of making acquisitions upon us, will not lightly hazard the giving us provocation; when we may choose peace or war, as our interest guided by justice shall counsel. Why forego the advantages of so peculiar a situation? Why quit our own to stand upon foreign ground? Why, by interweaving our destiny with that of any part of Europe, entangle our peace and prosperity in the toils of European ambition, rivalship, interest, humor or caprice?

'Tis our true policy to steer clear of permanent alliances with any portion of the foreign world. So far, I mean, as we are now at liberty to do it, for let me not be understood as capable of patronizing infidelity to existing engagements (I hold the maxim no less applicable to public than to private affairs, that honesty is always the best policy). I repeat it, therefore, let those engagements be observed in their genuine sense; but in my opinion, it is unnecessary and would be unwise to extend them. Taking care always to keep ourselves, by suitable establishments, on a respectably defensive posture, we may safely trust to temporary alliances for extraordinary emergencies.

Harmony, liberal intercourse with all nations, are recommended by policy, humanity, and interest. But even our commercial policy should hold an equal and impartial hand, neither seeking nor granting exclusive favors or preferences; consulting the natural course of things; diffusing and diversifying by gentle means the streams of commerce, but forcing nothing; establishing with powers so disposed in order to give trade a stable course, to define the rights of our merchants, and to enable the government to support them; conventional rules of intercourse, the best that present circumstances and mutual opinion will permit, but temporary—and liable to be from time to time, abandoned or varied—as experience and circumstances shall dictate; constantly keeping in view that 'tis folly in one nation to look for disinterested favors from another; that it must pay with a portion of its independence for whatever it may accept under that character; that by such acceptance, it may place itself in the condition of having given equivalents for nominal favors, and yet of being reproached with ingratitude for not giving more. There can be no greater error than to expect or calculate upon real favors from nation to nation. 'Tis an illusion which experience must cure, which a just pride ought to discard. In offering to you, my countrymen, these counsels of an old and affectionate friend, I dare not hope they will make the strong and lasting impression. I could wish that they will control the usual current of the passions or prevent our nation from running the course which has hitherto marked the destiny of nations. But, if I may even flatter myself, that they may be productive of some partial benefit, some occasional good; that they may now and then recur to moderate the fury of party spirit; to warn against the mischiefs of foreign intrigue; to guard against the impostures of pretended patriotism. This hope will be a full recompense for the solicitude for your welfare by which they have been dictated. How far in the discharge of my official duties I have been guided by the principles which have been delineated, the public records, and other evidences of my conduct must witness to you and to the world. To myself, the assurance of my own conscience is that I have at least believed myself to be guided by them.

In relation to the still subsisting war in Europe, my proclamation of the 22nd of April 1793 is the index to my plan. Sanctioned by your approving voice and by that of your representatives in both houses of Congress, the spirit of that measure has continually governed me, uninfluenced by any attempts to deter or divert me from it. After deliberate examination with the aid of the best lights I could obtain, I was well satisfied that our country, under all the circumstances of the case, had a right to take, and was bound in duty and interest to take a neutral position. Having taken it, I determined, as far as should depend upon me, to maintain it, with moderation, perseverance, and firmness. The considerations, which respect the right to hold this conduct, it is not necessary on this occasion to detail. I will only observe that according to my understanding of the matter, that right, so far from being denied by any of the belligerent powers, has been virtually admitted by all. The duty of holding a neutral conduct may be inferred, without anything more, from the obligation which justice and humanity impose on every nation, in cases in which it is free to act to maintain inviolate the relations of peace and amity toward other nations. The inducements of interest for observing that conduct will best be referred to your own reflections and experience. With me, a predominant motive has been to endeavor to gain time to our country, to settle and mature its yet recent institutions, and to progress without interruption to that degree of strength and consistency which is necessary to give it, humanly speaking, the command of its own fortunes.

Though in reviewing the incidents of my administration, I am unconscious of intentional error. I am, nevertheless, too sensible of my defects not to think it probable that I may have committed many errors. Whatever they may be, I fervently beseech the Almighty to avert or mitigate the evils to which they may tend. I shall also carry with me the hope that my country will never cease to view them with indulgence; and that after forty-five years of my life dedicated to its service with an upright zeal, the faults of incompetent abilities will be consigned to oblivion, as myself must soon be to the mansions of rest. Relying on its kindness, in this as in other things, and actuated by that fervent love toward it, which is so natural to a man who views in it the native soil of himself and his progenitors for several generations, I anticipate with pleasing expectation that retreat in which I promise myself to realize, without alloy, the sweet enjoyment of partaking in the midst of my fellow citizens; the benign influence of good laws under a free government; the ever favorite object of my heart; and the happy reward, as I trust, of our mutual cares, labors, and dangers.

Forty-Seven

THE END OF THE PRESIDENCY

(1796–1797)

While Washington's Farewell Address was in preparation, the foreign problems of the United States reversed direction. The British honored Washington's request that they withdraw the Provision Order, and they peaceably evacuated the northwestern forts on schedule. The commissions the Jay Treaty had established were with mutual toleration examining the claims of unpaid prerevolutionary British creditors on one hand and those of the more recently plundered American shipowners on the other. But when a copy of the Jay Treaty reached Paris, the French reacted with fury.

Washington had no specific knowledge of the correspondence that passed in cipher between opposition leaders at home (principally Madison and Jefferson) and Monroe, who was supposed to be representing Washington's government in Paris. However, Washington suspected that the French had been egged into protest "by communications of influential men in *this* country through a medium [Monroe] which ought to be the last to engage in it." He concluded that if war were to break out with France, "it originated here not there."

The French liked to feel that their relationship was with the American people rather than with Washington's government. Monroe was glad to describe that government as reactionary and regard himself as a representative of the people. He had begun his mission by presenting to the French National Convention an American flag with a statement that practically declared a new Franco-American alliance. This had embarrassed Jay's negotiation.

As soon as Monroe heard that a treaty had been signed, he asked Jay for a copy to give the French. If Jay had not refused, Paris would have had the treaty months before it reached the United States. When—it was after the Senate had approved—the treaty did finally reach France, Monroe was as outraged as was the government to whom he was supposed to justify his own government's acts. He felt that he himself had been perfidiously used as a decoy to keep the French passive while a treaty was negotiated which neither he nor the French would approve. The radical American citizen, Thomas Paine, was Monroe's houseguest, and both expressed their indignation to any Frenchman who would listen.

The official French protest against the treaty was dated March 11, 1796. It testified to Jay's skill as a lawyer by not even attempting to demonstrate specific legal infractions of the old Franco-American treaties. But it insisted that what had in essence been an all-out alliance with France had been replaced by an alliance with England. As was made manifest by another French reaction that was reported to Washington, the government in Paris believed that all those who were not altogether on their side were against them. They now regarded the government of the United States (although not the American people, whom they considered the victims of repression) as an active enemy.

Monroe and others notified Washington of a French threat to send a fleet to the United States with a special representative "directed to exact in the space of fifteen days a categorical answer to certain questions." Washington's relief when the issue faded away was quickly tempered by word that the French, popping in and out of their West Indian harbors, were violating provisions in the old Franco-American treaty by destroying the lucrative American trade to the British islands. American voices were not lacking to reinforce the claim which the French minister to the United States, Pierre Adet, released to the opposition press: the French depredations were an inevitable and legitimate result of the Jay Treaty.

To defuse the situation with France, Washington wished to appoint a special envoy, but felt he could not do so since the Senate, not being in session, could not give consent. However, his advisers ruled that he might, in the interim, replace one regularly appointed minister with another. Monroe was a liability; he would be recalled. But where would Washington find a replacement who "would not be obnoxious to one party or the other"? Seeking a reliable southerner who was *persona grata* to the Jeffersonians, he had the good fortune to secure, on his second try, the South Carolinian Charles Cotesworth Pinckney, whose older brother, Thomas Pinckney, had negotiated the triumphant treaty with Spain and recently resigned as minister to London.

As Charles Pinckney sailed, it was far from sure that he would be received by the French. They had been threatening to break off diplomatic relations with the United States. Their minister in Philadelphia was again in the newspapers, this time with a long list of decisions made in enforcing the Neutrality Proclamation which the French insisted violated the old Franco-American treaties.

Increasingly, Washington, who had formerly wished to control every executive act, shied away from attending to business.

From an opposition press, there roared a pamphlet, entitled *Letter to Washington,* by the author of *Common Sense,* whom Washington had during the Revolution supported and befriended. Paine now insisted that Washington had conspired with the French government to have him guillotined lest he expose the frightful tyranny that existed in the United States.* Paine went over all of Washington's career in a tone of insult, and insisted that every American act which displeased France was both illegal and damaging to the reputation of the United States. His peroration read, "As to you, sir, treacherous in private friendship (for so you have been to me and that in the day of danger) and a hypocrite in public life, the world will be puzzled to decide whether you are an apostate or an impostor; whether you have abandoned good principles or whether you ever had any."

Washington believed that this publication had been inspired by the French propaganda machine.

* Although Paine had served in the French National Convention, the English-born agitator had insisted that since he remained an American citizen, it was Washington's duty to extract him from the jail in which he had been placed for his activities in the French government. Washington, who felt that American neutrality prevented him from intervening even in favor of his spiritual son, Lafayette, made no exception for Paine.

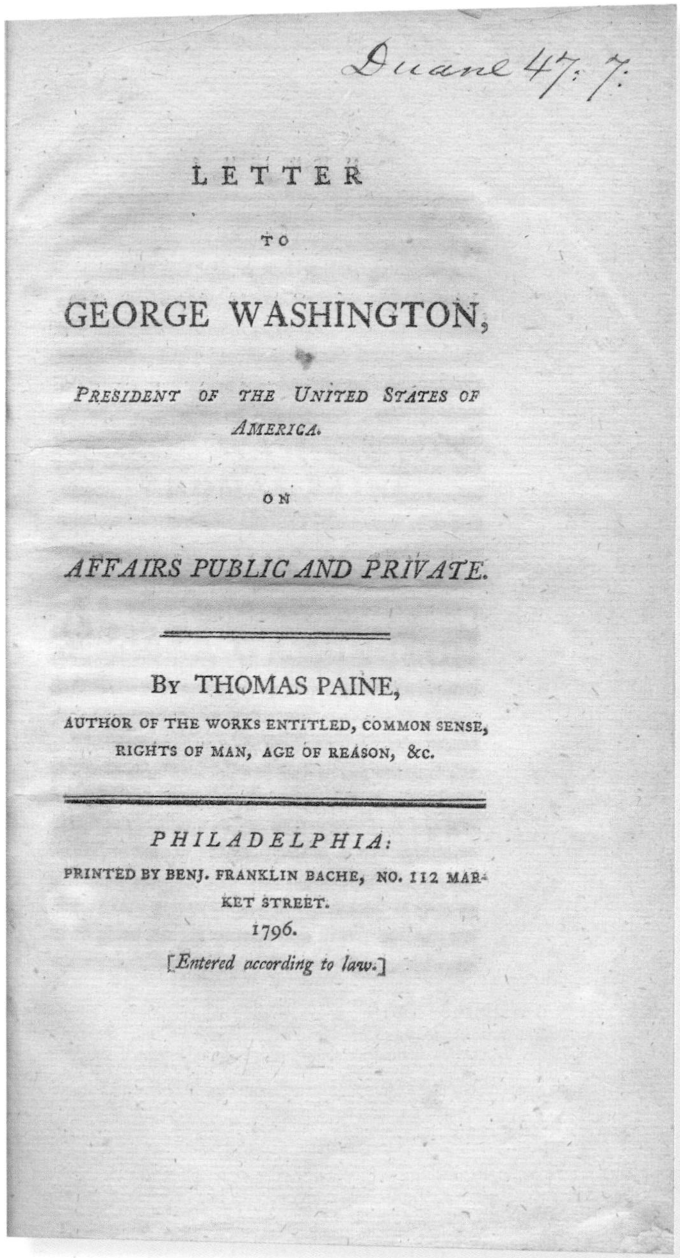

Duane 47: 7:

LETTER

TO

GEORGE WASHINGTON,

PRESIDENT OF THE UNITED STATES OF AMERICA.

ON

AFFAIRS PUBLIC AND PRIVATE.

BY THOMAS PAINE,

AUTHOR OF THE WORKS ENTITLED, COMMON SENSE, RIGHTS OF MAN, AGE OF REASON, &c.

PHILADELPHIA:

PRINTED BY BENJ. FRANKLIN BACHE, NO. 112 MARKET STREET.

1796.

[*Entered according to law.*]

Letter to George Washington *by Thomas Paine, Philadelphia, 1796.*

He was furious to have old forgeries, published by the Tories during the Revolution to prove him at heart a pro-British traitor, revived "with the highest emblazoning of which they are susceptible, with a view to attach principles to me which every action of my life have given lie to."

The Federalists around Washington were able to demonstrate that Monroe had, under false identification, been writing pro-French propaganda for the American opposition press. It was charged that he was secretly assisting a renewed effort to raise an army of Americans that would settle French power on the continent by capturing Louisiana. And Adet was clearly intervening, through his official statements as French minister, in the coming election, in order to insure the choice of Jefferson as president.

Aging men are often oversusceptible to suspicions. When a Philadelphia paper reported that Washington had been in a carriage accident, he believed the misinformation had been published for some "insidious purpose.... Evidence enough has been given that truth or falsehood is equally used and indifferent to that class of men."

Washington was now dwelling on the fact that, although the old Franco-American treaty had established between the signers the principle that free ships make free goods, the French were applying to American ships the much more stringent rules accepted in Anglo-American relations by the Jay Treaty. Since Washington had believed that nations could not rationally be expected to abide by treaties that were manifestly to their disadvantage, he would surely, as a younger man, have realized that the French could not be expected to allow the British so great an advantage. But now, since his own government had managed by legerdemain to adhere to the letter of the old treaties, he was tempted into accusing the French of perfidy. Furthermore, he warmed up personally to Jay, towards whom he had felt coldly since the treaty came in; and began to defend the treaty itself, concerning which he had not previously gone beyond the statement that under the circumstances he had no choice but to sign it.

Increasingly, Washington, who had formerly wished to control every executive act, shied away from attending to business. Back at Mount Vernon after publishing his Farewell Address, he wrote Secretary of State Pickering, whom he did not really trust, only to bother him if something momentous happened. And he broke off an important letter to Hamilton by stating that he was too "fatigued with this and other matters which crowd upon me" to write further.

Washington's final public appearance was to be his Eighth Annual Address, delivered on December 7, 1796, some three months before his term ended. That morning, his friend Eliza Powel sent to Martha a remedy for indigestion. She urged that the president "take a glass on his return from the Congress. I know his sensibility, diffidence, and delicacy too well not to believe that his spirits will be not a little agitated on the solemn and I fear last occasion that he will take of addressing his fellow citizens. He appears to have an invincible diffidence of his own abilities."

Another lady who admired Washington, the new British minister's blond and charming Scottish wife, Henrietta Liston, was present in the Senate chamber: "I happened to sit very near him and . . . I had an opportunity to see the extreme agitation he felt when he mentioned the *French*. He is, I believe, much enraged; this is the second French minister who has insulted him to the people."

He seemed, so Adams wrote, "to enjoy a triumph over me. Methought I heard him say, 'Ay, I'm fairly out and you're fairly in. See which of us will be happiest!'"

Washington's references to England showed the Jay Treaty being smoothly applied towards future amity. Very different were his references to France: "Our trade had suffered and is suffering extensive injuries in the West Indies from the cruisers and agents of the French republic, and communications have been received from its minister here which indicate the danger of a further disturbance of our commerce." Although he stated that he kept "unabated" his desire for harmony with France, he warned that he could not "forget what is due to the character of our government and nation."

Thus, in his very last address as president, Washington swerved from his invariable policy of balancing the hostile behavior of the two major European belligerents. During the final months of his presidency he was, indeed, inclining towards the anti-French, pro-Federalist position which he had been accused by his enemies of having always occupied.

During the election, however, Washington adhered to his highest principles. The stakes, he felt, were much higher than any partisanship, so high that risks would have to be taken concerning what would happen after the hand was played. He saw the election as a potential demonstration to all the world that republican institutions were, in their purity, viable.

He was, indeed, personally establishing a precedent that extended the Constitution. Despite much discussion of the issue, that document had not limited the number of terms a president could serve. The establishment of the vice presidency permitted succession in the monarchical manner: the president, again and again reelected if he pleased the people, would be, on his death, succeeded by his preestablished heir. Even Jefferson, during his period of closeness with Washington, had been content with the thought that the first president would serve out his lifetime. But Washington wished the succession to be determined, in an absolutely republican manner, by the ballot box. This would be the culmination of his own career, his final gift to the world.*

Perhaps it was Washington's realization of his own tremendous power that made him feel that if he intervened in an election he would prevent the people from making their own choice. In any case, he adhered to the resolution he had made when lesser offices were in the balance that he would play absolutely no role in the election. He had no intention of being publicly identified with either the Republicans or the Federalists. Although he believed that Jefferson had betrayed him personally and might well betray the nation to France, the old hero made absolutely no move to block Jefferson's road to the presidency.

The Federalist candidate, John Adams, won, but, owing to a confusion in the Federalist vote for vice president, Jefferson came into that office. Washington made no recorded comment.

If Washington had believed that because he had taken no part in the election, he would finally escape abuse, he was sadly disappointed. The Federalists had used every opportunity to point out that, unlike the Republicans, they had been loyal to Washington. Republican propagandists still felt that establishing the prestige of their party depended on demolishing the prestige of Washington.

In one of his last acts in the presidency, Washington wrote, "To the wearied traveler who sees a resting place and is bending his body to lean thereon, I now compare myself, but to be suffered to do *this* in peace is, I perceive, too much to be endured by *some*. To misrepresent my motives, to reprobate my politics, and to weaken the confidence which has been reposed in my administration are objects which cannot be relinquished by those who will be satisfied by nothing short of a change in our political system."

* The precedent Washington established, that a president should retire after two terms, held until it was breached by Franklin Delano Roosevelt. It was then formally written into the Constitution.

George Washington (The Athenaeum Portrait), *by Gilbert Stuart, oil on canvas, 1796. William Francis Warden Fund, John H. and Ernestine A. Payne Fund, Commonwealth Cultural Preservation Trust. Jointly owned by the Museum of Fine Arts, Boston, and the National Portrait Gallery, Washington, D.C. The most famous and celebrated of Gilbert Stuart's likenesses of Washington is known as the Athenaeum Portrait, and appears on the one-dollar bill. Stuart and his daughters painted a total of 130 reproductions of the Athenaeum, though he never completed the original version, which hangs still unfinished in Boston's Museum of Fine Arts.*

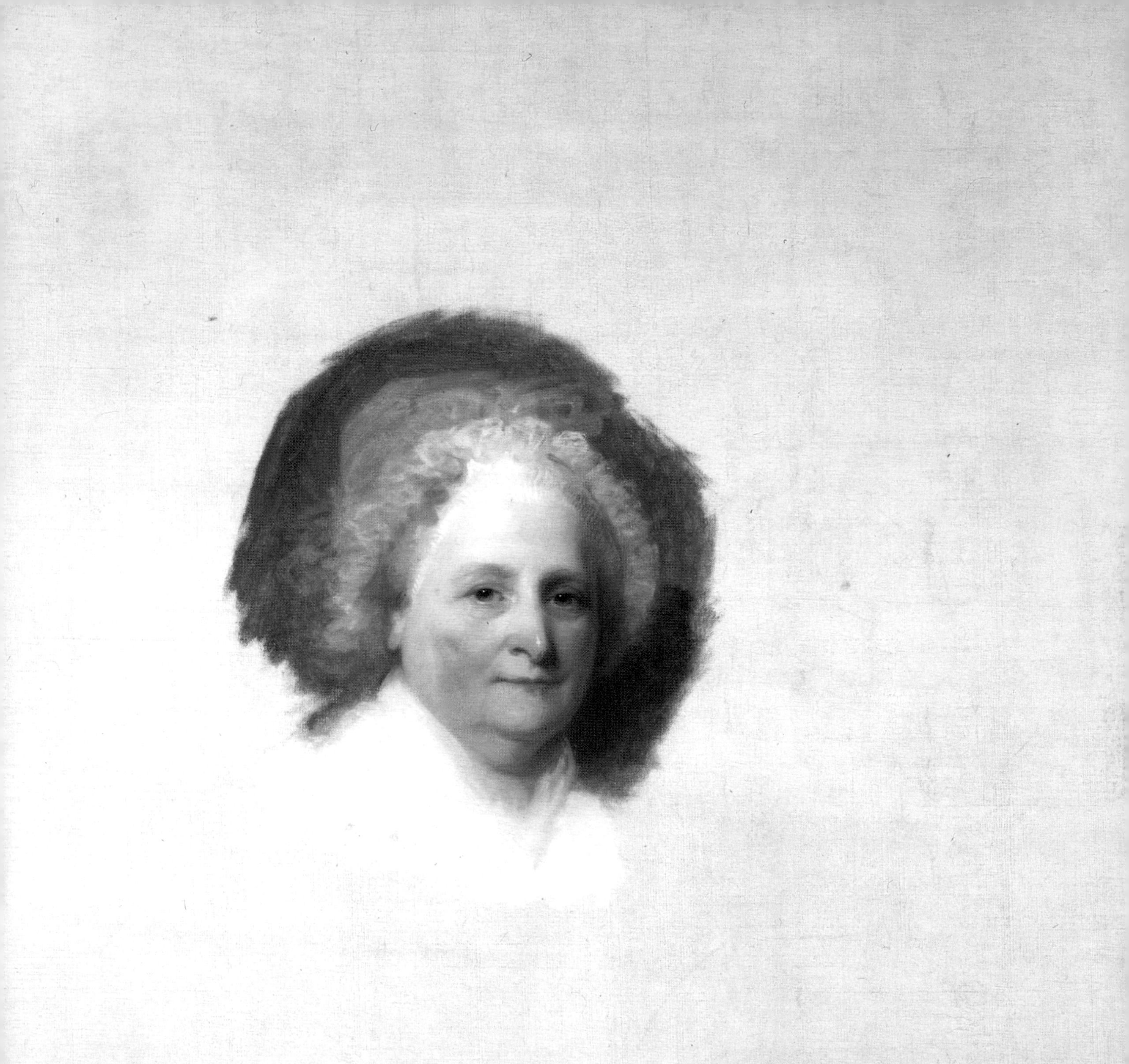

Martha Washington (The Athenaeum Portrait), *by Gilbert Stuart, oil on canvas, 1796. William Francis Warden Fund, John H. and Ernestine A. Payne Fund, Commonwealth Cultural Preservation Trust. Jointly owned by the Museum of Fine Arts, Boston, and the National Portrait Gallery, Washington, D.C. Though not as well known, Gilbert Stuart completed an Athenaeum portrait of Martha Washington as well.*

Adams's inauguration proved, however, that love for the hero had not died. No man in all probability had been so deeply jealous of George Washington for so long a time as the president-elect. He looked forward to having the spotlight turn to him at last, away from the tall Virginian whom he considered uneducated, unintellectual—and lucky. But when Adams, his short, rotund body resplendent in a pearlcolored suit, appeared in the chamber of the House to take the oath, most of the eyes that turned to him were wet. And in a moment, the eyes turned back to Washington, who was sitting, in an old-fashioned black coat, to one side of the dais.

Adams complained to his wife of "the full eyes, the streaming eyes, the trickling eyes, etc." Adams's situation was made even less satisfactory by the expression on the retiring president's face. He seemed, so Adams wrote, "to enjoy a triumph over me. Methought I heard him say, 'Ay, I'm fairly out and you're fairly in. See which of us will be happiest!'"

When Adams had taken the oath, made his speech, and departed, when the inauguration was over, the audience rushed after Washington to the street. They followed him towards the Francis Hotel, where he intended to congratulate the new president. As Washington went through the door and the door closed behind him, the crowd, seeing their hero pass from them, made "a sound like thunder."

Forty-Eight

HOME AGAIN

(1797–1799)

During Washington's eight years in office, almost all the "public" furnishings which Congress had supplied for the presidential mansion had been worn out or broken. He had replaced almost everything, sometimes several times, at his own expense, and usually elegantly. He believed in upholding the dignity of his office, and could not himself bear to live shoddily. Since Congress had given John Adams $14,000 to buy presidential furniture, Washington tried to sell what he had himself bought to his successor at what he said were bargain prices. The fine furnishings still seemed to the New Englander expensive. He confided to his wife that "everyone cheats as much as he can" and that Washington "says he must sell something in order to clear out." Yet Adams was so tempted that he allowed Washington to depart for Mount Vernon with the false hope that the basic furnishings of the main reception room would stay in place.

Washington was on the whole glad that Adams did not take the paintings. As a collector of art, Washington was several generations ahead of the taste of his time. Not that he set out to be pacemaking. Typically, he followed, indifferent to convention, his own interests.

One might assume that, being himself a historical hero, he would take naturally to what was then considered the "high style": elaborate compositions that depicted in an "elevated," supposedly inspiring manner great moments out of history or legend. Insofar as they reproduced the work of American artists resident in London—West, Copley, Trumbull—Washington did buy engravings after such compositions, but for the large oil paintings that were the most ambitious of his artistic purchases, he demanded a type of painting scorned by "correct" connoisseurs.

In his neoclassical time, when the proper study of man was considered to be man, to depict landscape was regarded as trivial and mean. Washington was indifferent to such theorizing. As he dreamed in a city of rivers, fields, and forests, the frontiersman and farmer limited his major patronage to landscapes. And he insisted that the painters—the Anglo-Americans William Winstanley and George Beck—play down those evidences of man-made refinements which gave the landscape art of his day what small value it was correctly admitted to have. Commissioning depictions of American scenery at its wildest, Washington anticipated by several generations the mid-nineteenth-century conceptions of the Hudson River School.

After he had got rid of everything that he could which he considered superfluous, Washington still had to hire a sloop to take the residue to his wharf on the Potomac. Breakables were stowed into his carriage around the bodies of his coachman and family. He wrote with the high spirits of a beleaguered family man, "On one side, I am called upon to remember the parrot; on the

Photographed by Israel & Biddle expressly for H. E. Hoyt & Co. No. 41 Baltimore Street, Baltimore Md.
THE
HOME OF WASHINGTON.
As it appeared May 14th 1859.
Gift No 139

This rare antebellum salted paper print by Israel and Biddle is the earliest known photograph of Mount Vernon. Still in its original mount with lithographed title and decorative border, it records the appearance of the mansion in May 1859, a year before the Mount Vernon Ladies' Association opened it to the public. Taken from a northeast perspective, it shows the masts of ships that were used to prop up the roof after several columns on the piazza rotted away.

other, to remember the dog. For my own part, I should not pine if they were both forgot."

On March 15, 1797, the coach rumbled up the bell-shaped drive to Mount Vernon. Washington promised himself "more real enjoyment than in all the business with which I have been occupied for upwards of forty years." All that business seemed to him now "little more than vanity and vexation." He would view the world "in the calm lights of mild philosophy."

But mild philosophy received a severe shock when "more by accident than design" he discovered that the great girder which supported his banquet hall was so decayed that "a company only moderately large would have sunk altogether into the cellar." Washington's "long forsaken residence at Mount Vernon" was dilapidated everywhere. He ordered such a flood of repairs "that I have scarcely a room to put a friend into or set in myself without the music of hammers or the odoriferous smell of paint." Seven months later he was still at it, and complaining: "Workmen in most countries, I believe, are necessary plagues. In this, where entreaties as well as money must be used to obtain their work . . . they baffle all calculation." He could fill several pages "with the perplexities I experience daily from workmen."

Washington's farms were in an even worse situation than his buildings, and that situation was much more difficult to remedy.

The workmen had their problems, too. Washington rose with the sun. "If my hirelings are not in their places at that time, I send them messages expressive of my sorrow for their indisposition. Then, having put these wheels in motion, I examine the state of things further," always finding more "wounds" in his structures that needed to be healed. At a little after seven o'clock, breakfast was ready. "This over, I mount my horse and ride round my farms, which employs me until it is time to dress for dinner, at which I rarely miss seeing strange faces, come, as they say, out of respect to me. Pray, would not the word curiosity answer as well? And how different this from having a few social friends at a cheerful board!

"The usual time of sitting at table, a walk, and tea, brings me within the dawn of candlelight, previous to which, if not prevented by company, I resolve that as soon as the glimmering taper supplies the place of the great luminary, I will retire to my writing table and acknowledge the letters I have received, but when the lights are brought, I feel tired and disinclined to engage in this work, conceiving that the next night will do as well. . . .

"Having given you the history of a day, it will serve for a year. . . . It may strike you that in this detail no mention is made . . . of reading. . . . I have not looked into a book since I came home, nor shall I be able to do it until I have discharged my workmen . . . when possibly I may be looking in doomsday book."

Doomsday book! Washington, so brave on battlefields, had always, in times of quiet, seen death stalking him. Now the fear was surely more than an insubstantial vision. He hoped, he wrote, that esteem of good men and his consciousness of having done the best for his country would "alleviate pain and soften any cares which are yet to be encountered—though hid from me at present."

Washington's farms were in an even worse situation than his buildings, and that situation was much more difficult to remedy. When, years before, he had taken over Mount Vernon, the soil had already been depleted. While he had been in residence, he had labored to enrich the land with crop rotation and fertilizers; he had tried, by perpetual attention to drainage ditches, to protect the thin topsoil from erosion. Now all was a shambles. Measly crops drooped in fields torn with gullies; the "live fences" were more gap than hedge; his horses, sheep, and cows had become smaller and weaker through inattention to breeding.

His plight was particularly brought home to Washington when the English author of *The Experienced Farmer,* Richard Parkinson, appeared in anticipation of renting one of the Mount Vernon farms. Washington expressed himself as "much flattered" by the visit of so celebrated an agriculturalist, but Parkinson noted that the general was soon "not well pleased with my conversation." The English farmer told the American hero that the barrenness of Mount Vernon was "beyond description." If Washington were to offer him twelve hundred acres as a present, he would not accept them.

To justify such strictures, Parkinson had, of course, to treat Washington "with a great deal of frankness. . . . I gave him strong proofs of his mistakes" by comparing Mount Vernon with English farms. Washington had on three thousand acres a mere one hundred sheep, while Parkinson's own father had only six hundred acres yet clipped eleven hundred sheep. The father got ten pounds of wool per fleece; the American, not three. The elder Parkinson grew ten times as much wheat per acre as the general did—and so on down through all Washington's farming activities and possessions, except his mules. Parkinson admired Washington's mules.

Upgrading Mount Vernon once more was made endlessly more difficult by a human hangover of Washington's presidency. When trapped in Philadelphia, Washington had yearned for an estate manager who would not sicken or move away and, towards the end of his second term, he had found one, an elderly Scot named James Anderson. Anderson had contributed to the cash income of Mount Vernon by getting Washington on a large scale into the distilling of whiskey. But in relation to the farms, he proved, after Washington's return, a thorn in the proprietor's side.

To Washington's comments on deficiencies everywhere, Anderson promised that all would be immediately rectified. Yet, as Washington rode around grimly, he could see nothing achieved. Turning on his estate manager all the lofty anger of an ex-commander in chief and ex-president, Washington thundered that such inefficiency "is not at all pleasant to a man who has practiced himself, and been accustomed to meet as much regularity as I have from others." Anderson replied unhappily that he would resign.

Washington considered it "strange and singular indeed" if a proprietor could not say anything without offending his manager. But he made a tactful effort to persuade the Scot to accept reduced responsibilities at no reduction of salary: he should manage the distillery, the commercial mill with its automated equipment, and some of the fisheries, leaving immediate supervision of the farms to Washington. Anderson replied that he was primarily a farmer. Washington yearned to discharge the troublesome subordinate but found himself "unwilling by any act of mine to hurt his feelings or . . . to lessen his respectability in the eyes of the public." He continued to accept the bumbling intervention that made even less possible the task of getting Mount Vernon back into shape during the few years that the proprietor assumed were left to him.

Even before the presidency, when Mount Vernon had been operating with maximum efficiency, Washington had been unable to live on the income it produced. Now the situation was, of course, much worse. He wrote in 1799, "Were it not for occasional supplies of money in payment for lands sold within the last four or five years to the amount of upwards of $50,000" (more than half a million in modern currency), he would be "in debt and difficulties."

During those economically troubled years, Washington's success as a land speculator was phenomenal. While he prospered, many of the nation's financial leaders, including the great Robert Morris himself, were carried by the collapse of their real estate schemes into debtors' prison.

During those economically troubled years, Washington's success as a land speculator was phenomenal. While he prospered, many of the nation's financial leaders, including the great Robert Morris himself, were carried by the collapse of their real estate schemes into debtors' prison. Not the least of the reasons that Washington was an exception was that he made no use of the financial facilities created by Hamilton. He did not expand his credit with the practice, so treacherous

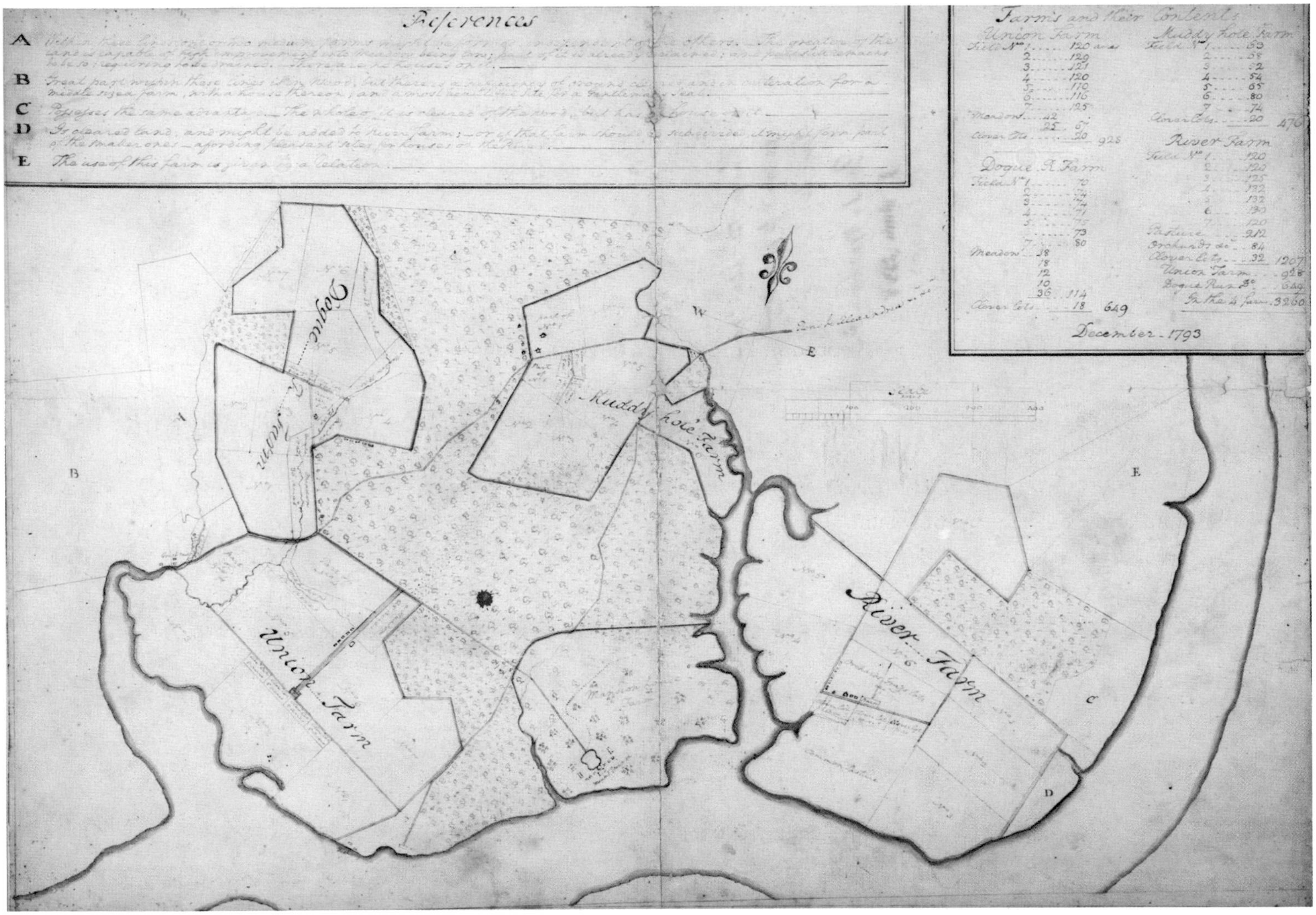

Washington's own survey of the Mount Vernon plantation, made in December 1793.

in time of sinking values, of "pyramiding": borrowing on assets that had themselves been purchased with the help of loans. Adhering to the economics of a farmer rather than a financial entrepreneur, Washington wrote, "It has been a maxim with me from early life never to undertake anything without perceiving a door to the accomplishment in a reasonable amount of time with my own resources."

An endemic problem of speculators in western land was how to find out about and successfully administer properties far from their countinghouses. But Washington could find in every community men glad to be in communication with so celebrated a man. Only a few years before, he had leaned over backwards not to take advantage of his eminence. Now he was completely shameless, asking government officials and private individuals to assess the value of tracts, see to surveying and improvements, advise him as to the reliability of respective buyers, collect sums due to

George Washington *by Charles Willson Peale, detail, oil on canvas, 1795.*

him, and so on. For the services of gentlemen, he never offered payment, but asked their permission to reimburse actual outlays. Only in matters too minor "to trouble my friends with," did he employ agents.

Washington was further helped by the fact that he had begun his purchases of western lands when he was a teenager almost a half century before. The tracts in the Shenandoah Valley where he had practiced as a surveyor and in western Pennsylvania where he had fought were now worth more than a hundred times what he had then paid.

Like all other possessors of western acres, Washington had great difficulty achieving sales. The war had blocked the flow of well-off European immigrants who had previously bought western land. And French depredations on American commerce had created a general depression. Since crops could not be exported safely, their value dropped. Few men desired more land to farm. Thus Washington usually could only sell to speculators who bought in expectation of a rise in values.

Such men were looking to the future rather than the present, and cash was, in any case, scarce. Thus Washington could not expect to get the whole purchase price in cash. The less credit he would give, the lower the amount he could ask. And a universal lack of liquid assets made it difficult to distinguish between reliable purchasers and those who could only complete their payments if fortune took a lucky turn.

In this welter, Washington operated with the dogged persistence which had stood him in good stead as general and president. He bought shrewdly and was an eager salesman, extolling his property. He kept a sharp eye on all details. Almost always unwilling to go to law—he disliked proceedings which distressed the helpless—he fired off many angry letters. He was often forced to accept a loss or take his land back, yet enough cash did come in to enable him to continue his style of living with only an occasional financial squeeze.

In July 1799, Washington assessed his still unsold land at $488,137 (several millions in modern currency). This estimate was based on what he considered foreseeable increases in value, and was thus optimistic, but it was not vaguely visionary.

Washington's financial success was based altogether on his own efforts. He had no business staff. And for many years he had been able to devote to his affairs only what little time he could disentangle from the most demanding of public pursuits. Clearly, he had great business gifts.

By temperament, Washington could never lie easy. For all his prosperity, he was perpetually worried about his finances. These worries were greatly enhanced during his very last years by an effort he made to help along that darling among his projects, the new national capital, which was now firmly named "Washington." The government was due to move there in 1800, but the general financial confusion had bankrupted the real estate operators who had agreed to build the necessary housing and had even contracted to advance money to complete the government buildings.

The former general could be high-spirited about the matter, as when he wrote: "Oh well, they can camp out. The Representatives in the first line, the Senate in the second, the president and his suite in the middle." However, he felt called upon to erect twin buildings, which he himself designed, intended to form a boardinghouse that would, in its sixteen bedrooms, accommodate twenty to thirty congressmen. He thought he had an innkeeper lined up to take over, but when the crucial moment came, the prospect did not even answer letters. Washington found that, to pay the builders, whose charges he considered wildly exorbitant, he had to enter "a new scene." He had to borrow money from a bank.

Again and again the ex-president expressed horror at having been forced into "a measure I never in the course of my life had practiced." The luxury of his mansion house, the spreading farms at Mount

Vernon, the deeds to extensive lands stowed away in his strongbox, all seemed, when the old farmer awoke in the nights, evanescent. He was terrified to think that he had been reduced to "a necessity of borrowing from the banks at a ruinous interest."

On leaving Philadelphia after the end of the presidency, Washington, feeling that a personal farewell "is not among the pleasantest circumstances of one's life," had said good-bye to Mrs. Powel in a letter. He soon heard from his flirtatious friend, to whom he had sold his personal desk: "I take up my pen to address you, as you have given me a complete triumph on the subject of all others on which you have I suppose thought me most deficient and most opposite to yourself." She had found in a secret drawer a packet of love letters from a lady. "What," Eliza asked, "will the goddess of prudence and circumspection say to her favorite son and votary for his dereliction of principles to which he has hitherto made such serious sacrifices?" Eliza kept Washington in suspense until she finally admitted that the letters were from Martha.

Washington replied that if he had had love letters to lose, Eliza's long preamble "might have tried how far my nerves were able to sustain the shock of having betrayed the confidence of a lady." If Eliza had not been too discreet to peek, she would have found Martha's letters "more fraught with expressions of friendship than of *enamoured* love." A reader "of the *romantic order*" could only have given the sheets "warmth" by setting them on fire.*

Below: *This book, owned by Washington, is a part of William Curtis's series of thirteen volumes of* The Botanical Magazine, *and carries Washington's signature on the title page. Its contents include the characteristics, history, and common names of a variety of plants, along with a hand-colored copper engraving of each one.*

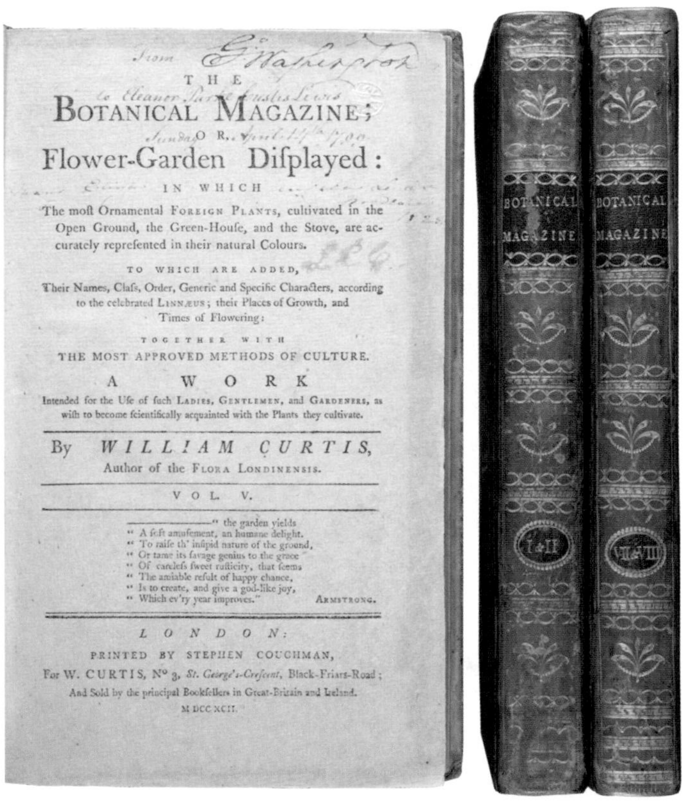
THE
BOTANICAL MAGAZINE;
OR,
Flower-Garden Difplayed:
IN WHICH
The moft Ornamental FOREIGN PLANTS, cultivated in the Open Ground, the Green-Houfe, and the Stove, are accurately reprefented in their natural Colours.
TO WHICH ARE ADDED,
Their Names, Clafs, Order, Generic and Specific Characters, according to the celebrated LINNÆUS; their Places of Growth, and Times of Flowering:
TOGETHER WITH
THE MOST APPROVED METHODS OF CULTURE.
A WORK
Intended for the Ufe of fuch LADIES, GENTLEMEN, and GARDENERS, as wifh to become fcientifically acquainted with the Plants they cultivate.
By WILLIAM CURTIS,
Author of the FLORA LONDINENSIS.
VOL. V.
———" the garden yields
" A foft amufement, an humane delight.
" To raife th' infipid nature of the ground,
" Or tame its favage genius to the grace
" Of carelefs fweet rufticity, that feems
" The amiable refult of happy chance,
" Is to create, and give a god-like joy,
" Which ev'ry year improves." ARMSTRONG.
LONDON:
PRINTED BY STEPHEN COUCHMAN,
For W. CURTIS, N° 3, *St. George's-Crefcent*, Black-Friars-Road;
And Sold by the principal Bookfellers in Great-Britain and Ireland.
M DCC XCII.

Opposite: *At the recommendation of his new farm manager, Scotsman James Anderson, Washington began building a rye and corn whiskey distillery at Mount Vernon in 1797. In operation by spring 1798, the distillery did a brisk business. This ledger records over eighty transactions in 1799, for a total sale of 10,942 gallons of whiskey valued at $7,674. It also lists the business details of a fishery located on the distillery site, where herring caught in the Potomac were salted and barreled for sale and shipment. These business ventures were little known but important aspects of Washington's later years.*

* This description of Washington's relationship with Martha may, of course, have been influenced by his attitude towards his correspondent: no man sends to a lady he admires expressions of passionate affection for his wife. However, what Washington wrote Eliza is our best information on the tenor of his correspondence with Martha. After his death, his wife, probably as a possessive reaction to having been forced to share her husband so extensively with the public, burned their letters to each other.

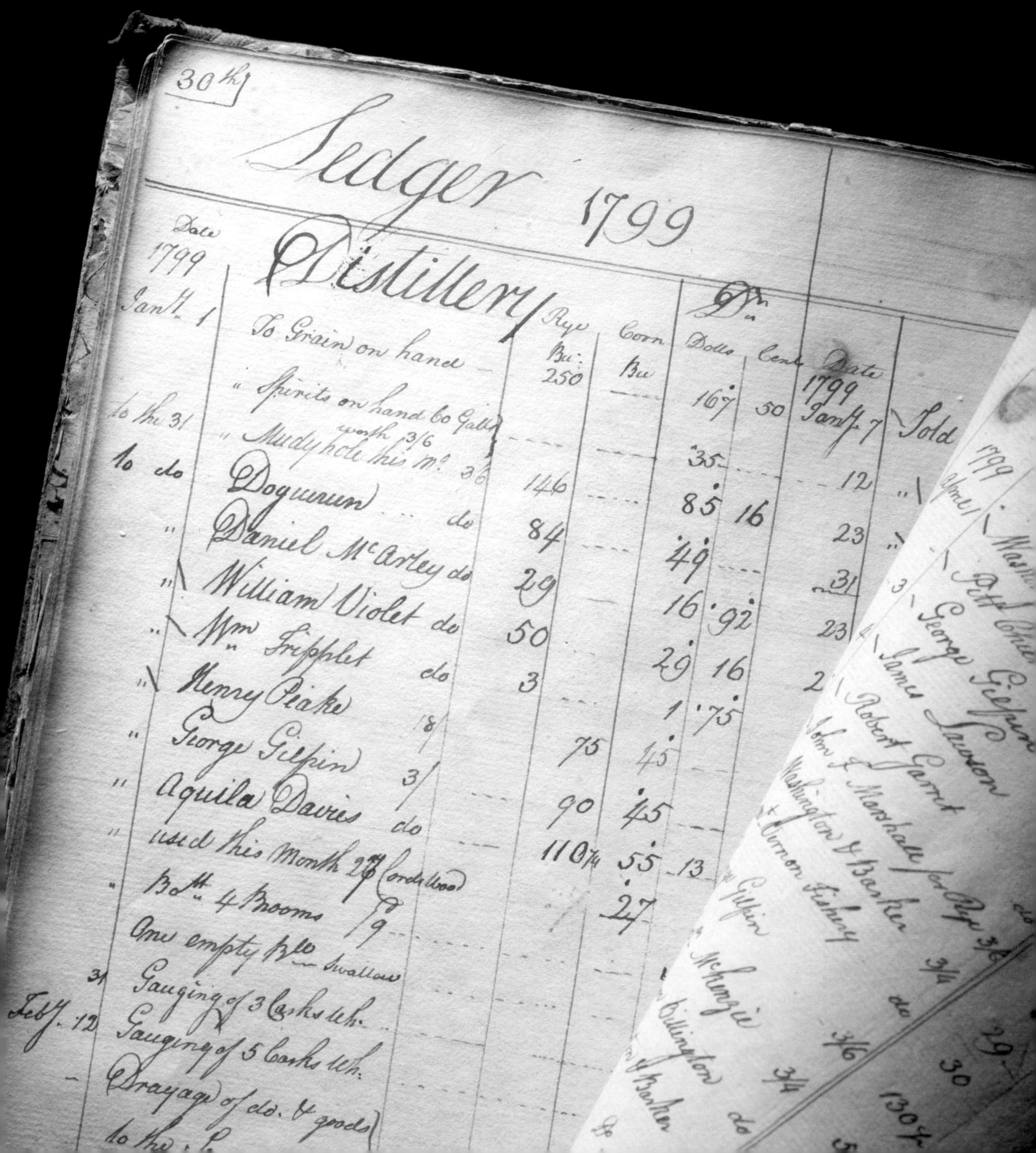

30th

Ledger 1799

Distillery Dr.

Date 1799			Rye Bu	Corn Bu	Dolls	Cents	Date 1799	
Jany. 1	To Grain on hand		250					
	" Spirits on hand 60 Gall worth 3/6				167	50	Jany. 7	Sold
to the 31	" Muddyhole this Mo.	3/6			35		12	
to do	Doguerun	do	146		85	16		
"	Daniel McCartey	do	84		49		23	
"	William Violet	do	29		16	92	31	
"	Wm. Tripplet	do	50		29	16	23	
"	Henry Peake		3		1	75	2	
"	George Gilpin	18/		75	45			
"	Aquila Davies	3/		90	45			
"	used this Month	do	110 3/4	55				
"	27 Cords Wood				13			
"	Bott. 4 Brooms	1/9			27			
	One empty Bbl. — Swallow							
31	Gauging of 3 Casks &c.							
Feby. 12	Gauging of 5 Casks &c.							
—	Drayage of do. & goods							
	to the 1							

1799

Jany. 1 — Washington
Pitt Chew...
3 — George Gilpin
4 — James Lawson
Robert Garrett
John & Marshall for Rye 3/6
Washington & Barker 3/4
& Vernon Fishery do
Gilpin 3/6 29
McKenzie 3/4 30
Billington do 130
& Barker

MARTHA AND GEORGE'S GRANDCHILDREN

DETAILS OF FAMILY PORTRAITS BY ROBERT EDGE PINE

Eleanor Parke Custis (Nelly)

George Washington Parke Custis (Washy)

Elizabeth Parke Custis

Martha Parke Custis (Patty)

Many legends circulate as to Washington's sexuality. The man who was probably sterile is said to have been a eunuch, even a woman in disguise; he is said to have been known as "the stallion of the Potomac." Eliza, who was surely in the best position to know, testifies to his continence in his later years. Although he undoubtedly had his fling when a young man, no one has ever discovered any authentic evidence that he was unfaithful to Martha. His lifetime battle for self-control included the sexual with other passions. However, both Eliza's letter and his reply make it clear that he was no prude. Eliza flirtatiously admitted her own shortcomings, and George implied that he would not have been concerned at being found in adultery but only at having "betrayed the confidence of a lady."

On an earlier occasion, Washington had contrasted unfavorably "the giddy rounds of promiscuous pleasure" with "domestic felicity." This graduate from an unhappy childhood was glad to achieve in marriage

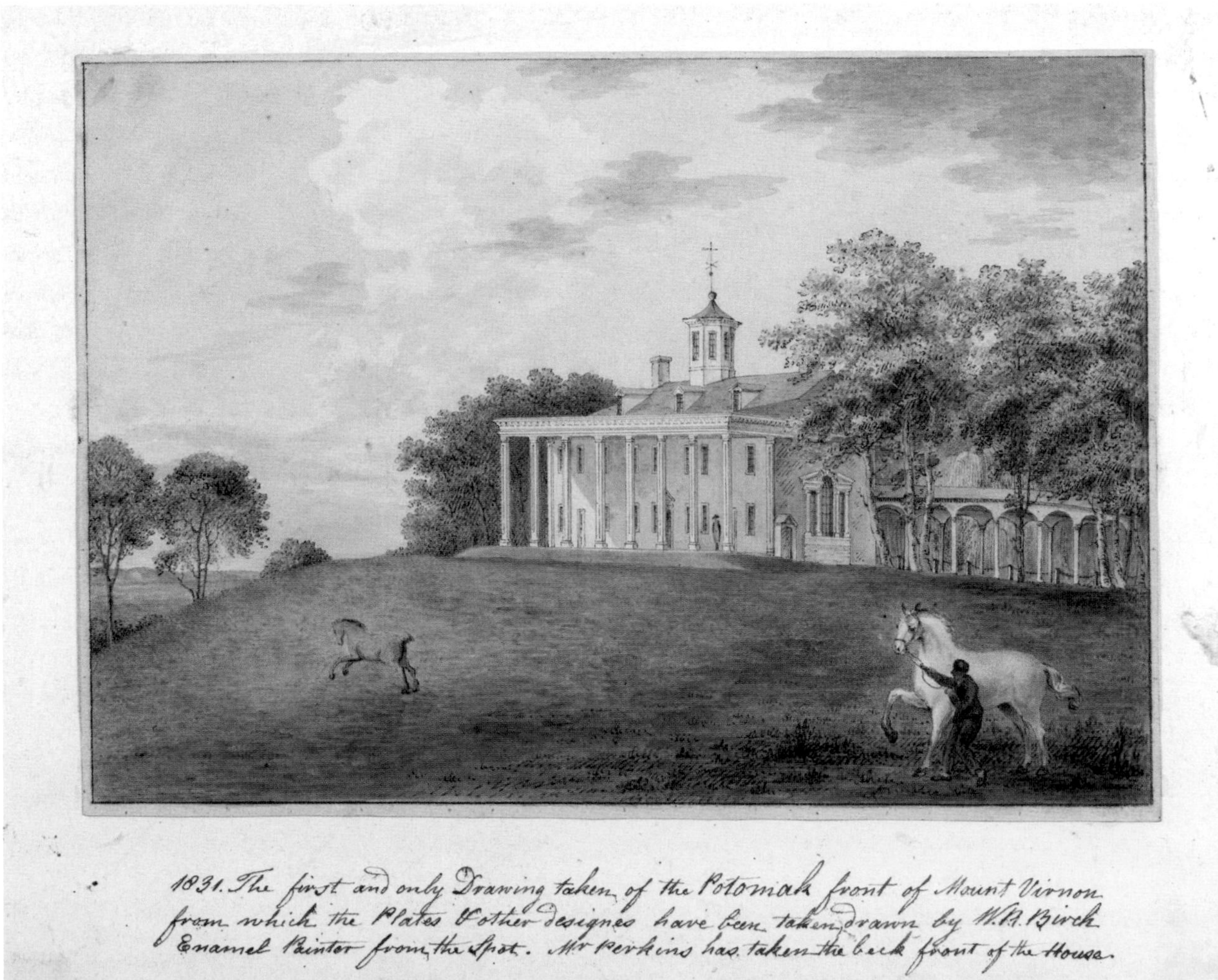

1831. The first and only Drawing taken of the Potomak front of Mount Virnon
from which the Plates & other designes have been taken drawn by W.R. Birch
Enamel Painter from the Spot. Mr Perkins has taken the back front of the House

Potomak Front of Mount Vernon *by William Birch, watercolor and graphite on paper, c. 1801–1803. This prospect of Mount Vernon's east front was one of the most widely circulated images of the estate in the nineteenth century. The English-born artist possibly executed this preparatory sketch, from which all the engravings are derived, as early as 1801, making it a very rare early view. Washington had died by this date, yet Birch included him standing on the piazza.*

tranquillity, not more excitement, of which he usually had plenty elsewhere.

But Martha was not much company in his retirement. She was slightly older than he and had gone downhill more rapidly. She was "greatly distressed and fatigued" by housekeeping details she had once enjoyed, and now preferred copying letters her husband had drafted to writing her own. Washington had been back at Mount Vernon only a few months when he sent a hurried invitation to a nearby friend. "Unless someone pops in unexpectedly, Mrs. Washington and myself will do what I believe has not been done within the last twenty years by us, that is to set down to dinner by ourselves."

Washington found himself a stranger in his own land. Almost all of the friends to whose houses he had ridden for a convivial night or a long stay had died or moved away. And the younger Virginians, following in the wake of Jefferson, were now his most passionate opponents. If he rode beyond his immediate neighborhood, he saw not smiles but frowns.

Mount Vernon was, of course, always crowded. Although Washington complained about the flow in and out of curious strangers, he would pounce eagerly on any individual who seemed to offer interest. He would hold such men in conversation for hours, beg them to stay the night. Wishing to have resident at Mount Vernon "a companion in my latter days," he tried to lure his former military aide David Humphreys, who was now American minister to Spain. However, the news that Humphreys was getting married "annihilated every hope." Washington (thinking perhaps of Martha and her niece Fanny Bassett) intended never again "to have two women in my house when I am there myself."

There was, however, one woman whom he particularly desired to have nearby. He wrote his old love, Sally Fairfax, that none of the "many important events" that had occurred since he had seen her "nor all of them together have been able to eradicate from my mind the recollection of those happy moments, the happiest in my life, which I have enjoyed in your company. Worn out in a manner by the toils of my past labor, I am again seated under my vine and fig tree. . . . It is a matter of sore regret, when I cast my eyes toward Belvoir [the deserted Fairfax estate] which I often do, to reflect that the former inhabitants of it, with whom we lived in such harmony and friendship, no longer reside there; and that the ruins can only be viewed as the memento of former pleasures." He often wondered why Sally, being now a widow, did not return, rebuild the house, and "spend the evening of your life" down the road from Mount Vernon.

But Sally Fairfax did not come to help relieve the old hero's loneliness.

Forty-Nine

MENTAL CONFUSION

(1797–1798)

When Washington had retired at the end of the Revolution, victory had rung down a curtain. If he had then remained on the national stage, it would have been in a different play. But now there was no such break. The drama in which he had starred was going on, although with a different actor in the presidential role.

Adams had inherited the French depredations against American shipping and the question of how Pinckney, whom Washington had appointed minister to Paris, would be received. On both scores, the news was bad. The attacks augmented and the Directory refused to receive Pinckney. Adams denounced the French to Congress more belligerently than Washington had ever done. He then did what Washington had contemplated: appointed two more delegates to form with Pinckney a special commission that could, if the French would talk to them, negotiate on an emergency basis.

Washington was trying to disentangle his emotions. He sometimes allowed several days to pass before he sent to Alexandria for the mails, and he did his best not to comment on public affairs. But the world would not leave him alone. After he had been at Mount Vernon for only two months, a letter from Jefferson surfaced in the press. Written to Philip Mazzei, an Italian radical, it summarized the American political scene towards the close of Washington's presidency as a struggle between "the main body of our citizens" and "an Anglican, monarchical, and aristocratic party" which controlled the executive along with most of the government. In a passage generally interpreted as referring to Washington, Jefferson had written, "It would give you a fever were I to name to you the apostates . . . men who were Samsons in the field and Solomons in council, but who have had their heads shorn by the harlot of Britain."

Two pamphlets appeared. In one, the former French minister to the United States, Fauchet, tried to demonstrate that Washington had as president always been anti-French. Washington was particularly angered by a false accusation that he had plotted secretly with an emissary of the French royal pretender. In the other pamphlet, the former American minister to France, Monroe, insisted (among many other charges) that Washington had cynically appointed him for the purpose of hoodwinking the French, and that the Jay Treaty had been a calculated surrender to Great Britain.

These public attacks were followed by one of the strangest events of Washington's entire career. He received a letter from Albemarle, Jefferson's home county, signed John Langhorne, which offered comfort to Washington for being subjected to "unmerited calumny." Although Washington diagnosed Langhorne as "a pedant who was desirous of displaying the flowers of his pen," he sent a courteous answer, as he did to all communications. He was soon informed by John Nicholas, one of the few Federalists resident in Albemarle, that the letter had been claimed by Jefferson's favorite nephew, Peter Carr. Nicholas insisted that Jefferson slandered Washington in conversation, and implied that he was responsible for the fraudulently signed Langhorne communication. Washington should beware of the "vile hypocrisy of *that man's* professions of friendship towards you."

Once he was out of office and intended to remain so for the rest of his earthly career, moderation ceased to be a matter of state. He permitted himself to espouse extremes. He became at last what he had for so long been accused of being: devotedly pro-Federalist.

Washington was deeply upset. He expressed reluctance to doubt "the sincerity of a friendship" which he had believed Jefferson had for him. However, "the attempts to explain away the Constitution and weaken the government are now become too open; and the desire of placing the affairs of this country under the influence and control of a foreign nation [France] is so apparent and strong, it is hardly to be expected that a resort to covert means to effect these objects will be longer regarded."

After the ex-president's able nephew, Bushrod Washington, had joined with Nicholas in inciting the old man, Washington wrote that if Jefferson could be demonstrated to have been "the *real* author or abettor, it would be a pity not to expose him to public execration for attempting in so dishonorable a way to obtain a disclosure of sentiments of which some advantage could be taken." And again, "If a *trick* so dirty and shabby as this is supposed to be [can be] *clearly proved,*" publication "would, in my opinion, be attended with a happy effect." But, "if it should be attempted and fail, the reverse would be the consequence." Bushrod was to use his own judgment.

Bushrod eventually and reluctantly decided not to make the matter public, since Jefferson's active involvement could not be proved.

Comparisons of handwriting have in more recent times demonstrated that the Langhorne letter was indeed written by Peter Carr. However, it seems extremely improbable that the astute Jefferson would have countenanced, whatever might have been his moral feelings, a maneuver so transparently indiscreet, so little promising of major results, and potentially so damaging. It seems most probable, since Carr was somewhat of a scapegrace, that the letter was a bilious prank intended to elicit a pompous, self-righteous reply that would raise renewed mirth among drinking companions. At the blackest, it can only be interpreted as a demonstration of the lack of respect for the old hero that was rife at Monticello.

To modern hindsight, Washington overreacted. That his able and much younger nephew Bushrod overreacted to an even greater extent reveals the hysteria of the times, but does not altogether explain away the frenetic behavior of a man who had been during so many years so notable (despite lapses) for withstanding hysteria, for striking the calm, the reasonable, the healing note.

Old men are naturally suspicious, and see plots. And it would require almost more than the fortitude of a saint not to be affected by the type of attacks which were made on Washington and his administration. Not only had his behavior been condemned because of entirely unfounded distrust of his motives, but what he did had been distorted; and not only had his acts been distorted, but he had been assailed by lies which the perpetrators often knew were total lies. And the vilification appeared in newspapers of national circulation that were semi-official organs of the Republican party.

As long as he had been in office he had tried, although towards the end with sometimes stumbling feet, to walk the path he had charted for himself, the path of complete neutrality between factions at home and belligerents abroad. Once he was out of office and intended to remain so for the rest of his earthly career, moderation ceased to be a matter of state. He permitted himself to espouse extremes. He became at last what he had for so long been accused of being: devotedly pro-Federalist. Since he doubted the intentions of all others, he communicated exclusively with Federalists. He could no longer palliate the efforts of the French government to interfere in American politics; he had become angrily anti-French. In his denunciations of French attacks on American commerce, he no longer pointed out that Britain was also guilty. He came to believe that the leaders of the opposition, patriots who had been his coadjutors and friends, were eager to make the United States a vassal of France: might indeed cooperate with a French invasion.

A French invasion! In 1798, that seemed possible.

During March and April, word came in that the French Directory, announcing themselves as "greatly exasperated" with President Adams, would not receive the American commissioners until Adams announced a complete change in policy. Then three mysterious agents, designated as X, Y, and Z (which led to the entire matter being called the XYZ Affair), appeared to state that if the commissioners would personally repudiate the policy of their government, give Foreign Minister Talleyrand a large bribe, and promise France a huge loan, the Directory might condescend to receive the mission.

When this was published in the United States, national anger flared. Congress authorized that the army be augmented by ten thousand men and that a further force of fifty thousand be organized on paper so that it could turn out instantly.

Many Federalists hoped for a declaration of war that would put the Republicans in the position of traitors. But Washington believed that America's injured pride should not drive her into initiating hostilities. He hoped that outrage, loudly and almost unanimously expressed by the American people, would persuade the French that an expeditionary force sent by them would not be welcomed by a horde of "democrats." Even if still riding high with the triumphs of Napoleon, the French would then draw back from mounting the "formidable invasion" which would force the United States into war.

Adams, whose government was made up of and supported by Federalists, found himself under extreme pressure to appoint Alexander Hamilton as commander in chief of the augmented army. Seeing a nefarious plot to exalt a schemer who might well use the army as an instrument of self-aggrandizement and tyranny, Adams made a convulsive move. Without consulting Washington, he appointed the ex-president lieutenant general and commander in chief, thus catapulting the old man back onto the public stage.

On hearing the news, Washington was surprised that he was not more upset. He had, he wrote, considered himself eager to "pass the remnant of a life (worn down with cares) in ruminating on past scenes and contemplating the future grandeur of this rising empire. But we little know ourselves much less the decisions of Providence."

Washington's main worry was that, in thus appointing him without notice, Adams had prevented him from making it a prior condition that he would not serve unless he were allowed to determine his top subordinates. This was in part a reflection of his typical wish to be master in his own house. But the issue seems to have been given desperate poignancy by his

WASHINGTON'S LETTER TO JOHN ADAMS

Upon hearing the news that Adams had appointed him lieutenant general and commander in chief of the Provisional army, Washington recorded how he, himself, was surprised to be willing to accept the hasty appointment. In the letter below, Washington humbly accepts Adams's commission, stating "how incumbent it is upon every person, of every description to contribute at all times to his country's welfare."

July 13, 1798
John Adams,
President of the United States

Dear Sir:

I had the honor, on the evening of the 11th instant, to receive from the hands of the Secretary of War your favor of the 7th, announcing that you had, with the advice and consent of the Senate, appointed me "lieutenant general and commander in chief of all the armies raised or to be raised for the service of the United States."

I cannot express how greatly affected I am at this new proof of public confidence and the highly flattering manner in which you have been pleased to make the communication. At the same time, I must not conceal from you my earnest wish that the choice had fallen upon a man less declined in years and better qualified to encounter the usual vicissitudes of war.

You know, Sir, what calculation I had made relative to the probable course of events on my retiring from office, and the determination I had consoled myself with of closing the remnant of my days in my present peaceful abode. You will therefore be at no loss to conceive and appreciate the sensations I must have experienced to bring my mind to any conclusion that would pledge me, at so late a period of life, to leave scenes I sincerely love to enter upon the boundless field of public action, incessant trouble, and high responsibility.

It was not possible for me to remain ignorant of, or indifferent to, recent transactions. The conduct of the directory of France toward our country, their insidious hostility to its government, their various practices to withdraw the affections of the people from it, the evident tendency of their acts and those of their agents to countenance and invigorate opposition, their disregard of solemn treaties and the laws of nations, their war upon our defenseless commerce, their treatment of our ministers of peace, and their demands amounting to tribute could not fail to excite in me corresponding sentiments with those my countrymen have so generally expressed in their affectionate addresses to you. Believe me, Sir, no one can more cordially approve of the wise and prudent measures of your administration. They ought to inspire universal confidence, and will no doubt, combined with the state of things, call from Congress such laws and means as will enable you to meet the full force and extent of the crisis.

GEO. WASHINGTON.
GIFT OF R. FRIDENBERG
JOHN ADAMS.
Born Feb. 22 1732, In. March 4.1789. Obt. Dec. 14.1799 Æ. 68.
Born Oct. 20.1735 In. 1797 Obt. July 4.1826 Æ. 91.

The best-known images of George Washington (left) and John Adams (right).

Satisfied, therefore, that you have sincerely wished and endeavored to avert war, and exhausted to the last drop the cup of reconciliation, we can with pure hearts appeal to Heaven for the justice of our cause, and may confidently trust the final result to that kind Providence who has heretofore, and so often, signally favored the people of these United States.

Thinking in this manner, and feeling how incumbent it is upon every person, of every description, to contribute at all times to his country's welfare, and especially in a moment like the present, when everything we hold dear and sacred is so seriously threatened, I have finally determined to accept the commission of commander in chief of the armies of the United States, with the reserve only that I shall not be called into the field until the army is in a situation to require my presence, or it becomes indispensable by the urgency of circumstances.

In making this reservation I beg it to be understood that I do not mean to withhold any assistance to arrange and organize the army which you may think I can afford. I take the liberty also to mention that I must decline having my acceptance considered as drawing after it any immediate charge upon the public, or that I can receive any emoluments annexed to the appointment before entering into a situation to incur expense.

The secretary of war being anxious to return to the seat of government, I have detained him no longer than was necessary to a full communication upon the several points he had in charge.

With very great respect and consideration, I have the honor to be, dear Sir, your most obedient and humble servant.

George Washington

From *The Writings of George Washington*, Volume XI, by Jared Sparks, 1848.

Washington's old friend and ally, Henry Knox, by Charles Willson Peale, from life, c. 1784.

fear that, being in fact too old, he would need the strongest possible shoulders to lean on.

The three major generals, Washington decided, should be Knox, Hamilton, and Charles Cotesworth Pinckney, who was on his way home from the abortive mission to France. On the issue of their relative rank, Washington became more confused than he had ever before been concerning any public matter.

Washington's most intimate emotions pled that Knox should be his second-in-command. He had no older and closer friend. Having been a major general during the Revolution, Knox far outranked Hamilton and Pinckney in that seniority which conventionally determined military rank. He would be deeply hurt if passed over. Since Knox was from Boston, his elevation would follow the time-honored convention of having in any national endeavor the two top figures come from the two main regions, preferably from Virginia and Massachusetts. But Knox, always overweight, was now fat and dull. He could be of little use as second-in-command.

Washington's judgment plunked for Pinckney, who he felt would be particularly valuable in the second post because he was a South Carolinian. Surely, if the French were "so insane" as to invade, they would strike the Deep South: because that was the weakest part of the nation; because they would expect to find the most friends in that region; because "there can be no doubt of their arming our own Negroes against us"; and because they could move on from South Carolina to capturing nearby Louisiana from Spain. Pinckney was not only a spirited, active, and judicious officer on whom Washington could rely, but Washington considered his connections more influential than any other group in the three southernmost states. If Pinckney led, his connections would follow. But were Hamilton put over him, Pinckney might well not serve, since he had outranked Hamilton in the Revolutionary army. This might cause "disgust" among the very leading families Washington would have to rely on to oppose the democrats and repel the French.

But Hamilton was pressing his claims hard. He had not been bothered by Adams's appointment of Washington, since he foresaw that the reins would slip from the old soldier's fingers to the man who held the posts he intended to occupy: both inspector general and second-in-command. He indicated to Washington and the Federalist leadership that he would not serve if denied this double role. Washington's correspondents, who were all Federalists, insisted that the loyal population of the United States, even in Knox's Massachusetts, wanted the reassurance of Hamilton in high rank. For his part, Washington admired Hamilton. He was used to working with him, and believed that, although Hamilton had never risen above colonel in the Revolution, he had had "as the principal and most confidential aide of the commander in chief," more opportunity to survey the whole military scene than either Knox or Pinckney. Washington was frightened by the thought that Hamilton might stay home.

Since that distant time when he was appointed commander in chief, Washington had been deeply concerned with fostering and preserving unity in the nation. Now he believed that the French would invade only if they judged the United States so divided that it could not or would not defend itself.

Adams, who had kept on all of Washington's cabinet, sent Secretary of War McHenry to Mount Vernon to persuade Washington officially to accept the command. Washington wished to make it a condition that he select his own general officers, but, realizing that this would be an unsuitable invasion of presidential prerogative, he accepted (this he was to forget) a half measure. In writing Adams, McHenry put it forward as his own belief that Washington would not be inclined to serve without general officers of his own choosing.

The conferees decided to request Adams to send to the Senate for confirmation as major generals the names of Hamilton, Pinckney, and Knox. They were listed in that order, but it was agreed (this Washington also forgot) that the sequence should not be taken to determine seniority; Adams would, in due course, solidify rank. Assuming that the president would do what Washington asked, the new lieutenant general welcomed the postponement, as it would give him time to try to persuade Hamilton to serve under Pinckney, and Knox to serve under both.

Washington's letter to Hamilton gave his prudential reasons for preferring Pinckney. He added, "My wish to put you first and my fear of losing him are not a little embarrassing." Then he passed the buck. "After all, it rests with the president to use his pleasure."

The letter to Knox was even more difficult. For whatever reasons, perhaps because Knox was such a disciple of Hamilton's, in this epistle Washington wrote that since "the public estimation" demanded Hamilton as second-in-command, he had agreed "with some fears, I confess, of the consequences." He then pointed out that Pinckney's services in the South would be very important. Knox would thus agree that, despite his seniority, he would have to be third. Washington could not write Pinckney, who was on the ocean.

Replies came in from both Knox and Hamilton on the same day. Knox stated that he was "much wounded" to discover that his faith of "more than twenty years" in Washington's friendship and admiration had been "a perfect delusion." Under such an insult, he could not serve.

Hamilton wrote that he believed he was the preference of "a real majority of the federal men," but if an "impartial decision" went against him, he would not allow his ambition and interest to stand in the way of the public good.

Washington's reply to Hamilton was a shocking demonstration of utter confusion. He said nothing of Hamilton's all-important offer to step down. He gave no hint as to how he wished to rank the eager New Yorker. He mourned Knox's hurt letter and wondered whether, after all, Pinckney would object to serving under Knox, who was so extremely his military senior.

Washington was thereupon "seized with a fever." Rapidly he lost twenty pounds, to the great concern of Dr. Craik, who labored to build up his system to a point where he could be treated for malaria. Finally, Craik administered "Jesuit's bark." Although Washington then improved, he remained for weeks "too much debilitated to be permitted to attend to much business."

President Adams was suffering and fuming. Suffering because his beloved wife seemed on the point of death; fuming because his Federalist advisers insisted that the order in which the general's names had been sent to and approved by the Senate—Hamilton, Pinckney, Knox—had determined beyond alteration their seniority. Adams was determined to accord Hamilton the lowest possible rank among combat generals. Adams had no intention of insulting his own state by ignoring the seniority that gave Massachusetts's Knox the claim to be second-in-command.

McHenry informed Washington that Hamilton would refuse to serve on these terms. McHenry quoted Adams as writing that if he consulted Washington, the only result would be that the problem would "come back to me at last after much altercation and exasperation of passions"—at which point he would decide as he did now: Knox first and Hamilton last. "There has been," Adams had continued, "much too much intrigue in this business with General Washington and me. If I shall ultimately be the dupe of it, I am much mistaken in myself."

The three cabinet ministers Washington had willed to Adams, men whom he had not trusted when he was in office, were now joining with other Federalists in sending the old man a barrage of letters insisting that Adams was insulting him; that Knox's elevation would bring in squads of superannuated generals with Revolutionary seniority; and that Hamilton was indispensable. In his perturbation, Washington got firmly fixed in his mind two misconceptions. One, that he had made it a firm condition, which the president had accepted, that he appoint his own general officers. And two, that the action of the Senate obliged Adams to put Hamilton first and Knox last. Feeling thus on sure ground, he struck out in a manner that belied his former convictions.

Since that distant time when he was appointed commander in chief, Washington had been deeply concerned with fostering and preserving unity in the nation. Now he believed that the French would invade only if they judged the United States so divided that it could not or would not defend itself. But, on September 25, 1798, he wrote President Adams a letter in which he threatened, by clear implication, publicly to resign from the army if the order of major generals were not Hamilton, Pinckney, Knox. He commented to McHenry, "You will readily perceive that even the *rumor* of a misunderstanding between the president and me, while the breach can be repaired, would be attended with unpleasant consequences." But, he added, "If there is no disposition on his part to do this, the public must decide which of us is right and which of us is wrong."

Imagination could hardly conceive the chaos into which both political power and public opinion would have been thrown had the old hero carried out his angry threat. Adams had no choice but to surrender.

Washington had blown up what was at its rational extreme a medium-size disagreement into an issue that threatened to convulse the nation. And at various moments in the controversy, the brilliant pragmatist had lost contact with reality.

Not even the most resplendent hero is immune to the passing of the years.

Fifty

POLITICS AT SUNSET

(1798–1799)

Washington, who had insisted that he would never again travel more than ten miles from his own lawn, set out for Philadelphia on November 5, 1798, to prepare a plan for the new army. On the road, he became worried because his nephew and houseguest, Lawrence Lewis, had not been in the group that had waved him good-bye. If Lewis had come down for breakfast, he had been rude; if he had not come down, why, he was sick and Washington had been rude in not going upstairs to say good-bye to him. Wrack his brains as he would, Washington could not remember where Lewis had breakfasted. Deciding that he would rather apologize than risk being discourteous, Washington wrote Lewis that he had been made absentminded by hurry.

The reemerging commander in chief had already made it clear that he did not suffer from that proverbial weakness of generals: the determination to fight new wars in the way that they won the old. He wished all Revolutionary seniority to be forgotten so that he could get an officer corps of young men. And he believed that the guerrilla tactics for which he was famous would not do if the French invaded. Any expeditionary force would have to be attacked before it could establish itself, which meant foreseeable and thus more formal battles. In conference with Hamilton and Pinckney (who had accepted being inferior to Hamilton as Knox had not), he sought information concerning French fighting methods so that the army could be organized to counteract them.

Washington had eagerly wished that the army he raised to put down the Whiskey Rebellion should represent all political opinions. But now he was unwilling to give commissions to men recommended by opposition congressmen lest, being pro-French, they "poison the army." If the old general were preparing a force that in the wrong hands—and had he selected the wrong hands?—could serve tyranny, the fears and suspicions rolling in his brain made him unconscious of it.

But he did arrange matters so that Hamilton would have little control. True, he did not intend, himself, to be active unless a crisis beckoned. However, the southern states were to be mobilized under Pinckney. Hamilton was to have charge in the rest of the Union, but, since he would make his headquarters close to Philadelphia, he was to be under the continual supervision of Adams and McHenry. Conscious certainly that some cautious men feared that Hamilton might try to carve out for himself an empire as the Napoleon of the Southwest, Washington arranged that, if French activity demanded a protective march into Louisiana, the intelligence should be sent not directly to Hamilton but first to the secretary of war. Washington had times of lucidity as great as his times of confusion.

Ever since he had been a little boy and his half brother Lawrence had set out resplendent in a British uniform for Cartagena, Washington had been fascinated with military regalia. He concerned himself with uniforms for his new army, designing particularly splendid regalia for himself. The commander in chief should wear "a blue coat with yellow buttons and gold epaulettes (each having three silver stars); linings, cape, and cuffs of buff; in winter buff vest and breeches; in summer a white vest and breeches of nankeen. The coat to be without lapels, and embroidered on the cape, cuffs, and pockets. A white plume in the hat to be a further distinction." He left the order with Philadelphia's leading tailor.

The reemerging commander in chief had already made it clear that he did not suffer from that proverbial weakness of generals: the determination to fight new wars in the way that they won the old.

Back at Mount Vernon, he was amazed to discover that his nephew Lawrence Lewis, whom he designated a major, had resolved that "before he enters the camp of Mars, he is to engage in that of Venus." To everyone's pleasure, as it would join the Washington and Custis families, Lewis had become engaged to Martha's resident granddaughter, Nelly Custis. Nelly announced that she would be married on the general's sixty-seventh birthday. She begged him to inaugurate his new uniform at her wedding. He enthusiastically agreed.

Opposite: Washington at Verplanck's Point *by John Trumbull, detail, 1790, oil on canvas.*

Washington wrote McHenry, "On reconsidering the uniform for the commander in chief, it has become a matter of doubt with me (although as it respected myself *personally* I was against *all* embroidery) whether embroidery on the cape, cuffs, and pockets of the coat and none on the *buff* waistcoat, would not have a disjointed and awkward appearance." He added that it was essential that he have the uniform before February 22.

Twelve days before the wedding, he reminded McHenry that the uniform should be "accompanied with cockades and stars for the epaulettes." Eleven days before the wedding, he wrote the tailor concerning a quick way to get the uniform to Mount Vernon. Finally, a package did arrive, but it was discouragingly small. It proved to contain eagles for the cockades but not even stars for the epaulettes. And nothing more came. When Nelly was married on the 22nd at "about candlelight," Washington wore his old uniform.

Washington now hoped to get his fine regalia for the Fourth of July. Letters poking up both McHenry and the tailor elicited the information that it had been impossible to find, in the entire United States, enough gold thread. But some was expected in the spring shipments from Europe. Four days before the Fourth, Washington wrote McHenry, "I shall send up to Alexandria on Wednesday but," he added bravely, "shall feel no disappointment if the uniform is not there." It was not there.

In final despair, the tailor sent the uniform off to Europe to be finished. Washington never had the pleasure of wearing it. Before it returned, he was dead.

In all American history, few pieces of legislation have had so obnoxious a reputation as the Alien and Sedition acts, passed by Congress during the XYZ hysteria in the same session that authorized the new army. The Alien Act greatly lengthened the period an immigrant would have to wait before he could apply for citizenship and empowered the president to expel

any alien he considered dangerous. The Sedition Act prescribed punishment for false and malicious writings aimed at bringing the government into disrepute.

That Washington would as president have done what Adams did, sign the acts into law, seems improbable. He had, it is true, suffered from attacks by aliens who, he believed, were venting European grievances on American institutions which they misunderstood. Yet his continuing attitude had been that one of the major roles of the United States was to be a haven for those unhappy or oppressed abroad. And, even when smarting under the most extreme newspaper libels, he had been an unvarying champion of freedom of the press (much more so than President Jefferson was to be).

But now the old man saw conspiracies. He wrote privately that there was no reason why aliens should be allowed to spread foreign poisons in the United States. Concerning a newspaper charge that the government was wallowing in British bribes, he commented that, if a fair and impartial investigation proved the accusations true, the editor would be "deserving of thanks and high reward for bringing to light conduct so abominable." However, "if it shall be found to be all calumny . . . punishment ought to be inflicted."

Having become a convinced Federalist, Washington finally broke—even if only behind the scenes—his rule of not intervening in an election. To weaken the Jeffersonian hold on Virginia, he set in motion a great political career by bullying John Marshall, the future trailblazing chief justice of the Supreme Court, to run for Congress. He also lured Patrick Henry out of retirement, even though the ailing patriarch did not live to serve in the Virginia assembly.

Although Adams had been defeated concerning Hamilton's rank, he found, as the XYZ fever abated, an effective way of protecting the nation against a man he considered so dangerous. He simply brought the organizing of the army to a halt—he had come to consider it unnecessary anyway. Hamilton fumed and tried to incite Washington. Washington admitted that he was in an embarrassing position in relation to officers who had been promised commissions they had never received, and that, if the army had been intended as more than a mere threat, the delay in recruiting "baffles all conjecture." But he added, "Far removed from the scene, I might ascribe these delays to the wrong causes, and therefore will hazard no opinion respecting them."

At the end of January 1799, Washington received a letter from Joel Barlow, a distinguished American resident in France, stating that the disagreements with the nation were all based on a misunderstanding, and that the Directory would now be happy to receive a minister from the United States. This epistle Washington forwarded to Adams, expressing the hope that it might lead to that "peace and tranquillity . . . upon just, and honorable, and dignified terms," which he was "persuaded" was "the ardent desire of all friends of this rising empire."

Adams's reply stated that, as a result of many such communications, and primarily because of a letter from Talleyrand, he had determined to break the diplomatic stalemate by appointing the American minister to Holland, William Vans Murray, as minister to France. Washington's pleasure was quickly submerged by a flood of Federalist communications: Talleyrand's letter had not been official. Furthermore, Adams had not consulted the Federalist leaders or his own cabinet.

Although, when president, Washington had avoided consulting the Federalist leaders and the very same crew of cabinet members, he allowed himself to be convinced that Adams had gone off half-cocked. He was relieved when the Senate placed roadblocks in the way of an immediate mission.

Opposite: *This portrait of Washington by Gilbert Stuart was begun in 1795 and was probably painted at least partly from life.*

In mid-July, Washington opened a letter from Governor Trumbull of Connecticut, which carried the marks of being the result of a general Federalist consultation. It stated that to prevent the election of "a French president," Washington would have to announce that he would again accept the office.

Washington's answer was a tragic demonstration of how completely he had lost his belief that he could lead the whole nation; of how utterly he had been disillusioned in his ideal that an administration could represent all or almost all the people. He now believed that the only effective qualification for election as president was that the candidate be the choice of the leading faction. Let the opposition "set up a broomstick and call it a true son of liberty, a democrat, or give it any other epithet that will suit their purpose, and it will command their votes *in toto*." Since the Federalists would be forced by self-defense to behave in the same manner, Washington was convinced that, despite all he had achieved, he would get no more votes than anyone else the Federalists designated. And in any case, Washington recognized that he was too old. If he allowed himself to be persuaded, he would be charged "with dotage and imbecility."

Nelson's great naval victory at the Battle of the Nile seemed so wildly to have swung the pendulum of the war that Federalists gleefully foresaw a restoration of the French monarchy. What was their horror when, at this very moment, Adams decided to unleash his embassy to the Directory! Washington himself was shocked and puzzled. "To those of us who are not behind the curtain," he wrote, the president's decision was "in the present state of European affairs, incomprehensible."

Frantic to block a move which they felt would encourage the Republicans in the United States and perhaps tie the nation to the seemingly sinking fortunes of France, the Federalists turned to the only force that could stop Adams. They importuned Washington to publish a protest.

In reply to McHenry's urging, Washington wrote: "I have for some time past viewed the political concerns of the United States with an anxious and painful eye. They appear to me to be moving by hasty strides to some awful crisis, but in what they will result, that Being who sees, foresees, and directs all things alone can tell. The vessel is afloat or very nearly so, and considering myself as a passenger only, I shall trust to the mariners whose duty it is to watch, to steer it into a safe port."

This refusal to intervene against what turned out to be one of the happiest strokes in all American diplomacy was Washington's last important political act.

Fifty-One

WASHINGTON AND SLAVERY

(1732–1799)

Ever since he had been called away to the Revolutionary War, Washington's dream, when embattled in the great world, was to recapture the relaxation and pleasure of the plantation world that was his hereditary environment. But gradually his dream became tainted with nightmare.

Almost all southern patriots had to find some personal resolution of the dilemma that their search for liberty for themselves and other whites was conducted while they continued to hold African Americans in slavery. They were likely to be most upset by this contradiction during their first flush of Revolutionary ardor. Thus, as the years passed, Jefferson shifted from active concern with emancipation to expressing high-sounding sentiments in letters, while he made use of his slaves as best suited his pleasure and profit.

Washington's growing passion for consistency, combined with his innate inability to separate theory from practice, made his horror of slavery increase as Jefferson's receded. Although his heart continued to yearn for peace in the world of his forebears and childhood, he began, during his second term as president, an active effort to tear, for the benefit of his slaves, Mount Vernon apart. He proved to be the only Virginia Founding Father to free all his slaves.

Historians, who have for so long looked nervously away from the role of slaves in American history, have failed to recognize the extremely important fact that Washington's repugnance to slavery was a major reason for his backing Hamilton's financial planning against Jeffersonian attacks. He could not accept the contention that agrarianism, as exemplified in Virginia, was so basic to free institutions that all other ways of life should be discouraged. The Hamiltonian system had no need for slavery. Washington felt that it was the Virginia institution that would have in the end to give way. "I clearly foresee," he told an English caller, "that nothing but the rooting out of slavery can perpetuate the existence of our union by consolidating it in a common bond of principle." To Randolph, he revealed a conclusion that tore at his most deeply seated habits and emotions. He stated that should the Union separate between North and South, "he had made up his mind to move and be of the northern."

Slavery had seemed as inherent a part of the world in which Washington was raised as the sun that rose every morning.* Throughout his young manhood he accepted the institution without question. His small inheritance had included slaves, and in the prosperity that followed his marriage, he had not only purchased

* Slavery stretches to the beginnings of human history. When Washington was a boy, it had not been officially challenged anywhere.

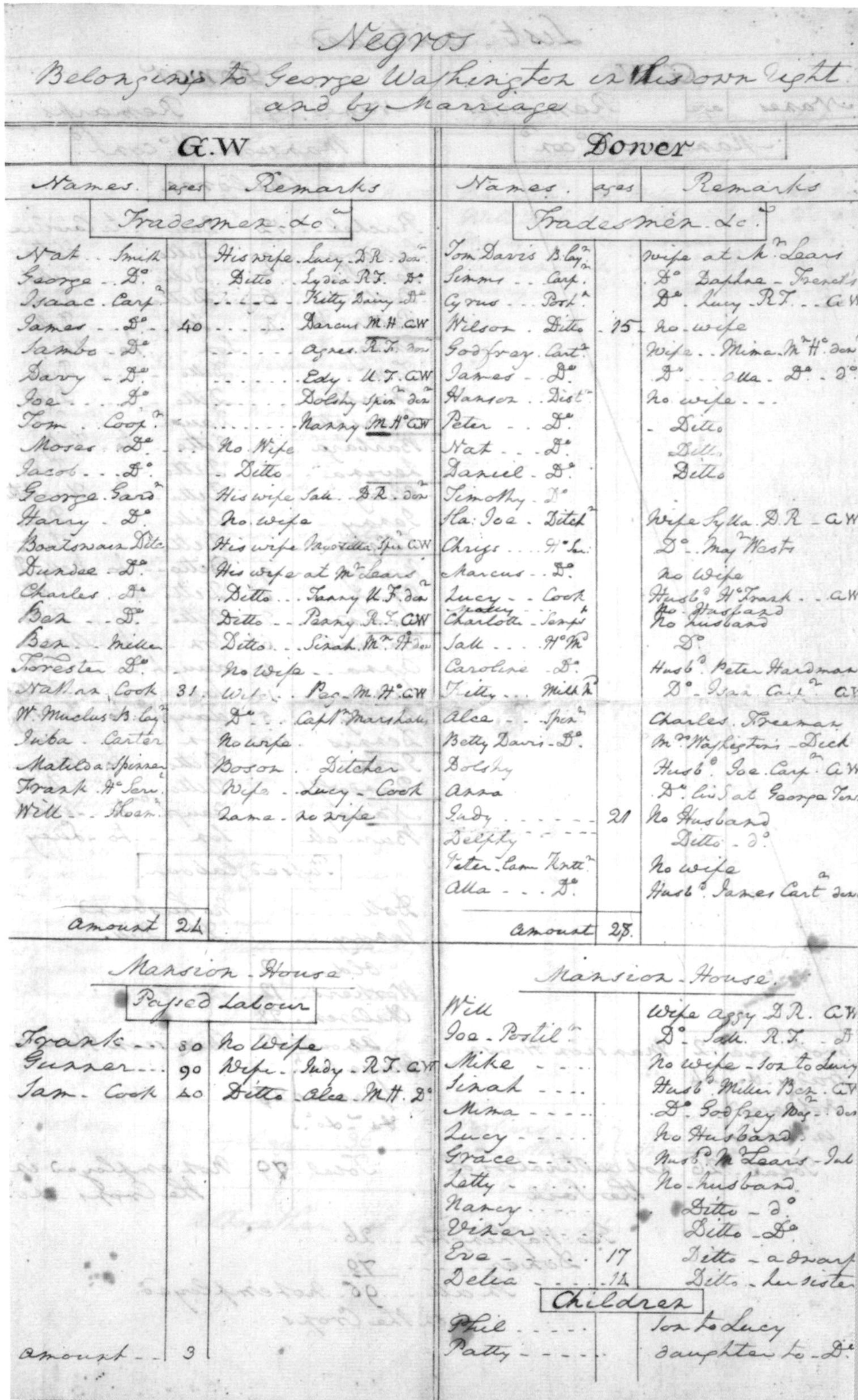

Negros

Belonging to George Washington in his own right and by Marriage

G.W

Names.	ages	Remarks
Tradesmen &c.		
Nat - Smith		His wife Lucy D.R. dow
George - Do		Ditto Lydia R.T. Do
Isaac Carpr		Kitty Dairy Do
James - Do	40	Darcus M.H. GW
Sambo - Do		Agnes R.T. dow
Davy - Do		Edy U.T. GW
Joe - Do		Dolshy Spinr dow
Tom Coopr		Nanny M.Ho GW
Moses Do		No Wife
Jacob - Do		Ditto
George Gardr		His wife Sall D.R. dow
Harry Do		No wife
Boatswain Ditr		His wife Myrtilla Spr GW
Dundee Do		His wife at Mr Lears
Charles Do		Ditto Fanny U.F. dow
Ben - Do		Ditto Penny R.T. GW
Ben Miller		Ditto Sinah Mn H. dow
Forester Do		No Wife
Nathan Cook	31	Wife Peg M.H. GW
W. Muclus B.Layr		Do Capt. Marshall
Juba Carter		No wife
Matilda Spinner		Boson Ditcher
Frank Ho Servt		Wife Lucy Cook
Will - Hostr		Lame no wife
Amount	24	
Mansion House		
Payed Labour		
Frank	80	No Wife
Gunner	90	Wife Judy R.T. GW
Sam Cook	40	Ditto Alce M.H. Do
Amount	3	

Dower

Names.	ages	Remarks
Tradesmen &c.		
Tom Davis B.Layr		Wife at Mr Lears
Simms Carp.		Do Daphne Frenchs
Cyrus Postn		Do Lucy R.T. GW
Wilson Ditto	15	No wife
Godfrey Cartr		Wife Mima Mn Ho dow
James - Do		Do Alla Do Do
Hanson Distr		No wife
Peter - Do		Ditto
Nat - Do		Ditto
Daniel - Do		Ditto
Timothy Do		
Ha. Joe Ditchr		Wife Sylla D.R. GW
Chriss Ho Servt		Do Mays Wests
Marcus - Do		No Wife
Lucy - Cook		Husbd Ho Frank GW
Charlotte Sempss		No Husband
Sall Ho Md		Do
Caroline Do		Husbd Peter Hardman
Kitty Milkm		Do Isaac Carpr GW
Alce Spinr		Charles Freeman
Betty Davis Do		Mrs Washington's Dick
Dolshy		Husbd Joe Carpn GW
Anna		Do lives at George Town
Judy	21	No Husband
Delphy		Ditto Do
Peter Lam Knittr		No wife
Alla - Do		Husbd James Cartr dow
Amount	28.	
Mansion House		
Will		Wife Aggy D.R. GW
Joe Postilr		Do Sall R.T. Do
Mike		No wife - son to Lucy
Sinah		Husbd Miller Ben GW
Mima		Do Godfrey Wagr dow
Lucy		No Husband
Grace		Husbd Mr Lears Ind
Letty		No husband
Nancy		Ditto Do
Viner		Ditto Do
Eve	17	Ditto a dwarf
Delia	12	Ditto her sister
Children		
Phil		Son to Lucy
Patty		daughter to Do

more land contiguous to Mount Vernon, but more slaves to work it. In a document shocking to modern eyes, he wrote a high-spirited letter to a sea captain asking him to sell in the West Indies a rebellious slave and invest the proceeds in "the best rum," "mixed sweetmeats," and other delicacies.

The first crack in Washington's armor seems to have come from the observation that slaves, deprived of other roots and with no property to take along, most dreaded being moved to a strange place from the plantation where they were part of a tight society of their own. Being, as he put it, "unwilling to hurt the feelings of anyone," Washington resolved, towards the end of his prerevolutionary stay at Mount Vernon, that he would not sell or move any slave without that slave's consent. Since consent was never (or hardly ever) given, Washington was soon carrying the economic liability of a work force larger than he could profitably employ. This was partly due to a high birthrate and partly because he had changed from tobacco to other crops that required much less labor.

In 1774, Washington made a statement the more revealing because it involved no conscious intention of expressing his opinion concerning slaves. He contended that if the Americans accepted British encroachments, "custom and use shall make us as tame and abject slaves as the blacks we rule over with such arbitrary sway." The final clause in this sentence reveals disgust at the behavior of the whites, but even more significant is the assumption that the "custom and use" which had debased slaves would debase whites equally. Never in all his writings did Washington express even by implication agreement with the belief of Jefferson and many other southern leaders that African Americans were racially inferior.

Opposite: *Washington probably prepared this eight-page document to accompany his will, which he drew up in June or July of 1799. It lists 317 slaves at Mount Vernon, including 124 he owned, 153 he managed as part of Martha's dower, and 40 he was renting from his neighbor, Mrs. Penelope French. The slaves' names, ages, relationships, and which of the five farms they resided at are also recorded. Washington's will freed his slaves upon Martha's death, although the Custis descendents inherited her dower slaves, tearing apart many of their families in the process.*

> Washington's growing passion for consistency, combined with his innate inability to separate theory from practice, made his horror of slavery increase as Jefferson's receded.

His role as commander in chief kept Washington for most of eight years in the North, away from slavery. He was at first shocked to find free slaves in the New England army, but he was soon urging desegregation for the large number of African Americans in the Rhode Island forces. As the war proceeded, he reached the point of urging that, even in the Deep South, slaves be enlisted with the promise of freedom at the war's end.

He came to regard his dependence at Mount Vernon on slave labor as a "misfortune." The economic education he was forced to give himself because of the plight of the army taught him not only the importance of manufacturing and financial credit, but also that a business economy was a viable alternative to the slavery society, which was the only economy he had previously known. When in Philadelphia during the winter of 1778–1779, he had seriously considered disentangling himself from what he could no longer justify, by selling his slaves and using the proceeds as investment capital. But such sales would have bothered his conscience, and he was buoyed up through his innumerable difficulties by his hope of returning to Mount Vernon. The plantation could not operate without slaves, since free farm labor was unprocurable in Virginia.

The Revolution won, Washington hoped that the American experiment would reveal to the world that kings and aristocracies were unnecessary, and that populations were capable of ruling themselves. This required national unity, and no issue was more divisive than slavery. Putting first what he considered the more comprehensive battle for freedom, Washington limited himself to stating that, if an authentic movement towards emancipation could be started in Virginia (none could), he would come to its support. Had Washington been more audacious, he would undoubtedly have failed to achieve the end of slavery, and he would certainly have made impossible the role he played in the Constitutional Convention and the presidency.

The best summary of Washington's attitude towards slavery between the Revolution and the presidency is found in a statement quoted by his intimate friend Humphreys: "The unfortunate condition of the persons whose labors I in part employed has been the only unavoidable subject of regret. To make the adults among them as easy and comfortable as their actual state of ignorance and improvidence would admit, and to lay a foundation to prepare the rising generation for a destiny different from that in which they were born, affords some satisfaction to my mind, and could not, I hoped, be displeasing to the justice of the Creator."

Washington remained, in fact, far from clear in his own mind concerning what he should, could, and would do concerning his slaves. On one thing he was determined: he refused to let anyone push him around. Already unsympathetic to the Quakers, whose pacifism had made him trouble during the Revolution, he was outraged by their efforts to separate Virginia slaves from their masters. Such extralegal intervention, he insisted, by "begetting discontent on one side and resentment on the other" induced "more evils than it could cure." Although there was no glimmer that any southern state would legislate to abolish slavery, Washington felt that emancipation could come only through legislative enactment. He wished to see some plan adopted that would free slaves "by slow, sure, and imperceptible degrees."

During 1791, Washington spirited a group of his slaves back to Mount Vernon from the presidential mansion in Philadelphia, lest his possession be undermined by a law that automatically freed slaves kept in Pennsylvania for a period of time. But all the while, his mind was seething. Between September 1 and December 12, 1793, probably at Mount Vernon while the yellow fever raged in Philadelphia, he reached a revolutionary conclusion.

In a letter of December 12 to the British agricultural reformer Arthur Young, Washington stated that "the thoughts I am now about to disclose to you" were not "even in embryo" when he had written Young on September 1. He "entertained serious thoughts," Washington explained, of renting, if he could secure as tenants expert English farmers, all the Mount Vernon plantation except the mansion house farm, which he would retain "for my own residence, occupation, and amusement in agriculture."

Describing his intentions to his intimate Lear, Washington explained in a paragraph headed "private" that his motive, "more powerful than all the rest" was "to liberate a certain species of property which I possess very repugnantly to my feelings, but which imperious necessity compels, and until I can substi-

Opposite: *The subject of this extraordinary portrait by Gilbert Stuart, oil on canvas, c. 1795–1797, has been identified as a slave named Hercules who served as Washington's cook, first at Mount Vernon and later at the presidential residence in Philadelphia, where he became one of the most famous cooks of his day. In March 1797, at the end of Washington's term and just a few days before his return to Mount Vernon, Hercules escaped. Officially a fugitive until 1801, he was granted freedom.*

tute some other expedient by which expenses not in my power to avoid (however well disposed I may be to do it) can be defrayed." Washington omitted from the copy of this letter he kept in his files the sentences which revealed his wish to free his slaves.

His intention, as he later revealed, was to have the renters of his farms hire, "as they would do any other laborers," slaves who had previously worked on the same farms as slaves.

"The unfortunate condition of the persons whose labors I in part employed has been the only unavoidable subject of regret. To make the adults among them as easy and comfortable as their actual state of ignorance and improvidence would admit, and to lay a foundation to prepare the rising generation for a destiny different from that in which they were born, affords some satisfaction to my mind, and could not, I hoped, be displeasing to the justice of the Creator."

Although he could look forward to collecting rent, Washington was preparing to accept a tremendous financial sacrifice. One good field hand was worth as much as a small city lot, three thousand pounds of beef, or three hundred gallons of whiskey. The many more than a hundred slaves Washington hoped to free constituted what was probably his largest financial asset and certainly (since slaves sold much more easily than land) his most negotiable. In addition, he would incur extra financial obligations. He would have to support the freed children until they were old enough to support themselves, and pension for life those too old or infirm to work. These two groups constituted almost half of the slaves he would liberate.

To the slave workers, Washington's plan offered a great advantage. They would not be "set adrift." The only dictated change in their situation would be their freedom. Now paid for their hire, those who wished could continue to pursue familiar tasks with their relations and old friends in familiar surroundings. This would help bridge what was perhaps the greatest transition a human being could experience.

The leap from slavery to freedom was so basic that (particularly in the case of the most numerous slaves, the field hands) there seemed no way to prepare people in the earlier condition for success (or even survival) in the later. A slave did not have any incentive to learn skills, become self-reliant, or in any way try to better himself. And without stirring up chaos or even insurrections, a slave could not, Washington believed, be encouraged to have the psychology of a free man until he was actually freed. On one recorded occasion, Washington asked despairingly how "the mind of a slave [could] be educated to perceive what are the obligations of a state of freedom?" As he had told Humphreys, he did not hope actually to prepare slaves for freedom but only to lay a foundation on which they could be prepared. According to Washington's plan, the crucial reeducation could take place after freedom but before the freed individual had to fly on his own wings.

Washington did not dare let move across his fields even the slightest hint of what he was trying to achieve, lest his slave quarters be completely disrupted. Secrecy was also essential in the white United States for reasons which Washington described as "of a political and indeed imperious nature."

Slave quarters at Mount Vernon, as preserved today.

He was already in enough trouble with the southern Republicans without word leaking out that he hoped to set an example towards undermining the institution of slavery. It was not only because he considered English farmers more skillful that he was seeking to bring in renters from abroad. They would have no predilection for slavery. And, ocean crossings being what they then were, offers could hardly reach Washington before he was safely out of the presidency. The storm would then only strike at him personally, not at the federal government.

When Washington left the presidency, he made use of the Pennsylvania law which he had previously taken care to evade. He slipped into freedom several of his house slaves so quietly, by simply leaving them behind, that no member of the southern opposition even guessed. Indeed, the secret remained undiscovered until this writer happened on a clue when examining a seemingly trivial letter to Washington's tailor.

Resident again at Mount Vernon, Washington found that what efforts he had made to improve the lot of his slaves had, like everything else on the plantation, gone backwards during his absence. In 1788, all five of his overseers had been African Americans, and now none were. His efforts to train the unmotivated slaves to trades—gardening, shoemaking, spinning, milling—had, it is true, never been particularly successful, but he was not happy to see that whites had slipped into many of the jobs. Since he was no longer familiar enough with the slave families to know where to look for promising youngsters, he could not mitigate the situation.

The frustration of slavery was all around him. Those slaves for whom the Washingtons had personal affection, the house slaves, lacerated their proprietors'

Mount Vernon on the Potomac River, 1860.

emotions by applying the sophistication and skills they had acquired in the family circle to running away. The only major effort Washington made—it proved vain—to recover an absconded slave was due to Martha's hurt feelings at being deserted by a slave girl, Oney Judge, whom she had brought up almost as her own child, but who had learned at her knee not only to be a fine seamstress but also to value freedom.

The field hands were a perpetual problem. Washington controlled, spread out over the five farms, the population of a large village: in 1799, more than three hundred. They were supposed to be under the management of the overseers, but the overseers were inefficient, stupid, and often drunken. Furthermore, there was on the plantation of a humane proprietor no effective way to punish a recalcitrant slave. Slaves could not be imprisoned without giving them vacations; they had no property with which to pay fines; they had been allowed no pride that would make them unhappy when upbraided. To use as a penalty sale to an unhappy environment was past Washington's sensibilities. The only visible punishment was whipping, and this Washington hated to authorize on practical as well as moral grounds: the overseers who administered the punishment were further brutalized, and the slaves made the more resentful.

There may have been Virginia estates on which slaves moved in lockstep to bellowed commands, but Mount Vernon was not one of them. Mount Vernon was a whirlpool of anarchy where all managerial efforts hardly sufficed to keep the confusion from overflowing the banks.

In their labors, the slaves, having nothing to gain, made an art of malingering and inefficiency. They demonstrated genius in breaking any machine that could be made useless by human hands. And when they temporarily slipped the moorings that were supposed to keep them on their farms, they found innumerable ways to harass their master to their own amusement and profit. If the doors were not sternly watched, the Mansion House would be awash with children smashing things. The flowers in the gardens were picked and trampled; vegetables and fruit disappeared, as did any portable object that was not nailed down or kept under strict surveillance. There were nearby stores and tippling houses where neither slaves nor overseers were ever asked where they had procured the goods they bartered.

Washington estimated that the services of a white farm hand (if one could be procured despite the lure of westward settlement) cost ten to fifteen pounds sterling a year. A slave cost only eight to twelve. Yet, because of their inefficiency and the superfluity he had to support, Washington believed that his slaves did not actually earn their keep. That their way of life, if anything but luxurious, was healthy is demonstrated by the high percentage of those too young or old to work. The profit of Virginia slaveholders came primarily from breeding slaves for sale. This Jefferson did, but Washington's conscience forbade it.

Slavery was for him uneconomic, and all the dark pleasures offered by slaveholding had for him no charms. Neither lust (despite legends to the contrary) nor sadism beckoned him on to his slave quarters. No otherwise unsatisfied yearning for power urged him to tyrannize over the helpless. He was temperamentally incapable of being indolent while others worked for him. Towards the mass of his slave possessions who had not individually caught his interest or affection, his emotions were unhappy: frustration, pity, anxiety concerning the possibility of a slave revolt,* and a deep personal sense of guilt.

Commonly, slaveholders opposed permanent marriage as an impediment to the mobility of individual slaves. Ownership of children being determined by the ownership of the mother, a family was defined as a woman and her offspring. At first, Washington accepted this conception with the other conventions of slavery. But he came to encourage slave marriages. When he listed his slaves in 1799, almost all were marked down as married to specific partners.

His intention, as he later revealed, was to have the renters of his farms hire, "as they would do any other laborers," slaves who had previously worked on the same farms as slaves.

This support of his family life created, as Washington looked forward to freeing his slaves, severe problems. He could free only about one-half the slaves in his cabins; the other half, which had come with his marriage to Martha, were entailed to the Custis estate and would on Martha's death become the property of her grandchildren. Since the two groups had intermarried, his freeing of those he controlled would divide many families. "To part, will be affecting and trying events," he mourned, "happen when it will." But he could see no way out.

Washington continued, whenever he had the opportunity, to offer his farms for rent on terms that did not include the slaves. However, as his declining years passed by, the end remained unachieved. When he drew up his will in July 1799, a final decision could

* This fear, as old in the slaveholding regions as slavery itself, had been given a new urgency by the slave revolt—an offshoot of the French Revolution—which bloodied Santo Domingo (Haiti) in 1791.

no longer be postponed. The provisions he worked out reveal that the old man was unable to visualize any practical solutions to the dilemmas involved in bringing freedom to slaves at Mount Vernon.

Having failed to establish a way to assure the adult slaves some employment congenial to their situation and experience, he saw no choice but to free them out of hand. He did require his heirs to make sure that all who were old or infirm would be "comfortably clothed and fed while they live." And he did his best to protect his former slaves from the harpies who kidnapped free slaves for sale further south or in the Indies. He specified that none be "under any pretext whatsoever" transported out of Virginia. But all this failed to ensure that slave workers, thrown unprepared into freedom, would not be worse off than before.

Children whose parents could not or would not take care of them were to be supported until they were old enough to be legally bound as if they were white apprentices. They were to serve until the age of twenty-five, "be taught to read and write, and brought up to some useful occupation agreeable to the laws of the Commonwealth of Virginia providing for the support of orphan and other poor children." They were thus not to be discriminated against but gathered into the white world.

The problem of separating the slaves he could free from their relations whom he could not produced Washington's lamest solution. He reasoned that the crises should pass more easily when the whole estate was broken up: the plantation was to be divided, after Martha's death, among three sets of heirs. Thus, he postponed the freeing of his slaves until "the decease of my wife." Although he had for years seen a danger of convulsing his slave quarters with premature hints of manumission, he chose to ignore the situation Martha would find herself in when some one hundred and fifty individuals were awaiting her death to set them free.

In December 1800, almost exactly a year after Washington died, Abigail Adams visited his widow at Mount Vernon. The Massachusetts abolitionist wrote her sister that "the estate is now going into decay. Mrs. Washington with all her fortune finds it difficult to support her family, which consists of three hundred slaves. One hundred and fifty of them are now to be liberated, men with wives and young children who have never seen an acre beyond the farm are now about to quit it, and go adrift into the world without horse, home, or friend. Mrs. Washington is distressed for them. At her own expense she has cloaked them all, and very many of them are already miserable at the thought of their lot. The aged she retains at their request; but she is distressed for the fate of others. She feels a parent and a wife." Those married to the Custis slaves would "quit all their connections—yet what could she do in the state in which they were left by the general, to be free at her death? She did not feel as though her life was safe in their hands, many of whom would be told that it was their interest to get rid of her. She therefore was advised to set them all free at the close of the year." This Martha did.

According to Washington's stepgrandson, the liberated slaves "succeeded very badly as free men: so true is the axiom that 'the hour that makes a man a slave takes half his worth away.'" The general's heirs did not limit their support to slaves who had been infirm at his death. Taking others back under the wing of his estate, they made their last pension payment in 1833. Washington's provisions for preparing the children for a white world could not be carried through because his Virginia neighbors passed laws against educating African Americans.

Fifty-Two

DEATH OF A HERO

(1799)

Washington did his best to cast an attractive aura about the creation of his will. He had special paper made, the watermark showing a goddess of agriculture seated upon a plow, holding in one hand a staff surmounted by a liberty cap, and in the other a flowering branch.

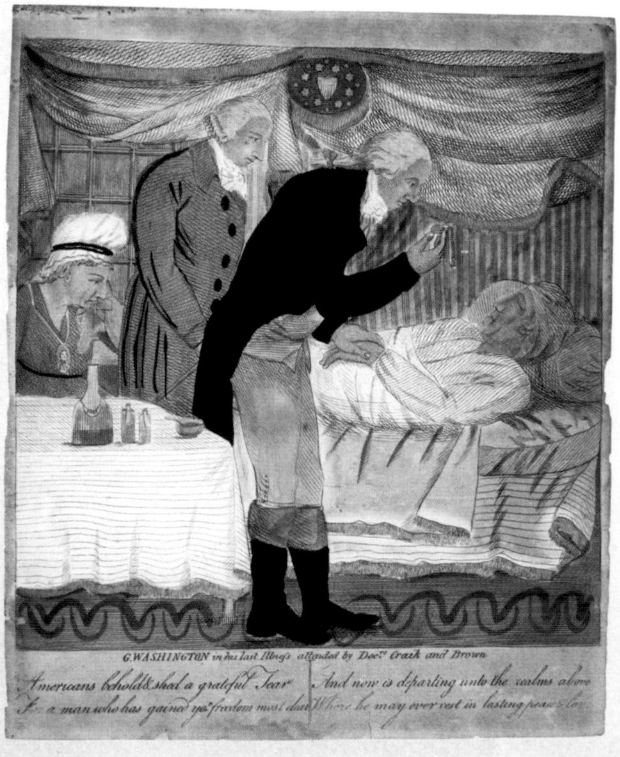

This hand-colored etching by an unknown artist depicts Washington in His Last Illness, *1800.*

He inscribed the text in his most careful hand, breaking the words without regard to syllabic structure so that the right-hand margin would be as straight as the left. He boasted that he had not called on the aid of any "professional character." Yet to the depression of every man facing disillusion there was added the fact that the only situation that would give the will meaning did not exist. He had no heirs of his body.

Nonetheless, Washington adhered (except for the provisions involved in freeing his slaves) almost altogether to the Virginia dynastic tradition. He did spread memorabilia and cash gifts to friends and faithful servants; he did make bequests for educational purposes, particularly to foster the establishment of a national university in the national capital; but no such provisions made more than a dent in the main body of his estate. Although he bequeathed to his longtime faithful secretary, Lear, lifetime use of the farm, he stipulated that it should return to his own estate at Lear's death. That estate was left altogether to his blood relations or Martha's.

Had he had children of his own, he would have died with the knowledge that the estate he had labored to amass would move down the years, augmenting the prosperity and the possibilities of his descendants. As it was, he sprinkled his holdings among more than twenty Washingtons, Custises, and Dandridges.

He did have the possibility of establishing, if not a physical, a political heir. The earl of Buchan had

In 1818 and 1819, landscape artist Joshua Shaw traveled the eastern seaboard to sketch the "most prominent beauties of notable scenery." Soon after, he commissioned John Hill to translate the scenes into prints. Of the eighteen images after Shaw's sketches, only one was dedicated to a burial site. It illustrates Washington's original tomb or "sepulchre," as he called it. Following the first president's interment in 1799, people from around the world traveled to visit his final resting place.

sent him a box, made of the oak that had sheltered Sir William Wallace after the Battle of Fallkirk, with the request that Washington would pass it, at his death, to the American who should merit it best. How Hamilton would have loved to be devised that box! Washington returned it to Lord Buchan.

Almost all the great rulers of history have wished to be enshrined in some grand edifice where their deeds could be emblazoned and posterity could come to worship. Almost all the great rulers of history have envisioned the pomp, the expressions of praise and of mourning, with which they would be interred. Washington did, it is true, decide that the old family vault at Mount Vernon was so cramped and decrepit that a better vault should be built. But he visualized no monumental structure dominating the streets of the national capital which bore his name.

In long-familiar ground near to his house at Mount Vernon, he had "marked out" an oblong "at the foot of what is called the Vineyard In-closure," which commanded a broad view of the land and the river he loved. Here, so he commanded in his will, a tomb was to be built of brick, large enough to accommodate "such others of my family as may choose to be entombed there," but yet no more than a modest family vault.

Preparing to be laid in his own soil with his relations around him, the hero stated "my express desire that my corpse may be interred in a private manner, without parade or funeral oration."

On December 12, 1799, Washington entered in his diary: "Morning cloudy. Wind to northeast and mercury 33. A large circle round the moon last night. At about ten o'clock it began to snow, soon after to hail, and then to a settled cold rain. Mercury 28 at night."

His secretary, Lear, remembered that the storm started shortly after Washington had ridden out to inspect his farms. "As he never regarded the weather, he kept out from about ten A.M. till three o'clock." After his return, Lear carried him some letters to frank. Having franked them, Washington said the weather was too bad for a servant to go to the post office.

"I observed to him," so Lear's account continues, "that I was afraid he had got wet. He said, No; his greatcoat had kept him dry—but his neck appeared wet and the snow was hanging on his hair. . . . He came to dinner without changing his dress. In the evening, he appeared as well as usual."

Washington's journal note for December 13 reads, "Morning snowing and about three inches deep. Wind at northeast and mercury at 30. Continuing snowing till one o'clock, and about four it became perfectly clear. Wind in the same place but not hard. Mercury 28 at night." These were probably the last words that George Washington ever wrote.

Washington admitted to a sore throat, "but," so Lear wrote his mother, "considering it as a trifling matter he took no measures to relieve it; for he was always averse to nursing himself for any slight complaint." He did take the precaution of not riding out again in the storm. After the sky had cleared, he walked on the lawn between the piazza and the river to mark some trees he wished to have cut down. His voice was hoarse, but he made light of it. During the evening, he sat in the parlor with Martha and Lear, reading some newspapers that had come from the post office. "He was very cheerful," Lear noted, "and, when he met with anything which he thought diverting or interesting, he would read it aloud, as well as his hoarseness would permit."

After Martha had retired, Washington asked Lear to read to him the report of some debates in the Virginia Assembly. When he heard that Madison was supporting Monroe for the Senate, he became upset. He "spoke with some degree of asperity," which Lear

Following page: George Washington on His Deathbed, *attended by family and friends, from the* Life of George Washington *series by Junius Brutus Stearns, c. 1853.*

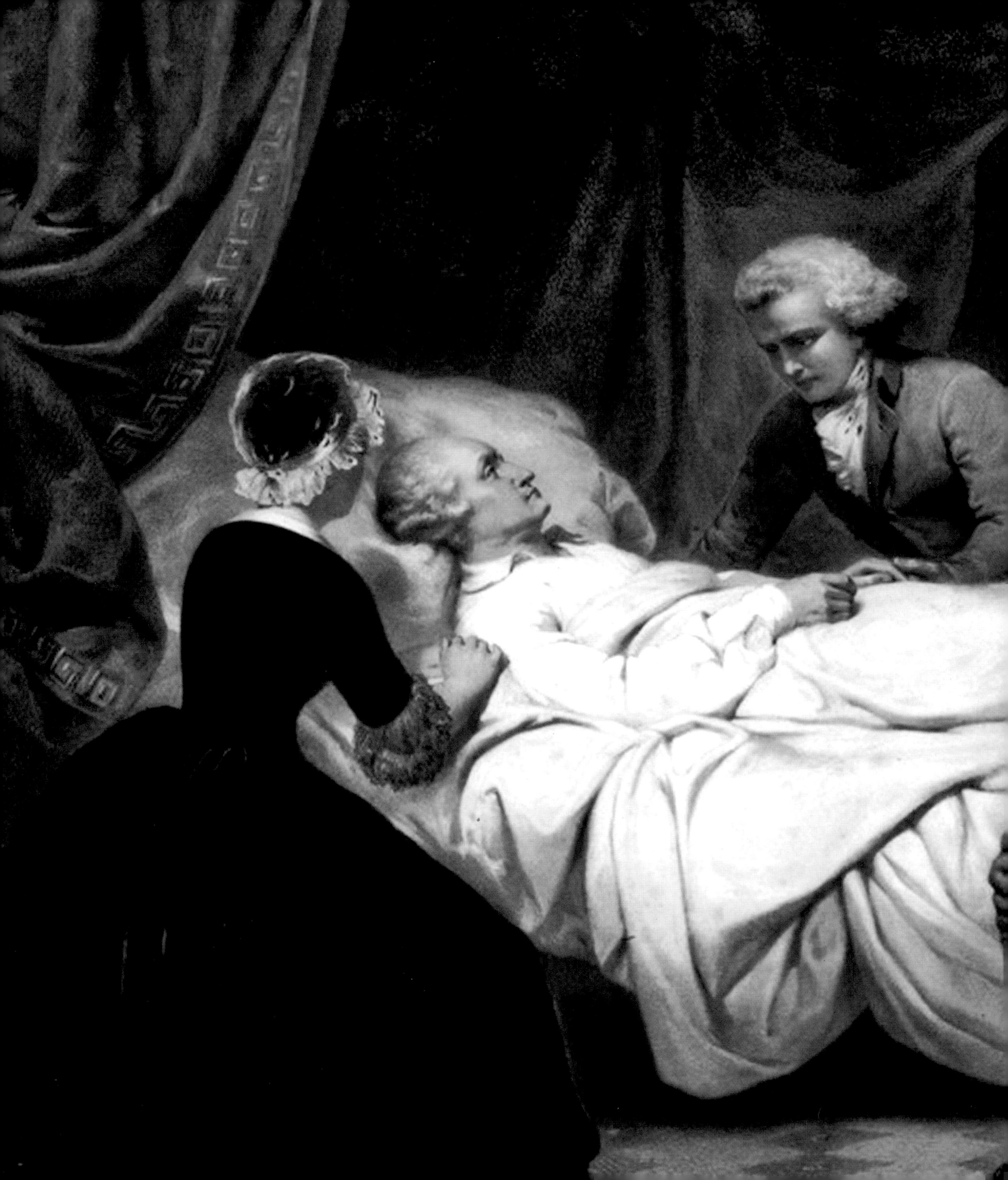

"endeavored to moderate, as I always did on such occasions." Eventually, Washington regained his cheerfulness and prepared to set off for bed. Lear urged him to use some medicine.

"No," said Washington. "You know I never take anything for a cold. Let it go as it came."

Between two and three in the morning, Washington awoke Martha to say that he had suffered an ague and was feeling extremely unwell. Observing that he could scarcely speak and was breathing with difficulty, Martha was alarmed. She wished to summon a servant, but Washington would not let her do so, lest by getting out of bed she should catch cold. It seems to have been at this point that the hero decided he was going to die. As two of his physicians later put it, "He was fully impressed at the beginning of his complaint . . . that its conclusion would be mortal; submitting to the several exertions made for his recovery, rather as a duty, than from any expectation of their efficacy."

At daybreak a maid came to make the fire. She was sent to get an overseer named Rawlins, who commonly ministered to sick slaves: Washington wished to be bled before the doctor (who had also been sent for) could get there. Lear was awakened. "A mixture of molasses, vinegar and butter was prepared, to try its effect in the throat; but he could not swallow a drop. Whenever he attempted it, he appeared to be distressed, convulsed and almost suffocated."

The sun was up by the time the overseer appeared. He had brought his lancet, but he was white and trembling. Washington bared his arm and, speaking with difficulty, said, "Don't be afraid." The incision having been made and the blood running pretty freely, Washington observed, "The orifice is not large enough."

At this, Martha, who was not sure that her husband was prescribing the right treatment, begged that too much blood should not be taken. She appealed to Lear "to stop it." Lear tried to intervene, but the general put out his hand in an arresting gesture. As soon as he could speak, he said, "More!" However, Martha continued to plead, and the bleeding was stopped after a pint had been taken. While Lear applied various poultices and soaked Washington's feet in warm water, Martha sent for a second doctor.

The first physician to arrive was his lifelong friend Dr. Craik. Craik used Spanish fly to draw blood into a blister directly from Washington's throat; he also took more blood from Washington's arm. The patient obediently tried to use a gargle of sage tea and vinegar, but the only result was that he was again almost suffocated. Craik urged him to cough. He tried, but could not do so. Craik sent for a third doctor and bled the general for a third time. "No effect however was produced by it, and he continued in the same state, unable to swallow anything."

Between three and four in the afternoon, two horsemen galloped separately up the driveway to Mount Vernon: Dr. Elisha Cullen Dick of Alexandria and Dr. Gustavus Richard Brown of Port Tobacco. Recollections become a little contradictory at this point, but it seems that the two new physicians each in turn examined Washington. Then the three doctors withdrew for a conference.

The facts on the conference are more precise. Drs. Craik and Brown agreed on the diagnosis of quinsy (an extreme form of tonsillitis) and urged further debilitating treatment—more bleeding and blisters and also purges. Dr. Dick, who at thirty-seven was by far the youngest of the three, argued that Washington was suffering from "a violent

Opposite: *Washington was a punctilious record keeper. Fifty-one diary volumes and fragments in his hand are known to exist, known as* The American Repository of Useful Information, *beginning in 1748 and ending with his death in December 1799. Washington recorded details of the last days of his presidency, his departure from Philadelphia, and his return to civilian life at his beloved Mount Vernon.*

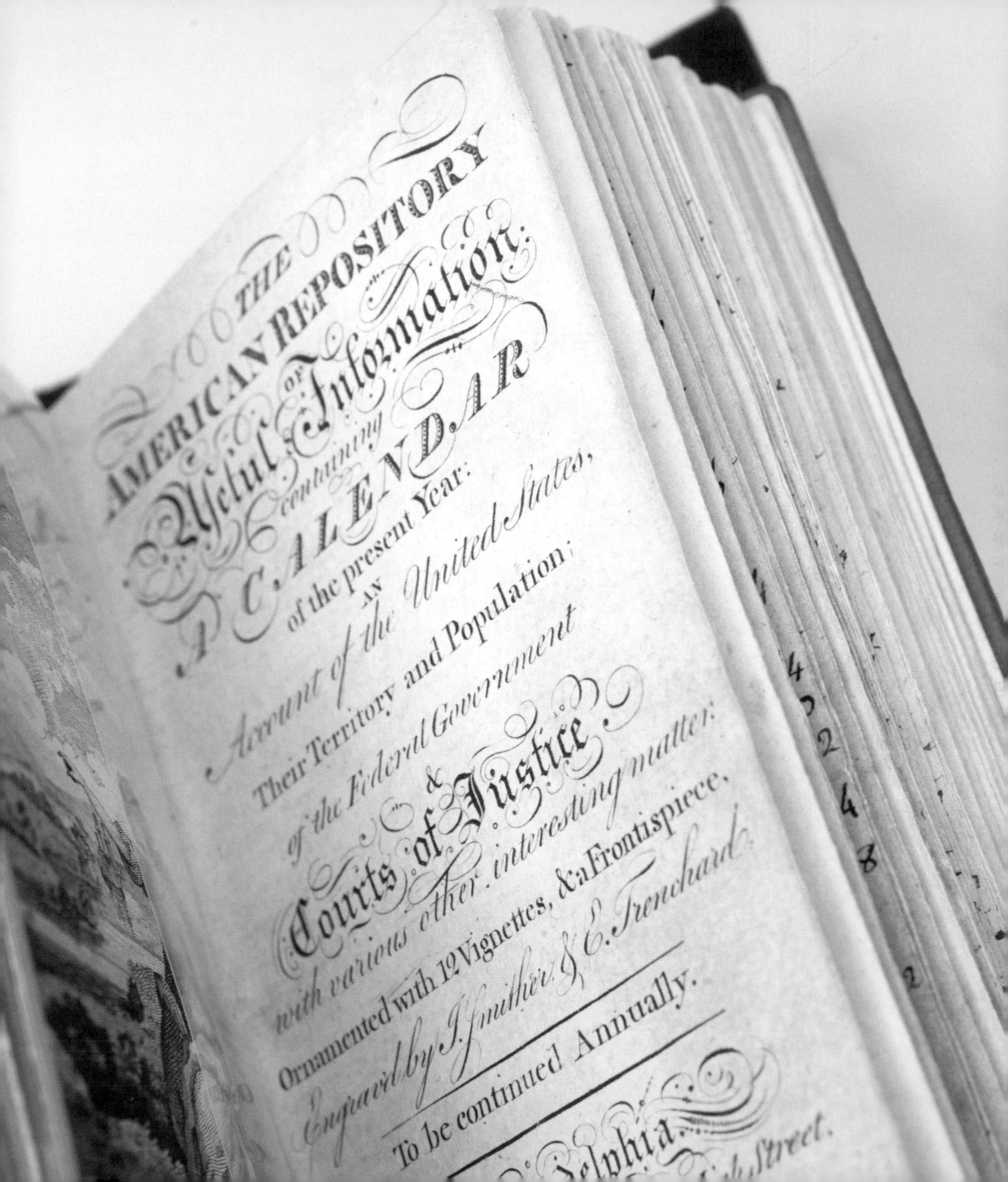
THE
AMERICAN REPOSITORY
of
Useful Information
containing
A CALENDAR
of the present Year:
AN
Account of the United States,
Their Territory and Population;
of the Federal Government
&
Courts of Justice
with various other interesting matter:
Ornamented with 12 Vignettes, & a Frontispiece,
Engraved by J. Smither & C. Trenchard.
To be continued Annually.

inflammation of the membranes of the throat, which it had almost closed, and which, if not immediately arrested, would result in death." He urged an operation that would open the trachea below the infection so Washington could breathe.

At first Craik seemed convinced, but Brown persuaded him that the operation might be fatal. Suspecting that his colleagues were afraid to assume such responsibility in the case of a patient so famous, Dick said that he would take all blame for failure on himself. Still Craik and Brown would not agree. Then Dick urged that the patient be not bled again. He did not deny the therapeutic efficiency of bleeding, but felt that it should be applied to the elderly only sparingly. Concerning Washington, he said, "He needs all his strength—bleeding will diminish it."

Later, after he had had time to think calmly, Craik wrote Brown they should have listened to Dick. Had they "taken no more blood from him, our good friend might have been alive now. But we were governed by the best light we had; we thought we were right, and so we are justified." (Down the years, doctors have speculated on the nature of Washington's illness. One guess is diphtheria; another, a virulent streptococcus infection of the throat. Either disease would, in the state of medicine at that time, have been fatal regardless of the treatment prescribed.)

As a result of the doctors' despairing conference, Washington was bled for the fourth time: "the blood ran very slowly—appeared very thick," but the operation "did not produce any symptoms of fainting." When, towards four in the afternoon, Washington proved able to swallow a little, the doctors took advantage of this situation by giving him calomel and other purges.

"About half past four o'clock," Lear recorded, "he desired me to ask Mrs. Washington to come to his bedside—when he requested her to go down into his room and take from his desk two wills which she would find there, and bring them to him, which she did. Upon looking at them, he gave her one, which he observed was useless, as it was superseded by the other, and desired her to burn it, which she did, and then [she] took the other and put it away into her closet."

Lear wrote his mother, "To the last moment he wished to be useful. As often as he could speak, he mentioned to me something he wished to have done."

Later, as Lear sat by his bed holding his hand, Washington said, "'I find I am going. My breath cannot continue long. I believed from the first attack it would be fatal. Do you arrange and record all my late military letters and papers—arrange my accounts and settle my books, as you know more about them than anyone else, and let Mr. Rawlins finish recording my other letters, which he has begun.'

"I told him this should be done. He then asked if I recollected anything which it was essential for him to do, as he had but a very short time to continue with us. I told him that I could recollect nothing, but that I hoped he was not so near his end. He observed, smiling, that he certainly was, and that, as it was the debt which we must all pay, he looked at the event with perfect resignation."

As the afternoon wore on, the pain in Washington's throat and his distress at his difficulty in breathing increased. He continually asked, "in so low and broken a voice as at times hardly to be understood," what time it was. He tried for a while sitting up by the fire, but, finding no relief, asked to be returned to his bed. Then he kept trying to shift his tall frame into a more comfortable position. The smaller Lear would lie down on the bed beside him "to raise him, and turn him with as much ease as possible." Washington would mumble the hope that he was not giving too much trouble. To one of Lear's assurances of his eagerness to help, Washington replied, "Well, it is a debt we must pay to each other, and I hope when you want aid of this kind, you will find it."

He asked when his nephew Lawrence Lewis and his stepgrandson George Washington Parke Custis would return from a trip. Lear said he believed about the 20th of the month. "He made no reply to it."

Craik came in and approached the bedside. "Doctor," Washington managed to enunciate, "I die hard, but I am not afraid to go. . . . My breath cannot last long." Lear noted: "The doctor pressed his hand, but could not utter a word. He retired from the bedside, and sat by the fire absorbed in grief."

The other two physicians entered. They ordered that the sufferer be painfully pulled up into a sitting position. "After repeated efforts to be understood," so wrote Craik and Dick, he "succeeded in expressing a desire that he might be permitted to die without further interruption." As Lear quoted him, "I feel myself going. I thank you for your attention. You had better not take any more trouble about me; but let me go off quietly; I cannot last long." Medical science, however, cannot give up trying. The doctors, although they admitted they were "without a ray of hope," applied blisters and also poultices of wheat bran to Washington's legs and feet.

Everyone noted that at no point in his illness did Washington complain or refer to his agony. As the evening lengthened into night, he limited his convulsive efforts at speech to asking what time it was. His breathing became a little easier, and then a fear struck him—the fear of being buried alive. Summoning all his powers, he managed, after several false starts, to say to Lear, "I am just going. Have me decently buried, and do not let my body be put into the vault in less than three days after I am dead."

Lear bowed assent, being too moved for words. Washington fixed his gaze. "Do you understand me?"

"Yes, sir."

"'Tis well." These seem to have been the hero's last words.

The night dragged slowly on. The two younger doctors, not being intimates of the family, waited downstairs. From the windows of the second-floor-room, lamplight threw glistening squares on meager snow. Within, Dr. Craik sat, as he had for hours, staring into the fire. Washington's body servant, Christopher, stood by the bed, a post he had not deserted since morning, although Washington had several times motioned him to sit down. A group of house servants—"Caroline, Molly, and Charlotte," and some others—stood near the door. Lear was hovering around the head of the bed, intently trying to interpret every gesture and do what he could to ease the sufferer. Martha was sitting near the foot of the bed.

No one thought to look at a clock, so we only know for sure that it was approaching midnight when Washington withdrew his hand from Lear's and felt his own pulse. Lear called Craik, who came to the bedside. Washington lifted his arm and then his "hand fell from his wrist." As Lear reached out for the limp hand, Craik put his own hand over Washington's eyes. There was no struggle, not even a sigh.

In a calm, controlled voice, Martha asked, "Is he gone?"

Unable to speak, Lear held up his hand in a signal of assent.

This mourning ring, c. 1800, weaves two types of hair believed to belong to George and Martha Washington.

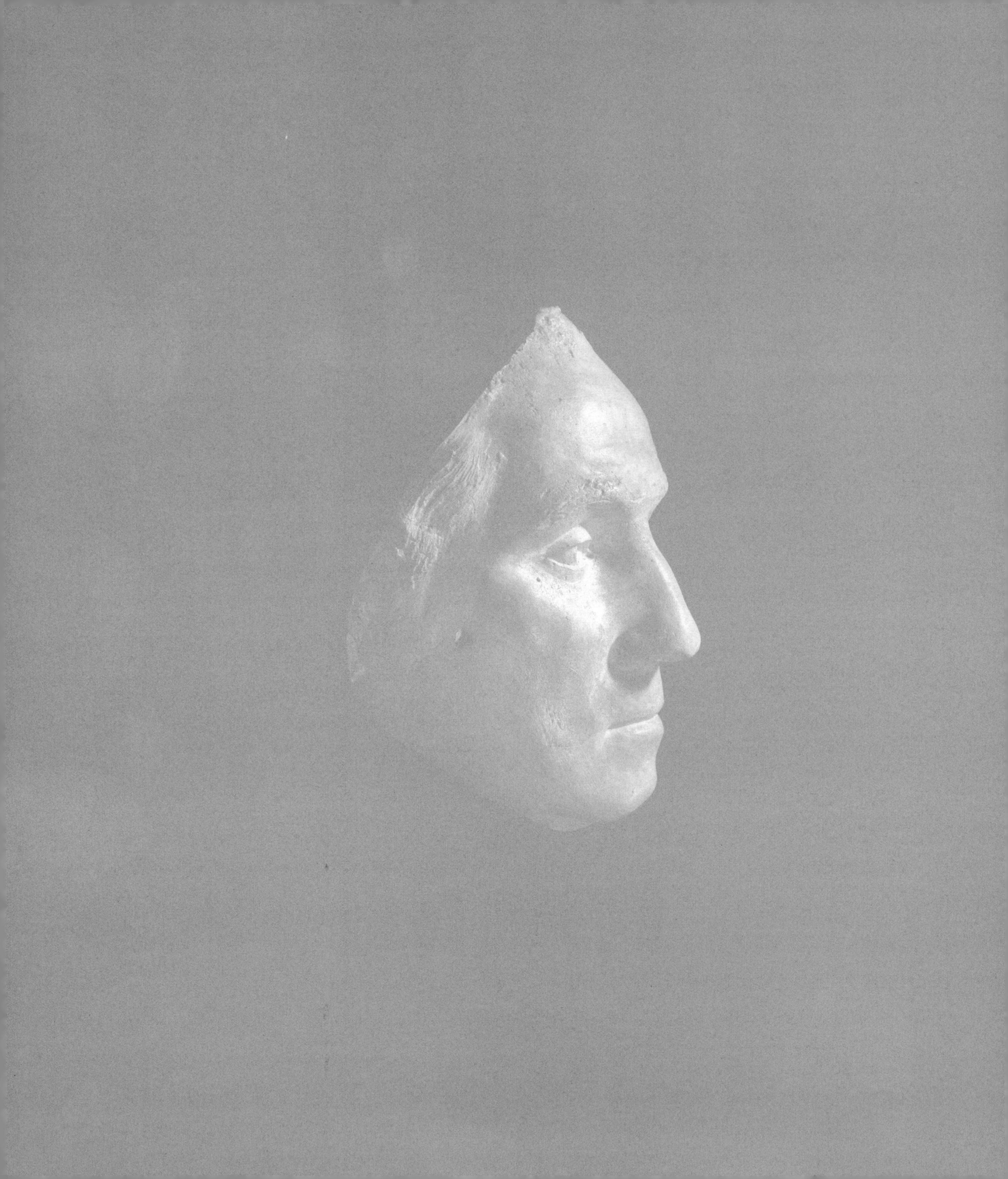

Acknowledgments

As has been my happy situation down the long years, I have been befriended and sustained from day to day by two of the libraries that are among the great cultural institutions of the United States: the New York Historical Society and the New York Public Library, which has permitted me to frequent the Frederick Lewis Allen Room.

The Mount Vernon Ladies' Association of the Union, which has preserved Washington's home with such grace and scholarship, continued its many helpful courtesies. I have also been assisted by the library of the Century Association, the Free Library of Cornwall, Connecticut, the Library of Congress, and the New York Society Library.

My wife, Beatrice Hudson Flexner, and my daughter, Helen Hudson Flexner, have helped in many ways.

I owe much to the staff of my publishers, Little, Brown and Company, and particularly to Arthur Thornhill Jr., Llewellyn Howland III, and that excellent copyeditor Jean Whitnack. Margaret Zweig has assisted greatly in the preparation of the manuscript. Ferdinand Lundberg suggested the subtitle, "The Indispensable Man."

I am also grateful to John A. Castellani, Thomas J. Dunnings Jr., Leon Edel, Sue Adele Gillies, James Gregory, James J. Heslin, Donald Jackson, Oliver Jensen, Mary-Jo Kline, Dumas Malone, Christine Meadows, Nancy Milford, Frank E. Morse, Harold C. Syrett, and Charles C. Wall.

Publisher's Note

The publisher would like to acknowledge the following for their valuable contributions to this edition:

New Editorial Content: Laura Ross

Historical Research: Ted Goodman

Photo Research: Susan Oyama

Historical Consultation & Content: Jimmy Napoli

Opposite: *Life mask of Washington by Jean-Antoine Houdon, plaster, 1785.*

Bibliography

My four-volume biography, on which this book is based, was published as follows: *George Washington: The Forge of Experience, 1732–1775* (Boston, 1965); *George Washington in the American Revolution, 1775–1783* (Boston, 1968); *George Washington and the New Nation, 1783–1793* (Boston, 1970); *and George Washington, Anguish and Farewell* (Boston, 1972). The reader is referred to the bibliography and source references of the apposite volume for documentation on specific matters discussed in this book.

This pin, c. 1791, bears a possible likeness of George Washington. He may have presented it to Catherine Littlefield Greene, the widow of Major General Nathanael Greene, during a visit to her home in 1791.

My desire to escape from the legends and misinformation that have accreted around Washington down the years, to determine what actually took place, dictated that I base my work as far as possible on original sources. For background, I have often relied on the writings and conclusions of others, but my picture of Washington is constructed almost completely from a new study of what he did and wrote.

Washington's own file of papers—diaries, financial accounts, letters and documents written or received by him, and other materials amount to about seventy-five thousand folios—is in the Library of Congress. The complete archive has been published by the Library on twenty-four reels of microfilm with a printed index: *Presidential Papers Microfilm: George Washington Papers* (Washington, D.C., 1965).

There have been a number of printed compilations of Washington's papers, but all previous such works were superseded by two sets edited by John C. Fitzpatrick: *George Washington's Diaries,* 4 vols. (Boston and New York, 1925) and *The Writings of George Washington,* 39 vols. (Washington, D.C., 1931–1944). Although containing only occasional quotations from letters to Washington, Fitzpatrick's edition of the *Writings* presents almost everything that Washington wrote which had come to light by 1944. Manuscripts discovered since then are in many collections. I have been assisted in finding them by the archives compiled at Mount Vernon, and more recently by a project that got under way in 1968. The University of Virginia and the Mount Vernon Ladies' Association of the Union are undertaking, under the editorship of Dr. Donald Jackson, a new and complete publication of Washington's papers. Including all communications sent to Washington, this set, which may well not be finished in this century, is expected to run to well over one hundred volumes. No volume of it has yet appeared. However, Dr. Jackson, on whose advisory board I serve, has been most helpful in answering my queries.

There are two important compendia of letters to Washington: *Stanislaus Murray Hamilton's Letters to Washington,* 5 vols. (Boston and New York, 1898–1902) quotes all such documents in the Library of Congress written between February 22, 1753, and July 1, 1775. Jared Sparks's *Correspondence of the American Revolution: Being Letters of Eminent Men to George Washington,* 4 vols. (Boston, 1853) is a selection tiny in relation to the vast archive that remains from this later period of Washington's activity.

Many publications contain papers of Washington's various coadjutors. The most important are included in the list of titles at the end of this statement. As the result would be too extensive, I have made no effort to particularize here the collections in which I found unpublished manuscripts.

Published biographies of Washington are as innumerable as the leaves in a forest. They fall into three major categories: the historically sound, the goody-goody, and the debunking.

The historically sound tradition began with John Marshall's *The Life of George Washington,* 5 vols. (London, 1804–1807). Important other works include *Henry Cabot Lodge's George Washington,* 2 vols. (Boston and New York, 1889); Paul Leicester Ford's *The True George Washington* (Philadelphia, 1898); Rupert Hughes's uncompleted *George Washington,* 3 vols. (New York, 1926–1930); Samuel Eliot Morison's brief *The Young George Washington* (Cambridge, Mass., 1932); John C. Fitzpatrick's *George Washington Himself* (Indianapolis, Ind., 1933); and Marcus Cunliffe's *George Washington: Man and Monument* (Boston, 1958). Standing alone as the most complete and most accurate documentary life of Washington is Douglas Southall Freeman's *George Washington: A Biography* (completed by J. A. Carroll and M. W. Ashworth), 7 vols. (New York, 1948–1957). This work, which is as close to a primary source as is possible for any such publication to be, has been extremely useful to me.

The goody-goody tradition was pioneered, directly after Washington's death, about 1800, by the inventor of the story about the cherry tree, that enticing fictionalizer Mason Locke (Parson) Weems. His *The Life of George Washington, with Curious Anecdotes Equally Honorable to Himself and Exemplary to His Young Countrymen* has gone into hundreds of editions and has been imitated by hundreds of other writers who, throughout the nineteenth and into the twentieth century, sought to edify the young and bolster their own moralizing by forging fictional Washingtons. Eventually this flood helped to create its equally fallacious opposite: the debunking tradition. The first truly influential biography in this mode was W. E. Woodward's *George Washington: The Image and the Man* (New York, 1926). Presenting Washington as stupid, dishonest, and venal is still an occupation of hack writers, whose effusions seemingly rise in the bestseller lists in exact relation to their inaccuracy.

To attempt to specify here the many thousands of printed sources to which I have been led by the ramifications of Washington's career would obviously create a list out of all proportion. The reader may turn to the bibliographies of my four original volumes, where some five hundred selected titles are listed. Or he may consult the bibliography in volume VI of Freeman's *Washington,* a list that runs to sixty-eight pages. I shall merely add to the sources already cited here the titles of some thirty other publications that I have found especially useful:

Adams, John, *Works,* ed. Charles Francis Adams, 10 vols. (Boston, 1850–1856). *American State Papers, Foreign Relations,* Vol. I (Washington, D.C., 1832); *Miscellaneous,* Vol. I (Washington, D.C., 1834).

Burnett, Edmund C., ed., *Letters of Members of the Continental Congress,* 8 vols. (Washington, D.C., 1921–1926).

Continental Congress, *Journals,* 1774–1789, 8 vols. (Washington, D.C., 1921–1926).

Custis, George Washington Parke, *Recollections and Private Memoirs of Washington* (New York, 1860).

Farrand, Max, ed., *Records of the Federal Convention of 1787,* 4 vols. (New Haven, 1937).

Force, Peter, ed., *American Archives,* 9 vols. (Washington, D.C., 1837–1853).

Hamilton, Alexander, *Papers,* ed. Harold C. Syrett, vols. I–XIX, all that have been published (New York, 1961–1973).

———, *Works,* ed. John C. Hamilton, 7 vols. (New York, 1851).

Humphreys, David, "The Life of George Washington," manuscript, Rosenbach Foundation, Philadelphia.

Jay, John, *The Correspondence and Public Papers of John Jay,* ed. Henry P. Johnston, 4 vols. (New York, 1890–1893).

Jefferson, Thomas, *Papers,* ed. Julian P. Boyd, vols. I–XVIII, all that have been published (Princeton, N.J., 1950–1971).

———, *Writings,* ed. Paul Leicester Ford, 10 vols. (New York, 1892–1899).

———, *Writings,* ed. A. A. Lipscomb and A. E. Berg, 20 vols. (Washington, D.C., 1903).

Lee, Charles, *The Lee Papers,* 4 vols. (New York, 1872–1875).

Madison, James, *Writings,* ed. Gaillard Hunt, 9 vols. (New York, 1900–1910).

Malone, Dumas, *Jefferson and His Time,* 4 vols. (Boston, 1951–1970).

Monroe, James, *Writings,* ed. Stanislaus Murray Hamilton, 7 vols. (New York, 1898–1899).

"Particulars of the Life and Character of General Washington," by an Old Soldier, reprinted from *Gentleman's Magazine* (London, August 1778) in William S. Baker, ed., *Early Sketches of George Washington* (Philadelphia, 1894), pp. 47–55.

Pickering, Octavius, *The Life of Timothy Pickering,* 4 vols. (Boston, 1867–1873).

Washington, George, *Account of Expenses while Commander in Chief,* with annotations of John C. Fitzpatrick (Boston, 1917).

———, *Calendar of the Correspondence of George Washington . . . with the Continental Congress,* ed. John C. Fitzpatrick (Washington, D.C., 1906).

———, *Calendar of the Correspondence of George Washington . . . with the Officers,* ed. John C. Fitzpatrick, 4 vols. (Washington, D.C., 1915).

———, *Calendar of the Washington Manuscripts in the Library of Congress,* ed. Herbert Friedenwald (Washington, D.C., 1901).

———, *Epistles Domestic, Confidential, and Official from General Washington* (New York, 1796). Forgery.

———, *The George Washington Atlas,* ed. Lawrence Martin (Washington, D.C., 1932).

———, *Last Will and Testament,* ed. John C. Fitzpatrick (Mount Vernon, 1939).

———, *Ledger A,* facsimile of the originals in the Library of Congress, 3 vols. (Boston, 1922).

———, *The Will of General Washington to which is Annexed a Schedule of His Property Directed to be Sold* (Alexandria, Va., 1800).

———, *Writings,* ed. Jared Sparks, 12 vols. (Boston, 1834–1837).

———, *Writings,* ed. Worthington Chauncey Ford, 14 vols. (New York and London, 1889–1893).

Wolcott, Oliver, *Memoirs of the Administrations of Washington and John Adams,* ed. George Gibbs, 2 vols. (New York, 1846).

Photography and Illustration Credits

Front cover: Top: *East Front of Mount Vernon, c. 1787–1792, detail of painting by Edward Savage.* Photograph by Harry Connolly, courtesy of Mount Vernon Ladies' Association. **Bottom:** *A map of General Washington's farm of Mount Vernon from a drawing transmitted by the General.* Library of Congress, Geography and Map Division. **Back cover:** *Washington at the Age of Twenty-Five by Thomas Addis Emmet, published 1851.* Emmet Collection, Miriam and Ira D. Wallach Division of Art, Prints and Photographs, The New York Public Library, Astor, Lenox and Tilden Foundations. **Back flap:** *Original Design of the Great Seal of the United States, 1782.* National Archives and Records Administration

Architect of the Capitol: 128, 180, 202–203

Art Resource, NY: 70, 163
- Erich Lessing/Art Resource, NY: 22
- Image copyright © The Metropolitan Museum of Art. Image source: Art Resource, NY: 113, 114, 326, 398
- National Portrait Gallery, Smithsonian Institution/Art Resource, NY: xi, xiii, 35, 104 right, 161, 193, 218, 221 top, left & right, 246, 253, 255, 271, 312, 353, 372, 373, 411
- The Pierpont Morgan Library/Art Resource, NY: 206, 420
- Réunion des Musées Nationaux/Art Resource, NY: xiv, 173, 293 right, 294, 296–297
- Scala/White Images/Art Resource, NY: 293 left
- Universal Images Group/Art Resource, NY: 408
- Yale University Art Gallery/Art Resource, NY: 120

Bridgeman Art Library
- Private Collection/Peter Newark American Pictures/The Bridgeman Art Library: 60, 247
- Private collection/Photo © Christie's Images/The Bridgeman Art Library: 140
- Chateau de Versailles, France/Giraudon/The Bridgeman Art Library: 147
- American Museum, Bath, Avon, UK/The Bridgeman Art Library: 192
- Private Collection/The Stapleton Collection/The Bridgeman Art Library: 305

©The British Library Board. Maps.K.Top.118.49.b: 198

The Colonial Williamsburg Foundation. Museum Purchase: 419

Corbis: © Bettmann/Corbis: 96, 139, 320, 328; © Richard T. Nowitz/Corbis: 141; © Bob Krist/Corbis: 146

Fine Arts Museums of San Francisco: Charles Willson Peale, American, (1741–1827), Self-Portrait, detail, 1822, oil on canvas, 29 1/4 x 24 1/8 in. ©Fine Arts Museums of San Francisco, gift of Mr. and Mrs. John D. Rockefeller 3rd, (1993.35.22): 55 left

Franklin D. Roosevelt Library: 300

Fraunces Tavern® Museum, New York City: 105 top

Getty Images: MPI/Archive Photos/Getty Images: 80

Houghton Library, Harvard University, Susan Dwight Bliss autograph collection, 1481-1915. MS Fr 167 (57): 20 left

Huntington Library, San Marino, California, HM 5995: 379

Independence National Historical Park: 76 2nd from top, 107, 125, 142 left, 158, 159, 170, 268, 273, 307, 346 right, 392

The Library Company of Philadelphia: 67

Library of Congress: 34, 191, 215, 299
- Geography and Map Division: 14, 26, 81–82, 100, 117–118, 132, 143, 177–178, 180, 183, 188
- Manuscript Division, The Thomas Jefferson Papers: 94, 267
- Manuscript Division, The James Madison Papers: 281
- Manuscript Division, George Washington Papers: 23, 74, 95, 167, 257
- Prints and Photographs Division: 5, 17, 44, 52, 62–63, 64, 76 top & bottom, 88, 101, 111, 137, 142 right, 186, 201, 221 bottom, 238, 239, 241 top, 248, 284, 318, 335, 358
- Rare Book and Special Collections Division: 61, 89, 199, 229, 338, 369
- Library of Congress, Serial and Government Publications Division: 105 bottom, 278 right

Courtesy of the Maryland Historical Society: 76 3rd from top, 135, 174

Morristown National Historical Park, Morristown, NJ, USA: 43

Mount Vernon Ladies' Association
Courtesy of Mount Vernon Ladies' Association: 1, 6, 8, 10, 42, 47, 48, 51, 54 top, 87, 127 #5 & 7, 251, 275, 288, 308, 349, 376, 383, 412, 422

Photograph by Gavin Ashworth: 99, 216, 217, 250 bottom, 385
Photograph by Ron Blunt: 407
Photograph by Harry Connolly: 3 right, 208 top & bottom, 250 top, 344, 350
Photograph by Hal Conroy: 212
Photograph by Conservation Center: 382, 402
Photograph by Mark Finkenstaedt: 241 bottom, left & right, 249, 417
Photograph by Mark Gulezian: 205
Photograph by Paul Kennedy: 54 bottom, left & center
Photograph by Robert C. Lautman: 211
Photograph by Edward Owen: 75
Photograph by Ted Vaughan: 233, 289, 384 top left & bottom right

© Museo Thyssen-Bornemisza, Madrid: 405

Photograph © 2012 Museum of Fine Arts, Boston: 84, 90

National Archives and Records Administration: 150, 151, 195, 224, 242, 262

Courtesy National Gallery of Art, Washington: 322

Courtesy, National Museum of the American Indian, Smithsonian Institution, catalog number 22/8915. Photo by Katherine Fogden: 272

National Park Service, George Washington Birthplace National Monument, Westmoreland County, Virginia: 2

© National Portrait Gallery, London: 11

Collection of the New-York Historical Society: 103, 104 left, 127 #6, 315, 323, 380

New York Public Library
Picture Collection, The New York Public Library, Astor, Lenox and Tilden Foundations: 3 left, 340
Emmet Collection, Miriam and Ira D. Wallach Division of Art, Prints and Photographs, The New York Public Library, Astor, Lenox and Tilden Foundations: 28, 85, 278 left, 306
Print Collection, Miriam and Ira D. Wallach Division of Art, Prints and Photographs, The New York Public Library, Astor, Lenox and Tilden Foundations: 134, 207, 391
I. N. Phelps Stokes Collection, Miriam and Ira D. Wallach Division of Art, Prints and Photographs, The New York Public Library, Astor, Lenox and Tilden Foundations: 108

Pennsylvania Academy of the Fine Arts, Philadelphia
Courtesy of the Pennsylvania Academy of the Fine Arts, Philadelphia. Gift of Mrs. Sarah Harrison (The Joseph Harrison, Jr. Collection): 57
Courtesy of the Pennsylvania Academy of the Fine Arts, Philadelphia. Bequest of Mrs. Sarah Harrison (The Joseph Harrison, Jr. Collection): 225
Courtesy of the Pennsylvania Academy of the Fine Arts, Philadelphia. Gift of Maria McKean Allen and Phebe Warren Downes through the bequest of their mother, Elizabeth Wharton McKean: 120
Courtesy of the Pennsylvania Academy of the Fine Arts, Philadelphia. Bequest of Henry C. Gibson: 124
Courtesy of the Pennsylvania Academy of the Fine Arts, Philadelphia. Bequest of Richard Ashhurst: 152
Courtesy of the Pennsylvania Academy of the Fine Arts, Philadelphia. Henry D. Gilpin Fund: 287

Redwood Library and Athenaeum: Gilbert Stuart, Self-portrait at 24. Bequest of Louisa Lee Waterhouse, from the collection of the Redwood Library and Athenaeum, Newport, Rhode Island: 55 right

The Royal Scots Dragoon Guards Collection: 31

Armed Forces History, Smithsonian Institution: 127 #1–4

SuperStock: © SuperStock/SuperStock: 126, 236–237; © Image Asset Management Ltd./SuperStock: 414–415

Virginia Historical Society (1990.5.2): 20 right

Washington-Custis-Lee Collection, Washington and Lee University, Lexington, Virginia: 54 right, 384 top right & bottom left

Courtesy, Winterthur Museum, 1957.856: 200
Courtesy, Winterthur Museum, 1964.2201: 396

Yale University
Courtesy Map Department, Sterling Memorial Library, Yale University: 37, 38–39, 79, 156
Yale University Art Gallery, Yale University Art Gallery: 162
Yale University Art Gallery, Gift of Ebenezer Baldwin, B.A. 1808: 165
Yale University Art Gallery, Gift of George Gibbs, M. A. (Hon.) 1808: 346 left

Index